BRIT GUI

D1149446

ORLANDU
& Walt Disney World

2012
Simon & Susan Veness

foulsham
LONDON • NEW YORK • TORONTO • SYDNEY

foulsham
The Oriel, 33 Bath Road, Slough SL1 3UF

Foulsham books can be found in all good bookshops or direct from www.foulsham.com

ISBN: 978-0-572-03664-5

Look out for the latest editions of Foulsham travel books:
Brit Guide to Las Vegas, Karen Marchbank with Jane Anderson
Brit Guide to Disneyland Resort Paris, Simon and Susan Veness
Brit Guide to New York, Amanda Statham

Dedication: To our special three-boy research team – Ben, Anthony and Mark – who help make our work fun!

SPECIAL THANKS
Special thanks for this edition go to: Visit Orlando, Kissimmee Convention and Visitors Bureau, The Walt Disney Company, Universal Orlando, SeaWorld Parks & Entertainment, St Petersburg/Clearwater Convention & Visitors Bureau, Seminole County Convention & Visitors Bureau, Mount Dora Chamber of Commerce, Florida Huddle, Daytona Beach Convention & Visitors Bureau, Mary Deatrick, Scott Joseph, Nigel Worrall, Allan Oakley and Bill Cowie, plus Matt and Debbie Churchill.
Our sincere thanks also go to all the hard-working people at Foulsham who help to bring our work to life every year.

Printed in Dubai

CONTENTS

FOREWORD   PAGE 4

1   **Introduction**
    (or, Welcome to the Holiday of a Lifetime).   PAGE 5

2   **Planning and Practicalities**
    (or, How to *Almost* Do It All and Live to Tell the Tale). PAGE 18

3   **Getting Around**
    (or, The Secret of Driving on the Wrong Side of the Road!). PAGE 47

4   **Accommodation**
    (or, Making Sense of American Hotels, Motels and Condos). PAGE 60

5   **The Theme Parks: Disney's Fab Four**
    (or, Spending the Day with Mickey and the Gang).   PAGE 101

6   **Five More of the Best**
    (or, Expanding Orlando's Universe).   PAGE 157

7   **The Other Attractions**
    (or, One Great Leap for Tourist Kind).   PAGE 213

8   **Off the Beaten Track**
    (or, When You're All Theme-Parked Out).   PAGE 245

9   **The Twin Centre Option**
    (or, To Orlando – and Beyond!).   PAGE 270

10 **Orlando by Night**
    (or, Burning the Candle at Both Ends).   PAGE 285

11 **Dining Out**
    (or, Man, These Portions are HUGE!).   PAGE 302

12 **Shopping**
    (or, How to Send Your Credit Card into Meltdown).   PAGE 325

13 **Going Home**
    (or, Where Did the Last Two Weeks Go?).   PAGE 339

14 **Your Holiday Planner**
    Example of how to plan for a 2-week holiday   PAGE 345

    INDEX   PAGE 347

    COPYRIGHT NOTICES   PAGE 352

    ACKNOWLEDGEMENTS   PAGE 352

FOREWORD

Simon says... Welcome to another feature-packed edition of the UK's best travel guide. And we don't just say that ourselves, we hear that from you, our readers, all the time. It isn't anything we take for granted, however, and we are continually striving to make the *Brit Guide to Orlando* even better and more user-friendly. Hence, with this edition, we are introducing another new feature, the **Brit Bonus**, which offers money off, special deals and other incentives on a wide range of attractions, accommodation and restaurants, in addition to our regular array of Partnership deals, which you see on the inside front and back covers. The Brit Bonus might offer you a free beer at Icebar on International Drive; 7 nights for the price of 5 at the Blue Heron Beach Resort; or $2 off a round of mini-golf. We know how expensive a 2-week holiday here can be – even though it remains fantastic value – so we are keen to highlight ways in which you can save money, too. And, of course, the *Brit Guide* continues to be the best possible 'good companion' for any visit to this amazingly exciting – but vast and complex – area that we call 'Orlando' but which actually covers most of Central Florida. It is a fabulous place to visit but it's easy to go wrong and end up tired, frustrated, lost or out of pocket. So stick with us and we'll steer you through all the delights in store. Disney may tell you 'It's a small world' but it's still a big place if you don't have the right guide!

Susan says... The name of the game in 2012 is 'savings', and as Simon has mentioned, we've searched high and low to bring you the best deals from the best attractions, dining and shopping centres Central Florida has to offer. In addition, there are countless ways of keeping the holiday affordable through the choices you make before and during your time in Orlando. Choose only as much ticketing as you can realistically use during your stay (that extra few pounds for days you 'might' use on an extended stay ticket does add up!), make use of online discounts and coupons (for savings of 50–90%), and pay attention to money-saving hints scattered throughout our Brit Tips. Tightening your belt a bit doesn't have to be painful and the *Brit Guide*, now more than ever, can help steer you in the right direction for the holiday of a lifetime that is friendly on the wallet, too. And, if you want to make sure you get the very best out of your holiday without wasting time or money, let us help with our Itinerary Planner Service (p45).

And now, on with the planning!

Simon and Susan Veness (visit us at **www.venesstravelmedia.com** or email **britsguide@yahoo.com**).

1 Introduction

Get ready for the world's most exciting holiday experience, because Orlando is all that and more besides. This area of Central Florida is actually a vast mix of theme parks, smaller attractions, sport, nature, amazing dining, world class shopping, fabulous nightlife and fun, fun, fun. It is adventure rides, thrills, excitement and fantasy without equal. It appeals to families, couples and singles; young and old alike. But you must be well prepared for what's in store.

First off, this is a BIG venture in every sense and it's vital you have an idea of the extensive and complex nature of this tourist wonderland. *Walt Disney World* is the leading attraction and is the size of a small city, and there is a strong supporting cast, led by Universal Orlando and SeaWorld. There's something for all tastes and ages, but it exacts a high toll. You'll walk a lot, queue a lot and probably eat a lot. You WILL have a fabulous time, but you'll probably end up exhausted, too. It is a holiday – but it's also something of a military campaign!

Eight theme parks

In simple terms, there are 8 essential major theme parks, and at least 1 will require 2 days to make you feel it has been done properly. Add a day at a water park, a trip to see one of the wildlife or nature attractions, and the lure of the nearby Kennedy Space Center, and you have 12 days of pure adventure mania. Then mix in the night-time fun of *Downtown Disney*, Universal's CityWalk and a host of dinner shows, plus superb shopping, and you start to understand the awesome scope of the place. Even with 2 weeks, something has to give – just make sure it isn't your patience, wallet – or sanity.

So, how do you get full value from this truly magical holiday? The basic answer is Good Planning – read, reflect and prepare. At the back of this book is a handy outline guide for all you might want to do. Be aware of the time demands of the parks and make sure you build in a quiet day or 2 by the pool or at 1 of the smaller attractions. With SO much on offer, it just isn't possible to 'do it all', so try to ensure you get full value from your choices. Also, don't underestimate the vast scale involved. Everything is well spread out and it takes time even to get from park to park. But do stop to admire the imagination and clever detail of what's on offer as it is all world class.

Orlando

In tourist terms, the name 'Orlando' has grown to encompass much of Central Florida, an area almost twice the size of Yorkshire. Yes, that big. The city itself is north of most of the parks and many people won't even see it as they charge from park to park, which is a shame as it is a bright and happening place.

When Walt Disney's dream of a

Florida

0 ——————— 50 miles

N

JACKSONVILLE

A t l a n t i c

O c e a n

St Augustine

Ormond Beach
Daytona Beach
New Smyrna Beach

Silver Springs
Ocala

Mount Dora
Sanford
Titusville

Homosassa Springs

Cape Canaveral
Kennedy Space Center

ORLANDO
Walt Disney World
Kissimmee
Cocoa Beach

New Port Richey

Winter Haven
Legoland Florida
Melbourne

Clearwater Beach
Lakeland

TAMPA

Lake Wales
Bok Tower Gardens

St Pete Beach

95

Vero Beach

Gulf of

FLORIDA

Bradenton

FLORIDA TURNPIKE

Mexico

Sarasota

Venice

*Lake
Okeechobee*

Charlotte Harbor

Fort Myers

Captiva

Sanibel

Palm Beach

Delray Beach
Boca Raton

Florida

Fort Lauderdale

How far from Orlando to . . .

	mls - km
Bradenton	130 - 210
Clearwater Beach	110 - 176
Cocoa Beach	40 - 64
Daytona Beach	60 - 97
Fort Lauderdale	205 - 330
Fort Myers	190 - 306
Jacksonville	155 - 250
Kay Largo	294 - 470
Key West	375 - 604
Miami	220 - 354
Naples	230 - 370
Sarasota	140 - 225
Silver Springs	80 - 129
St Augustine	120 - 193
St Pete Beach	105 - 169
Tampa	75 - 120
Venice	160 - 257
Winter Haven	40 - 64

Naples

Marco Island

Everglades

MIAMI

Key Largo

Key West

Florida Keys

© Steve Munns 2011

vast resort opened in 1971 with the *Magic Kingdom* (sadly, he never saw it realised as he died in 1966), it led to a massive tourist expansion in all directions. New attractions pop up all the time, varying from terrific to tacky, and both coasts also vie for attention.

There are 7 counties that make up Central Florida: **Orange County**, home to the city of Orlando, with *Walt Disney World* in the south-west corner, part of which is also in **Osceola County**, with Kissimmee its main town; **Seminole County**, home of Orlando Sanford International Airport, north-east of Orange County; **Lake County** to the north and west, with Mount Dora its principal town; **Polk County** lies to the south-west, home to many vacation villas and the new Legoland Florida; and **Brevard** and **Volusia Counties** to east, home to the Kennedy Space Center and Daytona Beach.

Each year, around 50 million people visit Orlando on holiday, and the area boasts some 115,000 hotel rooms, 26,000 vacation homes, more than 4,000 places to eat and 30 malls. Here's a taste of the main attractions.

Walt Disney World
This is where the 'magic' really starts – and the effect is vividly real. This vast resort actually consists of 4 separate theme parks, 20 speciality hotel resorts, a camping ground, 2 water parks, a sports complex, 4 18-hole golf courses, 4 mini-golf courses and a huge shopping and entertainment district (*Downtown Disney*). It covers 47ml²/122km². The likes of Alton Towers and Thorpe Park would comfortably fit into its car parks! At peak periods, there are estimated to be 200,000 visitors throughout the Resort. The Disney organisation does things with the most style, and there are always new projects on the drawing board. It maintains a high level of customer service, where everyone who works for them is officially a Cast Member, not just staff, and they take that ethic to heart.

Magic Kingdom: This is the essential Disney, including the fantasy of its wonderful films, the adventures of the Wild West and Africa, the excitement of thrill rides like Space Mountain (an indoor roller-coaster), the 3-D film fun of Mickey's PhilharMagic and splendid daily parades and fireworks.

Epcot: Disney's 2-part park, with the technology-inspired Future World, plus a potted journey around the globe in World Showcase. Though more educational than adventurous, it has some memorable rides, including Test Track and the superb Soarin', along with excellent dining options.

Disney's Hollywood Studios: Here you can ride the movies in style, meeting Star Wars™, the Muppets and Indiana Jones; drop into the fearsome Tower of Terror or the high-speed Rock 'n' Roller Coaster Starring Aerosmith; and learn the tricks of the trade at the epic Lights, Motors, Action!™ Extreme Stunt Show, try the Toy Story Mania ride and the American Idol Experience.

Disney's Animal Kingdom: This delivers another contrasting option, with realistic animal habitats, including a 100acre/40.5ha safari savannah, captivating shows and terrific rides, like the grand Expedition Everest.

Disney's Typhoon Lagoon Water Park: Bring your cozzie and spend a lazy day splashing down waterslides and learning to surf in the world's biggest man-made lagoon.

Disney's Blizzard Beach Water Park: The big brother of all the water parks, this has a massive spread of rides in a 'snowy' environment.

Downtown Disney: This incorporates a near mile-long spread of themed restaurants, bars, unique shops, a cinema multiplex, the DisneyQuest arcade of interactive games, House of Blues music venue and world-famous Cirque du Soleil® company.

Wedding Pavilion: Walt Disney World even boasts a fairytale venue overlooking Bay Lake for picture-perfect marriage ceremonies.

ESPN Wide World of Sports: This is a huge sporting venue to both play and watch top events.

The other parks

If you think Orlando is only about Disney, prepare to be amazed.

Universal Orlando: The other big resort development, this has 2 theme parks, an entertainment district and 3 speciality hotels. The parks are *Universal Studios*, where you Ride The Movies as you encounter The Simpsons, Jaws, the Shrek 4-D show, the Rip Ride Rockit roller-coaster and Revenge of the Mummy ride, plus Woody Woodpecker's KidZone and amazing Terminator 2: 3-D show; and *Islands of Adventure*, featuring the new Wizarding World of Harry Potter, with a superb blend of thrill rides, family attractions, shows, eye-catching design and high-tech features such as the Amazing Adventures of Spider-Man and Harry Potter and the Forbidden Journey.

Wet 'n Wild: On International Drive, this water park is Universal owned and offers plenty of fun rides and slides.

SeaWorld: This is THE place for creatures of the deep, with killer whales the main attraction, a bright, refreshing atmosphere, the amazing Blue Horizons and One Ocean shows and a serious ecological approach, thrill rides like the Manta 'flying' coaster and huge Kraken, plus an area of rides and activities just for kids.

Discovery Cove: Its exclusive neighbour offers the chance to swim with dolphins, among other things.

Aquatica: A fab water park that provides even more fun and animal encounters in a colourful South Seas environment.

BRITTIP
Be realistic about the tickets you need. You simply won't get full use out of, say, a 14-day Disney ticket and the Orlando FlexTicket Plus in a 2-week holiday.

Busch Gardens: In nearby Tampa, the sister park to SeaWorld offers creatures of the land, with a good mix of rides and shows. Highlights are the new Cheetah Hunt coaster, SheiKra 'dive-coaster', Myombe Reserve (a close-up look at endangered African gorillas), the Edge of Africa 'safari' experience and Jungala, another area of rides and animal exhibits. A family treat, plus a must for coaster fans.

Other key attractions

These include the **Kennedy Space Center**, the dramatically upgraded home of space exploration, with the Shuttle Launch Experience; the surprisingly fun and humorous **Gatorland**; **Legoland Florida**, brand new in 2011 and great for the 2–12 age group; **Silver Springs**, a look at Florida nature via various boat journeys on the crystal-clear Silver River; **Boggy Creek Airboats**, a real close-up with local nature in Kissimmee; and **Fantasy of Flight**, an aviation museum experience including the world's largest private collection of vintage aircraft. Plus there is great **mini-golf** almost everywhere and a variety of smaller-scale attractions along International Drive.

BRITTIP
Buy your theme park tickets in advance, NOT at the park gates. You will save time AND money, as most outlets offer an advance purchase discount.

Disney tickets

This is where things start to get complicated and it's important to work out what tickets you need. Most people buy 1 of 4 multi-day passes specifically for the UK market that allow visits to more than 1 park a day. They are great value for a 2 or 3-week visit and provide maximum flexibility. But they aren't cheap and, if you want to visit only 2 or 3 of the Disney parks, you have to buy a Magic Your Way ticket in Orlando. Be aware you can't walk between the parks (they can be miles apart) and trying to do more than 1 a day is hard work, especially in summer.

Disney's ticket system is called *Magic Your Way* and is horribly complicated (although there is a simplified choice, for UK visitors; see below). Multi-day tickets offer savings against 1-day tickets but unused days expire after 14 days of first use unless you buy an upgrade.

Magic Your Way: If you just turn up at the ticket booths (or buy in advance from a US broker), you must choose:

- The number of days you want (up to 10).
- If you want *Park Hopping* (the ability to move between parks on the same day) for $55/ticket.
- If you want the *Water Park Fun & More Option* (1–10 visits to the water parks, *DisneyQuest* and *ESPN Wide World of Sports*™) for $55/ticket. Disney also offers 1 free round at 9-hole Oak Trail golf course (book in advance on 407 939 4653); club hire NOT included.
- If you want the *Non-expiration Option* (at $25–225, depending on the number of days of ticket). This can be added *after* the initial purchase (but *before* the ticket's 14-day expiration). You pay based on the original length of the ticket, so, if you buy a 7-day ticket and decide after 4 days you won't use the rest of it on that visit, you can add non-expiration for $160 and save the remaining 3 days for the future.

Per-day ticket savings increase with the more days you buy: 1 day = $85 plus tax; 10 days = $291 plus tax, or $29.10/day.

BRITTIP
Use the **Guest Services** at Downtown Disney to save time and queuing if you need to buy Disney tickets in Orlando or exchange vouchers for tickets.

UK tickets: Pre-buy in the UK and there are only 4 tickets to consider (2 only in Britain). They are the 5 and 7-day Premium Ticket, and the 14 and 21-day Ultimate Ticket (see chart p11).

Other tickets

When it comes to Universal Orlando, Wet 'n Wild, SeaWorld, Busch Gardens and Aquatica, the choice can be equally complicated. Do check periodic special offers (see Orlando Ticket Deals, p10).

- The **Orlando FlexTicket** provides 14 consecutive days to both Universal parks, Wet 'n Wild, SeaWorld and Aquatica; add Busch Gardens with the **FlexTicket Plus**.
- For Universal alone, select from 1, 2, 3, 4 or 7-day Tickets either for **One Park** per day or park-to-park access to **Both Parks** each day.
- Look out in the UK for Universal's **2 and 3-Park Bonus Ticket** that offers 14 days at Universal Studios and Islands of Adventure or those 2 plus Wet 'n Wild.
- SeaWorld and Busch Gardens have **2 and 3-Park Tickets**, combining SeaWorld and Busch Gardens, or SeaWorld and Aquatica, or all 3, for a full 14 days.
- A day at **Discovery Cove** includes a **14-Day Pass** for SeaWorld, Busch Gardens or Aquatica; the **Discovery Cove Ultimate Ticket** includes SeaWorld, Busch AND Aquatica for 14 days for an additional $50–70.
- For Universal's CityWalk, there is also a **Party Pass** ($11.99 plus tax) or a **Party Pass with Movie** ($15 plus tax), as the centre has a 20-screen cinema.
- Many UK ticket brokers now offer a **14-Day Combo Pass** for Disney & Universal, Disney & SeaWorld parks or Universal & SeaWorld parks, plus a **Freedom Ticket**, or similar name, bundling all 8 parks (plus the water parks) together. This does NOT provide a single ticket but rather a bundle of 2 or 3 tickets.
- Another choice is the **Go Orlando Card**, which offers 1, 2, 3, 5 or 7 days of visits in the space of 14 days to more than 50 Florida attractions and activities, including Kennedy Space Center, Gatorland, WonderWorks, airboat rides, mini-golf, dinner shows and more ($74.99–229.99 adults, $62.99–184.99 3–12s). You'd have to work

hard to get full value for the 7-day card, but the 3 or 5-day ones are a good catch-all for some of the smaller attractions. It also comes with a handy guidebook to the attractions. See **www.goorlandocard. com**.

- By contrast, the new **Eat and Play Card** is a *discount* card for groups of up to 4, valid for 90 days from first use. Save 10–20% off 50-plus restaurants, from McDonald's, Denny's, Pizza Hut and TGI Friday's to upmarket choices like McCormick & Schmick, Crave and Pacino's, all in the main tourist areas; 10–30% on attractions like golf, mini-golf, Gatorland, Ripley's Believe It Or Not and more; and 10–15% off several shops like Macy's and Reebok Outlet Stores, plus dinner shows Arabian Nights and Outta Control Magic Show and even car hire with Avis or Budget. It costs a bargain $25 and covers the entire bill for up to 4 people each time, so there are significant savings possible. Buy it from **www. eatandplaycard.com** (or call 001 613 680 7109) or select ticket brokers and tour operators.

With annual price hikes, try to buy your tickets as soon as you can, being aware that some discounted tickets must be used for the first time in the year of purchase (e.g. 'first use by 31 Dec 2012'). Shop around, as many outlets have periodic sales and special offers, but use a reputable agent and use your credit card for added security. The following companies all come well recommended.

Attraction Tickets Direct: Britain's top direct-sell Florida ticket broker, with a sharp bookings team, has no credit card fees, free delivery in 7 days and a promise to match any other UK brochure price, plus a huge range of dinner shows, excursions, sports, theme park backstage tours and periodic special offers, as well as a keen online Florida Forum and info centre to which we also contribute (0800 975 0002, **www.attraction-tickets-direct.co.uk**).

Ocean Florida: This independent Florida holiday specialist also offers a well-priced ticket service, featuring all the theme parks, plus Kennedy Space Center and Miami Seaquarium (020 7939 7775, **www.ocean-florida.co.uk**).

Orlando Attractions: A UK-owned ticket service based in Orlando, it will happily post tickets to the UK and offers 3 and 4-day Disney tickets not usually available in Britain plus some good combo tickets. It is all fully ABTA-bonded. Shipping is free and price includes tax and no credit card fees (0800 294 9458, **www. orlandoattractions.com/tickets**).

Orlando Ticket Deals: A keenly priced and extremely helpful broker that also issues real tickets (not vouchers), has a next-day delivery service and offers a significant Price Promise for all its attractions, including all the parks, dinner shows and many excursions (0845 678 1682, **www.orlando-ticket-deals.co.uk**).

There are others, including the main tour operators (p20), while you can also visit the Official Visitor Center on International Drive (**www.visitorlando. com**) but beware of the lure of 'free' tickets in Orlando as these are usually timeshare scams. And NEVER buy resale tickets from a booth in Orlando – they are often unusable. Stick with one of the main brokers, who offer good products, service and local knowledge. And don't forget to plan with our sample Busy Day Guide (p346). You'll be exhausted if you try to do all the parks in one go!

BRITTIP

For all your theme park tickets, be sure to check out Brit Guide partner Orlando Ticket Deals first, as it features an exclusive money-saving offer for our readers (see inside back cover).

Another website to look for is the new **www.moreorlandocoupons.com**, a UK-orientated coupon option that offers a full book of money-off vouchers and various downloadable choices, including an iPhone app that provides an e-coupon discount for a variety of restaurants, attractions and shops.

Choosing a ticket

Ticket type	Park	Allowance
1-Day Ticket	Any Disney park, Universal Orlando parks, SeaWorld or Busch Gardens	Access to 1 park ONLY for 1 day; not available in advance
5-Day Premium Ticket	*Magic Kingdom Park, Epcot, Disney's Hollywood Studios, Disney's Animal Kingdom*	Access for 5 days, with multiple parks on same day; plus 5 visits to water parks, *ESPN Wide World of Sports*™ and *DisneyQuest*; and 1 round of at 9-hole Oak Trail golf course (clubs not included); valid for 14 days after first use; non-expiration option available
7-Day Premium Ticket	*Magic Kingdom Park, Epcot, Disney's Hollywood Studios, Disney's Animal Kingdom*	Access for 7 days, with multiple parks on same day; plus 7 visits to water parks, *ESPN Wide World of Sports*™ and *DisneyQuest*; and 1 round of at 9-hole Oak Trail golf course (clubs not included); valid for 14 days after first use; non-expiration option available
14-Day Ultimate Ticket	All Disney parks	Unlimited access to all Disney attractions, including water parks, *DisneyQuest*, *ESPN Wide World of Sports*™ and 9-hole Oak Trail golf course (clubs not included) for 14 days after first use; NO non-expiration option; available only in advance in the UK
21-Day Ultimate Ticket	All Disney parks	Unlimited access to all Disney attractions, including water parks, *DisneyQuest*, *ESPN Wide World of Sports*™ and 9-hole Oak Trail golf course (clubs not included) for 21 days after first use; NO non-expiration option; available only in advance in the UK
Annual Pass	*Magic Kingdom Park, Epcot, Disney's Hollywood Studios, Disney's Animal Kingdom;* plus discounts for shops, dining and tours	Unlimited admission and *free parking* for 365 days after purchase date. If ordered online, you get a voucher that must be activated at a park; the 365 days start on the first day you activate the pass
Premium Annual Pass	All Disney parks; plus numerous discounts for shops, dining and tours	Unlimited admission and *free parking* for 365 days after purchase date; plus discounts on sports and recreation
1, 2, 3, 4-Day 1-Park Ticket	Universal Studios, Islands of Adventure	Access to 1 of the Universal parks each day for 1–4 days, plus CityWalk on 2 days or more; valid for 14 days from first use
1, 2, 3, 4 or 7-Day 2-Park Ticket	Universal Studios, Islands of Adventure	Access to 1 of the Universal parks each day for 1–7 days, plus CityWalk on 2 days or more; valid for 14 days from first use
2-Park Bonus Ticket	Universal Studios, Islands of Adventure and CityWalk	14 consecutive days' access to both Universal parks, plus CityWalk clubs
3-Park Bonus Ticket	Universal Studios, Islands of Adventure, Wet 'n Wild and CityWalk	14 consecutive days' access to both Universal parks and Wet 'n Wild water park, plus CityWalk clubs
Orlando FlexTicket	Universal Studios, Islands of Adventure, SeaWorld, Wet 'n Wild, Aquatica	Access to all 5 parks, with multiple parks on same day, for 14 days from first use, plus CityWalk clubs
Orlando FlexTicket Plus	Universal Studios, Islands of Adventure, SeaWorld, Wet 'n Wild, Aquatica, Busch Gardens	Access to all 6 parks, with multiple parks on same day, for 14 days from first use, plus CityWalk clubs
2-Park Ticket	SeaWorld and Busch Gardens	14 consecutive days' access to both parks
2-Park Ticket	SeaWorld and Aquatica	14 consecutive days' access to both parks
3-Park Ticket	SeaWorld, Busch Gardens and Aquatica	14 consecutive days' access to all 3 parks

The climate

Florida's weather varies from bright but cool with the odd drizzly spell in winter (Nov–Feb), to furiously hot and humid punctuated by torrential tropical downpours in summer (May–Aug) . The most pleasant option is to go between the two extremes, in spring or autumn. You will also avoid the worst of the crowds in September and October. However, as most families are governed by school holidays, Easter and July–August remain the most popular months for British visitors, so we have plenty of advice on how to stay ahead of the high-season crush. If you do need to go in summer, opt for late August as some US schools have resumed by then and the crowds drop off somewhat.

BRITTIP

The tiring humidity levels – up to 100% – and fierce daily rainstorms in summer take a lot of visitors by surprise, so carry a lightweight rainproof jacket or buy a cheap plastic poncho locally.

The mood

Orlando is big, brash and fun, but above all it's American and that means everything is well organised, but with some cultural differences such as tipping (see below). It's clean, well maintained and eager to please: Floridians generally are an affable bunch, but they take affability to new heights in the theme parks, where staff are almost painfully keen to make sure you 'have a nice day'.

Tipping

A custom close to every American's heart, with the exception of fast-food restaurant servers, just about everyone who serves in hotels, bars, restaurants, buses, taxis, airports and public amenities will expect a tip; not least because all service industry workers are taxed on the basis of receiving 15% in tips, whether they're given or not.

- Bars, restaurants and taxis: 15%
- Porters: $1/bag
- Chambermaids: $1/day per adult.

BRITTIP

Tipping guide

Bill	Suggested tip
$15	$2.25
$20	$3.00
$25	$3.75
$30	$4.50
$40	$6.00
$50	$7.50

ESTA and immigration

Anyone flying to the USA on the Visa Waiver Programme MUST register online via the Electronic System for Travel Authorization (ESTA) no later than 3 days before departure. For all flights to the USA, this has now replaced the old green Visa Waiver form (I-94W).

ESTA: ESTA is a pre-authorisation process prior to arriving at US immigration. The fee is $10 per person (plus admin and credit card fees, taking the final cost to around $15) and is valid for any visits in a 2-year span (so you do NOT pay the $10 fee again in that time).

Apply at **https://esta.cbp.dhs.gov** and fill in your basic immigration info – passport, address in the USA, flight details, email address and a few security questions. Have your holiday address details available both for the ESTA and, later, for your flight check-in. Ask your tour operator if you don't have a specific address (e.g. for a villa allocated on arrival) as it will have a formula for this. Your application should generate an immediate response of 'Authorization Approved' or 'Pending'. If the response 'Travel Not Authorized' is generated, the applicant is unable to travel under the Visa Waiver Programme and must apply for a visa in advance. Remember to record or print your Application Number during the process so you can amend it for future visits within 2 years.

The ESTA speeds up the immigration process and also does away with much of the old form-filling. An ESTA must be completed for every member of your group or family travelling under the Visa Waiver Programme. Those who have a US visa because they are not eligible to travel under the Visa Waiver Programme (i.e. because of a criminal record – p15) still need to fill in a white I-94 form en route (fill in the front only) but they do NOT pay the $10 entry fee. However, anyone with a US visa for work purposes and who is travelling to America for a holiday, WILL need to fill in an ESTA and pay the fee.

BRITTIP
Beware unofficial websites that offer to fill in the ESTA form for you – for a fee. Stick with the official US government website and just pay the $10/person fee (or 'Travel Promotion Act fee').

Customs: You still need to complete a white customs form en route (it'll be given to you on the plane or at check-in and it's better to complete it in advance even though it is available on arrival). Only one customs form needs to be filled out per family, with some of the same basic info but also the value of any goods that will stay in the USA (put $0 unless you are arriving with gifts for friends). Hand the document(s) with your passports to the immigration official who checks you through and takes a fingerprint scan and photo. The customs form will be handed back to you to present to another official when you exit the baggage hall.

BRITTIP
If you need to fill in the white I-94 immigration form for visa holders, do so carefully in block capitals. Mistakes are often sent to the back of the queue. Please be courteous to immigration officials – they do a difficult job in demanding circumstances, and jokes about terrorism are NOT appreciated.

Visa requirements
Holiday visitors to America do not need a visa providing they hold a valid machine-readable passport (MRP) showing they are a British citizen. Any passport issued from 26 October 2005 must include a digital

photograph (not glued or laminated). All passports issued from 26 October 2006 must include the new biometric data. Each family member must have their own passport that does not expire for 90 days from the time of entry. However, British subjects, those without an MRP or those who fail to meet the photo/biometric data criteria DO need a visa ($131), and should apply at least 2 months in advance to the US Embassy.

BRITTIP
US immigration requires ALL visitors aged 14–79 to give fingerprint and photo ID on arrival. It is a simple process, though – first, left index finger then right index finger on the glass panel, then stand still for the camera. Some US gateways require a full 10-finger scan.

Some travellers may NOT be eligible under the Visa Waiver Programme and will have to apply for a special restricted visa or they may be refused entry. This applies to those who have been arrested in the past (even if it did not result in a conviction), have a criminal record (the Rehabilitation of Offenders Act does not apply to US visa law), have a serious communicable illness (and the US includes AIDS sufferers in this category), or have previously been refused admission into, been deported from, or have overstayed in the US on the Visa Waiver Programme. Minor traffic offences do not count.

Mad Tea Party at the Magic Kingdom

© Disney

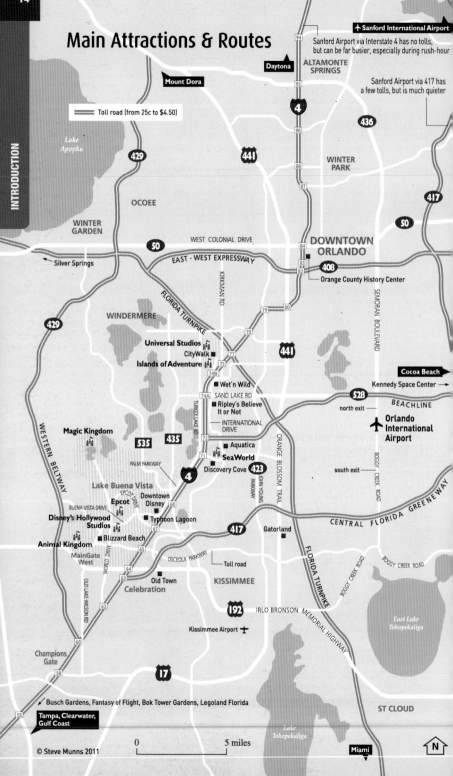

Main Attractions & Routes

✈ Sanford International Airport
Sanford Airport via Interstate 4 has no tolls, but can be far busier, especially during rush-hour

Sanford Airport via 417 has a few tolls, but is much quieter

Daytona

Mount Dora

ALTAMONTE SPRINGS

⬜ Toll road (from 25c to $4.50)

Lake Apopka

94

92

4

90

436

441

88

87

WINTER PARK

417

OCOEE

429

50

WINTER GARDEN

WEST COLONIAL DRIVE

50

84

DOWNTOWN ORLANDO

← Silver Springs

EAST - WEST EXPRESSWAY

83

82

87

408

Orange County History Center

FLORIDA TURNPIKE

KIRKMAN RD

79

80

78

441

WINDERMERE

429

Universal Studios
CityWalk
Islands of Adventure

77

75

74B

SEMORAN BOULEVARD

Cocoa Beach

Kennedy Space Center →

74A

SAND LAKE RD

Wet 'n Wild

Ripley's Believe It or Not

INTERNATIONAL DRIVE

528

BEACHLINE

north exit

Orlando International Airport

Magic Kingdom

535

435

72

71

Aquatica

SeaWorld

Discovery Cove

423

ORANGE BLOSSOM TRAIL

JOHN YOUNG PARKWAY

south exit

BOGGY CREEK ROAD

WESTERN BELTWAY

4

PALM PARKWAY

Lake Buena Vista

EPCOT DRIVE

Epcot

Downtown Disney

68

Typhoon Lagoon

CENTRAL FLORIDA GREENEWAY

BUENA VISTA DRIVE

Disney's Hollywood Studios

67

Animal Kingdom

Blizzard Beach

417

Gatorland

FLORIDA TURNPIKE

BOGGY CREEK ROAD

BOGGY CREEK ROAD

MainGate West

65

OSCEOLA PARKWAY

Toll road

64

OLD LAKE WILSON RD

63

Old Town

KISSIMMEE

East Lake Tohopekaliga

Celebration

62

192

IRLO BRONSON MEMORIAL HIGHWAY

Kissimmee Airport ✈

60

Champions Gate

58

17

↙ Busch Gardens, Fantasy of Flight, Bok Tower Gardens, Legoland Florida

ST CLOUD

53

◀ Tampa, Clearwater, Gulf Coast

Lake Tohopekaliga

© Steve Munns 2011

0   5 miles

Miami ▼

N

Simon and Susan say...

While Orlando remains a world-class destination, it is not getting any cheaper and there are increasingly little 'extra' charges that can mount up quickly if you're not aware of them. Some can be avoided with pre-planning – like taking a bottle of water with you and refilling as you go – but others need to be budgeted for.

Parking: Parking fees have soared – just $8 in 2006, but $14 in 2011 – and are hard to avoid. But you pay only once per day at all Disney parks so try NOT to visit Disney and Universal or SeaWorld on the same day.

Sun loungers and umbrellas: When you consider Disney never charged for these before 2010, to now put a $40 fee on 2 loungers, a table and umbrella and 2 towels at 'premium' spots around Typhoon Lagoon and Blizzard Beach seems unfair. You should still find a decent spot if you arrive early enough, but late-comers now risk not finding anywhere to base themselves.

Pushchairs: The price for pushchair hire is another example of over-pricing. Bring your own or even buy one in Orlando.

Peak price hikes: Peak-period price increases at some of the most sought-after restaurants (like Cinderella's Royal Table and Chef Mickey's) is another awful trick to play on your customers, especially if they can't visit outside those times. Better to have your main meals outside those parks where it can be MUCH cheaper to feed the family, or bring a picnic to the water parks.

Huge portions: Meal portions are far too large in many places. Split a main course or order a child's option. Most servers are happy to do this. Try to have your main meal at lunchtime rather than in the evening – dinner menus are often several dollars more expensive for the same things.

Souvenirs: Save big bucks by doing much of your shopping at the discount outlet shops rather than the Disney and Universal parks.

Otherwise, just go and have fun – it's all here waiting for you!

Contacts:

- England, Scotland and Wales: Visa Office, US Embassy, 24 Grosvenor Square, London W1A 2LQ (020 7499 9000).
- Northern Ireland: US Consulate General, Danesfort House, 223 Stranmillis Road, Belfast BT9 5GR (028 9038 6100).
- More detailed advice: 09042 450 100 (£1.23 per minute; 8am–9pm Mon–Fri, 9am–4pm Sat), **www.london.usembassy.gov**.

Travel information

Luggage is liable to random searches in the US and you are advised NOT to lock your suitcases at check-in for the flight home as TSA officials have the authority to break into them. Using zip-lock seals that can easily be snipped open is permissible and some airlines provide them free, while you can also buy TSA-approved reusable locks at some travel shops. Leave any gifts unwrapped in case screening requires them to be opened; don't put film in checked bags as screening equipment can damage it; and put scissors and other sharp items in checked bags, never in your hand luggage.

BRITTIP

Cabin baggage restrictions often change, so check with your airline in advance for up-to-date info.

Orlando Balloon Rides

What's new?

The biggest new feature for 2012 is right here in the *Brit Guide*! The **Brit Bonus** is a great way to help readers save a few extra dollars while they are dining out or playing. Here's how it works: throughout the book, as well as our trademark Brit Tips, you will now come across the Brit Bonus box that indicates a saving at various hotels, restaurants or attractions. Each one is different and indicates if it is a discount, 2-for-1, a free 'extra' or some other incentive for our readers. Each one is somewhere we're happy to recommend, and now there is an additional reason to visit. All you need to do is show your copy of the *Brit Guide* when you order (or use the special discount code included) – like this:

> **BRITBONUS**
>
> Receive an $8 discount on the regular Boat Tour price of $28 with Island Boat Tours in Cocoa beach by producing your copy of the *Brit Guide*. Remember to book in advance on 321 454 7414.

There are also plenty of new features throughout Orlando itself.

Magic Kingdom: The House of Mouse will unveil the biggest *Magic Kingdom* expansion since the park's opening in 1971 when the all-new *Fantasyland* makes its debut in late 2012. This 3-year project has used the old Mickey's Toontown Fair area to produce a much larger and more lavishly themed land, incorporating new rides, character meet-and-greets, shops and restaurants. Divided into 5 sections, it will offer an undersea adventure ride with The Little Mermaid; a grand Castle and Village for Beauty and the Beast, with shops and dramatic dining; Storybook Circus, a revitalisation of the Dumbo ride and kiddie-coaster The Great Goofini; the Seven Dwarfs Mine Train; and Princess Fairytale Hall (replacing the former Snow White ride).

Hyperion Wharf: Elsewhere in *Walt Disney World*, there is the redevelopment of the Pleasure Island area at *Downtown Disney* into a new entertainment-and-dining district called Hyperion Wharf. This should see things opening at different times

House of Blues at Downtown Disney West Side

© Disney

The Dragon coaster at the new LEGOLAND Florida

in 2012, including the new open-air Amphitheatre that will offer live music and other events, including a nightly light show (although, to be honest, the announced plans suggest it will be fairly small-scale and hardly a thrilling replacement for the many clubs and imaginative style of Pleasure Island).

Disney's Art of Animation Resort: By contrast, this will add almost 2,000 rooms themed in 4 areas around the films *The Little Mermaid, The Lion King, Cars* and *Finding Nemo*. Three-quarters of the resort will be devoted to family suites, sleeping up to 6, and there will be 4 courtyards featuring interactive icons and sculptures, as well as a main pool, 2 quiet pools, a food court and arcade. It is due to open by summer 2012.

Universal Orlando: Get ready for a new interactive, 3-D simulator experience in summer 2012 as Universal Studios replaces its Jimmy Neutron ride with an experience based on the hit 2010 film *Despicable Me*. With state-of-the-art projection systems, it promises to be a wild plunge into the chaotic world of Gru and his madcap minions.

Busch Gardens: Fresh from the debut of its amazing Cheetah Hunt coaster,

the Tampa park will offer a dramatic new ice show in 2012, along with a unique Animal Care and Nutrition Center open to live viewing.

LEGOLAND Florida: The latest park from the worldwide Legoland family was due to open on October 15th, 2011, giving Central Florida another major attraction. On the site of the former Cypress Gardens park in Winter Haven, 45mins south of Orlando, it features a great mix of 50 rides and other attractions purpose-designed for the 2–12 age group, as well as offering the heart of the original gardens and the trademark water-ski shows. In late 2012, they also hope to re-open the mini water park that was part of Cypress Gardens.

Fun Spot: The go-karts-and-more amusement park on International Drive has purchased the adjacent 10 acres/4ha of land and will begin tripling the size of the park in 2012.

Plan your visit

The next few chapters will tell you all you need to know to plan the ideal holiday. Make a rough itinerary and then fine tune it with this book. You can also take advantage of our unique Itinerary Planner Service (p45). Now read on and enjoy…

2 Planning and Practicalities

or How to *Almost* Do It All and Live to Tell the Tale

Good planning is the key to your Orlando holiday. This is not a place where you can 'make it up as you go along', and frustration and exhaustion lie in wait for all those without a sound plan of campaign.

This huge and demanding place can pull you in a dozen directions at once, with a dazzling array of options for practically *everything*. Nowhere else in the world can be so complex to navigate, so it's vital to do your 'homework' in advance. Start with WHEN you want to go; WHERE you'd like to stay; WHAT sort of holiday you want; WHO to book with; and finally HOW MUCH to try to do.

When to go

To avoid the worst of the crowds, the best times to go are Oct to Dec (but not Thanksgiving week in Nov or 20 Dec to New Year); early Jan to mid-Mar (avoiding President's Day in Feb); and the week after Easter to the end of May.

Busiest times: Orlando is seldom quiet but is busiest at:

- Christmas/New Year period (about 20 Dec–2 Jan).
- Mid-Mar to week after Easter.
- From Memorial Day (the last Monday in May, the official start of the summer season) to mid-Aug, notably week inc. 4 July.
- Labor Day weekend at the start of Sept, the last holiday of summer.

The parks can close to new arrivals by mid-morning at these times – especially at Christmas.

BRITTIP
Thanksgiving is the 4th Thurs in Nov; George Washington's birthday, or President's Day, is the 3rd Mon in Feb, and both make for above-average long-weekend crowds.

Best times: The best combination of good weather and smaller crowds is in Apr (after Easter) and Oct. Rain isn't a big factor (although outdoor rides and the water parks will close if lightning threatens), but the crowds will noticeably thin out when it does rain and you can take advantage by bringing waterproofs or buying a cheap plastic poncho (all the parks sell them, but they are cheaper from local supermarkets). In the colder months, take a few warm layers for early morning queues. Then, when it heats up, leave them in the park lockers. When it gets hot, take advantage of the air-conditioned attractions (and drink LOTS of water). The humidity alone will knock you sideways in summer and it's vital to re-hydrate at regular intervals.

Where to stay

This is equally important and, again, there's a huge choice. As a rough guide, 4 main areas make up the great Orlando tourist conglomeration.

Walt Disney World: Some of the most

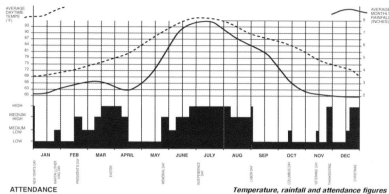

AVERAGE DAYTIME TEMPS (°F) — 93 90 87 84 81 78 75 72 69 66 63 60

AVERAGE MONTHLY RAINFALL (INCHES) — 8 7 6 5 4 3 2

HIGH | MEDIUM HIGH | MEDIUM LOW | LOW

JAN FEB MAR APRIL MAY JUNE JULY AUG SEP OCT NOV DEC

NEW YEAR'S DAY | MARTIN LUTHER KING DAY | PRESIDENTS' DAY | EASTER | MEMORIAL DAY | INDEPENDENCE DAY | LABOR DAY | COLUMBUS DAY | VETERANS' DAY | THANKSGIVING | CHRISTMAS

ATTENDANCE

Temperature, rainfall and attendance figures

sophisticated, convenient and fun places to stay are Disney's own hotels.

The same imagination that created the theme parks also worked on the likes of *Disney's Polynesian Resort* and *Animal Kingdom Lodge*. They all feature free transport, a resort ID card (so you can charge purchases to your room and have them delivered to the hotel), free parking and the BIG bonus of **Extra Magic Hours**. This allows Disney resort guests entry to 1 theme park each day, either an hour before official opening or for 3 hours after closing, so you can do many of the attractions with a fraction of the crowds (though evenings can still be busy). Many resorts also have great kids' clubs and babysitting services. However, with the exception of *Disney's All-Star* and *Pop Century Resorts*, its hotels are among the most expensive, especially to eat in, and are not close to other attractions you may wish to visit. They make a good 1-week base, though.

BRITTIP

Beware holiday homes (and some hotels) that insist they are 'just minutes from Disney World' – which may actually mean 30mins or more from the parks. Try to get the exact address and check it on **www.mapquest.com**.

Lake Buena Vista: On the eastern fringes of *Walt Disney World* and conveniently along Interstate 4 (I-4), this features a good mix of hotels. It is handy for Disney, with most hotels offering free transport to the parks,

plus there is excellent dining and shopping. Again, they do tend to be on the more expensive side.

International Drive: The ribbon development known as I-Drive lies mid-way between Disney and downtown Orlando, running parallel to I-4, and is an excellent central location about 20mins' drive from Disney and close to Universal and SeaWorld. It is a well-developed tourist area in its own right, with great shops, restaurants and attractions like Wet 'n Wild, Ripley's Believe It Or Not, WonderWorks and iFLY Orlando, plus its own handy transportation service, the I-Ride Trolley. The downside is it gets congested in peak times, especially in the evening, and parts of it – notably just north of Sand Lake Road – are looking a bit frowsy. But it is good value and one of the few areas with extensive pavement, making it easy to explore on foot. A sub-district off I-Drive is the Universal area of Kirkman Road and Major Boulevard.

Disney's Caribbean Beach Resort

© Disney

Kissimmee: Budget holiday-makers can be found in their greatest numbers along the tourist sprawl of Highway 192 (the Irlo Bronson Memorial Highway), an almost unbroken 20ml/32km strip of hotels, motels, restaurants and shops. It offers some of the best economy accommodation and is handy for Disney, though further from Universal and SeaWorld. A car is advisable here, although there is extensive pavement, landscaping, bus shelters and benches, so is better for getting around on foot or by bus. **Highway 27** is often referred to as 'Kissimmee' but is actually either in Lake County (to the north) or Polk County (to the south). This is prime holiday home territory, with numerous developments along its 13ml/21km (and growing!) extent.

Split holidays

Florida has so much to offer, many opt to spend a week or so in Orlando and a week somewhere else. The Atlantic coast has some great beaches only an hour to the east; the Florida Everglades are 3–4 hours to the south; and there are more wonderful beaches and pleasant coast roads to the west. There's great shopping almost everywhere, stunning golf courses and opportunities to play or watch tennis, baseball and basketball, go fishing, boating or kayaking. The tour operators all offer a huge variety of packages, plus some popular cruise-and-stay options. If you can afford it, the best option is to have 2 weeks in Orlando then a week relaxing on one of Florida's fabulous

The Dali Museum at St Petersburg

beaches. A 2-week, half-and-half split is popular, but can make for a hectic time in Orlando. Some companies offer a 10/4 Orlando/coast split, which is a better idea for 2 weeks. Fly-drives offer great flexibility, but there is a lot to tempt you and you may find it better to book a 2-centre stay that includes a car and accommodation so you can still travel but avoid too much packing and unpacking (see also Chapter 9).

Travel companies

There is serious competition for your hard-earned money – from the Big Boys, the Specialists and Online Agents – so choose an operator that best fits your needs on cost, flights, style and extras. We highlight the main features here. Always ensure they are ABTA (for travel agents) or ATOL (for flights) bonded.

The Big Boys

British Airways Holidays: A well-established and varied choice, although their website is distinctly clunky (0844 493 0759, **www. britishairways.com/travel/holidays-in-florida**).

- Direct, non-stop scheduled BA flights from Gatwick to Orlando International (9 a week) and Tampa (7).
- Twice daily Heathrow to Miami.
- Flexible holiday length, combination and style.
- Many 'free night' bonuses.
- Multi-centres, fly-drives and villas.
- Pre-bookable tours and excursions.
- Online check-in.

Cosmos Holidays: With a long history in Florida, Cosmos focuses on the key resort areas in Orlando and Gulf Coast (0871 423 8401, **www.cosmos-holidays.co.uk**).

- Cosmos use charter airline Monarch to Orlando Sanford May–Oct only from Gatwick, Manchester and Glasgow.
- A new winter programme will feature scheduled flights to Orlando International Airport and Tampa with Virgin and BA.

- Excellent range of properties in Clearwater, St Pete Beach, Sarasota, Newport Richey and Naples.
- Full range of hotels (including Disney and Universal), suites and villas.
- Package, fly-drive and flight-only for 7, 14 and 21-nights.
- Well priced for car hire.
- Early booking offers, low deposits and kids' prices from just £149.

First Choice: Reliable, family-friendly option (0871 200 7799, **www.firstchoice. co.uk /holidays/florida-holidays**).

- Thomson Airways flights from Birmingham, Bristol, East Midlands, Gatwick, Glasgow, Manchester and Newcastle to Orlando Sanford (6 days a week).
- Flights feature seat-back entertainment, more leg room, wider seats and meals included.
- Premier upgrades offer 92cm/36in pitch and leather seats, a 9in TV screen (with touchscreen and 42 channels), choice of meals and free Royal Palm Lounge access at Sanford Airport.
- Great range of accommodation, including the highly rated Lake Buena Vista Resort Village, the excellent value of CocoKey Hotel & Water Resort on I-Drive, Premier homes and 3 beach hotels on the Gulf Coast.
- Kids under 12 receive a Kids-eat-free card (limited offer).

Thomas Cook: One of the UK's biggest mainstream operators, including the Airtours brand (0844 412 5970, **www.thomascook.com**).

- Thomas Cook Airlines from Gatwick and Manchester from spring to late autumn (plus Belfast and Glasgow in summer) to Orlando Sanford.
- TC Premium upgrades add wider, more comfy leather seats, free bar service and headsets, upgraded menu, dedicated check-in and priority boarding, plus a 30kg luggage allowance instead of 15kg (extra 5kg can be pre-booked for £35).
- Wide range of packages.
- Good range of Disney's Value and Moderate resorts, plus a wide choice on I-Drive and in Kissimmee (including many villas, town homes and resorts).

Thomson: Another one of the reliable mainstream companies (0871 230 0900, **www.thomson.co.uk**).

- Thomson Airways from Birmingham, Bristol, Gatwick, Glasgow, Manchester and Newcastle to Orlando Sanford.
- Good in-flight entertainment and kids' packs. Day-before check-in at Gatwick and Manchester.
- 84cm/33in standard seat pitch (1 of the best) and great seat-back TV in-flight entertainment; options to pre-book seats together.
- Premium upgrade cabin has wider leather seats, improved entertainment choice, priority check-in and disembarkation, free drinks and enhanced meal service.
- Strong emphasis on its Thomson Villas with Pool brand and Disney hotel selection, plus twin-centre I-Drive/beach options in Clearwater, Fort Myers and St Pete's Beach.
- Other great choices include the Platinum-rated Hilton Bonnet Creek Resort and 2 fly-drive options.
- Free Kids-eat-free card for under-12s (limited offer).

Travel City Direct: Popular budget-minded brand under Virgin umbrella (0844 557 6969, **www.travelcitydirect. com**).

- Wide range of competitively priced packages.

Magic Carpets of Aladdin, Magic Kingdom

© Disney

- Virgin Atlantic flights from Gatwick, Manchester and Glasgow to Orlando Sanford, plus regional flights with BA, Delta, US Airways and Continental.
- Fly-drives, single and multi-centre stays (including St Pete Beach, Clearwater, Bradenton, Sarasota).
- Choice of 3, 4 and 5-bed villas with private pool, Disney Resort and Universal Orlando hotels, plus car hire or transfer options and competitive attraction ticket prices.
- All holidays for 14 nights (or more), with flexibility to mix and match from a wide choice of accommodation, including affordably priced favourites.

Virgin Holidays: Britain's leading tour operator to Florida and the official holiday company to Universal Orlando (0844 557 4000, **www.virginholidays.co.uk**).

- Virgin Atlantic non-stop scheduled flights to Orlando (13–15 times a week from Gatwick, 7–11 from Manchester and twice a week from Glasgow, May–Oct) and daily Heathrow–Miami.
- New A330 aircraft with all-new in-flight entertainment.
- Free drinks, kids' packs, meals, games.
- Upgrades to Premium Economy and Upper Class (including the

Virgin's V-Room

All Virgin Holidays passengers have the option of the V-Room private lounge at Gatwick and Manchester, a special hideaway that includes a dedicated kids' play area, video games, big-screen TV, internet access, relaxing adults-only area, free snacks, fruit, soft drinks and coffee, and a fast-track security channel. It costs £20 per adult and £12 per child (2–11), but is free with Platinum Collection bookings.

revolutionary fully flat beds; not on A330s).
- Twilight day-before check-in at Gatwick.
- Largest choice of accommodation, including all Disney resorts.
- Vast variety of combinations, with 150 properties, 2-centre options to Miami, Daytona Beach, Florida Keys and lesser-known resorts such as Vero Beach, Estero Island (Fort Myers) and Naples, plus the Caribbean and a variety of cruises.
- Favourite selection offering extra value, location or other benefits.
- Fly-drives, flying into Orlando and out of Miami, and vice versa.
- Platinum Collection features deluxe resorts such as Reunion in Orlando and Little Palm Island in the Keys.
- Disney soccer camp for kids each summer, training and learning skills

Kidani Village at Disney's Animal Kingdom Lodge

© Disney

Dining Plan options

Most tour operators offer the **Disney Dining Plan** as an optional extra with Disney hotel packages and it can be good value if you spend ALL your time in *Walt Disney World*, where there are few cheap dining outlets. But, because ALL members of the family must be included for the FULL length of your stay, even the Quick Service plan adds around £900 for a family of 4 (with children 3–9) staying for 2 weeks; the main Dining Plan would be £1,260; and the Deluxe Plan a whopping £1,900. It is a LOT of food to contend with, especially when it's hot, and you often need to book the full-service restaurants well in advance. You can certainly eat cheaper elsewhere, so consider if this is a good choice before you book. However, the Dining Plan is occasionally offered as a FREE perk by tour operators at quieter times of the year – a BIG bonus.

See more on Disney Dining Plan on p62.

with various well-known stars.

- Free Downtown Disney check-in service for return flights, 8.15am–1pm on the day of departure.
- Airport transfers, shuttle services, 2-centre transfers for non-drivers.
- Other useful extras: Single parent and single traveller offers, free upgrades to Premium Economy with select accommodations and free Kids-eat-free cards for under-12s at in-resort welcome meetings, free kids' places for early bookers.
- Extra perks to **Wizarding World of Harry Potter**, including early entry, free breakfast in the Three Broomsticks, free parking and a Potter keepsake.
- Early-entry packages to SeaWorld, with free Quick Queue and exclusive 20-min park tour.
- Direct bookings benefit from a unique concierge service to ask questions of Virgin reps in Orlando and tailor-make tours (call 0844 557 1042 after booking or email **orlandorep@virginholidays.com**).
- Platinum accommodation includes free access to Virgin's V-Room lounge at Gatwick Airport.

The specialists

Choose from the following small, specialist companies who all feature individual programmes to Florida:

- **Continental Airlines Vacations** (0844 557 4040, **www.covacations. co.uk**).
- **Funway Holidays** (0844 557 3333, **www.funwayholidays.co.uk**).

- **Jetsave** (0844 415 9880, **www.jetsave. com**).
- **Kuoni** (01306 747002, **www.kuoni. co.uk**).
- **Ocean Florida** (020 7939 7775, **www. ocean-florida.co.uk**).
- **Premier Holidays** (0844 4937 531, **www.premierholidays.co.uk**).
- **USAirtours** (0800 035 0149, **www. usairtours.co.uk**).

Online agents

The recent growth of online travel agents has been huge, and you will find some great deals in this group, for packages, flights or accommodation:

- **eBookers** (020 3320 3320, **www. ebookers.com**).
- **Expedia** (0330 123 1235, **www. expedia.co.uk**).
- **LastMinute** (0871 222 5952, **www. lastminute.com**).
- **Opodo** (0871 277 0090, **www.opodo. co.uk**).

Disney's Old Key West Resort

© Disney

- **Travel Supermarket** (0845 345 5708, **www.travelsupermarket.com**).
- **Trailfinders** (0845 054 6060, **www. trailfinders.com**).
- **Travelbag** (0871 703 4701, **www. travelbag.co.uk**).

For flights only, try:
- **Dial A Flight** (0844 811 4444, **www. dialaflight.com**).
- **Flight Centre** (0844 800 8660, **www. flightcentre.co.uk**).
- **NetFlights** (0871 703 8000, **www. netflights.com**).

Online search engines

The following selection search a number of travel agent sites at the same time:
- **Kelkoo** (http://travel.kelkoo.co.uk).
- **Kayak** (**www.kayak.co.uk**).
- **Travel Jungle** (**www.traveljungle. co.uk**).

For flight price comparison sites, try:
- **Cheap Flights** (**www.cheapflights. co.uk**).
- **Sky Scanner** (**www.skyscanner.net**).
- **NowFly** (**www.nowfly.co.uk**).

Scheduled flights

Apart from the 3 charter airlines (Monarch, Thomson and Thomas Cook), the only *direct* flights to Orlando are with **Virgin Atlantic** (Gatwick, Manchester and Glasgow), **British Airways** (Gatwick) and **Aer Lingus** (Dublin). BA also fly direct to Tampa and Miami and Virgin to Miami but you can often save money on indirect flights. Choose from **American Airlines** (from Heathrow

SheiKra at Busch Gardens

Complete Orlando

The highly rated Attraction Tickets Direct company has a full ATOL-bonded travel operator called Complete Orlando, which is well worth trying for packages, flights, hotels, car hire and travel insurance. It offers a wide range of accommodation (usually with some great deals on Disney hotels in particular), plus handy online videos, and promises no credit card fees or hidden extras. Call 0800 294 8844, **www. completeorlando.co.uk**.

via Boston, Chicago, Dallas, Miami, New York and Raleigh-Durham; Manchester via New York or Chicago; or Dublin via Chicago; **www. americanairlines.co.uk**); *Continental* (Heathrow via Cleveland, New York or Houston; Manchester, Birmingham, Belfast, Dublin, Glasgow or Edinburgh via New York; **www. continental.com**); **Delta/KLM** (Gatwick via Atlanta; Heathrow via Atlanta, Minneapolis, Detroit or New York; or Manchester via New York or Atlanta; **www.klm.com**); **United** (Heathrow via Washington or Chicago; **www. unitedairlines.co.uk**); and **US Airways** (Gatwick via Charlotte; Heathrow, Manchester, Glasgow or Dublin via Philadelphia; **www.usairways.com**). **Icelandair** (from Heathrow, Glasgow and Manchester; 0844 811 1190, **www. icelandair.co.uk**) also offers a scheduled transatlantic route to Orlando Sanford Airport via Reykjavik, Iceland.

The obvious drawback is the extra journey time, and the connecting flight may land you in Orlando late in the evening. However, it does break the journey and places like Detroit and Atlanta often process international passengers quicker than Orlando, meaning less hassle when you arrive in Florida.

What to see when

Once you arrive, the temptation is to head for the nearest theme park, then the next, and so on. Except this is the best way to end up exhausted. Some days at the parks are busier than others, while you'll also need a few rest days. So here's what to do.

Our must-do experiences

- Soarin' and IllumiNations show (*Epcot*)
- Cirque du Soleil® (*Downtown Disney*)
- Harry Potter and the Forbidden Journey, plus the Amazing Adventures of Spider-Man and The Hulk rides (Islands of Adventure)
- Boggy Creek Airboats (*Kissimmee*)
- Expedition Everest and Festival of The Lion King (*Animal Kingdom*)
- Wishes/Nightastic fireworks, Pirates of the Caribbean and Haunted Mansion rides (*Magic Kingdom*)
- Fantasmic! show and Star Tours II ride (*Disney's Hollywood Studios*)
- Shrek 4-D and The Simpsons Ride (*Universal Studios*)
- Shopping!
- One Ocean and Blue Horizons shows (*SeaWorld*)
- Cheetah Hunt and SheiKra coasters (*Busch Gardens*)
- Shuttle Launch Experience (*Kennedy Space Center*)
- A Disney character meal
- A day at a water park

Using the Planner on p345 as an example (or just use the *Brit Guide* Itinerary Planner Service, p45), make a note of the attractions you want to see. The most sensible strategy is to plan around the 8 'must-see' parks. If you have only a week, drop Busch Gardens and focus on Disney, Universal and SeaWorld. Space fans should also include the Kennedy Space Center, but it often bores young children.

- **Magic Kingdom:** 2 days – the biggest hit with children.
- **Epcot:** 2 days – only the most fleet of foot can do it in a day, and then only with low crowds, but there are fewer rides to amuse young 'uns.
- **Animal Kingdom:** 1 day – a little short on appeal for the youngest.
- **Disney's Hollywood Studios:** 1 day – plus the evening Fantasmic! show.
- **SeaWorld:** 1–2 days.
- **Islands of Adventure:** 1–2 days now the Harry Potter area is open.
- **Universal Studios:** 1 day – at least.
- **Busch Gardens:** 1 day – extremely popular with British families, it is 75mins away in Tampa.

Lights! Motors! Action! at Disney's Hollywood Studios

© Disney

The new Legoland Florida park, 45mins away in Winter Haven, is a good day's outing. Look at the detail in Chapters 5–8 before you pick up your pencil.

Smaller attractions

Of the other, smaller scale attractions, the nature park of Silver Springs is a full day out as it also involves a near 2-hour drive to get there but everything else can be fitted around your Big 8 itinerary. The water parks make for a relaxing ½-day, as does the quieter Bok Tower Gardens. Gatorland (requiring at least ½ a day) is a unique look at some of Florida's oldest inhabitants and is a good combination with Boggy Creek Airboats. Aviation fans will find Fantasy of Flight (further down I-4) a real delight for another novel ½-day experience. Then there are the likes of Ripley's Believe It Or Not museum and the WonderWorks house of fun, both offering several hours' entertainment, the thrills of iFLY Orlando (an indoor 'sky-diving' wind tunnel) and the lure of old-fashioned go-karts and other fairground-type rides at Fun Spot, Magical Midway and Old Town. Many stay open after the major theme parks close, too.

Disney also has *DisneyQuest*, an imaginative interactive arcade that guarantees several hours of fun (especially for older children) at *Downtown Disney*, while each main area is also well served with creatively designed mini-golf courses for that spare hour or 2.

Downtown Disney

Evenings

The evening entertainment features a similarly wide choice. By far the best, and worth at least 1 evening each, are *Downtown Disney* and Universal's CityWalk – the latter will keep you busy until the early hours! Dinner shows provide a lot of fun: 2-hour cabarets based on themes such as medieval knights, pirates, Arabian Nights, magic shows and murder mysteries that all include a hearty meal.

Shopping

Shopping in Orlando is world class (see Chapter 12) and your battle plan should include at least a day to visit the spectacular malls and discount centres, like the 2 excellent Orlando Premium Outlets centres, Mall at Millenia and the Florida Mall. They get busy at weekends, but handy if the rain sets in.

What to do when

There are several guidelines for avoiding the worst of the tourist hordes, even in high season.

Avoid busy days: Most Americans arrive at weekends and head for the main theme parks first, so Sun and Mon are often bad times to visit the *Magic Kingdom*, while Tues is usually also busy at *Epcot*. New rides like the reborn Star Tours (*Disney's Hollywood Studios*) also create longer queues, notably at weekends. The *Animal Kingdom* is the hardest to navigate when crowded, while *Epcot* handles the crowds best. *Disney's Blizzard Beach* and *Typhoon Lagoon* water parks hit high tide at weekends, and Thurs and Fri in summer. If *Walt Disney World* is humming early in the week, that makes it a good time to visit SeaWorld, Busch Gardens, Silver Springs or the Kennedy Space Center. Try to avoid Wet 'n Wild and Aquatica at weekends, too.

Disney's Extra Magic Hours: Allowing Disney guests early and late access (see p63) creates bigger crowds, too. So, if you are NOT staying at a Disney hotel, avoid these EMH days. For much of the year, they keep to the following regular weekly pattern: *Magic Kingdom*, Tues and Thurs in peak season, Thurs only off-peak; *Epcot*, Sun in peak, Tues off-peak; *Disney's Hollywood Studios*, Mon and Fri in peak, Sat off-peak; *Animal Kingdom*, Wed and Sat in peak, Mon off-peak. Be aware EMH days can still change from month to month at short notice, and the *Magic Kingdom* can often have multiple successive days at Easter and Christmas.

Universal Orlando: The picture is different here as only the Wizarding World of Harry Potter has daily early opening privileges (for guests at Universal's 3 hotels). This often means heavier crowds at Islands of Adventure early in the week, while both parks get busier at weekends when locals visit.

BRITTIP

If your hotel is not far away, take a mid-afternoon break from the park and return for a siesta or a swim. Your car park ticket is valid all day, and the evening is often the best time to be in the parks.

Arrive early: Getting the most out of your days at the parks is another art form, and there are several options. The opening times seldom vary from 9am (*Magic Kingdom* and *Animal Kingdom* can be 8am at peak times) but arriving early is highly advisable. Apart from being near the head of the queues (and they are SERIOUS queues, or 'lines'), the parks occasionally open early if the crowds build up. So you can be a step ahead by arriving at least 30mins before opening time (or an hour early during peak periods). You will also be better placed to park in the huge car parks and catch the tram to the main gates (anything up to ½ml/800m away).

Prioritise: Once you are in pole position, don't waste time on the shops, scenery and other frippery that will lure the unprepared first-timer. Instead, head straight for some of the main rides and get a few big-time thrills under your belt before the main hordes arrive. You will quickly work out where the most popular attractions are as the majority of early birds will flock to them. Use Chapters 5 and 6 to plan your park strategies.

Pace yourself: Disney's parks, notably the *Magic Kingdom*, stay open late for the main holidays, until midnight at times, and that can be a *l-o-n-g* day for kids. It's vital to pace yourself, especially if you arrive early. There are plenty of options to take time off for a drink or a sit-down somewhere air-conditioned, and these latter are vital in summer.

Meal breaks: Benefit from the American habit of dining en masse at lunchtime (noon–1.30pm) and dinner (5.30–7pm) by planning your own meals outside those times. It pays to take an early lunch (before noon), snack in mid-afternoon and then enjoy a relative drop-off in crowds in late afternoon. But try not to have all your meals in the parks; eating here can be expensive (at least $10/person for a basic meal). A good breakfast before you arrive and a light lunch will save you $$$s!

BRITTIP

The water IS safe to drink in the US but it may not taste great as it's heavily fluoridated. If you buy bottled water, do so at supermarkets, not at the parks, where it is exorbitantly expensive.

Comfort and clothing
You may feel jetlagged for the first day or so after your arrival, but this can be reduced by avoiding alcohol and coffee on the plane and drinking plenty of water.

Children will love the magic of the Mouse

© Disney

Shoes: The most important part of your holiday wardrobe is your footwear – you'll be on your feet a LOT, even at off-peak periods. The smallest park is 'only' 100 acres/40ha, but that is irrelevant to the time spent queuing. This is not the time to break in new sandals or trainers. Comfortable, well-worn shoes or trainers are essential (many rate Croc-type shoes as ideal park footwear).

> **BRITTIP**
> Look after your feet and avoid the onset of blisters by buying some moleskin footpads from a supermarket or 'drug-store' like Walgreens and CVS.

Casual clothes: You need dress only as the climate dictates. T-shirts and shorts are appropriate in all parks and nearly all restaurants will accept casual dress. However, swimwear is not acceptable away from pool areas. If you feel the need for a change of clothes or a sweater for the evening after a long day, use the handy lockers in all the parks (unlimited use all day for a small fee).

> **BRITTIP**
> Don't be tempted to pack a lot of smart or formal clothing – you really won't need it in hot, informal Florida.

Baby services: All the parks are well equipped with pushchairs, or 'strollers', for hire (although it pays to have your own), and baby services are located at regular intervals.

Sunscreen: It is VITAL to use high-factor sun creams at all times, even during the winter when the sun may not feel strong but can still burn. Few things will ruin your holiday like severe sunburn. Orlando has a subtropical climate and you need higher factor creams than in the Mediterranean. Use sun block on sensitive areas like nose and ears, and splash on the after-sun liberally at the end of the day. You'll also need waterproof sun cream for swimming. Skincare products are widely available and usually inexpensive (at the likes of Wal-Mart, Publix and Target). Wear a hat during the day, and avoid alcohol, coffee and fizzy drinks until the evening as they are dehydrating and make you liable to heatstroke. You must increase your fluid intake SIGNIFICANTLY in the summer, but stick to sports drinks, such as Gatorade, and lots of water.

> **BRITTIP**
> One of the best ways to keep cool in the sun is to buy a simple mist spray fan (about $7.99) from a supermarket.

Daniel Radcliffe and James Phelps enjoy riding the Hippogriff at Islands of Adventure

© Universal Orlando Resort

Medical aid

Should you require medical treatment, for sunburn or other first aid, consult your tour operator's info about local hospitals and surgeries. **In the event of a medical or other emergency, dial 911 as you would 999 in Britain.** It cannot be over-stressed, however, you should take out comprehensive travel insurance (p30) for any trip to America, as there is NO National Health Service and any form of medical treatment is expensive. Keep all the receipts and put in a claim on your return home.

BRITTIP
The summer is mosquito time and a spray-on or roll-on insect repellent is highly advisable away from the parks. Brands to look for locally are Cutter, Repel and Off!

Emergency outpatients: These can be found with Centra Care at Florida Hospital Medical Center in 16 central Florida locations and can provide hotel in-room services (407 238 2000) and free transport (407 938 0650; **www.centracare.org**). Open from 8am daily, Centra Care centres are at:

- 12500 S Apopka-Vineland Road near the Crossroads shopping centre and Downtown Disney at Lake Buena Vista (until midnight on weekdays, 8pm Sat and Sun; 407 934 2273);
- 7848 West Irlo Bronson Memorial Highway (192), in Formosa Gardens Village (until 8pm Mon–Fri, 5pm Sat and Sun; 407 397 7032);
- 6001 Vineland Road, near Universal Studios (7am–7pm Mon– Fri, 8am–6pm Sat and Sun; 407 351 6682);
- on Sand Lake Road, between John Young Parkway and Orange Blossom Trail (8am–8pm Mon–Fri, 9am–5pm Sat and Sun; 407 851 6478);
- 4320 West Vine Street, near Medieval Times (until 8pm Mon–Fri, 5pm Sat and Sun; 407 390 1888).
- Dr P Phillips Hospital, 9400 Turkey Lake Road, has an emergency outpatients (407 351 8500).
- East Coast Medical Network (407 648 5252, **http://themedicalconcierge. com**) makes hotel and villa 'house calls' 24 hours a day.

BRITTIP
If you take regular prescription drugs, check the name with your doctor or pharmacist as many have a different name in the US (e.g. adrenaline is known as epinephrine, paracetamol is acetaminophen). Find out and carry both names in case of an emergency.

Chemists: The two largest chemists ('drug stores' in the US) are Walgreens (www.walgreens.com) and CVS (www.cvs.com), and the Walgreens at 12100 S Apopka-Vineland Road (near Downtown Disney), 5935 W Irlo Bronson Memorial Highway (Highway 192 in Kissimmee), 6201, 8050, 8959 and 12650 International Drive (among others) are open 24 hours a day.

BRITTIP
Several Walgreens stores have walk-in Take Care Clinics that can treat patients (18 and over) 7 days a week, which can be quicker than visiting a hospital or other medical centre.

Popeye and Bluto's Bilge Rat Barges at IOA

© Universal Orlando Resort

Top things to do for FREE!

While Orlando has a magnificent array of paid-for attractions, there are still many things you can do that don't cost a cent.

Disney's Boardwalk Resort: Free nightly entertainment includes jugglers, comedians and live music. Time your visit to coincide with the 9pm IllumiNations fireworks extravaganza at nearby *Epcot.*

Fort Christmas Historical Park: 20ml/32km east of Orlando in the town of Christmas is this replica of an 1837 US Army fort from the Seminole Indian Wars, with tours, exhibits, video presentations and restored homes, and special events during some weekends; 8am–8pm summer, 8am–6pm winter (closed Mon and public holidays; **http://nbbd.com/godo/FortChristmas**).

Lake Eola Park: Take a walk on the mild side in downtown Orlando. The kids can play or feed the swans and summer sees live music at the Walt Disney Amphitheater.

Lake Tibet-Butler Preserve: Just 5mins from Disney but light years from the theme park bustle (on local highway 535, Winter Garden-Vineland Road) is this local nature preserve, with quiet trails, lake overlook and interpretive centre. Open 9am–dusk (not public holidays), it is on the Great Florida Birding Trail and is a minor gem of native wildlife).

Lakeridge Winery and Vineyards: Join one of its fun, free wine-tasting tours and you'll know why Lakeridge (in nearby Clermont) has won more than 300 awards. But designate a driver as sample sizes are generous! 10am–5pm Mon–Sat, 11am–5pm Sun (**www.lakeridgewinery.com**).

Morse Museum of American Art: This superb little museum in tranquil Winter Park, dedicated to American paintings, ceramics and representative arts from the 19th and 20th centuries, is free 4–8pm every Fri, Nov–Apr (**www.morsemuseum.org**).

Old Town, Kissimmee: The biggest vintage car parade in the US every Sat, with cars on display from 1pm and the parade at 8.30pm, and an American Classics line-up (classic and 'muscle' cars 1975–87) at 9pm on Fridays (**www.old-town.com**).

Peabody Duck March: Turn up at 11am or 5pm at the Peabody Hotel on International Drive to see its resident mallards get the red carpet treatment as they either arrive or leave their lobby fountain 'home' (**www.peabodyorlando.com**).

Downtown Orlando Skyline Tour: Take in the new Visitor Center on Orange Avenue and ask for 1 of their guided rooftop tours, which lays out the whole city. Better still, groups of 2 or 3 can take a free electric car tour of the whole area. Must call in advance to check availability on 407 246 3789 (**http://downtownorlando.com**).

Downtown Concert Series: 4 times a year, local radio station WMMO stages free open-air concerts in front of City Hall with the likes of Rick Springfield and Tears For Fears. Great day out, with festival atmosphere (**www.wmmo.com/s/dcs/**).

PLUS: Just watching the participants in action at **IFLY Orlando** on International Drive (p231); watch the NASCAR stock cars and IndyCar machines daily at the 1-mile tri-oval of the **Walt Disney World Speedway** (near the *Magic Kingdom*); the **Cornell Fine Arts Museum** at Rollins College in Winter Park (p254); and the many hiking trails of **Ocala National Forest**, north of Orlando (**www.stateparks.com/Ocala.html**).

Travel insurance

Having said you shouldn't travel without insurance, you shouldn't pay more than you need to either. Your travel agent may imply you need to buy its policy, which might be expensive, but you are free to buy elsewhere. Your policy should cover all these options.

- Medical cover of at least £2m.
- Personal liability up to £2m (this won't cover driving abroad; you still need Supplementary Liability Insurance with your car hire firm).

- Cancellation or curtailment cover up to £5,000.
- Personal property cover up to £1,500 (but check on expensive items, as most policies limit single articles to £250).
- Cash and document cover, including your passport and tickets.
- A 24-hour emergency helpline.
- If you want to go horse-riding, check your policy includes dangerous sports cover.

Shop around at reputable dealers such as:

- **American Express** (0800 028 7573, **www.americanexpress.com/uk**);
- **AA** (0800 975 5819, **www.theaa.com/insurance**).
- **Aviva** (0800 051 3606, **www.aviva.co.uk**).
- **Club Direct** (0800 083 2466, **www.clubdirect.com**).
- **Columbus** (0870 033 9988, **www.columbusdirect.com**).
- **Direct Travel** (0845 605 2700, **www.direct-travel.co.uk**).
- **Egg** (0800 519 9931, **http://new.egg.com**).
- **Worldwide Travel Insurance** (01892 833 338, **www.worldwideinsure.com**).
- **Money Supermarket** also compares travel insurers at **www.moneysupermarket.com/travel-insurance** (0845 345 5708).

Florida with children

We are often asked what we think is the right age to take children to Orlando, and there is no set answer. Some toddlers take to it instantly, while some 6 or 7-year-olds are overwhelmed. Very often, the best attractions for young children are the hotel swimming pool or the tram ride to a park's front gates! Some love the Disney characters instantly, while others find them frightening. There is no predicting how they'll react but, at 4½, Simon's oldest boy loved just about every second of his first experience (apart from the fireworks!) and still talks about it. A 3-year-old may not remember much, but will have fun and provide you with great memories, photos and videos. Here

are some top tips for travelling with youngsters.

The flight: Try to look calm (even if you don't feel it) and relaxed. Small children soon pick up on any anxieties and make them worse. Pack a bag with lots of little things for them (comics, sweets, colouring books, small surprise toys, etc.) and keep vital extras like Calpol (in sachets, if possible), a change of clothes, a small first-aid kit (plasters, antiseptic cream, baby wipes), sunglasses, a hat and sunscreen in your hand luggage.

BRITTIP

The handy Kids-eat-free card for Orlando offers a free child's meal (for 11 and under) with every adult meal or entrée purchased. It costs just $19.99/child and features more than 150 local restaurants – from the standard Chick-Fil-A and Dunkin' Donuts to upmarket Timpano Chophouse and Ming Court – with potential savings of $350. It is valid for 90 days from first use. See **www.kidseatfreecard.com** or buy from Attractions Tickets Direct, 0800 975 0002, for £10.

Once you're there: Take things slowly and let your children dictate the pace to a large extent. In hot, humid summer, only the most placid children (and few under-5s, in our

Wild Arctic at SeaWorld

Attractions with warnings for expectant mothers

Animal Kingdom: Dinosaur!, Expedition Everest, Kali River Rapids, Kilimanjaro Safari, Primeval Whirl.

Busch Gardens: Cheetah Hunt, Congo River Rapids, Crazy Camel, Gwazi, Kumba, Montu, Phoenix, Python, Rhino Rally, Sand Serpent, Sandstorm, Scorpion, SheiKra, Stanley Falls Log Flume, Tanganyika Tidal Wave, Ubanga-Banga Bumper Cars.

Epcot: Mission: SPACE, Soarin', Test Track.

Hollywood Studios: Rock 'n Roller Coaster, Star Tours II, Twilight Zone Tower of Terror.

Islands of Adventure: Cat in the Hat, Dragon ChallengeDudley Do-Right's Ripsaw Falls, , Flight of the Hippogriff, Harry Potter and the Forbidden Journey, Incredible Hulk Coaster, Jurassic Park River Adventure, Popeye & Bluto's Bilge Rat Barges, Storm Force Accelatron, Dr. Doom's Fearfall, The Amazing Adventures of Spider-Man.

Magic Kingdom: Big Thunder Mountain Railroad, The Great Goofini, Space Mountain, Splash Mountain, Tomorrowland Speedway,

SeaWorld: Journey to Atlantis, Jazzie Jellies, Kraken, Manta, Rock Wall, Shamu Express, Swishy Fishies, Trampoline, Wild Arctic (ride portion).

Universal Studios: Disaster!, ET Adventure, Jaws, Men in Black Alien Attack, Revenge of the Mummy, Shrek 4-D, Terminator 2: 3-D (stationary seats available), Twister – Ride it Out!, Woody Woodpecker's Nuthouse Coaster.

experience) will happily queue for an hour or more at a ride, so use Disney's FastPass system (p102) judiciously. The heat, in particular, can result in grizzly kids in no time, so take breaks for drinks and splash zones or head for attractions with air-conditioning. Remember to carry your small first-aid kit. Baby wipes always come in handy, and it's a good idea to take

California Grill at Disney's Contemporary Resort

© Disney

spare clothes, which you can leave in park lockers. Going back to the hotel for an afternoon snooze is a good idea – you will also dodge the worst of the heat and crowds.

In the sun: Carry sun cream and sun block at all times and use it often, in queues, on buses, etc. A children's after-sun lotion is also advisable. And make sure they drink a lot of water or non-fizzy drinks; tiredness and irritability are often the signs of mild dehydration.

Dining out: Look for Kids-eat-free deals in many places, as they can apply to children up to 12, and take advantage of the many buffet options (see Chapter 11, Dining Out) to fill up the family or for picky eaters. Many restaurants do Meals To Go if you want a quiet meal in your own accommodation without the worry of the kids playing up. And try to let your children get used to the characters (especially the size of them) before you go to one of the many wonderful character meals.

Having fun: Let your children do some of the decision-making and be prepared to go with the flow if they

© Disney

Disney's All-Star Sports Resort

find something unexpected – the many squirt fountains and splash zones in the parks are an example (bring swimsuits and/or a change of clothes!). The Orlando rule of 'You Can't Do It All' applies especially with kids. Be aware that some youngsters find the evening fireworks too loud. The 3 hotels around the Magic Kingdom offer ways to view the fireworks at a distance.

Baby centres: All the parks have facilities for nursing mothers and can provide baby food and nappies on request (locations are on the park map). The centres can even provide spare children's underpants for those little accidents. All Disney hotel gift shops stock baby food and nappies. Expectant mothers are strongly advised not to ride some of the more dynamic attractions and coasters, and there will be clear warnings on park maps and at the rides.

Pushchairs: 'Strollers' are essential, even if your children are a year or so out of them. The walking wears kids out quickly and a pushchair can save

a lot of discomfort. You can take your own, hire them at the parks or, better still, buy one for as little as $20 at a local supermarket.

Babysitting: Available through many Disney resorts and some of the bigger hotels elsewhere, while Kids Nite Out is a service providing parents with a chance to have an evening out on their own. It offers in-room sitters or helpers during your stay at a rate of $16/hour for the first child, $18.50 for 2, $21 for 3 and $23.50 for 4 (with an additional $2/hour after 9pm) for children 6 weeks to 12 years. There is a 4-hour minimum and reservations are required (1800 696 8105 or 407 828 0920; **www.kidsniteout.com**).

BRITTIP

Avoid making phone calls from your hotel – they're hugely expensive. It's cheaper to buy a local phone card and use a normal payphone. British tri-band mobiles are also costly to use in the US. To call the UK from the US, dial 011 44, then drop the first 0 from the UK area code.

Travellers with disabilities

The parks pay close attention to the needs of visitors with disabilities and Florida is extremely disabled-friendly (though Americans use the word 'handicapped' as we use 'disabled').

Access: Wheelchair availability and access is usually good (though there are a few rides that cannot cater for them) and most hotels now have disabled-accessible rooms. For hearing-impaired guests, there are assistive listening devices and reflective captioning at attractions where a commentary is part of the show. Braille guidebooks are available, plus rest areas for guide dogs, and there are special tape cassettes for blind guests. Disney, Universal and SeaWorld all offer Accessibility Guides for disabled guests in all their main parks (and online). Life-jackets are always on hand at water parks. For Disney disability assistance, call 407 824 4321 (TTY 407 827 5141); for Universal, call 407 224 4233.

Guest Assistance: If you require help with queuing or have children with special needs, visit any Disney theme park Guest Relations office, with the person in question, and request a Guest Assistance Card (GAC), which can be tailored to their needs. It doesn't provide front-of-the-line access (which many people believe), but it can make waiting more

Guest assistance at Animal Kingdom

comfortable. Universal, SeaWorld and Busch Gardens provide similar assistance through their Guest Services offices.

Parking permits: To use any of the plentiful designated disabled parking areas in all public areas (including the parks), UK drivers must obtain a **Temporary Disabled Parking Permit**, which costs $15. You can either go to a local tax collection office, with your UK blue badge and passport, when you arrive (most open 8.30am–4pm Mon–Fri only), OR apply by post, fax or email at least 4 weeks in advance. You need to send a photocopy of your Blue Badge (both sides), a copy of your passport ID page, your home address and address while in Florida, arrival and departure date and a money order (in US dollars) for $15, or your credit card details (for which there is a 2.5% service fee (not Visa cards; see below); do NOT send cash for safety reasons. The Osceola County tax office has a special service for UK visitors with a dedicated team to deal with all requests (8am–4.30pm Mon–Fri). By mail: Patsy Heffner Tax Collector, Attn Samantha or Sheryl, 1300 9th Street, Suite 101-B, St Cloud, Florida 34769, USA or by fax, 407 892 8076. By email: sjewell@osceola.org or srivera@osceola.org with a scanned copy of your details (as above, but NOT your credit card details) and they will email you back with a number to call to arrange payment. If you cannot reach them for any reason or don't get a response within 2 working days, try webinfo@oscoela.org or 407 742 4000.

NB: From Osceola Tax Office: 'Effective May 1, 2009, Visa regulations prohibit us from continuing to accept their credit or debit card.'

For a list of tax offices in Orange County (for the Orlando area), call 407 836 4145 (**www.ctaxcol.com**, and click on Office Locations); in Osceola County (for Kissimmee), call 407 742 4000 (**www.osceolataxcollector.com**). The temporary permits are issued for 90 days from issue date so it's best to apply no sooner than 5–6 weeks before travelling to ensure it will be valid for your stay. However, you may renew a permit within 12 months for no fee.

- **Special help:** Local company Suntastic Tours can help travellers with physical and mental disabilities in many ways, including travel, arranging tours of the parks and other accessibility issues (321 284 4507, **http://suntastictours.com**).
- **Walker Mobility** specialises in electric scooters and wheelchair rentals, with free delivery and pick-up, even from holiday villas (407 518 6000, **www.walkermobility.com**).
- **Wheelchair Vans of America** hires out full-size or mini vans equipped for wheelchair users (1800 910 8267 or 407 977 3799 **www.rainbowwheels. com**).
- **CARE Medical Equipment** are another company highly recommended for sale, rent or repair of powered scooters and wheelchairs and other medical equipment (407 856 2273 **www. caremedicalequipment.com**).

BRITTIP

'We used CARE Medical Equipment to hire a charger for our electric wheelchair as the 110v currency in the US does not work with a chair's 220v charging needs. They delivered to our villa within an hour and even stayed to make sure it worked. Some UK battery chargers will work but not all, so please check before you leave.' – Reader Lisa Smith, County Durham

The discussion forums on **www. wdwinfo.com** have a board geared to visitors with disabilities, while the excellent AllEars website has a big section on advice for a whole range of concerns, from children with ADD to vegetarian and vegan food. Visit **http:// allearsnet.com**, click on Walt Disney World Planning, then For Travelers With Special Challenges.

Orlando for grown-ups

You don't need to have kids in tow to enjoy Orlando. There is so much clever detail and imagination, it is usually the grown-ups who get the most out of the holiday experience.

In fact, as many couples and singles visit the parks as do families with children. Certainly, when you look at the entertainment at *Downtown Disney* and CityWalk and the great range of bars and fine restaurants, with a good number of romantic offerings, it is easy to see the attraction for those 21 and over. As well as Florida being a key honeymoon destination, its friendly, sociable atmosphere is ideal for singles, while couples without children can also take advantage of late opening at the parks and clubs like Jellyrolls and Atlantic City Dance Hall at *Disney's Boardwalk Resort*. Even better, the downtown area of the city of Orlando is coming back as a happening night-time venue, with a lot to recommend it for a lively evening out.

BRITTIP

If you have a fridge in your hotel, put drink cartons in the freezer overnight and they will be cool for much of the next day in your back-pack. Better still, buy a cheap coolbag, freeze it with some water bottles in, and leave it in the car – great after a day in the parks.

Accessibility is good throughout the parks

© Disney

Orlando for seniors

The more mature traveller can also benefit from a healthy dose of the Sunshine State. And, if our parents (all in their senior years) are any guide, they will have just as much fun, within slightly different parameters. Seniors can also take advantage of numerous discounts and special deals for their age group at the attractions, plus many restaurants and hotels. The official Visitor Center on I-Drive (p46) publishes a brochure of all the deals.

Hotels: For the older person, staying in a Disney hotel is highly recommended as it removes the stress of driving. The extra cost is offset, Simon's parents feel, by the beauty and convenience of their surroundings.

Parks: There is still plenty to do here, even if the thrill rides are not a draw –just watching can be entertainment enough! Both *Epcot* and *Disney's Animal Kingdom* have much to engage the older visitor, while the shows of *Disney's Hollywood Studios* make that a popular choice, too, and the *Magic Kingdom*, while 'probably the noisiest of all the parks', is still an essential experience.

Evenings: The *Downtown Disney* area can feel a bit frenetic for the senior crowd, but the *Boardwalk Resort* is popular and the whole of the *Epcot* resort area offers much in the way of fine dining and relaxation. In fact, this is often a prime area for seniors, notably the quieter *Disney's Yacht* and *Beach Club Resorts*, and the superb Swan-Dolphin complex.

Attractions: Simon's parents highlight the following for their age group.
- *Disney's Animal Kingdom Park:* Kilimanjaro Safaris, the Maharajah Jungle Trek, Pangani Forest Trail, Finding Nemo show and Festival of the Lion King.
- *Disney's Hollywood Studios:* Jim Henson's Muppet Vision 3-D, Indiana Jones Stunt Show, Beauty and the Beast and Fantasmic!.

There are no age limits

© Disney

At-a-glance kids' height requirements

Height	Park	Rides
2ft 8in/82cm	Disney's Blizzard Beach	Chairlift
Must be with a child 3ft–4ft 8in/91–142cm	Islands of Adventure	Pteranodon Flyers
3ft–4ft 8in/91–142cm	Wet 'n Wild	The Surge, Bubba Tub, Flyer, Disco H2O
3ft/91cm	Disney's Magic Kingdom	The Great Goofini (coming late 2012)
3ft 3in/99cm	Universal Studios	Woody Woodpecker's Nuthouse Coaster
	Busch Gardens	Rhino Rally (age 3 minimum)
3ft 4in/101cm	Disney's Animal Kingdom	DINOSAUR!
	Disney's Hollywood Studios	Star Tours II, The Twilight Zone Tower of Terror
	Disney's Magic Kingdom	Splash Mountain, Big Thunder Mountain Railroad
	Epcot	Test Track, Soarin'
	Islands of Adventure	The Amazing Adventures of Spider-Man
	Universal Studios	The Simpsons Ride
3ft 6in/106cm	Aquatica	Walhalla Wave, HooRoo Run, Taumata Racer
	Busch Gardens	The Wild Surge (3ft 2in/96cm with adult), Congo River Rapids, Ubanga-Banga Bumper Cars, Scorpion, Sandstorm, Sand Serpent (age 6 minimum)
	Disney's Animal Kingdom	Kali River Rapids
	Islands of Adventure	Jurassic Park River Adventure
	SeaWorld	Journey to Atlantis, Wild Arctic (Polar Express at Christmas
	Universal Studios	Men in Black: Alien Attack
3ft 8 in/111cm	Disney's Animal Kingdom	Expedition: Everest
	Disney's Magic Kingdom	Space Mountain
	Epcot	Mission: SPACE
	Islands of Adventure	Dudley Do-Right's Ripsaw Falls
3ft 10in/116cm	Busch Gardens	Stanley Falls
Under 4ft/122cm only	Aquatica	Kata's Kookaburra Cove
	Disney's Blizzard Beach	Tike's Peak
	Disney's Typhoon Lagoon	Ketchakiddee Creek
Under 4ft/122cm only (with adult)	Wet 'n Wild	Kids Park
4ft/122cm	Aquatica	Dolphin Plunge, Omaka Rocka
	Busch Gardens	Gwazi, Tanganyika Tidal Wave
	Disney's Animal Kingdom	Primeval Whirl
	Disney's Blizzard Beach	Summit Plummet, Slush Gusher, Downhill Double Dipper
	Disney's Hollywood Studios	Rock 'n' Roller Coaster Starring Aerosmith
	Disney's Typhoon Lagoon	Crush 'n' Gusher, Humunga Kowabunga
	Epcot	Sum of All Thrills (non-inversion)
	Islands of Adventure	Popeye And Bluto's Bilge-Rat Barges, Flight of the Hippogriff, Harry Potter and the Forbidden Journey
	Universal Studios	Revenge of the Mummy, Disaster! A Major Motion Picture Ride…Starring YOU (unless accompanied by adult), ET Adventure
	Wet 'n Wild	Bomb Bay, Der Stuka, Black Hole, The Storm, Brain Wash
4ft 3in/130cm	Universal Studios	Hollywood Rip Ride Rockit!
	Wet 'n Wild	Wild One
4ft 4in/132cm	Disney's Magic Kingdom	Tomorrowland Speedway (for child to drive alone)
	Epcot	Sum of All Thrills (with inversion)
	Islands of Adventure	Dr Doom's Fearfall
4ft 5in/143cm	Wet 'n Wild	Knee Ski Wake-Boarding
4ft 6in/137cm	Busch Gardens	SheiKra, Kumba, Montu, Cheetah Hunt
	Islands of Adventure	The Incredible Hulk Coaster, Dragon Challenge
	SeaWorld	Kraken, Manta
4ft 8in/145cm	Busch Gardens	Jungle Flyers

- *Epcot:* Spaceship Earth, Soarin', Universe of Energy, all of World Showcase and IllumiNations (plus the superb gardens and architecture).
- *Magic Kingdom:* The Haunted Mansion, Jungle Cruise, Pirates of the Caribbean, Mickey's PhilharMagic and the monorail ride.
- *Universal Studios and Islands of Adventure:* Most of US but less of IoA.
- Watching the children at the many parades and character greetings; dinner at the California Grill in *Disney's Contemporary Resort* (and other fine dining locations); shopping at Orlando Premium Outlets.
- *SeaWorld* remains hugely popular for seniors and even Busch Gardens, despite its many roller-coasters, has plenty to offer. The local Segway Tours (in Kissimmee, Mount Dora, St Petersburg and Clearwater Beach) are highly recommended for older visitors, while Mount Dora and Winter Park (see also Chapter 8) are also perfect senior fare.

Weather: Mar and late Oct/Nov are ideal times to visit, but the summer months are hard going for older folks. Good coats (and gloves) may still be necessary at times in winter.

Lego Store at Downtown Disney

© Lego

BRITTIP

Looking for essential travel accessories and useful knick-knacks, like TSA-approved locks, plug adapters and luggage scales (to avoid excess baggage on the trip home!)? Try www.tripneeds.com. Asda supermarkets also sell a good travel range.

Measurements

US clothes sizes are smaller than ours, hence a US size 12 dress is a UK 14, or an American jacket sized 42 is a 44. Shoes are the opposite: a US 10 should fit a British size 9 foot. The measuring system is imperial, not metric.

BRITTIP

Don't want to take your mobile with you for fear of high charges? Hire a phone for your holiday from Adam Phones and take advantage of its special local rates for the US (0800 123000, **www. adamphones.com**).

You've got mail

You won't find post boxes in many locations and some post offices don't seem to know the fees for postage to the UK. So here's what you need to know: all the parks have post boxes and you can get stamp books from most stamp machines and City Hall at the *Magic Kingdom.* A standard postcard or greetings card in an envelope to the UK both require a 98c stamp; standard postage within the US is 44c.

BRITTIP

Phonecards, which you need to make a call from a local payphone (much cheaper than using your hotel room phone), are available from most 7-Eleven stores or from your tour rep.

The main post office for the Disney area is at **10450 Turkey Lake Road** (just north of the junction of Palm Parkway and Central Florida Parkway; 8am–7pm Mon–Fri, 9am–5pm Sat); in Kissimmee, try **2600 Michigan Avenue** (8am–6.30pm Mon–Fri, 9am–4pm Sat) or 1415 W Oak Street (8.30am–5pm Mon–Fri, 9am–2pm

American-speak

Many words and phrases have a different meaning across the Atlantic. For instance, when Americans say the first floor, they mean the ground floor, the second floor is really the first, and so on. (NB: NEVER ask for a packet of fags; 'fag' is a crude, slang term for a homosexual.) Here are a few everyday words to help you:

American	English	American	English
Appetizer	Starter	Fender	Car bumper
Band aid	Plaster	Freeway	Motorway
Bathroom	Private toilet	Fries	Chips
Biscuit	Savoury scone	Gas	Petrol
Broiled	Grilled	Graham cracker	Digestive biscuit
Cellphone	Mobile phone	Hood	Car bonnet
Check	Bill	Intersection	Junction
Chips	Crisps	Nickel	5 cents
Collect call	Reverse charge phone call	No standing	No parking OR stopping
		'Pound sign'	The # on a phone keypad
Cookie	Biscuit		
Cot/rollaway	Fold-up bed	Purse	Handbag
Crib	Cot	Quarter	25 cents
Diaper	Nappy	Ramp	Slip road
Dime	10 cents	Restroom	Public toilet
Divided highway	Dual carriageway	Seltzer	Soda water
Eggplant	Aubergine	Shrimp	King prawn
Eggs 'over easy'	Eggs fried on both sides but soft	Soda	Fizzy drink
		Stroller	Pushchair
Eggs 'sunny side up'	Eggs fried on just 1 side (soft)	Trunk	Car boot
		Turn-out	Lay-by
Entrée	Main course	Yield	Give way
Facecloth/washcloth	Flannel	Zucchini	Courgette
Faucet	Tap		

Sat). You will also find a post office inside **Mall at Millenia**, off the lower level of the Grand Court.

Wedding bells

Florida is an increasingly popular choice for couples wanting to tie the knot (some 20,000 a year at the last count). Its almost guaranteed sunshine and lush, natural landscape make it a huge hit as a wedding backdrop. Orlando also has some terrific services, wedding co-ordinators and scenic venues like Magnolia Acres, Winter Park, Leu Gardens and the many resort hotels (like the Buena Vista Palace, *Walt Disney World Swan and Dolphin*, Bohemian Hotel and Wyndham Resort) and even the pristine golf courses (like Celebration Golf Club). More unusual ones include getting married at the Hard Rock Café, in a hot-air balloon or a helicopter, on the beach or a luxury yacht, in the pit-lane of the Richard Petty Driving

Wedding couple in a Cinderella carriage

© Disney

Hurricane alert?

June–Nov is officially hurricane season, but it is not anything to worry about. Even the unprecedented extremes of 2004, when 3 major storms hit Central Florida, caused no significant damage to the parks and the biggest inconvenience was losing electricity for a few days. In the unlikely event of a major storm, switch your TV to the Weather Channel or local news station WESH 2 and follow its advice.

Experience at *Walt Disney World* or even at 145mph/233kph around the speedway itself! All the tour operators feature wedding options and services and offer a variety of ceremonies, or you can pick a local specialist like **Get Married In Florida** (see opposite). Prices vary from around £300/couple (for a basic civil ceremony) to more than £2,000.

Walt Disney World's Wedding Pavilion: True fairytale romance, with the backdrop of Cinderella Castle, you can opt for traditional elegance in this Victorian setting with up to 260 guests or the full Disney experience, arriving in Cinderella's coach with Mickey and Minnie as guests. Disney's wedding planners can tailor-make the occasion for you (407 828 3400) but at a price – rates START at $3,000/couple for the basic ceremony and can top $20,000.

Cinderella Castle at Christmas

© Disney

Licence: To obtain a marriage licence, visit one of the local courthouses, which includes Osceola County Courthouse, Courthouse Square, Suite 2000, Kissimmee (just off Bryan Street in downtown Kissimmee) 8am–4pm Mon–Fri (407 343 3500); Orange County Courthouse, 425 North Orange Avenue (downtown Orlando) 7.30am–4pm Mon–Fri (407 836 2067); Clermont Courthouse, 1206 Bowman Street, Clermont (in Sunnyside Plaza) 8.30am–4.30pm (closed noon–1pm; 352 394 2018). All are closed on US bank holidays. Both parties must be present to apply for a marriage licence, which costs $93.50 (in cash, travellers' cheques or by credit card) and is valid for 60 days, while a ceremony (equivalent to a British register office) can be performed at the same time by the clerk for an extra $20. Passports and birth certificates are requested and, if you have been married before, you should bring your decree absolute. After acquiring a licence, a couple can marry anywhere in Florida. It is also possible to obtain a licence *before* arriving in Florida (see **www.floridamarriagelicencebypost. com**).

Get Married in Florida: This internet business dedicated to organising weddings for couples from the UK has specialised in Orlando marriages for many years and is ideally placed to deliver great personal service, with the complete package for the perfect wedding (407 226 3383, **www. getmarriedinflorida.com**).

Disney special occasions

Birthday badges: Free badges can be found at City Hall in the *Magic Kingdom Park* and Guest Services at *Epcot, Disney's Hollywood Studios* and *Disney's Animal Kingdom Park.* Cast Members like to make a fuss over children (and adults!) wearing a birthday badge.

Birthday cakes: Contact room service at your resort or Guest Services at one of the parks. All Disney restaurants can offer ready-made 15cm/6in cakes ($21 at each restaurant) or something larger ($32–120) if ordered 48 hours in

Top 10 romantic restaurants

1   Tchoup Chop, Universal's Royal Pacific Resort

2   California Grill, Disney's Contemporary Resort

3   Todd English's bluezoo, Walt Disney World Dolphin Resort

4   Zen, Omni Orlando Resort at Champions Gate

5   Jiko, Disney's Animal Kingdom Lodge

6   Seasons 52, Sand Lake Rd, Orlando

7   Old Hickory Steakhouse, Gaylord Palms Resort

8   Bice, Universal's Portofino Bay Hotel

9   Cala Bella, Shingle Creek Resort

10 Brio Tuscan Grille, The Mall at Millenia

advance on 407 827 2253. If someone in your group has a birthday, be sure to tell the Cast Member at check-in (or when you make your reservation), as well as hostesses and/or servers in restaurants. While not guaranteed, Disney staff often go out of their way to make the day special. If characters know it's a birthday when they sign a child's autograph book, they may add a special birthday wish.

Birthday cruise: The IllumiNations Celebration Cruise (to Epcot) provides snacks, drinks, streamers and balloons for a 90-minute tour, for up to 10, from Disney's Yacht and Beach Club Resort marina for $371 (407 939 7529).

Birthday parties: *Disney's Polynesian Resort* offers themed birthday parties with lunch options at its Neverland kids' club for ages 4 and over. A themed 2-hour Premium party with cake, pizza, drinks, party activities and one Disney character is $70/person, while the Basic version (without a Disney character) is $35/person (at least 1 week's notice required on 407 939 7529).

Winter-Summerland Miniature Golf: 2-hour birthday parties for 10 or more, including pizza, soft drinks, cake and a round of mini-golf at $19.95/head, plus tax (call at least a week in advance on 407 939 7529).

Goofy Party Central: This grand 90-minute experience for up to 12 takes place at Goofy's Candy Company in *Downtown Disney* and offers a choice of Goofy's Scien-Terrific Birthday Bash or the Perfectly Princess Party, each with themed

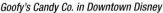

Goofy's Candy Co. in Downtown Disney

© Disney

events, games, gifts and treats, plus 2 party hosts for $370 (call 407 939 2329 up to 90 days in advance).

Disney's Pirate Cruise: This 2-hour adventure for kids 4–12 sails (on pontoon boats) from 4 of the resorts (Grand Floridian, Yacht/Beach Club, Port Orleans and Caribbean Beach at 9.30am) to find pirate 'booty' at different ports of call, with a final stop for lunch; $35 per child (407 939 7529, up to 180 days in advance).

Money matters

You'll need to carry ID for both cheques and some credit card purchases (take your UK driving licence card).

BRITTIP

American banknotes are all the same size and primarily green, with just the occasional splash of colour in the newer notes. The only real difference is the picture of the president and the denomination in each corner.

Cash: It is worth separating larger notes from smaller ones in your wallet to avoid flashing all your money in view. Losing £300 of travellers'

Two-way radio rentals

Two-way radios are popular in Orlando for safety and convenience. Many families buy 'walkie-talkies' to keep in touch around the parks in preference to mobile phones. You can pick them up locally for as little as $35 in stores like Wal-Mart, Best Buy, Radio Shack, Office Depot and Staples. However, they cannot be used in the UK as they use the same frequency as our emergency services.

cheques shouldn't ruin your holiday – but losing $600 in cash might. All the theme parks have ATMs.

Travellers' cheques: Dollar travellers' cheques can be used as cash almost everywhere (though a few places, like Golden Corral restaurants, no longer accept them) and can be replaced if lost or stolen, so it is not necessary (or advisable) to carry lots of cash. Sterling travellers' cheques can be cashed only in major banks.

Credit cards: Having a credit card is almost essential (especially for car hire) as they are accepted everywhere and provide extra buying security. Visa, Mastercard and American Express are all widely accepted.

Bibbidi Bobbidi boutique, Downtown Disney

Repeat visitors

Repeat visitors create a large part of the Orlando market and are always on the lookout for something new after they have done all the main parks. Chapters 8 and 9 (Off The Beaten Track and The Twin Centre Option) are largely designed with them in mind. Here are 10 things worth doing once you have Been There and Done That:

1 Behind the scenes tours at the Disney parks.

2 Dolphin watch cruise from Dolphin Landings at St Pete Beach.

3 Wildlife eco-tour with Island Boat Lines at Cocoa Beach.

4 The scenic boat ride and Morse Museum in Winter Park.

5 Bok Tower Gardens and lunch or dinner (plus a visit to the soup cannery!) at the eclectic Chalet Suzanne in Lake Wales.

6 St John's River Cruise in Blue Spring State Park, Seminole County.

7 Boggy Creek Airboats.

8 A zipline ride and buggy tour at Florida EcoSafaris.

9 Merritt Island National Wildlife Refuge at Titusville.

10 A visit to Mount Dora, north-west of Orlando.

FairFX card: Perhaps the best option is this convenient card, which you preload to a chosen amount (**www. fairfx.com**). The exchange rate is fixed at loading and you can save 5–10% on High Street currency rates.

Safety and security

While crime is not a serious issue in Florida, this is still big-city America, so don't leave your common sense at home. Tourism is such a vital part of the economy, the authorities have a highly safety-conscious attitude. However, it would be foolish to ignore the usual safety guidelines for travelling abroad.

BRITTIP

For your journey to the US, use a business rather than your home address on your luggage. It is less conspicuous and safer should any item be lost or stolen.

Commonsense tips: A bumbag (Americans say 'fanny pack'!) is better than a handbag or shoulder bag. Try not to look too much like a tourist – the map over the steering wheel is a giveaway, but other no-nos

are wearing loads of jewellery and carrying lots of camera equipment. The biggest giveaway is leaving a camera or camcorder on view in the car (which the heat may ruin).

The VERY strong police advice in the unlikely event of being confronted by an assailant is: DO NOT resist or 'have a go', because this can often make a bad situation worse. However, it is comforting to know Orlando does not have any no-go areas in the main tourist parts. The nearest is the portion of the Orange Blossom Trail south of downtown Orlando (a selection of strip clubs and 'adult bars' that can be downright seedy) and the Parramore area south-west of downtown.

Guests at Disney parks

© Disney

TOPS: International Drive has its own dedicated police unit (the Tourist Oriented Policing Squad, a division of the Orlando City Police), with officers patrolling this long tourist corridor, arranging crime prevention seminars with local hotels and ensuring I-Drive takes good care of its visitors. You will often see these police out on mountain bikes, and they are a polite, helpful bunch should you need assistance.

Hotel security: While in your hotel, always use door peepholes and security chains when someone knocks at the door. DON'T open the door to strangers without asking for identification, and check with the hotel desk if you are still not sure. It is stating the obvious, but keep doors and windows locked and always use deadlocks and security chains. Always take cash, credit cards, valuables and car keys when you go out (or put them in the room safe), and don't leave the door open, even if you just pop down the corridor to the ice machine. Most hotels now have electronic card-locks for extra security and can offer deposit boxes in addition to the standard in-room mini-safes. Don't be afraid to ask reception staff for safety advice for surrounding areas or if you are travelling somewhere you are not sure about. Safety is a major issue for the Central Florida Hotel/Motel Association and hotel staff are usually well briefed to be helpful.

BRITTIP

If your room has already been cleaned before you go out for the day, hang the 'Do Not Disturb' sign on the door. Always keep your valuables out of sight, whether in the hotel or the car.

Car safety: Make the basic safety checks of your hire car straight away and familiarise yourself with the car's controls BEFORE driving away. Try to memorise your route in advance, even if it's only a case of knowing the road numbers. Most hire firms now give good directions to all the hotels, so check them before you set off (or, better still, hire a GPS system). Make sure the fuel tank is well filled and never let it get near empty so you risk running out of 'gas' in an unfamiliar area. If you do stray off your pre-determined route, stick to well-lit areas and ask for directions only from official businesses like hotels and petrol stations, or the police. Try to park close to your destination where

Disney's Grand Floridian Resort & Spa

© Disney

Let us plan your holiday ...

...with our unique Itinerary Planner Service

The *Brit Guide* Itinerary Planner Service will ensure you get the very most out of your time in central Florida. This is a service no one else can offer. We will design an itinerary tailored to *your* plans for the parks and attractions of central Florida. In your planner (which usually runs to 40 pages for a 2-week itinerary), we will indicate the best days to visit the parks to avoid the crowds; all the main show and parade times; any rides that may be closed for refurbishment; and provide a touring plan for each park, a shopping guide, updates on new rides, etc., as well as up-to-the-minute advice right from the source of the fun, plus a host of Brit Tip Extras and Brit Picks (our special favourites) we can't fit into this book. All you have to do is visit the *Brit Guide* website and click on the Itinerary Planner link. Fill out the online form with your travel dates, hotel and family details, the tickets you have bought (or are buying) and what you want to fit into your visit. Submit the form, with your payment, and you'll receive an acknowledgement of your requirements. A few days before you go, you will receive, by email, your unique Itinerary Planner, which will consist of:

1   An official *Brit Guide* welcome from Susan and Simon Veness.

2   A full day-by-day plan for the length of your holiday.

3   A touring strategy for ALL of the parks, water parks and shopping centres you will visit, avoiding the crowds and taking advantage of the latest developments.

4   An alternative plan in case of bad weather.

5   All the main parade and fireworks times with your daily plans.

6   A note of any rides/shows that are closed during your visit.

7   A special selection of Brit Tip Extras and local advice specifically for you.

8   Our Brit Picks – a guide to a range of personal favourites, from restaurants to shops.

9   The ultimate insider knowledge, as Susan an Simon are based in the heart of the Orlando magic and are fully up to date on all developments.

10 Our special bonus: an EXCLUSIVE Platinum VIP Passport for Orlando Premium Outlets (not available to the public), with extra savings at select stores at this great shopping venue (in addition to its free VIP Coupon Book we offer to all readers – see inside back cover).

All in all, it adds up to the most comprehensive package of specialised holiday info anywhere, and it represents the secret to the most fun, in the most hassle-free way, in the most exciting place on earth. What more could you ask for? Just check us out on **www.britguideorlando.net** and we'll do the rest for you.

Please note: There is a minimum order period, so check online and apply in good time before your holiday (at least 2 weeks). Book owners receive a discount on the price of the Itinerary Planner, so have it with you when you register as you'll need a password from the book. *The password is random and expires on 31 Dec of the edition's year, no exceptions.* We are not a travel agency or ticket service and you MUST know your ticket requirements in advance.

there are plenty of lights and DO NOT get out if there are suspicious characters around. Always keep windows closed (and air-con on), and don't hesitate to lock the doors from the inside if you feel threatened (larger cars have doors that lock automatically as you drive off). Don't forget to lock the car when you leave it – not all rental cars have central locking.

More info: For more info on safety, contact the Community Affairs office of Orange County Police (407 836 3720) or the International Drive police team office (407 351 9368).

Emergencies

Emergency services: For police, fire department or ambulance, dial 911 (9-911 from your hotel room). Make sure your children know this number.

General: For smaller-scale crises (e.g. mislaid tickets, lost passports or rescheduled flights), your holiday company should have an emergency contact number in the hotel reception.

Independent travellers: If you run into passport or other problems that need help from the British Consulate, its office is at 200 South Orange Avenue, Suite 2110, Orlando, Florida, 32801, with walk-in visitor hours Mon-Fri 9am–noon and 2– 4pm, or call 407 254 3300 (**http://ukinusa.fco. gov.uk**).

You'll find masses of info on all things Orlando on the fun-packed discussion forums at **www.attraction-tickets-direct.co.uk**, **www.thedibb.co.uk** and **www.wdwinfo.com**, to which we also contribute. They also have great features, theme park info, restaurant advice, news, weather, facts and tips.

Know before you go

Here are the best sources for additional info before you go.

- **Fan websites:** The biggest and best of these is **www.thedibb.co.uk** ('Disney with a British accent'), the

Downtown Orlando

fully comprehensive **http://allearsnet. com** (notably for its Disney dining section) and **www.disboards.com**.

- **Orlando Attractions** magazine (which we also write for) offers a superb website full of newsy features and videos at **www. attractionsmagazine.com**, plus a weekly magazine-style programme called *The Show*.

- **Official sites:** These aren't bad for opening hours, rides, parades, etc. and bookings, though Disney's can be hard work. Visit **www.disneyworld. co.uk**, **www.seaworld.com**, **www. universalorlando.com** and **www. buschgardens.com**.

- **Orlando Sentinel:** The online local paper (**www.orlandosentinel.com**) is packed with info (especially for shopping, dining and nightlife), while the free *Orlando Weekly* is also worth checking (**www. orlandoweekly.com**).

- **Orlando Visitor Center:** It's worth checking Orlando's ONLY official Visitor Center, 8.30am– 6.30pm daily at 8723 International Drive (407 363 5872 or email **info@ visitorlando.com**) for discounted attraction tickets, and free brochures, accommodation advice, info pamphlets and maps.

- **Visit Florida:** Offers a free info pack, as well as many online ebrochures (01737 644 882, **www.visitflorida.com/ uk**).

- **Visit Kissimmee:** more useful online info and an eguide to download (**www.visitkissimmee.com**).

- **Visit Orlando:** has a 24-hour info line, plus a website where you order its free Holiday Planning kit (0800 018 6760, **www.visitorlando.com/uk/**).

Now, on to the next step of the holiday, your transport…

3 Getting Around

or The Secret of Driving on the Wrong Side of the Road!

Arriving and driving in Orlando are two of the biggest concerns for visitors, especially first-timers, but there's no need to worry. Although most people begin their holiday by leaving the airport in a newly acquired, automatic, left-hand-drive hire car on roads that can appear bewildering, driving here is a lot easier and more enjoyable than in the UK. Anyone familiar with the M25 should find Florida FAR less stressful.

Before you get to your hire car, though, you need to be aware of the arrival process at either of the airports.

Orlando International

This is one of the most modern and enjoyable airports in the world, but it can be confusing for newcomers. All flights arrive at one of 4 satellite terminals and you then take a shuttle tram (like a mini monorail) to the main terminal. Allow around an hour from landing to ground transportation.

International arrivals: If you arrive with British Airways or Virgin Atlantic, you disembark at the satellite for Gates 60–99. First, you go through Immigration. Join one of the 2 main queues which feed into the individual immigration kiosks, and wait for the official to call you to the next open kiosk. Once through Immigration,

collect your baggage from the carousel and go through the Customs check.

Then you have a choice. Option 1: deposit your checked luggage on a second conveyor belt to take it to the main terminal while you go upstairs to the shuttle with your hand luggage only. Once in the main terminal you are on Level 3 and you follow signs down to Baggage Claim B (unless you took a Virgin flight, in which case you cross over to Baggage Claim A) on Level 2.

BRITTIP
Visit www.orlandoairports.net for a photo preview of the arrival process at Orlando International Airport (click Airport Guide, then Arrivals Guide) and other info.

Option 2: If you can manage your luggage without a trolley, take it on the escalator up to the shuttle and go straight to pick up your transport on Level 1 (or, if a specific driver is meeting you, Level 2).

BRITTIP
Don't forget you must have filled in your ESTA form and immigration details online before you travel (see p12). For country of residence put UNITED KINGDOM; for Passport Issuing Country, put UK – BRITISH CITIZEN. You must give a valid US address for your accommodation.

Domestic arrivals: For anyone arriving on a US domestic flight (from another US gateway), you disembark at the satellite terminal and proceed straight to the main terminal on the shuttle to collect your baggage on Level 2 (either A or B side, depending on arrival gate). Once at the main baggage claim, porters can help you to Level 1 (for a $1/bag tip) for all car hire, shuttles and buses. Trolleys need $3 in change (or you can use a credit card) to operate – they are not free here.

Transfers: Kerbside pick-up is just outside the doors on Level 2. If a driver is meeting you, he or she will wait on Level 2, either at the bottom of the escalators or by your baggage reclaim. Several tour operators have help desks here, too, while Virgin has a reception desk on Level 1. The public bus system, Lynx (p50), operates ONLY from the A side of Level 1 (from 6am–10.30pm; 9.30pm on Sundays and public holidays), in spaces 38–41. Links 11, 41 and 51 depart every ½hr (less often on Sundays and bank holidays) for Orlando city centre (about 45mins away), while Link 42 serves International Drive (about a 1hr journey) and Link 111 goes to *Walt Disney World* (Hotel Plaza Boulevard and the Transportation & Ticket Center) via the Florida Mall and I-Drive (Canadian Court). Fares are $2 one-way.

Car hire: All the main hire companies are now on site at the airport (with another 15 off-airport). The main 11 to choose from include Dollar, National, Thrifty, Hertz, Avis and *Brit Guide* partner Alamo, and all offer a

Krustyland at Universal Studios

full service (look out for Alamo's new automated self-service kiosks). Dollar is used for packages with Thomson, Travel City and First Choice; Alamo is the main client for Funway, Jetsave, Kuoni, BA Holidays, Virgin and Thomas Cook. After completing your paperwork, simply walk out of Level 1, across the road to the multi-storey car park to collect your car.

If you arrive late, consider staying overnight at the **Hyatt Regency** hotel inside the airport itself rather than driving tired. You will be far more ready to drive next day (and the car hire queues will be shorter). Several tour operators also offer an arrival-day transfer, with car hire pick-up arranged the next day.

BRITTIP

If you are hiring a car from one of the on-airport companies, save time by sending the driver to complete the paperwork BEFORE collecting your luggage on Level 2.

Leaving the airport: When you drive out of the airport, DON'T follow signs to 'Orlando'. The main tourist areas are south and west of the city proper, so follow the respective signs for your accommodation.

BRITTIP

The Martin Andersen Beachline (formerly Beeline) Expressway (528) and Greeneway (417) are both toll roads, so make sure you have some US currency before leaving the airport. Toll booths hate to change notes above $20, while some auto-tolls take ONLY coins.

- For International Drive (or I-Drive), take the **North Exit** and the Beachline Expressway (Route 528) west until it crosses I-Drive just north of SeaWorld (you will need $1.75 in toll fees). Most hotels on I-Drive are to the north, so keep right at the exit.
- For Kissimmee, Disney and villas in Clermont/Davenport, take the **South Exit** for 3ml/5km and pick up the Central Florida Greeneway (Highway 417) west.
- For most Disney resorts, take exit

6 and follow the signs; for *Animal Kingdom* resorts, use exit 3 and take Osceola Parkway west.

- For eastern Kissimmee, come off Highway 417 at exit 11, the Orange Blossom Trail (Highway 17/92), and go south.
- For west Kissimmee and Clermont/Davenport (Highway 27), take exit 2, turn right on Celebration Avenue and left (west) on Highway 192 all the way to Highway 27 (you will need around $2.75 in toll fees).

Orlando Sanford International Airport

Arriving at Sanford (in Seminole County) couldn't be easier. The list of airlines visiting this easy-to-use airport currently includes Thomson Airways, Monarch, Thomas Cook Airlines and Icelandair. It generally takes only 30–40mins from arrival to leaving the baggage hall, but there may be delays in peak season when several planes arrive at once, as its handling capacity is limited. It's a short walk from the plane to the immigration hall (where there are 2 queues that feed through to the kiosks); you then collect your baggage, pass through Customs and walk straight out to car hire, shuttle or taxi pick-up.

BRITTIP

Don't want to drive? Consider a multi-centre stay within Orlando itself, staying first at, say, I-Drive or Universal Orlando and then a Disney resort, to get the best of the free or cheap transport options.

Car hire: You will find the tour operator welcome desks and Dollar car hire offices immediately in front of you, while our *Brit Guide* partner **Alamo** has a large welcome centre via a covered walkway and boardwalk behind this, and its British-dedicated operation is pretty smooth. Avis, Budget, Enterprise, National, Thrifty and Hertz are also on-airport (turn right out of Customs then take the first door on the right). Look up more on **www.orlandosanfordairport.com**.

BRITTIP

For traffic news and reports, tune to 660AM (WORL) or 580AM (WDBO). Dial 511 on a tri-band mobile phone for traffic info on I-4.

Leaving the airport: It may be 35ml/56km to the north and involve more driving (and taxis and shuttles are much more expensive – a town car service would be around $130 one-way to Walt Disney World and a taxi $100), but you usually save time by your quicker exit. There is just one main road out, on to Lake Mary Boulevard, and you then take Seminole Expressway (Highway 417, which becomes Central Florida Greeneway in Orange County) south. The slip road to this toll motorway is just under the flyover on your LEFT, and you need $6.25 to reach Disney or Kissimmee or $5.25 for I-Drive (via the Beachline Expressway). You can avoid the tolls by staying on Lake Mary Blvd for 6ml/10km until you get to I-4, but you're likely to hit heavy traffic through the city centre. The Expressway/Greeneway is an excellent, easy-driving introduction to Orlando, even if it does cost a few dollars.

BRITTIP

If you suspect you may need more boot space in your car, upgrade when you book at home as it is usually more expensive to upgrade when you arrive.

Characters in Flight at Downtown Disney

© Disney

ORLANDO WITHOUT A CAR

Although being mobile is advisable, it is certainly possible to survive without a car. However, few attractions are within walking distance of hotels, and taxis can be expensive. You also need to plan with greater precision to allow for extra travelling time (and with children, taking buses can be tiring). For non-drivers, your best base is either *Walt Disney World* itself (free transport throughout, but harder to get to the rest of Orlando) or International Drive for its location, 'walkability' and the great I-Ride Trolley. Many hotels have free shuttles to some of the parks or a cheap, regular mini-bus service. There are 4 main options: public transport; shuttle services; town cars and limousines; and taxis.

Public transport

Lynx bus system: Reliable and cheap but slightly plodding, it covers much of metro Orlando. Its online system map shows all its routes (or 'links') and main attractions (407 841 5969, **www.golynx.com**).

- **Link 18:** From Kissimmee to downtown Orlando (from Osceola Square Mall, east on Highway 192 and north on Boggy Creek Road, Buenaventura Boulevard and Orange Avenue).
- **Link 38:** I-Drive to downtown Orlando (from the Convention Center via Wet 'n Wild, Kirkman Road and I¬4).
- **Link 42:** From Orlando International Airport to I-Drive.

Hard Rock Live at Universal CityWalk

© Universal Orlando Resort

- **Link 50:** From the TTC via SeaWorld and I-4.
- **Link 55:** Kissimmee's Highway 192 from Osceola Square Mall west to Four Corners via the Summer Bay Resort.
- **Link 56:** From Kissimmee to Disney (from Osceola Square Mall, along Highway 192 via Old Town and Celebration to Disney's Transportation & Ticket Center (TTC) by the Magic Kingdom).
- **Link 300:** From Downtown Disney via I-4 to downtown Orlando.
- **Link 304:** To Disney from the top of I-Drive (Oak Ridge Road to Downtown Disney, via Sand Lake Drive).

> **BRITTIP**
> Lynx buses use the Downtown Disney West Side Transfer Center as their Disney hub, with Links 301, 302 and 303 spreading out from there to the theme parks and resorts.

Lynx fares are $2 a ride (transfers are free) or $16 for a weekly pass (children 6 and under go free with a full-fare passenger). The service is every 30mins in the main areas, every 15mins 6–9am and 3.30–6.30pm, but you must have the right change. Lynx stops are marked by pink paw-print signs and all buses are wheelchair accessible. There can be long queues for buses at Disney at closing time, so you could take Disney transport to *Downtown Disney* (via one of the resorts or the TTC), then get a taxi back to your hotel (about $30 to I-Drive).

I-Ride Trolley: Great-value service for the I-Drive area, it operates 2 routes along a 14ml/23km stretch of this tourist corridor.

- **The Main/Red Line:** With 77 stops, this runs from the Orlando Premium Outlets at the top of I-Drive to SeaWorld and Aquatica via Westwood Boulevard and Sea Harbor Drive, and on to Orlando Premium Outlets (Vineland Ave).
- **The Green Line:** With 33 stops, this goes from the Universal resort area (Windhover Drive and Major

Boulevard) south to Orlando Premium Outlets via Universal Boulevard, the Convention Center and SeaWorld.

Running every day, 8am–10.30pm at roughly 20-minute intervals (30mins on the Green Line), it costs $1.25/trip (25c for seniors) – please have the right change – or you can buy Unlimited Ride Passes for 1, 3, 5, 7 or 14 days at $4, $6, $8, $10, $17. If you need to transfer between routes, ask for a transfer coupon when you board (not needed with Unlimited Ride Passes). Kids 12 and under go free with an adult, and all trolleys have hydraulic lifts for wheelchairs. Passes are sold at more than 100 locations in the I-Drive area, including the Official Visitor Center and most hotel desks but NOT on the trolleys themselves (407 248 9590 or US freephone 1866 243 7483, **www.iridetrolley.com**).

> **BRITTIP**
> The cheapest way to get from I-Drive to Disney is the $2 Lynx bus Link 50 from SeaWorld – 6600 Sea Harbor Drive – to the Transportation & Ticket Center next to the Magic Kingdom Park. All Disney transport then operates from there. Use the I-Ride Trolley to get to SeaWorld.

Busch Shuttle Express: Another regular service is from SeaWorld to Busch Gardens in Tampa, with 7 departure points, 8.15–9.40am daily. It costs $10/person but is FREE if you have Busch tickets in advance (included in the FlexTicket Plus or 3-Park Ticket with SeaWorld and Aquatica). For more info, call 1800 221 1339 toll-free.

Shuttle services

An alternative to public transport are the well-organised firms offering set-fee shuttles to the attractions that pick up at hotels. There are more than a dozen, with everything from stretch Hummer limos to buses.

Mears: The most comprehensive service, with a 1,000-vehicle fleet from limousines to town cars and coaches. Typical round-trip shuttle fares would be: airport to *Walt Disney World*, $35 adults, $27 under-12s, under-4s free ($22 and $17 one way); airport to I-Drive, $30 and $24 ($20 and $15 one way); airport to Highway 192 in Kissimmee $46 and $37 ($27 and $22 one way); *Walt Disney World* to Universal Orlando, $20 round trip; I-Drive to *Walt Disney World*, $20; I-Drive or *Walt Disney World* to Kennedy Space Center, $36. You can book a shuttle on arrival at the Mears' desks in the luggage halls, but it can be a longish trip if it has a full van stopping at several hotels before yours (407 423 5566, **www.mearstransportation.com**).

MagicCity National Transportation: Goes to all the main attractions (e.g. $12 each for a family of 4 from I-Drive to Walt Disney World; $10 each for 4 from I-Drive to Orlando International Airport; 407 678 8888, **www.magiccitynationaltransportation.com**).

Maingate Transportation: Another option from the Highway 192 area ($16 round-trip to Universal or Wet 'n Wild, $13 to SeaWorld and $12 to Disney parks; 407 870 5553, **www.maingatetaxi.com**).

Omega Transportation: with a full range of shuttle and airport transfer services from most hotels (1800 997 9489, **www.shuttlesinorlando.com**).

Shopping mall shuttles: Lake Buena Vista Factory Stores collects guests free each day from 54 hotels in the Orlando and Kissimmee areas (407 363 1093, or **www.lbvfs.com**); **Orlando Premium Outlets** has a free shuttle from 15 Lake Buena Vista area hotels or for $10 a round trip from Kissimmee hotels (call at least 2hrs in advance on 407 390 0000).

One Fish, Two Fish at IoA

© Universal Orlando Resort

Excursions: There are also excursion services offered by the likes of *Brit Guide* partners **Florida Dolphin Tours** (407 352 5151, **www.floridadolphintours.com**) and **Gray Line Tours** (p262).

Town cars and limos

When it comes to limousine, town car and other transport services, there is again a huge choice (more than 150 at the last count). The following all earn a *Brit Guide* recommendation:

BRITTIP
A 'town car' means a deluxe saloon, such as a Cadillac or Lincoln.

Quick Transportation: A good bet for airport transfers and tailor-made transport packages, its town cars comfortably cope with a family of 4, while luxury vans cater for larger parties and all offer a ½hr grocery stop for an extra $20. Luxury van rates (for up to 7) 1-way from Orlando International Airport range from $60 to the I-Drive area up to $95 for the farthest parts of *Walt Disney World.* Up to 11 can use a van for a small additional fee per person. Larger parties may need a luggage trailer for $25 extra each way. Town car rates are $120 from the airport to anywhere in Greater Orlando and $230 for a round trip, while stretch limos are $195 and $380. It serves all the parks and attractions and offers online quotes for all services, while it can also supply vehicles for the disabled (407 354 2456 or 1888 784 2522, **www.quicktransportation.com**).

Reunion Resort

Skyy Limousine: This company has one of the largest selections of vehicles in town, from Lincolns and executive vans to the amazing Hummer limo. One-way airport transfers from $70 (plus a 20% driver gratuity), and vehicles can also be hired by the hour from $55/hour. Other options cover much of central Florida, offering cruise transfers, a night on the town, all-day services, beach trips, concerts and tailor-made excursions (407 352 4644, **www.skyylimousine.com**).

FL Tours: This well-established and popular company specialises in both airport–Disney routes and Port Canaveral transfers. One-way trips start from $65 and round trips from $110 ($119 and $229 from Orlando Sanford International Airport), plus gratuity; it also offers a free ½hr grocery stop, free kids' booster and car seats, 24-hour online reservation access, and no extra charge for late pick-ups (407 857 9606, **www.fltours.com**). Look up the full airport list at **www.orlandoairports.net/transport/vfh.htm**.

Taxis

For groups of 4 or 5, taxis can be more cost-effective than the shuttles. Orlando International Airport to I-Drive would be around $35 (plus tip); $50–60 for the Kissimmee area; $60 to *Magic Kingdom* resorts and $55 for the *Epcot* resort area; $15 from I-Drive to Universal Orlando; and $25-30 from I-Drive to *Downtown Disney.* You'll find plenty of taxis in ranks at the parks, hotels and shopping centres, but they don't cruise around looking for fares, so it's often best to book in advance. You also need to ensure you choose a reliable, fully insured company. Check the name and phone number of the cab company is clearly displayed on the side, the driver's ID and insurance are visible and the rates are shown on the window or inside the car. Some drivers look for fares in the airport baggage hall, which is strictly illegal; all legitimate taxis should be in the rank on Level 1.

Mears: A group of 3 firms – Checker Cabs, Yellow Cabs and City Cabs (407 422 2222) – all of which are reliable. Mears is the main taxi company for Orlando Sanford International Airport, and you can pre-book cabs for around $85 to I-Drive, $105 to Lake Buena Vista and $115 to Disney hotels. Most taxis are metered but it is also acceptable to ask in advance what the fare will be.

Other reputable firms: Ace Metro/ Luxury Cab (407 855 1111), Star Taxis (407 857 9999) and Diamond Cab Co. (407 523 3333). Several hotels have town cars at their ranks and these won't have meters, so you can either ask for the fare or call one of the companies listed above.

THE CAR

Ultimately, having a car is the key to being in charge of your holiday and, on a weekly basis, car hire tends to be quite reasonable: weekly rates can be as low as $110 for the smallest car. The scale of the car hire operation is huge, with as many as 1,000 visitors arriving at a time.

> **BRIT**TIP
> Your first call for car hire should be to *Brit Guide* partner Alamo. See inside the front cover for our special offer.

The cars will be mainly American - Chevrolet, Dodge, Buick, Chrysler, Ford, Mercury and Lincoln, plus some other makes like Kia, Hyundai and Nissan.

> **BRIT**TIP
> Check you have both parts of your driving licence BEFORE you leave home. You will simply NOT be given a hire car without all of it.

- **Economy:** Also called a sub-compact, the smallest cars are usually a Vauxhall Corsa-sized hatchback.
- **Compact:** Next up is a small family saloon like a Nissan Versa.
- **Midsize:** The Intermediate is a more spacious 4-door, 5-seater like a Toyota Corolla.
- **Fullsize:** This would be a larger-style executive car like a Ford Fusion.
- **Premium, Luxury, Convertible, SUV and Minivan:** All more upmarket options, while the Minivan is a Ford Galaxy or Renault Espace type.

Most holiday companies offer 'free car hire', but that doesn't mean it won't cost you anything. Only the *rental* cost is free and you must still pay the insurances and taxes (which makes the all-inclusive packages more attractive).

> **BRIT**TIP
> Be firm with the car hire company check-in clerk. Some can push you into having extras, like car upgrades, you simply won't need.

Also beware low starting rates – there are essential insurances, taxes and surcharges that can take the weekly rate above $300. However, all the big rental companies now offer all-inclusive rates, which can work out cheaper if booked in advance in the UK, and you also benefit from easier processing in Orlando, making the whole business quicker.

> **BRIT**TIP
> The boot (trunk) size of American cars tends to be slightly smaller than the British equivalent. Plus you won't get 7 adults AND all their luggage in a 7-seat people carrier ('van')!

Car rental companies: Alamo is our *Brit Guide* partner and offers excellent rates and service (see inside front cover). You also benefit with Alamo

Disney's Wedding Pavilion

© Disney

from being able to choose your own car from the different ranges – Compact, Intermediate, etc. – where the other companies assign you a specific car. For alternatives, try **Dollar** (0808 234 2474), **Avis** (0844 581 0147), **Budget** (0844 544 3439) or **Thrifty** (01494 751 500).

BRITTIP

Unless you have accepted the SunPass pre-pay auto-toll option from the car rental firm, you **cannot** drive through the toll booths marked 'Sunpass' or 'E-Pass' only. You must stop at the booths marked 'Change Given' (in green) or 'Exact Change Only' (in blue).

Insurance: Having a credit card is essential, and there are two main kinds of insurance, the most important being the Loss or Collision Damage Waiver (LDW or CDW). This costs $24–26/day and covers you for any damage to your hire car. You can do without it, but the hire company will insist on a deposit around $1,500 on your credit card (and you are liable for ANY damage). You will also be offered Supplemental Liability Insurance (SLI) or Extended Protection at $13–15 a day, which is not essential but does cover you for most damage you might cause. Another option is Underinsured Motorists Protection (in case someone with minimal cover runs into you) at around $7 a day.

Those on a budget can cut costs by taking insurance through specialists like **Insurance4CarHire** (0844 892 1770, **www.cdwsli.com**), whose Worldwide cover offers LDW and SLI at £7 a day. You may still need to leave a credit card imprint with the

Simon at Gatorland

Enter Mapman

By far the best and most up-to-date area map is a British production, created by Disney fan and cartographer Steve 'Mapman' Munns. It is superbly detailed for the I-4 corridor, Highway 192 and Walt Disney World, with special sections on I-Drive and villa locations. All the main attractions, hotels and even many restaurants are clearly indicated and there is accompanying text and photos, while the website adds updates and insider tips. The latest edition is also ultra hard-wearing. We think it's the perfect companion to the *Brit Guide* and you won't go wrong with it at only £7.40 (plus 78p p&p). Go to **www.orlandomaps.co.uk** (online orders only). It's also available as an iPhone/iPod/iPad App from the iTunes store for £2.99. Called iOrlando Tourist Map, it is offline so there are no roaming charges, but it does include a searchable database to find places quickly. Even better, Steve is our resident 'mapman' for the *Brit Guide*.

hire firm, but it should accept these policies (check in advance).

Other costs: Drivers must be at least 21, and those under 25 have to pay an extra $25 a day. Other costs include local and Florida state taxes, which can add $25–30 a week. Many companies also offer a Roadside Plus (around $5/day), which covers breakdowns, flat tyres, running out of fuel or locking your keys in the car, but this is again totally optional.

Fuel: Then there is 'gas', though this is still cheaper than in the UK. You can either *pre-pay* for a full tank (so you bring it back empty; the charge is usually slightly under the local rate/gallon for this); *fill it up yourself* so you have a full tank on return; or pay a *fuel surcharge* at the end for the company to refill the tank (the most expensive option).

Pre-pay tolls: You can also opt for the SunPass auto-pay system (Dollar calls it Pass24) for toll roads, so you just drive through without stopping; all your tolls are auto-recorded for payment when you return the car (plus a $2/day convenience fee).

The satnav solution

The best way to navigate is by a GPS or SatNav system. All car hire companies offer this as an extra (at around $70/week) or you can bring your own. If your system has only the base-level (i.e. UK) maps loaded, download the maps for south-east USA for around £35. If you are thinking of buying a GPS system, the likes of Wal-Mart offer new systems, fully loaded for the US, for less than $200.

Getting used to your car

Most people soon find driving in America is a pleasure, mainly because nearly all hire cars are automatics and nearly new. And, because speed limits are lower (and rigidly enforced), you won't often be rushed into taking a wrong turn.

- All cars have air-conditioning, which is essential for most of the year. Turn on the fan as well as the A/C button or it won't work! A small pool of liquid will form under the car from condensation from the A/C unit.
- Power steering is universal.
- Larger cars have cruise control, so you can set the desired speed and take your foot off the accelerator. There will be 2 buttons on the steering wheel, one to switch on cruise control, the other to set the speed. To cancel, either press the first button or touch the brake.
- Some cars have an extra pedal to the left of the brake, and you need to push this to engage the handbrake. To release it, you pull the tab just above it, if there is one, or give a second push on the pedal.
- Keep your foot on the brake when you are stationary as automatics tend to creep forward. Always put the gear lever in 'P' (Park) when switching off.
- The car probably won't start unless the gear lever is in 'P'. To put the car in 'D' for Drive, depress the brake pedal. D1 and D2 are extra gears for steep hills (none in Florida!).
- Not all cars have central locking, so make sure you lock ALL the doors before leaving it. With an automatic, you won't be able to take the keys out of the ignition unless you put the gear lever in 'Park'.

Fuel: All local 'gas' stations are self-service and most require you to pay before filling up. However, the pumps should allow you to pay by credit card without having to visit the cashier (some stations ask for a local zip code with a credit card swipe, which means you DO need to go inside). To activate the petrol pump, you may need first to lift the lever underneath the pump nozzle. **RaceTrac** and **Hess** petrol stations are often the cheapest. The 2 Hess stations in *Walt Disney World* are, surprisingly, among the cheapest in the area, while the **Wal-Mart** on Vineland Road is also a cheap option. Petrol stations just outside Disney and the airport are the MOST expensive.

Finding your way

Your car hire company should provide you with a basic map of Orlando, plus directions to your hotel – insist they do as all the hire companies make a big point of this in their literature.

BRITTIP

Be organised – get your directions in advance off the internet at sites like **www.mapquest.com** or use Google Earth to source maps, directions and even check out the lie of the land in advance. Download it free from its website at **http://earth. google.com**.

Christmas fireworks at the Magic Kingdom

© Disney

Signposting: You can't fail to find the main attractions, but retracing your steps can be tricky as the exit road may be different from the way in. It is vital to familiarise yourself with the main roads in advance and learn to navigate by road numbers (as it's mainly those that are given on the signposts), exit numbers off the main roads, and directions around the attractions so you know where you're heading (i.e. if you want I-4 east or west or 192 as you exit *Walt Disney World*).

Lanes and exits: Exits off motorways can be on EITHER side of the carriageway, not just on the right, but you can overtake in ANY lane on multi-lane highways. Therefore, you can sit in the middle lane until you see your exit. You don't get much advance notice of turn-offs, though.

BRITTIP

Just after exit 34, the Greeneway (417) heading south appears to split into two where it meets Highway 408. Keep RIGHT to stay southbound.

Road names: It helps that none of the main attractions is off the beaten track, but the support of a front-seat navigator can be useful. Around town, road names are displayed at every junction suspended ABOVE the road underneath the traffic lights. This road name is NOT the road you are on, but the one you are CROSSING. Once again there is little advance notice of each junction and the road names can be hard to read as you approach, especially at night, so keep your speed down if you think you are close to your turn-off to allow time

Winter-Summerland Mini-Golf

© Disney

to get into the correct lane. If you do miss a turning, most roads are on a grid system, so it's easy to work back.

Occasionally you will meet a crossroads where no right of way is obvious. This is a 4-Way Stop, and the priority goes in order of arrival. So, when it's your turn, just indicate and pull out slowly (America doesn't have many roundabouts, so this may be the closest you get to one).

Local maps: Orlando has yet to come up with a comprehensive tourist map of its streets, and the maps supplied by the car rental companies are pretty basic. The best of the free maps is the bright orange *Welcome Guide Map* (also full of discount coupons), available in the main tourist areas, and the pull-out map inside the *Kissimmee Visitors' Guide* (or see it online at **www. visitkissimmee.com**; go to Travel Guide and then Maps). AA members are also well catered for (p57).

Rules and regulations

As well as the obvious difference of driving on the 'wrong' side of the road, there are several differences in procedure.

Tolls: For toll roads, have some change handy in amounts from 25c to $2. They all give change (in the GREEN lanes), but you will get through quicker if you have the correct money (in the BLUE lanes). On minor exits of Osceola Parkway and the Greeneway, there are auto-toll machines only, so keep some loose change to hand.

BRITTIP

On nearly all toll roads, for the manned toll booths you have to pull in to a slip road on the *right* to pay. It is SunPass/E-Pass only on the main carriageway. This can catch you out when you have just left the airport.

Traffic lights: The most frequent British errors occur at traffic lights (which are hung above the road). At a red light, you can still turn RIGHT providing there is no traffic coming from the left. Come to a complete stop, check there are no pedestrians crossing and make your turn - unless there is a sign indicating 'No turn on red'. Turning left at the lights, you have the right of way with a green ARROW but must give way to traffic from the other direction on a SOLID green.

Left turns: The majority of accidents involving overseas visitors take place on left turns, so take extra care. There is also no amber light from red to green, but there IS from green to red. A flashing amber light at a junction means proceed but watch for traffic joining the carriageway, while a flashing red light indicates it is okay to turn if the carriageway is clear.

BRITTIP

The Osceola Parkway toll road (522) that runs parallel to Highway 192 is a better route in to *Walt Disney World* from eastern Kissimmee and costs only $1.75. Use Sherberth Road for Disney access from west 192 or the new Western Beltway (Highway 429).

Speed limits: Speed limits are always well marked with black numbering on white signs and the police are pretty hot on speeding, with steep on-the-spot fines. There are varying limits of 55–70mph (88–113kph) on the Interstates, where there is also a 40mph (64kph) minimum speed limit. It can also be just 15–25mph (24–40kph) in built-up areas.

Seat belts: These are compulsory for all passengers, while child seats must be used for under-4s and can be hired from the car companies at $10–15 a day (better to bring your own or buy one locally for $70–80). Children aged 4 or 5 must use a seat belt, in the front or back, or have a child seat fitted.

Parking: It is illegal to park within 3m/10ft of a fire hydrant or a lowered kerb, and never park in front of a yellow-painted kerb – they are stopping points for emergency vehicles and you will be towed away. Never park ON a kerb, either. Park bonnet first – reverse parking is frowned upon because number plates are only on the rear of cars and

police then can't see them. If you park parallel to the kerb, you must point in the direction of traffic.

Other traffic laws: Flashing orange lights over the road indicate a school zone and school buses must NOT be overtaken in either direction when they are unloading and have their hazard lights on. U-turns are forbidden in built-up areas and where there is a solid line down the middle of the road. You must pull to the side of the road to allow emergency vehicles to pass, in either direction, when they have lights and/or sirens going. Also, on multi-lane highways in Florida, the Move Over law means you must pull into an adjacent lane if you see a police car on the hard shoulder, or slow down if you can't move over. And you must put on your lights in the rain.

Finally, DON'T drink and drive. Florida has strict laws, with penalties of up to 6 months in prison for first-time offenders. The blood-alcohol limit is lower than in Britain, so it is safer not to drink at all if you are driving. It is also illegal to carry open containers of alcohol in the car.

Bonus for AA members: Your membership is recognised by the equivalent AAA in the US and you benefit from various special offers. Take your AA card and produce it where you see the AAA 'Show & Save'

Taumata Racer at Aquatica

signs in to enjoy the same discounts as the locals. Visit **www.aaasouth.com** and click AAA Discounts for the full range, which includes shopping and dining, like 10% off at Hard Rock Cafe and Dennys restaurants (use the zip code 32819 when prompted).

BRITTIP
You won't encounter any fixed speed cameras like those in the UK, but police cars will often be stationed in busy areas with hand-held cameras (notably on Sherberth Rd in Kissimmee). But there are now cameras on many traffic lights to catch red-light runners, so don't take any risks.

Accidents
In the unlikely event of an accident, no matter how minor, you must contact the police before the cars can be moved (except on the busy I-4). Car hire firms will insist on a full police report for the insurance. If you break down, there should be an emergency number for the hire company in its literature or, if you are on a main highway, raise the bonnet and wait for one of the frequent police patrol cars to stop (or dial *FHP on your mobile). Always carry both parts of your driving licence and your car hire forms in case you are stopped by the police.

Bert and Ernie's at Busch Gardens

Key routes
All main motorways are prefixed I, the even numbers going east–west and odd numbers north–south. Federal Highways are the next grade down, with black numerals on white shields, while state roads are prefixed SR (black numbers on white circular or rectangular signs).

All American motorways have their junctions numbered in mileage terms, which makes it easy to calculate journey distances. I-4 starts at exit 1 in Tampa and goes to exit 132 at Daytona, 132mls away. In Orlando, the main junctions run from exit 55, at Highway 27, to exit 83 (downtown Orlando) and exit 101 for the Seminole Expressway (417) and Orlando Sanford International Airport.

Interstate 4: I-4 is the main route through Orlando, a 4, 6 or 8-lane motorway linking the coasts. Interstates are always indicated on blue shield-shaped signs. For most of its length, I-4 travels east–west but, around Orlando, it swings north–south, though directions are still given east (for north) or west (for south). All the attractions of *Walt Disney World*, plus SeaWorld and Universal Orlando are well signposted from I-4. Legoland Florida in Winter Haven, Lake Wales and Bok Tower Gardens are a 45min drive from Orlando west on I-4 and then south on Highway 27, while Busch Gardens is 75–90mins down I-4 to Tampa. Be aware I-4 can be packed with traffic for long sections in the morning and evening rush hours. You can check for major roadworks on **www.trans4mation.org**.

International Drive: I-Drive is the second key local roadway, linking a 14½ml/24km ribbon of hotels, shops, restaurants and attractions like Wet 'n Wild, Pointe Orlando and Orlando Premium Outlets (I-Drive South, from Highway 192 in Kissimmee north to Route 535 is NOT the main stretch and the 2 sections are linked via Route 535 and World Center Drive). From I-4, take exits 71, 72, 74A or 75A going east, or 75B, 74A or 72 going west. To the north, I-Drive runs

Manta at SeaWorld

into Oak Ridge Road and the South Orange Blossom Trail, which leads to downtown Orlando (junctions 82C–84 off I-4). I-Drive is also bisected by Sand Lake Road and runs into World Center Drive (536) to the south, also convenient for Disney.

I-Drive is a major tourist centre and makes an excellent base, especially around the Sand Lake Road junction, as it is fully pedestrian-friendly. It's a 20min drive to Disney and 10mins from Universal. However, at peak times, heavy traffic means it's best to avoid the stretch from the Convention Center north. Use Universal Boulevard instead.

Kissimmee: The other main tourist area, south of Orlando and south-east of Disney, its features are grouped along a 20ml/32km stretch of the Irlo Bronson Memorial Highway (192), which intersects I-4 at junction 64B, and is close to *Walt Disney World* (though a good 25mins from SeaWorld and Universal). Downtown Kissimmee is off Main Street, Broadway and Emmett Street, and is ideal for walking.

A handy visual along Highway 192 is the **Marker Series** from Formosa Gardens (number 4) to just past Medieval Times (number 15). These highly visible signs are good locators for hotels, restaurants and attractions, and much of this stretch is also walkable (though few places are close together). Try to avoid the area of the 192 east of Marker 15, though; it is becoming increasingly run-down

and unappealing. If you're heading to downtown Kissimmee (which we DO recommend) use the Osceola Parkway and S Orange Blossom Trail (441). The unique Disney-inspired town of Celebration is also here (just south of *Walt Disney World*).

Highway 27: This is at the west end of Highway 192, running north to Clermont and south to Davenport (and Haines City). A major area of holiday villa developments, these are generally quite convenient for Disney. However, many home owners claim they are only '5mins from Disney', which is extremely misleading. It is usually at least 10mins from Highway 27 to the edge of Disney property; often more. The area is also starting to add shops and restaurants, notably in the Cagan Crossings junction (just north of where 192 meets 27), where there is also a large Wal-Mart, and Berry Town Center (to the south).

Western Beltway: The new 429 provides a western Orlando by-pass, avoiding the often-crowded I-4 and linking with the Florida Turnpike and Apopka to the north. More importantly, it offers an alternative west gateway to Walt Disney World at Exit 8 (Western Way), which is handy for the Davenport/Clermont areas. This junction is also destined for development in the next 10 years as an area called Flamingo Crossings at the junction of the 429 and Western Way (**www.flamingocrossings.com**).

Now, let's go on to the next vital step – your holiday accommodation…

Metro Orlando has the second highest concentration of hotels in the world (after Las Vegas) and more are being built all the time. There are currently 115,000 rooms, and counting, not to mention 26,000 villas for rent. Therefore, what follows is only a general guide to the various types, plus our recommendations and favourites.

The main choice is between a traditional hotel option and one of the many self-catering types of accommodation, which can be villas/vacation homes, town homes or condos.

BRITTIP

Don't make calls from your hotel – most add a 45–70% surcharge (Disney resorts even add a connection fee), while you can be charged for an unanswered call if it rings 5 or more times. Buy a phonecard instead (p33 and 38).

Disney's Fort Wilderness Resort and Campground

© Disney

HOTELS

Many American hotels, particularly in the tourist areas, tend towards the motel type, where everything is not necessarily located in one main building. Your room may be in one of several blocks sited round the pool, restaurant or other amenities. Room size rarely alters, even from 2 to 4-star hotels; their amenities and services form the basis of their star ratings. A standard room usually has 2 double beds and will accommodate a family of 4 (couples without children should ask for a king room, with an extra-size bed). All hotels should offer non-smoking rooms. Motel-type accommodation can also lack a restaurant as they operate on a room-only basis, so you may have to drive to the nearest restaurant (many are within walking distance on I-Drive). Ask about the dining facilities before you book.

Most hotels are big, clean, efficient and great value. You'll find plenty of soft-drink and ice machines (though it's cheaper to buy drinks from a supermarket), with ice buckets in all rooms. All accommodation will be air-conditioned and, when it is hot, you have to live with the drone of the A/C unit at night. If you need a more spacious room, look for one of the many suite hotels, which provide sitting rooms and mini-kitchens, as well as 1, 2 or even 3 bedrooms.

Deals and bookings: If you've just arrived and need a hotel, visit the official Visitor Center on I-Drive just north of Pointe Orlando (on the corner of Austrian Court; 8.30am–6.30pm daily; 407 363 5872), where they have brochures on all current deals. If you're keen on auction websites like **www.priceline.co.uk**, you may land a bargain. Other hotel agents are **Expedia** (0871 226 0808, **www.expedia.co.uk**), **Hotel Anywhere** (01444 410555, **www.hotelanywhere.co.uk**), **Hotels.com** (020 3027 8146; **www.hotels.com**), **Orbitz** (1888 656 4546 in the US or 001 312 416 0018 from the UK, **www.orbitz.com**) and **Hotwire** (**www.hotwire.com**).

BRITTIP

Buy soft drinks at the supermarket, and a polystyrene cooler for about $5 that you can fill from your hotel ice machine to keep drinks cold.

Prices: Hotel prices are always per room (not per person) and they will be cheaper out of the main holiday periods, with special deals at times. Always ask for rates if you book directly and check if special rates apply during your visit (don't be afraid to ask for their 'best rate' at off-peak times, which can be lower than published or 'rack' rates). There may be an additional charge ($5–15/person) for more than 2 adults sharing a room, plus there is state tax and, sometimes, a sneaky resort fee that can add $10–15/day.

There is no widely accepted star rating, so (with the exception of Disney's resorts), we group hotels into 4 ranges: *Budget, Value, Moderate* and *Deluxe*, where the (rough) price groups/night will be:

- Budget   =   up to $50
- Value   = $51–99
- Moderate   = $100–160
- Deluxe   = $161 plus

The main factor is the extra facilities. Thus, a Deluxe rating will include the highest level of facilities and service, while a Budget will be a basic motel-type. A key pricing factor is location (the closer to Disney and other parks, the higher the price), so you can save if you don't mind a longer journey.

Suite things

Suites hotels, virtually unknown in the UK, provide a combination of hotel and apartment, with extra value for large families or groups. Typically, a suites room gives you a living room and kitchenette, including microwave, coffee-maker, fridge, cutlery and crockery, while many offer a complimentary continental breakfast (or better). All have pools and grocery stores or snack bars and several have restaurants. They vary only in the number of bedrooms and can usually sleep 6–10.

Disney hotels

Our review of Orlando's hotels starts with *Walt Disney World*. Sited conveniently for all its attractions – and linked by an excellent free transport system of monorail, buses and boats – Disney's hotels, suites and campsites are all magnificently appointed and maintained. It also groups them into 5 types: *Value, Moderate* and *Deluxe Resorts*, then the *Deluxe Villas* (Disney's timeshare properties) and the *Campground* of Fort Wilderness (with a strong element of self-catering for the latter 2). They range from the swanky *Grand Floridian Resort & Spa* to the more basic but still fun style of the *Pop Century Resort*. And Disney's imagination and attention to detail here are as good as at the parks. There are more than 22,000 rooms, while **Fort Wilderness** has 1,195 campsites and cabins.

Grand accommodation comes at a price, though. A regular room at the *Grand Floridian* can be $700 a night

Disney's Grand Floridian Resort & Spa

© Disney

Disney Dining Plan

One other possible perk of staying onsite with Disney is its **Dining Plan**. This allows its hotel guests to pre-pay most meals during their stay at a set fee per day. However, it is an EXPENSIVE option if you are staying for a week or more. There are three different Plans to choose from: (prices shown as of summer 2011):

Quick Service Dining Plan: Provides 2 counter-service meals and 2 snacks a day, plus 1 refillable resort mug/person. Counter-service meals are defined as 1 entrée or combo meal, plus 1 dessert and 1 (non-alcoholic) drink for lunch or dinner, and 1 juice, 1 entrée or combo meal and 1 drink for breakfast. Snacks can be any item such as an ice-cream, popcorn, pastry, a piece of fruit, a bag of crisps, a bottled drink, a medium soda or tea/coffee. Cost: $34.99/day for adults, $11.99 for 3–9s (children must also order off the Children's Menu).

Disney Dining Plan: Provides 1 table-service meal, 1 counter-service and 1 snack per person per day. Table-service meals are 1 appetiser, 1 entrée, 1 dessert and 1 (non-alcoholic) drink, or 1 juice, 1 entrée and 1 drink OR a full buffet for breakfast. Cost: $45.99 and $11.99/day (but $47.99 and $12.99 in peak season).

Deluxe Dining Plan: Provides 3 meals (either table or counter-service) and 2 snacks per person per day, plus 1 refillable resort mug per person. Cost: $78.99 and $21.99/day.

All meals do NOT have to be used per day and can be spread over the full duration of your stay, so you can miss a table-service meal one day, then use 2 table-service credits another day for a signature restaurant or dinner show. Gratuities are NOT included, though. When you check in at a Disney hotel, you're given a 'Key to the World' card you then use for all your Dining Plan meals and that monitors your daily usage. The Dining Plans CAN be used for Character Meals, when 1 table-service meal is required per person (2 at ultra-popular Cinderella's Royal Table in *Magic Kingdom*), and for the 9 Signature Restaurants in *Walt Disney World* (notably Jiko at *Animal Kingdom Lodge*, California Grill at the *Contemporary Resort* and Citricos at the *Grand Floridian Resort*), which all require 2 table-service meals. They can even be used at Disney's Dinner Shows (p293), subject to availability, at 2 table-service meals per person.

However, ALL members of the group must book the Plan for the *full* duration of the stay and inclusive of park tickets. It is also advisable to pre-book (on 407 939 3463) full-service meals well in advance as the sit-down restaurants usually book up early. Not all restaurants are on the Plan but you still have 100 options. Be aware there were substantial increases in Dining Plan prices in 2011, making this even more expensive, in our view. More info at **www.disneyworld.co.uk**, where you can book all table service restaurants online.

in high season (suites can top $2,000) and even the Moderate *Caribbean Beach Resort* can be $180 a night. Dining at resort hotels is not cheap either, and you'll find few fast-food outlets on site. However, staying with the Mouse is one of the great thrills, for the style, service and extras. The 20 resorts offer a superb array of facilities that children especially love. The benefits are:

- **Resort ID card:** Every guest receives a card with which to charge almost all on-site purchases.
- **Package delivery:** Park purchases can be sent back to your hotel.

- **Free parking:** No charge at any of Disney's car parks.
- **Refillable mugs:** All Disney resorts sell collectable drinking mugs, which are well worth buying ($13) as you then get free refills at their self-service cafés.
- **Dining priority:** Many Disney restaurants hold tables for resort guests, while you can also book 180 days in advance *plus* the length of your stay (i.e. 194 days if you're going for 2 weeks). Call 407 939 3463 (non-Disney hotel guests can book only 180 days in advance).
- **Priority golf:** The best tee times are

reserved for resort guests and can be booked 90 days in advance on 407 939 4653.

- **Children's services:** All resorts have in-room or group babysitting (subject to availability) and 8 of the 9 Deluxe resorts have supervised activity centres and dinner clubs (around $13/child per hour), usually open until midnight.
- **Mickey on call:** What better way to wake than with an alarm call from the Mouse himself?
- **Extra Magic Hours:** This is the BIG bonus, the chance to get into 1 of the parks each day either 1 hour early or for 3 hours after regular park closing, and enjoy many rides with reduced crowds.
- **Disney's Magical Express Service:** The free airport transfer service for guests at Disney hotels. Book at least 10 days before arrival through **www.disneyworld.co.uk** or a travel agent.

Value resorts

Disney's All-Star Resorts: Here you can stay in one of the 5 **Sports**-themed blocks centred around a massive food court, 2 swimming pools, a games arcade and shops; the **Music**-themed version; or the **Movies** complex. The latter is possibly the most imaginative, with its Fantasia pool and kids' play areas, and the most popular blocks are Toy Story and 101 Dalmatians (both non-smoking).

Standard rooms are bright and compact (read 'tight' for families with older children), but well designed for those who want the Disney convenience but not the price. The *All Star Music Resort* (Jazz and Calypso buildings) also has 192 impressive 2-room Family Suites (combining 2 standard rooms) that sleep up to 6. Each suite has 2 bathrooms, a well-stocked kitchenette, a lounge and private master bedroom, making the space much more flexible.

All 3 centres, with 5,568 rooms, have pool bars, shops, laundry facilities, video games rooms and a pizza delivery service. Close to the entrance is a large McDonald's if the resort's food courts don't appeal. All resort transport is provided by an efficient bus service.

⚓ BRITTIP

To make a reservation at any Walt Disney World hotel, call 407 934 7639, or visit **www.disneyworld.co.uk**.

Disney's Pop Century Resort: In a similar vein, themed round the decades of the 2nd half of the 20th century, here are 5 blocks with giant icons – such as yo-yos, Rubik's cubes and juke-boxes – and a riot of period sayings and visual gags. Opened in 2003, it features a pool fashioned like a 10-pin bowling lane (others are shaped like a computer and a flower), a huge table football set-up and open-air Twister mats. Blocks are grouped around a main building housing the check-in area (with a large-screen TV showing Disney films), an imaginative food court, a lounge (with quick-breakfast bar), a Disney store and games arcade. The 177-acre/72ha complex also features a central lake and lots of bright landscaping. It also has a well-organised bus service to the parks. The drawbacks? Long queues to check in and a rather hectic feel, even late in the evening. You need to request a hairdryer from reception and rooms are, again, rather small.

Disney's Art of Animation Resort: Opening in summer 2012 is this new development for Disney, a budget-priced suites-style resort, building on the popularity of the Family Suites at the *All Star Music Resort*. Originally intended to be part of the *Pop Century*

Disney's Pop Century Resort

© Disney

Resort, it will instead be a 4-part, 1,984-room complex (1,120 suites, 864 standard rooms) based around classic animated films *The Lion King*, *The Little Mermaid*, *Finding Nemo* and *Cars*, completely non-smoking and with an elaborate main pool, 2 'quiet' pools, an animation-themed food court, games arcade and shop. The 4 different courtyards will be heavily themed for each of the films, with larger-than-life icons, interactive sculptures, fountains and other play features, and theming in all the rooms, with the suites offering a master bedroom, 2 bathrooms and 3 separate sleeping areas in the living space, including the 'Inovabed' – a piece of furniture that converts from a table or work-desk into a bed. Like *Pop Century*, all park transport is by bus.

Moderate resorts

Disney's Caribbean Beach Resort: This 2,112-room complex is spread over 5 Caribbean 'islands' (with an inter-island bus service). Rooms are relatively plain, but comfortably sleep 4, and the Market Street food court, main restaurant Shutters and outdoor activities (with a lakeside recreation area with themed waterfalls, slides, games arcade, bike and boat rentals) are a big hit with kids. The 6 Market Street outlets at the Old Port Royale resort hub can get busy in the morning, and the Trinidad South and Barbados 'islands' are a fair walk from the centre. Trinidad South rooms feature some fun pirate theming (for a supplement) and there are other imaginative touches, like Parrot Cay Island with its tropical birds and play

Disney's Port Orleans Resort

© Disney

area. Transport to all the parks is solely by bus.

Disney's Coronado Springs Resort: Possibly the best value of this trio, it has slightly more facilities for its 1,921 rooms spread over 125 acres/50ha: 4 pools (including the massive Lost City of Cibola activity pool with waterslide), 2 games arcades, a boating marina, bike rentals, restaurant, food court and café/ convenience store, lounge bar, gift shop, beauty salon and health club, business centre and 2 launderettes. The chic and upscale Rix Lounge – a bar/nightclub serving unique cocktails and appetisers – gives the resort another claim to fame. Constructed on a scenic Mexican/ Spanish theme in 3 'villages' (Casitas, Ranchos and Cabanas), Coronado is an often-overlooked treasure. Check out the Maya Grill and its New Latino cuisine; sample the offerings of the tempting Pepper Market food court; or just grab a drink and soak up the splendid lake views from the outdoor terrace. Coronado Springs is only 5mins from *Disney's Animal Kingdom* and is well served by the bus network.

BRITTIP

Disney resort restaurants can (and, we think, should) be visited even if you aren't staying there. Advance book at any of the parks, call 407 939 3463 or visit **www.disneyworld.co.uk**.

Disney's Port Orleans Resort: This is a 2-part complex (formerly Port Orleans and Dixie Landings) split into the 2,048-room *Riverside* – with a steamboat reception area, a great Riverside Mill food court, Boatwright's full-service restaurant, the River Roost lounge (with live entertainment on certain nights) and an old-fashioned General Store (gift shop) – and the 1,008-room *French Quarter*, which has the Sassagoula Floatworks and Food Factory court, 2 bars, a games room and shopping arcade. The Riverside includes the magnificent Ol' Man Island, a 3½-acre/1.5ha playground with swimming pool, kids' area and a fishing hole, while the French Quarter has Doubloon

Kidsuites = happy families

Orlando has pioneered a great family accommodation style, worth seeking out if you have kids who enjoy bunk beds. Basically, a kidsuite is a separate area within the hotel room that gives the kids their own 'bedroom' (with bunks), usually also with their own TV and games console.

Lagoon, with Mardi Gras dragon slide, alligator fountains and a play area. The eye-catching landscaping and design vary from rustic Bayou backwoods to turn-of-the-century New Orleans. Transport for both is by bus to the parks and bus or boat to Downtown Disney.

Deluxe resorts

More than anything, Disney specialises in high-quality hotels with all manner of grand design features, amenities and restaurants. All 9 offer a Concierge level, which adds an exclusive, personalised service, and a private lounge with meals and snacks.

Disney's Animal Kingdom Lodge:
This stunning 'private game lodge' is set on a 33-acre/13ha animal-filled savannah, which many rooms overlook. The pervasive African theme and the effect of opening your curtains to a vista of giraffes and zebras is immense. The lavishness and detail are superb, right down to the guides who can tell guests about the animals and their habitats, the African folklore stories around the outdoor firepit and the chance for children to become junior safari researchers while Mum and Dad do some wine-tasting (the hotel boasts a huge collection of South African wines).

All this creativity comes before you consider the amenities: 2 restaurants, café, bar, elaborately themed 'watering-hole' main pool (with waterslide) and kids' pool, massage and fitness centre, large gift shop, children's play area and an awesome 4-storey atrium.

The main restaurant, Jiko, is spectacular, but there is also the superb buffet-style Boma, a 'marketplace' restaurant featuring African-tinged dishes from a wood-burning grill and rotisserie for breakfast and dinner.

◀️🇬🇧 **BRITTIP**

Jiko at Disney's Animal Kingdom Lodge offers an imaginative New World cuisine menu, attentive service and authentic ambience, and is a wonderfully romantic choice.

Rooms range from standard doubles to 1 and 2-bedroom suites, some of which have bunk beds. Part of the main building, Jambo House, has been converted into studios and 1 and 2-bed villas (the latter with full kitchens) for Disney Vacation Club guests, sleeping 4–12, but these are also available to regular guests when not in use by DVC. The new **Kidani Village** wing adds still more (p71). Simba's Cubhouse is for 4–12s (4.30pm– midnight), and all transport is by bus (with the *Animal Kingdom* barely 5mins away).

Disney's Boardwalk Inn and Villas:
One of the Crescent Lake resorts next to *Epcot* is this 45-acre/18ha extravagant Inn and entertainment 'district'. It features a 512-room hotel, 383 villas, 4 themed restaurants, a TV sports club and 2 nightclubs, plus an array of shops, sports facilities and a huge, free-form pool with a waterslide, all on a semi-circular boardwalk around the lake. The effect is stunning, and the in-room attention to detail excellent, notably in the 'summer cottage' Villas (also part of the Disney Vacation Club).

Disney's Animal Kingdom Lodge

© Disney

Equally excellent is the Mediterranean-themed restaurant Kouzzina by celebrity chef Cat Cora (breakfast and dinner) and Big River Grille Brewing Company (lunch and dinner) for some great beers from its own micro-brewery. Top of the lot is the expensive but superb seafood of the Flying Fish Café (dinner only). You can also try the Boardwalk Bakery for a snack. It's a delightful place to visit for a meal, the nightlife (especially Jellyrolls piano bar and ESPN Club) or just to wander along the boardwalk. Transport is by boat to *Epcot* and *Disney's Hollywood Studios* and bus to the other parks.

Disney's Contemporary Resort:

Situated on the monorail next to the *Magic Kingdom*, this 15-storey resort boasts 655 rooms, a cavernous foyer, 5 shops, 4 restaurants, 2 lounges, a real sandy beach, a marina, 2 pools (1 with waterslide), 6 tennis courts, a video games centre and health club – and fabulous views, especially from the superb, hotel-top California Grill (one of the most romantic settings in Orlando; try to get a reservation to coincide with the park's fireworks). Don't miss Chef Mickey's for a breakfast or dinner buffet with your favourite characters, while the monorail runs right *through* the hotel – great for kids. Rooms are some of Disney's largest and were all renovated from 2006-09, adding elegant new decor, dark-wood furniture and comfy duvets. Chic restaurant/lounge The Wave features a modern bar and dining area with a highly varied menu and is well worth

Disney's Bay Lake Tower

trying for dinner or just a cocktail (or 2!), while the Contempo Café adds a light meal option 6am–midnight. In 2011, the 14th floor was converted to offer a full health-and-wellness theme, with a private yoga studio, spa cuisine, bamboo floors, low-allergen bedding, massage tables and 'rainwater' showers. Within walking distance of the *Magic Kingdom*, transport to other parks is by bus.

Disney's Grand Floridian Resort & Spa:

This true 5-star hotel is built like an elaborate Victorian mansion, with 867 rooms, an impressive domed foyer and staff in period costume. Again on the monorail, 1 stop from the *Magic Kingdom*, the rooms and facilities are truly luxurious – hence the mega prices, though it's worth a look even if you're not staying. Its 6 restaurants include the top-of-the-range Victoria and Albert's (where the set 6-course dinner with wine costs $185), the chic seafood-based Narcoossee's (one of our favourites), with its excellent view over Seven Seas Lagoon, and Mediterranean-styled Citricos. There are also 4 bars and impressive sports and relaxation facilities, notably the fabulous spa and Salon. There's a wonderful second pool area, complete with zero-depth entry and waterslide. The Mouseketeer Club caters for 4–12s (4.30pm–midnight) and the 1900 Park Fare restaurant is hugely popular for character breakfasts and dinners, plus the children's Wonderland Tea Party with Alice and friends (1.30–2.30pm Mon– Fri, $42.60/child) and Captain's Shipyard Cruise (9.30–11.30am, Mon, Wed, Thurs and Sat, $36/child). For young princesses, the Garden View Lounge hosts My Disney Girl's Perfectly Princess Tea Party (10.30am–noon daily except Tues and Wed), featuring Princess Aurora from Sleeping Beauty and with storytelling, singalongs and a princess parade, plus a princess doll and gifts for each child (3–11). The cost for 1 adult and child is a steep $250 ($165 each additional child, plus $85 for an extra adult), but reservations (on 407 939 3463) are still advisable. The Garden View Lounge serves a variety of traditional Afternoon Teas 2–4.30pm daily, $10.50–25.50/person. Transport to the *Magic Kingdom* is by boat and monorail; by bus to the other parks.

BRITTIP

Watch out for the free nightly Electrical Water Pageant on Bay Lake and Seven Seas Lagoon, on view from all the Magic Kingdom resorts.

Disney's Polynesian Resort: This is a South Seas tropical fantasy – with modern sophistication and comfort. Beautiful beaches, lush vegetation and architecture are home to 853 rooms built in wooden long-house style, all with balconies and superb views. Also on the monorail opposite the *Magic Kingdom*, it boasts a lovely 3-storey atrium, with 75 varieties of tropical plants, koi ponds and a waterfall. The large rooms, like those of the Contemporary Resort, have been extensively refurbished to revive the Pacific isles theme, with custom-made furniture, tapestries and warm, earth colours. The resort offers excellent eating: 'Ohana is an entertaining and stylish dinner venue that has lively character breakfasts, while the Kona Café is slightly less formal but still with an extensive menu and Captain Cook's Snack Company has more basic counter-service fare. Then there are canoe rentals, a beautiful 'Volcano' pool area with waterslide, games room, shops and children's playground. The Neverland Club caters for 4–12s (4pm–midnight). Catch the monorail or boat to the *Magic Kingdom* and buses to the other parks. The Poly is also home to the *Spirit of Aloha* dinner show (p293), which is open to non-resort guests and makes a great evening among the torchlit gardens. The Resort's beach is a great area from which to view the nightly *Magic Kingdom* fireworks.

Disney's Wilderness Lodge: One of the most picturesque resorts, this is also a great romantic destination. It is a detailed re-creation of a National Park lodge, from the stream running through the massive wooden balcony-lined atrium into the gardens, past the swimming pool (with hot and cold spas) to a geyser that erupts each hour. Offering authentic backwoods charm with luxury, the resort is connected to the *Magic Kingdom* by boat and bus (and buses to the other parks). Rooms are all spacious with some lovely furniture, while the Courtyard View rooms are the best of the regular rooms (though at a slight premium). Deluxe rooms sleep up to 6 and the suites (at up to $900/night) are sumptuous. It also has 2 restaurants: the brilliant Artist's Point (lunch and dinner) and the Whispering Canyon Café (lively breakfast and huge all-you-can-eat buffets) – plus a snack bar and pool bar. The Cubs' Den is for 4–12s (4.30pm–midnight). The Villas at Wilderness Lodge is a Disney Vacation Club development of 136 studios and 1f and 2-bed villas. Facilities include living areas, kitchens, private balconies and whirlpool baths. There is a quiet pool area, a spa and health club.

Disney's Yacht and Beach Club Resorts: Disney added more refined quality with this duo, featuring 630 and 580 nautical-themed rooms respectively. Set around Crescent Lake next to the *Epcot* park, they help to form a massive resort area that is a delight to walk around at any time but especially at night. For dinner, the Yachtsman Steakhouse offers friendly, polished and elegant dining at the Yacht Club, while the sister hotel features Cape May Café for lovely character breakfasts and a nightly New England-style clambake buffet. Beaches & Cream can also be found here, a classic 1950s-style diner

Disney's Yacht Club Resort

© Disney

for burgers, shakes and sundaes. Both resorts are set along a white-sand beach like a tropical island paradise and share water fun at Stormalong Bay, a superb 2½-acre/1ha recreation area with waterslides and a sandy lagoon. You can go boating or catch a water-shuttle to *Epcot* or *Disney's Hollywood Studios*; other park transport is by bus. The Sand Castle Club here caters for youngsters aged 4–12 (4.30pm–midnight).

◀◗▶ **BRITTIP**

Look out for the nightly Disney film shows on the big outdoor movie screen by the beach at the Yacht and Beach Club Resorts.

Walt Disney World Swan and Dolphin Resort: These unmistakable twin hotels, while not actually owned by Disney, still conform to the same high standards. They have some of the most extensive facilities, a wonderful location, fab restaurants and a night-time view second to none, while they are usually slightly cheaper than most Deluxe resorts. They're within walking distance of *Epcot* and *Disney's Hollywood Studios, Disney's Boardwalk Resort* and the *Fantasia Gardens Miniature Golf Courses*, but also have a boat service to both parks (and bus to the others). The unique architecture is extensive, with the Swan topped by a 45ft/14m statue, as well as 756 large rooms (including 55 suites), while the Dolphin (1,509 rooms, 112 suites) is crowned by 2 even bigger statues. Both have been extensively refurbished to include the Westin Heavenly Bed® and high-speed wi-fi. The Dolphin also boasts the Balinese-inspired Mandara Spa, with a relaxing tea garden and authentic Meru Temple. This resort has 17 restaurants and lounges, 4 tennis courts, 5 pools (1 an amazing grotto pool with hidden alcoves and waterslide), a kids' pool and white-sand beach, 2 health clubs, bike and paddle boat rentals, a great range of shops, a video arcade and the Camp Dolphin centre for 4–12s (5.30pm–11pm, $10/hour per child). Even for non-guests, Shula's Steak House and celebrity chef Todd English's bluezoo (both Dolphin) are worth seeking out, along with Il Mulino Trattoria, New York's top Italian restaurant (in the Swan). Fresh, the Dolphin's Mediterranean-style market, serves breakfast and lunch, featuring all made-to-order menu items and both à la carte and tableside dining. The decor and atmosphere at the Swan's Garden Grove Café is inspired by the gardens of Central Park, and it serves à la carte or buffet breakfasts, with Disney characters, at the weekend. Those who like authentic sushi will enjoy the intimate Kimonos, in the Swan, which also features a karaoke bar. Picabu Buffeteria in the Dolphin is open 24 hours with all-American favourites. With its ideal location and amenities, this is possibly the perfect resort (407 934 3000, **www.swandolphin. com**).

Campground and cabins

Disney's Fort Wilderness Resort & Campground: This is possibly the best value of all the Disney properties. Situated on Bay Lake across from the Magic Kingdom, it offers impressive camping facilities and chalet-style cabins housing up to 6 in a 750-acre/304ha spread of countryside. Two 'trading posts' supply fresh groceries and there are 2 bars and cafés plus a range of on-site activities, including 2 swimming pools, the thrice-nightly Hoop-Dee-Doo Musical Revue, Mickey's Backyard Barbecue (a seasonal character buffet dinner), campfire programme, open-air films, sports, games and a prime position to view the nightly Electrical Water Pageant. You can rent bikes or boats or take horse rides around the country trails, while the Tri-Circle D ranch has a small petting zoo. There is even a Segway Tour (the amazing 2-wheeled personal transports), the *Wilderness Back Trail Adventure*, providing a unique 2-hour trundle around the many trails ($90/person, Tues, Fri and Sat, over-15s only). The Trails End restaurant (sit-down and takeaway) offers a great value buffet breakfast, a la carte lunch and buffet dinner, while

Walt Disney World and Lake Buena Vista Accommodation

Big Sand Lake

Toll road

Hilton Garden Inn
Residence Inn
Embassy Suites
Hampton Inn
Clarion Inn
Holiday Inn Express
Quality Suites Lake Buena Vista
Floridays
Hilton Grand Vacations Club (I-Drive)
Extended Stay America Deluxe
Hawthorn Suites
Courtyard Orlando
Celebrity R
Crossroads Center
Marriott Village
Radisson Lake Buena Vista
Courtyard by Marriott, Fairfield Inn, SpringHill Suites
Bryan's Spanish Cove
Embassy Vacation Resort
Caribe Royale
Buena Vista Suites
Blue Heron Beach Resort
Sunspree
Marriott Vacation Club
Nickelodeon Family Suites

APOPKA - VINELAND ROAD

Cypress Pointe Resort
Staybridge Suites
Country Inn & Suites
Sheraton Safari
Hyatt Regency Grand Cypress
Orlando Vista
Doubletree Guest Suites
Best Western LBV
Wyndham LBV Resort
Royal Plaza Resort
Holiday Inn
Hilton Orlando Resort
Vistana Resort
Orlando World Center Marriott Resort

LBV
BUENA VISTA DRIVE

Buena Vista Palace
Saratoga Springs Resort & Spa
Old Key West Resort
Treehouse Villas
DOWNTOWN DISNEY
Typhoon Lagoon

Four Seasons Hotel Resort and Disney's Golden Oak Villas [opening 2011/12]

Port Orleans Riverside Resort
Port Orleans French Quarter Resort
Caribbean Beach Resort
Waldorf-Astoria and Hilton Orlando Bonnet Creek
Pop Century Resort

Fort Wilderness Resort & Campground

Walt Disney World

Epcot
Car Park
Beach Club
Yacht Club
Dolphin
Swan
Boardwalk
Disney's Hollywood Studios
Disney's Art of Animation Resort
Car Park

Bay Lake
Contemporary Resort & Bay Lake Tower
Wilderness Lodge
Transportation & Ticket Center
monorail
Seven Seas Lagoon

Magic Kingdom
Grand Floridian Resort & Spa
Polynesian Resort

BAY LAKE

Coronado Springs Resort
Blizzard Beach

WORLD DRIVE

Animal Kingdom
Animal Kingdom Lodge Resort & Kidani Village
All-Star Resorts

© Steve Munns 2011

N

Crockett's Tavern serves pizza and appetisers (dinner only). Buses and boats link the resort with other areas (and the short boat ride to the *Magic Kingdom* is a great start to the day). If you need a break from the *Magic Kingdom*, hop on the boat here and try the family-friendly Trail's End for lunch or the dinner buffet ($22.99 for adults, $12.99 3-9s).

BRITTIP

Most Disney hotel rooms will accommodate only 4, with the exception of Port Orleans Riverside (which can take an extra child on a trundle bed). For larger groups, consider Old Key West, Saratoga Springs, the Boardwalk Villas, the villas at *Animal Kingdom* Lodge, Wilderness Lodge Villas, Fort Wilderness cabins or 2-room suites at the *All Star Music Resort* and new *Art of Animation Resort*.

Disney Vacation Club resorts

Disney's Old Key West Resort: Disney's first Vacation Club resort, this is primarily a 5-star holiday ownership scheme (one of 8 such 'timeshare' properties), but the 1, 2 or 3-bed studios in a Key West setting can also be rented nightly when not in use by members. Facilities include 4 pools, tennis courts, a games room, shops and a fitness centre, plus the lovely Olivia's restaurant. Transport to all parks is by bus.

Disney's Saratoga Springs Resort & Spa: The most extensive DVC resort, this 65-acre/26ha apartment complex is opposite *Downtown Disney*, has some wonderful views over the lake and is next to scenic Lake Buena Vista Golf Course. It boasts 828 units, from standard 2-bed hotel-style studio rooms to massive 2-storey, 3-bed apartments sleeping 12. The theme is the 1880s' New York resort of the same name, with a peaceful, gracious look and a great array of facilities, from the free-form, zero-depth entry main pool (with waterslide and squirt-fountains), a smaller quiet pool, the health-conscious dining room (the Artist's Palette, offering breakfast, lunch and dinner, plus food shop),

'Green' hotels

Florida hotels take environmental issues seriously and Orlando has many resorts that submit to the **Florida Green Lodging Certification Program**, with initiatives to protect and preserve the local environment. It highlights hotels that demonstrate water and energy conservation, waste reduction, recycling and pollution prevention.

All Disney hotels are in the FGLCP, as are those of Universal Orlando and the Give Kids The World Village in Kissimmee. Others are the Rosen trio of the Plaza, Centre and Shingle Creek hotels, Grande Lakes Resort, local Marriott and Renaissance hotels, Embassy and Hawthorn Suites, Buena Vista Palace and Gaylord Palms. Also the Hilton Garden Inn and Homewood Suites just off Palm Parkway in Lake Buena Vista conform to the highest standards for eco-friendly hotels. See also **www.dep.state.fl.us/greenlodging/**. For info on environmental travel options, visit **www.greentravelhub.com**.

a large video arcade, tennis courts and a wonderful full-service spa and gym. All but the hotel-style studios have a kitchen (with dishwasher and microwave), washer-dryer, whirlpool bath and DVD player, with TVs in each living room and bedroom. The resort includes room service, babysitting and childminding services plus a water taxi to the shops and entertainment at *Downtown Disney*. Rates for the 3-bed villas top $1,000 a night, but the 1-bed units are more modestly priced and, although it is a Vacation Club property, rooms are usually available to the public.

Also here are 60 3-bed **Treehouse Villas**, beautiful chalets raised 10ft/3m off the ground and set among a heavily wooded area next to Sassagoula River. Sleeping up to 9, they feature some sumptuous furnishings, including granite counter-tops and flatscreen TVs, as well as 2 full bathrooms and outdoor barbecue grills. They also have their own leisure pool and whirlpool spa. Transport to all parks is by bus.

Bay Lake Tower at Disney's Contemporary Resort: This resort is linked to the *Contemporary Resort* by a 5th-floor bridge and features its own pool, waterslide and whirlpool spa, plus kids' water-play area, shuffleboard and bocce courts. The 14-storey, 295-room Tower offers modern decor throughout, including the studio rooms and spacious 1, 2 and 3-bed villas. The studios (sleeping up to 4) all have small fridges, microwaves and coffee-makers, while the villas (sleeping up to 12) have full kitchens and laundry facilities. The Tower superbly complements its neighbour resort and affords wonderful views over the Magic Kingdom and nightly fireworks from its exclusive rooftop lounge and viewing deck (DVC members only). There is also a gourmet coffee bar and easy access to the restaurants of the Contemporary Resort. Transport by monorail or bus (or on foot to *Magic Kingdom*).

Disney's Animal Kingdom Lodge – Kidani Village: An addition to the *Animal Kingdom Lodge*, this is divided into hotel-room studios (sleeping up to 4) and 1, 2 and 3-bed villas (sleeping 5, 9 or 12), all offering full kitchens and laundry facilities. The low-rise architecture and decor continue the resort's eye-catching African theme and the 3-bed villas are magnificently spacious. There is a separate wildlife preserve in 4 animal savannah areas, a fabulous pool and kids' play area, and another restaurant, Sanaa, which continues the Lodge's reputation for fine dining. The stunning Samawati Springs – a 4,700ft^2/437m^2, zero-depth entry pool – is also open to guests at the Lodge, while children will make a beeline for Uwanja Camp, a 3-part interactive water playground (for ages 4 and under, 5–7s, and 8 and over). Other amenities include a video arcade, basketball court, fitness centre, gift shop and animal programmes, from flamingo-feeding to campfire story-telling. Transport to all parks is by bus.

Disney Hotel Plaza

If Disney's hotel prices are just out of your range, consider the 7 'guest' hotels that are still on site but come with a less hefty price-tag, on Hotel Plaza Boulevard on the doorstep of *Downtown Disney*. There's a free bus service to the parks, guaranteed admission (even on the busiest days), and you can make reservations for shows and restaurants before the general public. The convenience of being able to walk to Downtown Disney and the Crossroads shopping plaza is also handy.

Best Western Lake Buena Vista: This 18-storey, tropically themed hotel has 325 rooms (all with high-speed internet access) with views over the Marketplace, in-room coffee-makers and hairdryers, while the huge top-floor suites are magnificent. Garden-themed Traders Island Grill is pleasant for breakfast or dinner,

The Sanaa Restaurant at Kidani Village

© Disney

plus there is a Pizza Hut Express and deli-style Parakeet Internet Cafe, as well as a large pool, video arcade and small gym, with a Garden Gazebo for special occasions, including weddings (407 828 2424; *Value*).

Buena Vista Palace Hotel & Spa: Arguably the outstanding property here, this has been extensively renovated, with an all-new lobby, including bar and lounge, totally remodelled rooms (with chic decor, flatscreen TVs, ergonomic chairs, new bathrooms and plush bedding) and extra amenities. The elegant 27-storey cluster offers 1,012 rooms and suites (in 8 categories, many with a view over much of *Walt Disney World*), plus a blissful European-style spa, 3 heated pools, a tennis court, jogging track, basketball and sand volleyball court and no fewer than 5 restaurants. The ultra-spacious 1 and 2-bed Island Suites offer great family style with upgraded design and amenities. The Australian-themed Outback Restaurant (not part of the Outback Steakhouse chain) is an ideal venue for a memorable meal, while Kook Sports Bar has a network of 38 TVs. The smart Watercress Café offers a lovely lake view, breakfast buffet and Sunday breakfast with Disney characters (407 827 2727; *Moderate*).

Doubletree Guest Suites: For extra spacious rooms, this modern choice offers 229 family suites with every convenience, from in-room safe to cookies, high-speed internet, wet bar, 2 TVs, fridge and microwave. There are excellent kids' facilities, with their own check-in area, pool,

Andiamo at the Hilton Orlando

playground and video arcade, and a casual restaurant, the Evergreen Café & Lounge, plus a large main pool (though next to noisy I-4), an exercise room and tennis court (407 934 1000; *Moderate*).

Hilton Orlando Resort: Another high-quality choice is this 10-storey, 814-room hotel, with 2 excellent pools, 7 restaurants and lounges and a state-of-the-art health club. It is the only 'outside' hotel to enjoy Disney's Extra Magic Hours, while there's a babysitting service and Disney character breakfast on Sundays. The ultra-plush rooms all have high-speed wi-fi. Dining choices feature the superior Benihana restaurant for sushi, sashimi, chicken and great steaks; Covington Mill for a casual breakfast and lunch; Andiamo Italian Bistro; the 24-hour Mainstreet Market deli; a pool bar and grill; and a coffee/wine bar (407 827 4000; *Moderate*).

> **BRITTIP**
> Stop by the **Holiday Inn at Walt Disney World** for an excellent lunch or dinner and sample the Asian-fusion style of lauded local chef Leon Teow. It has all the flavour of some of the bigger name restaurants hereabouts but less of the price tag.

Holiday Inn: This 323-room, 14-storey hotel reopened in 2010 after a dramatic $35m rebuild to give it a fresh Miami South Beach vibe. Rooms have been comprehensively upgraded with fresh décor, flatscreen TVs, mini-fridges, room safes and wi-fi, while there is a fabulous tropical pool area with a zero-depth entry pool and whirlpool. The Palm Breezes Restaurant offers all-day dining, from a breakfast buffet to an elegant dinner, with an eye-catching pool bar/lounge adjacent to the pool and appetising fare from star chef Leon Teow. There is then a Grab & Go snack shop and a Kids-eat-free programme for 2–12s. A stylish gym, business centre and Disney gift shop complete the amenities of a stylish hotel that offers real competition to the next door Hilton but at slightly less than their prices (407 828 8888; *Moderate*).

Wyndham Lake Buena Vista Resort: This has 619 recently modernised rooms and 7 suites, all with smart decor. There are 2 main pools, a large hot tub and an excellent children's pool with water playground, as well as a fitness centre and volleyball, tennis and basketball courts. There is a Disney character breakfast Tues, Thurs and Sat at the graceful LakeView Restaurant, plus a new lobby bar, poolside bar and grill and 24-hour café, Sundial 24/7 (407 828 4444; *Moderate*).

Royal Plaza Resort: This spacious 394-room hotel (in 5 categories of rooms and suites accommodating up to 5) features plush Royal Beds and excellent personal amenities. There is a full-service diner-restaurant (the Giraffe Café and Lounge, with a great breakfast buffet; free for under-11s), Grab 'n Go deli-café, landscaped pool and pool bar, 4 tennis courts, health club, fitness centre and Disney gift shop. Standard rooms have a sitting area and balcony and the magnificent 2-room suites boast large private patios (407 828 2828; *Moderate*).

For more info on these 7 hotels, go to **www.downtowndisneyhotels.com**.

Beyond Disney

Once you move away from *Walt Disney World*, your hotel choice becomes more diverse. The Budget and Value types are most common, and the area you stay in also has an effect on price: the further you go from Disney on Kissimmee's Highway 192, the cheaper (and more basic) the hotel/motel, while parts of I-Drive are more expensive than others (north of Sand Lake Road is usually cheaper).

Facilities vary little and what you see is usually what you get. All the chain hotels can be found here, with rates as low as $30/room off-peak (but remember the local sales tax). Some also have rooms with a kitchenette (an 'efficiency'). Be prepared to shop around, especially on Highway 192, where many hotels advertise their rates, and feel free to ask to see a room before you book. Here are the main options.

Budget hotels

Chain hotels can be found at their most numerous in this category and you'll find few frills. All have pools but not many have restaurants, bars or lounges (though some provide a free continental breakfast and many offer fridges and microwaves).

- **Days Inn:** Chain that varies widely from tired older hotels to smart newer ones, and with free continental breakfast (1800 329 7466, **www.daysinn.com**).
- **Econo Lodge:** Also with free wi-fi and continental breakfast (1877 424 6423, **www.econolodge.com**).
- **Howard Johnson:** Mainly older properties, many with a Kids-eat-free option and free breakfast, but rooms are often more spacious (1800 446 4656, **www.hojo.com**).
- **Knights Inn:** Several smarter choices in the Orlando area (1800 843 5644, **www.knightsinn.com**).
- **Masters Inn:** Free continental breakfast, plus lower rates for a week or more (1800 633 3434, **www.mastersinn.com**).
- **Microtel Inn & Suites:** Chain of newer properties plus free wi-fi and breakfast (1800 771 7171, **www.microtelinn.com**).
- **Motel 6:** A basic, 'bargain basement' choice (1800 466 8356, **www.motel6.com**).

- **Red Roof Inn:** Several renovated properties in Orlando, plus free wi-fi (1800 733 7663, **www.redroof.com**).
- **Rodeway Inn:** Chain that has slipped from Value to more Budget territory but still offers a free breakfast (1877 424 6423, **www.rodewayinn.com**).
- **Super 8 Motel:** Chain varies a lot but has several newer motels (notably on American Way, just off I-Drive) and all offer free breakfast; look for its 'Pride' hotels, which are all above average (1800 800 8000, **www.super8.com**).
- **Travelodge:** With an excellent property on American Way, plus free breakfast and wi-fi (1800 578 7878, **www.travelodge.com**).

There are dozens of smaller, independent outfits that offer special rates periodically, especially a battery of cheap and cheerful motels along Highway 192 in Kissimmee (but try to stay west of Marker 14).

BRITTIP

Hotels designated Maingate East or Maingate West should be close to Disney's main entrance on Highway 192, though it is wise to check.

Of the few individual Budget choices in the area, these are worthy of note.

- **Magic Castle Inn & Suites:** Maingate East, where amenities include free continental breakfast and Disney transport, in-room fridge and microwave, kids' playground and guest laundry (1800 446 5669, **www.magicorlando.com**).
- **Golden Link Motel:** On Highway 192, a quaint little retro motel with free breakfast and wi-fi (407 496 0555).
- **Sevilla Inn:** A neat, above-average small motel-style offering in Maingate East with microwave and fridge in all rooms and a heated pool (407 396 4135, **http://sevillainn.net**).
- **Super 8 Kissimmee/Maingate:** Well above average for this low-cost chain, with good customer feedback (407 396 88883, **www.super8.com**).

- **Champions World Resort:** Converted Howard Johnson on west Highway 192, a sound budget choice with free Disney transport and wi-fi (1800 638 7829, **www.championsworldresort.com**).
- **Econo Lodge Inn & Suites I-Drive:** Above-average, with free wi-fi and shuttles to Universal and SeaWorld (407 345 8195, **www.econolodge.com**).
- **Ramada Gateway Hotel:** Smart option in Kissimmee, exceptional value in 2010–11 for this brand (407 396 4400, **www.ramadagateway.com**).
- **Travelodge Suites East Gate Orange:** Higher quality from a basic chain motel, with wi-fi, microwave and fridge in all rooms, a good pool and kiddie pool (407 396 0696, **www.travelodge.com**).

Value hotels

At first glance there may not seem much difference here, as some are still motels, and the big chains dominate. They should have smarter facilities, but not all have their own restaurant.

- **Baymont Inn & Suites:** Highly worthwhile group, boasting several new properties in the area, all with free breakfast and wi-fi (1877 229 6668, **www.baymontinns.com**).
- **Choice Hotels:** Group comprising Comfort Inn, bland chain but offers a free breakfast; Comfort Suites, with some smart, newer properties; Quality Inn, with a reputation for good value, some with an exercise room and free continental breakfast; and the smarter Clarion Inn (and Suites), often including restaurants, though age of properties varies (1877 424 6423, **www.choicehotels.com**).
- **Extended Stay America and Extended Stay Deluxe:** No-frills, clean and consistent chains with more space than many in this group (and fully equipped kitchens); sister brand Homestead Studio Suites offers extra facilities (1800 804 3724, **www.extendedstayamerica.com**).
- **Fairfield Inns:** Budget version of the Marriott chain, usually with newer hotels, many with gyms and most

Kissimmee Accommodation

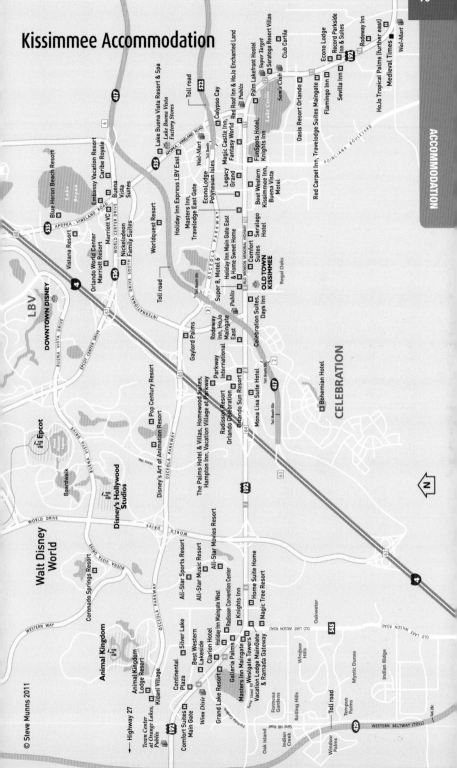

© Steve Munns 2011

with free breakfast (1800 1927 1927 in the UK, 1888 236 2427 in the US, **www.marriott.com**).

- **Hampton Inns and Suites:** Usually above average in this category, with free wi-fi, hot breakfast and tea/coffee in the lobby 24hrs (1800 426 7866, **www.hamptoninn.com**).

- **Ramada:** Good value at this level, many have free wi-fi and breakfast or a restaurant (1800 272 6232, **www.ramada.com**).

> ◀️ **BRITTIP**
> Not all hotels provide hairdryers, though they can often be ordered from the front desk. For your own, you will need a US plug adaptor (with 2 flat pins). The voltage is 110–120AC (ours is 220) so UK appliances will be sluggish.

There are more options at the upper end of the category.

- **Best Western:** Good, family-style facilities with more amenities (0800 393 130 in UK, 1800 780 7234 in US, **www.bestwestern.com**).

- **Holiday Inn and Holiday Inn Express:** Rebranded to go upmarket, but there's still bargains in Value/Moderate as they offer Kids-eat-free (with parents) at all properties and many include sophisticated pools and extra facilities like games rooms (0800 405060 from the UK, 1888 465 4329 in the US, **www.holidayinn.com**).

- **La Quinta Inn and Suites:** Some notably smart hotels in Orlando (1800 753 3757, **www.lq.com**).

- **Radisson:** Possibly the best overall value here, this group has some

Radisson Lake Buena Vista

excellently priced hotels, all with above-average amenities and services, free wi-fi and well situated for the parks (1800 395 7046, **www.radisson.com**).

- **Wingate Inn:** Modern chain, with gyms, free breakfast and wi-fi (1800 228 1000, **www.wingatehotels.com**).

Individuals worthy of note include:

- **Enclave Suites:** Reliable 1 and 2-bed suites in great location on Carrier Drive, just off I-Drive, are excellent value as there's a Kids-eat-free option (with parents), free breakfast and transport to Universal and SeaWorld as well as a good array of facilities (407 351 1155, **www.enclavesuites.com**).

- **Palms Hotel & Villas:** Just off Highway 192 in Kissimmee (close to I-4), resort with spacious 1 and 2-room suites with full kitchens, 2 large pools and kiddie pool, sports court, free shuttle to Disney parks and free breakfast (407 396 2229, **www.thepalmshotelandvillas.com**).

- **Seralago Inn Hotel and Suites Maingate East:** 2-room suites and kidsuites, great pools and kids' facilities (with free films in their own cinema) make it a family 'old faithful'. It's handy for Old Town and under-11s with their parents get free breakfast (407 396 4488, **www.seralagohotel.com**).

> ◀️ **BRITTIP**
> It is usual to tip hotel chambermaids by leaving $1/adult each day before your room is made up.

Moderate Hotels

This is a category with fewer of each brand, so we highlight a few worthy individuals as well as the chains. All properties provide a good pool (often with extras like a waterslide, kids' pool and/or playground), at least 1 restaurant, bar and café, and extra in-room comfort.

Main chains:

- **Country Inn & Suites:** A smart choice, with spacious rooms and a pleasant country-house lobby, with an extensive free breakfast (1888

Our Value recommendations

Notable properties in this range:

Extended Stay Deluxe Orlando-Universal Studios: A high-quality in this chain in a great location for Universal and I-Drive (407 370 4428, **www.extendedstayhotels.com**).

Galleria Palms Hotel: In Kissimmee at Maingate West, just off Highway 192, has a smart, contemporary look, ultra-comfy rooms, a great location close to Disney, free shuttle to the parks, free breakfast and wi-fi, and a relaxing pool area (there is no restaurant but plenty nearby; 407 396 6300, **www. galleriakissimmeehotel.com**).

Holiday Inn Maingate East: In Kissimmee (between Markers 8 and 9), offering well-maintained rooms (including kidsuites) in 2 high-rise towers, plus an oversized pool, kids' pool, waterslides, gym, children's theatre, food court and lobby lounge, plus a Kids-eat-free programme (407 396 4222, **www. holidayinnmge.com**).

Ramada Inn I-Drive Lakefront: Top value-for-money choice in a good I-Drive location with a free continental breakfast, wi-fi and Disney transport, plus over-sized rooms all with fridge, microwave and coffee-maker (407 345 5340, **www.michotel.com**)

Orlando Sun Resort: Formerly the Ramada Celebration, this ideal location in Kissimmee (on Parkway Boulevard, close to the Highway 192 junction with I-4), in landscaped tropical grounds has 3 pools, a state-of-the-art fitness centre, comfy rooms and great dining choices (407 396 7000, **www. orlandosunresort.com**).

Orlando Vista Hotel: Fun style on Apopka-Vineland Road in Lake Buena Vista, at the entrance to Downtown Disney, which features great kidsuites, a pleasant bar and café, large pool deck and spacious, airy rooms, with free breakfast, wi-fi and transport to the Disney parks, making this something of a bargain (407 239 4646, **www.orlandovistahotel.com**)

Wyndham Orlando Resort: In the heart of I-Drive, with great facilities (3 pools, 2 restaurants, 3 bars, a deli, ice-cream shop, tennis courts, kids' club, games arcade and health club) in landscaped grounds but without the high price tag you might expect. The resort covers 42 acres/17ha and takes some getting around, but is a good all-round choice (407 351 2420; **www.wyndham.com**).

201 1746, **www.countryinns.com**).
- **Hyatt Place:** A chic, contemporary choice with stylish, comfortable rooms, free continental breakfast (or hot breakfast upgrade), 24-hour café and evening bar service, plus free wi-fi (1888 492 8847, **www.hyatt.com/hyatt/place**).
- **Residence Inns:** Identikit but consistent, with free breakfast and exercise rooms, plus microwave, fridge and tea/coffee-making facilities (1800 331 3131, **www.marriott.com/residence-inn/travel.mi**.
- **Springhill Suites:** Also part of the Marriott group, they offer reliable, comfortable value (1888 287 9400, **www.marriott.com/springhill-suites/travel.mi**).

More upmarket
- **Crowne Plaza Hotels:** Some eye-catching properties featuring great pool areas, smart restaurants, fitness centres and ultra-comfy rooms (**www.ichotelsgroup.com**). The **Crowne Plaza Orlando-Universal** is a fine example, with 398 rooms and suites in 2 stylish blocks and a spectacular atrium. Two restaurants, a cocktail lounge and fitness centre, plus a huge heated pool add up to quality and value in an ideal location on Universal Boulevard's junction with Sand Lake Road (407 355 0550, **www.cporlando.com**).
- **Doubletree by Hilton:** A contemporary, upscale choice with fewer frills but spacious,

Coming up Rosen

One notable non-chain operator in Orlando is the **Rosen Hotels & Resorts** group, with a good variety of 7 well-run, value-conscious properties. Four are budget-minded, the Brit-popular **Rosen Inn at Pointe Orlando** (formerly the Quality Inn Plaza), **Quality Inn International** and **Rosen Inn** (ex Rodeway Inn) on I-Drive, and the **Clarion Inn Lake Buena Vista** (formerly a Comfort Inn). All have been impressively refurbished and offer standard amenities but thoughtful touches, like family-style buffet restaurants, kids facilities, plenty of quiet choice and free wi-fi. The other hotels are the flagship Deluxe **Rosen Shingle Creek Resort**, and the Moderate pair of **Rosen Centre Hotel** (p83) and **Rosen Plaza Hotel**, a distinctive 800-room property with excellent resort facilities – including 2 restaurants, a pizza shop, deli, fitness centre and nightclub – and spacious, recently redecorated accommodation (1800 627 8258, **www. rosenhotels.com**).

ultra-comfy rooms featuring their Sweet Dreams sleep experience and signature welcome cookies, plus a rare B&B option (1800 445 8667, **http://doubletree1.hilton.com**). A good example is the **Doubletree by Hilton Orlando at SeaWorld**, a recently remodelled hotel just off I-Drive set in 28 acres/11ha. It offers 3 pools, 2 kids' pools, a playground, mini-golf and extra-large suites. Limited dining options, but tropical grounds give it a luxury feel (407 352 1100, **www. doubletreeorlandoidrive.com**).

- **Hilton Garden Inn:** The Hilton chain has really struck the right note with this modern, comfortable and family-friendly brand, with

Crowne Plaza Orlando Universal

a number of attractive, modern hotels (1877 7829 444, **www. wiltongardeninn.com**).

- **Hyatt group:** Rare in tourist territory, but a prime example is the Hyatt Regency at Orlando International Airport. It has 2 excellent restaurants and a smart pool deck, plus a fitness room, lounge and business centre. Rooms are ultra-spacious, particularly the corner rooms, and many feature internal balconies overlooking the airport atrium. There is no noticeable aircraft noise and none of the bustle you expect at an airport hotel. Staying there gives the distinct advantage of collecting your hire car in the morning rather than straight after a long flight (407 825 1234, **http://orlandoairport.hyatt. com**).

- **Marriott:** Another well-represented group, with some of the smartest hotels in this category, often providing extra facilities and more landscaped grounds, a choice of restaurants and some of the largest standard rooms. Features include its signature Revive beds for a guaranteed good night's sleep (1800 380 6751, **www.marriott.com**).

- **Sheraton hotels:** These boast a smart, revamped look. Several are themed and feature extra facilities and good dining (1888 625 5144, **www.starwoodhotels.com/sheraton**). NB: the popular **Sheraton Safari Hotel** in Lake Buena Vista was due to undergo a major renovation in late 2011, completely restyling the rooms, adding a spectacular new

The Sky's the limit

For a good cross-section of 7 contrasting properties (6 in Orlando, 1 in Daytona Beach), from Value hotels to villas and community resorts, try **Sky Hotels & Resorts**, a specialist management company. Its one-stop shop includes the reliable Enclave Suites just off I-Drive (p76), 2 Hawthorn Suites properties, the excellent Lake Buena Vista Resort Village & Spa (p92) and the highly-rated **Coral Cay Resort** in Kissimmee, a well-designed gated development of 3 and 4-bed town-homes (terraced villas), plus the spectacular views of the 3-star **Hawaiian Inn Beach Resort** at Daytona Beach. Arguably its crown jewel, though, is the smart new **Palisades Resort** at the western end of Highway 192 in Kissimmee, an upmarket and quality-conscious self-catering resort, with 2 and 3-bed condos (p93; 1866 455 4062, **www.staysky.com**).

pool complex and fitness centre, and upgrading the restaurant and lounge. It should be completed by spring 2012 (407 239 0444, **www.sheratonsafari.com**).

BRITTIP

Need a value hotel that will keep the kids amused? Consider the new **CoCo Key Hotel and Water Resort**. One of the most thoughtful and family-friendly hotels we've seen in ages.

Notable individuals: There are only a few non-chain properties in the Moderate category.

- **Monumental Hotel:** A converted Crowne Plaza hotel and still ultra-stylish, with a Key West theme, 94 spacious, well-equipped rooms, beautiful pool area and Pineapple Grill Restaurant (1877 239 1222, **www.monumentalhotelorlando.com**).
- **CoCo Key Hotel & Water Resort Orlando:** New on I-Drive is this ultra-family-friendly option with excellent amenities, notably the extensive water park. It has been transformed from an old Ramada in every respect, from the chic new lobby area to the 391 rooms (all with flatscreen TVs, smart bedding and furniture, coffee-maker and free wi-fi). There is a quiet adults' pool, with fountain and Jacuzzi, buffet breakfast room (Tradewinds), food court (Callaloo Grill, featuring Pizza Hut), indoor sports bar and outdoor Tiki Bar overlooking the Key West-themed water park, with a canopy roof to protect from the sun (but also an uncovered play area and terrace). There is a fitness centre, extensive games arcade, gift shop and convenience store, private rooms for birthday parties and a kids' club. The water park is a marvel, with 4 areas: Parrot's Perch, an interactive jungle-gym; Minnow Lagoon, for pre-school kids, with a zero-depth entry pool and water cannons with mini-slides and other small-scale fun (with life-jackets, and life-guards on duty); Coral Reef Cove, the teen activity pool, with the Cyclone body-slide; and the outdoor Water-Park, with nine different slides, including the Over The Falls and Surfer Splash body-slides and Boomerango double-rider tube slide. There is a 'resort fee' for use of the water park, but at $19/room per day, it isn't unreasonable. Day guests are also allowed when the resort is not full, at $15–20/person. This is easily 1 of the most imaginative resorts in the area and really enhances this part of I-Drive (1877 875 4681, **www.cocokeywater resort.com**).

Deluxe hotels

When it comes to the best hotels, it is largely a question of individuals. The growing selection of genuinely deluxe properties in this area are all highly distinctive, with excellent facilities, outstanding service and, usually, at least one 5-star restaurant. They can be divided into 5 main areas: Universal Orlando, International Drive, Lake Buena Vista, Kissimmee and Further Afield.

Our Moderate recommendations

Embassy Suites International Drive South: Consistently gets good reader feedback and is exceedingly smart, with excellent service and spacious rooms (either standard 2-room suites sleeping 4 or double-doubles for 6) providing 2 TVs, coffee-maker, fridge and microwave. There's a great outdoor pool deck, kids' splash pool and indoor pool, plus a sauna and gym and good dining options, with a free breakfast. It is rare in this area in offering a free shuttle service to both Disney and Universal (407 352 1400, **www.embassysuitesorlando.com**).

Four Points By Sheraton Orlando Studio City: A 21-storey I-Drive icon near Universal Orlando, this features a heated tropical pool and paddling pool, games room, mini-golf, fitness room and free shuttle to Disney and Universal. All 301 well-appointed rooms have coffee-makers, Nintendo games and free wi-fi, plus superb views (ask for a Universal view if possible). The Tropical Palms restaurant is a minor gem, with a fun ambience for breakfast, lunch or dinner, and an imaginative dinner menu, while you can also grab a drink at the Oasis Lounge or Tropical Breezes patio pool bar (407 351 2100, **www.starwoodhotels.com**).

Radisson Hotel Lake Buena Vista: A dramatically remodelled property, convenient for Disney and the Crossroads area, with sleek rooms and furnishings, the stylish Liquid Bar & Grill, small gym and free wi-fi. Extra-spacious rooms feature a fridge, microwave, coffee-maker, large, flatscreen TV and the signature comfy Sleep Number bed (407 597 3400, **www.radisson.com**).

Rosen Center Hotel: This spectacular 24-storey property, one of the area's largest, caters mainly for conventions (it's next door to the huge Convention Center) but also offers excellent facilities with 1,334 rooms and 80 suites. It has a huge swimming grotto, tennis courts, an exercise centre, high-quality restaurants (the excellent steak-and-seafood Everglades and casual 24-hour deli, Café Gauguin), the chic Banshoo Sushi bar and new 89Forty Tapas & Tequila bar. The style is luxurious, yet the prices aren't (1800 204 7234, **www.rosencenter.com**).

We also rate the renovated **Holiday Inn at Walt Disney World** (p72) very highly.

Universal Orlando

Universal teamed up with the Loews group to create its fine threesome, and they come with the **Universal Express** bonus, front-of-queue access to the main attractions by showing your key card. Universal resort guests also benefit from other benefits, like a resort ID card (for buying food, merchandise, etc. throughout the resort), priority seating at most restaurants (show your room key card), package delivery to your room, special golf privileges at 4 nearby courses, early entry to the Wizarding World of Harry Potter in the Islands of Adventure park and the chance to buy a *Length of Stay* pass (for unlimited park access while you're at the resort). All 3 feature excellent kids' activity centres with a meal option (for 4–14s; 5–11.30pm Sun–Thurs, to midnight Fri and Sat; $16/hour per child, plus $15 for meal). For all Universal hotels, call 1888 273 1311 or visit **www.universalorlando.com**.

Hard Rock Hotel: Possibly the coolest hotel in Orlando, this icon of rock chic is themed as a former rock star's home, with 650 rooms and suites in California mission style. High ceilings, wooden beams, marble floors and eclectic artwork give an eye-catching style, with a rock-star theme to most

Rosen Center Hotel

public areas, music memorabilia, black-suited foyer staff and fairly constant music. The 14-acre/6ha site includes 3 bars (including the ultra-cool Velvet Bar), 2 restaurants (the full-service The Kitchen and the 5-star, dinner-only Palm Restaurant), plus a takeaway café, fitness centre, gift shop and games room. The lido area features a huge, free-form pool and 240ft/73m waterslide, 2 Jacuzzis, a beach volleyball court, shuffleboard and life-size chess and draughts. The pool even has an underwater sound system! The 650 rooms (including 12 kidsuites and 10 king suites) are big, beautifully furnished in the hotel's chic style and superbly comfortable.

BRITTIP
Hard Rock Hotel guests – and music fans – should make a note of the monthly Velvet Sessions at the hotel, live gigs by well-known bands ('rock 'n roll cocktail parties' as they call them), on the last Thurs of each month. There's music, free drinks and finger foods. Book tickets at www.velvetsessions.com.

Portofino Bay Hotel: The stunning jewel in Universal's crown is a splendid re-creation of the famous Italian port. The elaborate porticos, trompe l'oeil painting, harbourside piazza and faithful ornamentation of the waterfront make it one of Florida's most memorable settings. The 750 rooms are impeccably appointed, with lashings of Italian style. Standard rooms are sumptuous, with huge beds, spacious bathrooms, mini-bar and coffee facilities, ironing board and hairdryer, while the 94 Club Rooms feature concierge service with private lounge, extra room amenities and free entry to the Mandara Spa fitness centre. There are 18 kidsuites (including 6 wacky Dr Seuss-themed suites) with separate bedrooms each with their own TV. The resort facilities are equally breathtaking – a Roman aqueduct-style pool with waterslide (and poolside films on Sat evenings), an enclosed kids' play area and wading pool, a separate quiet pool, Jacuzzis, the beautiful Mandara Spa, business centre, an array of

gift shops and a video games room. The Portofino also has an amazing 8 restaurants and lounges, including the 5-star (and very romantic) Bice Ristorante (p321), the boisterous Trattoria del Porto (with themed character dinners on Fri 6.30–9.30pm), Mama Della's, an authentic Italian family dining experience (watch out for Mama herself!), an aromatic deli, a pizzeria, gelateria and swanky Bar American. It is only a short boat ride to the parks, but is lightyears away in terms of its tranquil ambience.

BRITTIP
For some wonderful gift shopping, check out the Portofino Bay's Galleria Portofino for art and jewellery.

Royal Pacific Resort: This 53-acre/21ha, 1,000-room resort has an exotic 1930s South Seas style, and you feel as if you have stepped into another world as you cross the bamboo bridge into the elegant lobby, faced by the splendid Orchid Garden courtyard. Extensive use of rich, dark woods, cool stone floors and masses of greenery give the place an opulent, colonial feel. Standard rooms feature hand-carved Balinese furniture among many refined touches, and there is also a Club level, with separate lounge and extended facilities, and 51 superlative suites – including 8 Jurassic Park-themed kidsuites (dinosaurs not included!). The Islands Dining Room offers breakfast, lunch and dinner in a setting of oriental simplicity (children have their own buffet area with TV screen, plus character

Portofino Bay Hotel

Suite choice

To our mind these are best suites hotels.

Embassy Suites: With smart interior courtyards, good restaurants and relaxing pool areas (1800 362 2779, **http://embassysuites1.hilton.com**).

Homewood Suites: Provide extra room for larger families in 1 and 2-bed suites with full kitchens, free breakfast and an upmarket feel with mid-range pricing (1800 222 4663, **www.homewoodsuites.com**).

Hawthorn Suites by Wyndham and Staybridge Suites: Both feature spacious 1 and 2-bed suites that sleep up to 6 and fully fitted kitchens, plus a hearty free breakfast, wi-fi and free local phone calls (1800 527 1133, www.hawthorn.com or 1877 238 8889, **www.ichotelsgroup.com**).

Sister properties the **Buena Vista Suites**, a well-appointed and more individual choice and **Caribe Royale Resort** (1800 823 8300, **www.cariberoyale.com**) are on World Center Drive just off the lower end of I-Drive. The former is the more basic type, with spacious 2-room suites, a free full breakfast, heated pool, whirlpool, tennis courts, gift shop, mini-market and the Vista Bistro. The Caribe Royale is more luxurious, with a choice of 1-bed suites and 2-bed villas, a tropical pool with waterslide, tennis courts and 2 fitness rooms. Award-winning Venetian Room restaurant is a treat for lovers of fine continental cuisine, and there are 4 other cafés and lounges.

Nickelodeon Family Suites: Not so much a hotel as a theme park resort is this striking, kid-friendly choice on I-Drive South. Characters from Nickelodeon TV adorn strategic points and there is plenty of live interaction (notably at breakfast). Activities include scavenger hunts and arcade tournaments, while Studio Nick stages shows in its mini-theatre and a daily **Birthday Celebration** with Spongebob and Team Nick (plus a host of birthday upgrades involving slime, cake, slime, video games, slime, face painting, slime, karaoke and more slime), open to children with birthdays within 30 days of their stay. The 4-D Experience is an interactive 3-D cinema and there is even a Kids' Spa. Suites come with bunks or twin beds and a TV and video console. The water features form 2 huge play areas, complete with all manner of sprays, slides and flumes, and there are poolside games, video arcade, mini-golf and various shops. Rooms come in 1-bed kitchen suites and 2 and 3-bed kidsuites, with living room and bathroom, microwave and fridge (and full kitchen with some). Nicktoons Café offers buffet dining (plus à la carte in the evening), while the popular character breakfast costs $12/under-13s and $22/adults. Plus there is a food court, pool bar and grill, and adult-friendly Nick@Nite Lounge. It all adds up to a striking (if somewhat raucous) holiday base in an excellent location close to Disney (1866 462 6425; **www. nickhotel.com**).

dining on select nights), while fine dining is taken to a new dimension by a magnificent restaurant run by celebrity chef Emeril Lagasse called Tchoup Chop (possibly the best in Orlando; p324). There's a pool snack bar and luau garden area, with the **Wantilan Luau** Saturday nights, featuring an eye-catching Polynesian feast and dinner show ($60 adults, $33 under-13s; 407 503 3463 to book). The huge freeform pool is ideal for kids, with zero-depth entry at one end and a boat-shaped interactive play area of squirting fountains. Add a health club (with Jacuzzi, sauna and gym), kids' club (with computer games, TVs and organised activities), video arcade and 2 shops and you have superb value, even at this end of the scale.

International Drive
There are 4 superb hotels here that take advantage of I-Drive's great location.

Hilton Orlando: This impressive 1,400-room hotel on I-Drive next to the big Convention Center and set in 26 acres/10.5ha boasts superb leisure facilities. It features upscale steakhouse, Spencer's, along with David's Club bar and grill, casual dining at The Bistro, a 24hr Marketplace and an inviting pool

International Drive Accommodation

Steve Munns 2011

bar and grill. A full-service spa, a large state-of-the- art fitness centre, 2 pools, lazy river (in a wonderful 'tropical island' setting), tennis, volleyball and basketball courts, and a neat 9-hole putting golf course complete the impressive amenities. The Resort pool boasts a waterslide and kids' fountain, while the Quiet pool has several Jacuzzis and both have cabanas, with fridges and TVs, for hire. Rooms feature Hilton 'Serenity' bedding, 37in HD TVs and high-quality toiletries, while an executive level adds a superb private lounge and extra services (407 313 4300, **www.thehiltonorlando.com**).

BRITTIP
Spencer's at the Hilton Orlando offers some of the best dry-aged steaks in Florida, and a unique monthly cooking class with Chef John O'Leary, including wine from its exclusive cellar.

Peabody Orlando: Classy and hugely stocked for holiday fun, this used to be primarily an upmarket convention hotel but their big $450m 2010 expansion has added real family appeal to this I-Drive icon. The original 891-room tower, also been refurbished as part of the rebuild, has an Olympic-size pool, tennis courts and 3 superb restaurants, notably the gourmet Italian of Capriccio and the amazing B-Line Diner (with its signature Sunday brunch; p315). Service is superb and the style is a cut above normal tourist fare – just check

Peabody Orlando

out the Royal Duck Palace! Larger-than-average rooms and huge suites add to the quality, but conference business can make this side of the hotel a bit hectic.

BRITTIP
The impressive 2,178m²/22,000ft² The Spa at The Peabody features a superb array of treatments and make-up services, plus a full-service nail and hair salon, teen treatments and all-day spa packages with lunch, all open to non-hotel guests on a daily basis (407 345 4431).

Proper afternoon tea is served Mon–Fri 3–4.30pm. The new 34-storey tower adds real cutting-edge sophistication and holiday appeal, with another 1,641 luxurious rooms; a lushly landscaped 3-acre recreation area with 3 pools (and you'll feel a million miles from busy I-Drive), with tropical pool bar and cabanas; a Napa Valley wine-themed restaurant; a chic cocktail bar, Rocks (superb in the evening, with live music); a grab-and-go Café; lobby coffee bar; and a superbly stylish spa and fitness centre. All the new rooms (and 193 massive suites) come with LED motion-censored night lights, 42in LCD TVs, iPod docking stations, a Peabody Dream Bed®, fridges, cordless phones and even mini LCD TVs in bathroom mirrors! (407 352 4000, **www.peabodyorlando.com**).

BRITTIP
Don't miss Peabody's twice-daily red-carpet Duck March at 11am and 5pm, when its trademark ducks take up residence in the lobby fountain.

Renaissance Orlando Resort: This superb resort (788 rooms on Sea Harbor Drive, behind SeaWorld) is notable for its style, service and hospitality. It has a massive 10-storey atrium lobby and some equally large rooms and suites, an extensive pool area with bar and grill, tennis courts, lavish Neu Lotus Spa and fitness centre, plus kids' play areas and activities. All rooms have been renovated to a high standard, with extra bathroom amenities, flatscreen

ACCOMMODATION

Condo hotels

A condo-hotel is a cross between a villa and a hotel. People buy 'rooms' in these big properties (which look like resort hotels), which they then own – unlike timeshare, where you just 'own' a time period for a resort. All rooms are identically furnished, unlike villas, and feature 1, 2 or 3 bedrooms, living/dining room and kitchen or kitchenette. They are then rented out by a management company on behalf of the owners. For guests, they are booked as you would for any hotel. Some are owned by hotel groups such as Starwood while others are just managed by hotel specialists to ensure they maintain the right standards. They are usually built in tower blocks around communal facilities like the Clubhouse check-in and swimming pool (often with elaborate water features), and can include restaurants, fitness centres and even spas.

TVs and Marriott's Revive bedding. The dining line-up consists of Mist Sushi & Spirits (cocktails and full-service dining, plus an amazing 'aquarium' video wall), Boardwalk Sports Bar, the upscale but casual Tradewinds for breakfast, lunch and dinner, Palms Pool Bar & Grill and a Starbucks café. The hotel offers great packages in conjunction with SeaWorld, which is a 2-minute walk across the car park, and its rates are often the best in Deluxe territory (1800 327 6677, **www. renaissanceseaworldorlando.com**).

Rosen Shingle Creek Hotel: This 230-acre/93ha resort ranks among the grandest for its location, quality and style. In the middle of the award-winning Shingle Creek Golf Club on lower Universal Boulevard, it boasts 1,500 rooms and suites, all with sumptuous decor and comfort, as well as a full-service spa and fitness centre. Rooms vary from standard doubles to presidential suites, but all with fabulous flatscreen TVs, wi-fi, fridges and first-class toiletries. Amenities include 5 restaurants, 4 bars, a lounge, coffee house, deli and ice-creamery, plus 3 outdoor pools, tennis, basketball and volleyball courts and nature trails.

There is also a shopping gallery and babysitting service. The resort is built in a 1900s Spanish revival style and offers flawless service (especially at concierge level). Don't miss A Land Remembered, one of the best steakhouses in the state, in the Golf Clubhouse, and Cala Bella, a fine-dining Italian restaurant, with heavenly desserts from its renowned pastry chef (407 996 9939, **www. shinglecreekresort.com**).

Westin Imagine Orlando: Also on Universal Boulevard, this chic condo-hotel property features 315 king rooms and 1 and 2-bed suites, with either kitchenettes or full kitchens, and the trademark Westin Heavenly bed and bath, plus distinctive decor and extras like flatscreen TVs and marble-topped desks. Signature Italian restaurant Fiorella's Cucina Toscana features delicious casual lunches and upmarket dinners surrounded by unique decorative glass designs, with the option of al fresco dining. The bar area is equally distinguished plus there is a huge South Beach-style pool with Tiki Bar and a modern fitness centre to complete a very fresh and modern offering (407 233 2200, **www. starwoodhotels.com**).

BRITTIP
Try lunch at Fiorella's Cucina Toscana and sample some stylish cuisine at very modest prices.

Rosen Shingle Creek

Lake Buena Vista

Moving to the next major resort area, there is a growing range of Deluxe choice here, too.

Orlando World Center Marriott: We love this impressive landmark on Disney's outskirts, set in landscaped 200 acres/810ha and surrounded by a beautiful golf course. With 2,000 rooms and suites (most boasting fabulous views up to 28 storeys high), 9 restaurants and 6 pools (including 2 kids' pools and a superb freeform tropical main pool with waterfalls), it is a monumental prospect, set among landscaped foliage and with fabulous facilities, including a Bill Madonna Golf Academy, tennis courts, volleyball, basketball, spa and state-of-the-art gym. Highlights are the Mikado Japanese Steakhouse, Hawk's Landing Steakhouse, Ristorante Tuscany and High Velocity Sports Bar, while there are also excellent children's amenities and programmes. It gets busy with convention business, but the picturesque pool complex offers true relaxation bliss (407 239 4200, **www.marriottworldcenter.com**).

Hilton at Bonnet Creek Resort: This rare and extensive development is in a unique position inside *Walt Disney World* but privately owned (the only piece of land Walt was unable to buy from the original landowners in 1966). It is part of a 482-acre/194ha resort complex with the Waldorf-Astoria (see below) and shares some of the same facilities. The Hilton features 1,000 rooms, 4 restaurants, a lagoon pool complex with lazy river and waterslide, 18-hole golf course, tennis courts and the adjoining full-service European spa and fitness centre. Fine dining is provided by the chic modern Italian-themed La Luce restaurant, while the Harvest Bistro offers the main alternative (with kids 12 and under eating free with a full-paying adult), along with the Muse grab-and-go deli (with coffee bar), Zeta bar/lounge and Beech Pool Bar and Grill. One of its prime draws, though, is that it is just minutes from the Disney parks, and benefits from the full Hilton package of stylish accommodation and excellent kids' activity programmes, as well as some blissfully comfy rooms (407 597 3600, **www.hilton.com**).

Waldorf-Astoria: The second part of the huge Bonnet Creek development, this 497-room hotel is the first US Waldorf outside New York and added a new level of luxury to the Orlando scene when it opened in 2009. Stately and serene, the famous-name hotel features 313 standard rooms with Italian marble bathrooms and HD

Waldorf-Astoria

flat-screen TVs, plus 185 truly grand suites with butler service. The zero-entry pool boasts cabanas and waiter service, while the dining choice is superb, from the poolside grille and classic Bull & Bear Steakhouse to the small-plate cuisine of Peacock Alley, gourmet style of signature Oscar's brasserie and private club atmosphere of Harry's Lounge. The Spa by Guerlain is also unashamedly 5-star. Other amenities include basketball and tennis, jogging trails, bike rentals, a state-of-the-art fitness centre (with personal trainers), yoga and aerobics classes and boutique shops on a par with the Waldorf's luxury cachet. Even children aren't forgotten, with the WA Kids Club providing active, creative fun for 5-12s (10am–9pm, $15/hour per child) and the After Dark programme with dinner and games from 7–10pm at $75/child (407 597 5500, **www.waldorfastoriaorlando.com**).

Hyatt Regency Grand Cypress: The area's first genuine Deluxe hotel in 1984, this is still one of the best. A mature 1,500-acre/608ha resort with a unique mix of facilities, it has a rare 9-hole pitch-and-putt golf course, 27 holes of regular golf (designed by Jack Nicklaus), a golf academy, boating lake and superb pool complex. A $50m refurbishment in 2009 added to its appeal. The elegant lobby boasts Zen-inspired décor with some very relaxing touches, while all 750 rooms have been given a bright, contemporary finish, with large, flatscreen TVs, large shower units and elaborate lighting. The dining choice is among the best of any Orlando resort, and the location remains ideal, almost on the doorstep of Disney yet blissfully reclusive (on Winter Garden-Vineland Road, around the corner from the Crossroads area). The huge freeform swimming pool boasts Jacuzzis, waterfalls and slide, while the white sand beach and magnificent restaurants make for a sumptuous stay, especially Hemingway's, its Key West-styled dinner spot, and La Coquina, with a novel Chef's Table inside the kitchen on Sat and a sensational Sunday Brunch (not in summer). There is also the stylish White Horse sports bar and grill; pool bar and deli-style café; an inviting lobby lounge and sushi bar; and an eye-catching art gallery. Watersports – such as boating, kayaking or fishing on scenic Lake Windsong with its white-sand beach – and other activities like tennis and bike rentals are covered by the one-off resort fee. And, once among its richly landscaped grounds, you could easily be light years from the theme-park bustle (407 239 1234, **http://grandcypress.hyatt.com**).

Kissimmee

The more budget-oriented area of Osceola County also now has its share of upmarket properties.

Bohemian Hotel: In the Disney-inspired town of Celebration just off Highway 192, this unique hotel offers refreshing small-town America style that is a long way from the usual tourist hurly-burly. With just 115 rooms in its 1920s' wood-frame design, it has a classy ambience and a wealth of high-quality touches, notably in the ultra-comfy rooms. These come in a choice of an attic-like Retreat, Traditional (with either a king or 2 queen-size beds), Studio or a 2-room suite and are all beautifully furnished. Lovely artwork, courteous staff and a good array of facilities – pool, Jacuzzi and fitness centre, plus the highly-regarded Bohemian Bar & Grill (excellent for breakfast, it becomes a signature steakhouse at night) – mark out this hotel as a real gem. In addition, it is within a short stroll of the town's shops, restaurants

Hyatt Regency Grand Cypress

and lakeside walks and makes a great romantic choice (407 566 6000, **www.celebrationhotel.com**).

Gaylord Palms Resort: One of the most dramatic hotels, with 1,406 rooms, is on the junction of I-Drive South and Osceola Parkway (ideal for Disney). A cross between a convention centre and a vast turn-of-the-century Florida mansion, it features 4½ acres/2ha of indoor gardens, fountains and 'landscaped' waters under a glass dome, with live entertainment nightly. Three themed indoor areas bear witness to great creativity and the resort offers every creature comfort, with an array of restaurants and bars, full-service spa, children's centre and 10 shops. Its imaginative Clearwater Cove water play area has a huge zero-entry pool, waterfall, octopus waterslide and kids' splash area, while the sophisticated adults-only area, Coquina Dunes, offers a quiet pool, bocce court, volleyball, croquet lawn and a realistic 9-hole putting challenge. Standard rooms are some of the smartest and most spacious, while the suites are enormous. The central Emerald Bay offers even more choice with a concierge level. One area is landscaped like the Everglades (with alligator feeding!); another copies St Augustine's old-world charm, with a replica Spanish fort; and the third is eclectic Key West, with

Gaylord Palms Resort

a mock-up marina and sailboat. To walk into the resort's marbled lobby and cavernous interior at night is like entering a future world. Then there is the signature fine dining, with the choice of Old Hickory Steakhouse, Sunset Sam's (fine seafood), the Mediterranean buffet-style Villa de Flora (with an excellent Sunday brunch) and a Sushi Bar. The Relâche Spa is one of the area's largest, with 25 treatment rooms, fitness centre and beauty salon. There are 13 shops, plus the Java Coast coffee shop, Auggie's Jammin' Piano Bar and H2O Sports Bar. The hotel stages regular special events and is a great wedding venue (407 586 2000, **www.gaylordhotels.com/palms-home.html**).

BRITTIP

The Gaylord Palms features the stunning Christmas celebration ICE!, a wonderland of ice sculptures, snow scenery and ice slides, plus skating and other festive touches. Early Nov–3 Jan, tickets $20-30/adults, $18/over-55s and $13/4–12s, or combo tickets (ICE! plus skating) for $32, $22 and $15.

Mona Lisa Suite Hotel: One of the finest condo-hotels, on Highway 192 at the entrance to Celebration, this is a luxury 5-storey, 240-unit property set around a spectacular 'vanishing edge' swimming pool and boasting upmarket dining at The Galerie Restaurant and Bistro Restaurant & Bar (with its Stone Hearth Oven). The 1 and 2-bed suites feature beautifully furnished living areas, full kitchens and ultra-comfy bedrooms, with L'Occitane toiletries. Balconies overlook the infinity pool or lush landscaping. There is a free shuttle to all the theme parks and privileged use of the Celebration Day Spa and Golf Club (1866 404 6662; **www.monalisasuitehotel.com**).

BRITTIP

Don't miss the signature pizzas and flatbreads at The Bistro at the Mona Lisa Hotel, a wonderful tropical hangout in which to enjoy a drink, snack or sample its fresh, traditional dishes in an inviting ambience.

Further afield

Beyond the main tourist areas you'll find more high-quality offerings.

Grand Bohemian Hotel: Sister property to the Bohemian Hotel, this adds a touch of class to the downtown scene. It features an early 20th-century Austrian theme, with the accent on fine art, fine dining and good service. Its 14 storeys make it a major landmark and it boasts the wonderful Bohème restaurant and über-stylish Bösendorfer Lounge – with great live entertainment nightly – plus a 14th-floor concierge suite, heated pool, spa, fitness centre and Gallery of Fine Art. The Sunday Jazz Brunch is another outstanding feature. Rooms are superbly appointed, with wi-fi, mini-bars, CD players and interactive TVs, plus there are 36 superb suites. Every room features the ultra-comfy Sumptuous Bed (407 313 9000, **www. grandbohemianhotel.com**).

Grande Lakes Orlando: You'll find extensive luxury at this 500-acre/200ha combination of a 584-room, 5-star Ritz-Carlton Hotel, a 1,000-room JW Marriott Hotel, grand spa, 18-hole Greg Norman-designed golf course, tennis centre and an upscale range of shops and restaurants, like the outstanding Norman's, featuring the 'new world' cuisine of celebrity chef Norman Van Aken. Located on the edge of a forestry preserve, it feels secluded and remote – quite a feat in this area. It is slightly off the beaten track – at the junction of John Young and Central Florida Parkway – yet is only 10mls/16km from Disney and Orlando International Airport.

JW Marriott: This flagship hotel of the Marriott group has Spanish-Moorish design, a formal restaurant featuring fresh, organic produce, an American brasserie, Starbucks lounge, Sushi Bar and a pool bar and grill. It has a great 'lazy river' mini-water park, plus a kids' pool and splash fountain. Rooms are plush and ultra-comfortable; 70% have balconies and there are 64 grand suites.

Ritz-Carlton: This offers a wonderful blend of scale and detail, with lush gardens, abundant lakes and streams, Venetian-inspired architecture and a wealth of genuine antiques. It has a large, sloped-entry pool, kids' pool, 3 floodlit tennis courts, a signature shop and 5 dining choices, plus a separate children's check-in and

Ritz-Carlton

the excellent Ritz Kids Club (5–12s; also for JW Marriott guests), while all restaurants offer child menus. Apart from highly rated Norman's, the restaurants include The Vineyard Grill steakhouse (try its excellent Sun champagne brunch at $65/adults and $29/children), Fairways Pub and Bleu pool bar and grill. The rooms are beautifully furnished, with high-quality products in the marbled bathrooms, plasma-screen TVs, radio/CD, mini-bar, slippers and robes, and all have balconies. There are 66 spacious suites and 92 Club rooms on the top 2 floors, with concierge and butler service, food and drink presentations in the Club Lounge and Bvlgari amenities. Two kidsuites feature a separate bedroom and bathroom, with toys, games, TV and video games for 100% child appeal. The golf course is immaculate and offers a Caddie Concierge programme for the ultimate in service. The beautiful citrus-tinged spa boasts a huge fitness centre and aerobics studio, lap pool (all free to guests at both hotels), lovely spa-cuisine restaurant and a huge array of massages and therapies. The pricing is suitably upmarket, but it is a rare treat (407 206 2300/2400, **www.grandelakes.com**).

◀◼▶ BRITTIP

Head for the Ritz-Carlton's lobby lounge for afternoon tea or drinks in style with a magnificent view, especially at sunset.

Bahama Bay Resort

Omni Orlando Resort at Champions Gate: A real golfing paradise, this offers 720 rooms and suites overlooking a superb golf set-up with 2 Greg Norman-designed courses. An imposing hotel with impressive facilities, including the HQ of the renowned David Leadbetter golf academy, main swimming pool and activity pool (including a 'lazy river' feature, fountains and waterslide), 4 restaurants (notably the superb Asian cuisine of Zen and the chic David's Club bar-restaurant), coffee bar, deli, 3 lounge bars, state-of-the-art health club and full-service spa. Just 15mins south of Disney off I-4, this is well situated yet off the beaten track for those (especially golfers) looking for something different. Set in 1,500 landscaped acres/607ha and with a magnificent vista as you walk in, it suits both business travellers and leisure-seekers. It also has 59 superb 2 and 3-bed villas, affording a more private stay, with full kitchens and opulent furnishings (407 390 6664, **www.omnihotels.com**).

SELF-CATERING

Once you venture beyond pure hotel territory, your choice varies through a range of 'Resorts' to timeshares, villa communities, studios and condos, all of which are essentially self-catering (although some still offer restaurants and other hotel-type amenities). They all tend to be further away from the parks, but they represent a flexible option, especially for larger groups.

Bahama Bay Resort: A wonderful location on Lake Davenport in Davenport (west on Highway 192, then south on Highway 27 to Florence Villa Grove Rd, or via Westside Rd), this is spread over 70 acres/28ha, with 498 condos in 38 2 and 3-storey buildings. The community is woven with tropical landscaping that includes water features, a recreation centre and clubhouse, restaurant and snack bar, internet café, fitness centre, fabulous Eleuthera Spa & Salon, tennis, basketball and volleyball, 4 heated pools and kiddie pools. You can fish in the lake, which has a sandy beach, plus there is a

Our definitions

To avoid confusion, here's the correct terminology for self-catering accommodation (but check with the operator for the exact type if it's not clear):

Villa: Detached vacation home, usually with its own screened-in pool, in self-contained residential communities.

Townhome: 2-storey terraced-style house, rarely with its own pool; found in many Resorts.

Condo: 1, 2 or 3-bed apartment-style unit, usually in a low-rise block but sometimes 10 or more storeys.

Studio: 1-room accommodation unit that includes kitchen facilities.

Resort: Collection of condos (or townhomes) built around central features like pools, recreation facilities and (sometimes) a restaurant/bar or 2.

video arcade and small cinema. A shuttle runs to theme parks for a small charge. The 4 types of condo offer 2-bed, 2-bath (sleeping 6, with a sofa-bed in the lounge) and 3-bed, 2-bath (sleeping 8, again with sofa-bed), with fitted kitchen, laundry room/washer-dryer, living room and dining area. The Grand Bahama 3-bed condo has 1,739ft^2/162m^2 of space and is one of the most elegant (1877 299 4481 or **www.bahamabay.co**m).

Barefoot'n Resort: This boutique timeshare of 40 1-bed condos is nicely tucked away next to Old Town in Kissimmee and was dramatically enhanced in 2009 with another 42 1 and 2-bed units. There's a main pool, kids' pool, whirlpool, children's play area, volleyball and barbecue stations. (407 589 2127, **www.barefootn. com**).

Blue Heron Beach Resort: A superb complex of 2 high-rise towers (16 and 21 storeys) on Apopka-Vineland Rd (Highway 535) in Lake Buena Vista, this features 283 beautifully furnished 1 and 2-bed condos, all with 2 bathrooms, a balcony and fully equipped kitchen, including washer-dryer. There are bunk beds for kids in

the spacious 1 and 2-bed units, which can comfortably sleep 6–8. All master bedrooms also include a whirlpool tub in the en-suite bathrooms. One side has a Disney view (including the fireworks at night) while the other overlooks scenic Lake Bryan.

BRITTIP
If you prefer a tranquil Lake View room at the **Blue Heron Beach Resort**, you can still get a view of Disney's fireworks at night from the outdoor corridor/terrace on each floor.

There is a superb lido deck, with a large freeform pool, kids' pool and hot tub, plus a boardwalk fronting the lake and watersports (jet-skis and water-skiing, for an extra charge), with the 36-hole Hawaiian Rumble mini-golf course outside. There is a video games room and 2 fitness centres, but no restaurant (but plenty nearby, including a CiCi's Pizza, Starbucks and Dunkin' Donuts in front, plus a supermarket). As a self-catering resort, daily house-keeping is available only for a charge, but there is a free daily shuttle to the parks (407 387 2200, **www. blueheronbeachresort.com**).

BRITBONUS
Get 7 nights for the price of 5 or 14 for the price of 10 at the **Blue Heron Beach Resort**. Book online or call 407 387 2200, extension 4, and use booking code "BRIT75." Valid until 31 December 2012; not valid with any other discount or coupon. Based on availability and certain blackout dates.

Blue Heron Beach Resort

Floridays Resort Orlando: One of the smartest of the area's condo-hotels, this is well situated in a quieter part of I-Drive, but close to Orlando Premium Outlets and with a free shuttle service to the parks. The full site consists of 6 condo blocks (each with 72 rooms), 2 pools (including the elaborate main zero-depth entry pool and great water-play area), a pool bar and grill, fitness centre, stylish Welcome Center, kids' activity centre and games room, a small grocery store, plus concierge services, business centre and meeting facilities. The 2 and 3-bed grand suites are beautifully furnished, sleep 6–10, and have either a balcony or patio. Living rooms include large plasma TVs, high-speed internet, games console and stereos, while each bedroom also has a TV. There's also a delivery service from the Marketplace, which also serves Starbucks coffee. All rooms are wheelchair-accessible and some are adapted for the disabled with roll-in showers (1866 797 0022, **www.floridaysresortorlando.com**).

Fountains Resort: This high-quality timeshare set-up is also on the quieter stretch of I-Drive (south of SeaWorld). It has superb 2-bed, 2-bath condos, all with full kitchens, plus an huge pool area with waterslides and poolside bar, all in a beautiful tropical environment, complete with the large Clubhouse boasting a games room, kids' activity centre, bar and coffee lounge (1800 456 0009, **www.bluegreenrentals.com**).

Floridays Resort

Hapimag Resort: An unusual combination of vacation home and resort, this is the Swiss timeshare operator's only US property (but with NO timeshare solicitation), inside the mature Lake Berkley villa community in Kissimmee (almost behind Medieval Times). It encompasses a self-contained circle of 2 and 3-bed town-homes, grouped around a busy clubhouse with pool, volleyball court, small fitness centre and gift shop. There are also a handful of fully furnished 4-bed villas elsewhere in the community, which also has its own clubhouse and smart pool area with kids' pool, plus another gym, games room and internet room. There is then a scenic walkway around the lake, with 2 white-sand beaches (407 390 9083, **www.orlando-hapimag.com**).

BRITBONUS

$ Stay 6 consecutive nights at the **Hapimag Resort** and the 7th night is free. Special rates for 1, 2 and 3-bed units of $70, $80 & $90/night low season; $80, $90 & $100/night high season; and $90, $100 & $110/night holiday season (all plus tax) also apply. All offers valid to end 2012; subject to availability; some blackout dates apply. Just quote the code 'Brit Guide 2012' when booking on 407 390 9083.

Lake Buena Vista Resort Village & Spa: This stylish condo-hotel features 5 tower blocks of 2, 3 and 4-bed condos, next to Lake Buena Vista Factory Stores on Highway 535. The current phase includes a superb freeform swimming pool, with pirate play-ship, a second quiet pool, a state-of-the-art fitness centre, video games room and Kids' Club. There is a convenience store and gift shop, a Pizza Hut Express, specialist bar-restaurant Frankie Farrell's Irish Pub & Grille, and a 5-star spa, as well as a free shuttle to the main theme parks. The rooms (all with full kitchens, Jacuzzi tubs, digital TVs and internet) are comfortable and stylish, with the 4-bed condos very spacious. The blissful Reflections Spa & Salon offers some wonderfully relaxing treatments (407 956 6103, **www.lbvorlandoresort. com** or **www.staysky.com**).

BRITTIP

Visiting Lake Buena Vista Factory Stores? Relieve aching limbs by popping next door to the **Resort Village & Spa** for a soothing pedicure, massage or other spa treatment (407 597 1695).

Liki Tiki Village: On the western fringe of Highway 192, this timeshare set-up often has good-value condos to rent on a weekly basis. Its newest blocks offer huge 1 and 2-bed units, with well-equipped kitchens (all with coffee and ice-makers), while the 64-acre/26ha complex boasts 2 pools, a mini water park, tennis courts, paddle boats, bikes, pool-bar and grill and free continental breakfast Mon–Fri (407 239 5000, **www.likitiki.com**).

Mystic Dunes Resort & Golf Club: Holiday ownership property tucked away in a quiet corner of Kissimmee offering hotel rentals, often at terrific rates. It is a luxurious resort with just about every facility, plus an impressive array of beautiful 1, 2 and 3-bed villas that sleep up to 12 (1877 747 4747, **www.mystic-dunes-resort. com**).

Orange Lake Resort: This vast resort on west Highway 192 offers a mixture of well-furnished 1, 2 and 3-bed condos (NB: Orange Lake refers to them as 'villas' but they are definitely apartment-type) and studios that sleep 4–12, plus golf, watersports and cinema. Then there are kids' activities, exercise classes, tennis, racquetball, mini-golf and a Marketplace of general store, pizzeria and golf shop. The amazing River Island water park has a lazy river, 2 zero-depth entry pools, mini-golf, whirlpool tubs, waterfalls and a clubhouse, arcade and fitness centre, while the Water's Edge beach Club adds a restaurant, pool bar, cabañas, stage and gift shop, plus an Olympic-size pool with beach-style entry. There is also a Publix supermarket, and this resort gets consistently good feedback, if occasionally a bit strong on the timeshare sales (407 239 0000, **http://orangelake.com/home.html**).

Palisades Resort: A real find out at the rural western end of Highway 192 in Kissimmee, this smart condo-hotel features spacious 1, 2 and 3-bed condos that sleep 4–8, with fully equipped kitchens, including washer-dryers, and private balconies. Each unit offers generous living and dining areas, 2 bathrooms (master bed with oversized bath) and flatscreen TVs. The tropical lido deck has a large outdoor pool in lush surroundings, plus there is a sauna, cinema, fitness centre, video games room and free wi-fi. It is close enough to benefit from the shops and restaurants along Highway 192 (and be just 10mins from Disney), but still be tranquil.

Mystic Dunes Resort & Golf Club

Reunion Resort

There are free pastries, coffee and tea at breakfast and, at busier times of the year, spa facilities. There is no bar or restaurant but a Publix supermarket is only 5mins away and its rates in 2011 ($95/night for a 3-bed condo in low season) were amazing (321 250 3030, **www.palisadesresortorlando.com** or **www. staysky.com**).

Regal Oaks at Old Town: This mix of stylish town-homes, from 3-bed, 2-bath units to grand 4-bed, 3-bath villas, follows the successful blueprint of accommodations set around an elaborate clubhouse, with fabulous water features (zero-entry pool, waterslide, whirlpool and lazy river), Tiki Bar and other facilities. Right next to all the fun and shopping of Old Town in Kissimmee, it offers terrific value (407 997 1000, **www. regaloaksresort.com**).

Regal Palms Resort & Spa: Next door to the serene Highlands Reserve villa community on Highway 27 is this mix of 3 and 4-bed townhomes and 4–6-bed villas set around a beautiful Clubhouse that includes a mini water park (with lazy river and waterslides), pools, Jacuzzis and extensive sun terraces. The sister resort to Regal Oaks, it also features a pub that shows live UK sports, a business centre, gym and gift shop/grocery store, plus an indulgent Spa & Health Club (863 424 6141, **www.regalpalmsorlando.com**).

Reunion Resort & Club: Arguably the grandest of all the resorts, this will be of keen interest to golfers who appreciate the 5-star touch. On Highway 532 in Kissimmee (just off exit 58 of I-4 south of Disney), this fledgling 'community' boasts a vast line-up of condos, town-homes and luxury villas set around 3 superb golf courses (designed by Arnold Palmer, Tom Watson and Jack Nicklaus). The choice is deluxe: immaculate 1, 2 and 3-bed condos (many with stunning golf course views); a range of private homes, from modest 3-beds to mansion-style 8-beds; a stylish golf clubhouse with excellent bar and restaurant; a full-service spa, with a superb array of treatments; the scenic Seven Eagles pool, complete with Pavilion Bar & Grille, Jacuzzis, fitness room and kids' play centre; floodlit tennis courts; an amazing water park consisting of lazy river, slides, pools, waterfalls and interactive kids' area; and miles of biking and hiking trails. High-rise condo, the Reunion Grande, features 82 luxurious 1 and 2-bed suites, magnificent fine-dining chophouse Forte, a state-of-the-art fitness facility and ultra-chic rooftop pool and bar, Eleven, offering tapas, cocktails and panoramic views. It all comes with concierge service and even private in-room dining that marks this out as one of Florida's most upmarket resorts. Only those staying here or members can play on the courses, but the scale and imagination of the resort are superb (407 662 1000, **www.reunionresort.com**). Reunion is also home to the state-of-the-art ANNIKA Academy, created under the direction of top golfer Annika Sorenstam.

BRITTIP
At both Sheraton Vistana properties, for a nominal fee, you can arrange to have your condo pre-stocked with food and laundry products.

Sheraton Vistana Resort: This sprawling family-friendly timeshare set-up in Lake Buena Vista, close to *Walt Disney World*, is a mature development of roomy 1 and 2-bed/2-bath condos (sleeping 4–8; again, they are called 'villas' but are definitely apartment-type) with fully equipped kitchens and magnificent resort facilities. Furnishings and facilities are all modern, with multiple TVs, DVD player and a screened-in private patio or balcony, plus large washer-dryers, which all serves to underline the great self-catering value of this type of accommodation. There are 7 giant pools, 9 floodlit tennis courts, smart Marketplace deli (with Starbucks coffee), Food Court (with KFC, Pizza Hut and A&W), Zimmie's Casual Eatery & Sports Bar and 3 pool bars, plus massage treatments and even a Tues evening 'picnic in the park' session with live music. There is free scheduled transport to the Disney parks and lots of family-orientated activities, including cookouts and storytelling (407 239 3100, **www.sheraton.com/vistanaresort**).

BRITBONUS
Stay at the **Sheraton Vistana Resort** and receive $50 in vacation dollars to use in the resort, plus valuable money-off coupons. Just quote the special Brit Guide code 'BBG' when booking.

Sheraton Vistana Villages: The sister, newer property, located on I-Drive south of SeaWorld, this upmarket family resort offers spacious 1 and 2-bed/2-bath condos with fully equipped kitchen or kitchenette,

dining area, washer-dryer and more, all in 5 and 6-storey blocks and all set around scenic landscaping or pool areas. The beautiful lobby opens on to a stunning main pool boasting waterfalls, Jacuzzis and children's play areas, while there is also the smart Flagler Station Bar & Grill for breakfast, lunch and dinner. Less than 6mls/10km from Disney, guests enjoy extensive amenities like free scheduled transport to the parks, 3 pool areas, a state-of-the-art fitness centre, games room, basketball and tennis courts and a grocery store, plus there is a big Publix supermarket nearby (407 238 5000, **www.sheraton.com/vistanavillages**).

BRITTIP
As the Sheraton Vistana resorts are both timeshare properties, you may well be asked if you'd like to take their property tour, but there is no pressure to sign up or hard-sell if you do.

Summer Bay Resort: Out on west Highway 192 is a mix of Budget motel (The Inn at Summer Bay), Standard hotel (Holiday Inn Express), some 3-bed vacation homes and new 1, 2 and 3-bed timeshare condos. The 700 rooms spread over 64 acres/26ha are all smart, while the facilities include outdoor heated pools and kiddie pools, an elaborate children's water-play area, mini-golf, clubhouse with volleyball, tennis, basketball, shuffleboard and fitness room, video arcade, gift shop and snack bar. The lake provides jet-skis, paddleboats, waterskiing and more, plus daily kids' activities and organised sports. Even

Summer Bay Resort

those in The Inn and Holiday Inn (which has its own pool and breakfast area) benefit from the clubhouse facilities, while next door is a Denny's diner and Publix supermarket. (1888 742 1100, **www.summerbayresort.com**).

Tuscana: This Mediterranean-inspired condo-resort bordering the Champions Gate golf courses offers 288 elegant, oversized 2 and 3-bed condos, each with 2 full baths, balcony, fully equipped kitchen, washer and dryer. The excellent clubhouse boasts the Tuscana Tavern bar and grill, tiki snack bar, elegant pool, kiddie pool, cabanas, fitness centre and a 24-seat movie theatre (407 787 4800, **www.tuscana.net**).

Villas at Grand Cypress: Arguably Orlando's top golf resort, this is also a wonderfully upmarket option in a beautiful setting behind *Walt Disney World*. It offers 186 single-room club suites and 1, 2, 3 and 4-bed condo-style villas, all luxuriously furnished, with fully equipped kitchens and patios or balconies. There is a blissful Villa Pool, with poolside saunas and bar, bike rentals and 2 restaurants (The Club sports bar and fine-dining Nine18 overlooking the North-South golf course), plus 24hr room service. Villa guests also get full use of all the amenities of the nearby Hyatt Regency Grand Cypress (p87), a 5min ride on the free on-demand shuttle service (407 239 4700, **www. grandcypress.com**).

Grand Cypress

Vista Cay Resort: This recent timeshare development offers some of the most extensive facilities in the I-Drive/ Universal Boulevard area (behind the Convention Center North). Convenient for all the attractions but away from the main bustle, it has beautiful accommodations (2 and 3-bed executive suites and 3-bed town-homes), plus a large clubhouse with a pool set in lush, tropical landscaping; whirlpool spa, kids' pool and basketball court; games room, business centre and fitness centre. Apartments range from 1,500ft^2/140m^2 to 2,300ft^2/214m^2 and offer fully-equipped kitchens, large HD TVs with DVD players and Sony PlayStations, dining rooms, master bedrooms (with separate Roman tubs and showers), private balconies and free wi-fi (407 996 4647, **www. vistacayholidays.com**).

Windsor Palms Resort: Just off west Highway 192 in Kissimmee, this popular gated community has a mix of 2-bed condos, 2 and 3-bed town-homes, and 3–6-bed private pool villas. Amenities include a large clubhouse and fitness centre, tennis courts, an Olympic-sized pool, a kiddie pool and spa, basketball, billiard room, volleyball court, video arcade, playground and a 58-seat cinema showing recent films. The (slightly newer) sister resort **Windsor Hills** on Old Lake Wilson Road offers the same accommodation choice and impressive amenities, like its huge lagoon-style pool with waterslide and state-of-the-art fitness centre and is even closer to the Disney parks (1888 426 0427, **www.globalresorthomes.co**m).

HOLIDAY HOMES

This is in many ways the biggest area of accommodation in Orlando, especially for UK visitors, as there has been a huge development of holiday homes, or villas, in the last 20 years. Generally speaking, they provide a valuable way for large families and groups to stay together – the largest can sleep 16 – and cut costs by self-catering. The homes – individual or groups in residential

Rental Accommodation

Remington

Windsor Park

Buena Ventura Lakes

Magic Landings

Winn Dixie

Kissimmee Pines

Whispering Oaks

Oscola Square Mall *Publix*

The Hamlets
Chatham Park
Montego Bay
Sweetwater Club
Siesta Lago
Bella Vida
Lake Berkley
Indian
Point

Villas at Somerset
Royal Bay
Windward Cay
Seasons
Terra Verde

Bass Lakes
Country Creek
Creekside

Eagle Point
Liberty Village
Fiesta Key
Cumbrian Lakes

Publix

Kissimmee

Wal-Mart

Publix

Crystal Cove
Laguna Bay

Indian Wells *Publix*

Cane
Island

Barefoot'n &
Regal Oaks

Hamilton's Reserve

Poinciana Boulevard

St James Park
Trafalgar Villas
Doral Woods

Blackstone Landing

Crescent Lakes
Countryside Manor

Poinciana

SEAWORLD

Winn Dixie

TOLLS

**Walt Disney
World**

EPCOT

HOLLYWOOD STUDIOS

Celebration

Old Lake Wilson Road

* Terrace Ridge & Lake View
also at Town Center

Ronald Reagan Parkway /
Loughman Road

Aviana
Providence
Watersong

Davenport, Haines City

0   3 miles

MAGIC KINGDOM

TOLLS

**ANIMAL
KINGDOM**

Winn Dixie

Winn Dixie

Publix

Arcadia Estates

Formosa Gardens
Windsor Hills
Rolling
Hills
Tempus Palms
Mystic Dunes
Oakwater

Indian Ridge

Lake Wilson
Terraces at Reunion

Reunion

Bridgewater
Crossing

Sandy
Ridge
Town
Center

Thousand Oaks
Paradise Woods

Oak Point
Grand Reserve
Robbins Rest

Wildflower
Ridge

Westchester Villas

Siena Ridge
Mission Park
Weston Hills

Greater Groves

Sawgrass Bay

Orange Tree

Clermont

Eagle Ridge

Glenbrook Resort
Sunrise Lakes
Woodridge, Clear
Creek, Silver Creek

Summer Bay,
Lighthouse Key,
Liki Tiki Resort
Palisades

Riverside Bank
Wal-Mart

Orange Lake
Publix

Vista del Lago

Lake Davenport
Estates

Windsor Palms

Cagan Crossings
High Grove

Publix

Legacy Dunes
Grand Palms
Lindfields

Oak
Island
Encantada
Emerald
Island
Indian Creek
Bahama Bay

Berry Town Center

Wal-Mart

Polo Park East
Esprit

Davenport
Lakes
Sunset Lakes

Publix

The Ridge
Hampton Lakes
Palm Key
Solana

**Champions
Gate**

Publix

Bentley Oaks
Loma Linda

West
Haven

Windwood Bay
Sunridge Woods

Briargrove

Ashley Manor

Posner Park
Target

Arrowhead Lakes
Royal Palms
Aylesbury

Ridgewood Lakes
Marbella

Highlands Reserve

Westridge
(Durango Loop)

Florida Pines
Calabay Parc
The Preserve
Four Corners
West Stonebridge
Tuscan Ridge
Pines West

The Gardens
Santa Cruz
Loma Del Sol

Walgreens

Bella Toscana
Loma Vista
Dunston Hills

Polo Park
Windmill Village
Bass Lake
Tuscan Hills
Legacy Park
Wellington

Tivoli Manor
Westbury
Sunset Ridge
Silver Palms
Regency Place

Vizcay

Haines City

Tampa

Poinciana

Davenport, Haines City

© Steve Munns 2011

N

communities, often newly built – are sometimes gated, and most have a private pool, while some have access to communal facilities like pools and recreation areas. They are always equipped with microwaves, multiple TVs and washer-dryers. Some are classed as 'executive', and this usually means more facilities (games rooms, barbecues, Jacuzzis, etc.) rather than an increase in size. A hire car is usually essential, but the savings can be significant. Prices can be as low as $450/week off-peak, but expect to pay at least $1,500/week for a 5 or 6-bed villa in high season. A word of warning: once you've experienced pool-at-home life, you may never go back to a hotel!

If you book independently, there are several key questions to ask. Do you need to go to an office some way away to pick up the keys or is there a combination lockbox at the house? Is there a local contact if anything goes wrong (most owners do not live in Florida) and is the property maintained by a local company? Does it offer a secure bonding for your booking, and is it a member of a reputable organisation, such as the Better Business Bureau of Central Florida? In winter, is the pool heated, and what is the charge for heating? Finally, is it as close to Disney as it says (some can be in Polk County, 30mins away)?

There are more than 20,000 villas on offer, spread across Kissimmee and out in Polk and Lake Counties to the west and south-west of

Advantage Vacation Homes

Disney, most in well established developments (Highlands Reserve is a good example). Be aware homes within a particular community can still vary in quality depending on the care and attention of owners and/or property managers, hence just being in, say, stylish Cumbrian Lakes, is not a guarantee of executive quality. You can rent direct from the owners (on sites like **www.vrbo.com**, **www.lastminutevillas.net** and **www. thedibb.co.uk**) or from a property management company, which will look after multiple villas. Ironically, there are increasing numbers of town-homes (so developers can fit in more); for a 'detached' house, ask for a 'single family home'. The bottom line is you must do your homework, shop around as you would for any big purchase, and check with organisations like the Central Florida Vacation Rental Managers Association. This is the only acknowledged umbrella organisation for the holiday home business and helps to provide a level of credibility.

The following companies all pass the *Brit Guide* credibility test.

Advantage Vacation Homes: In the villa rental business for more than 20 years and one of the largest companies, few of its 2–6 bed homes (the majority on west Highway 192 and Highway 27 in Clermont and Davenport) are more than 10yrs old, while many are 4–5yrs at most. It also manages a range of condos (in the Bahama Bay and Sun Lake resorts) and town-homes. It offers 24hr management, with courteous and efficient staff at its office just off west Highway 192 (plus an attraction ticket service), open 9am–10pm daily. Its holiday homes are rated Silver, Gold or Platinum, with the difference measured in the extras rather than size (larger-screen or plasma TVs, tiled floors rather than carpeting, a Jacuzzi or games room, etc), though some of the more exclusive villas might be situated on a golf community or have tennis courts (0871 711 9531 in the UK, 1866 544 5301 in the US, **www. advantagevacationhomes.com**).

Alexander Holiday Homes: Family-owned Alexander manages more than 200 properties in Kissimmee, from standard 2, 3 and 4-bed condos to luxury 7-bed executive homes sleeping 14, all with pools and immaculately furnished, within 15–20mins of Disney, including some of the closest to the parks. This company was the first of its kind in Orlando (in 1981) and still offers a personable, efficient service. It was only the third management company to earn the distinguished AAA (American Automobile Association) 3 Diamond rating and definitely gets our approval. It shows prices in UK and US currency and even offers an airport meet-and-greet service to ensure you get to your home, as well as arrival grocery packages, barbecue rentals, scooter and wheelchair hire. Its informative website provides photo tours of all its homes, useful blogs and other features (0871 711 5371 in the UK, 1800 621 7888 in the US, **www.floridasunshine.com**).

Florida Choice Vacation Homes: Provides town-homes (3 or 4-bed with communal pools and recreation facilities), standard and executive homes (3–7 bed private properties) in Orlando and Naples, some with heated pools and with free local phone calls. There is optional maid service and cot and highchair rentals (407 397 3013, **www.floridachoice.com**).

Florida Leisure Vacation Homes: Another company we know well and can recommend, it is British-owned and pays great attention to detail. With 100 homes (3–7 beds) in the Kissimmee area, most just a few years old and many in the highly regarded Cumbrian Lakes community, it prides itself on a personal touch (even down to providing personal chef, massage and concierge services) and offers some of the biggest and newest properties, as well as a full online booking system. Many are in the Executive range, with the fullest array of amenities in addition to their private, screened pools, and often in gated communities. All properties have lock-boxes, so you don't need to visit the management office to check in. You can see all its homes online (in extended photo and video) plus lots of local info, while its new testimonial sections provide first-hand feedback. The website includes a regular blog, free newsletter and other useful features. Its office is handily placed on Highway 192 in Kissimmee, at the junction with Apopka-Vineland Road, SR 535 (407 870 1600; **www.floridaleisure.com**).

Florida Vacation Shop: Another local British specialist, it features a select range of new homes in some of the smartest local developments. Options include Formosa Garden Estates, Emerald Island Resorts, Legacy Park and Crescent Lakes, plus the Regal Oaks resort. Its concierge service offers the chance to arrange other services in advance (like dining), while there are optional maid services, Welcome Packs and Tailor-Made Shopping (specific goods delivered to your villa prior to arrival). Pushchairs, cots, high-chairs and barbecue grills can all be hired on a weekly basis. Its website has a useful Vacation Guide and downloadable handbooks for the various accommodations (1866 394 2583; **www.floridavacationshop.com**).

BRITTIP
The Central Florida Vacation Rental Managers Association website promotes villa rentals and makes booking easier (**www.vacationwithconfidence.com**). Another website that offers insights is **www.discovervacationhomes.com**.

Florida Choice Vacation Homes

Loyalty Homes: For a luxury touch, all these homes (2–6 bedrooms) are no more than 4mls/6.5 km from Disney and all offer the true 'executive' style, with the likes of digital door locks (so no key collection required), cable TV and many with games rooms. The website offers video tours, too (call 0121 468 0016 in the UK or 407 397 7475 in the US, **www.loyaltyusa.com**).

Park Square Homes: This is actually operated by the home builder, hence it features the complete resort communities of Encantada and Bella Vida, both just off Highway 192 in Kissimmee, with a series of well-built and beautifully furnished 3 and 4-bed town-homes, plus larger villas at Bella Vida, all with private pools. The 2 tropically styled resorts benefit from a central clubhouse, with a large pool, cyber café, exercise room and lakefront gazebo, while Encantada also has a video games room and café (1866 930 0444, **www.bellavidavacationhomes.com** and **www.encantadaresorthomes.com**).

✠ BRITTIP

One of the most frequent questions we hear about pool-villas is: will we need pool heat? Typically, you'll probably need to pay for pool heating from late October-early May but most pools will be warm enough from mid-May to mid-October without any heating.

Premier Vacation Homes: A good range of spacious properties with 2–6 beds, sleeping up to 14, in secure residential communities within a

Premier Vacation Homes town option

15–20min drive of Disney. All are privately owned and have been furnished as holiday homes, with screened pools, 2 TVs, fully equipped kitchens (including dishwasher, washer-dryer, microwave and coffee-maker), at least 1 king or queen bed and free local phone calls. Maid service can be added for a fee. The Luxury homes (2–4 beds) are standard accommodation, while Executive homes (3–6 beds) are bigger, with an extra TV, VCR and barbecue, and there's also a town-home and condo choice (407 396 2401, **www.pr-vacation.com**).

Prestige Vacations Direct: Another British-owned and run company, this agency specialises in renting out a wide variety of 3–6 bed vacation homes, most just a short drive from Disney. It can provide special monthly rates and UK sterling prices, has periodic special offers, and features 26 different villa communities, from Windsor Palms to Westridge and Highlands Reserve on Highway 27. Rates in 2011 were as low as $99/night for a 3-bed villa with pool (1877 462 4424, **www.prestigevacationsdirect.com**).

✠ BRITTIP

You'll find Marmite, Ribena, McVities and a handful of other British groceries at Publix and Winn-Dixie supermarkets, and most Wal-Marts (International aisle), but your best bet is the British Supermarket on Vineland Rd (1 block east of its Kirkman Rd junction, just north of Universal; p338).

Villa Direct: Another major Orlando specialist, and one of the biggest, with an extensive range of properties in the area, from 2-bed condos to luxury 7-bed villas, and a good user-friendly website, plus an excellent range of guest services, including arrival groceries and even mobility equipment rental. Its welcome centre is easily found on west Highway 192 in Kissimmee while the head office is close by in Celebration, just off I-4 (407 397 1210, **www.villadirect.com**).

OK, that's enough accommodation advice. Now it's on to the parks…

5 The Theme Parks: Disney's Fab Four

or Spending the Day with Mickey and the Gang

By now you should be prepared to deal with the main business of any visit to Orlando: *Walt Disney World.* This is the heart of all the excitement and fun in store (along with the other big theme parks of Universal Orlando, SeaWorld and Busch Gardens).

In our opinion, 2 weeks is barely enough to see all this vast resort has in store. So, when you add in the other 4 theme parks and the array of smaller-scale attractions, you start to realise the awesome scope of an Orlando holiday!

BRITTIP
Make a photocopy of the back of your park passes, and of your passport, before leaving home. If your tickets are lost during your holiday you will need the information on the back of each ticket to have them replaced. A copy of your passport will suffice as photo ID in the parks, or if your passport becomes lost.

Buying your tickets in advance is highly advisable (it saves time and is often better value), but work out your requirements first – you won't get full use out of, say, a 7-day Premium ticket AND an Orlando Flex Ticket Plus in just a fortnight. Once you're ready to buy, check what security the ticket outlet offers (ABTA bonding, etc.) and what it does in case of tickets lost or stolen during shipping or during your holiday. Try to use your credit card for all purchases – there is built-in additional security (for our list of recommended ticket outlets; p8–9).

Discount options: You will find a welter of discount coupons for many of the smaller attractions in tourist publications distributed in Orlando (or from your hotel Guest Services desk – it's often worth asking), while the tour operators' welcome meetings usually have special offers and tickets for the latest excursions.

BRITTIP
Offers of 'free' Disney tickets usually mean timeshare firms, which also claim to have 'official' visitor centres. I-Drive has the only genuine Official Visitor Center.

Cinderella Castle

© Disney

Check out the **Official Visitor Center** for discounts at 8723 International Drive in the Gala Center on the corner of Austrian Row (407 363 5872, **www. visitorlando.com/uk**; see map on p69). The **Universal Attractions** booths at several shopping malls also have great deals (3 days for the price of 2, 2-for-1 drinks etc.) from time to time. It IS possible to bag free tickets by attending timeshare presentations but they can easily take half a day of your precious holiday and do you really want the hard-sell hassle?

If you DO want to check out timeshare options, look first at **Disney Vacation Club** for the guarantee of memorable holidays. A tour (for which you will be picked up) will take around 3 hours, but you will be given some FastPasses in return to save time back at the parks. Call 407 566 3300, 1800 500 3990 or visit **http://dvc. disney.go.com/dvc/index**.

BRITTIP

Smoking is not permitted in the parks, apart from in a handful of designated areas. Check park maps for their exact locations. All restaurants are strictly non-smoking.

Ratings

We judge all the rides and shows on a unique rating system that splits them into thrill rides and scenic rides. Thrill rides earn **T** ratings out of 5 (hence a

TTTTT is as exciting as they get) and scenic rides get **A** ratings out of 5 (an **AA** attraction is likely to be twee and missable). It is obviously a matter of opinion but you can be sure a **T** or **A** ride is not worth your time, a **TT** or **AA** is worth seeing only if there is no queue, a **TTT** or **AAA** should be seen if you have time, but you won't miss much if you don't, a **TTTT** or **AAAA** ride is a big-time attraction that should be high on your 'must do' list, and a **TTTTT** or **AAAAA** attraction should not be missed! The latter will have the longest queues, so you should plan your visit around them. Some rides have height restrictions and are not advisable for people with back, neck or heart problems or for expectant mothers. Where this is the case we say, for example, '**Restrictions:** 3ft 6in/106cm'. Height restrictions (strictly enforced) are based on the average 5-year-old being 3ft 6in/106cm tall, those aged 6 being 3ft 9in/114cm and 9s being 4ft 4in/132cm. You can also refer to our **Height Restriction Guide**, p37.

Disney's FastPass

One essential aid to queuing is **Disney's FastPass** system **FP**. Many of the main attractions have this, allowing you to roam while you wait for an allotted time to ride. How it works: insert your main park entrance ticket into the FP machine (to the

Welcome to the magic

© Disney

Character dining

Having a meal with Mickey and Co (or Winnie the Pooh, Cinderella or Mary Poppins) is one of the great Disney experiences – even if you don't have children! It is also often the best way to meet your favourite characters without a wait, as they come to YOU. Reservations can be made up to 180 days in advance by phoning 407 WDW DINE (939 3463), calling at any Guest Services desk in a hotel, or by touching *88 on any Disney pay phone or 55 from a Disney resort room phone.

Some meals are difficult to get. Breakfast at Cinderella's Royal Table at the *Magic Kingdom* usually sells out within minutes of the 180-day window being open. Chef Mickey's and the Princess Storybook meals also go quickly. If you cannot book in advance, try calling the day you'd like to dine or, as a last resort, show up to see if there have been any cancellations. You must check in at the podium 10mins prior to your time and you will be given the next available table. Some characters don't enter the restaurant so, if they are in the lobby, you'll want to meet them before you are seated. Dining is all-you-can-eat, served buffet, pre-plated or family-style. Inside the restaurant, characters circulate among the tables giving attention to each group (particularly when children are holding the camera!). Character interaction is top-notch, especially if you dine off-hours when the restaurant is quieter. Be sure to bring your autograph book, a fat pen or marker (easier for the characters to hold) and plenty of film or an extra digital card for your camera. Some characters are huge, and children may be put off by them. If you aren't sure how they'll react, see how they are with the characters in the park before booking a character meal. Price range: breakfast $20.99-49 adults, $10.99-32 children; lunch $28.99-53 and $14.99-33; dinner $34.99-59 and $16.99-36 (NB: beware the peak season price rises – Disney has started the dubious practice of raising its restaurant rates in high season).

side of the attraction's entrance) and you get another ticket giving you a period of time in which to return for your ride with only a minimal wait (NB: you need a FP ticket for every person who wants to ride, not just 1 per group). You can hold only 1 FP ticket per 2-hour period, though once you've used it you can get another straight away. If you start by going to one of the FP rides, collecting your ticket and returning later, you can by-pass a lot of queuing. You can also get another FP as soon as your 'window' opens: e.g., if your time slot for Space Mountain is 10–11am, you could get another FP for, say, Buzz Lightyear's Space Ranger Spin at 10.01 and then go and ride Space Mountain. Many people miss this, but it is FREE (FastPass rides are indicated by FP in descriptions). If you miss your FP 'window', you will still be allowed on, but you can't ride *before* your time period.

BRITTIP

Purchase a lanyard for your park tickets if you plan to use FastPass often. This keeps your tickets together and easily accessible.

With young ones

All Disney's parks offer pushchair ('stroller') hire, and you can save money by purchasing a multi-day rental at your first park. Children of ALL ages seem to get a big thrill from collecting autographs from the various Disney characters, and most shops sell handy **autograph books**.

PhotoPass

This unique and worthwhile scheme is available in all Disney's parks and (occasionally) in *Downtown Disney*. Disney photographers take photos of guests and, instead of

Meet Tigger and Pooh

Character Dining: the meals

MAGIC KINGDOM: Crystal Palace for breakfast, lunch or dinner with Winnie the Pooh and Co – especially good for smaller children; and **Cinderella's Royal Table** for the (expensive) *Once Upon A Breakfast*, with Cinderella and her Princess Friends; *Fairytale Lunch* (Cinderella and Friends); and *Dreams Come True Dinner* (Fairy Godmother only). Breakfast is $49 adults, $32 children; lunch $53 and, $33; dinner $59 and $36. Payment in full on your credit card is required to book, $10/person may be charged for no-shows (photo package and gratuity included, additional photos for a fee).

EPCOT: Garden Grill for lunch or dinner with Farmer Mickey, Pluto, Chip and Dale; **Princess Storybook Dining** at Restaurant Akershus (Norway) for breakfast, lunch and dinner; an alternative to Cinderella's, with some of Belle, Jasmine, Snow White, Mulan, Aurora (Sleeping Beauty) and Mary Poppins. Breakfast $39 adults, $23 children; lunch $41 and $24; dinner $46 and $25. Credit card needed to book, $10/person charged for no-shows.

DISNEY'S HOLLYWOOD STUDIOS: Hollywood & Vine for breakfast or lunch with the Disney Junior Pals, including JoJo and Goliath from JoJo's Circus and Leo from Little Einsteins.

DISNEY'S ANIMAL KINGDOM: Donald's Safari Breakfast at Tusker House with Donald, Goofy, Pluto and sometimes Mickey.

DISNEY RESORTS: Chef Mickey's at *Contemporary Resort*, breakfast or dinner with Mickey, Minnie, Goofy, Pluto, Chip and Dale – peak times book up quickly; **1900 Park Fare** at *Grand Floridian*, breakfast with Alice, Mary Poppins and Mad Hatter; dinner with Cinderella, Anastasia, Drizella, Lady Tremaine and, sometimes, Prince Charming – again, book early; **Wonderland Tea Party** at *Grand Floridian*, 1.30–2.30pm Mon-Fri, 4-12s only, $42.60, meal, activities and storytelling with Alice and friends ($10 no-show); **Perfectly Princess Tea Party** with Princess Aurora at *Grand Floridian*, 10.30am–12pm, ages 3–11 with an adult, $250 for 1 adult with 1 child age 3–11. Meal (tea, cake, finger sandwiches), singalong, story time, My Disney Girl doll, bracelet, tiara, scrapbook page, and Best Friend certificate. **'Ohana** at *Polynesian Resort*, breakfast with Lilo, Stitch, Pluto and Mickey; **Cape May Café** at *Beach Club Resort*, breakfast with Goofy, Minnie and Donald; **Mickey's Backyard Barbecue** at *Fort Wilderness*, $45 and $26, games, storytelling, live entertainment, music and dancing with Mickey, Minnie and Co; chicken, hot dogs, burgers, ribs, beer, wine, iced tea and lemonade (Thurs and Sat only, 6.30pm, Mar– Dec); **Garden Grove Café** at *Walt Disney World Swan*, Mon-Fri, Timon and Rafiki; Sat and Sun breakfast with Goofy and Pluto.

receiving a paper claim ticket, they receive a *Disney PhotoPass* that links all their photos on one online account for easy viewing. There is

Inside The Land pavilion at Epcot

© Disney

no charge for obtaining a *PhotoPass* or for viewing (though there is if you want to download and print them), while each photo can be enhanced with Disney characters and special borders. Guests typically have 30 days after the photos were taken to decide if they want them (visit **www. disneyphotopass.com**), or you can view one of 3 PhotoPass shops – at the *Magic Kingdom*, the *Epcot* park or *Disney's Grand Floridian Resort*. Collect as many as you want (up to 300!) and have them burned on to one CD for a bargain $149.95. There are a huge range of other products you can have your photos transferred on to, including mugs, mouse pads and calendars!

Triceratop Spin at Animal Kingdom

Cast Members

Disney employees are called Cast Members or CMs (never 'staff' as they all play a 'role' in the entertainment) and they're renowned for their helpful, cheerful style, always willing to assist, offer advice or just chat. Interaction with CMs often provides some of the best memories of a visit. So, if you've had exceptional service or a CM has gone out of their way to help, let Disney know as it values such feedback (plus CMs get credit for it). Call in at Guest Relations (or City Hall at the *Magic Kingdom*) to record your thanks.

Child Swap

Where families have small children, but Mum and Dad still want to try a ride with height restrictions, you DON'T have to queue twice. When you reach the entrance to the queue, tell the operator you want to do a Child Swap. This means Mum can ride while Dad looks after junior in a quiet area and, on her return, Dad can have his go. At some attractions you may be given a Child Swap ticket while you wait.

Park security

All visitors with bags are required to go through a security bag-check before reaching the turnstiles. This is a fairly cursory (but compulsory) inspection but there is a separate lane for those without bags. When you put your ticket through the turnstile, you are also required to give a finger scan (which stops others from using your ticket).

Disney has an App for that

Get all the latest Disney Parks updates on your mobile phone, including park hours, wait times, dining and attraction info, plus games and more. Visit **www.disneyparksmobile.com**.

Jedi training

Magic Kingdom Park

The starting point for any visit has to be the *Magic Kingdom*, the park that best embodies the genuine enchantment Disney bestows on its visitors. It's the original development that sparked the Orlando tourist boom in 1971. In comparative terms, the *Magic Kingdom* is similar to the *Disneyland Park* at *Disneyland Resort Paris*® and *Disneyland California*. Outside those, it has no equal as a captivating day out for all the family. However, although a few rides are the same as those in Paris or LA, there are key differences, notably on Pirates of the Caribbean, Big Thunder Mountain Railroad and Haunted Mansion. And Space Mountain is a completely different ride from the one in Paris. And, even if a couple of attractions are closed for refurbishment, you won't be short of things to do! We will now attempt to steer you through a typical day at the park, with a guide to the rides, shows and places to eat; how to park, how to avoid the worst of the crowds – and how much you should expect to pay. The *Magic Kingdom* takes up just 107 acres/43ha of Disney's near 31,000 acres/12,555ha but attracts almost as many as the rest put together. It has 6 separate 'lands', like slices of a cake, centred on Florida's most famous landmark, Cinderella Castle. More than 40 attractions are packed into the park, plus numerous shops and restaurants (though the eating opportunities are less impressive than in *Epcot* and *Disney's Hollywood Studios*). It's easy to get overwhelmed, especially as it gets so busy (even the fast-food restaurants have big queues in high season), so plan around what most takes your fancy.

Magic Kingdom Park at a glance

Location	Off World Drive, Walt Disney World		
Size	107 acres/43ha in 6 'lands'		
Hours	9am–7pm off peak; 9am–10pm public holidays (see Brit Tip, p18), Spring school holidays; 8 or 9am–11pm or midnight high season (Easter, summer holidays, Thanksgiving and Christmas)		
Admission	Under-3s free; 3–9 $79 (1–day base ticket), $342 (5–day Premium), $358 (7-day Premium); adult (10+) $85, $361, $377. Prices do not include tax.		
Parking	$15		
Lockers	Next to stroller and wheelchair hire $12 small; $14 large ($5 deposit)		
Pushchairs	$15 and $30 (Stroller Shop to right of main entrance); length-of-stay, $13 per day single, $27 per day double		
Wheelchairs	$12 or $70 ($20 deposit refunded) at Main Ticket Centre		
Top attractions	Splash Mountain, Space Mountain, Mickey's PhilharMagic, Big Thunder Mountain Railroad, Pirates of the Caribbean, most rides in Fantasyland		
Don't miss	Celebrate A Dream Come True Parade, Main Street Electrical Parade or SpectroMagic (certain nights) and Wishes fireworks (most nights)		
Hidden costs	**Meals**	Burger, chips and coke $10.92 3-course dinner (Tony's Town Square) $28.50–48 Kids' counter service meal $4.99	
	T-shirts	$19.95–39.95	
	Souvenirs	$.99–450-plus	
	Sundries	Chalk colour portraits $17.95-35.95, or silhouettes $8, with oval frame $15.95	

Location

The *Magic Kingdom* is situated at the innermost end of *Walt Disney World*, with its entrance Toll Plaza three-quarters of the way along World Drive, the main entrance off Highway 192. World Drive runs north–south, while the Interstate 4 (I-4) entrance, Epcot Drive, runs east–west. Unless you are staying at a Disney resort, you must pay the $14 parking fee at the Toll Plaza to bring you into the massive car park.

BRITTIP
For the smoothest entry by road from Highway 192, take Seralago Boulevard (opposite the Seralago Hotel & Suites next to Old Town), turn left on to a non-toll stretch of Osceola Parkway and follow the signs to your chosen park. On West 192, turn off on Sherberth Road, go north to the first traffic lights and turn right, then pick up the Disney signs.

The majority arrive between 9.30 and 11.30am, so the car parks are busiest then, which is another good reason to get here EARLY. If you can't make it by 9am during peak periods, you might want to wait until after 1pm, or even later when the park is open as late as midnight. Remember to note exactly where you park, e.g. Mickey, Row 30; otherwise you'll be struggling, because many hire cars look the same!

A motorised tram takes you from the car park to the Transportation and Ticket Center at the heart of the operation. Unless you already have your ticket (which will save valuable time), you visit the ticket booths here. Then, either the monorail or ferryboat will bring you to the *Magic Kingdom* itself. The monorail (straight ahead) is quicker if there isn't a queue, otherwise bear left and take a slower ferryboat. If you're staying at a Disney hotel, the resort buses deliver you almost to the front door (or the monorail or boat will if you are staying at one of the *Magic Kingdom* resorts). Finally, the *Magic Kingdom* is the only 'dry' park – that is, there's NO alcohol on sale.

BRITTIP
An easy way to remember where you parked is to take a picture of the Section and Row number on your digital camera or phone. Then simply delete it when you get back to your car.

Main Street USA

Right, we've finally reached the park itself… but not quite. Hopefully, you've arrived early and are among the leading hordes aiming to swarm through the entrance. The published opening time may say 9am, but the gates can open up to 45mins earlier.

Main Street is the first of the 6 'lands' and, at opening time, there is an informal Welcome Parade, with costumed singers and dancers, and the Character Train arrives at Main Street Station to bring a variety of characters for a meet-and-greet in Town Square (get those autograph books ready!). A family is then chosen at random to sprinkle some 'pixie dust' to open the park officially for the day. Immediately on your right is **Town Square Theater**, the new location to meet Mickey and Minnie and temporary home to the Princesses until they move to a new purpose-built location in Fantasyland's big redevelopment.

BRITTIP
Meet Mickey without the long wait by using the NEW meet-and-greet **FastPass** system, located to the left of Tony's Town Square restaurant.

Main Street, USA

© Disney

ADVENTURELAND
1 Swiss Family Treehouse
2 Jungle Cruise
3 Magic Carpets of Aladdin
4 The Enchanted Tiki Room
5 Pirates of the Caribbean

FRONTIERLAND
6 Splash Mountain
7 Big Thunder Mountain Railroad
8 Country Bear Jamboree
9 Raft to Tom Sawyer Island

LIBERTY SQUARE
10 Liberty Tree Tavern
11 Liberty Square Riverboat
12 The Haunted Mansion
13 The Hall of Presidents

FANTASYLAND
14 'it's a small world'
15 Prince Charming Regal Carrousel
16 Mad Tea Party
17 The Many Adventures of Winnie The Pooh
18 Princess Meet-and-greet

19 Dumbo The Flying Elephant
20 Mickey's PhilharMagic
21 Peter Pan's Flight
22 Castle Forecourt Stage
23 Cinderella's Royal Table
24 Tangled Meet-and-greet

TOMORROWLAND
25 Space Mountain
26 Tomorrowland Indy Speedway
27 Tomorrowland Transit Authority
28 Walt Disney's Carousel of Progress
29 Astro Orbiter
30 Stitch's Great Escape!
31 Buzz Lightyear's Space Ranger Spin
32 Monsters Inc. Laugh Floor
33 Club 626 Dance Party

TRANSPORT
34 Walt Disney World Railroad
35 Boat Dock
36 Monorail Station
37 Bus Station

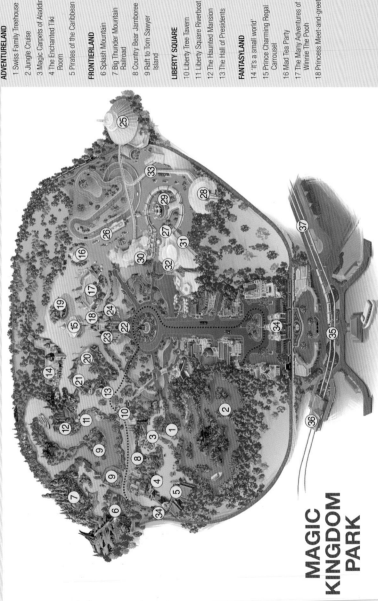

MAGIC KINGDOM PARK

On your left is **City Hall**, where you can pick up a park map and daily schedule (if you haven't been given them at the Toll Plaza) and book restaurants (highly advisable at peak periods). You can also find out where and when the characters will appear. Ahead is **Town Square**, where you can take a 1-way ride on a horse-drawn bus or fire engine, or visit the **Car Barn** mini museum. The Street itself houses the park's best shopping (check out the massive Emporium), and the *Walt Disney World Railroad AAA*, a Western-themed steam train that circles the park and is one of the better attractions when queues are long elsewhere (though Town Square station is often the busiest).

Dining: The Italian-style **Tony's Town Square Restaurant** serves lunch and dinner; **The Plaza Restaurant** offers salads and sandwiches (lunch and dinner); and **The Crystal Palace** (breakfast $24.99 adult, $13.99 ages 3–9; lunch $26.99 & $14.99; dinner $36.99 & $17.99) is buffet-style food with Winnie the Pooh and Co. Quick bites can be bought from **Casey's Corner** (hot dogs, chips and soft drinks), **Main Street Bakery** (coffee and pastries), **Main Street Confectionery** (chocolate and sweets) and the **Plaza Ice Cream Parlor**. Disney characters also appear periodically throughout the Square.

Info: Check the **Guest Information Board** at the top of Main Street (on the left) as it gives waiting times for all the attractions. The **Baby Center** (for nursing mothers) is also at the top of Main Street, to the left next to Crystal Palace, along with the **First Aid** station.

BRITTIP

Can't find Mickey and Co? This is often one of the main laments of those who arrive unprepared. At City Hall they can tell you where to find the characters. In fact, City Hall is your best friend for many queries, from baby facilities to meal bookings (but there are NO baby facilities at City Hall itself). Character meet-and-greets are also shown on all park maps with a 'Mickey glove' icon.

Beating the queues: Unless you are a late arrival, give Main Street no more than a passing glance and head for the end of the street to the *real* entrance to the park. This is where you await the official opening hour *Rope Drop*, and you should adopt 1 of 3 tactics, each aimed at doing some of the most popular rides before the queues build up (wait times of 2 hours for Splash Mountain are not unknown). 1: If you fancy the 5-star, log-flume ride Splash Mountain, keep left in front of the Crystal Palace with the majority, who will head for the same place. 2: If you have young children who can't wait to try the Fantasyland rides, stay in the middle and pass around the Castle. 3: If the thrills of indoor roller-coaster Space Mountain appeal, move to the right by The Plaza Restaurant and go straight into Tomorrowland. Now you'll be in pole position for the initial rush (and it will be a rush; take care with children).

Other entertainment: Watch out for the **Move It! Shake It! Celebrate It! Street Party** up to 3 times daily, from Town Square, along Main Street, ending up in the Hub area as Disney characters, stilt walkers and dancers lead guests in a high-energy street party. The fun barbershop quartet the **Dapper Dans**, brass band **Main Street Philharmonic** and **Main Street Saxophone Four** add lively musical interludes throughout the day, as does **Casey's Corner Pianist**, and don't miss the **Glass Blowing Demonstrations** at Crystal Arts Shop.

BRITTIP

The Move It! Shake It! Celebrate It! Street Party begins in Town Square, but the real action takes place around the Castle Hub. Stake out a spot in advance if you want an up-front view.

Adventureland

If you head left (going clockwise round the park), you enter Adventureland. If you're going to Splash Mountain first, pass the Swiss Family Treehouse on your left and bear right through an archway (with toilets) into Frontierland, where you turn left and Splash Mountain is ahead. Stopping in Adventureland, these are the attractions.

Swiss Family Treehouse: This imitation banyan tree is a clever replica of the treehouse from Disney's 1960 film *Swiss Family Robinson*. It's a walk-through attraction where the queues (rarely long) move steadily if not quickly, providing a neat glimpse of the ultimate tree house, complete with kitchen, rope bridges and running water. AA

Jungle Cruise: It's not so much the scenic, geographically suspect boat ride (where the Nile suddenly becomes the Amazon) that is so amusing here as the patter of your boat's captain, who spins a non-stop yarn about your adventure that features wild animals, tropical plants, hidden temples and sudden waterfalls. Great detail but long queues, so visit either early morning (opens 10am) or late afternoon (evening queues are shortest, but you'll miss some of the detail in the dark). AAAA FP

BRITTIP

Look for the special deal on autograph book and fat pen combo, which can be cheaper than purchasing them separately.

Pirates of the Caribbean: One of Disney's most impressive attractions that involves Walt's pioneering work in audio-animatronics, life-size figures that move, talk and, in this instance, lay siege to a Caribbean island! Your 8-minute underground

Jungle Cruise

© Disney

boat ride visits a typical pirate adventure and the world of Captain Jack Sparrow and nemesis Captain Barbossa as they search for buried treasure. It's terrific family fun (though perhaps a bit spooky for young children, with one small drop in the dark). Queues are longest from late morning to mid-afternoon. AAAAA (**TTTT** under-10s).

The Enchanted Tiki Room: A classic bird-laden, South Seas audio-animatronic show (re-themed to its original version in 2011) starring various parrots, macaws and other tropical feathered friends – plus the angry Tiki Gods! Queues are rare and it is air-conditioned. AAA

Magic Carpets of Aladdin: Here, in an Agrabah-themed area, this ride spins you up, down and around as you try to dodge the spitting camel! Your 'flying carpet' tilts as well as levitates, simple stuff geared for younger children (virtually identical to the Magic Carpets of Agrabah in the *Walt Disney Studios in Disneyland Paris*). TT (**TTTT** under-5s).

Shrunken Ned's Junior Jungle Boats: This costs an extra $2 for kids to try their hand at steering rather tame toy boats. T

Other entertainment: Outside the Pirates of the Caribbean ride (and a must for young swashbucklers), **Captain Jack Sparrow's Pirate Tutorial** runs several times daily. Captain Jack and sidekick Mack invite youngsters to join them in sword fights and treasure hunting, ending with the Pirate Oath to become honorary buccaneers. **Disney characters** also turn up near Pirates of the Caribbean and Magic Carpets rides and on the Adventureland Veranda. Ariel the Little Mermaid makes this a temporary home until her new realm in Fantasyland is ready later in 2012.

Shopping and dining: The best shopping is in the **Pirates Bazaar**. Here, the **Pirates League** (9am–4pm) offers a macho version of the Bibbidi Bobbidi Boutique that lets young swashbucklers transform into fully-fledged pirates. Choose from 2 packages ($29.95): *First Mate* includes face painting, an official pirate name, participation in the Pirate Parade and the official Pirate Oath; the *Empress Package* is the same but with 'shimmering' face paint and nail polish. Accessories, including bandanas, earrings, eye patches, swords, removable teeth (!), coin necklaces, temporary tattoo and photos, are sold separately. For food, you have **Aloha Isle** (yoghurt and ice-cream), **Sunshine Tree Terrace** (fruit, snacks, yoghurt, tea and coffee), and the more substantial beef or vegetarian tacos, empanadas and taco salads of **Tortuga Tavern**.

Frontierland

This Western-themed area is one of the busiest and is best avoided from late morning to late afternoon.

Splash Mountain: Based on the 1946 classic Disney cartoon *Song of the South*, this is a watery journey into the world of Brer Rabbit, Brer Fox and Brer Bear. The first part is all jolly cartoon scenery and fun with the main characters and a couple of minor swoops in your 8-passenger log boat. The conclusion, a 5-storey plummet at 45° into a mist-shrouded pool, seems like you are falling off the edge of the world! A huge adrenalin rush, but busy almost all day (try it first thing or during one of the parades to avoid the longest queues). Some riders also get VERY wet! **Restrictions:** 3ft 4in/101cm. TTTT FP

Big Thunder Mountain Railroad: When Disney does a roller-coaster it will be one of the classiest, and here it is – a runaway mine train that swoops, tilts and plunges through a mock abandoned mine filled with clever scenery. You have to ride it at least twice to appreciate all the detail, but again queues are heavy, so go first thing (after Splash Mountain) or late in the day. R 3ft 4in/101cm. TTTT FP

Country Bear Jamboree: Now here's a novelty: a 16-minute musical revue presented by audio-animatronic bears! It's great family fun with plenty of novel touches (watch for the talking moose head). Crowds are rare, so it's a good one when it's busy elsewhere. AAA

Frontierland Shootin' Arcade: The other of the park's two attractions that cost extra ($1 for 35 shots), as you take aim at a series of animated targets. TT

Tom Sawyer Island: Take a raft over to an overgrown playground of mysterious caves, grottos and mazes, rope bridges and Fort Sam Clemens, where you can fire air guns at passing boats (opens 10am). A good choice in early afternoon when the queues are long elsewhere. **Aunt Polly's Dockside Inn** allows time off your feet, but the only drinks here are from a vending machine. TT

Other entertainment: Musical interludes are provided by the comic trio of **The Notorious Banjo Brothers and Bob**, and the **Frontierland Hoedown**, with the **Country Bears**, plus Woody and Jessie from the *Toy Story* films can be found here.

Shopping and dining: Frontierland shops sell cowboy hats, guns and badges as well as Native American and Mexican crafts. Look out for the nicely themed **Briar Patch** and **Prairie Outpost** for interesting gifts. For food, try **Pecos Bill Tall Tale Inn & Café** (salads, sandwiches and burgers), **Golden Oak Outpost** (chicken nuggets, chicken sandwich, desserts, flatbread, fries and drinks) or **Turkey Leg Cart** (massive, smoke-grilled turkey legs).

Big Thunder Mountain Railroad

© Disney

Liberty Square

The clockwise tour brings you next to a homage to post-independence America. A lot of the historical content will go over the heads of British visitors, but it still has some great attractions.

Liberty Square Riverboat: Cruise America's 'rivers' on an authentic paddle steamer, be menaced by river pirates and thrill to the stories of How the West Was Won (opens 10am). This is also good at busier times of the day, especially early afternoon. AAA

The Haunted Mansion: A clever delve into the world of Master Gracey's ghostly bride that is neither too scary for most kids nor too twee for adults. Not so much a thrill ride as a scenic adventure. Watch out for the fun touch at the end when your car picks up an extra 'passenger'. Longish queues for much of the day, however, so try to visit late on. AAAA (**TTTT** under-6s).

The Hall of Presidents: This is the attraction likely to mean least to us, a 2-part show that is a film about the Constitution and an audio-animatronic parade of all 44 US presidents (opens 10am). Technically impressive, but it may bore young 'uns (though it is air-conditioned). AAA

Shopping and dining: Shopping includes **Ye Olde Christmas Shoppe** and **The Yankee Trader**; eating options are the full-service **Liberty Tree Tavern** (hearty soups, salads, and traditional dishes like roast turkey, carved beef and smoked ham), **Columbia Harbor House** (counter-service fried chicken or fish and some

The Haunted Mansion

good soups, salads and sandwiches, notably for vegetarians) and **Sleepy Hollow** (a picnic area serving snacks, fruit and drinks).

Fantasyland

Leaving Liberty Square, you come into the park's spiritual heart, the area with which young children are most enchanted. The attractions are designed with kids in mind, but the shops are quite sophisticated.

'It's a Small World': This could almost be Disney's theme ride, a family boat trip around the world, each represented by hundreds of dancing, singing audio-animatronic dolls in delightful set-piece pageants. If it sounds twee, it actually creates a surprisingly striking effect, accompanied by an annoyingly catchy theme song that young children adore. Crowds peak in early afternoon. AAAA

BRITTIP

Get more value for your money at the parks by ordering sodas 'without ice' to get a full cup.

Prince Charming Regal Carrousel: The Fantasyland centrepiece shouldn't need any more explanation other than it is a vintage carousel that kids love. Long queues for much of the day, though. T (**TTT** under-5s)

Mad Tea Party: The kids will insist you take them in these spinning, oversized tea cups that have their own 'steering wheel' to add to the whirling effect. Actually, they're just a heavily disguised fairground ride. Again, go early or expect crowds. Characters from *Alice in Wonderland* also visit periodically. TT (**TTTT** under-5s).

The Many Adventures of Winnie the Pooh: Building on the timeless popularity of Pooh, Piglet and Co, this family ride offers a musical jaunt through Hundred Acre Wood with some clever effects (get ready to 'bounce' with Tigger!) and an original soundtrack. Wait times are made easier by hands-on elements throughout the queue. AAA (AAAAA under-5s) **FP**

Snow White's Scary Adventures: This lively indoor ride tells the cartoon story of Snow White with a few ghost train effects that may scare young children. Good fun, though, for parents and kids. Again, you need to go early or late (or during the main parade) to beat the queues. TTT (TTTTT under-5s). NB: This attraction will close in early 2012 to make way for a new Princess meet-and-greet location.

Mickey's PhilharMagic: This fun-tastic 10-minute 3-D film show has a host of special effects as Donald tries to conduct the Enchanted Orchestra – to comic effect. It features a 150ft/46m wide screen to immerse guests in the 3-D world of *Beauty and the Beast*, *The Little Mermaid*, T*he Lion King*, *Peter Pan* and *Aladdin*, with hapless Donald surviving a string of adventures before Mickey brings him back to earth. The lavish theatre, artistic animation, special effects (you can 'smell' the food!) and all-round family entertainment make for a hugely enjoyable attraction. There is no scare factor (though the sudden plunge into darkness at one point and noise of the 'orchestra' can spook young children), while you'll be enchanted when Tinker Bell seems to fly out of the screen in front of you. AAAAA FP

Peter Pan's Flight: This may seem a rather tame ride but is another Walt classic and a big hit with kids. Its novel effect of flying with Peter Pan is good fun and there's a lot of clever detail as your ship sails to Neverland. AAA (AAAAA under-6s; FP).

New in late 2012 will be several attractions that greatly expand the Fantasyland area and its theming.

The Seven Dwarfs Mine Train: It's 'off to work we go' with the Seven Dwarfs in this charming dark ride (that becomes a child-friendly coaster!) through gem-laden mines. This delightful indoor/outdoor adventure has all the swaying sensation of a real mine train and all the charm of the fairytale from which it originates. Expect a gift shop here, too. TTT (TTTTT under 12s).

Under the Sea – Journey of the Little Mermaid: Be a part of her world as you journey under the sea with Ariel in this lovely, gentle ride aboard stylised clamshells, past colourful scenes from the much-loved animated movie. Ariel, Prince Eric, Flounder, Scuttle, Sebastian, King Triton and evil sea witch Ursula, all make appearances, while favourite songs from the hit movie add to this charming adventure (with some surprising special effects!) that is sure to have a happy ending. AAAA

Beast's Castle and Belle's village: Take a scenic stroll through Belle's famed Provincial town, where you can visit her quaint cottage, nestled in the shadow of Beast's Castle. Here, guests are magically transported to an interactive *Enchanted Tales with Belle* story-time experience. AAAA

Princess Fairytale Hall: (In the former site of Snow White's Scary Adventures.) This is the place to meet the Disney Princesses, including Cinderella, Aurora, Tiana, Rapunzel and others. Look for the convenience of FastPass to will save significant wait time. AAA FP

Liberty Square Riverboat

© Disney

The former Toontown area of the park is now gone and is being incorporated into Fantasyland as **Storybook Circus**. Twin Dumbo rides and a re-themed child's coaster add huge kid-appeal.

Dumbo the Flying Elephant: Young children cannot pass this one by, and thankfully, with duo Dumbos (doubling the capacity!) and an all-new interactive queue, parents should be less put off by the prospect of a long wait. It's a 2-minute ride on the back of a swooping, circling, flying elephant, and its charm is undeniable. **TT** (**TTTT** under-5s).

The Barnstormer – starring The Great Goofini: This re-themed ride (from the original Toontown Fair) will be a child-sized coaster with a surprisingly whizzy punch! And, because it's Goofy, you know it's going to be one wacky ride! **TTT** (**TTTTT** 4–8s). Look for new gift shops and circus-style entertainment here, too.

Other entertainment: The superb **Dream Along With Mickey** show is staged up to 6 times a day on the Castle Forecourt Stage, a 20-minute fantasy featuring Donald, Mickey, Minnie, Goofy and various Princesses and their Princes. Peter Pan and Wendy join the battle against Maleficent and Captain Hook to help Donald remember the power of believing in your dreams (**AAA**). The **Fantasyland Woodwind Society** plays up to 4 times daily, while the **Fairy Godmother at Cinderella's Fountain Meet and Greet** happens twice a day. Another worthwhile character experience, with games and dancing, is **Rapunzel and Flynn Rider** from *Tangled* in the Fairytale Garden, on the Castle corner facing Tomorrowland.

Shopping and dining: Shop at **Castle Couture**, the excellent **Sir Mickey's**, **Fantasy Faire** and **Pooh's Thotful Shop**. There is also an outlet of the **Bibbidi Bobbidi Boutique** here (the other is in *Downtown Disney*), where 'little princesses' who are over 3 can choose from 3 make-over packages ($49.95–239.95) and hairstyles – the Disney Diva, Pop Princess or Fairytale Princess from 9am–7pm. Eating opportunities are at **Pinocchio Village Haus** (fairly uninspired pizza, chicken nuggets and salads), the **Enchanted Grove** (iced drinks and juices) and **Friar's Nook** (hot dogs, French fries, carrot cake, apple dippers and drinks). **Cinderella's Royal Table** is a fine setting for the popular character breakfast and lunch (dinner is also

Bibbidi Bobbidi Boutique

© Disney

served, but with the Fairy Godmother only). The majestic hall, waitresses in costume and well-presented food – salads, seafood, roast beef, prime rib and chicken – provide a memorable experience. It's pricey, though ($164 for a family of 4 for breakfast; $172 for lunch and a massive $192 for dinner).

Also new later in 2012 will be the 550-seat counter-service by day, full-service by night **Be Our Guest** restaurant inside the Beast's Castle (sure to be a sought-after dining location), plus nearby quick service **Gaston's Tavern** and **Bonjour! Village Gifts**, as part of the ongoing Fantasyland expansion.

Tomorrowland

The last of the 'lands', this has a cartoon-like space-age appearance that has guaranteed appeal for youngsters, while it also boasts some original shops.

Space Mountain: One of the 3 most popular attractions, its reputation is deserved. Launching from Starport 75, this is a high-thrills, tight-turning roller-coaster, completely in the dark save for occasional flashes as you whizz through the galaxy. Don't do this on a full stomach! The only way to beat the crowds is to go either first thing, late in the day or during one of the parades (or, of course, get a FastPass). Ride photos are available for $18.95-32.95; digital photos $14.95-24.95. **Restrictions:** 3ft 8in/111cm. **TTTTT FP**. Children are also likely to gravitate towards the Tomorrowland Arcade as you exit.

Tomorrowland Speedway: Despite the long queues, this is a rather tame ride on supposed race tracks that just putt-putts along on rails with little real steering required (children must be 4ft 4in/132cm to drive alone). **T (TTTT** under-6s).

Astro Orbiter: A jazzed-up version of Dumbo in Fantasyland, this ride is a bit faster and higher and features rockets. Long, slow-moving queues are a reason to give this a miss unless you have young children. **TT (TTTT** under-10s).

Walt Disney's Carousel of Progress: This will surprise, entertain and amuse. It is a journey through 20th-century technology with audio-animatronics in a revolving theatre that reveals different periods in history. Its 22-minute duration is rarely threatened by crowds (open only at peak periods). **AAA**

Tomorrowland Transit Authority: A neat 'future transport system', this offers an elevated view of the area, including a glimpse inside Space Mountain, in electro-magnetic cars. Queues are usually short. **AAA (TTT** under-8s).

Stitch's Great Escape!: This 15-minute experience receives mixed reviews – some like it for the audio-animatronic prequel to Disney's *Lilo & Stitch*, with visitors being recruited into the madcap Galactic Federation prison service (where things go hilariously wrong as Stitch arrives and causes havoc), while others find it puzzling and rather lame. Young children can also be scared by the complete darkness at times. There are 2 pre-show areas before recruits are ushered into the sit-down chamber (with shoulder restraints) where Stitch is let loose to bounce, dribble and even belch over the unwary audience. **R**: 3ft 2in/101cm. **AA FP**

Buzz Lightyear's Space Ranger Spin: Kids won't want to miss joining the great *Toy Story* character in his battle against evil Emperor Zurg. Ride into action against the robot army – and shoot them with laser cannons! A sure-fire family winner, especially as you get to keep score. **TTT (TTTTT** under-8s) **FP**

Space Mountain

Monsters Inc Laugh Floor: This innovative show is based on the hit Pixar film *Monsters Inc*. With 'live' animation, special effects and high-tech voice links, guests can meet and match wits with the likes of Mike, Sulley and Roz and be entertained by their patter and amusing antics. Billy Boil opens the show, introducing various comedians (including 2-headed jokester Sam-n-Ella), with the aim of capturing the audience's laughter. Guest interaction is integral to the show. Watch the screen – you may be featured! AAA

Other entertainment: Stitch fans should enjoy the **Club 626 Dance Party** (high season), a chance to bop along with a live VJ and various Disney characters, led by the mischievous alien, while **PUSH, the Talking Trashcan** makes hilarious regular appearances. **Disney characters** are often on hand by the Carousel of Progress.

Shopping and dining: Shopping highlights are provided by **Mickey's Star Traders** and **Merchant of Venus**. For food, try **Cosmic Ray's Starlight Café** (burgers, chicken, pasta, soups and salads, flavoured iced coffees),

the **Plaza Pavilion** (pizza, subs and salads), **Auntie Gravity's Galactic Goodies** (ice-cream and juices), the **Lunching Pad** (smoked turkey legs, snacks and drinks) or **Tomorrowland Terrace** (burgers, fried chicken, lobster roll, salads; open seasonally).

Having come full circle you're now back at Main Street USA and it's best to return here in the afternoon to avoid the crowds and enjoy the impressive shops.

Disney parades

If there is one thing Disney knows how to do well, it's a parade. Coupled with its range of special seasonal events, there is always much more to look forward to than just the rides.

> **BRITTIP**
>
> To watch a parade, sit on the left side of Main Street USA (facing the Castle) to stay in the shade if it's hot. People start staking out the best spots an HOUR in advance.

Celebrate A Dream Come True Parade: This truly enchanting multi-float presentation featuring all the favourite characters is the

Main Street at night

MAGIC KINGDOM PARK with children

Here is a rough guide to the attractions that appeal to different age groups (height restrictions have been taken into account):

Under-5s

Buzz Lightyear's Space Ranger Spin, Prince Charming Regal Carousel, Country Bear Jamboree, Dream Along With Mickey, Dumbo the Flying Elephant, The Enchanted Tiki Room, 'It's a Small World', Jungle Cruise, Liberty Square Riverboat, Main Street Vehicles, Many Adventures of Winnie the Pooh, Mickey's PhilharMagic, Monsters Inc Laugh Floor, Move It! Shake It! Celebrate It! Street Party, Peter Pan's Flight, Tomorrowland Speedway (with a parent), Tomorrowland Transit Authority, Walt Disney World Railroad, Main Street Electrical Parade.

5–8s

Astro Orbiter, The Barnstormer – Starring The Great Goofini, Big Thunder Mountain Railroad, Buzz Lightyear's Space Ranger Spin, Country Bear Jamboree, Dream Along With Mickey, The Enchanted Tiki Room, Haunted Mansion, Jungle Cruise, Liberty Square Riverboat, Mad Tea Party, Magic Carpets of Aladdin, Many Adventures of Winnie the Pooh, Mickey's PhilharMagic, Monsters Inc Laugh Floor, Move It! Shake It! Celebrate It! Street Party, Pirates of the Caribbean, Space Mountain (with parental discretion), Splash Mountain, Stitch's Great Escape!, Swiss Family Treehouse, Tom Sawyer Island, Tomorrowland Speedway (with a parent), Tomorrowland Transit Authority, Walt Disney World Railroad, Walt Disney's Carousel of Progress, Main Street Electrical Parade.

9–12s

Astro Orbiter, Big Thunder Mountain Railroad, Buzz Lightyear's Space Ranger Spin, Country Bear Jamboree, The Haunted Mansion, Mad Tea Party, Mickey's PhilharMagic, Monsters Inc. Laugh Floor, Move It! Shake It! Celebrate It! Street Party, Pirates of the Caribbean, Space Mountain, Splash Mountain, Stitch's Great Escape!, Tomorrowland Indy Speedway (without a parent), Main Street Electrical Parade.

Over-12s

Astro Orbiter, Big Thunder Mountain Railroad, Buzz Lightyear's Space Ranger Spin, Haunted Mansion, Mad Tea Party, Mickey's PhilharMagic, Move It! Shake It! Celebrate It! Street Party, Pirates of the Caribbean, Space Mountain, Splash Mountain, Stitch's Great Escape!, Main Street Electrical Parade.

daily highlight. With clever themes, lively music and non-stop (and hard-working!) dancers, the parade halts at regular intervals to reveal some eye-catching special effects. Mickey, Minnie and a host of Disney Princesses all make an appearance, plus some of the classic villains, and it is sure to captivate the whole family (though it is especially popular with children). At Easter and Christmas, the parade takes on seasonal charm with appearances by the Easter Bunny and Father Christmas. AAAAA

Move It! Shake It! Celebrate It! Street Party: Up to 3 times daily, with 5 floats featuring Mickey and Friends, characters from *Aladdin, Beauty and the Beast, Toy Story, The Little Mermaid* and *The Incredibles*. Heavy on guest participation, it's a song and dance fest around the Hub that will have you moving, shaking and celebrating!

Move It! Shake It! Celebrate It! Street Party

Main Street Electrical Parade: A mind-boggling light and sound festival full of glitter and razzamatazz, with the Disney characters at the centre of a multitude of fibre-optic effect floats. It is classic Disney, using the latest technology to enhance the heart-tugging impact of this sparkling cavalcade. Tinker Bell leads the procession, with each successive float a visual and audio treat, and the music a real highlight. A true must-see end to any *Magic Kingdom* day. When the park is open late (during peak periods and weekends), there are 2 showings per night, and the second is less crowded. AAAAA

BRITTIP

Main Street USA closes 30mins after the rest of the park, so you can avoid the inevitable mad rush for the car parks by lingering here to shop or enjoy an ice-cream.

Wishes: Most nights also finish with this spectacular fireworks show over the Castle. With a clever soundtrack narrated by Jiminy Cricket and featuring memorable moments from various Disney classics, it is magnificently choreographed and culminates in a sequence of dazzling pyrotechnic explosions (many designed especially for this show). Starting with an appearance by Tinker Bell (from the Castle's top turret), it continues for 12mins of typical Disney emotional appeal; the perfect pixie-dust farewell to a memorable day. AAAAA

Main Street Electrical Parade

The Magic, The Memories, and You!: This stunning new (in 2011) state-of-the-art projection show uses Cinderella Castle as its backdrop, incorporating pictures and videos of the day's guests framed against changing animated backgrounds. The Castle seems to come alive, transforming again and again, from a vine-covered fantasy to a fiery inferno, and at one point even launching one of its turrets into space! Set to the original theme song, Let the Memories Begin, this must-see display is pure Disney magic. AAAA

BRITTIP

After the fireworks crowd exits, you are allowed to take the Resort Only monorail back to the Transportation & Ticket Center, rather than queue for the main Express monorail.

Wishes Cruises: If you prefer not to fight the crowds for a fab view of Wishes, book one of 3 speciality cruises to view the fireworks from Seven Seas Lagoon. The *Basic Cruise* holds up to 8 guests onboard a 21ft/6m pontoon boat and costs $292 (includes water, soft drinks and snacks); the *Premium Cruise* holds up to 10 on a 25ft/7.6m pontoon boat (for $346), including water, soft drinks, snacks and an audio feed to the Wishes music; or splash out for the *Celebration Cruise*, which adds special occasion decorations to the Basic Cruise for a total of $325 and the Premium Cruise for $375. All can be booked 90 days in advance.

BRITTIP

For a final bit of typical Disney entertainment, head outside the *Magic Kingdom* at 10.25pm and catch the **Electrical Water Pageant** passing by on Seven Seas Lagoon in front of the park.

Pirate and Pals Fireworks Voyage: This kid-friendly Wishes cruise includes meeting Mr Smee and Capt Hook before cruising the Seven Seas Lagoon to view the Electrical Water Pageant and Wishes. Snacks and

© Disney

Wishes

drinks are provided while you enjoy a retelling of the Peter Pan story, then meet Pan himself at the end of your voyage ($57/adult, $33/3–9; can be booked 180 days in advance).

Leaving the park: When it comes to leaving, the monorail is quicker than the ferry but it can still take up to an hour to get back to your car. Also, if the crowds get too heavy during the day, you can escape by leaving in the early afternoon (your car park ticket is valid all day) and returning to your hotel for a few hours' rest or a dip in the pool. Alternatively, catch a boat to one of the Disney resorts. Fort Wilderness is especially fun for kids and boasts the good value Trails End Buffet for lunch or dinner.

Halloween & Christmas

Two additional annual events in the *Magic Kingdom* provide a separate, party-style ticketed event 7pm–midnight, with most of the rides open and extra themed fun and games.

Mickey's Not So Scary Halloween Party: Sept–Oct sees many visitors dress up for the typical American trick-or-treat fun, with plenty of treats for youngsters along the way. With special music, storytelling, parades and the HalloWishes fireworks (plus some wonderful lighting effects), tickets go on sale about 5 months in advance and sell out quickly.

Mickey's Very Merry Christmas Party: The Christmas party (Nov–Dec) sees 'snow' on Main Street and an array of magnificent festive decorations and theming. There is free hot chocolate and cookies, as well as a special parade and more fireworks. The atmosphere is truly enchanting, though the evening can be prone to unfriendly weather.

> **BRITTIP**
> Although the special evening parties don't start officially until 7pm, you can use the ticket to gain entry to the park from 4pm, which gives you 8 full hours to enjoy all the attractions.

Park tours: Finally, one of the park's little-known secrets is the Keys to the Kingdom, a 4–5-hour guided tour of many backstage areas, including the service tunnel under the park, and entertainment production buildings. It's an extra $78 (including lunch; not available for under-16s) but is a superb journey into the park's creation. **Disney's Family Magic Tour** is a 2-hour guided adventure that takes you on a search for clues throughout the park at $34/person, or you can experience the 3-hour **Steam Trains Tour** ($52/person; no under-10s) as you join the crew that prepares the park's trains each day. **Walt Disney: Marceline to Magic Kingdom** is a 3-hour tour focusing on how the inspiration of Walt's early years in Marceline, Missouri, culminated in the creation of the *Magic Kingdom* ($32/person; no under-12s).

Epcot

Epcot actually stands for 'Experimental Prototype Community of Tomorrow', but it might be more accurate to say Every Person Comes Out Tired. For this is a BIG park, with a lot to see and do, and much legwork required to cover its 300-acre/122ha extent. Actually, it is not so much a vision of the future as a look at the world and technology of today, with a strong educational and environmental message. At almost 3 times the size of the *Magic Kingdom* Park, it is more likely to require a 2-day visit (though under-5s might find it less entertaining) and your feet in particular will notice the difference!

Location

Epcot opened in October 1982 and its giant car park can hold 9,000 vehicles, so a tram takes you from your car to the main entrance (though if you are staying at a Disney hotel you can catch the monorail, boat or bus service to the gates; International Gateway is a separate entrance for guests at the Epcot resort hotels). Don't forget to note where you have parked (e.g. Create, row 78). If you have your ticket, you pass through the turnstiles and wait in the immediate entrance plaza for Rope Drop, which is signalled by Mickey and Co arriving to greet guests.

Beating the queues: *Epcot* is divided into 2 distinct parts arranged in a figure of 8 and there are 2 tactics to help you avoid the worst of the crowds. The first or lower half of the '8' consists of **Future World**, with 6 pavilions arranged around Spaceship Earth (which dominates the skyline) and the 2 Innoventions centres.

Epcot at a glance

Location	Off Epcot Drive, Walt Disney World
Size	300 acres/122ha in Future World and World Showcase
Hours	9am–7pm Future World (except Test Track, Mission: SPACE, Soarin'™, 9am–9pm), 11am–9pm (World Showcase)
Admission	Under-3s free; 3-9 $79 (1-day base ticket), $342 (5-day Premium), $358 (7-day Premium); adult (10+) $85, $361, $377. Prices do not include tax.
Parking	$15
Lockers	Through the main entrance to the right hand side and at International Gateway $12 small; $14 large ($5 deposit)
Pushchairs	$15 and $31 to the left after the main entrance and at International Gateway; length of stay $13 per day single, $27 per day double
Wheelchairs	$12 or $70 ($20 deposit refunded) with pushchairs
Top attractions	Mission: SPACE, Test Track, Spaceship Earth, Soarin'™, Universe of Energy, American Adventure
Don't miss	IllumiNations: Reflections of Earth, Disney Character Spot, Turtle Talk With Crush, live entertainment (including Off Kilter in Canada, JAMMitors in Innoventions plaza, Miyuki in Japan and Voices of Liberty in America), and dinner at any of the World Showcase pavilions
Hidden costs	Meals	Burger, chips and coke $10.58 3-course dinner $35-45; child's meal $7.75 (La Hacienda, Mexico) Kids' meal $4.99
	T-shirts	$21.95-39.95
	Souvenirs	$.99-495-plus
	Sundries	Epcot 'Passport' $9.95

Future World

1 Universe of
   Energy
2 Mission: SPACE
3 Test Track
4 Odyssey Center
5 Imagination!
   (including
   Captain EO)
6 The Land
   (including
   Soarin'™)
7 The Seas with
   Nemo and Friends
8 Spaceship Earth
9 Innoventions West
10 Innoventions East

World Showcase

11 Mexico
12 Norway
13 China
14 The Outpost
15 Germany
16 Italy
17 The American
   Adventure
18 Japan
19 Morocco
20 France
21 International
   Gateway (to Epcot
   resort hotels)
22 United Kingdom
23 Canada
24 Friendship Boats
   to Italy and
   Morocco
25 America Gardens
   Theater
26 Showcase Plaza
27 Monorail Station
K Kidcot Fun Stops

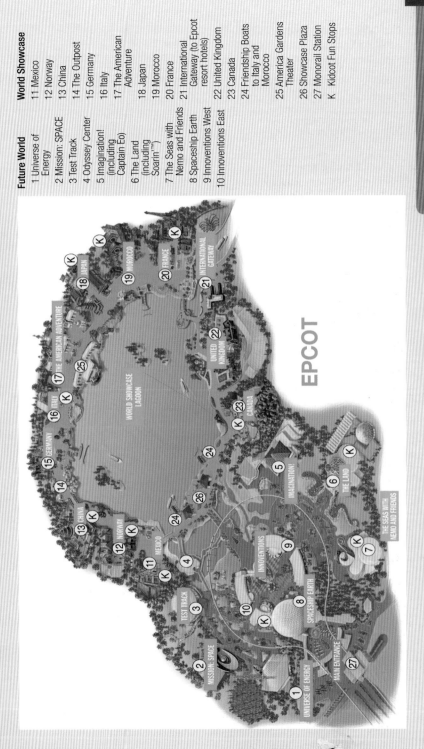

The second part, or top of the '8', is **World Showcase**, a potted journey around the world via 11 international pavilions that feature a taste of each country's culture, history, entertainment, shopping and cuisine. Once through the entrance plaza, aim to get the 3 big-time rides – Test Track, Mission: Space and Soarin'™ – under your belt first, then move into World Showcase for its 11am opening. Continue around World Showcase until 4 or 5pm, then return to Future World to catch up on the other attractions there, as the majority will have moved on (apart from at the 3 main rides). As a general tactic, head first for the magnificent **Soarin'™** –, then go across to the other side of Future World and grab a FastPass for **Test Track**. While you wait for your ride time, you can queue for **Mission: SPACE** and perhaps even take in **Universe of Energy**. Alternatively, if the rides don't appeal quite so much as a visit to such diverse cultures as Japan and Morocco, spend your first couple of hours in the Innoventions centres (busy from mid-morning), then head into World Showcase at 11am and you'll be ahead of the crowds for several hours. The other thing you should do early on is book lunch or dinner at one of the fine restaurants around World Showcase (Mexico, Italy and Japan are all highly recommended). The best reservations go fast, but check in at Guest Relations (on the left after Spaceship Earth) for advice and bookings.

Mission: SPACE

Planning your visit

If you plan a 2-day visit, it makes sense to spend the first day in World Showcase, arriving by 11am and going straight there while the majority stay in Future World, booking your evening meal for around 5.30pm, then lingering around the lagoon for the evening entertainment. For your second visit, try arriving in mid-afternoon and then doing Future World in a more leisurely fashion. Queues at most of the pavilions are almost non-existent for rides like Universe of Energy, Spaceship Earth and Journey into Imagination, though Test Track, Soarin'™ and Mission: Space stay busy all day. You CAN do *Epcot* in a day – if you arrive early, put in some speedy legwork and give some detail a miss. But, of all the parks, it is a shame to hurry this one. Browse in the shops (almost 70 in all), when the rides are busiest.

Kidcot Fun Stops: At 11 activity centres around *Epcot* (each country in World Showcase), children can play games and collect a special Epcot Passport to get stamped as they visit each Stop.

Future World

Here's what you'll find in the first part of your *Epcot* adventure.

Universe of Energy: There is just the one attraction here but it is a stunner. **Ellen's Energy Adventure** is a 35-minute show-and-ride with comedienne Ellen DeGeneres and Bill Nye the Science Guy exploring the creation of fuels from the age of dinosaurs to their modern-day usages. The film elements make it seem you are in a conventional theatre, but then your seats rearrange themselves into 96-person solar-powered cars and you are off on a journey through the prehistoric era, with some realistic dinosaurs! Queues are steady but not overwhelming from mid-morning. AAAAA

Mission: SPACE: This is more high-tech Disney imagination, a journey into the future at the International Space Training Center. The space-age building prepares you for a major adventure as you enter through Planetary Plaza, with its giant replica planets (check out the model showing the moon landings). At the entrance you have a choice of 4 queues – FastPass Collection, Standby (the main queue), Single Riders and FastPass Return, and the clever organisation keeps queues moving. As you enter the training facility, there are some superb models and graphics (like the giant revolving Gravity Wheel) to look at while you queue to reach Team Dispatch. Here, the 4 ready rooms form you into teams of 4 for the ride, and you will be either Navigator, Engineer, Pilot or Commander, each with different functions to perform. You also have the choice of either the full, dynamic version of the ride (the 'orange' version) or a toned-down alternative that avoids the 'spinning' effect (the 'green' version). Once briefed (by actor Gary Sinise), you enter the Preparation Room to learn your mission – a flight to Mars. And then it's into the ride vehicle – capsules that close down tightly with outer doors, shoulder restraints and screens that move forward to just 18in/46cm from your face (this is NOT a good ride for those with claustrophobia or prone to motion sickness). The sense of realism, with the control consoles, individual speakers and countdown is magnificent. For those on the full version, the blast-off feels VERY real as you experience some of the genuine forces of a rocket launch (thanks to its huge centrifuge, which is part-ride and part-simulator). Each member of the team has to perform their duties on cue and you experience a simulated sling-shot around the moon and on to Mars, where the landing is an adventure in itself. It's a truly original, aggressive ride, but you should heed the advice to keep your head still and look straight into the screen or you WILL feel sick (unless you are on the tamer version, where the capsules just tilt and turn). We think the full-on experience is too intense for young children, and there is no backing out

once you blast off (parents could try it first), while it is definitely not for expectant mothers. Restrictions: 3ft 8in/112cm. TTTTT FP

BRITTIP

Even if you don't ride Mission: Space, you (and your children) should visit the post-ride area of games and fun. Just enter through the Cargo Bay gift shop to the left of the pavilion.

As you exit the ride, there is an elaborate post-show and activities. **Space Base** is an excellent play area for children who can't ride (and those who just like to climb, slide and crawl); **Space Race** is a great game for 2 teams of 60 players to propel a rocket back to Earth via a series of on-screen challenges; **Expedition Mars** is a computer game to rescue stranded astronauts; and, in **Postcards from Space**, you can email a 'space video' to friends and family. There is then the inevitable (and well-stocked) gift shop. All in all, it's a terrific experience.

Test Track: Another big production – a 5½-minute whirl along Disney's longest and fastest track. It starts with an elaborate queue that demonstrates car-testing techniques and quality control, and prepares riders for a taste of the ride to come as the cars whiz around the outside of the building at up to 65mph/104kph. The reality is good, too, as you are taken on a tour of a proving ground, including a hill climb test, suspension test (hold on to those fillings), brake test, environment chamber, barrier test (beware the crash test dummies!)

Test Track

and the steeply banked, high-speed finale. Along with a smart gift store and ride photo opportunity, it makes for an involving exhibit. It does draw HUGE queues, though, topping 2 hours at times, while the available FP service often runs out by late morning. Head straight here when it opens or come back in the evening to keep your queuing to bearable levels. If you are on your own or don't mind being split up, save time by using the Single Rider Queue. **Restrictions:** 3ft 4in/101cm. **TTTT** (TTT teens) FP

BRITTIP

Innoventions East and West are good places in which to spend time if you need to cool down, or if it's raining. They are usually quiet in the afternoon, too.

The Odyssey Center: See here for baby-care and first-aid facilities, telephones and restrooms.

Imagination!: The 2-part attraction here starts with **Journey into Imagination with Figment**, an uneven but quirky ride into experiments with imagination in the company of Eric Idle (as Dr Nigel Channing of the Imagination Institute) and the cartoon dragon Figment. The sight laboratory sees Figment having fun with a vision chart, the sound lab is a symphony of imaginative melodies and Figment's house is a truly topsy-turvy world (watch out for the skunk in the smell lab!). It's gentle fun and rarely draws a crowd. AAA You exit into **Image Works – The Kodak 'What If' Labs**, an interactive playground of sight and sound, which usually amuses kids

Soarin'™

more than adults (though you might be tempted to buy various cartoon images and select-your-own CDs).

Captain EO: Come out and turn right for an encore presentation of this fun 3-D musical film show starring Michael Jackson, which originally debuted in *Epcot* in 1986 but was replaced by *Honey I Shrunk The Audience* in 1994. Now digitally remastered and sound enhanced, it is a 17-minute romp through space as Captain EO and his band of ragtag renegades set out to save the universe by bringing a special gift to the evil Supreme Leader: the key to unlocking the 'beauty within'. Jackson's signature dancing and the show's *We Are Here To Change The World* message keep the tone upbeat, but some of the darker thematic elements may frighten young children. It's a visually thrilling trip down memory lane for Disney fans, as good conquers evil – naturally! AAAA FP Outside, kids are always fascinated by the **Jellyfish** and **Serpentine Fountains** that send water squirting from pond to pond. Have your cameras ready!

The Land: This pavilion combines 3 elements to make an entertaining but educational experience on food and nutrition – plus the spectacular Soarin'™ ride, which is a pure thrill. **Living with the Land** is an informative 14-minute boat ride well worth the usually long queue. A journey through various types of food production may sound dull, but it is informative and enjoyable, with plenty to make children of all ages sit up and take notice through the 3 ecological communities, especially the greenhouse finale. AAAA FP Having ridden the ride, you can also take the **Behind the Seeds** 1hr guided tour through the greenhouse complex and learn more about Disney's horticultural projects ($18 adults, $14 3–9s).

The Circle of Life: This is a 15-minute animation story, featuring characters from *The Lion King*, which explains environmental concerns and is easily digestible for kids. Queues are not a problem. AAA

Epcot

Soarin'™: *Epcot's* latest and greatest, this imaginative 'flight simulator' offers an exhilarating ride for all ages, with a breathtaking swoop over the landmarks of California, complete with 'aromavision' (smell those orange groves!). An elaborate queuing area leads to the departure lounge, with passengers embarking on rows of seats that are then hoisted into the air over a giant screen. The feeling is somewhat akin to taking a hang-glider ride as the special film, sounds and scents become all-encompassing. Feet dangling, you soar above the Golden Gate Bridge, sweep through a redwood forest and glide above Napa Valley. The finale includes a close encounter with a certain Disney theme park in Los Angeles! The ride's realism, magnificent music and superb technology ensure a 5-star experience – but also long, slow-moving queues. FastPasses often run out by 11am, so visit early and use FP for a second ride. **Restrictions:** 3ft 4in/101cm. AAAAA FP

Dining: The **Sunshine Season Food Fair** offers the chance to eat some of Disney's home-grown produce, while the **Garden Grill** restaurant is a slowly revolving platform that offers more traditional food, including roast meats, pasta, seafood and a vegetarian selection, all in the company of Mickey, Goofy, Pluto and Chip 'n' Dale.

The Seas with Nemo & Friends: This pavilion does for the oceans what The Land does for terra firma, in the company of the characters from the Pixar film *Finding Nemo*. You start with the signature ride, **The Seas With Nemo and Friends**, which takes riders on an underwater journey in 'clamobiles' to meet Nemo and Co (who are brilliantly interwoven into the huge aquarium, apparently swimming with the real fish!). Nemo has gone missing (again), hence the ride becomes a quest to reunite him with teacher Mr Ray and the rest of the class in a rousing musical finale. AAAA You then exit into **Sea Base**, a 2-level development offering 6 modules presenting stories of undersea exploration and marine life, including a research centre that provides a close encounter with the endangered manatee. Plenty of interactive elements and educational touch-screens are on offer, plus additional tanks displaying Caribbean reef fish, jellyfish and cuttlefish, while there is an excellent demonstration of a diving chamber. Crowds are steady, but queues rarely get too long – with one exception. **Turtle Talk With Crush** is a splendidly interactive and original meet-and-greet with the

Turtle Talk with Crush

cartoon surfer dude turtle and his friend Dory from the film *Finding Nemo*. Crush is literally the star of the show as he swims up and engages children in the audience with some genuinely fun live banter. AAAA Next door, **Bruce's Sub House** is a fun kids' play area including some great photo opportunities with more of the *Finding Nemo* characters (TTT under-6s). **Nemo and Friends** is more hands-on fun for kids, while **Mr Ray's Lagoon** showcases some real stingrays.

Dining: The pavilion includes the highly recommended **Coral Reef Restaurant** that serves great seafood, as well as providing a grandstand view of the massive aquarium. Dinner for 2 will be around $55 (starter and main) up to $100, depending on your choices, which isn't cheap, but the food is first class.

Spaceship Earth: Spiralling up 18 storeys, this attraction is a convincing time-travel story into various technologies narrated by Dame Judi Dench. From cave paintings to the internet (with a superb depiction of Michelangelo's Sistine Chapel), the gentle ride unfolds in imaginative historical stages, culminating in an interactive finale that invites riders to 'predict' the future. Sponsor Siemens (the electronics giant) has added a post-show interactive demonstration area (including predictive surgery and a driving challenge), which makes for an entertaining diversion after the 15-minute ride. Queues are heavy all morning, but almost non-existent late in the day. AAAA

Innoventions: These 2 centres of hands-on exhibits and computer games – subtitled **The Road to Tomorrow** – include a glimpse of Disney's latest work with virtual reality entertainment and other demonstrations of current and future technologies, especially the internet and computers, presented by the likes of IBM, T. Rowe Price and Liberty Mutual. You can also take a look at the latest transport – the wonderful 2-wheeled Segway Human Transporter (which you can also pay to ride – p137). Both sides are routed like a journey into the future and reward enquiring minds.

Innoventions East: Don't miss **The Sum of All Thrills** interactive experience, where budding mathematicians and engineers can design and create their own ride using

Spaceship Earth

physics principles and touch-screen technology. Then, hop aboard the motion simulator for a hair-raising ride! **Restrictions:** 4ft/122cm for non-inversion ride, 4ft 6in/138cm with inversions. **TTT**. Other novelties include **Test the Limits Lab** and **Don't Waste It** (a recycling challenge), **House of Innoventions** (a 15-minute walking tour through new home technologies, due to reopen after a long closure) and **Storm Struck** (experience a violent storm from a special viewing theatre). A small **Environmentality Corner** focuses on Earth awareness.

Innoventions West: Kids gravitate to **Smarter Planet**, where they're quizzed on ways to save the planet before creating a personalised avatar for a fun romp through their own video game world! Worth waiting for are the 20-minute **Where's The Fire?**, an interactive game exploring home fire hazards, and a section with free Disney video games. For those concerned about their finances, the humorous **Great Piggy Bank Adventure** teaches the importance of setting financial goals and saving money.

Other entertainment: Both Innoventions pavilions feature a **Team Possible Recruitment Center** (11am–8pm) where you can sign up for super secret agent missions as part of the family-friendly *Disney's Kim Possible World Showcase Adventure* interactive game, which sends guests on special tasks around World Showcase. Some of the 'missions' – using your handy Kim-unicator – are genuinely challenging and we think this is WAY too good just for kids! Live fun is also provided periodically in the Innoventions plaza with the unique **JAMMitors** percussion group, while the **Epcot Character Spot** (across from Innoventions West, 9am–9pm at peak times, 10am–6pm off-peak) offers a meet-and-greet with many Disney characters. Daisy Duck and Stitch can often be found just inside the main entrance. The majestic **Plaza Fountain** choreographs to musical performances every 15 minutes.

Dining and shopping: Food outlets include the counter-service **Electric Umbrella Restaurant** for lunch and dinner (sandwiches, burgers and salads) and the **Fountain View Ice Cream** for Edy's ice-cream and drinks. Look out also for **Club Cool** presented by Coca-Cola®, where you can check out the latest Coke-inspired products and souvenirs, along with various free soft-drink tastes from around the world (beware the Beverly!). For shopping, **Mouse Gear** in Innoventions East features a massive variety of *Epcot* and Disney merchandise (and do check out the wacky ceiling architecture!), while the **Art of Disney** features superb signature art and animator drawings.

World Showcase

If you found Future World amazing, prepare to be astounded by the equally imaginative pavilions around the World Showcase Lagoon. Each features a glimpse of a different country in dramatic settings. Several have rides or films to showcase their main features, while the restaurants offer some outstanding fare. There is also a third **Team Possible Recruitment Center** on the bridge from Future World to World Showcase and at International Gateway, while many Disney character meet 'n' greets can be found in each country (check the daily *Times Guide* for locations and timings).

Meeting Cinderella

© Disney

Mexico: Starting at the bottom left of the circular tour of the lagoon and moving clockwise, your first encounter is inside the spectacular pyramid of Mexico. Here you have the amusing boat ride **Gran Fiesta Tour Starring The Three Caballeros**, a 9min journey through the people and history of the country with Donald Duck, Panchito and José Carioca as your guides. Queues build up in mid-afternoon but are usually light otherwise. AAA

Other entertainment: As in all of the World Showcase pavilions, there is live entertainment, with periodic 25min music shows from **Mariachi Cobre**, while Donald Duck puts in character appearances.

Dining and shopping: Much of the pavilion comprises market-style gift shops, while the **San Angel Inn** is a romantic Mexican restaurant and **La Cava del Tequila** has tempting cocktails, light bites and signature tequilas. Outside, choose from the revamped counter service **Cantina de San Angel** (open air lunch from 11am,

China Pavilion

serving tacos, nachos and tortillas) and full-service **La Hacienda de San Angel** (dinner from 4pm) serving a rich variety of authentic Mexican fare with a superb lagoon view and grandstand seat for the nightly IllumiNations show. This gets our thumbs-up as a stand-out choice.

Norway: Next up is the best ride in World Showcase, the Viking-themed **Maelstrom**. This 10-minute longboat journey through Norway's history and scenery features a short waterfall drop and a North Sea storm. It attracts longish queues from early afternoon, so the best tactic is to go soon after World Showcase's 11am opening. TTT FP There are periodic Norwegian-themed exhibits in the reconstructed **Stave Church** and twice-daily guided tours (sign up at the Tourism desk). The pavilion also contains a reproduction of Oslo's Akershus Fortress.

Dining and shopping: The **Akershus Royal Banquet Hall** offers the Princess Storybook dining for breakfast, lunch and dinner, complete with a host of Disney Princesses, while the **Kringla Bakeri Og Kafé** serves sandwiches, pastries and drinks. **Puffin's Roost** is a large gift shop for all things Norwegian.

China: The spectacular landscapes of China are well served by the main attraction of this pavilion, the stunning *Reflections of China*, a 360° film in the circular Temple of Heaven. Here you are surrounded by the sights and sounds of one of the world's most enigmatic countries in an eye-catching production. Queues build up to half an hour during the main part of the day (but it is fully air-conditioned). AAAA

Other entertainment: Don't miss the periodic shows from classical Chinese musicians **Si Xian** on the plaza in front of the temple and the 20-minute **Lion Dance** show. Disney characters from *Mulan* also appear in the afternoon.

Dining and shopping: Two restaurants, the **Nine Dragons** and the counter-service **Lotus Blossom**

© Disney

Germany pavilion

Café offer tastes of the Orient, while **Yong Feng Shangdian Dept Store** is a warehouse of Chinese gifts and artefacts.

The **Outpost** between China and Germany features hut-style shops and snacks, with entertainment from Africa and the Caribbean.

Germany: This provides more in the way of shopping and eating than entertainment, though you still find a magnificent recreation of a Bavarian **Biergarten**, with lively Oktoberfest shows featuring the resident **Musikanten** brass band at regular intervals. It also offers hearty portions of German sausage, sauerkraut and rotisserie chicken. The **Sommerfest** is fast food German-style (bratwurst and strudel), while there are more shops (8 in all) than anywhere else in *Epcot*, including chocolates, wines, crystal, porcelain, toys and cuckoo clocks.

BRITTIP

With seating for 400, **Biergarten** often takes walk-ups even when Disney's reservations system indicates the restaurant is full.

Other entertainment: An elaborate outdoor model railway is popular with children, and look out for **character appearances** from Snow White and Dopey.

Italy: Similarly, Italy has pretty, authentic architecture, including a superb reproduction of Venice's St Mark's Square, 3 gift shops stocking wine, chocolates, Armani collectables, fine crystal, porcelain and Venetian masks, and 2 full-service restaurants. **Tutto Italia** is the fine dining option, while the superb **Via Napoli** is a delightfully authentic pizzeria, featuring wood-burning ovens and genuine Neapolitan style, with 300 seats, including an outdoor terrace.

Other entertainment: Watch out for the fun entertainment of **Sergio**, a madcap juggler who loves to involve his audience, and the comedy of **The Ziti Sisters** – with audience 'guest' stars!

The American Adventure: At the top of the lagoon and dominating World Showcase is this huge edifice, not so much a pavilion as a celebration of the country's history and Constitution. A colonial Fife & Drum Corps and wonderful singing group add authentic sounds to the 18th-century setting, overlooked by a reproduction of Philadelphia's Liberty Hall. Inside, you have the **American Adventure** show, a magnificent ½hr film and audio-animatronic production that details the country's founding, its struggles and triumphs, presidents, statesmen and heroes. It's a glossy, patriotic display, featuring

Italy pavilion

© Disney

some outstanding technology and, while some of it will leave foreign visitors fairly cold, it's difficult not to be impressed. A good choice at most times of the day – and it's all in the cool! If you have time to spare, check out the special exhibitions in the **American Heritage Gallery**.

Other entertainment: Superb *a capella* group **Voices of Liberty** appear in the pavilion's rotunda several times a day, while the **Spirit of America Fife & Drum Corps** put on a show out front. The **America Gardens Theater**, next to the lagoon, presents concerts from international artists during the Flower & Garden Festival, Sounds Like Summer series and Food & Wine Festival.

Dining and shopping: Antiques and handcarts provide touches of nostalgia, along with the **Heritage Manor Gifts** store, while **Liberty Inn** offers fast-food lunch and dinner.

Japan: Next up on the clockwise tour, you are introduced to typical Japanese style and architecture, including the breathtaking Chi Nien Tien, a round ½-scale reproduction of a temple, some magnificent art exhibits, notably in the **Bijutsu-kan Gallery**, featuring art and insights into Japanese history and culture, a tranquil Bonsai garden (complete with carp pond) and landmark Torii gate.

Other entertainment: Live shows are key here, with periodic presentations from the superb **Matsuriza** *taiko* drummers and the eye-catching artistry of child-friendly **Miyuki**, a lovely lady who spins amazing sweet creations out of toffee sugar.

Dining and shopping: Great food is a real highlight, and the restaurant line-up consists of the wonderful fine dining of **Teppan Edo** (with its traditional chefs at each table) and **Tokyo Dining**, a venue featuring typical cuisine and ingredients, showcasing sushi and innovative presentation. **Yakitori House** is its fast-food equivalent, with great soups, teriyaki and tempura dishes. The huge **Mitsukoshi** store adds fascinating shopping, from traditional calligraphy, tea kettles and wind chimes to Hello Kitty souvenirs.

Morocco: As you would expect, this is another shopping experience, with bazaars, alleyways and stalls selling a well-priced array of carpets, leather goods, clothing, brass ornaments, pottery and antiques. All the building materials were faithfully imported for the pavilion, which was hand-built to give Morocco a greater degree of authenticity, even by World Showcase's high standards. **The Gallery of Arts and History** offers more historical and cultural insights, while the **Fez House** depicts a typical Moroccan home.

Morocco

© Disney

EPCOT with children

Here is our rough guide to the attractions that appeal to different age groups:

Under-5s
Circle of Life, Gran Fiesta Tour Starring The Three Caballeros, Journey into Imagination with Figment, Kidcot stops, Living with the Land, The Seas with Nemo and Friends, Soarin'™ (if tall enough), Spaceship Earth, Turtle Talk with Crush, Universe of Energy.

5–8s
All the above, plus The American Adventure, Captain EO (with parental discretion), Image Works, Innoventions, JAMMitors, Maelstrom, Miyuki the Candy Lady, Test Track, Kim Possible World Showcase Adventure.

9–12s
All the above, plus Impressions de France, Matsuriza Drummers, Mission: SPACE, O Canada!, Sergio, Le Serveur Amusant, Reflections of China.

Over-12s
Living with the Land, The Seas with Nemo and Friends, Soarin'™, Spaceship Earth, Universe of Energy, The American Adventure, Captain EO, Innoventions, JAMMitors, Maelstrom, Test Track, Impressions de France, Matsuriza Drummers, Mission: SPACE, O Canada!, Reflections of China, Bijutsu-kan Gallery, Off Kilter (Canada).

Other entertainment: Characters from Disney's *Aladdin* appear from time to time, while live musical show **MoRockin'** presents a variety of Arabic rhythms in fun style, including an eye-catching belly-dancer!

Dining: Restaurant Marrakesh provides a full dining experience, complete with traditional musicians and their own belly dancer. It's rather pricey ($45/person for the Taste of Morocco Marrakesh Royal Feast and $42 for the Marrakesh Feast), but the lively atmosphere is entertaining. Better value can be had at **Tangierine Café**, with its healthy array of roast lamb, hummus, tabbouleh, couscous, lentil salad and Moroccan breads ($8.99–14.99; kids' meals $7.99).

BRITTIP

The **Tangierine Café** in Morocco is a peaceful haven in which to enjoy a quiet, healthy lunch, especially if you are vegetarian, plus there is a tempting coffee and pastry counter.

France: Predictably overlooked by a replica Eiffel Tower, this is a clean and cheerful pre-World War I Paris, with comedy street theatre adding to the rather dreamy atmosphere and pleasant gardens, plus stylish shopping. Don't miss **Impressions de France**, a big-film production that serves up all the grandest sights of the country to the music of Offenbach, Debussy, Saint-Saëns and Satie. Crowds get quite heavy from mid-day. **AAAA**

Other entertainment: Look out for the visual comedy and amazing balancing act of **Serveur Amusant** (not when it's too windy), while Princess Aurora (Sleeping Beauty) makes regular appearances, along with *Beauty and the Beast* characters and Marie from *The Aristocats*.

Dining and shopping: This is also the pavilion for a gastronomic experience provided by 3 restaurants, of which **Les Chefs de France** (where Remy from the movie *Ratatouille* appears 4 times daily until 6:30pm) and **Bistro de Paris** are major discoveries. The former is an award-winning, full-service (but expensive) establishment featuring top-quality cuisine created by French chefs on a daily basis, while the latter, upstairs, offers more intimate bistro dining and plenty of style (starters $12–15; mains $33–42; Bistro 3 Course Tasting Menu $54, with wine pairings $89). The Bistro books only 30 days in advance. Alternatively, the **Boulangerie Patisserie** is a sidewalk café offering more modest fare (and wonderful pastries). Shopping is suitably chic, with an authentic **Wine Shop** and elegant **Guerlain** and **Givenchy** perfumeries (ask about the free perfume tour during the Flower and Garden Festival).

United Kingdom: The least inspiring of all the pavilions, and certainly with little to entertain those who have ever visited a pub or shopped for Royal Doulton or Burberry goods, it is partly offset by some good live entertainment and pleasant gardens, but that is about it.

Other entertainment: Sadly, the super Beatles tribute band the **British Invasion** finished a 15-year run at *Epcot* in 2011 and the live music is now provided by **British Revolution**, offering the sounds of the 60s, 70s and 80s up to 5 times a day, while **The Hat Lady** is the pub pianist and the **World Showcase Players** add periodic street theatre. Mary Poppins, Winnie the Pooh, Alice in Wonderland and Friends can also be found here.

Dining and shopping: The **Rose and Crown Pub** is antiseptically authentic but you can get better elsewhere at these prices (grilled sirloin $23.99, bangers and mash or fish and chips $15.99, and a pint of Bass, Harp or Guinness for a whopping $8). There's also a takeaway **Yorkshire County** fish and chippie. The best shops are the **Tea Caddy**, the **Queen's Table**, **Crown and Crest** (perfumes and heraldry), **Sportsman Shoppe** (sweaters, kilts, football shirts) and **Toy Soldier** (traditional games and toys), but prices are WAY above what you'd pay at home.

Canada: Completing the World Showcase circle, the main features here are **Victoria Gardens**, based on the world-famous Butchart Gardens on Vancouver Island, some spectacular Rocky Mountain scenery, a replica French gothic mansion, the Hôtel de Canada, and another stunning 360° film, **O Canada!** As with China and France, this showcases the country's sights and scenery in a terrific, 17-minute advert for the Canadian Tourist Board led by comedian Martin Short. It's at its busiest in late afternoon. AAA

Other entertainment: Resident band **Off Kilter** are one of the most entertaining acts we've seen anywhere and they perform 30-minute sets up to 5 times a day. Want to hear rock 'n' roll bagpipes? This is the group for you!

BRITTIP

Best way to tour World Showcase? Start in Canada and continue anticlockwise or jump on the Friendship Boats and go straight to Italy or Morocco.

Dining and shopping: Le Cellier Steakhouse is an excellent dining room, offering great steaks, prime rib, seafood, chicken and several vegetarian dishes for lunch and dinner. **The Trading Post** and **Northwest Mercantile** provide a range of Canadian clothing and souvenirs, notably wonderful glass ornaments, Deauville perfume – and Off Kilter CDs!

IllumiNations: Reflections of Earth

The day's big finale and an absolute show-stopper, this firework and special-effects extravaganza is awesome even by Disney standards. British composer Gavin Greenaway provided the original music for a 15-minute performance of vivid brilliance. Some 2,800 firework shells are launched as a celestial backdrop to a series of fire-and-water effects on the World Showcase Lagoon. The central icon is a 28ft/9m video globe of Earth that opens in a spectacular climax of choreographed pyrotechnics. However, people start staking out the best lagoon-side spots up to 2 HOURS in advance. The ultimate way to view IllumiNations is by private boat on one of 2 **speciality cruises** from *Disney's Boardwalk* or *Yacht and Beach Club Resorts*, and the *Grand Floridian* (for non-residents, too). The price range is $325–1040 per boat (holding 4–10 guests) and can be used for special celebrations. The *Basic Cruise* costs $325 and the boat holds up to 10. It includes water, soft drinks and snacks. The classic Sea Ray yacht *Grand I* costs $520 for 60mins, $780/90min, $1040/120min (up to 17 adults; call 407 824 2682 up to 90 days in advance to book). Be aware cruises launch regardless of whether fireworks are taking place.

Behind-the-scenes tours

Epcot also has a big range of tours. Book all tours on 407 939 8687.

Dolphins in Depth: This is a 3hr dip into the research areas of The Seas pavilion, including a chance to meet the dolphins ($206, with refreshments, photo and T-shirt; 13–17s must be accompanied by an adult).

Undiscovered Future World: A 4½hr journey into the creation of *Epcot*, Walt's vision for the resort and backstage areas like IllumiNations ($58).

Behind the Seeds: This 1hr tour, every 45mins from 9.45am–4.30pm at The Land pavilion, looks at Disney's innovative gardening practices ($16 adults, $12 3–9s).

Dive Quest: A 3hr experience, with a 40min dive into The Seas aquarium, plus a backstage look at the facility at 4.30 and 5.30pm daily, Must have scuba certification; park admission not required ($186/person, 10 and over, includes T-shirt and certificate).

Seas Aqua Tour: A similar tour without the scuba diving, daily at 12.30pm ($149/person, 8 and over; under-18s must be accompanied by an adult).

Around the World at Epcot: For those who enjoy new technology, a World Showcase 2hr tour 4 times each morning on the amazing, innovative 2-wheeled Segway Human Transporter ($105/person, not including park admission; min age 16).

Nature-Inspired Design: Going backstage at The Land and Seas pavilions, including a detailed look at the Soarin' ride and greenhouses, plus an off-road experience on a Segway at 8.15am Tue, Wed, Thur and Sat ($132/person).

Backstage Magic: The most comprehensive tour goes behind the scenes of *Epcot*, *Magic Kingdom* and *Disney's Hollywood Studios* on a 7hr foray into little-seen aspects, such as the backstage areas of the Studios and the tunnels below *Magic Kingdom* ($243, 16 and over).

Annual festivals

There are 2 main annual *Epcot* events to watch out for.

International Flower and Garden Festival: This literally puts the whole park in full bloom with an amazing series of set-pieces, seminars and mini-exhibitions from early Mar to mid-May. All the exhibits and lectures are free and they add a beautiful aspect to an already scenic park.

Food and Wine Festival: Runs from 1 Oct through mid-Nov and showcases national and regional cuisines, wines and beers, with the chance to attend grand Winemakers' Dinners and Tasting Events, or just sample the offerings of more than 20 food booths dotted around World Showcase. Both also offer free concerts several times a day at the America Gardens Theater.

International Flower and Garden Festival

Disney's Hollywood Studios

Welcome to a journey into the world of film and TV, an epic voyage of adventure, creation – and fun. Here you will learn plenty of tricks of the trade; movie-making secrets and behind-the-scenes glimpses that have been cleverly turned into rides, shows and other attractions with guaranteed entertainment appeal. Rather bigger than the *Magic Kingdom* at 154 acres/62ha but smaller than *Epcot*, *Disney's Hollywood Studios* is a different experience yet again with its rather chaotic combination of attractions, street entertainment, film sets and smart gift shops. Like the *Magic Kingdom*, the food may not win awards, but some of the restaurants (notably the Sci-Fi Dine-in Theater and 50s Prime Time Café) have imaginative settings. The park also has more to occupy smaller children than *Epcot*, but you can still easily see most of it in a day unless the crowds are heavy.

Location

The entrance arrangements will be fairly familiar if you have already visited the other parks. Disney's Hollywood Studios is located on Buena Vista Drive (which runs between World Drive and Epcot Drive) and parking is $14. Remember to make a note of where you park before you catch the tram to the main gates, where you must wait for the official opening time. If the queues build up quickly, the gates will open early, so be ready for a running start.

Once through the gates, you are into Hollywood Boulevard, a street of gift shops, and you have to decide which

Disney's Hollywood Studios at a glance

Location	Off Buena Vista Drive or World Drive, Walt Disney World		
Size	154 acres/62ha		
Hours	9am–7pm off peak; 9am–10pm high season (Easter, summer holidays, Thanksgiving and Christmas)		
Admission	Under-3s free; 3-9 $79 (1-day base ticket), $342 (5-day Premium), $358 (7-day Premium); adult (10+) $85, $361, $377. Prices do not include tax.		
Parking	$15		
Lockers	From the Crossroads kiosk through the main entrance; $12 small, $14 large		
Pushchairs	$15 and $31 Oscar's Super Service Station; length of stay $13 per day single, $27 per day double		
Wheelchairs	$12 or $70 ($20 deposit refunded), from Oscar's		
Top attractions	Toy Story Mania, Twilight Zone™ Tower of Terror, Rock 'n' Roller Coaster Starring Aerosmith, Star Tours II, The Great Movie Ride, Voyage of the Little Mermaid, Jim Henson's Muppet*Vision 3-D, Lights, Motors, Action!™ Extreme Stunt Show		
Don't miss	Pixar Pals Countdown To Fun parade, Indiana Jones™ Epic Stunt Spectacular, American Idol Experience, Fantasmic!		
Hidden costs	Meals	Burger, chips and coke $10.58 3-course lunch $22-43 (Mama Melrose's) Beer $5.50–6.25 Kids' meal $4.99	
	T-shirts	$21.95-39.95	
	Souvenirs	$1.95–2,350	
	Sundries	Temporary tattoo $5–10	

of the main attractions to head for first, as these are the ones where the queues will be heaviest most of the day. Try to ignore the lure of the shops as it is better to browse in the early afternoon when the attractions are at their busiest.

BRITTIP

People begin queuing for the Lights, Motors, Action!™ Extreme Stunt Show a good ½hr before seating, but may end up sitting in the sun the whole time. Go for the first performance, or wait until the day cools down.

Incidentally, if you thought Disney had elevated queuing to an art form in its other parks, wait until you see how clever they are here. Just when you think you have reached the ride itself, there is another twist to the queue you hadn't seen or an extra element to the ride that holds you up. The latter are 'holding pens', which are an ingenious way of making it seem you are being entertained instead of queuing. Look out for them in particular at the Great Movie Ride, Twilight Zone™ Tower of Terror and Jim Henson's Muppet*Vision 3-D.

The main attractions

The park is laid out in a rather more confusing fashion than its counterparts, with their neatly packaged 'lands', so you should have your map handy to keep your bearings.

Beating the queues: The opening-gate crowds will all surge in one of 3 directions, which will give you a pretty good idea of where you want to go. By far the biggest attraction here is the **Twilight Zone™ Tower of Terror**, a magnificent haunted hotel ride that ends in a 13-storey drop in a lift, where queues hit 2 hours at peak periods. So, if the Tower appeals to you, do it first! Head straight up Hollywood Boulevard, turn right into Sunset Boulevard and you'll see it at the end, looming ominously over the park. It's a FastPass FP ride (p102), as is another huge draw, the **Rock 'n' Roller Coaster Starring Aerosmith** (at the end of Sunset Boulevard on the left), so you can get a FP for 1 and ride the other.

Star Tours, the remodelled *Star Wars*™ simulator ride, and **Toy Story Midway Mania** are also serious

Star Tours

© Disney

1 Parade Route Pixar Pals Countdown to Fun
2 The Great Movie Ride
3 American Idol Live!
4 ABC Sound Studio 'Sounds Dangerous' starring Drew Carey
5 Indiana Jones™ Epic Stunt Spectacular
6 Star Tours
7 Jim Henson's Muppet*Vision 3-D
8 Honey, I Shrunk the Kids Movie Set Adventure
9 Catastrophe Canyon on Disney's Hollywood Studios Backlot Tour
10 Studio Backlot Tour
11 Journey into Narnia: Prince Caspian
12 Toy Story Mania
13 Walt Disney: One Man's Dream
14 Voyage of the Little Mermaid
15 The Magic of Disney Animation

16 Disney Junior – Live on Stage!
17 Rock 'n' Roller Coaster Starring Aerosmith
18 The Twilight Zone™ Tower of Terror
19 Beauty and the Beast – Live on Stage
20 Fantasmic!
21 Guest Information Board
22 Toy Story Pizza Planet
23 Lights, Motors, Action!™ Extreme Stunt Show
24 Premier Theater
25 '50s Prime Time Café
26 Hollywood and Vine
27 Hollywood Brown Derby
28 Mama Melrose's
29 Sunset Ranch Market
30 Sci-Fi Dine-in Theater Restaurant

DISNEY'S HOLLYWOOD STUDIOS

queue-builders and FP attractions. If you are not up for the really big thrills, grab a FP for Toy Story Mania (straight up Hollywood Boulevard, pass right of the giant Mickey Hat and into the new Pixar Place area), then head for Star Tours (back across the main square past the Indiana Jones™ show). After Star Tours and Toy Story Mania, another gentler experience (and also worth doing early on) is the hysterical **Muppet*Vision 3-D** show, which is another big draw later in the day. It has the benefit of being air-conditioned, too, for when you need a rest. The park's big stunt show, **Lights, Motors, Action!**™ **Extreme Stunt Show**, plays 2–3 times a day and is a good one to catch early on or later in the day.

Hollywood Boulevard

Moving around the park in a (roughly) clockwise direction, you start in the Hollywood Boulevard area. As with the *Magic Kingdom*, your entry here is along a street of shops and services that are best visited in early afternoon when it's busier elsewhere. Immediately to the left through the turnstiles are the **Guest Relations** and **First Aid** offices, plus the **Baby Care** centre. An up-to-the-minute check on queue times at the attractions is kept on a **Guest Information Board** on Hollywood Boulevard, just past its junction with Sunset Boulevard, where you can also book restaurants. To the right is **Oscar's Station** for pushchair and wheelchair hire, while locker hire is obtained at the Crossroads kiosk in front of you.

The Great Movie Ride: This faces you (behind the Hat icon) as you walk in along Hollywood Boulevard and is a good place to start if the crowds are not too serious. An all-star audio-animatronics cast re-creates a number of box office smashes, including Jimmy Cagney's *Public Enemy*, Julie Andrews in *Mary Poppins*, Gene Kelly in *Singin' in the Rain* and many more masterful set-pieces as you undertake your conducted tour. Young children may find the menace of *The Alien* too strong, but otherwise the ride

has universal appeal and features some clever live twists (there are 2 variations on this ride, a cowboy and a gangster version – ask a Cast Member if there's one you especially want to do). AAAA

Other entertainment: Showing up to 6 times daily in front of the Sorcerer's Hat, **Disney Channel Rocks** pits the guys against the gals in a dance-off featuring music from favourite Disney artists such as Hannah Montana, JONAS, Star Struck and Camp Rock. And you might be chosen to show off your best moves, too! AAA. A series of **Citizens of Hollywood** acts also enliven Hollywood Boulevard throughout the day, staging impromptu movie shoots, casting calls or even detective investigations. Have fun with them – you just might end up the star of the show! Also by the Hat, look out for Disney characters during the morning.

Shopping and dining: Hollywood Boulevard has the best of the park's shopping (9 of the 21 stores), including **Sid Caheunga's One-of-a-Kind** (rare movie and TV items, including celebrity autographs), **Keystone Clothiers** (some of the best apparel), **Mickey's of Hollywood** (all your souvenirs and gift items) and **The Darkroom** (for camera items). **The Brown Derby** is the park's signature restaurant, offering fine dining in best vintage Hollywood style (reservations usually necessary).

The Disney Channel Rocks show

Indiana Jones™ Epic Stunt Spectacular

Echo Lake

Turn left out of Hollywood Boulevard and you find another area that pays homage to the movie world of the 1930s and '40s.

American Idol Experience: An exciting audience participation show based on the TV reality series. Guest performers undergo the full Idol experience, from audition to preparation (with a vocal coach and hair and make-up artists) to the performance, with those who score highest returning for an end-of-day Grand Finale show. The show features 3 contestants with varying degrees of talent (from 'exceptional' to 'good sport') and, while the judge's critiques are a bit canned, the experience is suitably realistic and die-hard Idol fans will love it. AAA

ABC Sound Studio 'Sounds Dangerous' Starring Drew Carey: A sound FX special that features American comedian Drew Carey in an instalment of a spoof undercover police show *Sounds Dangerous*. Most of the 12-minute show is in the dark – which upsets some children – and is centred on your special headphones as Carey's stakeout goes wildly wrong. Clever and amusing – if a bit tame for older children – you exit into the Sound Works Studio to try out some well-known sound effects. AAA

Indiana Jones™ Epic Stunt Spectacular: Consult your park *Times Guide* for the various times this stunt cavalcade hits the stage. A special movie set creates 3 different backdrops for Indiana Jones'™ stunt people to put on a dazzling array of scenes and special effects from the films. Audience participation is an element and there are some amusing sub-plots. Queues for the 30min show begin up to ½hr beforehand, but the auditorium holds more than 2,000 so everyone usually gets in. TTTT FP

Star Tours: The popular *Star Wars*™ simulator ride has had a complete revamp, returning in 3-D as The Adventure Continues. Climb into your StarSpeeder 1000 for a stunning high-speed journey through the worlds created by George Lucas in his award-winning films, including Coruscant, Naboo, Kashyyyk (the Wookiee planet) and Tatooine, where riders blast into the Boonta Eve Classic Podrace with convincing and dramatic results. New robot characters AC-38 ('Ace') and Aly San San prepare you for your flight, but predictably it all goes wrong, and droids R2-D2 and C-3PO must save your Speeder from disaster as they evade the Imperial Forces and a very determined bounty hunter. Master Yoda, Boba Fett, Darth Vader and a new branch of stormtroopers, called 'Skytroopers', join the pursuit, and you never know how it will all work out. With the option to change the story at various points, making for more than 50 ride options, the repeat factor here is huge! The realism of the *Star Wars*™ world, from the queue to the post-ride gift shop, is brilliant and lots of fun. **Restrictions:** 3ft 4in/101cm, no under-3s. **TTTT** (plus **AAAAA**; **FP**).

Other entertainment: Kids should make a beeline for the **Jedi Training Academy**, on the stage outside the Star Tours ride up to 8 times a day. Here, young Jedi hopefuls get to try their light sabre technique under the eyes of a Jedi master, before taking on Darth Vader himself. Great fun just to watch, too (**TTTT** for under-12s).

Shopping and dining: Shop for *Star Wars*™ goods at **Tatooine Traders** (at the exit to Star Tours) and Indiana Jones souvenirs at the **Indy Truck and Adventure Outpost**. There are also 3 good dining choices: the **'50s Prime Time Café** is a fun experience as you sit in mock stage sets from 1950s American TV sitcoms and eat meals 'just like Mom used to make' (the waiters all claim to be your aunt, uncle or cousin and warn you to take your elbows off the table – good fun!); the **Backlot Express** features superb burgers, hot dogs and sandwiches, while a varied buffet dinner is served up at **Hollywood & Vine** in addition to the **Play 'n Dine** character meal with the Disney Junior Pals, available from 8am–2.25pm ($32.99 adults, $17.99 3–9s).

Streets of America

Three of the park's bigger attractions can all be found here, along with an often-overlooked gem of a restaurant.

Muppet*Vision 3-D: The 3-D is crossed out here and 4-D substituted in its place, so be warned strange things are about to happen! A wonderful 10-minute holding-pen pre-show takes you into the Muppet Theater for a 20min experience with all of the Muppets, 3-D special effects and more – when Fozzie Bear points his squirty flower at you, prepare to get wet! It's a gem, and the kids love it. Queues build up through the main parts of the day, but Disney's queuing expertise makes them seem shorter. **AAAAA FP**

Honey, I Shrunk the Kids Movie Set Adventure: This adventure playground gives youngsters the chance to tackle massive blades of grass that turn out to be slides, crawl through caves, investigate giant mushrooms and more. There can be long queues here, so arrive early if the kids demand it (and bring plenty of film or a spare memory card). **TTTT** under-10s.

Premier Theater: This fully enclosed theatre is used for the *Star Wars*™ Weekend meet and greets and other set-piece special events.

Lights, Motors, Action!™ **Extreme Stunt Show:** A direct import from the *Walt Disney Studios* in Paris, this is one of the most remarkable shows you will see anywhere, full of genuine

Muppet*Vision 3-D

high-risk stunts featuring cars, motorbikes, jet-skis and stuntmen of all kinds, that will leave you shaking your head in amazement. The magnificently crafted set is based on a Mediterranean village and seating starts 30min prior to a show. There is some amusing pre-show chat before the serious stuff starts, when you are treated to a 33min extravaganza of daredevil stunts, with a Car Ballet sequence, a Motorbike Chase and a Grand Finale that features some surprise pyrotechnics to complete an awesome presentation (keep your eyes on the windows below the video screen at the end). Each scene – featuring a secret-agent and various baddies – is explained by a movie director and the results of each shoot are played back on screen to show how the effects were created.

BRITTIP

If you have young children, be aware there is some (loud) mock gunfire in the Lights, Motors, Action!™ Extreme Stunt Show, which can upset sensitive ears, while the motorbike scene includes a rider catching fire, which can be frightening for them, too.

All the cars were specially built by Vauxhall and there are some extra tricks between the main scenes. It was all designed by Frenchman Rémy Julienne, the doyen of film car stunt sequences from James Bond films *Goldeneye* and *Licence to Kill* and other action epics like *The Rock*, *Gone in 60 Seconds* and *Enemy of the State*. The exit can be quite a scrum, though, as 5,000 people have to leave together, and it can take 15mins to clear the auditorium, hence if you can sit towards the front, you will be out quicker. Because it involves so much live co-ordination, it makes for a thrilling experience and you may want to see it more than once – another reason to see it early on. TTTTT

Studio Backlot Tour: Before you board the special trams for a look at the off-limits part of the studios in this 35min walk-and-ride tour, you are treated to some special effects (involving an amusing water tank with a mock Pearl Harbor attack). The tram takes you round the production backlot and then to **Catastrophe Canyon** for a demonstration of special effects that try both to drown you and blow you up! AAA (plus TTTT). You exit into the **American Film Institute** showcase of costumes and props from recent films.

BRITTIP

Don't queue for the Backlot Tour when Lights, Motors, Action! has just ended – it will be far too crowded.

Other entertainment: Live music is provided periodically on the main street by the spectacular comedy rock band **Mulch, Sweat and Shears** (AAA; sometimes in front of the Sorcerer's Hat at the top of Hollywood Boulevard), while this is also a great place to meet Disney characters – look for *Cars* friends Lightning McQueen and Tow Mater at **Luigi's Garage** in front of the Backlot Tour, and *Monsters Inc.* in the building to the right of Lights, Motors, Action! Show.

Lights! Motors! Action! ™ *Extreme Stunt Show*

Catastrophe Canyon

Shopping and dining: Shop for Christmas items at **It's A Wonderful Shop, Stage 1 Company Store** for Muppet and *Sesame Street* souvenirs and **Writer's Stop** for books and speciality coffees. **Mama Melrose's Ristorante Italiano** is a wonderful table-service Italian option (one of our favourites), while there are also the counter-service offerings of **Toy Story Pizza Planet** (average pizza, salads and drinks) and **Studio Catering Co.** (sandwiches, chicken wraps, salads and its own bar).

Commissary Lane
This is just a small link between the Streets of America and the central plaza by the Sorcerer's Hat, and contains only 2 eating opportunities. **The Sci-Fi Dine-In Theater Restaurant** is a big hit with kids as you dine in a mock drive-in cinema, with cars as tables, car-hop waitresses and a big film screen showing old black-and-white science-fiction movie clips. The menu features gourmet burgers ($14), ribs, chicken, pasta and sandwiches, as well as the signature milkshakes and sodas ($28 for 3-course lunch, $8.99 kids' meal).

The counter-service option **ABC Commissary** serves up a multi-ethnic choice that includes a chicken curry, Cuban sandwich and Asian salad.

Pixar Place
This area has undergone a complete transformation from the old Mickey Avenue to the new-look Pixar Studios (styled after the Pixar Film Studios in California) after the opening of the *Toy Story* ride in 2009.

Toy Story Midway Mania: A real family fun fiesta, a 3-D ride into a fantasy fairground of games with the *Toy Story* characters. To start with you are 'shrunk' to toy-size and board

Buzz Lightyear on parade

carnival vehicles (each equipped with individual spring-action shooters) to go through Andy's Bedroom, where the toys have set up a Midway Games Play Set with 5 challenges, plus a practice round. Thanks to a pair of 3D glasses, riders can 'see' everything their shooter fires at the sequence of targets (while, with the magic of Disney's special effects, they might also 'feel' objects whirring past as they burst out of the screens; and, if you hit a water balloon, watch out!). Throw virtual eggs at barnyard targets, launch darts at prehistoric balloon targets, break plates with baseballs, land rings on Buzz Lightyear's alien friends and finish up in Woody's Rootin' Tootin' Shootin' Gallery (with a bonus roundup) before totting up your scores and comparing with fellow riders. All the time, the *Toy Story* characters cheer you on (and pass on hints to boost your score, so it works for all abilities) and provide some amusing commentary. At times it is a touch raucous and chaotic, but kids are sure to love the shooting game element and the whole family can enjoy the amusing ride through the toys' world. Even the queuing area is fun, with a huge animatronic Mr Potato Head acting as a fairground barker to entertain while you wait (**AAA TTTT; FP**). As a recent ride, it draws some HUGE queues, so you should use the FastPass option here early on (as they usually run out by mid-day).

Disney guests

Other entertainment: Look out for the *Toy Story* characters meet-and-greet here, plus the audio-animatronic **Luxo Jr** – the amusing lamp character from all Pixar films – who makes regular appearances on a courtyard balcony.

Shopping and dining: For souvenirs and gifts from your favourite Pixar films visit the **Camera Dept**, while **Hey Howdy Hey Take Away** offers counter-service ice-cream, snacks and drinks.

Animation Courtyard

Get ready for a series of wonderful family-friendly shows in this area of the park, starting with **Voyage of the Little Mermaid**, a 17min live performance that is primarily for children who have seen the Disney cartoon. It brings together a mix of actors, animation and puppetry to re-create the film's highlights. Parents will still enjoy the special effects, but queues tend to be long, so go early or late. There is also the likelihood you will get a little wet. **AAA** (**AAAAA** under-9s; **FP**).

Journey into Narnia: Prince Caspian: This walk-through experience features a dramatic entryway into a Narnian fantasy world and multimedia show. Set in Aslan's stone temple chamber, it tells the story of the second Narnia film and provides a highlight reel and various re-created scenes from the saga. You then exit into an exhibit of original art, props and costumes. **AA**

BRITTIP
Try to sit at least halfway back in the Mermaid Theatre, especially if you are with young children, as the stage front is a bit high.

Walt Disney: One Man's Dream: This interactive show-and-tell exhibit chronicles Walt himself and his lifetime of accomplishments. From archive school records to a model of the Nautilus from *20,000 Leagues Under the Sea*, the story of the man behind the Mouse comes to vivid life. The homage ends with a preview of

© Disney

DISNEY'S HOLLYWOOD STUDIOS with children

Here is our guide to the attractions that appeal to the different age groups in this park:

Under-5s
Beauty and the Beast – Live on Stage, Pixar Pals Countdown To Fun parade, Fantasmic!, Honey I Shrunk the Kids Movie Set Adventure, The Magic of Disney Animation, Disney Junior–Live On Stage!, Voyage of the Little Mermaid.

5–8s
Beauty and the Beast – Live On Stage, Pixar Pals Parade, Fantasmic!, Honey I Shrunk the Kids Movie Set Adventure, Indiana Jones™ Epic Stunt Spectacular, Journey Into Narnia: Prince Caspian, Lights, Motors, Action!™ Extreme Stunt Show, The Magic of Disney Animation, Muppet* Vision 3-D, 'Sounds Dangerous' Starring Drew Carey, Studio Backlot Tour, Toy Story Mania, Voyage of the Little Mermaid.

9–12s
American Idol Experience, Beauty and the Beast – Live on Stage, Fantasmic!, The Great Movie Ride, Indiana Jones™ Epic Stunt Spectacular, Journey into Narnia: Prince Caspian, Lights, Motors, Action!™ Extreme Stunt Show, The Magic of Disney Animation, Muppet*Vision 3-D, Rock 'n' Roller Coaster Starring Aerosmith, 'Sounds Dangerous' Starring Drew Carey, Star Tours, Studio Backlot Tour, Twilight Zone™ Tower of Terror, Toy Story Mania.

Over-12s
American Idol Experience, Fantasmic!, The Great Movie Ride, Indiana Jones™ Epic Stunt Spectacular, Lights, Motors, Action!™ Extreme Stunt Show, The Magic of Disney Animation, Muppet*Vision 3-D, Rock 'n' Roller Coaster Starring Aerosmith, Star Tours, Studio Backlot Tour, Toy Story Mania, Twilight Zone™ Tower of Terror, Walt Disney: One Man's Dream.

Disney's future developments, plus a 10min film encapsulating all Walt achieved and dreamed about. AAAA

The Magic of Disney Animation: An amusing and entertaining 30min show-and-tour through the making of cartoons. It starts with a theatrical performance by Mushu, the Eddie Murphy-voiced dragon from the film *Mulan*. From there, you exit into a hands-on area of interactive fun (especially for children); *Ink & Paint* is a colouring challenge; at *Sound Stage* you can try a voiceover; and *You're a Character* will tell you which Disney character you most resemble. From there, you have the choice of joining the Animation Academy for a tutored class in cartoon art or stopping for a meet and greet with Disney characters, including Mickey Mouse and The Incredibles. You exit via the *Animation Gallery*, which has some fabulous gifts. Queues are rarely serious, so it's a good afternoon choice. AAAA

Disney Junior – Live on Stage!:
Mickey, Goofy, Donald, and Daisy are throwing a surprise birthday party for Minnie, but need the help of friends like Handy Manny, Jake and the Neverland Pirates, and Little Einsteins to make this the best celebration ever. It's colourful and entertaining and pre-schoolers just love it. AA (AAAAA under-5s).

Rock 'n' Roller Coaster entrance

© Disney

Other entertainment: Youngsters can meet all their favourite Disney Junior characters in Animation Courtyard, several times daily.

Sunset Boulevard

The final part of the park contains the 2 high-thrill rides, and the big night-time finale, but it's also the busiest area from midday on, so try to visit here first or use the FastPass options.

Rock 'n' Roller Coaster Starring Aerosmith: Disney's first big-thrill inverted coaster is a sure-fire draw for the adrenalin ride addicts, with a magnificent indoor setting and nerve-jangling ride. It features a clever holographic-style film show starring rock group Aerosmith in their recording studio. That leads to the real fun, set to specially recorded tracks from the band itself and with outrageous speaker systems, as riders climb aboard Cadillac cars for a memorable whiz through a mock Los Angeles (watch out for a close encounter with the Hollywood sign!). The high-speed launch and inversions ensure a dynamic coaster experience. Go first thing or expect serious queues, and don't forget to check out your ride photo ($18.95-32.95). **Restrictions:** 4ft/124cm. TTTTT FP

BRITTIP

If only 1 or 2 in your group want to ride Rock 'n' Roller Coaster, or you want to save significant time waiting, opt for the Single Rider queue. You will be split up, but the wait will be much shorter.

The Twilight Zone™ Tower of Terror: This 199ft/60m landmark invites you to experience another dimension in the strange Hollywood Tower Hotel that time forgot. The exterior is intriguing, the interior is fascinating, the ride is scintillating and the queues are huge! Just when you think you are through to the ride, there's another queue, so spend your time inspecting the superb detail. There's a lot more to this than just the big 13-storey drop, however, as the 'Twilight Zone' theme adds a real element of invention. Your elevator car twists and turns unexpectedly before it is time to 'drop in', and the random drop sequence provides hair-raising thrills before you exit! **Restrictions:** 3ft 4in/101cm. TTTTT FP

Beauty and the Beast – Live on Stage: An enchanting live musical song and dance performance of the highlights of this Disney classic will entertain the whole family for 30min in the Theater of the Stars. Check the daily schedule for show times, which are up to 5 times a day, usually starting at 11.45am. AAA

Fantasmic!: This special-effects spectacular is simply not to be missed. Staged 2-5 times a week

The Twilight Zone™ Tower of Terror

© Disney

(twice a night at peak periods) in a 6,900-seat amphitheatre, it features the dreams of Mickey, portrayed as the Sorcerer's Apprentice, through films such as *Pocahontas*, *The Lion King* and *Snow White*, but hijacked by the Disney villains, leading to an epic battle with Our Hero emerging triumphant. Dancing waters, shooting comets, animated fountains, swirling stars and balls of fire combine in a breathtaking presentation – but beware of the giant, fire-breathing dragon! The 25-minute show begins seating up to 2 hours in advance and it's best to head there at least 30 mins before (watch out for the splash zones!). AAAAA

Other entertainment: Sunset Boulevard is also home to more of the park's **Citizens of Hollywood** characters.

Shopping and dining: The best shopping here is provided by **Legends of Hollywood**, **Planet Hollywood Super Store** and the **Sunset Boulevard** shops (for limited edition watches, clothing and other collectibles). **Rosie's All-American Café** (chicken, burgers and salads) and **Catalina Eddie's** (pizza) are the best of Sunset Boulevard's 5 market-style eateries.

Daily parade

It's a real character-fest in the entertaining **Pixar Pals Countdown to Fun Parade** as favourites from *The Incredibles, Bugs Life, Ratatouille, Monsters INC, UP* and *Toy Story* make their way through the Studios in cavalcade style on a series of imaginative floats and on the ground, with plenty of Disney dancers to add energy to proceedings. Have the camera ready for some great looks at this colourful extravaganza with its catchy tunes. AAAA

BRITTIP

You can get a plain burger without all the trimmings at Backlot Express and Rosie's. Just ask when you reach the cashier. It's not on the menu, but it is available.

Studios at Christmas

At Christmas (late Nov–1 Jan), one of the most amazing spectacles anywhere is the **Osborne Family Spectacle of Dancing Lights**, which are switched on every evening in the Streets of America area. This stunning display of 5 million twinkling, themed fairy lights draws huge crowds all evening (go during a Fantasmic! performance to avoid the worst of the throngs).

Skywalker and Co

Star Wars™ film fans will want to make a beeline for the Studios during weekends in late May and early June when the park becomes a playground for characters, film stars, photo-opportunities, competitions and other memorabilia based on anything to do with Luke Skywalker and Co. Much of the event is scheduled in and around the Premier Theater in the Streets of America area. There is no additional fee to rub shoulders with (and get autographs from) various *Star Wars™* personalities, and the Studios take on an extra dimension each weekend (though the park is also at its most crowded).

Park tours

Inspiration: Through Walt's Eyes: This gives insight into how Walt Disney influenced film making, and how ideas are transformed into the elements, large and small, that we see in the parks. Tour Hollywood Studio's Sunset Boulevard, go backstage to see Event and Decorating Support, then visit the famous utilidors in **Magic Kingdom** (9am Mon, Fri, Sun; $105/person, no under-16s).

Pixar Pals Countdown to Fun

Disney's Animal Kingdom Theme Park

Disney's newest and smartest theme park opened in 1998 representing a completely different experience. With an emphasis on conservation and nature, it largely eschews the non-stop thrills and attractions of the other parks and instead offers a change of pace, a more relaxing motif, as well as Disney's usual seamless entertainment style, but still with some excellent rides, including 1 of its very best. The attractions are relatively few, with just 6 out-and-out rides, but there are then 2 elaborate wildlife trails, 4 shows (including 2 that are almost worth the entry fee alone), an extravagant adventure playground, conservation station and petting zoo, and a Disney character greeting area.

It is also outrageously scenic, notably with the 145ft/44m Tree of Life, the Kilimanjaro Safaris and the Asian village of Serka Zong (home to the gigantic Expedition: Everest™ ride), but it won't overwhelm you with Disney's usual grand fantasy. Rather, it is a chance to explore and experience; to learn and understand; and to soak up the gentler more natural ambience. It is not a zoo in the conventional sense, but it is home to 200-plus species of birds and animals (in some wonderfully naturalistic settings). The educational tone is fairly strong, but children in particular may pick up easily on the essential conservation undertones of things like Kilimanjaro Safaris and Maharajah Jungle Trek. However, the park does get crowded, the walkways can be congested and there are also fewer places to cool down. It is definitely a good idea to be here on time and use FastPass to minimise queuing.

Disney's Animal Kingdom Theme Park at a glance

Location	Directly off Osceola Parkway, also via World Drive and Buena Vista Drive		
Size	500 acres/203ha divided into 6 'lands'		
Hours	9am–5 or 6pm off peak; 8am–7pm in high season		
Admission	Under-3s free; 3–9 $79 (1–day base ticket), $342 (5–day Premium), $358 (7-day Premium); adult (10+) $85, $361, $377. Prices do not include tax.		
Parking	$15		
Lockers	Either side of Entrance Plaza; $12 small; $14 large ($5 deposit)		
Pushchairs	$15 and $31 at Garden Gate Gifts, through entrance on right; length of stay $13 per day single, $27 per day double		
Wheelchairs	$12 or $70 ($20 deposit refunded) with pushchairs		
Top attractions	DINOSAUR!, Kilimanjaro Safaris, It's Tough To Be A Bug!, Kali River Rapids, Festival Of The Lion King, Finding Nemo – The Musical, Expedition: Everest™		
Don't miss	Pangani Forest Exploration Trail, Maharajah Jungle Trek, Rafiki's Planet Watch, Mickey's Jammin' Jungle Parade, dining at Rainforest Café		
Hidden costs	**Meals**	Burger, chips and coke $10.58 3-course meal at Yak & Yeti $33-47 (kid's entrée and dessert $9.48) Beer $6.25 and $7.25 Kids' meal $6.49	
	T-shirts	$19.95-39.95	
	Souvenirs	$1–225-plus	
	Sundries	Face painting $10–15	

The Oasis

1 The Oasis Tropical Garden

Discovery Island

2 The Tree of Life
3 It's Tough To Be A Bug
4 Discovery Island Trails
5 Flame Tree Barbecue
6 Pizzafari

Camp Minnie-Mickey

7 Character Greeting Trails
8 Festival Of The Lion King

Dinoland USA

9 DINOSAUR!
10 The Boneyard
11 Finding Nemo – The Musical

12 Chester And Hester's Dino-Rama!
13 TriceraTOP Spin
14 Primeval Whirl
15 Restaurantosaurus

Africa

16 Harambe
17 Kilimanjaro Safaris
18 Rafiki's Planet Watch
19 Pangani Forest Trail
20 Tusker House Restaurant

Asia

21 Flights Of Wonder
22 Kali River Rapids
23 Maharajah Jungle Trek
24 Expedition: Everest™
25 Yak 'n Yeti Restaurant
26 Rainforest Café

DISNEY'S ANIMAL KINGDOM

Rafiki's Planet Watch

Asia

Dinoland U.S.A.

Discovery Island

Oasis

ENTRANCE

Africa

Camp Minnie-Mickey

Serengeti Safari

Location

If you are staying in the Kissimmee area, *Disney's Animal Kingdom* is the easiest of the parks to find. Just get on the (toll) Osceola Parkway and follow it all the way to the toll booths. Alternatively, coming down I-4, take exit 65 on to Osceola Parkway. From West Highway 192, come in on Sherberth Road and turn right at the first traffic lights. If you arrive early (which is advisable), you can walk to the Entrance Plaza. Otherwise, the usual tram system takes you in, so make a note of the row you park in (e.g. Unicorn, 67). The entrance plaza is overlooked by the **Rainforest Café**, with its 65ft/20m waterfall, which is open for breakfast, lunch and dinner

Anandapur Forest Trail

(but is busy 12.30–3.30pm and an hour before closing). With Orlando so hot in summer, you need to be here as early as possible to see the animals before they hide in the shade.

BRITTIP

An early start is especially advised for Kilimanjaro Safaris. You will see far more animals in the first few cooler hours of the day than during the hotter afternoon when they seek the shade.

Beating the queues: For the early birds, here is your best plan of campaign. Once through the gates, animal lovers should head first for Kilimanjaro Safaris, through the Oasis, Discovery Island and Africa. After the Safari, go straight to Pangani Forest Exploration Trail and you will have experienced 2 of the park's best animal encounters before it gets too hot. Alternatively, thrill-seekers should walk straight through Discovery Island for Asia, where the Expedition: Everest™ ride is the big draw. Then head to Kilimanjaro Safaris or the nearby Kali River Rapids raft ride, followed by the scenic Maharajah Jungle Trek. The best combination for the first arrivals is to get a FastPass for Expedition:

Everest™, then ride Kilimanjaro Safaris and, once you have done that (and depending on your FP time), either do your Everest ride or go straight to Kali River Rapids. Check your show schedule for Festival of the Lion King and try to catch one of the first 2 performances, as the later ones draw sizeable queues. The wait time board at the entrance to Discovery Island is helpful. Those are your main tactics – here is the full rundown.

The Oasis

Tropical Garden: A gentle, walk-through introduction to the park, this is a rocky, tree-covered area featuring animal habitats, streams, waterfalls and lush plant life. Here you meet miniature deer, a giant anteater, exotic boars, macaws, sloths, iguanas and kangaroos in an understated environment that leads you across a stone bridge to the main park area. Visit in early afternoon when many of the rides are busy. AAA

Other entertainment: Look out for a host of **Disney characters** – including Mickey, Minnie, Rafiki and King Louie – here throughout the morning.

Shopping and dining: Stop at **Garden Gate Gifts** (on the right) for pushchair, wheelchair and locker hire, while **Guest Relations** is on the left. The fun **Rainforest Café** also has an entrance inside the park here. If you haven't seen the one at *Downtown Disney*, you should call in to view the amazing jungle interior with its audio-animatronic animals, waterfalls, thunderstorms and aquariums. A 3-course meal costs $29–$59, but the setting alone is worth it and the food is above average. Try breakfast or an early dinner to avoid the crowds.

Discovery Island

This colourful village is the park hub, themed as a tropical artists' colony, with animal-inspired artwork, nature trails, 4 main shops and 2 eateries. You will also find the **First Aid** station here (look for the 'ladybird' lights) and the **Baby Center**.

The Tree of Life: This arboreal edifice is the park centre-piece, an awesome creation that seems to have a different perspective from wherever you view it. The trunk and roots are covered in 325 carvings representing

The Tree of Life

the Circle of Life, from the dolphin to the lion. **Trails** lead round the tree, interspersed with habitats for flamingos, otters, ring-tailed lemurs, macaws, axis deer, cranes, storks, ducks and tortoises. The tree canopy spreads 160ft/49m, the trunk is 50ft/15m wide and the diameter of the roots is 170ft/52m. It has 103,000 leaves (all attached by hand) on more than 8,000 branches! AAAA

It's Tough To Be A Bug!: Winding down among the Tree's roots brings you 'underground' to a 430-seat theatre and another example of Disney's artistry in 3-D films and special effects. This hysterical 10min show, in the company of Flick from the Pixar film *A Bug's Life*, is a homage to 80% of the animal world, featuring grasshoppers, beetles, spiders, stink bugs and termites (beware the 'acid' spray!) as well as several tricks we couldn't possibly reveal. Sit towards the back in the middle (allow a good number of people in first as the rows are filled up from the far side) to get

the best of the 3-D effects. Queues build up from midday, but they do move quite steadily. Don't miss the 'forthcoming attractions' posters in the foyer for some excruciating bug puns on famous films. AAAAA FP

> **BRITTIP**
>
> The dark, special effects and mock creepy-crawlies in **It's Tough To Be A Bug!** can be *extremely* scary for young 'uns. Use caution.

Other entertainment: The Island is home to live music and **Disney characters** are also on hand – Winnie the Pooh and friends at Character Landing (opposite Flame Tree Barbecue) and Lilo and Stitch next to Island Mercantile.

Shopping and dining: You will find a huge range of merchandise, souvenirs and gifts here, notably in **Disney Outfitters** (artwork and collectables) and **Island Mercantile**. Counter-service restaurants **Pizzafari** (pizza, salads and sandwiches) and **Flame**

Festival of the Lion King

© Disney

Tree Barbecue (barbecued ribs, beef and pork, chicken sandwiches and salads) are both good choices. If it's not too hot, the Flame Tree is a picturesque option, set among pretty gardens and fountains on the Discovery River; the air-conditioned Pizzafari is better in summer months.

Camp Minnie-Mickey

This is a woodland retreat featuring winding paths and more of Disney's clever scenery, plus a superb show, a real character fest, plus the ever-popular (with kids!) squirt fountains.

Character Greeting Trails: A series of trails lead to 4 different pavilions that are home to a variety of jungle encounters with Disney characters such as Mickey and Minnie (naturally), Winnie the Pooh and friends plus, occasionally, Pocahontas, Brother Bear, Jungle Book and Song of the South characters. AAAAA (for kids).

Festival of the Lion King: Not to be missed, this high-powered 25min production (up to 8 times a day at peak periods; 5 a day at others) brings the hit animated film to life in spectacular fashion, with giant moving stages, huge animated figures, singers, dancers, acrobats and stilt-walkers, plus some fun audience participation. All the well-known songs are given an airing in a fiesta of colour and sound, and it underlines the quality Disney brings to its live shows. However, queuing often begins 45mins in advance for the 1,000-seat (air-conditioned) theatre, so try to take in one of the early shows. AAAAA

Other entertainment: The kids' favourite animal songs periodically get an airing with the wonderfully amusing **Gi-Tar Dan**.

Africa

The largest land in the park, it recreates the forests, grasslands and rocky homelands of East Africa's most fascinating residents in a richly landscaped setting that is part rundown port town and part savannah. The central area, **Harambe Village**, is a superb Imagineer's eye-view of a Kenyan port town, complete with white coral walls and thatched roofs, and is the starting point of your adventure. The Arab-influenced Swahili culture is also depicted in the native tribal costumes and architecture.

> **BRITTIP**
>
> The best (i.e. the most jolting) ride with the Kilimanjaro Safaris is at the back of the truck. There is much less to see from midday to late afternoon when many of the animals take a siesta.

Kilimanjaro Safaris: The queuing area alone earns high marks for authenticity, preparing you for the sights and sounds of the 110-acre/45ha savannah beyond. You board a 32-passenger truck, with your driver relaying information about the flora and fauna on view and a bush ranger-pilot overhead relaying facts and figures on the wildlife, including the dangers threatening them in the real world. Scores of animals are spread out in various habitats, with no fences in sight (the ditches and barriers are all well concealed) as you splash through fords and cross rickety bridges, and you should get good close-ups of lions, rhinos, elephants, giraffes, antelope, zebras, hippos and ostriches. Once again, the authentic nature of all you see (okay, some of the tyre 'ruts' and termite mounds are concrete and the baobab trees are fake) is breathtaking, with the spread of the vegetation and landscaping. The animals roam over a wide area,

Kilimanjaro Safaris

though, and can disappear from view. Not recommended for expectant mothers or anyone with back or neck problems. **AAAAA FP**

Pangani Forest Exploration Trail: As you leave the Safari, you turn on to a serious nature trail that showcases gorillas, hippos, meerkats and rare tropical birds. You wander the trail at your own pace and visit 'research' stations to learn more about the animals, including the underwater view of the hippos (check out the size of a hippo skull and those teeth!) and the savannah overlook, where giraffes and antelope graze and the meerkats frolic. The walk-through aviary gives you the chance to meet the carmine bee-eater, pygmy goose, African green pigeon, ibis and brimstone canary, among others, but the real centre-piece is the silverback gorilla habitat (in fact, 2 of them). The family group is often just inches away from the plate-glass window, while the bachelor group further along can prove more elusive. Again, the natural aspect of the trail is fabulous and it provides a host of photo opportunities. Do this early or save it for late in the day when most of the crowds will have moved on. **AAAAA**

Rafiki's Planet Watch: This subsection of Africa involves a (rather dull) rustic train ride, with a peek into some of the backstage areas, as a preamble to

Pangani Forest Exploration Trail

the park's interactive and educational exhibits (especially for children). The 3-part journey starts with **Habitat Habit!**, where you can see cotton-top tamarins and learn how conservation begins in your own back garden. **Conservation Station** offers a series of exhibits, shows and information stations about the environment and threats to its ecology. Look out for *Sounds of the Rain Forest*, the story of endangered species, at the Mermaid Tales Theater and the Eco-Heroes (who can be quizzed on-screen) trying to redress the balance, then observe the park's veterinary treatment centre, hatchery and neonatal care. You can easily spend an hour absorbing the information here, inspired by **Disney's Worldwide Conservation Fund**. Finally, the **Affection Section** petting zoo consists of a herd of friendly goats and a rather shy calf. **AAA**

Other entertainment: There's plenty more to enjoy here, with the splendid percussion of **Mor Thiam**, the pageantry and rhythms of **Tam Tam's of Congo**. With luck you'll also spot the wonderful **DiVine**, a 'moving' part of the foliage (also in The Oasis at times). **Disney characters** can be found in Harambe and Rafiki's Planet Watch.

Shopping and dining: Harambe is home to the **Mombasa Marketplace/ Ziwani Traders**, where you can suit up safari-style, while Rafiki's Planet Watch has **Out of the Wild** for more gifts and souvenirs. **Tusker House Restaurant** (featuring *Donald's Safari Breakfast* at $26.99 adults, $14.99 children, and non-character buffets at lunch and dinner) is one of the best diners in the park, with a mouth-watering array of salads, a hot carvery, rotisserie chicken, stews and vegetarian dishes ($25.99 adults, $13.99 children for lunch; $32.99 and $16.99 for dinner). There are also 4 snack and drink bars, most notably the **Kusafiri Coffee Shop** (muffins, pastries, coffee), while **Tamu Tamu Refreshments** offers the standard burgers, sandwiches, salads and drinks.

Maharajah Jungle Trek

Asia

The next 'land' is elaborately themed as the gateway to the imaginary south-east Asian city of Anandapur, with temples, ruined forts, landscape and wildlife. The element of reality is startling and the architecture is full of faithful representations of genuine locations.

Flights of Wonder: Another wildlife show, this portrays the talents and traits of the park's avian inhabitants. A trainer showcases the behaviours of various birds, including macaws and hawks, before being interrupted by a bumbling tour guide, who needs to be reminded of key conservation issues. This is the cue for some frolics with our feathered friends, including vultures, eagles, toucans and a singing parrot. The Caravan Stage is not air-conditioned, though, and can be hot in summer. AAA

Kali River Rapids: Part thrill-ride, part scenic journey, this bouncy raft ride will get you pretty wet (not great for early morning in winter). It starts out in tropical forest territory before launching into a scene of logging devastation, warning of the dangers of clear-cut burning. Your raft then plunges down a waterfall (and one unlucky soul – usually the one with their back to the drop – gets seriously damp) before you finish more sedately. Queues can be long through the main part of the day, so use FastPass here. **Restrictions:** 3ft 6in/106cm (a few rafts have adult-and-child seats allowing smaller children to ride). TTT AAAA FP

Maharajah Jungle Trek: Asia's version of the wildlife trail is another picturesque walk past decaying temple ruins and animal encounters. Playful gibbons, tapirs, Komodo dragons and a bat enclosure (including the flying fox bat, the world's largest) lead to the main viewing area, the 5-acre/2ha Tiger Range, whose pool and fountains are a popular playground early in the day for these magnificent big cats. An antelope enclosure and walk-through aviary complete this breathtaking trek (which rarely draws heavy crowds). AAAAA

Expedition: Everest™: A major attraction, this clever roller-coaster takes you deep into the Himalayas for an encounter with the mythical Yeti. The queuing area alone will convince you of its authentic location (try to do the main queue at least once rather than FastPass to appreciate all the fine detail) as it delivers you to an old abandoned tea plantation railway station. Here you undertake the ride to the foothills of Mount Everest, but you must first brave the perils of

Kali River Rapids

the Forbidden Mountain – lair of the Yeti. Will the beast be in evidence? You bet! The ride becomes a typically fast-paced whiz (but no inversions), forwards AND backwards, as you attempt to escape the creature's domain. The final encounter with a massive audio-animatronic Yeti is jaw-dropping and underlines the splendidly creative nature of this ride. It has proved to be a fabulous attraction but draws equally impressive crowds all day, so make it one of the first things you do. You can also take advantage of a Single Rider queue here (at the FP entrance) if you don't mind your group being split up. You can get ride photos here too ($18.95-32.95). **Restrictions:** 3ft 8in/115cm. TTTTT FP

🇬🇧 **BRITTIP**

Although Expedition: Everest™ is a FastPass ride, its popularity means FPs often run out, so don't leave it too late.

Shopping and dining: The retail options are limited in Asia (just 2 minor kiosks), but it is also home to the fab **Yak and Yeti** combination diner. Outside is the counter-service Local Foods Café (honey chicken, orange beef, egg rolls, chicken salad and sweet and sour chicken), while inside the 2-storey structure is the full Restaurant. Yak and Yeti offers some imaginative cuisine, from a Dim Sum basket to Maple Tamarind Chicken and a Malaysian Seafood Curry, as well as more standard Asian-fusion dishes. A good range of drinks and cocktails complement this outstanding eatery. Extra incentive to visit: a full range of bar drinks 'to go'!

DinoLand USA

The final area of the park is somewhat at odds with the natural theme of the rest, a full-scale palaeontology exercise, with the accent on a 'university fossil dig'. Energetically tongue-in-cheek (the students who work the area have the motto 'Been there, dug that', while you enter under a mock brachiosaurus skeleton, the 'Oldengate Bridge' – groan!), it still features some glimpses into genuine research and artefacts.

DINOSAUR!: Renamed after Disney's big animated film (it was initially called *Countdown to Extinction*), this is a herky-jerky ride experience, rather dark and intense (and often too scary for young children). It is also a wonderfully realistic journey back to the end of the Cretaceous period, when a giant meteor put paid to dinosaur life. You enter the high-tech Dino Institute for a multimedia history show that leads to a briefing

Expedition Everest

© Disney

DISNEY'S ANIMAL KINGDOM THEME PARK with children

Here is our guide to the attractions that appeal to the different age groups in this park:

Under-5s

Affection Section, The Boneyard, Character Greetings Trails, Discovery Island Trails, Festival of the Lion King, Finding Nemo – The Musical, Kilimanjaro Safaris, Maharajah Jungle Trek, Pangani Forest Exploration Trail, TriceraTOP Spin, Mickey's Jammin' Jungle Parade.

5–8s

All the above, plus Conservation Station, DINOSAUR! (with parental discretion), Flights Of Wonder, Habitat Habit!, It's Tough To Be A Bug (with parental discretion), Kali River Rapids, Primeval Whirl.

9–12s

All the above, plus Expedition: Everest™.

Over-12s

DINOSAUR!, Expedition: Everest™, Festival of the Lion King, Flights Of Wonder, It's Tough To Be A Bug!, Kali River Rapids, Kilimanjaro Safaris, Maharajah Jungle Trek, Pangani Forest Exploration Trail, Primeval Whirl, Mickey's Jammin' Jungle Parade

room for your 'mission' 65 million years in the past. However, one of the Institute's scientists hijacks your trip to capture a dinosaur, and you career back to a prehistoric jungle in a 12-passenger Time Rover. The threat of a carnotaurus (quite frightening for children; try to sit them on the inside of the car) and the impending doom of the meteor add up to a breathtaking whirl through a menacing environment. You will need to ride at least twice to appreciate all the detail, but queues build up quickly, so go either first thing or late in the day. **Restrictions:** 3ft 4in/101cm. **TTTT** AAAA FP

The Boneyard: A hugely imaginative adventure playground, it offers kids the chance to slip, slide and climb through the 'fossilised' remains of triceratops and brontosaurs, explore caves, dig for bones and splash through a mini waterfall. The amusing signage will be wasted on most kids, but it's ideal for parents to let their young 'uns loose for up to an hour (though not just after the neighbouring Finding Nemo show has finished). **TTTT** (kids only).

Finding Nemo – The Musical: This lovely show is a first for Disney entertainment, taking a non-musical animated feature and turning it into a fully fledged all-singing extravaganza.

The show combines colourful puppets, dancers, acrobats and animated backdrops with innovative lighting, sound and special effects. The basic idea remains faithful to the story of Nemo, his dad Marlin and friends Dory and Crush and features larger-than-life puppetry, plus rod, bunraku and shadow puppets, all designed by Michael Curry, who created the award-winning Broadway version of Disney's *The Lion King* show. It's a spectacular combination of music and grand staging, and the 30min show performs up to 5 times a day. **AAAA**

BRITTIP

Finding Nemo – The Musical is a popular addition, but although it draws long queues, the theatre seats 1,500, so most people usually get in.

Dinosaur!

© Disney

Chester & Hester's Dino-Rama!:
This mini-land of rides, fairground games and stalls adds a rather garish element to the park. Its main icon is a towering concretosaurus (!), and it is designed to have a quirky, tongue-in-cheek style reminiscent of 1950s' American roadside attractions. The rides are: **TriceraTOP Spin:** another version of the Dumbo/Aladdin rides in the *Magic Kingdom*, where a flying, twirling, spinning top bounces you up and down with a surprise at the top. AA (**TTTT** under-5s); and **Primeval Whirl:** coaster fans will get a laugh out of this wacky offering that sends its riders through a maze of curves, hills and (quite sharp) drops that make it seem faster than it actually is. It's basically a lampoon of the DINOSAUR! ride, a mock journey 'way back in time', with plenty of cartoon frippery. Extra fun is provided by the fact that the cars spin, which gives an unpredictable element to each 3min ride. The queuing area is a riot of visual gags, but the ride is not recommended for anyone with back or neck problems. **Restrictions:** 4ft/122cm. **TTTT** FP

Other entertainment: Dino-Rama also features the **Fossil Fun Games**, 6 fairground-type stalls (costing a rather hefty $4–15) designed to tempt you into trying to win a large cuddly dinosaur. Caribbean steel drum band **The Tropicals** perform up to 5 times a day and there are **Disney character** meet-and-greets across from TriceraTop Spin.

Wild Africa Trek

© Disney

Shopping and dining: Chester and Hester's Dinosaur Treasures (the 'Fossiliferous Gift Store' – groan!) offers a wide range of dino-related souvenirs. You can get a counter-service meal at the (you've guessed it!) **Restaurantosaurus** (burgers, hot dogs and salad) or grab a snack at **PetriFries**.

Parades and tours

Mickey's Jammin' Jungle Parade: The daily highlight is a tour de force in which the Imagineers have created a series of fanciful 'Expedition Rovers' that give Disney characters the chance to celebrate all the animals that live here. The parade is enhanced by stilt-walkers, puppets, mobile sculptures and different 'party animals', plus live percussionists as it snakes down a narrow path from Harambe, around Discovery Island and back. With memorable musical backing, it sounds as good as it looks, while 25 park guests are chosen to take part every day, travelling on the back of amusingly designed rickshaws that follow each of the character jeeps. AAAAA

Tours: Finally, for a behind-the-scenes look at the park, **Backstage Safari** is a wonderful 3hr journey into the handling and care of all the animals ($77, no under-16s), while **Wild By Design** offers a 3hr tour of the park's art, architecture and history and how it was all created ($64, no under-14s). For something really different, try the new **Wild Africa Trek**, a 3hr ride-and-trek into the African savannah. From a precarious rope bridge crossing high above Harambe Reserve to a VIP safari and a visit to Harambe's private camp, this exclusive experience is open to ages 9 and up, 6 times daily. Closed toe shoes required, weight limit 350lb/158kg. Seasonal pricing $189–249. Book tours on 407 939 8687.

That's the full Disney theme park story, but there is still PLENTY more in store…!

It's time to leave the wonderful world of Disney and venture out into the rest of Central Florida's great tourist attractions. And, believe us, there's still a terrific amount in store.

For a start, they don't come much more ambitious than Universal Orlando. The area that used to consist of just 1 theme park, Universal Studios Florida, is now a fully fledged resort in its own right. Second park Islands of Adventure opened in 1999, as well as the CityWalk entertainment district. The first hotel, Portofino Bay, also opened in 1999, followed by the Hard Rock Hotel and Royal Pacific Resort in 2000 and 2002 respectively. Other recent additions include **Blue Man Group** in 2007 (p290), the amazing **Hollywood Rip Ride Rockit** coaster in 2009, and the biggest thing to hit Orlando in more than 10 years, 2010's **The Wizarding World of Harry Potter**.

A waterway network connects the hotels to the CityWalk hub, while the multi-storey car parks, for more than 20,000 vehicles, have done away with the need for any other transport system, as it is easy to move between parks. The Orlando FlexTicket tie-up with SeaWorld and Busch Gardens, plus the purchase of the Wet 'n Wild water park, has also proved a success – not to mention great value. It's certainly a multi-day experience these days and there are periodic special ticket deals. In 2011, UK ticket outlets featured a Universal 2-Park Bonus ticket with unlimited admission for 14 days for little more than the cost of 2 1-day tickets and a 3-Park Bonus (with Wet 'n Wild) also valid for unlimited admission over 2 weeks. Sadly, Universal does not offer a free system like Disney's FastPass, only the paid-for **Universal Express Plus**, a day pass providing 1-time access to all their rides (with the exception of Hollywood Rip Ride Rockit in Universal Studios, and Harry Potter and the Forbidden Journey and Pteranodon Flyers in Islands of Adventure) with minimal queuing – for an extra $20–80 ($26–90 for both parks) per person, depending on time of year. A limited number go on sale after park opening and are snapped up, but they can also be bought online for a specific day at **www. universalorlando.com** or in the parks themselves for another day. The new **Park to Park VIP Ticket** provides park admission AND unlimited **Express Plus** front-of-queue access for 1, 2, 3, 4 or 7 days, from $160-380/adult, $150–360/child (online only). It does save time, but at quieter times of the year it can be unnecessary. Universal hotel guests benefit from Express ride priority all day by showing their room key. In addition, some rides have Single Rider queues, which save time if you want to go by yourself or don't mind splitting up your group. Once again, height/health restrictions are noted in ride descriptions.

Universal Studios Florida®

Universal opened its first Florida park in June 1990 (its original Los Angeles movie site opened to the public in 1917!) and quickly became a serious rival to Disney. For the visitor, it means a consistently high standard and good value (though the choice can be bewildering), but there are few similarities to the LA Studios. Universal is also a different proposition to Disney, with a more in-your-face style that appeals especially to teens. Younger children are still well catered for, though. Universal parks can also need more than a full day in high season. Strategies are the same, though: arrive EARLY (up to 30mins before opening), do the big rides first, avoid main meal times and take time out for an afternoon break (try shopping, dining or visiting the cinemas at CityWalk) if it gets too crowded.

Location

Universal Studios Florida® is divided into 6 main areas, set around a large, man-made lagoon, but there are no great distinguishing features, so you'll need your map. The main resort entrance is just off Interstate 4 (I-4 eastbound take exit 75A; westbound take exit 74B) or via Universal Boulevard from I-Drive by Wet 'n Wild. Parking is in its massive multi-storey car park and there is quite a walk (with moving walkways) to the front gates.

Beating the queues: Once through, your best bet is to turn right on to Rodeo Drive, along Hollywood Boulevard and Sunset Boulevard and into World Expo for The Simpsons, followed by Men In Black – Alien Attack. From there, head across the bridge to Jaws, then go back along the

Universal Studios Florida® at a glance

Location	Off exits 75A and 74B from I-4; Universal Boulevard and Kirkman Road		
Size	110 acres/45ha in 7 themed areas		
Hours	9am–6 or 7pm off peak; 9am–10pm high season (Washington's birthday, Easter, summer holidays, Thanksgiving, Christmas)		
Admission	Under-3s free; 3–9 $74 (1-day Ticket), $122 (2-day Park to Park Ticket), $255 (FlexTicket), $295 (FlexTicket Plus); adult $82, $134.99, $275, $315. Prices do not include tax.		
Parking	$15 (preferred parking $20; valet parking $25)		
Lockers	Immediately to left in Front Lot $8		
Pushchairs	$14 and $24, kiddie cars $17.99 and $27.99 next to locker hire		
Wheelchairs	$12 and $50 (with photo ID as deposit), with pushchairs		
Top attractions	Revenge of the Mummy, Men in Black, Jaws, ET Adventure, Shrek 4-D, The Simpsons, Terminator 2: 3-D, Hollywood Rip Ride Rockit!		
Don't miss	Universal 360: A Cinesphere Spectacular (peak season only), Curious George Playground (for kids), The Blues Brothers		
Hidden costs	Meals	Burger, chips and coke $8.88 3-course dinner $21–32 (Lombard's) Kids' meal $5.49 ($4.99–7.99 in Finnegan's)	
	T-shirts	$21.95–28.95	
	Souvenirs	95c–$1,500	
	Sundries	Hair braiding from $25 for 5 braids no beads to $175 whole head with beads	

Embarcadero for Disaster! and into New York for Revenge Of The Mummy. This will get most of the main rides under your belt before the crowds build, and you can then take it a bit easier by seeing some of the shows. Alternatively, try to be among the early birds flocking to the Shrek 4-D film show in Production Central and Revenge Of The Mummy in New York to avoid the queues that build up, then visit the likes of The Simpsons and Men in Black. Thrill-ride seekers should head first for the tremendous Hollywood Rip Ride Rockit. Here's a full guide to the Studios (for CityWalk, see Chapter 10, Orlando by Night). Watch out for the helpful mobile electronic **Wait Times** boards around both parks, too.

Production Central

Coming straight through the gates brings you into the administrative centre, with a couple of large gift stores (have a look at these in mid-afternoon) plus **Studio Sweets**. Call at **Guest Services** for guides for disabled visitors, TDD and assisted listening devices, and to make restaurant bookings, which can also be made at

a kiosk to the right after the turnstiles, next to the Beverly Hills Boulangerie. **First aid** is available here (and on Canal Street between New York and San Francisco), while there are facilities for nursing mothers at **Family Services** by the bank through the gates on the right. In addition, Universal Studios hosts **Total Non Stop Action Wrestling** (specific dates April–July), with free tickets available on a first-come, first-served basis (call 407 224 6000 for more details). Coming to the top of the Plaza of the Stars brings you to the business end of the park.

Shrek 4-D: This adds a new dimension to the genre of 3-D films as the original cast of the Oscar-winning *Shrek* movies (Mike Myers, Eddie Murphy, Cameron Diaz and John Lithgow) return for a 13-minute prequel to *Shrek 2*. The evil Lord Farquaad is back in ghost form to welcome visitors to his dungeons and ruin the honeymoon of Shrek and Princess Fiona. The amusing 7min pre-show leads into the 500-seat main theatre, where you don your Ogre Vision 3-D glasses and prepare to enter a new world. The film is

Shrek 4-D

Production Central

1 Main Entrance
2 Shrek 4-D
3 Despicable Me (coming 2012)
4 Hollywood Rip, Ride, Rockit!
5 Donkey's Photo Finish
6 Monsters Café

New York

7 Twister
8 Revenge Of The Mummy
9 The Blues Brothers
10 Alley Climb
11 Finnegan's Bar and Grill
12 Louie's Italian Restaurant

San Francisco/Amity

13 Disaster! A Major Motion Picture Ride ... starring YOU
14 Jaws
15 Beetlejuice's Graveyard Revue
16 Central Lagoon
17 Lombard's Seafood Grille
18 Fear Factor Live

World Expo

19 The Simpsons Ride
20 Men In Black – Alien Attack

Woody Woodpecker's Zidzone

21 Animal Actors On Location!
22 Fievel's Playland
23 A Day In The Park With Barney
24 ET Adventure
25 Woody Woodpecker's Nuthouse Coaster
26 Curious George Goes To Town

Hollywood

27 Universal's Horror Make-Up Show
28 Terminator 2: 3-D Battle Across Time
29 Lucy: A Tribute
30 Guest Services
31 Mel's Drive-In
32 Café La Bamba

Hollywood Rip Ride Rocket

funny enough as Shrek and Donkey save the Princess, but the special effects (watch out for the spiders!) and moving seats add a startling extra element that is hugely entertaining. State-of-the-art digital projection and audio systems, lighting effects and smoke (plus a hilarious finale featuring an out-of-control Tinker Bell) ensure a real laugh-fest. A major draw, so try to go first thing or expect waits of an hour-plus. AAAAA+.

Despicable Me: coming in summer 2012 is this new attraction based on the big 2010 animated film starring Steve Carell, taking the place of the former **Jimmy Neutron** simulator ride. With state-of-the-art new 3-D film projectors, guests are invited to visit super-villain Gru and his laboratory, being shrunk to the size of Minions along the way. Next it's time to get some training in the inimitable Gru style – but be ready for things to go wrong. There are some dastardly twists and turns along the way, with the evil Vector lurking to ruin Gru's plans, so hang on tight – things are going to get bumpy! Those with heart, neck, or back problems should ask for the stationary seats. TTT (TTTTT under-10s).

Hollywood Rip Ride Rockit!: This iconic ride is a high-tech colossus, a roller-coaster packed with unique

features and audio-visual gizmos that allow you to select your own ride music – then take home the DVD afterwards. The dimensions alone are daunting – at 167ft/51m it is Orlando's highest coaster and, at almost 70mph/113kph, it is also the fastest. You can't miss it as it loops out of the front of the park by the Blue Man Group theatre in CityWalk and runs to the back of the park, too, curling around and through the buildings of the New York area – a vivid red steel beast that dares you to ride it! It starts with a video intro while you queue that reveals 5 music choices (Rap/Hip Hop, Country, Classic Rock/Metal, Pop/Disco and Club Electronica), with 6 tracks in each category. You're then strapped into an open-sided car that goes straight up a vertical lift-hill 17-storeys high. Breathless yet? You soon will be – the ride goes into a

Jaws

© OCVB

steep dive and then the signature Double Take, the world's first non-inverted loop (you don't actually go upside-down but it feels like it!). Two more first-of-a-kind features follow – the Treble Clef (a twisting manoeuvre shaped like the musical symbol) and Jump Cut (a spiralling zero-gravity roll that feels like a corkscrew but again without an inversion) – with another 3 breathtaking manoeuvres before you return to the station. You will soar over the heads of people in the queue, dive below ground level and fly around a 150° banked turn, all in the course of the 1min 40sec ride. The innovative open cars make the whole experience feel even faster and more dynamic than it actually is, while the mix of pounding music (from your headrest and speakers along the track) and concert-style lighting (flashy enough during the day, stunning at night) ensure this is a ride that really rocks. You can then opt to buy the ride video, complete with your musical selection that is captured by multiple cameras both in your car and along the track (for $35; ride photo $19.95). In truth, it looks more frightening than it actually is, and it is truly exhilarating. **Restrictions:** 4ft 3in/130cm. TTTTT+ Our music choice? *Bring Me To Life* by Evanescence in the Rock/Metal category. Kicking!).

BRITTIP

If you don't empty your pockets before riding Rip Ride Rockit, you'll find them empty by the end of the ride! Put ALL loose items in the free lockers.

Other entertainment: Meet Shrek, Fiona and Donkey on 8th Avenue for **Donkey's Photo Finish**, well worth catching for the amusing patter. And look for a **SpongeBob** photo opportunity in the Nickstuff Store.

Shopping and dining: You'll find some of the best of the shops here, including **On Location** (film, apparel, sundries and 2-way radio rentals), **Nickstuff** (Toon merchandise with Jimmy Neutron, SpongeBob SquarePants and Dora the Explorer), the massive **Universal Studios Store** (the full range of gifts, plus Harry Potter merchandise, including wands) and **It's A Wrap** (discounted items). The main eating outlet is the wonderful **Monsters Café**, offering salads, pasta, ribs, pizza and chicken (peak season only). The counter-service area is themed like Frankenstein's lab, with the dining areas subdivided into Swamp, Space, Crypt and Mansion Dining, all accompanied by old black-and-white horror film clips.

Woody Woodpecker's Nuthouse Coaster

© OCVB

Twister

New York

From Production Central, you head to New York and some impressive architecture and detail. It's too clean to be authentic, but the façades are first class.

Twister: This experience, based on the hit film, brings audiences 'up close and personal' with the awesome destructive forces of a tornado. The 5-storey terror shatters everything in its path (OK, it's pretty tame compared to the real thing), building to a shattering climax of destruction (watch for the flying cow!). The noise can be a bit much for under-10s, so parental discretion is advised. The pre-show area is a work of art but do it early or late in the day. TTT.

Revenge Of The Mummy: This superb offering in Orlando's roller-coaster catalogue is a high-thrill, high-fun journey into the world of The Mummy film series. It features an indoor spin into Ancient Egypt, fusing coaster technology with space-age robotics and special effects. It starts out as a dark ride (a slow journey through the shadowy, curse-ridden interior of Hamunaptra, The City of the Dead) but soon evolves into something far

more dynamic – with a breathtaking launch.

BRITTIP

For the best ride experience on Revenge Of The Mummy, try to get a back row seat. You are not allowed to carry anything on the ride – loose items must be left in the (free) lockers provided.

The basic premise of the film studio becoming a full archaeological discovery is a good one, and the transition from dark ride to coaster is ingenious, with a host of special effects and audio-animatronics as you brave the Mummy's realm. The high-speed whiz in the dark

Revenge of the Mummy

New York

(backwards to start with) doesn't involve inversions but is still a thrill with its tight turns and dips, while there are several clever twists (the front row may get slightly damp!). It is a hugely immersive experience and, with the elaborate queuing area, is a real 5-star attraction. However, it is probably too scary for under-8s. Be sure to preview your ride photos ($24.95–39.95) as you enter the gift shop. **Restrictions:** 4ft/122cm. TTTT½.

The Blues Brothers

The Blues Brothers: Fans of the film will not want to miss this live show as Jake and Elwood Blues (or pretty good doubles anyway) put on a stormin' performance on New York's Delancey Street several times a day. They cruise up in their Bluesmobile and go through a series of the film's hits before heading off into the sunset, stopping only for autographs. AAAA.

Other entertainment: The energetic can try the **Alley Climb** (rock wall) on 5th Avenue ($5). New York also boasts the inevitable amusement arcade.

Shopping and dining: Check out **Sahara Traders** for Mummy souvenirs, as well as jewellery and toys, **Rosie's Irish Shop** for all things Irish and **Aftermath** for Twister souvenirs. For dining, you have 2 main restaurants: **Finnegan's Bar and Grill** offers shepherd's pie, fish and chips, corned beef and cabbage, along with steak, burgers, fries and a good range of beers, plus Irish-tinged entertainment and Happy Hour 4–7pm ($3.50 Bud and Bud Light; $4.50 imported beers), while **Louie's Italian Restaurant** has counter-service pizza and pasta, ice-cream and tiramisu. There's also a **Ben and Jerry's** store for ice-cream and smoothies, and a **Starbucks** for coffee and pastries.

San Francisco/Amity

Crossing Canal Street brings you right across America to San Francisco/Amity and 2 more serious queues.

Disaster! A Major Motion Picture Ride... Starring YOU: This hugely funny 3-part adventure gets busy from mid-morning until late afternoon and goes behind the scenes into film special effects in the mythical Disaster Studios. You go first into the Screening Room, where your tour host interacts with a creative projection of actor Christopher Walken (playing Studios boss Frank Kincaid in high style) to set the scene for the Sound Stage (a sequence of amusing set-pieces using audience volunteers) and then the Disaster Set – an underground train ride into a San Francisco earthquake, with YOU as the 'extras'. Tremble as walls and ceilings collapse, trains collide, fire erupts and a tidal wave of water pours in. Finally, check out how you did on the screen at the end, which reveals some hilarious results! It's probably a touch scary for small children, while those with bad backs or necks or expectant mothers should not ride the final scene. Restrictions: 4ft/122cm (unless accompanied by an adult, with parental discretion). AAAA and TTT.

Jaws: The technical wizardry alone will amaze you here, and queues of an hour are common as you head out into the waters of this mini 'Amity'. This is no ordinary ride, and its 6-minute duration will seem a lot longer as your hapless boat guide steers you through a spectacular series of stunts, explosions and menace from the Great White. You WILL be impressed – and just a little scared. It can also be a wet experience for those sitting on the right! TTTT.

Beetlejuice's Graveyard Revue: Disney's Hollywood Studios has *Beauty and the Beast* and *The Little Mermaid*: Universal goes for *Dracula, Frankenstein, The Wolfman* and *Frankenstein's Bride* in this 20-minute 'shock 'n' roll' extravaganza, compèred by Beetlejuice himself. The raucous concert shuns the prettiness of Disney's attractions yet still comes up with a fun family show, as the graveyard characters perform specially adapted rock and pop anthems (like Dancing in the Dark and Jump) with a mock-horror theme in a great setting. AAAA.

Fear Factor Live (high season only): This live action version of the reality TV show asks audience volunteers to take part in some hair-raising (and stomach-churning!) challenges, with a head-to-head competition to find the biggest daredevil. Auditions take place 70mins before each show, and the audience then gets to see the chosen few battle it out, with clips from the TV show interspersed with live action. Some of the stunts are distinctly off-colour (anyone for a maggot milkshake?) and may not be good for young children (or anyone of a weak disposition!), but it is a well-staged production. TTT.

Other entertainment: A **Boardwalk** of fairground games (for additional cost to play) includes an amusing Guess Your Weight stall.

San Francisco

Shopping and dining: Visit **Quint's Surf Shack** (beach apparel and other clothing), **Oakley** (sunglasses and accessories), **Amazing Pictures** (have your photo superimposed on a variety of film backgrounds; $29–49.99) and the **San Francisco Candy Factory** (great pick-n-mix!). This area also has the park's best dining choices, with **Lombard's Seafood Grill** the highlight (high season only; reservations accepted). Great seafood, pasta and sandwiches are accompanied by a good view over the Central Lagoon. **San Francisco Pastry Co** offers desserts and coffee, **Richter's Burger Co** has some tempting burger options and **Midway Grill** provides hot dogs and fries.

World Expo

Crossing the bridge brings you to a rather nondescript area, but home to 2 of the park's most amusing attractions.

The Simpsons Ride: This brings the world of Springfield to vibrant life in a colourful and amusing production, even if you're not a fan of The Simpsons. It is themed as Krustyland amusement park, brainchild of irascible Krusty the Clown, a bizarre funfair that is the setting for a hectic,

Men in Black

The Simpsons Ride

breathtaking ride in the company of Homer, Bart, Lisa, Marge and Maggie. A wicked sound system and state-of-the-art motion simulator technology ensure a frantic race through outlandish attractions (watch out for the Tooth Chipper!) with the Simpsons by your side. The feel of the 'ride' is amazing and the huge domed screen ensures an outrageously comical sensory experience. All the characters have been voiced by the original stars and even the queuing area is a riot of visual hilarity. However, this can also be the park's biggest draw, hence you need to do this early or expect a LONG queue. **Restrictions:** 3ft 4in/101cm. TTTTT.

Men in Black – Alien Attack: This combination thrill/dark ride takes up where the hit films, starring Will Smith, left off. Visitors are secretly introduced to the MIB Institute in an inventive mock-futuristic setting and enrolled as trainees for a battle around the streets of New York with a horde of escaped aliens. Your 6-person car is equipped with laser zappers for an interactive shoot-out that is like a real-life arcade game, as the aliens can also shoot back to send your car spinning. The finale features a close encounter with a 30ft/9m bug

A Day in the Park with Barney

that is all mouth. Will you survive? Only your collective shooting skills can save the day, and there are numerous ride variations according to your accuracy. Will Smith and Rip Torn are your on-screen hosts, and Will returns at the end to reveal if your score makes you Galaxy Defenders, Cosmically Average or Bug Bait! Fast, frantic and a bit confusing, you'll want to come back until you can top 250,000 (for Defender status). **Restrictions:** 3ft 6in/106cm. **TTTT.**

BRITTIP
For a big score in Men In Black, when you meet the Big Bug – push the big red button!

Shopping and dining: To complete the Springfield effect, visit the **Kwik-E-Mart** for a range of Simpsons souvenirs (plus more trademark humour), while **MIB Gear** has more themed gifts and clothing. **The International Food and Film Festival** is a food court offering Italian, American, Asian and salads (in air-conditioned comfort), while Expo Eats offers drinks and snacks.

BRITTIP
Along the lagoon in the World Expo/KidZone area is East Green, a quiet spot where you can stop to take a break for a while.

KidZone

This is great place to let the kids loose for a while, but it does also feature several great family attractions.

Animal Actors On Location!: An amusing mix of video, animal performance and audience interaction, several children are invited to help present some unlikely feats and stunts featuring a range of wildlife, from a raccoon to a snake, and on to cats and dogs. Many have been rescued from animal shelters and gone on to feature in films before finding a home at Universal. The theatre also provides an escape from the queues. AAAA.

Fievel's Playland: Strictly for kids, this playground, based on the enlarged world of the cartoon mouse, offers the chance to bounce under a 1,000-gallon hat, crawl through a giant boot, climb a giant spider's web and shoot the rapids (a 200ft/61m waterslide) in Fievel's sardine can. TTTT (young 'uns only!).

A Day in the Park with Barney: Again strictly for the younger set (2–5), the purple dinosaur from kids' TV is brought to super-dee-duper life in a large arena that features a pre-show before the 15-minute main event, plus an interactive post-show area. Parents will cringe but the youngsters

Curious George Goes to Town

love it. NB: Check out the amazing loos! AA (AAAAA under-5s).

ET Adventure: This is as glorious as scenic rides come, with a picturesque queuing area from the film and then a spectacular leap on the trademark flying bicycles to save ET's home planet. Steven Spielberg has added some special effects and characters, and you have an individual ET greeting at the end. The masses often overlook this corner of the park, hence it is worth saving for later in the day. **Restriction:** 4ft/122cm to ride alone, but smaller children can ride with parents. AAAAA

Woody Woodpecker's Nuthouse Coaster: Anchoring the excellent under-10s adventure land is this child-sized but still quite racy roller-coaster. The ride reaches only 28ft/8m high and 22mph, but it seems the real deal to young 'uns. However, the height restriction is still 3ft/91cm. TTTT (juniors only).

Curious George Goes To Town: Kids of all ages love this amazing adventure playground and huge range of activities – with plenty of ways to get wet. It combines toddler play, water-based play stations and a huge interactive ball pool, and is a real bonus for harassed parents. The town theme includes buildings to climb, pumps and hoses to spray water, a ball factory in which to shoot, dump and blast thousands of foam balls and – the tour de force – 2 huge buckets of water that dump their contents on the street below at regular intervals. TTTTT (under-12s). Curious George himself roams the KidZone from time to time, while other characters make regular appearances.

BRITTIP

If you want to let your youngsters loose in the Curious George playground, it is advisable to bring swimsuits or a change of clothing.

Other entertainment: Check out the **Star Toons Show** up to 6 times a day, with music and dance from the 1980s, and a **Madagascar** meet-and-greet with the stars of the cartoon films.

Shopping and dining: Shop at the **Cartoon Store**, **Barney Store** or **ET's Toy Closet** and **Photo Spot**. For a quick bite, **Kidzone Pizza Company** offers pizza and chicken fingers.

UNIVERSAL STUDIOS with children

Our guide to the attractions that generally appeal to the different age groups:

Under-5s
Animal Actors On Location!, Curious George Goes To Town, A Day In The Park With Barney, ET Adventure, Fievel's Playland.

5–8s
All the above (minus Barney), plus Disaster! (with parental discretion), Despicable Me, Men In Black, Shrek 4-D, The Simpsons and Woody Woodpecker's Nuthouse Coaster.

9–12s
All the above, plus Hollywood Rip Ride Rockit, Beetlejuice's Graveyard Revue, Fear Factor Live!, Jaws, Revenge Of The Mummy, Terminator 2: 3-D Battle Across Time, Twister, Universal 360: A Cinesphere Spectacular.

Over-12s
Hollywood Rip Ride Rockit, Beetlejuice's Graveyard Revue, The Blues Brothers, Disaster!, ET Adventure, Fear Factor Live, Jaws, Despicable Me, Men In Black – Alien Attack, Revenge Of The Mummy, Shrek 4-D, The Simpsons, Terminator 2: 3-D Battle Across Time, Twister, Universal 360: A Cinesphere Spectacular, Universal's Horror Make-Up Show.

Hollywood

Finally, your circular tour of Universal returns you to the main entrance via Hollywood (where else?).

Universal's Horror Make-Up Show: Not recommended for under-12s, this demonstrates some of the often amusing ways in which films have attempted to terrorise us, with clips from modern additions to the genre like Van Helsing. It's a 20min show, queues are rarely long and the special effects are well worth discovering. AAA

Terminator 2: 3-D Battle Across Time: Another first-of-its-kind attraction, this is part film, part show, part experience but all action, and usually leaves its audience in awe. The 'Wow!' factor works overtime as you go through a 10min pre-show representing a trip to the Cyberdyne Systems company from the *Terminator* films and then into a 700-seat theatre for a 'presentation' on its latest robot creations. The show is interrupted, though, by John and Sarah Connor and mayhem ensues, with the audience subjected to an array of (loud) special effects, including real actors interacting with the screen and the audience, indoor pyrotechnics and a climactic 3-D film finale that takes the Terminator story a step further. Arnold Schwarzenegger and other members of the original cast collaborated on the 12min movie and the overall effect is dazzling, but you should arrive early or expect queues to top an hour (parental discretion for under-12s). TTTTT.

Lucy: A Tribute: The last attraction (or first, depending on which way you go round) will mean little to all but devoted fans of the late Lucille Ball and her 1960s TV comedy *The Lucy Show*. Classic shows, home movies, costumes and scripts are paraded, but youngsters will find it tedious. AA.

Terminator 2

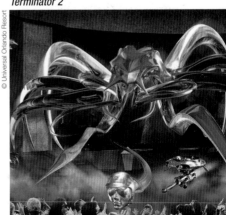

© Universal Orlando Resort

Other entertainment: The Hollywood Character Zone provides numerous character appearances throughout the day along Hollywood Boulevard, from Scooby Do and Shaggy to Dudley Do-Right, The Flintstones and Lucille Ball.

BRITTIP

Budding magicians should make a bee-line for the small Theater Magic shop next to Mel's Drive-In, with merchandise and some terrific small-scale magic shows several times daily.

Shopping and dining: Look for Terminator gifts and clothing in **Cyber Image**, all manner of headgear in **The Brown Derby**, Hollywood legends' jewellery in **Studio Styles** and movie memorabilia in **Silver Screen Collectibles**. There are 4 contrasting eateries: **Mel's Drive-In**, a re-creation from the film *American Graffiti*, serving all manner of burgers and hot dogs (though Richter's has better burgers); **Café La Bamba** for rotisserie chicken, ribs, salad and burgers, plus margaritas and beer (Happy Hour 3–5pm; high season only); **Schwab's Pharmacy**, with traditional ice-cream, milkshakes and sundaes; and **Beverly Hills Boulangerie** for a range of sandwiches, cheesecake, pastries, juices and Seattle's Best coffee.

Special programmes

Universal Studios features some brilliant extra seasonal entertainment for **Mardi Gras**, with a hectic, bead-throwing parade, plus music, street entertainment and authentic New Orleans food each Saturday at 6pm from mid-Feb to late May (and free with park admission). The day culminates in a live concert with well-known acts (like Beach Boys, Foreigner and KC and the Sunshine Band in 2011), but it does draw HUGE crowds. Universal also throws a major party for the **4th of July**, when the park presents a stunning fireworks spectacular, while the **Summer Concert Series** runs on Saturdays in June and July, with stars such as Earth, Wind and Fire, Counting Crows and Train.

Finally, **Universal 360: A Cinesphere Spectacular** brings down the curtain each night in peak season and at special events with a blaze of fireworks and 4 gigantic 'cinespheres' that allow for cinema projection. The overall effect places guests in the middle of their favourite films, with a dramatic musical score (on 300 outdoor speakers), lasers and other pyrotechnics, using the spheres as video screens. It's a stunning performance, so check your park map to see if it's showing during your visit.

Café La Bamba

Islands of Adventure

You could be forgiven for calling this Harry Potter Land since 2010. The much-heralded opening of the Wizarding World gave Universal's second park a huge shot in the arm and massive public appeal (although it has always been a favourite of ours). The Islands of Adventure opened in 1999 under the supervision of creative consultant Steven Spielberg, and it provided 1 of the most complete and thrilling theme parks you could imagine; brilliantly conceived and executed, containing an upbeat collection of high-adrenalin rides, shows and other entertainment, plus some fine dining. Then The Wizarding World of Harry Potter opened in June 2010, adding a whole new land and a world of excitement unlike anything seen in Orlando for years.

Islands of Adventure has a full range of attractions, from the real adrenaline overloads to pure family entertainment, and it even sounds good – with some 40 pieces of original music, you can buy the CD of the theme park! OK, so they aren't really islands (the areas form a chain around the central lagoon), but that's the only illusion. And you get a lot for your money here, unless you have extremely timid children or under-5s. Seuss Landing will usually keep preschoolers amused for several hours, while Camp Jurassic is a clever adventure playground for the 5–12s, but the rest of the park, with its 8 5-star thrill rides and other attractions, is primarily geared to kids of 8 and over, their parents and especially teenagers. There are 6 elements that look alarming, but don't

Islands of Adventure at a glance

Location	Off exits 75A and 74B from I-4; Universal Boulevard and Kirkman Road		
Size	110 acres/45ha in 6 'islands'		
Hours	9am–7pm off peak; 9am–10pm high season (Washington's birthday, Easter, summer holidays, Thanksgiving, Christmas)		
Admission	Under-3s free; 3–9 $74 (1-day Ticket), $122 (2-day Park to Park Ticket), $255 (FlexTicket), $295 (FlexTicket Plus); adult (10+) $82, $134.99, $275, $315. Prices do not include tax.		
Parking	$15 (preferred parking $20; valet parking $25)		
Lockers	Immediately to left through main gates; $8		
Pushchairs	$14.99 and $24.99; next to locker hire.		
Wheelchairs	$12 and $50 (with photo ID as deposit)		
Top attractions	Harry Potter and the Forbidden Journey, Amazing Adventures Of Spider-Man, Dragon Challenge, Incredible Hulk Coaster, Jurassic Park River Adventure, Dudley Do-Right's Ripsaw Falls, The Cat In The Hat		
Don't miss	Eighth Voyage Of Sindbad, Jurassic Park Discovery Centre, If I Ran The Zoo playground (for toddlers), Three Broomsticks restaurant and Ollivander's Wand Shop		
Hidden costs	Meals	Burger, chips and coke $8.88 3-course lunch $19–35 (Confisco Grill) Kids' meal $5.99–6.99 (drink not included)	
	T-shirts	$19-28.95	
	Souvenirs	95c-$500-plus	
	Sundries	Caricature drawings $15–36 (black and white and airbrush colour); Butterbeer $3.25 regular, $4.25 frozen	

Port of Entry
1 Ocean Trader Market
2 Confisco Grille

Marvel Super-Hero Island
3 Incredible Hulk Coaster
4 Dr Doom's Fearfall
5 Café 4
6 Captain America Diner
7 The Amazing Adventures Of Spider-Man
8 Storm Force Accelatron

Toon Lagoon
9 Popeye And Bluto's Bilge-Rat Barges
10 Dudley Do-Right's Ripsaw Falls
11 Me Ship, The Olive
12 Comic Strip Café
13 Toon Lagoon Amphitheater

Jurassic Park
14 Jurassic Park River Adventure
15 Pteranodon Flyers
16 Camp Jurassic
17 Discovery Center
18 Thunder Falls Terrace

The Wizarding World of Harry Potter
19 Harry Potter and the Forbidden Journey
20 Filch's Emporium
21 Flight of the Hippogriff
22 Olivander's
23 Dervish and Banges
24 Three Broomsticks
25 Zonko's
26 Dragon Challenge

The Lost Continent
27 Mythos Restaurant
28 Mystic Fountain
29 The Eighth Voyage of Sindbad
30 Poseidon's Fury

Seuss Landing
31 Seuss Landing Dining
32 High In The Sky Seuss Trolley Train Ride
33 Caro-Seuss-el
34 If I Ran The Zoo
35 The Cat In The Hat
36 One Fish, Two Fish, Red Fish, Blue Fish

Main Entrance

ISLANDS OF ADVENTURE

be put off – they all deliver immense fun as well as terrific spectator value! If any one ride sums up IoA, it is Harry Potter and the Forbidden Journey, which took theme park ride technology to a whole new level.

Private nursing facilities, an open area for feeding and resting (with high chairs) and nappy-changing stations, can be found at the **Family Service Facility** at Guest Services (to the right inside the main gates), while ALL restrooms throughout the park are equipped with **nappy-changing** facilities. **First aid** is provided in Sindbad's Village in the Lost Continent, just across from Oasis Coolers, and in Port of Entry.

Port of Entry

You arrive for IoA as you do for Universal Studios, in the big multi-storey car parks off I-4 and Universal Boulevard and pass right through the CityWalk area, where you come to the main entrance plaza (head for the huge Pharos Lighthouse). As with Universal Studios, you can purchase the **Universal Express Plus** pass for Islands of Adventure ($20–80, depending on time of year) at various locations throughout the park and at Guest Services. Once through the gates, the lockers, pushchair and wheelchair hire are on your left as the

Port of Entry opens up before you. This elaborate 'village' consists of shops and eateries, so push straight on until you hit the main lagoon.

Shopping and dining: Later in the day, return to check out the extensive retail experience at places like **IoA Trading Company** and **Ocean Trader Market**. Enjoy a snack at **Cinnabon** (cinnamon rolls and pastries) or **Croissant Moon Bakery** (excellent coffee, croissants and sandwiches), or chill out with a soft drink or ice-cream from **Arctic Express**. Alternatively, sit down for lunch or dinner (good steaks, pasta, fish, pizza, burgers and salads) at **Confisco Grille** and grab a beverage or snack at the **Backwater Bar** (Happy Hour 4–7pm). There is also a **Character Breakfast** at Confisco Grille (9–10.30am Thurs and Sun) with Universal characters like Spider-Man and The Cat In The Hat, plus The Grinch at Christmas ($21 adults, $13 children; 407 224 4012 for reservations). Above all, take in the wonderful architecture, which borrows from Middle East, Far East and African themes and uses bric-a-brac from all over the world.

Beating the queues: At the end of the street, you will need to decide which way to head first as there are 9 attractions where the queues build up quickly and remain that way most of

Despicable Me

the day. If you are among the majority lured by the massively popular **Wizarding World of Harry Potter** and its outstanding Forbidden Journey and Dragon Challenge rides, turn right (through Seuss Landing and The Lost Continent; bear in mind you may be directed into Jurassic Park to queue just to get into Wizaring World, especially in peak season, which underlines the need to arrive early). If you're after the big thrill rides, turn left into **Marvel Super-Hero Island** and head straight to Spider-Man, then do Dr Doom's Fearfall and the Incredible Hulk Coaster.

> **BRITTIP**
>
> There are 2 entrances to the Wizarding World of Harry Potter: from Jurassic Park and The Lost Continent. The latter is much more dramatic and offers the full Hogsmeade Village panorama.

Dinosaur fans should head straight around the lagoon (turn left) to Jurassic Park, where you can do the River Adventure before the majority arrive. Once you are nice and wet, go back to Toon Lagoon for Ripsaw Falls and the Bilge-Rat Barges. Or, if you have younger children, turn right into the multicoloured world of Seuss Landing and enjoy The Cat In The Hat and High In The Sky Seuss Trolley Train Ride prior to the main crowd build-up.

Turning right, in an anti-clockwise direction, here's what you find.

Green Eggs and Ham

Seuss Landing

There is not a straight line to be seen in this vivid 3-D working of the books of Dr Seuss. The characters may not mean much to those unfamiliar with the children's stories, but everyone can relate to the fun here (though queues build up quickly). Take your time and try not to miss the clever detail, from squirt ponds to beach scenes.

Caro-Seuss-el: This intricate carousel ride on some of the Seuss characters – cowfish, elephant-birds and dog-a-lopes, for example – has rider-activated features that are a big hit with children. AA (AAAA under-5s).

One Fish, Two Fish, Red Fish, Blue Fish: A fairground ride with a twist as you pilot these Seussian fish up and down according to the rhyme that plays while you ride. Get it wrong and you get squirted! More fun for the younger set. TTT (TTTTT under-5s).

The Cat in the Hat: Prepare for a ride with a difference as you board these crazy 6-passenger 'couches' to meet the world's most adventurous cat and friends Thing One and Thing Two. You literally go for a spin through this storybook world, and it may be a bit much for very young children. The slow-moving queues are a bit of a drag, so try to get here early or leave it until later in the day. AAAA/TTT.

If I Ran the Zoo: Interactive playgrounds don't get much better for the pre-school brigade than with these different Seuss character scenarios, some of which can be pretty wet! Hugely imaginative and great fun to watch. TTTTT (under-5s).

The High in the Sky Seuss Trolley Train Ride: This fun family adventure high above Seuss Landing has terrific appeal to youngsters as you board a trolley to journey into the world of the Sneetches, visiting the Inking and Stamping Room, the Star Wash Room and a tour inside the Circus McGurkus Café Stoo-pendous. It is slow-paced and scenic, but it does draw slow-moving queues, so head here early on if your children are 2–8. AAAA.

Other entertainment: Look out for **character appearances** by The Cat In The Hat, Thing One and Thing Two and The Grinch outside the Circus McGurkus, and the character-filled celebration of the **Oh! The Stories You'll Hear** street show.

Shopping and dining: If you have been captivated by the land, you can buy the books at **Dr Seuss' All The Books You Can Read Store**, or a full variety of character merchandise at the **Mulberry Street Store**. **Snookers and Snookers Sweet Candy Cookers** is a super sweet shop, while snacks and drinks can be had at **Hop On Pop Ice Cream Shop**, **Moose Juice Goose Juice** and **Green Eggs and Ham Café** (sandwiches and burgers). The **Circus McGurkus Café Stoo-pendous** is a mind-boggling eatery for fried chicken, lasagne, spaghetti and pizza – with clowns and pipe organs.

The Lost Continent
This land underwent a rather drastic reduction to accommodate Harry Potter. However, it still offers some great attractions.

The Eighth Voyage of Sindbad: This stunt and special effects show is fun for both elaborate staging and performance. Mythical adventurer Sindbad and side-kick Kabob tackle evil witch Miseria in a bid to rescue Princess Amoura, and the action

springs up in surprising places. There are several loud bangs that could scare young children but otherwise it's good family fun. There is also a post-show feature where the cast reappear for photos and autographs. TT/AAAA.

Poseidon's Fury: A walk-through show that puts its audience at the heart of the action as a journey in the company of a hapless young archaeologist takes a turn for the worse in the lost temple of Poseidon. You pass through an amazing water vortex before your expedition awakens an ancient demon. There is an element of suspense, but the special effects showdown between Poseidon and the demon is amazing. Queuing is tedious, but it is inside. TTT.

Other entertainment: For an extra fee, try the **Pitch and Skill Games** or a bit of mystic manipulation with **Psychic Readers**. But beware **The Mystic Fountain**; it can strike up a conversation – and then soak you!

Shopping and dining: Find some original souvenirs at **The Coin Mint** (watch coins forged and struck) and **Historic Families** (explore the history of your family name and coat of arms), **Treasures of Poseidon** (jewellery, apparel), and **The Pearl Factory** (pick an oyster). Food options include **The Fire-Eater's Grill**

Poseidon's Fury

Hogwarts

(sausages, chips and drinks) and **Frozen Desert** (sundaes and sodas). The ornate **Mythos Restaurant** provides the best dining in IoA; the food (seafood, salads, grills, pizza and pasta) is first class, but the setting (inside a dormant volcano with fountains and clever lighting) is a real attraction (3-course meal $18-33, kids' meals $5.99–10.99).

The Lost Continent

Wizarding World of Harry Potter

This 'Island' is now THE big draw in Orlando and has significantly boosted the park's attendance since it opened in June 2010. The magnificent edifice of Hogwarts Castle looms large over the 20-acre spread of the famous Wizarding World but *everything* you see here takes you fully inside this incredible creation, which owes much to the design genius of the film series but is also faithful to the books. Entering from The Lost Continent area provides the grand view, through Hogsmeade and with Hogwarts seemingly towering above (the use of architectural perspective is masterful), and you are drawn into an all-encompassing realm where chimneys smoke, icicles glitter, owls roost, visitors are warned to 'Observe the spell limits' and Butterbeer is real!

Hogsmeade Village: Walk through the grand archway into the Wizarding World and a powerful sense of realism envelops you. This is a shimmering, ancient, snow-covered extravaganza, a fully immersive and interactive version of the magical settlement Harry, Ron and Hermione inhabit. It is the shopping and dining heart of the Wizarding World, but is an attraction in itself. Here you will find the **Hogwarts Express**, puffing and steaming as it awaits its passengers, and, while you can't board Engine 5972, it makes a wonderful photo opportunity. Nearly all the shop windows feature clever 'wizardly' animatronic touches; the **Owl Clock** comes to life every 15mins; the wooden-raftered **Owlery** is a work of art; and you may just encounter Moaning Myrtle in the loos! Numerous other clever effects and design touches all help to transform this corner of Florida into J K Rowling's authentic creation (see also Shopping and dining). **AAAAA+**

Dragon Challenge: This towering coaster sees riders delve into the *Goblet of Fire* story involving the big contest between the wizarding schools of Hogwarts, Durmstrang and Beauxbatons, represented by the billowing banners at the entrance. The long, elaborate queuing area (we LOVE the Corridor of Candles!) sets the scene for your 'flight' on either a Chinese Fireball or Hungarian Horntail dragon, with perils aplenty. You choose which dragon to ride (the tracks differ slightly) and this is a suspended coaster, so your legs dangle free – the initial drop is therefore like going into free-fall! Coaster aficionados reckon the best ride is in the back of the Hungarian (blue) dragon, but both offer an awesome experience. The coaster features a 100ft/30m drop,

multiple loops, twists and 3 near-miss encounters at almost 60mph/96kph. **Restrictions:** 4ft 6in/137cm; all loose items *must* be left in the lockers by the entrance. **TTTTT+**.

BRITTIP
The lockers for Dragon Challenge are in the Hogsmeade train station, but are free only for the duration of your ride. Make a note of your locker number!

The Flight of The Hippogriff: This junior-sized coaster is aimed primarily at youngsters and features a journey into Hagrid's realm, where his love of outlandish creatures gives rise to this swooping ride. Hagrid offers instructions and warnings as you wind through the queue, and you may even hear Fang barking from inside his hut. There are no big drops, but it delivers a surprisingly fast-paced whirl. Be sure to bow to the Hippogriff at the start of the ride, though! **Restrictions:** 3ft 4in/92cm. **TTT** (**TTTT** for 6–12s

Harry Potter and the Forbidden Journey: This is the Big One: a trip inside the legendary halls of Hogwarts, and a breathtaking plunge on a state-of-the-art ride, Quidditch and all. The basic premise is that 'muggles' (non-wizarding types, i.e.

Portrait Gallery at Hogwarts

you!) have been invited to tour the school for the first time and you get to see much of the castle's interior. The queuing area is part discovery, part story-telling, part entertainment – and wholly mind-blowing (especially as it winds through, out, around and back in again for some 400 metres before you even get to the ride!). Be ready for a LONG time on your feet as you traverse the corridors, traipse through the greenhouse, tiptoe along the Portrait Hall (where the paintings of the 4 founders of Hogwarts come to life in magical fashion) and tread the stone floors of the Gryffindor common room. Along the way, you'll be greeted by Professor Dumbledore in his study (complete with more talking portraits), be accosted by the Fat Lady (another painting-come-to-life) and enter the Defence Against the Dark Arts classroom, where Harry, Ron and Hermione urge visitors to abandon their 'boring' tour and come to the Quidditch match (with the aid of a magic spell).

BRITTIP

Once again, this is an unpredictable, dynamic ride, with sudden twists, turns and tilts. You are strongly advised to leave all loose items in the free-to-use lockers just inside the castle.

Finally, you reach the Room of Requirement (past the Sorting Hat), where your mode of transport to the match is revealed – magical flying benches. With some pre-ride warnings ('It flies like a dragon with its tail on fire!'), you are then strapped in to your 'bench' and (with the aid of some Floo-powder) are up, up and away. Only things don't go as planned and, before you can say 'Expecto Patronum' you're on a crazy dash through some of the young wizard's most dangerous adventures. Your unique ride vehicle – which moves on a giant robotic arm – sweeps you through dramatic settings that combine clever film technology with full-scale, all-encompassing scenery,

Harry Potter and the Forbidden Journey

© Universal Orlando Resort

creating a totally convincing effect as you move up, down, backwards, forwards and even sideways.

A close encounter with a fire-breathing dragon sends you off course into the Forbidden Forest, where an army of giant spiders lays in wait before Hermione comes to the rescue, via a narrow escape with the clutches of the Whomping Willow. That only paves the way for a battle with the Dementors, who try to grab you and deliver their deadly kiss in a spooky underground cavern. Naturally, Harry is there to save the day and bring you safely back to Hogwarts for a warm welcome from all the main characters. The 4-minute whirl will seem a LOT longer as the ride's breathtaking sequence of special effects make this an eye-popping extravaganza of sound, movement and high-tech dynamics. It is genuinely one of the most astounding theme park experiences anywhere in the world but it WILL scare small children (and those with arachnophobia!), and it draws HUGE queues – in excess of 3 hours at times in summer 2011 – so you are strongly advised to do this early in the day. **Restrictions:** 4ft/122cm. **TTTTT+** You exit through **Filch's Emporium of Confiscated Goods**, where you'll find plush Hedwig owls, Crookshank cats, Scabbers rats and 3-headed dogs (watch out, he growls!), plus a range of tempting Azkaban and House-related clothing and gifts. You also pick up your ride photos here ($16.99–35.99).

BRITTIP

Look out for the Marauders Map in Filch's Emporium, plus other clever Hogwarts signature gadgets and gizmos among the merchandise.

Other entertainment: Hogwarts' students work in the shops and restaurant, and wander the streets, but the real entertainment in Hogsmeade is the **TriWizard Spirit Rally**, celebrating the upcoming tournament. Witches from the Beauxbatons Academy of Magic perform ribbon dances and wizards from Durmstrang Institute pose staff-fighting challenges. Hogwarts is represented by the **Frog Choir** (4 students and 2 enormous, hilarious frogs!), an ensemble whose unique vocal talents result in an immensely entertaining show.

BRITTIP

Butterbeer is non-alcoholic and comes in 2 sweet varieties, 'regular' and frozen (slushie style). Try both, as they taste quite different!

Shopping and dining: As with all things here, the level of detail given to shopping and dining locations is so intricate they are really attractions in their own right. Many items can be found only here in Hogsmeade, but whether you pull your wallet out or not, be sure to have a wander through each to soak up the atmosphere.

When shopping, be sure to visit, **Zonko's**, George and Fred Weasley's favourite stomping ground, which predictably sells novelty items and joke gifts, such as the Sneakoscope, Extendable Ears and Screaming YoYo. **Sweetshop Honeydukes** is the place for Cauldron Cakes, Bertie Bott's Every Flavour Beans and Chocolate Frogs! Find 136 varieties of sweets, many from the Harry Potter films or well-known British favourites (including jelly babies, humbugs

Zonko's

© Universal Orlando Resort

Michael Douglas and Catherine Zeta-Jones at the first anniversary

and sherbet lemons). **Dervish and Banges**, Hogsmeade's general store, supplies 'students' with Quidditch gear and school related clothing and robes, Luna Lovegood's 3-D Quibbler, and even the Nimbus and Nimbus 2001 broomsticks. **Owl Post:** Purchase your wand here after visiting Ollivander's, and don't miss sending a letter by owl! Your mail will receive 1 of 4 different Hogsmeade postmarks, a wonderful little detail friends and family back home can enjoy. Also here are stationery and owl-related gifts. Every wizard needs a wand, and incredible **Ollivander's** has 13 varieties to choose from. Here, 'the wand also chooses the wizard,' with surprising special effects similar to those Harry experienced when choosing his wand. Because the environment is interactive and the shop is small, a limited number of guests are allowed inside for each 'show'. Queue up early here as wait times are long all day. AAAAA.

There is only 1 sit-down dining location here, but it's a corker. A 'Cathedral to Butterbeer', **The Three Broomsticks** menu features British favourites such as shepherd's pie, fish and chips and Cornish pasties, along with the Great Feast, a family-style meal of salad, ribs, chicken, roast potatoes and corn on the cob ($49.99

party of 4; $12.99 per extra person). Entrées range from $7.99–13.99, with desserts $3.49–3.99, including strawberry and peanut-butter ice cream, found only in the Wizarding World. Next door is the **Hogs Head Pub** where you'll find Hogs Head Brew ($6.50), created especially for the Wizarding World, and complete with animatronic boar's head!

BRITTIP

Of all the buildings, The Three Broomsticks is a must-see experience of dramatic interior design and special effects. Look up in the rafters for arriving owls, magical maids and Dobby the House Elf!

All in all, it's an immense collection of vivid and charming elements (witness the animated *Prisoner of Azkaban* poster in Hogsmeade) that add up to a vivid portrayal of J K Rowling's work. You don't need to be a fan to enjoy the Wizarding World and the only snags are the crowds it draws for much of the day, as most of the shops are quite small and quickly feel crowded. Arriving early is highly advisable, but you should also try to see it after dark, when the lighting effects make it even more dramatic. But just take your time and wander the area, and we're sure you'll feel quite magical.

Jurassic Park

Leaving the comic-book lands behind, you travel back to the Cretaceous age and the make-believe dinosaur film world. Again, the immersive style is first class and the extravagant scenery will have you looking over your shoulder for stray dinos.

Jurassic Park River Adventure: From scenic splendour, the mood changes to hidden menace as your journey into this magnificent waterborne realm brings you up close and personal with some seriously realistic dinosaurs. Inevitably, your passage is diverted from the safe to the hazardous, and the danger increases as the 16-person raft climbs into the heights of the main building – with raptors loose everywhere. You are aware of something large lurking in the shadows – will you fall prey to the T-Rex, or will your boat take the 85ft/26m plunge to safety (plus a good soaking, down the longest water descent in the world)? Queues usually move briskly but will top an hour in mid-afternoon. **Restrictions:** 3ft 6in/106cm. The ride photo comes in various packages ($16–24). **TTTT**

> ◆ **BRITTIP**
> Automobile Association members receive a 10% discount on all ride photos at Universal Orlando.

Pteranodon Flyers: The slow-moving queues are a major turn-off, especially for a fairly average ride, which glides gently over much of Jurassic Park (though it reaches a height of almost 30ft/9m). **Restrictions:** It is designed mainly for kids, and anyone OVER the height range of 3ft–4ft 8in/91–142cm (usually 11+) must be accompanied by a child of the right height. **TT** (**TTTT** under-9s).

Camp Jurassic: More excellent kids' fare with the mountainous jungle giving way to an 'active' volcano for youngsters to explore, climb and slide down. Squirt guns and spitter dinosaurs add to the fun (for kids, but parents can explore!). **TTTT**

Discovery Center: This indoor centre offers various interactive games, like creating a dinosaur via DNA sequencing, mixing your own DNA with a dino on a touch-screen, seeing through the eyes of various large reptiles and handling 'dino eggs', plus other hands-on exhibits. It's ideal in summer as it's fully air-conditioned (10am–5pm; 7pm peak season). **AAA**

Other entertainment: The more adventurous can try the **Rock Climbing Wall** (just outside River Adventure) for an extra $5.

Shopping and dining: Visit **Dinostore** for the best shopping, while you can try **Burger Digs** (huge burger platters), **Pizza Predattoria**, **Thunder Falls Terrace** (counter service for rotisserie chicken and salads, plus a great view of River Adventure) or the **Watering Hole** bar (Happy Hour 3–5pm).

Toon Lagoon

The thrills continue here with a watery theme and more comic-book elements as the (US) newspaper cartoon characters take a bow. Children will also love the fountains, squirt pools and overflowing fire hydrants!

Popeye And Bluto's Bilge-Rat Barges: Every park seems to have a variation on the white-water raft ride, but this is one of the wettest! Fast, bouncy and unpredictable, it has water coming at you from every direction, a couple of sizeable drops and a whirl through the Octoplus Grotto that adds to the fun. If you don't want to get wet, don't ride, because there is no escaping

Jurassic Park River Adventure

the deluge here. This is also one of the top 5 for long queues (at least when it's hot), but it's worth the wait. **Restrictions:** 4ft/ 122cm. Look for the Water Blasters (for 25c) on the bridge to give riders a wet start. TTTTT

BRITTIP
A change of clothes is often advisable after the Barges, unless it's so hot you need to cool down in a hurry. Bring a waterproof bag for your valuables or leave them in a locker.

Dudley Do-Right's Ripsaw Falls: Universal's designers also hit the jackpot with this flume ride that sends its passengers on a wild (and steep!) journey in the company of guileless Mounties Dudley Do-Right, bidding to save girlfriend Nell from the evil Snidely Whiplash. The action builds to an explosive finale at the top of a 75ft/27m abyss that drops you through the roof of a ramshackle dynamite shack to the lagoon below. Just awesome – as are the queues from mid-morning to late afternoon. Wet? You bet! **Restrictions:** 3ft 8in/111cm. TTTTT There are more Water Blasters here (25c) on the bridge overlooking the final drop to get riders even wetter.

Me Ship, The Olive: This purpose-built kids' playland is designed as a 3-storey boat full of interactive fun

and games, including water cannons, bells and slides (ideal for squirting riders on the Bilge-Rat Barges below), in best Popeye style. TTTT (for youngsters)

Other entertainment: The **Toon Lagoon Amphitheatre** stages seasonal live shows (like the high-flying skateboard, roller-blade and BMX bike stunts of **Mat Hoffman's Aggro Circus** in spring and summer 2011), while **Toon Character Zone**, on King's Row and Comic Strip Lane, is the place to meet the area's many characters like Beetle Bailey, Hagar the Horrible, Betty Boop, Popeye, The Flintstones and Dudley Do-Right.

Shopping and dining: There is the usual array of character shops, like **Gasoline Alley**, **Boop Oop A Doop** and **Toon Extra**, while you can grab a humongous sandwich at **Blondie's** (home of the Dagwood), a trademark burger at **Wimpy's**, sample the food court of **Comic Strip Café** (Mexican, Chinese, American and Italian), something cool at **Cathy's Ice Cream** or a cold beverage at **Ale To The Chief**.

Marvel Super-Hero Island
Finally, you arrive at total immersion in the elaborate comic-book pages of the super-heroes. The amazing façades of this world surround you with an utterly credible alternative

Marvel Super-Heroes

ISLANDS OF ADVENTURE with children

Our guide to the attractions that generally appeal to the different age groups:

Under-5s

Caro-Seuss-el, The Cat In The Hat, High In The Sky Seuss Trolley Train Ride, If I Ran The Zoo, Jurassic Park Discovery Center, Me Ship, The Olive, One Fish, Two Fish, Red Fish, Blue Fish.

5–8s

All the above, plus Amazing Adventures Of Spider-Man, Camp Jurassic, Eighth Voyage of Sindbad, Flight of the Hippogriff, Jurassic Park River Adventure (with parental discretion), Pteranodon Flyers, Storm Force Accelatron, Harry Potter and the Forbidden Journey (if tall enough).

9–12s

Amazing Adventures Of Spider-Man, Camp Jurassic, The Cat In The Hat, Dr Doom's Fearfall, Dudley Do-Right's Ripsaw Falls, Dragon Challenge, Eighth Voyage Of Sindbad, Flight of the Hippogriff, Harry Potter and the Forbidden Journey, Incredible Hulk Coaster, Jurassic Park Discovery Center, Jurassic Park River Adventure, Popeye And Bluto's Bilge-Rat Barges, Pteranodon Flyers, Storm Force Accelatron.

Over-12s

Amazing Adventures Of Spider-Man, Dr Doom's Fearfall, Dudley Do-Right's Ripsaw Falls, Dragon Challenge, Eighth Voyage Of Sindbad, Harry Potter and the Forbidden Journey, Incredible Hulk Coaster, Jurassic Park Discovery Center, Jurassic Park River Adventure, Popeye And Bluto's Bilge-Rat Barges, Storm Force Accelatron.

reality that is one of the park's triumphs – and that's before you have tried the rides.

The Incredible Hulk Coaster: Roller-coasters don't come much more dramatic than this giant green edifice that soars over the lagoon, blasting 0– 40mph/64kph in 2 seconds, and reaching a top speed of 65mph/105kph. It looks awesome, sounds stunning and rides like a demon as you enter the gamma-ray world of Dr David Banner, aka the Incredible Hulk, and zoom into a weightless inversion 100ft/30m up.

BRITTIP

At the Hulk Coaster, keep left where the queue splits up and you will be in line for the front car for an even more extreme Hulk experience.

Just watching is mind-boggling, and the effects are distinctly brain-scrambling! You will need to deposit ANY loose articles in the lockers at the front of the building as the ride is guaranteed to shake anything out of your pockets. Crowds build up rapidly but queues move reasonably

quickly. **Restrictions:** 4ft 6in/137cm. You can also buy the DVD of your ride for $24.95, with extra park footage, or photo packages from $16.95–$39.95. TTTTT+

Dr Doom's Fearfall: This is where, oh hapless visitor, you wander into the lair of the evil Dr Doom – arch-enemy of the Fantastic Four – and his sinister cohorts. His latest creation is the Fearfall, a device for sucking every iota of fear out of his victims, and YOU are about to test it as 16 riders at a time are strapped into chairs at the bottom of a 200ft/60m tower. The dry ice rolls, and whoosh! Up you go at breakneck speed, only to plummet back seemingly even faster, with an

Dr Doom's Fearfall

© Universal Orlando Resort

amazing split second in between when you feel suspended in mid-air. Summon up the courage to do this and we promise an astonishing (if brief!) experience. There are substantial queues from mid-day. **Restrictions:** 4ft 4in/132cm. **TTTTT+**

The Amazing Adventures Of Spider-Man: Get ready for another signature ride, which will be even more amazing in 2012 after a technical overhaul to add new digital film and 3-D projectors (it may close for a few weeks for the upgrade to take place). A visit to the Daily Bugle, home of ace reporter Peter Parker (aka Spider-Man), turns into a mission in a 'Scoop' vehicle – and an audio-visual extravaganza as the roving 3-D motion simulator takes you into a battle with various super-villains that includes a convincing 'drop' off a skyscraper as the contest hots up. There are special effects aplenty and the whole ride is loaded with the 'wow' factor. Go early on or wait until late in the day – queues often top an hour by mid-morning. **Restrictions:** 3ft 4in/101cm. **TTTTT+**

BRITTIP
You can beat some of the queues on the Spider-Man ride at busy times by opting for the Single Rider queue.

Storm Force Accelatron: This ride, primarily for kids, puts you in the middle of a battle between X-Men heroine Storm and arch-nemesis Magneto. It's basically an updated spinning-cup ride but with some neat twists (like a 3-way rotation where the cars look set to collide). **TTT (TTTTT under-12s)**

BRITTIP
For some of the park's best shopping bargains, visit Port Provisions right by the exit gates (to the left as you come through) where all the merchandise is 30–50% off.

Other entertainment: The **Marvel Super-Heroes** appear here periodically for photos and autographs, while **Spider-Man** has his own meet 'n' greet booth at The Marvel Alterniverse Store. A high-energy **video arcade** can be found at the exit to Dr Doom's Fearfall.

Shopping and dining: Each ride has its own character merchandise, while the **Comic Book Shop** and **Marvel Alterniverse Shop** sell other souvenirs. For a bite to eat, try the Italian buffeteria **Café 4** (pizza, spaghetti, sandwiches and salads) or a burger, chicken fingers or salad at the **Captain America Diner**.

And that, folks, is the full low-down on arguably the world's most thrilling and complete theme park. Not to be missed!

The Amazing Adventures of Spider-Man

SeaWorld

SeaWorld is firmly established with British visitors as one of the most popular parks for its more peaceful and naturalistic aspect, the change of pace it offers and the general lack of substantial queues. Like Disney's Epcot park, it is large enough to handle big crowds well (though it still gets busy in peak season) and is a big hit with families in particular, but it has some dramatic rides and imaginative attractions too, including the park's newest coaster Manta. It is one of the SeaWorld Parks & Entertainment group, along with sister parks **Busch Gardens** in Tampa, with its emphasis on animal encounters (p201), **Discovery Cove**, an exotic tropical 'island' with dolphin, stingray and snorkelling adventures (p197) and **Aquatica** (p243). These latter have added huge appeal, along with new 2 and 3-day tickets and Discovery Cove's

Ultimate Ticket, which includes all 4 parks. SeaWorld's recent new shows and other enhancements mean this remains a wonderfully fresh and invigorating place to visit.

Happily, this is still a park where you can proceed at a relatively leisurely pace, see what you want without too much jostling and yet feel you have been well entertained (even if the restaurants get crowded at mealtimes). SeaWorld is a good starting point if this is your first Orlando visit as it gives you the hang of negotiating the vast areas, navigating by the various maps and learning to plan around the show times. There are special offers for booking online at **www.seaworld.com**, where you can print your tickets to save waiting in the queue, plus a website for UK visitors – **www. seaworldparks.co.uk**.

SeaWorld at a glance

Location	7007 SeaWorld Drive, off Central Florida Parkway (Junctions 71 and 72 off I-4)		
Size	More than 200 acres/81ha, incorporating 26 attractions		
Hours	9am–6pm off peak; 9am–10pm high season (Easter, summer holidays, Thanksgiving, Christmas)		
Admission	Under-3s free; 3–9 $72 (1-day Ticket), $106 (2-Park Ticket, w/Aquatica or Busch Gardens), $122 (3-Park Ticket inc Aquatica and Busch Gardens), $255 (Orlando FlexTicket), $295(Orlando FlexTicket Plus); adult (10+) $80, $115, $130, $275, $315.		
Parking	$14, $20 preferred parking		
Lockers	Inside Entrance Plaza (next to Sweet Sailin' Candy), $7 and $10 (rent from Pushchair and Wheelchair location)		
Pushchairs	$14 and $19, to right of Guest Services inside park		
Wheelchairs	$12 and $45; with pushchairs		
Top attractions	One Ocean at Shamu Stadium, Shark Encounter, Journey To Atlantis, Kraken, Manta, Wild Arctic, Blue Horizons		
Don't miss	Reflections (high season), Manatee Rescue, behind-the-scenes tours, A'Lure Call of the Ocean show, dining at Sharks Underwater Grill		
Hidden costs	**Meals**	Burger, chips and coke $12.27 3-course lunch $39.00 (Sharks Underwater Grill) Kids' meal $5.99, including souvenir Shamu lunchbox; $8–10 at Sharks Underwater Grill	
	T-shirts	$18–38	
	Souvenirs	$.99–1,000-plus	
	Sundries	Manta ride photo $19.99, combo with Kraken $24.99	

1 Entrance plaza
2 Key West at SeaWorld
3 Stingray Lagoon
4 Turtle Point
5 Dolphin Cove
6 Blue Horizons
7 Garden of Discovery
8 Manatee Rescue
9 Journey To Atlantis
10 Kraken
11 The Manta
12 Penguin Encounter
13 Pacific Point Preserve
14 Sea Lion and Otter Stadium
15 Xtreme Zone
16 The Waterfront
17 Seaport Theater
18 Seafire Inn/ Makahiki Luau
19 Sky Tower
20 Dolphin Nursery
21 Voyager's Smokehouse
22 Shark Encounter
23 Nautilus Theater – A'lure
24 Sharks Underwater Grill
25 The Terrace
26 Animal Connections at Sea Garden
27 Shamu Stadium
28 Shamu's Happy Harbor
29 Wild Arctic
30 Mango Joe's Café
31 Atlantis Bayside Stadium
32 Dine with Shamu

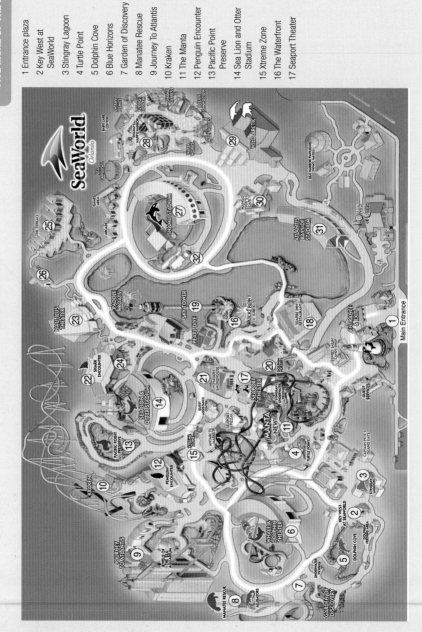

Backstage programmes: This park has a strong educational and environmental message. The 10 behind-the-scenes tours provide great insight into SeaWorld's conservation and research programmes, as well as its entertainment resources. Book in advance online, call 1888 800 5447, or visit the Guided Tours counter first thing when you arrive.

VIP Tour: 7hr tour with individual tour guide and back-door access to rides, shows, lunch and animal feeding ($100/adult, $75 3–9s;).

Elite VIP Tour: Similar to the above but just for your family or group, including a penguin meeting and lunch at Sharks Underwater Grill ($275/person).

Summer Nights VIP Tour: 7hr tour featuring animal feedings, front-of-line access to popular rides, priority seating for Shamu Rocks and Sea Lions Tonight, plus dinner at Sharks Underwater Grill. Available during Summer Nights only ($125 adult, $100 3–9).

Dolphins Up-Close Tour: Fascinating 1hr glimpse backstage at the training and care of the stars of the Blue Horizons show, as well as a look into the dolphin-care facilities, finishing with a Q&A session with a trainer at Dolphin Cove and the chance to touch one of the residents ($50 adults, $30 3–9s).

Penguins Up-Close Tour: 1hr tour highlighting penguin and puffin care, including limited encounters with these delightful birds ($40 and $20).

Sea Lions Up-Close Tour: A 90min walking tour focusing on the care and training of the stars of the Clyde & Seamore show, including a photo with them and a chance to feed the Pacific Point Preserve sea lions ($40 and $20).

Behind The Scenes Tour: 90min look at what goes on in the turtle and manatee rescue areas, with the chance to meet a small shark, check out a polar bear den and touch a penguin ($30 and $10).

Family Fun Tour: A 4hr guided walking tour of the top children's attractions, feeding dolphins and sea lions, touching a penguin, reserved seats at the Believe show, a light meal and select rides in Shamu's Happy Harbor, finishing with an exclusive meet 'n' greet with the cuddly Shamu character and a gift ($75 and $55).

Marine Mammal Keeper Experience: The first of 3 interactive programmes, this takes 2 visitors daily to discover

Manatee Rescue

the care needed to rehabilitate injured manatees, plus bottle-feed some of them, meet the seals and walruses and prepare meals for the beluga whales (starts at 6.30am; lasts around 8hrs; $399/person including lunch, T-shirt, special book, souvenir photo and 7-day SeaWorld pass; must be 13 or older).

Beluga Interactive Program: a unique chance to meet some of the park's biggest but most benign denizens in their own environment. Swimming isn't necessary but guests must be comfortable in the water as touching, feeding and using hand signals are part of this informative tour ($99/person, $149 with photo package; no expectant mothers; must be 10 or older).

Location
SeaWorld is located off Central Florida Parkway, between I-4 (exit 71 going east or 72 heading west) and I-Drive, and parking is $14 ($20 for preferred parking, closer to the entrance). It is still best to arrive a bit before the official opening time

Blue Horizons

so you're in a good position to book one of the backstage tours, dash to one of the few attractions that draws a crowd, like Manta, or purchase **Quick Queue**, the park's queue-beating, paid-for pass that entitles bearers to the unlimited access to Manta, Kraken, Journey to Atlantis, and Wild Arctic, plus unlimited use of the Skytower and paddle boats (pricing is seasonal at $14.95–$24.95 for one-time use per day, $19.95-34.95 unlimited use per day; quantities limited).

The park covers more than 200 acres/81ha, with 6 shows, 4 major rides, 10 large-scale continuous viewing attractions and 7 smaller ones, plus a smart range of shops and restaurants (a notable feature of the SeaWorld group). As in the other parks, try to eat before midday or after 2.30pm for a crowd-free lunch, and before 5.30pm if you want a leisurely dinner (better still, book Sharks Underwater Grill).

SeaWorld is not organised into neat 'lands' like the others, though, and it often requires much to-ing and fro-ing to catch the various shows, which can be wearing. Keep a close grip on your map and entertainment schedule and try to establish a programme to allow regular breaks. Going in a clockwise direction, here's what you find.

Entrance plaza
Coming through the turnstiles brings you to the park's main business area, including the **Guest Information** kiosk, **Lost & Found**, **Behind The Scenes** tour desk, lockers and pushchair and wheelchair rental. You will also find some good shopping and snack options here. Look for **Shamu Emporium** for the full range of SeaWorld souvenirs, while **Keyhole Photos** provides all your park pictures taken by the SeaWorld photographers. You can grab a quick breakfast (tasty pastries and coffee) at **Cypress Bakery** or something colder from the **Polar Parlor Ice Cream**. This is also the place for a photo opportunity with **Shamu and friends**.

South Seas Extravaganza

Another SeaWorld show well worth considering is the splendid nightly Makahiki Luau at the Seafire Inn, a 2hr South Seas dinner extravaganza with island music, songs, great costumes and the eye-opening fire-dance, as well as a huge feast. It costs an extra $46 adults, or $29 3–9s (nightly, times vary; special Christmas Luau available; call 407 351 3600 or book online) but adds more style to the park's entertainment.

Key West at SeaWorld

A whole collection of exhibits is grouped together here under the clever Key West theme. **Stingray Lagoon**, where you can feed (for $5) and touch fully grown rays, includes a nursery for newborn rays, while the park's rescued and rehabilitated sea turtles can be seen at **Turtle Point**. The centre-piece, the 2.1-acre/0.8ha **Dolphin Cove**, is a more spectacular, naturalistic development and offers the chance to feed this community of frisky Atlantic bottlenose dolphins (for $7 at specified periods through the day). There is also an excellent underwater viewing area, and park photographers are ready to snap you at play with the dolphins (a 6 x 8 photo will set you back $19.99; frames are $12 and $20).

Garden of Discovery

BRITTIP

If you drop your fish on the ground when feeding the dolphins, seals or sea lions you are asked to throw it away, for the animals' health and safety.

Garden of Discovery: A lovely, semi-secluded walk-through nature cove, with bench seats, just right for some time off your feet. Occasional small animal encounters occur here, adding to the delightfully relaxing atmosphere.

The whole Key West area is designed in the eclectic, tropical flavour of America's most southerly city, but it also underlines the environmental message of conservation through interactive graphics and video displays adjacent to the animal habitats, and children will find it a fun, educational experience. AAAA

Shopping and dining: There are 5 gift shops and kiosks here, the best being **Coconut Bay Trader** (apparel and soft toys) and **Sandcastle Toys 'n Treats**. You can grab a hot dog or chicken tenders at **Captain Pete's Island Eats**.

BRITTIP

Seek out **Gulliver's** store in Key West for a range of heavily discounted SeaWorld and Discovery Cove apparel and gifts.

Manta

Whale & dolphin theater

The first large-scale encounter is the setting for a magnificent show, plus the Manatee rescue exhibit.

Blue Horizons: This wonderful production serves up a big helping of dramatic animal behaviour in best Broadway style. It features dolphins, false killer whales and exotic birds (including an Andean condor), but a lot more besides as the general (and rather abstract) theme of a girl's dream about maritime wildlife is brought to life. The elaborate set design has a 40ft/12m sea-meets-sky backdrop that also conceals the setting for a host of additional performers, from high divers to bungee jumpers and trapeze-like aerialists. There is no obvious interaction between trainers and animals as the show moves from one scene to the next, both above and below the water, but there is plenty to admire as the stage is filled with graceful and daring action. The complex staging and Broadway-style costumes are underpinned by a stirring score by the Seattle Symphony Orchestra and it makes for a magnificent 25mins that often draws a huge ovation. AAAAA

Manatee Rescue: Next door is an exhibit to tug at your heartstrings as you learn the plight of this endangered species of Florida's waterways. Watch these lazy-looking creatures (half-walrus, half-cow?) lounge in their man-made lagoon, then walk down the ramp to the circular theatre where a 5min film with 3-D effects reveals the dangers facing the harmless manatee. Pass on into the underwater viewing section, with hands-on TV screens offering more information. It's a magnificent animal conservation exhibit. Try to avoid going just after a Blue Horizons show as it can get congested. AAA½

Shopping and dining: Look to **Manatee Cove** for a kids' wonderland of cuddly toys, while there are also 2 drinks carts.

Ride central

Continue past Whale & Dolphin Theatre and you come to the park's serious thrill quotient.

Journey to Atlantis: Unique in Orlando, this terrific water-coaster gave SeaWorld its first 5-star thrill attraction in 1998. The combination of extra elements makes it a one-off, with some illusory special effects giving way to a high-speed water ride that becomes a runaway roller-coaster. The discovery of Atlantis in your 8-passenger 'fishing boat' starts gently through the lost city. But evil spirit Allura takes over and riders plunge into a dash through Atlantis, dodging gushing fountains and water cannons, with hundreds of dazzling holographic and laser-generated illusions before the 60ft/18m drop, which is merely the entry to the roller-coaster finale back in the candle-filled catacombs. Be ready to get soaked, which is great in summer but not so clever first thing on a winter morning. **Restrictions:** 3ft 6in/106cm. **TTTTT**.

Kraken: This is one of Florida's most breathtaking roller-coasters. Based on the mythical sea monster, Kraken is an innovative pedestal ride (you are effectively sitting in a chair without a floor – pretty exposed!) that plunges an initial 144ft/44m, hits 65mph/105kph, dives underground 3 times, adds 7 inversions (including a vertical loop, a diving loop, a zero-gravity roll and a cobra roll) and a flat spin before riders escape the beast's lair. The ride from the front row, especially down an opening drop at an angle best described as ludicrous, is positively blood-curdling, and sitting in the rear is thrilling, too. **Restrictions:** 4ft 6in/137cm. **TTTTT+**

Manta: This ride is a triumph of the designer's art, turning a high-tech coaster into a unique mixture of ride and animal encounter. The elaborate queuing area winds through cool, rocky caverns, passing waterfalls and floor-to-ceiling windows showcasing some 300 rays and thousands of fish, which lead through to the 'undersea world' of the manta ray. Themed like a giant ray, riders are strapped into a face-down position before being launched into an exhilarating series of 4 inversions along 3,359ft/1,024m of track, reaching nearly 60mph/96kph and 140ft/43m high as well as skimming the surface of the lagoon. The 'flying' nature of the coaster and smooth ride vehicles make this a true original. It is a visual treat and a breathtaking ride, and even non-riders can enjoy the nearby walk-though aquarium with its own entry. Lockers located near the queue entry are available for use during your ride (50c). **Restrictions,** 54in/137cm. **TTTTT**

BRITTIP
Not sure if your youngster is tall enough for the bigger rides? A height check measuring stick is available at the small **Guest Assistance Center** between Manta and Sea Lion and Otter Stadium.

Shopping and dining: Don't miss the **Sea Aquarium Gallery** as you exit Journey to Atlantis, a combination gift shop and aquarium full of tropical fish (remember to look upwards), while there are more animal-orientated souvenirs in **Kraken Gifts**. **Manta Market** and **High Seas Market**, each near their namesake coaster, offer convenient grab-and-go snacks and drinks. Find **Sea Spray** games nearby at $5 each.

Penguins and sea lions

Getting back to the animal side of the park brings you to 2 more outstanding natural habitats, and a hilarious show.

Penguin Encounter: Always a hit with families (and one of the more crowded exhibits), the ever-comical penguins are brilliantly presented in

Journey to Atlantis

this chilly showpiece. You have the choice of going close and using the moving walkway along the display or standing back and watching from a non-moving position. Both afford fascinating views both above and below the water of the 17 different species. The 5 or so daily feeding times are also popular, so arrive early if you want a prime spot. There is a Q&A session at 2pm every day – the winner gets to pet a penguin! AAAA

Pacific Point Preserve: This carefully re-created rocky coast habitat shows the park's seals and sea lions at their most natural. A hidden wave machine adds the perfect touch, while park attendants provide informative talks. You can also buy packs of smelt ($5 per tray or 5 trays for $20) to throw to these ever-hungry mammals. AAA

Sea Lion and Otter Stadium: The venue for a wonderful show, *Clyde And Seamore Take Pirate Island*, it features the resident sea lions who, with their pals the otter and walrus (plus a couple of humans as the fall guys), put on a hilarious 25min performance of watery stunts and gags. Arrive early for some first-class audience mickey-taking from the resident pirate 'mime'. AAAA

Other entertainment: Xtreme Zone offers a 2min **Trampoline Jump** for an extra $6.

Shopping and dining: Pets Ahoy Gifts is the best of the shops here, along with the large **Friends of the Wild**. Grab a meal at **Antarctic Market** (a good range of fresh sandwiches,

Penguin Encounter

salads and chilli) or the **Seaport Pizza** (cheese and pepperoni pizza), while there are also 3 drinks carts and an ice-cream counter.

The waterfront
Backtracking slightly (or turning right after the Entrance Plaza area) brings you to this beautiful 5-acre/2ha seafront 'village' of restaurants and shops, which is a great place to spend some time when other parts are busy, especially for lunch or dinner.

Pets Ahoy!: Just inside the Waterfront is the air-conditioned haven (during the hottest part of the day) of the Seaport Theater, which hosts this cute 25min giggle featuring the unlikely talents of a menagerie of dogs, cats, birds, rats, pot-bellied pigs and others, the majority of which have come from local animal rescue shelters. AAA

Other entertainment: The Tower is the centrepiece of the Waterfront, with a 400ft/122m landmark offering (at an extra $4) slowly rotating rides for a bird's-eye view of the park and surrounding areas. The **Dolphin Nursery** provides close-up views with some of the park's younger dolphins.

Shopping and dining: This has some of the best in SeaWorld, starting with 4 interlinked boutique-style shops that offer a stylish range of souvenirs and other gift items (check out **Allura's Treasure Trove** and **Artisans Hall**, as well as the brand name fashions at **Currents**). The unique **Oyster's Secret** shop features resident pearl divers who can be viewed underwater as they collect the pearl-bearing oysters on request, to be incorporated into jewellery pieces by the shop's artisans. The 3 excellent eateries are: **Seafire Inn** (gourmet burgers, salads, Cuban sandwich and fish and chips); **Voyagers** (smoked chicken, barbecue ribs, salad, children's menu with chicken tenders, hot dog, or macaroni and cheese); and **The Spice Mill** (flame-grilled burgers and grilled chicken with a range of seasonings). There are also 3 snack bars: **Café de Mar** for pastries, coffees, smoothies and soft drinks;

Smugglers Feast for smoked turkey legs; and **Freezas** for frozen yoghurt and other drinks. The **SandBar** is a water's edge cocktail bar, serving snacks and speciality drinks – the place to watch the sun go down!

Sharks and co

Continuing the clockwise tour brings you towards the back of the park (which usually doesn't open until 11am). Here you find more animal encounters – and a wonderful show.

BRITTIP

Grab an evening meal at **The Spice Mill**, then head out on to its open-air terrace for one of the best seats in the house to experience the Reflections summer nightly finale.

Shark Encounter: Top of the bill, the world's largest collection of dangerous sea creatures can be found here, brought dramatically to life by the walk-through tubes that surround you with more than 50 prowling sharks (including sand tigers, black tips, nurse sharks and sand bars), sawfish, tropical fish and gigantic groupers. It's an eerie experience, but brilliantly presented and, again, highly informative. Queues build up here at peak times, though. AAAA TTTT

A'Lure, the Call of the Ocean: This imaginative 30min show in the Nautilus Theater features creative acrobatic feats, engaging live music, yo-yo artists, clever lighting and special effects. The show tells the story of a fisherman who is pulled into the ocean to an undersea world ruled by a tyrant queen. He becomes the unwilling pawn in her battle against a beautiful Siren for control of the ocean kingdom. AAAA

The theatre is also home to weekend events throughout the year, notably **Jack Hanna's Animal Adventure**, the **Bud and BBQ Country Music Festival**, and **Viva La Musica** Latin weekends.

BRITTIP

Looking for a quiet spot for a break? Seek out the terrace along the lagoon (with tables and chairs) directly behind **Fins** gift shop and across from Sharks Underwater Grill.

Other entertainment: The flamingo pedal-boats on the lagoon rent for $5 per 20min (for 2 people). You can also **feed the sharks** and stingrays outside Shark Encounter ($5 per tray). Also nearby is the new **Sea Garden** area, a lovely spot for some time off your feet. **Animal Connections** small animal

SeaWorld's main entrance

encounters can be found here several times daily. Bring your camera, as photo ops are also available.

Shopping and dining: The 3 shops here (**Ocean Treasures**, **Shark Photo** and **Gulf Breeze Trader**) are relatively small-scale but, at the entrance to Shark Encounter is the top dining choice, **Sharks Underwater Grill**. Not only do you have an amazing backdrop for your meal in a clever, subterranean environment (check out the mini-aquarium bar), but the upmarket menu features appetising 'Floribbean' cuisine, blending local and spicy Caribbean fare. The emphasis is on seafood – wonderful creations with scallops, king prawns, grouper and sea bass – plus pasta, filet mignon, chicken and pork – and desserts to die for, plus refreshing (non-alcoholic) cocktails and menus for under-10s and teens. Open from 11am to park closing, it's busy at lunch but quieter in late afternoon, so we advise booking (at the restaurant itself) as soon as you arrive. The **Terrace Café** offers deli sandwiches, salad, beef stew, bratwurst and hot dogs, while the **Terrace Bar** has a selection of beers. Sadly, it no longer offers free tastes of Anheuser-Busch products.

Shamu central

The other main area of the park features the iconic Shamu Stadium and a fabulous kids play area, plus another engaging ride/animal attraction.

Swishy Fishes at Shamu's Happy Harbor

BRITTIP

The first 14 rows at Shamu Stadium get VERY wet (watch out for your cameras) – when a killer whale leaps into the air in front of you, it displaces a LOT of water on landing. In fact, the Splash Zones should be renamed Soak Zones!

Shamu Stadium: 'What can 1 person do?' That is the message One Ocean brings to SeaWorld in a spectacular new show filled with brilliant splashes of colour – especially of the black and white variety! In the past, the whales' relationship with their trainers was the main focus, and while that bond remains strong, the heart of One Ocean lies with the relationship between the whales themselves. Behaviours common to whales in the wild combine with learned behaviours in a celebration of joyful play, reminding us we are all connected and, when we pull together, we can do amazing things. And if the biggest thrills in past Shamu shows came from seeing these magnificent animals jump, spin, and cover the Soak Zone in a wall of water, you're in for a real treat! Even better, the charming Side By Side scene features the connection between mother and baby, so have those cameras ready. Shamu Stadium is extremely popular, so try to take in 1 of the early shows. And, if you think it looks good during the day, return in the evening (in high season) for an even more dramatic presentation under the lights. AAAAA+

BRITTIP

Be sure to arrive early for **One Ocean**, especially if you have a smartphone. You may get a sneak peek behind the scenes during the pre-show!

All guests can then enjoy the backstage **Underwater Viewing** area.

Shamu's Happy Harbor: 4 acres/1.6ha of brilliantly designed adventure playground and rides await youngsters of all ages here. Activities include a 4-storey net climb, 2 tented ball rooms to wade through, a giant trampoline tent, a mock pirate ship

SEAWORLD with children

The following gives a general idea of the appeal of the attractions to the different age groups:

Under-5s
One Ocean, Blue Horizons, Clyde And Seamore Take Pirate Island, Clydesdale Hamlet, Elmo Show, Manatee Rescue, A'Lure, the Call of the Ocean, Pacific Point Preserve, Penguin Encounter, Pets Ahoy!, Shamu's Happy Harbor, Waterfront entertainment, Wild Arctic (without the ride).

5–8s
All the above, plus Reflections, Shark Encounter, Wild Arctic (with the ride).

9–12s
All the above, plus Journey to Atlantis, The Manta and Kraken.

Over-12s
One Ocean, Blue Horizons, Clyde And Seamore Take Pirate Island, Journey To Atlantis, The Manta, Kraken, Reflections, A'Lure, Shark Encounter, Wild Arctic.

and a splashy water play area, **Water Works** (great on a hot day). The signature junior-sized coaster **Shamu Express** offers mild thrills over more than 800ft/245m of track. The **Jazzy Jellies** is a jellyfish-themed samba tower ride that lifts and spins, while **Swishy Fishes** features oversized seats that spin round a giant waterspout. **Flying Fiddler** (a 20ft/6.1m tower ride on a jumping giant crab), **Ocean Commotion** (a rocking tug ride) and **Sea Carousel** (a traditional carousel featuring 65 sea creatures) complete the line-up. The area gets busy from midday, but the kids seem to love it at any time. Next door is the arcade and **Games Area**, a series of fairground-type stalls ranging from $1–10 as you head toward Penguin Encounter. TTTT. At the back of the Harbor is a well equipped, comfortable **Baby Care Center** and the park's **First Aid** station.

Wild Arctic: This interactive ride-and-view experience provides a realistic environment that is both educational and thrilling. It's an exciting simulator jet helicopter journey into the white wilderness, arriving at 'Base Station Wild Arctic' where passengers disembark into a frozen wonderland to see polar bears, beluga whales and walruses. This one is not to be missed (but avoid just after One Ocean when the hordes descend). Restrictions: 3ft 6in/106cm. TTTT/AAAAA. Those who

don't want to do the (quite dynamic) ride can just walk to the Base Station.

Shopping and dining: The **Wild Arctic Gift Shop** is the best of the

Wild Arctic

3 stores here. For dining, **Mango Joe's Café** offers grilled fajitas, speciality salads and sandwiches, while **Coconut Cove** offers drinks and snacks in Shamu's Happy Harbor. Weary parents will enjoy the convenience of **Harbor Market** grab-and-go snacks and drinks.

◀✦▶ **BRITTIP**

Any purchases can be forwarded to Package Pick-up in Shamu's Emporium to collect on your way out, provided you give them at least an hour's notice.

Dine with Shamu: A VIP experience 'backstage' with the killer whales and their trainers. A huge all-you-can-eat buffet on a covered terrace by the main pool allows the trainers to display their unique bond with and care for the animals (you may also get a little wet). Offered daily (times vary) but book in advance online or on 1888 800 5447 *(Note: This experience was suspended in 2010, but is expected to return in a modified form without prior notice. Be sure to call in advance to check availability).*

The **All Day Dining Deal** is a set fee for a special wristband that gives unlimited visits to 6 restaurants (Spice Mill, Voyager's Terrace Café, Mango Joe's, Seaport Pizza and Seafire Inn), claiming an entrée, side dish and drink each time ($29.99 and $14.99).

The One Ocean show

Atlantis Bayside Stadium

The final part of SeaWorld is this large outdoor arena facing the central Lagoon. It's home to an array of seasonal entertainment but is most susceptible to any bad weather.

Elmo and Abby's Treasure Hunt: Each summer sees a special *Sesame Street* live show on stage here, from late May to Sept 1. Guaranteed to appeal to the pre-school set, the musical presentation features Elmo, Cookie Monster, Rosita, Grover, Abby Cadabby and others in a 25min song and dance fest, encouraging youngsters to use their imagination in a mock treasure hunt. There is also a post-show character meet and greet. AA (or AAAAA, depending on age).

Summer extras

During the official summer season, SeaWorld has extended hours to 10pm and offers an array of extra live entertainment as part of its **AfterDark** programme. The 'rock 'n' roll' party atmosphere is generated by live DJs and other entertainers and features extra shows, notably **Shamu Rocks**, which adds a more high-energy, free-form version of the main show, including live music and dramatic lighting. Then, over at Sea Lion & Otter Stadium, there is a second evening show, **Sea Lions Tonite**, which serves up a fun parody of other SeaWorld shows.

◀✦▶ **BRITTIP**

Learn more about SeaWorld's conservation and environmental efforts at **www.seaworld.org**.

It all leads up to the big **Reflections** finale on the Waterfront lagoon. This is a neat mix of pyrotechnics and special effects, with towering fountains (up to 100ft/30m high), mist sprays, unique fireworks and an epic soundtrack. View from the Waterfront, or arrive early for seating at the Bayside Stadium. AAAA.

Discovery Cove

Fancy a day in your own tropical paradise, with the chance to swim with dolphins, encounter sharks, snorkel in a coral reef and dive through a waterfall into a tropical aviary? Well, Discovery Cove is all that and more. The only drawback is the price. This mini theme park comes at a premium because it is restricted to just 1,000 guests a day, creating an exclusive experience that is reflected in the admission fee.

The weather can get distinctly cool in the winter, but the water is always heated (apart from the dolphin lagoon, which remains at 72ºF/22ºC) and full wetsuits are available to keep out the chill. The attention to detail is superb, guest ratings are extremely high and it is hugely popular with British visitors. However, if any element falls below expectations, it's worth bringing it to the attention of a manager as they are always keen to rectify any oversights.

The costs

In 2011, the flat-rate entrance fee was $199–299, depending on season. The only reduction is $100 off for those not wishing to do the Dolphin Swim, and under-3s (free). So, just what do you get for your money? Well, as you would expect, it's a supremely personal park. You check in at the beautiful entrance lobby as you would for a hotel rather than a theme park, and you have a guide to take you in and get you set. All your basic requirements – towel, mask, snorkel, wet-jacket, lockers, beach umbrellas, food and drink – are included, and the level of service is excellent. A pass for SeaWorld, Aquatica, or Busch Gardens is also included (valid for 14 consecutive days before or after your Discovery Cove visit), or you can upgrade to the **Ultimate Experience**, which provides 14 days at SeaWorld, Aquatica AND Busch Gardens for an extra $80 (superb value). Continental breakfast, snacks, beverages (including Anheuser-Busch products) and an excellent buffet

at the **Laguna Grill** are all included. But gift shop and photo prices reflect the entry fee – expensive. It is also an extra $100-$200 (seasonally) to hire one of their swanky **cabañas** for the day (which include tables, chairs, loungers, towels and drinks service). In addition to the basic cabaña, Pool view cabañas are available for $125–225, Premium cabaña (with upgraded furniture and concierge service) $175–275. Ultimate cabañas are also available for $600 (year round), available only by advance reservation.

Therefore, for all its style and dolphin appeal, Discovery Cove will take a BIG bite out of your holiday budget. A family of 4, with children old enough to do the Dolphin Swim, would pay $1,196 in peak season. Even with a free SeaWorld pass, it's a big outlay. The charge for ages 3–5 is also pretty steep, in our opinion. Your sundries can add up, too. A 6x8 photo is $20; then there are various photo packages at $60, $139 and $219, while the DVD of your experience (which includes 30mins of park highlights) costs $50 and the Ultimate Package (7 6x8 photos, 1 4x6 photo, 2 key chains, digital photo CD, Interaction video, photo album, 16x24 poster) is $219. Poster-size photos (24x36) are available for $25. However, despite the costs, the feedback we get is almost unfailingly positive and most people are totally captivated by the experience. One handy free perk, though, is the **Horticulture**

Dolphin Interaction

Tour, twice a day, which takes guests through the care and maintenance of the park's rich tropical plant and tree life.

There is also an additional programme that adds a great deal of appeal to the basic day, but at more cost. **Trainer for a Day** is an exciting opportunity to go behind the scenes into the park's training, feeding and welfare. You get to work with the experts as they interact with dolphins, birds, sharks, stingrays and tropical fish, including a behavioural training class, the chance to experience a double-foot push (ride on the front of 2 dolphins), a souvenir shirt, dolphin book and waterproof camera. Participants must be at least 6 and in good health, and it costs $389-$488 (seasonally). For all Discovery Cove bookings, call 407 370 1280 (freephone 0800 3344 1818 in the UK) or visit **www.discoverycove.com**.

Location

Situated on Central Florida Parkway, almost opposite the SeaWorld entrance (open year-round 9am–5.30pm; parking free), the whole 30-acre/12ha park is magnificently landscaped, with thatched buildings, palm trees, lush vegetation, white-sand beaches, gurgling streams – even hammocks to chill out in. The overall effect is of being transported to a relaxing tropical paradise away from the hurly-burly. The 5-star resort feel is enhanced by a high staff-to-guest ratio, there are no queues (though the restaurant may get busy at lunchtime), and the highlight Dolphin Encounter is world class. Visitors with disabilities are well catered for, with special wheelchairs that can move in sand and shallow water, and an area of the Dolphin Lagoon that allows those who can't enter the water still to touch a dolphin.

The Grand Reef

The main attractions

Tropical Reef: Prior to 2011 this was the main snorkelling reef, but with the opening of the Grand Reef, this one has closed. It is due to open again as a fresh-water feature late in 2012.

Ray Lagoon: A carefully sculpted pool provides the opportunity to paddle among several dozen southern and cownose rays – harmless, but with a genuine fascination. AAAA

Wind-away River: This 800yd/732m circuit of gently flowing bath-warm water is a variation on the lazy river feature of many of the water parks, though with a far more naturalistic aspect and none of the inner tubes. It is primarily designed for snorkellers and features rocky lagoons, caves, a beach section, a tropical forest segment, and sunken ruins. The lack of fish makes it a bit bland after the Grand Reef and Ray Lagoon, but it is as much about relaxing as having fun. It is up to 8ft/2.4m deep at points, so non-swimmers are advised to use a flotation vest. It finishes in the freeform Serenity Bay Pool, which provides more idyllic relaxation. AAA

Explorer's Aviary: This 3-part adventure is both an area in its own right and a 120ft/37m section of the Tropical River. You can walk in off the beach or swim in through the waterfall from Wind-away River, which is a beautifully scenic touch and fun for snorkellers. Some 250 tropical birds (plus tiny muntjak deer) fill the main enclosure and, if you stand still, they are likely to use you as a perch. There is a small-bird sanctuary – full of finches, honeycreepers and hummingbirds – and a large-bird enclosure, featuring toucans and the red-legged seriema. Guides will introduce you to specific birds (which you can hand-feed) and tell you about their habitats and conservation issues. AAAAA

Dolphin Swim: The park's headline attraction is the encounter with the park's Atlantic bottlenose dolphin community. A 20-minute orientation programme in one of the beach cabañas, with a film and instruction from 2 trainers, sets you up for this thrilling experience. Groups of 6–8 go into the lagoon with the trainers and, starting off standing in the waist-deep (slightly chilly) water as one of the dolphins comes over, you gradually become more adventurous until you are swimming with them. Timid swimmers are well catered for and there are flotation vests for those who need them. The lagoon is up to 12ft/3.6m deep so there is a real feeling of being in the dolphins' environment. You learn how trainers use hand signals and positive reinforcement to communicate, and get the chance to stroke, feed and even kiss your dolphin. The encounter concludes dramatically as you are towed ashore by one of these awesome animals (which weigh up to 600lb/272kg), though activities vary according to the dolphins' attention span. You spend around 30mins in the water and it is totally unforgettable. Under-6s are not allowed in the lagoon. TTTTT+

The Grand Reef: And grand it is! This new area of Discovery Cove features a massive 2.5 acre/1ha artificial reef with 125 species of sea creatures, including fish, rays, eels, sharks, urchins, and lionfish (the dangerous ones are behind glass!). White sand beaches, meandering pathways and scenic bridges lead to shallow wading areas, waist-deep paddling pools and deep-water snorkelling lagoons, while underwater canyons and inviting grottos combine with brightly coloured artificial coral reefs for a convincing and utterly exhilarating experience. It's like paradise, only better!

Ray Lagoon

For an extra element of relaxation, stake out a hammock on the central island or consider hiring one of 8 private waterside cabañas (with table, chairs, loungers and towels). There is a drinks kiosk here but no food outlets. AAAAA

Sea Venture: One of the most innovative features of the Grand Reef is this underwater walking tour. Equipped with special dive helmets, guests make a 20min trek along the bottom of the reef, passing sharks and lionfish and interacting with schools of fish and gentle rays. This is a totally immersive experience and a sensation like no other (how often can you explore underwater while standing up straight?). There are handrails throughout the journey, which takes groups of 4-9 at a time. Total tour time is 1hr, including preparation and underwater trek (for an extra $59 per person). Ages 10 and up only. TTTT

BRITTIP

The Sea Venture area is not accessible to snorkellers during tours, but you can swim there when a tour is not running.

The Grand Reef

The beach

Discovery Cove 'extras'

This isn't a cheap day out, but the extra quality is everywhere. The **Laguna Grill** lunch is excellent and you can visit as often as you want, while a Calypso band adds to the tropical paradise feel. **Conservation Cabaña** allows guests to meet a neat selection of the park's small mammals (like an anteater and tree sloth); **parking** is free and you also receive an 8 x 6 **welcome photo**. And, while official opening time is 9am, they will check you in as early as 8am to take advantage of the free breakfast.

Special occasions

For that special birthday or anniversary, or for somewhere different to propose marriage, Discovery Cove has a range of options that involve dolphin interaction and private beach cabañas.

The **Celebration Package** ($129) includes 6x8 photo, photo frame or plush toy, bag, T-shirt, souvenir buoy, and 25% off Ultimate photo package, while a **Premium Package** version ($229) adds a private cabañas and disposable underwater camera.

The **Elite Package** ($449) includes all the amenities of the Premium Package, plus a private animal meet-and-greet in your cabaña, champagne, souvenir toasting flutes, a dozen roses, and luscious chocolate truffles.

Park admission and dolphin swim package are required with all special occasion packages. You are advised to book at least 3 months in advance as special packages do sell out in peak periods. There is also a 10% advance discount periodically for online bookings. See **www.discoverycove.com**.

Busch Gardens

While the Orlando parks may get more publicity, the 335-acre/136ha Busch Gardens in Tampa offers just as much in terms of attractions and – especially – Brit appeal. In fact, the sister park to SeaWorld, which started as a mini-menagerie for the wildlife collection of the brewery-owning Busch family in 1959, is often 1 of the most popular of all Florida attractions with UK visitors for its nature appeal – and superb roller-coasters. It is a major, multi-faceted family park, the biggest outside Orlando and just an hour from International Drive. It is rated among the top 4 zoos in America, with more than 2,700 animals representing over 320 species of mammals, birds, reptiles, amphibians and spiders. But that's just the start. It boasts a safari-like section of Africa spread over 65 acres/26ha of grassy veldt, with special tours to hand-feed some

of the animals. Interspersed among the animals are more than 20 bona fide theme park rides, including the mind-numbing coasters **Kumba**, **SheiKra**, **Montu** and **Gwazi**, and the new **Cheetah Hunt**, which opened in summer 2011, with guaranteed fun for coaster addicts, plus plenty of scaled-down rides for children. Then there are animal shows, musicians and big-stage show productions.

The overall theme is Africa, hence the park is divided into areas like Nairobi and Congo, and dining and shopping is equally as good as the other theme parks. It doesn't quite have the pizzazz of *Epcot* or Universal, and the staff are a bit more laid back, but it has guaranteed 5-star family appeal, especially with its selection of rides just for kids. In a way, it is like the big brother of Chessington World of Adventures in Surrey, though

BUSCH GARDENS at a glance

Location	Busch Blvd, Tampa; 75–90mins' drive from Orlando
Size	335 acres/136ha in 11 themed areas
Hours	9 or 10am–6 or 7pm off peak; 9am–8pm Easter, Thanksgiving, Christmas; 9 or 9.30am–10.30pm summer
Admission	Under-3s free; 3–9 $70 (1-day Ticket), $85 (2-Park Ticket inc Adventure Island water park), $107 (2-Park Ticket inc SeaWorld), $140 (3-Park Ticket inc Aquatica and SeaWorld), $295 (Orlando FlexTicket Plus); adult (10+) $78, $93, $115, $150, $315.
Parking	$13, $20 preferred, $26 valet
Lockers	$7, in Morocco, Congo, Egypt and Stanleyville
Pushchairs	$15 and $20
Wheelchairs	$15 and $45, with pushchairs
Top attractions	Congo River Rapids, Gwazi, Kumba, Montu, Cheetah Hunt, Rhino Rally, SheiKra, Tanganyika Tidal Wave
Don't miss	Cheetah Run, Jungala, Edge of Africa, Animal Keeper talks, Myombe Reserve, Mystic Sheikhs band
Hidden costs	**Meals**	Burger, chips and Pepsi $9.58 3-course meal $17.99–24.95, family-style diner $14.95 and $8.45 (Crown Colony House) Kids' meal $7.79
	T-shirts	$15.92-32.00
	Souvenirs	99c–$899
	Sundries	Face Painting $13–17

Morocco
1 Marrakesh Theater
2 Moroccan Palace Theater
3 Myombi Reserve
4 Gwazi

Cheetah Hunt
5 Cheetah Run
6 Cheetah Hunt and Skyride Station

Bird Gardens
7 Garden Theatre
8 Lory Landing
9 Walkabout Way

Sesame Street Safari of Fun
10 Air Grover
11 Sunny Day Theater
12 Big Bird's 123-Smile With Me

Stanleyville
13 SheiKra
14 Stanley Falls
15 Tanganika Tidal Wave
16 Stanleyville Theater
17 Skyride Station
18 Zambia Smokehouse

Jungala
19 Jungle Flyers, The Wild Surge and Treetop Trails
20 Tiger Habitat
21 Orang Outpost

Congo
22 Kumba
23 Congo River Rapids
24 Ubanga-Banga Bumper Cars

Timbuktu
25 Timbuktu 4-D Theater
26 Sand Serpent
27 The Phoenix
28 Scorpion
29 Sahara Go-Round

Nairobi
30 Rhino Rally
31 Serengeti Plain
32 Jambo Junction
33 Edge of Africa
34 Elephant Habitat

Egypt
35 Tut's Tomb
36 Montu

on a grander scale (and in a better climate). Busch Gardens is the only park to offer 1-day Tickets with a rain guarantee, which means if you get rained out on your visit, you can return FREE within 7 days. Look for self-serve ticket machines to the right of the park entrance to save time at ticket booths.

BRITTIP

Like SeaWorld, Busch Gardens offers **Quick Queue**, for priority entry into shows and front-of-queue access to rides. Price varies (seasonally) from $15.95–32.95 for One-time use, $44.95–46.95 for Unlimited use.

All Day Dining Deal: For just $29.99 ($14.99 3–9s) you can enjoy all-you-care-to-eat-and-drink privileges at 7 restaurants throughout the park. With your special wristband, choose 1 entrée, 1 side or dessert and a soft drink each time you pass through the dining queue (child's price valid for kids' meal only; baby back ribs excluded).

Look out also for **Meet The Keeper** sessions around the park, where the animal handlers explain various features of animal husbandry, notably with the gorillas, elephants and hippos. You will find them at the Alligator Habitat, Myombe Reserve, Edge of Africa, Jungala, Elephant and Rhinoceros Habitats and Jambo Junction (where they feature various small-animal encounters).

Location

Busch Gardens can be hard to locate on the sketchy local maps as the sign-posting is not as sharp as it could be, but from Orlando the directions are simple. Head west on I-4 for almost an hour (it is 55mls/88km from I-4's junction with Highway 192) until you hit intersecting motorway I-75. Take I-75 north for 3½mls/5.5km to the exit for Fowler Avenue (Highway 582). Go west on Fowler for another 3½mls/5.5km, then, just past the University of South Florida on your right, turn LEFT into McKinley Drive. A mile/1.6km down McKinley Drive, the car park is on your *left*, where it

costs $13 to park (those with disabled badges should continue on then turn right).

Those without a car can use the **Busch Gardens Shuttle Express** bus, which makes several $10 round trips a day from Orlando (FREE if you have a multi-day ticket). You board at SeaWorld, Orlando Premium Outlets, Universal Studios, Ramada Maingate West, Best Western Lakeside or Old Town in Kissimmee and pick-up times range from 8.30 to 9.40am, returning at 6 or 7pm. Book at **Guest Services** at SeaWorld or call 1800 221 1339.

Beating the queues: You may think you've left the crowds behind in Orlando but, unfortunately, in high season you'd be wrong. It's still advisable to be here at opening time, if only to be first in line to ride the dazzling roller-coasters, which all draw big queues (especially SheiKra and the new Cheetah Hunt). The Congo River Rapids, Stanley Falls Log Flume ride and Tanganyika Tidal Wave (all opportunities to get wet) are also prime draws in peak season. But queues take longer to build here, so for the first few hours you can enjoy a relatively crowd-free experience.

On your left through the main gates is the **Adventure Tour Centre**, and you should go there first (better still, book in advance on 1888 800 5447 or online at **www.buschgardens.com**) if you'd like to do the wonderful Serengeti Safari or other Adventure Tours (p211). Busch Gardens is divided into 11 main sections, with the major rides all a bit of a hike from the main entrance. Check your park map for times and locations of various small-animal encounters throughout the park – then watch for passing flamingos as they take the first of their twice-daily promenades in the main courtyard!

Coaster fans flock in serious numbers to **SheiKra**, the world's highest and fastest dive coaster, and queues can hit 2 HOURS by mid-afternoon in peak season. So, if you are tempted by this first, bear left through Morocco past the Zagora Café, through the Bird Gardens and up into Stanleyville.

Gwazi, the rattlin' wooden coaster, is another to draw a crowd quickly, and you could do this en route to SheiKra. Then continue through Stanleyville to Congo for **Kumba**, and retrace your steps to do **Congo River Rapids** and the other 2 water rides. If you would like to start with the superb new **Cheetah Hunt** coaster, veer right into Morocco and go past the Moroccan Palace Theater, where the loading area for the ride faces Crown Colony. After riding the Cheetah, you should take the SkyRide to Stanleyville and take on the other big rides there. Here is the full layout of the park in a clockwise direction (usually the optimum route).

Morocco

Coming through the main gates brings you into the home of all the guest services and a lot of good shops. *Epcot*'s Moroccan pavilion sets the scene better, but the architecture is still impressive and this version won't tax your wallet as much as Disney's! Turning the corner brings you to the first animal encounter, the alligator pen. Morocco is also home to 2 of the park's biggest shows.

Marrakesh Theater: In summer 2011, this live venue presented **Sweet Music: Sounds of the Motor City**, a song and dance tribute to the Motown Sound. Back in the 1960s, Detroit grooved to the sounds of Smokey Robinson, Diana Ross and the Supremes, Marvin Gaye and

The new Cheetah Hunt

others, and their music lights up the stage several times daily. AAA.

Moroccan Palace Theater: The former home of lavish stage show KaTonga and Cirque Dreams Jungle Fantasy, this will now showcase a long-awaited Ice Show set to debut in 2012, with eye-catching costumes and special effects to maintain the park's standards for high-quality live productions. Expect first-of-its-kind staging, with performers coming out into the audience at times. AAAA (expected)

Myombe Reserve: One of the largest and most realistic habitats for the threatened highland gorillas and chimpanzees of Central Africa, this 3-acre/1.2ha walk-through has a superb tropical setting where the temperature is kept high and convincing with the aid of lush forest landscaping and water mist sprays. Take your time, especially as there are good, seated vantage points, and be patient to catch these magnificent creatures on their daily routine. It is also highly informative, with attendants on hand to answer any questions. AAAAA

Cheetah Hunt: Like a cheetah in hot pursuit of its prey, this new beast of a coaster re-creates the thrill of a high-speed chase, not once, twice but 3 times. Launching from the loading station out across the savannah, the hunt is on. A second launch spirals you 10 storeys up the ride's signature figure-of-8 tower (with an astonishing view of the landscape) before taking an exhilarating 130ft/40m plunge into a subterranean gorge. Then you're off again, low and fast along the Serengeti. A final launch zips back across the grasslands (leaping over the heads of onlookers below and above the SkyRide!) and, just before you're completely out of breath, the hunt comes to an end. It lasts just 1min 20secs but the effect is sensational. The smooth nature of the coaster, extensive theming and superb eye-appeal mark this out as possibly Florida's finest but it draws BIG queues, so try to do it early on. Restrictions: 4ft/120cm; TTTTT+

Cheetah Run: For the first time, Busch Gardens is home to the planet's most agile animal, and here you have the chance to see these magnificent cats up close in a 250ft sprint (chasing their favourite toy alongside Cheetah Hunt!), or just lounging around the splendid new habitat designed especially for them. Sprints occur up to 6 times daily (check park map for times). Then, take time to learn more about cheetahs and the park's conservation efforts through nearby touch-screen technology.

Gwazi: Busch's second largest roller-coaster is a massive 'duelling' wooden creation in the classic style (i.e. no going upside-down). The 2 sets of cars, the Gwazi Lion and Gwazi Tiger, each top 50mph/80kph and generate a G-force of up to 3.5 as they career around nearly 7,000ft/2,134m of track with 6 fly-by encounters. You get to choose your ride in the intricately themed village plaza and then you are off up the big lift hill for a breathtaking 2½mins. The shake, rattle 'n' roll effect of a classic wooden coaster has been softened slightly with new trains in 2011, and the Lion and Tiger rides are slightly different, so you should try both. **Restrictions:** 4ft/122cm. **TTTTT**

Gwazi Gliders: This gentle circling 'hang-gliding' ride is purely for the pre-school crowd. **T** (**TTT** under-6s)

Other entertainment: The great fun of the marching, dancing, 8-piece brass band **Mystic Sheikhs** can be found in Morocco at regular intervals, along with Men of Note, a strolling 4-piece a cappella group with Motown specialities, and **park characters** like TJ the Tiger, Gina the Giraffe and Hilda Hippo. Basketball fans can try the Hoops Challenge (extra fee applies) next to Gwazi.

Shopping and dining: Choose from 7 different shops, with **The Emporium** and **Marrakesh Market** the pick of the bunch. For a quick meal, try **Zagora Café**, especially at breakfast. Alternatively, the enticing **Sultan's Sweets** serves coffee and pastries.

Bird Gardens

The most peaceful area and the original starting point of the park in 1959, it is possible to unwind here from the usual theme-park hurly-burly. The exhibits and shows are all family-orientated, too, with live shows, an elaborate kids' playground and more animal exhibits.

BRITTIP
The Bird Gardens area is a good place to visit in mid-afternoon when most of the rides are busy.

Garden Theater: This hosts the amusing 25min **Critter Castaways** show featuring numerous animals (almost 80 in all) in a light-hearted desert island romp. Dogs, cats, birds and even kangaroos all get in on the act with their human co-stars. AAA

Lory Landing: Walk through this tropical aviary featuring lorikeets, hornbills, parrots and more, with the chance to become a human perch and feed the friendly lorikeets. A cup of nectar costs $5, but makes for a great photo opportunity. AAA

Walkabout Way: This charming Australia-themed animal attraction offers the chance to feed the free-roaming kangaroos and wallabies ($10, ages 5 and up only) and meet other Down Under denizens. It is a surprisingly captivating area, perfect for a relaxed stroll. AAA. Other encounters include the lush, walk-through **Aviary**, **Flamingo Island**, the **Living Dragons** and **Eagle Canyon**, plus the **Backyard Wildlife Habitat**.

Other entertainment: Gwazi Park is home to the seasonal live musical entertainment during summer and other special events.

Shopping and dining: A real novelty here is the eye-catching **Xcursions** eco-friendly gift shop. Its live frog and gecko displays and conservation info on interactive touch-screens make it worth visiting whether you buy or not (but all proceeds contribute to the Busch Gardens Conservation Fund). **Garden Gate** is another imaginative shop. A new pizza-and-pasta buffet with salad, dessert and non-alcoholic drinks (beer and wine extra) is on offer at the pleasant **Garden Gate Café** (excellent value at $9.99 per person).

Sesame Street Safari of Fun

This impressive children's interactive play area is the cheerful 'home away from home' for much-loved *Sesame Street* characters, dressed in best African Safari finery. You will be hard pressed to get pre-schoolers away when they catch sight of this land's 7 rides (including a junior-sized coaster, a gentle flume ride and character-themed fairground style rides), entertaining stage show and the wonderfully extensive water play and climb-and-slide areas. The huge treehouse climb, ball pools and adventure play structures alone will keep most kids busy for hours! But there's more:

Air Grover: A whizzy little dip-and-turn coaster packing plenty of junior-sized thrills, piloted by everyone's favourite blue guy, Grover. **Restrictions:** 2ft 9in/97cm accompanied; 3ft 5in/104cm unaccompanied.

Sunny Day Theater: Elmo, Abby, Zoe, Grover and Cookie Monster star in *A is for Africa*, a delightfully zany stage show that brings tales of adventure to life, with a gently uplifting message. Children (and adults!) can't help but sing and clap along, and it is a great photo opportunity as the characters arrive and then come out for a meet-and-greet afterwards.

> **BRITTIP**
> Arrive early and find a seat in the first 5 rows for an unobstructed view at the Sunny Day Theater. Seat children on the ends for the best character interaction.

Big Bird's 1-2-3 Smile with Me: Big Bird and friends have their own meet-and-greet area, near Air Grover. The big bonus here is 1-on-1 time with the character in a quiet, air conditioned room (photo $15; add a special background for $10).

Bert and Ernie's Watering Hole: Thoughtfully designed with even the smallest guests in mind, this gentle water-play area is filled with bubblers, water jets, dump buckets, geysers and splash tubs. Swimwear and sun block are available at Cookie Monster's Trading Post if you forgot yours. Convenient seating surrounds the area. TTTTT (young 'uns only!)

Shopping and dining: Look for **Abby Cadabby's Treasure Hut** and **Cookie Monster's Trading Post** for *Seasame Street* gifts and souvenirs. For a quick bite here, try **Snack-n-Getti Tribal Treats**. The big opportunity, though, is **Dine with Elmo & Friends**, where visitors can enjoy breakfast or lunch with Elmo and his chums in an outdoor covered dining area. A kid-friendly buffet along with a character song-and-dance show make this a delight for the younger set, with loads of time to meet their favourite characters (breakfast $18 adults, $13 children; lunch $22 and $15; both include 6x8 photo per family.

> **BRITTIP**
> Dine with Elmo has a great Birthday Package option, with photo, decorated table and special Happy Birthday song, Muppet-style. Call 1888 800 5447 or visit **www.SesameStreetSafariofFun.com**.

Stanleyville

This brings you back into true ride territory, with the park's biggest coaster, as well as several water rides. You'll also find one of the 3 **Train Stations** here (next to SheiKra), for a gentle 35min journey round the park.

SheiKra: The park's outstanding big-thrill attraction is the giant steel structure of this monstrous coaster. A world first at 200ft/62m tall and hitting 70mph/112kph, this is the ride to put Alton Towers' fearsome Oblivion in the shade. Higher, longer and faster, it features an initial drop at an angle as near vertical as makes no difference (with a delicious moment of stop-go balance as you teeter on the edge!), a second drop of 138ft/42m into an underground tunnel, an Immelman loop (an exhilarating rolling manoeuvre) and a water splashdown over 0.6mls/1km of smooth-as-silk track. As if all that isn't enough, a 2007 modification removed the coaster's *floor*, so there is nothing between you and track but air! The whole ride lasts less than 3min and is almost as much fun to watch as to ride. It also draws massive quques, so get here early or expect a long wait (or use the paid-for Quick Queue system). You can buy the video of your ride for $25 or 6x8 photo for $15. **Restrictions:** 4ft 6in/137cm. **TTTTT+**

Stanley Falls: Almost identical to Log Flume rides at Chessington, Legoland, Thorpe Park and Alton Towers, this guarantees a good soaking at the final 40ft/12m drop. **Restrictions:** 3ft 10in/116cm. **TTT**

Tanganyika Tidal Wave: A distinctly more scenic ride, this takes you on a journey along 'uncharted' African waters before tipping you down a 2-stage drop that lands with tidal-wave force. **Restrictions:** 4ft/122cm. **TTTT**

✠ BRITTIP

Don't stand on the bridge by Tanganyika Tidal Wave or by the SheiKra splashdown – unless you want to get seriously wet!

Stanleyville Theater: A good place to put your feet up as you watch the resident entertainers turn on the style. This varies seasonally and includes musical acts, acrobats and family-style comedy, plus occasional animal encounters. **AAA½**

Skyride: The other end of the park's cable-car ride (from Morocco), it offers spectacular views over the Serengeti Plain (with a thrilling moment as Cheetah Hunt races above!). However, it closes when it's windy and queues can build up here in late afternoon. **AA**

Other entertainment: Test your skills at **Bahati Hoops** (next to SheiKra) for a small fee.

Shopping and dining: The **Kariba Marketplace** has the best of the shopping, while, for a hearty meal (and a great view of SheiKra), try **Zambia Smokehouse**, where its wood-smoked ribs platter is a delight among a heavily barbecue-orientated menu (also with salads, sandwiches and kids' meals).

Jungala

One of the park's biggest expansions, this 4-acre/1.6ha land opened in 2008 adding a couple of small-scale rides, some superb animal habitats and a hugely elaborate children's play area, designed with older children in mind (where Sesame Street Safari of Fun is primarily for under-6s). It also gets busy in the afternoon, so visit either early on or late in the day.

Jungle Flyers: This kids' ride (6–13s) is a junior-sized zipline journey over part of the Jungala area, a 1-seat there-and-back trip from the upper level of Treetop Trails. Great fun for kids, but a rather short ride, and queues build up quickly and move slowly most of the day. **Restrictions:** Maximum height 4ft 8in/145cm. **TTT**

The Wild Surge: Get ready to 'surge' 4 storeys into the air on this tower ride from inside a giant waterfall providing a (brief!) glimpse over Jungala before bouncing back down again. Queues are also long and slow-moving as the ride takes just 14 at a time. **Restrictions:** 3ft 6in/106cm to ride solo (3ft 2in/96cm with a parent). **TTT (TTTTT under-12s)**

Stanley Falls

Treetop Trails: Climbing nets, elaborate bridges, crawl tubes and a multi-level maze are the basis of this fab 3-storey childen's playground, with smaller-scale adventures at ground level, including squirt fountains and other watery fun (swimsuits or a change of clothes are advisable). It cleverly mixes in 2 different animal habitats, for the fun-loving gibbons, flying fox-bats and the rare tomistoma (an Asian crocodile). TTTT (young 'uns only)

BRITTIP

It's worth knowing for parents with younger children that the toddler play area in Treetop Trails is very thoughtfully in the shade.

Tiger Habitat: One of the park's most creative animal environments is this multi-level tiger exhibit (including its rare white tigers). It is divided into **Tiger Lodge**, an air-conditioned overlook including conservation info and issues, and **Tiger Trail**, a walkthrough section with various close-up opportunities, including a unique pop-up turret (which has a separate queue) in the main enclosure and a rope-pull for guests to 'test their strength' (periodically) against the big cats. Huge windows provide maximum viewing of the animals at play, especially in their plunge pool. AAAA

Orang Outpost: Another brilliant animal habitat, this showcases the park orangutans, who love to look in on guests, viewing them as much

Tiger Habitat

as vice versa. A series of close-up windows, including a glass floor over a hammock play area and a kids' tunnel, provide superb observation of the specially designed forest environment. AAAA

Other entertainment: Look out for **Kareebu Jungala**, colourful stilt-walkers around the village area periodically (see map for times).

Shopping and dining: Shop for gifts at **Tiger Treasures** (organic cotton T-shirts and conservation-related items) and **Cubs Closet** (kids' clothing), and then stop to eat at **Bengal Bistro** (fish, burgers, veggie wraps, salads and sandwiches) or the more snack-orientated **Orang Café** (chicken strips, hot doges, fries, and funnel cakes).

Congo

As you continue into the Congo, this is primarily about just 3 rides, plus a stop on the Serengeti Railway.

Kumba: Another of the park's signature coasters, this unmistakable giant turquoise structure looms over the area. It's one of the largest and fastest in south-east USA and, at 60mph/97kph, features 3 high-thrill elements: a diving loop plunging a full 110ft/33m; a camel-back, with a 360º spiral; and a vertical loop. For good measure, it dives underground! It looks terrifying close up but is absolutely exhilarating, even for non-coaster fans. **Restrictions:** 4ft 6in/137cm. TTTTT

Congo River Rapids: These look pretty tame after Kumba, but don't be fooled. The giant rubber rafts will bounce you down some of the most convincing rapids outside of the Rockies, and you will end up with a fair soaking. **Restrictions:** 3ft 6in/106cm. TTTT

Ubanga-Banga Bumper Cars: Fairly typical fairground dodgems, you won't miss anything if you pass them by. **Restrictions:** 3ft 6in/106cm. TT

Shopping and dining: There is just the **Congo River Outfitters** gift shop here, plus 3 refreshment kiosks.

Timbuktu

Passing through Congo brings you to another heavily ride-dominated area. Here in a North African desert setting you will find many typical funfair elements, with a couple of brain-scrambling rides and 2 good shows.

Sesame Street presents Lights, Camera, Imagination!: New in 2010, this kid-orientated show is a 3-D film romp with all the TV series characters as they try to save the Sesame Street Film Festival. It all goes wrong when the films unravel, cuing a multitude of in-theatre special effects, visual gags and sensory surprises, so be ready to get wet (beware Grover the fireman!) and even tickled. Wind, bubbles and stampeding vermin are all part of the '4-D' experience, which is sure to thrill pre-schoolers, but is lively enough to engage older children and adults, particularly those who grew up with Big Bird, Elmo and Cookie Monster. AAA (**TTTT** for under-6s)

Alternating with Lights, Camera, Imagination! in the Timbuktu 4-D Theater is **Pirates 4-D**, a fun romp that appeals to all children, as the story centres on a band of hapless pirates lead by an incompetent captain (the late Leslie Nielson) and blundering first mate (Eric Idle). Treasure and mutiny cue a riot of 3-D visuals and special effects – think water and lots of it! AAA

BRITTIP

Water effects during Lights, Camera, Imagination! are rather more than just a light misting. Ladies in light coloured tops beware (and children at eye-level with the chair-backs)!

Sand Serpent (formerly Cheetah Chase): This family-orientated 'Crazy Mouse' style coaster is surprisingly energetic, rising as it does some 46ft/14m and adding tight turns and swift drops. Top speed is only 22mph/35kph, but it seems faster and thrills younger kids. **TTT** (**TTTTT** under-10s)

The Phoenix: A positively evil invention that involves sitting in a gigantic, boat-shaped swing that eventually performs a 360º rotation in dramatic, slow-motion style. Don't eat just before this one! Restrictions: 4ft/122cm. **TTTT**

Scorpion: A 50mph/80kph roller-coaster, this features a 62ft/19m drop and a 360º loop that is guaranteed to dial D for dizzy for a while. It lasts just 120secs, but seems longer. Queues build here from late morning. Restrictions: 3ft 6in/106cm. **TTTT**

Sandstorm: A fairly routine whirligig contraption that spins and levitates at high speed (hold on to your stomach). Restrictions: 3ft 6in/106cm. **TTT**

Sahara Go-Round: This offers the opportunity to ride a genuine Mary Poppins-type carousel. **TT**

Other entertainment: As well as the big rides, there are scaled-down Kiddie Rides geared to under-10s. The **Sultan's Arcade** and **Games Area** offers sideshows and stalls that require a few extra dollars, or buy a Games Pass (it can be loaded in the Games Area) and simply swipe your card to play. The **Desert Grill Theater** is home to regular live entertainment in air-conditioned comfort (a lively song-and-dance cabaret that changes on a regular basis). In 2011 it was **Let's Dance**, a Broadway-style international dance festival.

Shopping and dining: Desert Grill is an excellent themed café-diner (serving great sandwiches, salads, pasta, ribs, fried chicken and kids' meals in souvenir buckets), while Timbuktu also has 2 snack kiosks.

The Phoenix

Nairobi

It's back to the animals as we enter this area, with 5 different habitats, plus one of the park's top rides, which also includes an animal adventure.

Rhino Rally: This dramatic and scenic ride is an imaginative off-road jeep safari that has been extended to include even more animal encounters (although the original water-raft part of the ride has been removed to make room for Cheetah Hunt). The 8min whirl through the wilds of Africa encounters elephants, rhinos, crocodiles, antelope and more, as the safari nature of the ride is about as real as they can make it. Your driver adds to the fun with some amusing spiel about the rally and your Land-Rover vehicle, but it does draw slow-moving queues from mid-day, so try to arrive early to beat the crowds. **Restrictions:** 3ft 3in/99cm. AAAA

Serengeti Plain: A 49-acre/20ha spread of African savannah, this is home to buffalo, antelope, zebras, giraffes, wildebeest, ostriches, hippos, rhinos and many exotic birds, and can be viewed for much of the journey on the Serengeti Express, a full-size, open-car steam train that chugs slowly from its main station in Nairobi to the Congo, Stanleyville and back. AAA

BRITTIP
Take the Serengeti Railway from Nairobi (or Congo or Stanleyville) in mid-afternoon to give your feet a rest when it's busy elsewhere.

Jambo Junction: The park's field hospital and nursery is an interesting

animal encounter, with some friendly flamingos, small critters (lemurs, sloths, possums and various babies needing extra care) on view through the large windows. This is the place to meet the park's well travelled Animal Ambassadors, who make media appearances and aid in educating the public about conservation issues. AA

A new **Animal Hospital & Nutrition Center** will be open in late 2012, featuring a unique insight into the care of the park's animals. Keepers will be on hand to answer questions and you may see medical procedures in progress, with an audio link to ask questions of the vets working behind the glass.

Nairobi incorporates the park's **Edge of Africa** area (which can also be accessed through Egypt), a 15-acre/6ha 'safari experience' that guarantees a close-up almost like the real thing. The walk-through puts you in an authentic setting of native wilds and villages from which you can view giraffes, lions, baboons, meerkats, crocodiles, hyenas and vultures, and even an underwater hippo habitat. Look out for the abandoned jeep – you can sit in the cab while lions lounge in the back! Wandering naturalists offer informal talks, and the attention to detail is superb.

BRITTIP
Edge of Africa offers some fantastic photo opportunities but, in the hot months, come here early in the day as many animals seek refuge from the heat later.

Other entertainment: Look out for the **Elephant Habitat** and periodic sessions with animal staff (notably the afternoon Elephant Wash), while you can see more park inhabitants at the **Reptile House**, **Curiosity Caverns** (nocturnal animals) and **Tortoise Habitat**. The new meeting area for the **Serengeti Safari** is also here, next to Kenya Kanteen.

Shopping and dining: Caravan Crossing (safari apparel and hats) has the best shopping here while **Kenya Kanteen** offers drinks and snacks.

The Elephant Habitat

Egypt

The final area of Busch Gardens is somewhat tucked away, so it's best visited either first thing or late in the day (sooner rather than later if you want to ride Montu). It sits in the park's bottom right corner and much of it is carefully re-created pharaoh country, dominated by suspended coaster Montu, named after an ancient Egyptian warrior god. You can also take the **SkyRide** cable car to Stanleyville (with a great look at Rhino Rally en route).

Tut's Tomb: This re-creation of the Tutankhamen discovery by famous archaeologist Howard Carter is now missing most of its lighting and audio effects, hence is pretty unremarkable. A

Montu: You cannot miss the area's other main attraction, another breathtaking inverted coaster, covering nearly 4,000ft/1,219m of track at up to 60mph/97kph and peaking with a G-force of 3.85! Like Kumba, it looks terrifying but really is a 5-star thrill as it leaves your legs dangling and twists and dives (underground at 2 points) for almost 3min of brain-scrambling fun. Restrictions: 4ft 6in/137cm. TTTTT

Other entertainment: Youngsters can make their own excavations in the **Shifting Sands**, a neat sand play area.

Shopping and dining: The high-quality **Golden Scarab** offers hand-blown glass and cartouche paintings while you can grab souvenirs at **Edge of Africa Gift Shop** and **Montu Gifts**. For dining, Victorian-style **Crown Colony Restaurant** overlooks Serengeti Plain and offers counter-service salads, sandwiches and pizzas in the Café downstairs (with a pub bar, too) or full-service dining upstairs, with magnificent views of the animals. For a memorable meal (11.30am until an hour before park closing), head here for lunch (it doesn't take bookings) or, even better, come back at early evening and see the animals visit the waterhole.

BRITTIP

We find **Crown Colony Restaurant** a blissful lunch stop in the hotter months when its cool interior and elegant ambience offer a welcome change of pace after a lot of the rides.

Special tours

Busch Gardens features a wide range of behind-the-scenes tours and adventure expeditions that add an extra dimension to the park. For all tours, book at the Adventure Tour Center in Morocco or, better still, book in advance on 1888 800 5447 or at **www.buschgardens.com**.

Serengeti Safari: A 30min excursion (5 times a day, up to 20 at a time) aboard flat-bed trucks, takes you to meet some of the Serengeti Plain's residents and feed the beautiful giraffes while learning about the park's environmental efforts. It tends to fill up quickly and costs $33.95/person (children must be at least 5; 5–15s must be accompanied by an adult); the **Sunrise Safari** adds a continental breakfast to this experience at park opening ($39.95). There is even a **Serengeti Night Safari** (park admission not required) for a 2hr after-dark excursion into the Serengeti, with appetisers and hot and cold drinks ($60/person, 21 and over only)

Guided Adventure Tour: This takes just 15 at a time on a 5hr VIP trek, with your own guide, reserved seating at the Moroccan Palace Theater, front-of-line access for major rides like Gwazi and Rhino Rally, counter-service lunch at one of the restaurants and close encounters with many of the animals, including the Serengeti Safari ($94.99 adults, $84.99 children)

Montu

Elite Adventure Tour: A personal, exclusive park tour with front-of-line access to all rides, the Serengeti Safari, reserved seating at shows, free bottled water throughout and lunch at Crown Colony ($199.99/person, 5 and over).

Endangered Species Safari: A 45min meet-and-greet with various animal specialists (notably a close-up with the rhinos), learning about their work and conservation issues, including how Busch is involved with worldwide wildlife projects ($39.95; no under-5s).

Sunset Safari: 45mins, beginning at the Crown Colony, then heading out on the Serengeti Plain to hand-feed giraffes, meet the wildlife and enjoy a beer or 2 as you tour ($39.99/person, 21 and over only, with valid photo ID).

Keeper for a Day: An exclusive 6hr behind-the-scenes tour where you join the keepers as they feed, train and care for giraffes and antelope, then move on to assist the avian team on the Serengeti ($249.95/person, including park admission; 13 and over only).

Tiger and Orang-utan Keeper Experience: A 90min backstage tour into the care and health of Jungala's animals ($199.95 for group of 6).

Elephant Keeper Experience: A similar 90min opportunity with the park's elephants ($199.95 for up to 6; no under-10s, sturdy footwear required).

Tut's Tomb

Elephant Insider: A 45min group walking tour behind the scenes with the elephant handlers and their charges ($19.95/person).

Roller Coaster Insider: Unique 45min look at how the park builds and maintains its amazing array of rides, with front-row seats for Montu to finish with (14 and over only, $19.95/person).

Jungala Insider: A fascinating 45min group visit behind the scenes in Jungala to meet the keepers, see how they care for the magnificent tigers (you might even help to weigh one!) and orang-utans, and learn a few zoo husbandry secrets ($19.95/person).

Special programmes

Busch Gardens is open until 10pm for the **Summer Nights** programme (June–Aug), featuring outdoor food and drink, live entertainment (notably at the Desert Grill Theater and Gwazi Pavilion), music and DJs, plus clever lighting effects on coasters like SheiKra. A nightly high-energy finale, **Kinetix**, brings together live musicians, singers, dancers and original artists for a 30min contemporary rock show enhanced by innovative lighting. There is also a huge **fireworks spectacular** 2–4 July.

For a really full family day out, you can combine Busch Gardens with sister water park **Adventure Island** (on McKinley Drive), which is blissful when it hots up. The 25 acres/10ha of watery fun, in a Key West theme, offer a full range of slides and rides, such as the **Wahoo Run** raft ride, a 210ft/64m plunge on the body slide **Gulf Scream**, the exciting 4-lane mat slide **Riptide** and spiralling tube ride **Calypso Coaster**. Adventure Island is open mid-Mar to late Oct (weekends only Sept and Oct) 10am–5pm (9pm in summer). Tickets are $43 (adults) and $39 (3–9s), while a Busch Gardens-Adventure Island combo is $93 and $85

Well, that's the low-down on all the main theme parks, but there is still MUCH more to discover…

7 The Other Attractions

If you think you can 'do' Orlando just by sticking to the main theme parks, think again! There is still a LOT more to discover, starting with Kennedy Space Center, which we rate as an essential place to visit these days. It will easily demand a day of your attention.

Then there are the new Legoland Florida and Silver Springs, which offer a taste of the more natural Florida, while Gatorland provides another great-value experience with its alligators and shows. Then you have fun venues like WonderWorks, Orlando Science Center and Ripley's Believe It Or Not. For more individual attractions, there is the unique aviation museum Fantasy of Flight, the amazing 'skydive' experience of iFLY Orlando, plus some magnificent water parks. The choice is yours, but it's an immense selection. Let's start with One Giant Leap for Mankind.

Kennedy Space Center

Welcome to the past, present and future of NASA's space programme, and one of the most enjoyable, and fascinating places in Florida. The KSC has undergone huge redevelopment in recent years, culminating with the opening of the stunning **Shuttle Launch Experience**, part of a complete overhaul of the main Visitor Complex. This has really put it among the front rank of local attractions and

there is even more now to justify an all-day visit. The process will continue in 2012 with the overhaul of the Space Shuttle Plaza to showcase the grand acquisition of the shuttle **Atlantis**, one of the 3 surviving space vehicles now the programme is officially over. This will also see more dramatic development of the KSC in the coming years.

There are 5 continually running shows (including 2 splendid IMAX films and a live theatre presentation for kids), 6 static showcases, a children's play area, an art gallery, the captivating Astronaut Encounter and moving Astronaut Memorial, and a bus tour of the Space Center, which add up to great value. Plus there are 2 additional programmes, the **Astronaut Training Experience** and **Family Astronaut Experience** that provide outstanding extras.

Shuttle Launch

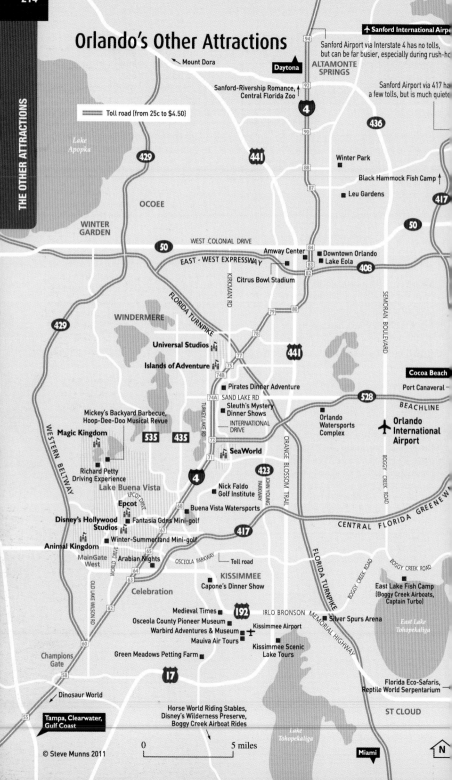

Orlando's Other Attractions

✈ Sanford International Airpo

Sanford Airport via Interstate 4 has no tolls, but can be far busier, especially during rush-ho

Sanford Airport via 417 ha a few tolls, but is much quiete

Mount Dora

Daytona

ALTAMONTE SPRINGS

Sanford-Rivership Romance, Central Florida Zoo

Toll road (from 25c to $4.50)

Lake Apopka

Winter Park

Black Hammock Fish Camp

Leu Gardens

OCOEE

WINTER GARDEN

WEST COLONIAL DRIVE

EAST - WEST EXPRESSWAY

Amway Center

Downtown Orlando
Lake Eola

Citrus Bowl Stadium

FLORIDA TURNPIKE

KIRKMAN RD

SEMORAN BOULEVARD

WINDERMERE

Universal Studios

Islands of Adventure

Cocoa Beach

Port Canaveral

Pirates Dinner Adventure

SAND LAKE RD

BEACHLINE

Sleuth's Mystery Dinner Shows

Mickey's Backyard Barbecue, Hoop-Dee-Doo Musical Revue

INTERNATIONAL DRIVE

Orlando Watersports Complex

Orlando International Airport

WESTERN BELTWAY

TURKEY LAKE RD

Magic Kingdom

Richard Petty Driving Experience

SeaWorld

Lake Buena Vista

Nick Faldo Golf Institute

ORANGE BLOSSOM TRAIL

JOHN YOUNG PARKWAY

Epcot

EPCOT DRIVE

Buena Vista Watersports

Disney's Hollywood Studios

Fantasia Gdns Mini-golf

CENTRAL FLORIDA GREENEW

BOGGY CREEK ROAD

Animal Kingdom

Winter-Summerland Mini-golf

WORLD DRIVE

MainGate West

Arabian Nights

OSCEOLA PARKWAY

Toll road

FLORIDA TURNPIKE

BOGGY CREEK ROAD

Celebration

KISSIMMEE

Capone's Dinner Show

East Lake Fish Camp
(Boggy Creek Airboats, Captain Turbo)

OLD LAKE WILSON RD

Medieval Times

Osceola County Pioneer Museum

IRLO BRONSON

Silver Spurs Arena

East Lake Tohopekaliga

Warbird Adventures & Museum

Kissimmee Airport

Mauiva Air Tours

MEMORIAL HIGHWAY

Green Meadows Petting Farm

Kissimmee Scenic Lake Tours

Champions Gate

Dinosaur World

Horse World Riding Stables, Disney's Wilderness Preserve, Boggy Creek Airboat Rides

ST CLOUD

Tampa, Clearwater, Gulf Coast

Lake Tohopekaliga

Florida Eco-Safaris, Reptile World Serpentarium

0   5 miles

Miami

N

© Steve Munns 2011

KENNEDY SPACE CENTER at a glance

Location	Off State Road 405 in Titusville	
Size	Visitor Complex 70 acres/28.3ha	
Hours	9am–5 or 6pm) year-round (except Christmas Day)	
Admission	Under-3s free; 3–11 $31; adult (12+) $41. Prices do not include tax but include admission to US Astronaut Hall of Fame.	
Parking	Free	
Lockers	No	
Pushchairs	Available on a complimentary basis (with photo ID as deposit) inside the Information Center	
Wheelchairs	Available on a complimentary basis (with photo ID as deposit) inside the Information Center	
Top attractions	Shuttle Launch Experience; IMAX films; Astronaut Encounter; KSC Bus Tours	
Don't miss	Apollo-Saturn V Center on Bus Tours; Astronaut Memorial; Rocket Garden; Space Shuttle Plaza; Sci Fi Summer	
Hidden costs	Meals	Burger, chips and coke $10.18 Kids' meal $4.99
	T-shirts	$14.99–30.99
	Souvenirs	69c–$450
	Sundries	Lunch with an Astronaut $16.95 children, $26.49 adults

You enter through the futuristic ticket plaza and can spend several hours just wandering around the exhibits and presentations of the Visitor Complex. But, with the huge draw of its latest attraction, you should head here first and save your meandering for later on.

Shuttle Launch Experience: This is the BIG one in every sense, a dramatic presentation into a real-life shuttle launch – with you on board! You enter the huge building along a life-like gantry and there is then a clever pre-show, with dry ice, atmospheric lighting and some clever sound and vibration effects to provide the 'feel' of a launch. Then you enter the high-tech 'ready room' to prepare for your own blast-off into space. There are 4 'capsules' of 44 passengers each, designed to look like crew cabins in the cargo hold of the Shuttle, and, once aboard you go through the full launch procedure as the vehicle moves into a near-vertical position for take-off. On the command 'Go for engine start' the fun really begins as you are at the heart of an awesome

5-minute simulation that provides all the features of a realistic launch, with the use of massive vibration generators, sound effects, cabin and seat movements and screen visuals. You get a taste of the G-forces involved, the Rocket Booster and External Tank separations, and a moment of 'weightlessness' as you

Shuttle Launch Experience

enter earth's orbit. Finally, the cargo hold doors open above you to provide a truly awe-inspiring view. To make sure you don't get your breath back for a while, you exit the Shuttle to 'walk' back to earth via a spiral walkway surrounded by the stars and more satellite views of the planet.

Don't miss the plaques to mark every Shuttle flight – and the memorials to the tragic Challenger and Columbia missions. Even the Gift Shop is a cut above average! TTT and AAAAA

BRITTIP

All of the Shuttle Launch Experience is fully wheelchair-accessible, and there is a seat outside for potential riders to test their comfort level. For anyone wary of the full ride (although there is no need to be), there is a bypass room where you can experience the attraction without the motion.

Bus tours: The KSC's signature air-conditioned coaches depart every 15mins from 10am and are fully narrated throughout to provide the full overview of the Space Center. They make 2 important stops in addition to driving around much of the working areas (including the massive Vehicle Assembly Building). The first stop is the **LC39 Observation Gantry**, just 1ml/1.6km from shuttle launch pad 39A, a combination 4-storey observation deck and exhibition centre. The exhibits consist of a 10min film into how launches were prepared plus models and videos of a countdown and touch-screen info on the shuttle programme. Next, you stop at the **Apollo/Saturn V Center**, one of the KSC's great exhibits, where you can easily spend 90mins. It highlights the Apollo missions and first moon landing with 2 impressive theatrical presentations on the risks and triumphs (complete with vibrating seats and other special effects for a real you-are-there feeling), a full-size 363ft/111m Saturn V rocket and a hands-on gallery that brings space exploration into sharp focus. Allow 2–3hrs to do the tour justice, but be aware the last bus leaves the Visitor Center at 2.20 or 2.50pm, depending on time of year. AAAAA

IMAX films: Back at the Visitor Complex are the IMAX cinemas – two 55ft/17m screens that give the impression of sitting on top of the action. **Space Station 3-D**, narrated by Tom Cruise, is a breathtaking slice of science fact, living with the crew of the International Space Station and affording a heart-stopping look at the construction process. **Hubble 3-D** (narrated by Leonardo DiCaprio) is a breathtaking 43min journey through the universe as seen by the Hubble Space Telescope. Float beside

Apollo/Saturn V Center

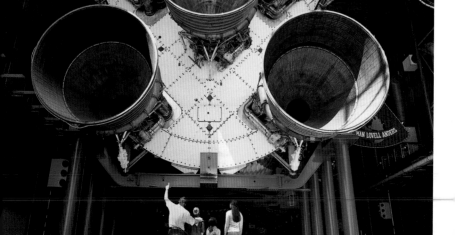

Lunch with an astronaut

For another fully engrossing feature at the Kennedy Space Center, book its special Lunch With An Astronaut, where a small group gets to dine with the star of the daily Astronaut Encounter. The featured person gives their own special briefing, adding extra insight into their space missions, plus answers individual questions, gives autographs and poses for photos. It is $24.37 adults and $16.95 children at 12.15pm daily, and tickets may be bought online or by calling 321 449 4400. It's a highly worthwhile opportunity and 1 we strongly recommend. The buffet-style lunch is pretty good, too!

astronauts as they adjust and repair Hubble, marvel at the sensation of moving through galaxies and experience the profound dynamics of the cosmos. This presentation truly dazzles with the spirit of human achievement and you may feel the urge to stand up and cheer at the end! AAAA Also in the IMAX building, you'll find *Eye on the Universe: The Hubble Telescope Exhibit*, featuring still images taken by Hubble.

Astronaut Encounter: This engaging feature is a daily talk and Q&A session, along with personal observations and stories from various veterans of the space programmes, including regular Shuttle astronauts. It is an insightful and engrossing programme, up to 3 times a day at the Astronaut Encounter Theater. AAAA

Robot Scouts: This walk-through display-and-show is done in the company of Starquester 2000, your 'robot host', who explains the history of NASA's unmanned space probes in a surprising and amusing style. AAA

Shuttle Explorer will be closing some time in 2012 as part of the thrilling addition of the Space Shuttle Atlantis, which will make a permanent home at Kennedy Space Center. The Center will undergo a major redesign making Atlantis the focal point, so watch out for some exciting changes here.

Early Space Exploration: A clever and coherent walk-through trip into the space programme's recent past, including the Hall of Discovery, the Mercury Mission Control Room – the original consoles from America's first manned space flights – and the Hall of History. AAA

Exploration Space: A new interactive exhibit and showcase featuring the Explorers Wanted show, an engaging NASA presentation geared toward children. Check out the computer photo stations for a neat souvenir. AAA

Star Trek Live: Showing several times daily in the Astronaut Encounter Theater, this 30min interactive show encourages the audience to become Starfleet cadets experiencing their first day of training at the Academy. Living and working in space, space travel, communication, and technology are among the challenges cadets must deal with, all under the threat of intergalactic chaos when a pesky Romulan launches an attack on Earth. Captain Kirk and Mr Spock make on-screen appearances and cutting edge special effects add to the excitement, with science and (of course!) logic being the keys to success. AAA

Astronaut Encounter

Other exhibits: Try **Nature and Technology** (which showcases early Florida settlement and the unique balance the Center maintains with the local environment), the **Center for Space Education** (an interactive learning and teacher resource centre), the **Space Walk of Honor** and **NASA Art Gallery** (exhibits and artwork).

Youngsters have their own playground, the covered **Children's Play Dome**, which has a range of climbing/ crawling/sliding elements. Finally, head out to see the hardware of space flight in the **Rocket Garden**, which has a kids' splash fountain and an Apollo capsule gantry, to give the feel of astronauts boarding the Saturn V rocket. Free tours are given twice a day (9.30am and 10.30am). Don't forget to stop at the **Astronaut Memorial**, a sombre but moving tribute to the men and women who have died in the cause of the space programme. AAA

Shopping and dining: The Visitor Complex has an excellent **Space Shop** (the world's largest store for space memorabilia and gifts – enter at your peril!), the smaller **Space Shop II** by the main exit and **The Right Stuff Shop** at the Apollo/Saturn V Center. Stop for a bite to eat at the **Orbit Food Court**, a cafeteria-style diner serving a fresh range of salads, burgers, pasta, pizza and sandwiches. Quick bites can be found at **G-Force Grill** (hot dogs, turkey legs, fries, drinks) plus **Shuttle Plaza Snacks** and various kiosks for snacks and drinks. You'll

Astronaut Training Experience

also find the **Moon Rock Café** at the Apollo/Saturn V Center on the bus tour. The Center then has 2 optional extra tours and its Astronaut Training feature.

Cape Canaveral: Then and Now: If you want to learn more about NASA past and present, here is a 2hr-plus guided journey (daily at noon) into the early days of space exploration around the older part of the facility. Highlights include the Air Force Space and Missile Museum, Mercury launch sites and Memorial, original astronaut training facility and several active launch pads, all of which are otherwise off-limits. Photo ID is required for all visitors on this tour ($21 adults, $15 3–11s).

Discover Kennedy Space Center: Today & Tomorrow: This 2hr tour (departing between 10am and 1.50pm daily) takes visitors as close to the launch pad as possible in the company of an expert guide. Tour the Shuttle Landing Facility, view the launch area and stop outside the Vehicle Assembly Building ($21 adults, $15 3–11s; all tours require Space Center admission. Book online or call 321 449 4400).

Astronaut Training Experience (ATX): Away from the main attractions, you have the choice of the thrilling, full-day programme into the training required for a Shuttle mission. You progress through a sequence of simulated hands-on preparations, with the input of various NASA veterans. The training provides a range of activities, from the multi-axis trainer and one-sixth gravity chair, to operating a Shuttle mock-up and taking the helm in Mission Control. The ATX Half-Day Core experience (morning or afternoon) is limited to a few participants each day and you must be at least 14 (under-18s must be accompanied by a parent). Hard-wearing clothes and athletic shoes are advised, and 'recruits' should be free of neck and back injuries. It costs $145 (including ATX gear) but guarantees a memorable day for 'space cadets'.

Kennedy Space Center

US Astronaut Hall of Fame

While the Space Center tells you primarily about the machinery of putting men and women in space, the Astronaut Hall of Fame (on SR 405, just before the main entrance to KSC) gives the low-down on the people involved, with engaging memorabilia, exhibits and explanations. A chronological approach divides it into 5 sections.

Entry Experience introduces the visions of space flight, with an 8min video of the astronauts as modern explorers, and leads into **Race to the Moon**, the stories of the *Mercury*, *Gemini* and *Apollo* missions (where you can see how incredibly small the first space capsules were). The Museum's heart and soul is the **Space Shuttle: The Astronaut Experience** exhibit, a unique collection of astronaut testimonials, personal experiences and authentic artefacts, which create a personal connection for visitors with the enduring stories and endeavours of the Space Shuttle men and women honoured in the Hall of Fame. The **Astronaut Adventure** room then features space-walk 'chairs', a G-force simulator, moon exploration, interactive

Family Astronaut Training Experience: A chance for children as young as 7, with a parent, to participate in a half-day course. The morning session is spent building and launching rockets, riding realistic simulators, meeting an veteran NASA Astronaut and working together on a realistic shuttle mission to the International Space Station in the full-scale orbiter mock-up and Mission Control. It's $145/person and includes an ATX t-shirt and cap. Book in advance on 321 449 4400 or online (see below).

> **BRITTIP**
> Although there are no more Shuttle launches, the KSC still has an active rocket launch programme. Look for 1 during your visit at **www.nasa.gov** and **www.spacecoastlaunches.com**.

Getting there: Take the Beachline Expressway out of Orlando (Route 528, and a toll road, see map p214) for about 45mins, bear left on SR 407 (don't follow signs to Cape Canaveral or Cocoa Beach at this point) and turn right at the T-junction onto SR 405. The Visitor Center is located 9mls/14km along on the right. Tours and IMAX presentations start at 10am (**www.KennedySpaceCenter.com**).

Astronaut Hall of Fame

computers (try to 'land' a Shuttle) and Mars Mission experience. **Science on a Sphere:** This fascinating 3-D exhibit explores the Earth, the moon, and the planets in our solar system as if you are viewing them from space. Watch hurricanes, see ocean currents move and weather patterns change, and learn about space technology's role in understanding global climate trends.

Admission: Included with Kennedy Space Center or $20 adults, $16 3–11s on its own. Open 9am–6 or 7pm. If you enjoyed the KSC, try to spend a couple of hours here (it is busiest towards the end of the day). **AAA**

LEGOLAND Florida

With Merlin Entertainments Group's purchase of the former Cypress Gardens in 2010, Europe's biggest attraction operator opened **LEGOLAND Florida** in 2011. This is Merlin's second Legoland park in the USA and the world's largest, and features its trademark rides and attractions geared primarily for the 2–12 age group, all with a unique Floridian flair. The park in Winter Haven (south-west of Disney and Kissimmee) includes 50 rides, shows and attractions, plus their wonderfully creative Lego models and interactive elements.

The Beginning: Start your adventure here (where else!) for the ticket centre, Guest Relations, and functional elements of the park. There are no shows or attractions here, but the fun starts in the next area, just a short walk away.

Legoland

Shopping and dining: Immediately to the left of the entrance is **The Big Shop** (one of the largest Lego merchandise stores in the world). Dining is found at **The Garden Restaurant** (soups, salads, sandwiches; gluten free, vegetarian, and healthy options available) with quick bites at **The Market** (pastries, yoghurt, ice cream, espresso, drinks).

Fun Town: Here is where the squeals of delight begin! In true Legoland style, you have entered a charming village complete with a working factory, 4-D cinema and a carousel. Immediately to your right is the **Factory Tour**, where guests can watch working machinery as it goes through the process of making Lego bricks, from moulding to packaging. Just beyond is **Fun Town Theater**, featuring 3 4-D movies daily.

Shopping and dining: All of your favourite Lego merchandise can be found at **Studio Store**, including Star Wars, SpongeBob, Indiana Jones, and Batman. **Granny's Apple Fries** serves up the park's signature dessert (apples, cinnamon and a creamy sauce).

Miniland USA: Continuing in clockwise fashion, enter this iconic area, featuring 8 specially themed US locations in miniature. **Florida** shows off some of the state's gems, including a large area devoted entirely to **Kennedy Space Center**. It even has its own version of Daytona International Speedway, where youngsters can race Lego cars. **Las Vegas** boasts the glittering luxury resorts and other icons of Nevada's most famous city. **Washington DC** re-creates the White House, US Capitol building, the Smithsonian museum and the Washington and Jefferson monuments. Look closely and you'll see an animated parade and the beautiful cherry trees that bloom each spring. No mini-land would be complete without **New York City**, and Legoland's representation includes Rockefeller Plaza (complete with squirt fountains!), Times Square, Lady Liberty, the Empire State building, Bronx Zoo, and Grand Central Station.

Aquazone Wave Racers

For authenticity, there's an army of Yellow Cabs, which no New York street would be without. Finally, there is a section devoted to the ever-popular subject of **Pirates**, and another miniland that highlights the state of **California**.

Pirates Cove: Veer to the left as you head out of Miniland and you'll find swashbuckling meets water in an exciting battle on the 'high seas' of Lake Eloise. Lego characters and a life-sized pirate ship add to the fun of this water stunt show that children will not want to miss.

Botanical Gardens: Just beyond and to the right of the stadium are the beautiful gardens that Cypress Gardens was known for, lovingly restored and now a peaceful haven perfect for strolling (and yes, that banyan tree is real!).

Imagination Zone: The creative heart of the park, here children put their imaginations to work at 4 hands-on stations. **Game Space** features 13 Lego-themed video games; build and race a Lego car at **Build & Test** or assemble a computerised robot at **Lego Mindstorms**. **Kid Power Towers** burn off excess energy as kids (and adults!) use ropes and pulleys to ascend colourful towers, then let go for a 'free fall' back down. **Restrictions:** 4ft/122cm or 3ft 4in/130cm with adult. Child swap available, guests in wheelchairs must transfer.

Shopping and dining: Lego Clubhouse offers ice cream, popcorn, drinks and snacks, along with bulk Lego bricks and Make & Create kits. **Pizza Mania** has pizza, snacks, ice cream and drinks.

LEGO City: At the far end of the park, youngsters may want to make a bee-line for this. Scaled down to kid-size are all the important elements of a working town. And your muscles will be put to work at **Fun Town Rescue Academy**, as families race each other to 'put out the fire'. But these fire trucks only move when you pump the levers! **Restrictions:** 4ft/122cm, or 2ft 10in/with adult. Child Swap; guests in wheelchairs must transfer. Legoland's popular **Driving School** (ages 6–12) and **Junior Driving School** (3–5s) and **Boating School** are here too, giving kids the chance to navigate electric cars and small boats to earn official Legoland driving licences. For something more dynamic, try **Flight School**'s inverted steel coaster. Arguably the biggest thrill in the park and a big hit with coaster fans! **Restrictions:** 3ft 8in/111cm expected. When your feet hit the ground again, head into **The Big Test** for a humorous show featuring would-be fire fighters from Fun Town Fire Department as they learn a thing or two about fire safety.

Xtreme: Next is where riders race, break and bank in life-size Lego Technic cars onboard the steel

coaster Lego Technic Test Track.
Restrictions: 3ft 6in/99cm expected.
Ride the waves and dodge soaking
blasts of water on **Aquazone Wave
Racers**, a ride so cool you'll want to
queue up straight away for another
go! **Restrictions:** 4ft 4in/132cm.

Land of Adventure: Circling back,
you come upon another big thrill in
the form of **Coastersaurus**, a classic
wooden coaster that zips through a
prehistoric jungle and past animated
dinosaurs (made from Lego, of
course!). **Restrictions:** 3ft expected.
The excitement continues at **Lost
Kingdom Adventure** as you hunt for
treasure while fighting off baddies
with laser blasters. Kids will want
to ride several times to better their
score. **Restrictions:** 4ft 6in/137cm,
2ft 10in/86cm with adult. Child Swap,
ride photos available. Let young 'uns
loose at **Pharaoh's Revenge** multi-
level climbing structure, with the
added fun of being able to shoot soft
foam balls at each other. **Restrictions:**
Under-5s must be accompanied by
an adult. **Beetle Bounce** shoots riders
15ft/4.5m high on this kid-friendly
tower ride. **Restrictions:** 3ft/91cm

Dining: BBQ Restaurant is a good
choice for ribs, chicken, salads,
desserts and beverages.

Castle Hill: Your final destination
has just 2 attractions, both of which
are real draws. Climb aboard **The
Dragon** for a backstage view of life in
an enchanted castle, then take off on
a thrilling flight on this scenic dark
ride that becomes a dynamic outdoor
coaster! **Restrictions:** 4ft 4in/132
or 4ft/122 with adult. Child Swap.
Ride photo available. Then, saddle
up on Lego themed horses for **The
Royal Joust**, where youngsters gallop
though an enchanted forest, jousting
with Lego knights along the way.
Restrictions: 3ft/91cm; Min 4yrs, max
12; max 169lb/76kg.

DUPLO® Village: And lastly (or first,
if you veer right out of Fun Town) you
enter the perfect place for toddlers to
let their imaginations run wild as they
explore a village sized just for them.

Tickets cost $65 3–12s and seniors,

$75 adults. Hours 10am–5pm, 7pm
peak season. Legoland will initially
be **closed** Tues and Wed, but that may
change at some point in 2012. Check
the website for current hours (1877
350 5346 **www.legolandfloridaresort.
com**).

Silver Springs

Silver Springs, just under 2hrs' drive
to the north of Orlando, makes
a restful break from the hectic
theme park pace. This peaceful
350-acre/142ha nature park
surrounds the headwaters of the
crystal-clear Silver River, and the
real highlights are its famous Glass-
bottomed boats, which take you to
watch the world's largest artesian
springs, along with plenty of wildlife.

> **BRITTIP**
>
> Silver Springs and Wild Waters are
> both busy at weekends, but you
> shouldn't encounter many queues on
> weekdays, especially in summer. NB: The
> park continues to experiment with autumn/
> winter hours, closing Mon–Thurs at times.
> Check **www.silversprings.com** for the full
> opening hours.

Expect close encounters with
alligators, turtles, raccoons and lots
of waterfowl, while the park also has
a collection of more exotic animals
such as bears, panthers and giraffes.
Five animal shows, an alligator and
crocodile encounter, a large bear
exhibit, a petting zoo, kids' adventure
playground, a tower ride and a
white alligator exhibit complete the
attractions. To destroy a few more film
illusions, this was the setting for the
1930s and '40s Tarzan films starring
Johnny Weissmuller (a long way from
Africa!). In all, you'd probably want at
least half a day here.

Tours and shows: The park's main
attraction (dating back to 1878) is
the **Glass-bottomed Boat Ride**, a
20min tour that goes down well with
all the family and gives a first-class
view of the 7 different springs and
water life. Similarly, the **Lost River
Voyage** is another 20min boat trip
down one of the unspoilt stretches

A Lion break

Heading to Legoland Florida? The friendly **Red Lion Pub** on Hwy 27 in Lake Hamilton makes a perfect dinner stop after a day there. The menu features American and British favourites (cod and chips, bangers and mash, shepherd's pie, plus steaks, liver and onions, wings, burgers and more) and the pub serves up 4 British beers and 5 American ones, plus there are darts and a pool table. There is live music on Fri evenings and karaoke on Sats. They also have a country-style restaurant next door. Lunch specials (from $4.99) 11am–4pm; Early Bird specials from 4–6pm Mon–Fri; Happy Hour 4–9pm daily. Pub open 11am–11pm Sun–Thurs, 11am–1am Fri and Sat (863 439 1700).

of the Silver River, with a visit to the park's wildlife outpost. The 3rd boat trip, the **Fort King River Cruise**, takes you back to pioneer Florida, the Seminole wars and a reconstruction of Fort King. With sightings of native wildlife, an archaeological dig, movie set and Florida Cracker Farm, it is another gentle 20min historical perspective, with some storytelling from the boat captain as a bonus. The **Wilderness Trail** features a tram ride towed behind a Wrangler Jeep into a wilderness area populated by assorted local wildlife (including gators!). Then there are the 2 **Ross Allen Island Animal Shows**, each lasting 15min and featuring an entertaining – and occasionally hair-raising – look at the worlds of reptiles and non-venomous snakes and **Wings of the Springs**, a 25min bird show, with dramatic free-flight demonstrations that showcase a diverse collection of parrots, ducks, hawks, falcons and vultures.

Animal Attractions: On Ross Allen Island, take time to explore the **Big Gator Lagoon** in a cypress swamp habitat, viewed from a raised boardwalk. See the largest American crocodile in captivity, the 2,000lb/900kg Sobek, as well as a collection of alligators, turtles and Galapagos tortoises (with gator feeding daily at 2.30pm). The **Florida Natives** attraction features snakes, turtles, spiders, otters and other

local denizens. Other large-scale exhibits are the **World of Bears**, an educational presentation including conservation information in a 2-acre/0.8ha spread devoted to bears of all kinds, from grizzly to black bears; **Panther Prowl**, with a unique look at the endangered Florida panther and Western cougar; and the **White Gator** exhibit, which shows why these creatures are known as swamp ghosts. All 3 have educational presentations several times daily. Petting zoo **Kritter Korral** (with sheep, rabbits, donkeys, llamas, pot-bellied pigs, ponies and goats) is a big draw for the little 'uns, while the Giraffe enclosure allows close-up encounters with these gentle giants, plus a feeding option (for a small fee).

Rides: In addition to its boat tours, Silver Springs also boasts a child-friendly **Carousel**, next to the imaginative **Kids Ahoy** playland, with its centrepiece riverboat featuring slides, rides, air bounce, ball crawl, 3D net maze, bumper boats and games. Older children will gravitate to the **Lighthouse Ride**, a combined carousel and gondola lift rising almost 100ft/30m above the park (and magnificently lit at night). By contrast, the **Floral Gardens** provide a peaceful haven in which to sit and watch the world go by.

Shopping and dining: Springside Mall provides an array of shops and eateries, with the Deli offering pleasant sandwiches and the **Springside Café** also above average, while shopping can be found at **Swampy's Emporium**.

Glass-bottomed boats at Silver Springs

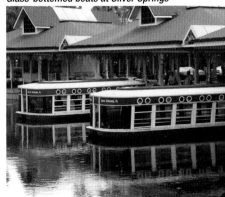

Special events: Silver Springs also offers a regular concert series at the **Twin Oaks Mansion** stage (included with admission) through the spring and autumn, with artists like Blue Oyster Cult, Foreigner and a variety of well-known country and western acts. Other special events include 4th July celebrations, themed weekends (like the Ocala Scottish Highland Games in October), special events (such as Cirque Shanghai Bai Xi and several speciality car shows in 2011), plus Halloween **Fright Nights** (on specific dates in Oct), with haunted houses and the Gatorman River Cruise. The Christmas **Festival of Lights** (late Nov–30 Dec, dusk–8.30pm), features a huge display through the park and other festive touches.

Wild Waters: Worth at least a couple of hours, the neighbouring 9-acre/4ha water park offers slides such as the Alligator Ambush (a daring tube ride into a 35ft/10.7m bowl with water-spraying gator!), Bunyan's Bend (a winding body slide), the 220ft/67m Silver Bullet and the helter-skelter Osceola's Revenge, as well as a 400ft/122m tube ride on the turbocharged Hurricane, a huge wave pool, and various kid-sized fun in Cool Kids Cove and Tad Pool for tots.

> **BRITTIP**
> Check Silver Springs' website for current discounted admission offers, or buy an annual (Silver) pass for multiple visits for less than the cost of 2 days' admission.

Gatorland

Getting there: On SR40 in Ocala, 72mls/116km north of Orlando. Take the Florida Turnpike (a toll road, see map p6) until it turns into I-75. 28mls/45km further north, go east on SR40 for 10mls/16km, just past Wild Waters on your right. Admission: $29.99 adults, seniors (55+), $24.99 3–10s (under-3s free); parking $7; 10am–5pm most days, Mar–July; closed some Mon and Tues in Aug and Sept (Oct–Jan hours vary; see website for details). Wild Waters $29.99 adults and $22.99 3–10s (under 48in/122cm). A joint Silver Springs/ Wild Waters ticket is $44.99 (352 236 2121, **www.silversprings.com**). AAA½.

Gatorland

For another taste of 'real' Florida wildlife, this is as authentic as it gets and is popular with children of all ages. The 'Alligator Capital of the World' was founded in 1949 and is still family owned, so it possesses a home-spun charm and naturalism few of its big-name rivals can match. And, when the wildlife consists of several thousand menacing alligators and crocodiles in various natural habitats and 4 fascinating shows – plus a fabulous new Zip Line attraction – you know you're in for a different experience. Overall, Gatorland is something you're unlikely to get anywhere else, though encounters with these living dinosaurs may not be everyone's cup of tea.

> **BRITTIP**
> If you have an evening flight home from Orlando International, visit Gatorland for half a day on your final day as it is just 20mins' drive from the airport.

Tours and attractions: Start by taking the 15min **Gatorland Express** railway around the park to get an idea of its 110-acre/45ha expanse. This has a small added fee but is good for multiple rides, is fully narrated (usually in amusing style) and is especially fun for kids. You also get a good look at the native animal habitat, which features whitetail deer, wild turkey and quail. Wander the natural beauty of the 2,000ft/610m

Swamp Walk, as well as the **Alligator Breeding Marsh Walkway**, where a 3-storey observation tower gives a close-up view of these reptiles. Ask yourself: are they hanging around in the hope someone might 'drop in' for lunch?

BRITTIP

If you are at Gatorland first thing in the morning, take the Swamp Walk straight away. There will be far more wildlife activity then and the peaceful ambience is quite invigorating.

Breeding pens, baby alligator nurseries and rearing ponds are also situated throughout the park to provide an idea of the growth cycle of the gator and enhance the overall feeling that it is the visitor behind bars here, not the animals. **Jungle Crocs** features some of the deadliest animals of Egypt, Australia and Cuba, with authentic lairs and brilliant presentation (look out for Sultan and his 'harem' of lady crocs from the Nile). Many of the small-scale attractions have been designed with kids in mind and there is plenty to keep everyone amused. **Allie's Barnyard** is a petting zoo, while you can feed some friendly lorikeets at the **Very Merry Aviary**, and view the pink inhabitants of **Flamingo Lagoon**.

Don't miss the **White Gator Swamp**, showcasing 4 rare and completely white alligators. They are leucistic (without pigment), hence they have startling blue eyes, not pink like albinos. A remarkable exhibit and superbly presented. Other animals to see include bats, iguanas, turtles, turkey vultures, tortoises, snakes, emus, deer and 2 cute tree porcupines from South America. The park is also home to hundreds of wading birds, providing a fascinating close-up of the nests during Mar–Aug. However, the gators and crocs are the main attraction and the shows are the real draw (though you will never find yourself on the end of a queue here).

Shows: The 800-seat **Wrestling Stadium** sets the scene for some real cracker-style feats (a 'cracker'

is a Florida cowboy) as Gatorland's resident 'wranglers' catch a medium-sized gator and proceed to point out the animal's features, with the aid of some daredevil stunts that will have you questioning their sanity. The **Gator Jumparoo** is another eye-opening spectacle as some of the park's biggest creatures use their tails to 'jump' out of the water and be hand-fed tasty morsels, like whole chickens! **Upclose Animal Encounters** is another amusing showcase of creatures, from the expected snakes to less obvious cockroaches and scorpions. Great photo opportunities for brave children! **Critters On The Go** features Ms Vera, trail boss Gabe and other Gatorland entertainers who host Orlando's cuddliest character meet-and-greet, with the chance to stroke some of the park's furrier residents. Watch out for these small animal encounters as they crop up around the park.

Gator Gully: This superb little water park features numerous ways for kids to cool down, get wet and generally have fun. The ½-acre/0.2ha park features 5 elements, including a giant jalopy with water jets for spokes and a fountain radiator, an old shack that 'explodes' with water, and giant gators with squirt guns. The neighbouring dry play area and chairs and tables allow parents to sit and watch their offspring expend some energy, perhaps with a drink from one of the kiosks.

But wait…that's not all!

Screamin' Gator Zip Line: Gatorland has fixed its eyes firmly on the brave of heart, introducing a first-of-its-kind zip line experience, with 4 zips soaring high above the park's most notorious residents. At 1,200ft long and up to 56ft high, the lines afford spectacular views of jumping Cuban Crocodiles and the scenic Alligator Breeding Marsh. Start at Tower One, where the 'bunny hill' builds up your courage (and your excitement). Tower Two soars over 2 croc pools (look down – the view is outrageous!); Tower Three is the tallest launch point at 75ft/23m, and its 600ft/182m run zips straight over the breeding marsh at up to 35mph/56kph (are you feeling the adrenaline rush? Yes, you are!). Take the walking bridge over to Tower Four where you're met by a double zipline for a final (and utterly thrilling) race to the finish. The experience includes orientation, a nature walk through the swamp, the zip line and a trek across a swinging bridge. There is a separate fee, but at $69.99/person, it includes all-day admission to the park. **Restrictions:** Min weight 75lb/34kg, max 250/113. Must be able to climb stairs. Wear closed toe shoes and long trousers.

◀️▶️ **BRITTIP**

Book Gatorland's zip line experience at least 3 months in advance to avoid disappointment. Capacity is limited to 12, and demand is high. Reserve by phone or online.

Shopping and dining: In addition to 3 gift stores around the park and the amusing **Gator & Snake photo opportunity**, you should visit the **Gift Shop** complex (rebuilt after a 2006 fire) at the entrance, which incorporates the trademark Gator Mouth entryway. You can grab a bite or drink at 3 snack bars, try **Gator Jake's Fudge Kitchen** or dine on smoked gator ribs and fried gator nuggets (as well as burgers and hot dogs) at **Pearl's Smokehouse**, with excellent kids' meals at $5.99.

Special events: Three unique options if you really want to get to know your gators are: **Trainer for a Day**, with the chance to work behind the scenes at the park 8am–10am, finding out what it takes to handle such dangerous animals, behavioural training and novice gator wrangling ($125 12s and over, max 5 people; includes park admission); **Gator Night Shine**, which takes guests into the Breeding Marsh after dark for a 1hr tour with one of the park's senior gator experts, with torches and gator food to lure the 'locals'. You can then marvel at how gator eyes shine like red beacons in the torchlight and learn more about the habits of these amazing animals

– a real family treat, which kids seem to love (dusk, apx 8.15pm summer, 6.30pm autumn and winter; $20 all ages; bug spray provided; reservations required); and **Adventure Hour**, a chance to go truly 'behind-the-scenes' in the Breeding Marsh to feed and pose for photos with the gators here ($10/person). **Rookie Wrestling** is every kid's chance to show their bravery and have the picture to prove it ($10 to kneel over a gator's back, extra for the photo).

Getting there: Gatorland is on the South Orange Blossom Trail, 2mls/3km south of the Central Florida Greeneway and 3mls/5km north of Highway 192 (see map p14). **Admission:** $22.99 adults, $14.99 3–12s, 9am–5pm (6pm summer), parking free. Annual passes are only $43.99 and $29.99 if you plan more than one visit (407 855 5496, **www. gatorland.com**). AAAA

Fantasy of Flight

Another wonderful and fresh alternative on the central Florida scene – voted No 1 'Best Kept Secret' by the locals – is this aviation attraction that offers a 4-part adventure with the world's largest private collection of vintage aircraft. Even those not usually interested in aviation or the glamour of flying's golden age should be fully captivated.

History of Flight: You start by entering this series of expertly re-created 'immersion experiences' into memorable moments in aviation history. The entrance alone is eye-opening – along the fuselage of a DC-3 Dakota as if for a parachute drop, stepping out into a moonlit night. Then you visit set-pieces that include a dogfight over the trenches in World War I and a bomber mission with a Flying Fortress in World War II. The latter includes a walk-through of an actual B-17 as it prepares for its bombing run! Audio-visual effects and film clips give everything an awe-inspiring feeling of authenticity. You exit into the **Vintage Aircraft** displays in 2 huge hangars, with the exhibits ranging from a replica *Spirit* *of St Louis* to a Ford Tri-Motor, a Mk-XVI Spitfire and the world's only fully airworthy Short Sunderland flying boat, which you can actually board. One aircraft is selected from the collection of more than 40 vintage planes each day for an **Aerial Demonstration** (weather permitting), with the pilot holding a Q&A session about that plane before going on to perform a series of manoeuvres over Fantasy of Flight.

Fun with Flight: More family-orientated entertainment is provided by this hands-on interactive area where guests can test their paper aeroplane-making skills in The Fly Zone and learn about the principles of lift with Bernoulli's Ball. Kids will want to try the hang-glide simulator while the mock balloon flight is also great fun.

Special exhibits and tours: Other special exhibits include **They Dared To Fly**, a tribute to the Tuskegee airmen of World War II. A variety of **guided tours** is given each day, with a tram tour of the restricted areas (including the Maintenance Hangar and Wood Shop, where specialists restore and rebuild wooden aircraft), a walking tour of the Backlot, and a visit to the Restoration Shop, highlighting in detail what it takes to restore and maintain these magnificent machines. The whole experience is crafted in 1930s art deco style and includes a full-service diner (the excellent **Compass Rose**; 11am–3pm) and an original gift shop. There is strong Brit appeal, too, with the exhibits of both World Wars. Then there is Fantasy of Flight's 3hr balloon ride for $175 (up to 4 passengers; seasonal operations, reservations required). Want a private flight for 2? Opt for the Exclusivity For Two **balloon flight** ($475/couple).

Fantasy of Flight is the brainchild of American entrepreneur and aviation whiz Kermit Weeks – who still shows off his pilot skills occasionally for the aerial demonstration – and we have yet to encounter an attraction put together with more genuine affection. In fact, it is as much a work of art as a tourist attraction, and the masses have yet to discover it.

Getting there: 20mins west of *Walt Disney World* on I-4 at exit 44 (Polk City), turn first right, then left on SR 559 for ½ml/800m to the entrance on the left. Admission: $28.95 adults, $14.95 6–15s (under-6s free); 10am–5pm (parking free; closed Thanksgiving and Christmas Day; 863 984 3500, **www.fantasyofflight.com**). AAAA

Waldo Wright's Flying Service

Flying daily from the Fantasy of Flight airfield is this wonderfully authentic biplane experience. If you ever fancied yourself as a silk-scarf-and-leather-jacket-wearing flying ace, this is definitely the place for you (even if you don't, try it anyway – it's terrific fun). There are 2 distinct rides: in an open-cockpit 1929 **New Standard D25** biplane (where the front seats can hold up to 4) for $69.95/person; or the more daring, hands-on, 2-seater 1942 **Boeing Stearman PT-17** biplane trainer, where your pilot takes you up and then lets you take the controls! The 30min experience costs $229. There is a $5 fuel surcharge for the D25, $10 for the PT-17. Both rides are fairly gentle (and just a little thrilling) as you get a slow, bird's-eye view of this pretty part of Florida. The way the planes seem able to turn on a wingtip gives you a deep respect for the pilots of these wonderful machines (863 873 1339, **www.waldowrights.com**).

Simon and Susan at Waldo Wright's

INTERNATIONAL DRIVE

The 14½ml/23km tourist corridor of I-Drive (see maps p83 and 214) continues to be an ever-changing source of hotels, restaurants, shopping and, more importantly, fun. There are more than 33,000 hotel rooms, 150 restaurants and 500-plus shops, as well as 14 attractions, including 6 mini-golf courses. The **I-Ride Trolley** links it together in transport terms and **www.International DriveOrlando.com** highlights all the options. Its Official Visitors Guide has an I-Ride map and valuable money-off coupons, which you can download to get you started. There is also a hotel booking facility.

Here's a look at the area's top attractions (see also Chapter 10, Orlando By Night, and Chapter 12, Shopping, to get the complete picture).

 BRITTIP

Ripley's, Titanic, and WonderWorks are all handy retreats to keep in mind for a rainy day.

Ripley's Believe It Or Not

You can't miss this particular attraction and its extraordinary tilted appearance as it's designed to seem as if it's falling into a Florida 'sinkhole'. However, once inside you soon get back on the level and, for an hour or two, you can wander through this quirky museum dedicated to the weird and wonderful. Robert L. Ripley was an eccentric explorer and collector (a real-life Indiana Jones) who for 40 years travelled the world in his bid to assemble a collection of the greatest oddities known to man. The Orlando branch of this chain features 8,900ft²/830m² of displays, including authentic artefacts, interactive exhibits, illusions, video presentations and music. The elaborate re-creation of an Egyptian tomb showcases a mummy and 3 rare mummified animals, while the Primitive Gallery contains artefacts (some quite gruesome) from tribal societies around the world. There are then Human and Animal

Oddities, Big and Little galleries, Illusions and Dinosaurs, plus extra interactive elements. The collection of miniatures includes the world's smallest violin and a single grain of rice hand-painted with a tropical sunset. Larger-scale exhibits include a portion of the Berlin Wall, a ⅔-scale 1907 Rolls-Royce built in matchsticks and a 26ft/8m tall 'painting' of Van Gogh made out of postcards! New in 2011 were a dozen new exhibits, including a portrait of Beyonce made of sweets, a 25ft portrait of Jimi Hendrix made from playing cards, and the fossilised leg of a T-Rex.

Admission: $19.99 adults, $11.99 4– 12s; 9.0am–12am daily (last admission 11pm; 407 345 0501, **www. ripleysorlando.com**). AAA

 BRITTIP

Receive a $3 discount/adult, $2/ child (age 4–12) on the regular admission price at Ripley's Believe It Or Not by visiting their website.

Titanic – The Experience

Go back in time at this fascinating attraction just north of Sand Lake Road. Weave through the redesigned Experience featuring full-scale re-creations of the *Titanic*'s famous rooms, including her grand staircase, first class parlour suite, Veranda Café and the newly added Marconi Room, third class cabin and bridge. Actors in period costume portray such notables as Captain Smith and Molly Brown, sharing stories of passengers and crew during a 1hr guided journey of the famous ship. The 18-room attraction features an interactive Underwater Room, including a 15ft/4.5m 'iceberg' and a detailed replica of the vessel as she appears on the bottom of the Atlantic today. More than 200 artefacts and treasures, including memorabilia from James Cameron's blockbuster movie *Titanic* are also on display here.

Admission: $21.95 adults, $12.95 4– 12s (under-4s free); tours 10am–9 pm daily (**www.titanictheexperience.com**). AAAA

For something special, try the exclusive **Titanic Dinner Event** (Fri and Sat only), a set-piece theatre/dining occasion with the impressive cast of the Experience. Starring Molly Brown, Captain Smith and Thomas Andrews, it offers each table a front row seat for the whole *Titanic* story, setting the scene and delivering a dinner party with a difference, all in period style. A sumptuous 3-course meal, featuring roast sirloin and chicken, is served, along with tea, coffee and soft drinks (add $15 for unlimited beer and wine), and the ambience is one of genuine maritime splendour. The 3hr performance costs $64.95 for adults, $39.95 for 6–11s (not recommended for under-6s) and must be booked in advance on 407 248 1166.

Fun Spot Action Park

Here's another choice for full-scale, family fun, just off I-Drive on Del Verde Way (look for the 100ft/31m Big Wheel past the junction with Kirkman Road). The main focus is the go-karts, with 4 challenging tracks, including the max thrills of the 1,600ft/488m **Quad Helix**, the 1,000ft/305m **Conquest**, with its triple level corkscrew, the fiendish 800ft/244m **Thrasher** and the multi-level **Commander**. Then there are bumper cars and boats, 4 daring fairground-type rides (including the whizzy **Scrambler** and **Paratrooper**), an impressive 2-storey video arcade (one of the largest in Florida), 7 Kid Spot rides and a Cadet track for the little ones. This 4.7-acre/2ha park promises hours of fun! The **Oasis Snack Bar** serves hot dogs, pizza, nachos, popcorn and ice-cream and the arcade games include some of the latest. Passes are geared around children's height (above and below 4ft 4in/1.32m), with younger children getting free run of all the rides (and as a passenger on the 2-seater go-karts with an adult) and older children (and grown-ups!) having unlimited access to all the rides, go-karts and games. Watch for new developments in 2012, as they have a 10-acre/4ha expansion in the works that will more than double their size.

Ripley's Believe It Or Not

Admission: Free; then Go-Kart Armband (all day on all 4 tracks, plus all rides and unlimited Free Play arcade) $34.95; Rides Armband (all day on all rides plus unlimited Free Play arcade) $24.95; Kid Spot Armband (all day on Kid Spot rides plus unlimited Free Play arcade) $14.95; and Free Play Armband (unlimited play in upstairs Free Play arcade) $4.95. Go-kart rides $6, ride tickets $3, Track Sampler $19.95. Height requirements: over 4ft 4in/1.32m for Quad Helix, Conquest and Commander; 4ft 6in/1.37m for Thrasher. Open daily 10am–midnight, noon–midnight Mon–Fri in low season (407 363 3867, **www.fun-spot.com**). TTTT

Magical Midway

In a similar vein, **Magical Midway** back on I-Drive (just north of Sand Lake Road) offers more go-karts, games and thrill rides, including the **Slingshot** (400ft straight up!) and the amazing **StarFlyer**, a 230ft/70m tower with chair swings that lift and rotate up the full height for a dizzying view of the surrounding area at 54mph (the only ride of its kind in America). The 2 elevated kart tracks, the double uphill corkscrew of **The Avalanche** and the sharply banked **Alpine Jump** are its signature rides (you must be at least 12 and 4ft 8in/147cm tall to drive, at least 16 to drive a passenger, and at least 5 and 3ft/91cm to be a passenger). **Fast Track**, a flat concrete track with a 25° bank turn (riders must be 12 and 4ft 8in/147cm to drive; single cars only) complete the

WonderWorks

line-up. There are also bumper cars, bumper boats, 3 more fairground-type rides, a large arcade, a pizza parlour and ice-cream counter.

Admission: Free, then 3hr Armband (unlimited go-karts and midway rides for 3 hours, not SlingShot) $25; Package 1: SlingShot or Starflyer plus T-shirt and DVD, $50; Package 2: SlingShot and Starflyer, plus DVD and t-shirt $75. Individual ride tickets are $25 SlingShot or $7 Starflyer (ride DVD $15), $7 for go-karts, and $3 for other rides; must be 4ft/121cm for Bumper Cars, and 3ft 6in/106cm for Bumper Boats and Kiddie Track. 2–10pm Mon–Tues, 2pm–midnight Wed-Fri, 10am–midnight Sat-Sun (407 370 5353, **www.magicalmidway.com**). TTTT

WonderWorks

This interactive entertainment centre is I-Drive's most unmistakable landmark, a 3-storey chamber of family fun with a host of novel elements. Unmistakable? How many upside-down buildings do you know? That's right, all the 82ft/25m edifice is constructed from the roof up! The basic premise (working on the theory that every attraction must have a story) is that WonderWorks is a secret research facility into unexplained phenomena that was uprooted by a tornado experiment and dumped in topsy-turvy fashion in the heart of this busy tourist district (yeah, right!). Well, you have to give full marks for imagination and, with various enhancements since it opened in 1998, there's a lot here, especially for 6–12s.

> **BRITTIP**
>
> WonderWorks, Fun Spot and Magical Midway are open until midnight in high season, long after most theme parks are shut, so you can have a day at the park, then let the kids loose here for a while to tire them out!

You enter through an 'inversion tunnel' that orientates you the same way round as the building (look out of the window to check!) and then progress to various chambers of entertaining and mildly educational hands-on experiences that demand several hours to explore fully. Without ever using the words 'science' or 'museum', WonderWorks steers you through various 'labs' of interactive activities, including **natural disasters** (earthquakes, hurricanes, famous disasters and the new **Global VR** – a virtual reality trek into the Desert War); **physical challenges** (virtual basketball and soccer, virtual 'swim with the sharks', Bed of Nails and the chance to make an impression of your entire body in 40,000 plastic nails at Wonderwall!); **illusions** (with a computer ageing process and 'elastic surgery', ethnicity changer and a 'couple's morph' that combines 2 faces to see what the resulting children would look like!); and **The Control Room**, where you have **Jet Fighters** (virtual reality F18 fighter jet), **Shuttle Landers** (your chance to pilot the Discovery Space Shuttle), a Mercury capsule mock-up, an astronaut spacesuit and **Wonder Coaster** (a pair of enclosed 'pods' that let you design and ride your own coaster). Recent additions include biofeedback game of Mindball, a 3-storey indoor rope climbing structure with 20 obstacles, and the new **XD Theater 4-D Extreme Motion Experience** simulator ride. Plus there is the **WonderWorks Gift Shop and Café**. A **Lazer Tag** game on the top floor adds even more appeal for kids. If you have already seen DisneyQuest, WonderWorks may seem tame, while it isn't as educational as the Orlando Science Center, but it also offers fun dinner-show option **The Outta Control Magic Comedy Dinner Show** (p310), with a good value combo ticket.

Admission: $24.99 adults, $19.99 seniors (55+) and 4–12s; $6.99 for Lazer Tag; $24.99 and $16.99 for The Outta Control Dinner Show; $43.99 and $33.99 for WonderWorks/ dinner show combo; $27.99 and $22.99 for WonderWorks/ Lazer Tag combo; $44.99 and $34.99 for all 3; 9am– midnight (407 351 8800, **www.wonderworksonline.com**). TTT

iFLY Orlando

At the junction with I-Drive and Kirkman Road is this unmistakable blue and yellow funnel that houses one of the most fun 'rides' in town. Formerly SkyVenture, now iFLY Orlando, it is billed as a 'free-fall skydiving adventure' but it is much more than that – a fun, addictive, difficult but exhilarating 'flying' experience, with the bonus of being a great spectator sport! It's basically a huge vertical wind tunnel, which provides the feeling of a freefall parachute jump without the hassle of having to leap out of a plane, wrestle with a parachute and possibly hit the ground too hard. The standard 1hr programme provides a full briefing with an instructor, then you're provided with your equipment - helmet, pads, goggles, earplugs and flight suit - and your group of 8–12 returns to the flight deck, where you get 2 1min 'flights' (which seem a lot longer!) with your instructor helping all the way. Just watching makes it seem all too easy but, as soon as you hit the tunnel, you discover how fiendishly tough it is to just 'hang' in this 125mph/200kph column of air. However, before long it becomes a fun and absorbing experience and it's almost guaranteed to make you want to try again. There is no fee for non-participating members of your group to watch from the observation deck, and you can also just turn up to see for yourself at any time (you might even get to see sky-dive groups practising).

iFLY Orlando

Admission: Standard flight, which includes a certificate, is $49.95/person; add a DVD and photo CD for $19.99. Discount coupons and gift certificates can be found on its website. Try a Family Package for up to 5 flyers at $239.95 or a Spread Your Wings Package (double your flight time) for $89.95. Reservations recommended (407 903 1150, **www.iflyorlando.com**). **TTTT**

Helicopter rides

These are another local staple, and you can try any one of 9 tours with **Air Florida Helicopters** at 8990 International Drive (just north of the big Convention Center). A minimum of 2 people are required, and then it's just a question of whether you want the local 8ml/12.87m tour, a trip over Universal and SeaWorld, the chance to see Disney from the air, a view of Downtown Orlando or a mega 30ml/48km grand journey that adds flying over the homes of the rich and famous in Windermere. Prices vary from $25 for the short flight to $335 for the longest ($20–325 for children; see website for discounts). No need to book; just turn up and go. They fly 9.30am–7pm daily (407 354 1400, **www.airfloridahelicopter.com**).

Mini-golf

For those in need of more holiday fun, don't miss the 6 mini-golf outlets along International Drive (see p265).

Old Town Kissimmee

Kissimmee

Old Town: In the heart of tourist Highway 192 in Kissimmee is this shopping and entertainment attraction. The shopping part is covered in Chapter 12 but there are many associated attractions worth noting. Old Town itself features 14 out-and-out rides, from the standard and rather tame **Happy Days** bumper cars, go-karts and large **Ferris Wheel** to the **Windstorm** roller-coaster, the **Super Shot** (a free-fall-style ride of over 140ft/43m). There is a **Fun Town** area of junior rides, plus a **Laser Tag** game, and tickets are sold separately for most rides ($2 each), but if you plan to do several, go for the Valuepak at $25 for 30, or $35 for 45. There are 2 All You Can Ride Wristbands, the Mega Saver ($35, 14 rides plus bumper cars, go karts and laser tag) or Super Saver ($25, 14 rides plus bumper cars). There are separate fees for bumper cars ($5), Laser Tag ($5) and go-karts ($6). For a different kind of fun, try the 2-storey Grimm Haunted House ($10 adults, $6.75 children). The rides have varying opening times: Kid Town open Mon-Fri 2pm-11pm, Sat-Sun noon-11pm; Swing Town open Mon-Fri 4pm-11pm, Sat-Sun 2pm-11pm; Bumper Cars/Laser Tag/Go-karts open noon–11pm (later at peak periods; 407 390 0906, **www.old-town.com**). **TTTT**

Fun Spot USA: Next door to Old Town (but not connected) is another area of rides and fun owned by Fun Spot of I- Drive. There are a good selection of thrill rides, a Kid Spot of junior-sized rides, 2 high-adrenalin signature rides (which are real one-offs) and 4 go-kart tracks. **Power Trip Roller Coaster**, a coaster formerly in Cypress Gardens, made its new home here in 2011, adding another terrific ride to the line-up. But the big daddy of them all is the amazing **SkyCoaster**, a 300ft/90m tower that sends up to 3 riders at a time on a free-fall plunge (for the first 120ft/ 37m) that turns into a giant swing – at 85mph/136kph! The more down-to-earth rides consist of 2 flat go-kart tracks, **Slick** and **Road Course**, and 2 multi-level tracks, the labyrinthine **Chaos** and

Vortex, with its challenging banked bowl section. The other rides are almost as much fun – like the **Extraordinary Bike** (pedal your way upside-down!), **Double Ferris Wheel**, the more fairground style of **Flying Bob's Bobsleds** and the **Paratrooper**, the giant swing of the **Hot Seat** and the tower-ride **Screamer**. There is a well-stocked **Snack Bar** (with free soft drinks) in the outdoor rides section; drinks and snacks at **SkyCoaster**. Children will also gravitate to the new arcade, with 60 games (perfect for a wet day or the heat of summer).

Admission: Free, then Go-Kart Armband $34.95 (unlimited go-karts and other rides), Rides Armband (unlimited rides) $24.95, Kid Spot Rides Armband $14.94 and Track Sampler $20 (4 goes on go-karts or rides); regular tickets $3 each or 15 for $40 (Go-Karts 2 or 3 tickets each). The SkyCoaster is $40 for 1 rider ($25 for a second ride), $70 for 2, $90 for 3. 10am–midnight; (407 397 2509, **www.funspotusa.com**). There is also a special 2-park Armband for Fun Spot and Fun Spot USA at $54.95.

BRITTIP
Visit **www.funspotusa.com** for discount coupons off Fun Spot USA's Ride Armband, or save your armband from 1 Fun Spot location for money off the other.

DOWNTOWN ORLANDO

The last few years have seen a major revamp of Orlando's city centre ('downtown'), with new offices, apartments, shops and restaurants. This has also enhanced some notable tourist attractions and is well served by the new Information Center on Orange Avenue (9am–6pm, Mon–Fri; 407 246 3789, **www.downtownorlando. com** – click *Visit Downtown*). Start here to get a full overview, with interactive info kiosks, a 3-D city model and ultra-helpful staff (plus free wi-fi). They can provide free maps of the area, a Historic Walking Tour guide and info on riding the free **Lymmo** bus service around downtown. There is also a free guided tour at 9:30am on the first Fri of each

month with local historian Richard Forbes (not June–Sept).

Skyline Tours: The other must-try opportunity is these free guided rooftop tours of the city with 1 of its tourist Volunteers, who can provide essential city history and other info while pointing out the main sights from the top of 1 of the city's high-rise buildings. You can also tour downtown (with a guide) onboard a 4-seater **Smart Car** (ladies, pull long hair back; it gets breezy!). These are provided daily, often on a turn-up-and-go basis (although it is best to call in advance for the Skyline Tour and the Smart Car requires reservations – 407 246 3789) and are a real 'high'-light of any downtown visit!

BRITTIP
Visiting the downtown Orlando Information Center? Take exit 82B off I-4 and there are 4 multi-storey car parks nearby, the best being the Library park (take 4th right on Central Boulevard).

Orange County History Center

This smart, modern addition to the downtown scene offers an imaginative journey into central Florida history, from the wildlife and Native Americans to today's tourist issues and space programme. Again, the accent is on the interactive, with hands-on exhibits and audiovisual presentations, and it is very much a journey through time, starting outside in renovated Heritage Square, complete with cypress trees and

The History Center

fountains. The Center itself is in the former 1927 County Courthouse, with the foyer converted into a dome featuring more than 150 icons unique to central Florida (see how many you can identify before and after your tour).

The 4-storey adventure starts at the top with the **Orientation Theater**'s 14min multimedia presentation as you sit in rocking chairs on the 'front porch'. Then you visit the **Natural Environment** and **First Peoples** exhibits (12,000 years ago), before **First Contact** brings in the European element. Jump into the 1800s and visit a Seminole settlement, a pioneer 'cracker' home, hear tales of the ranching days, the Seminole wars and learn about the citrus industry. The story of tourism before Walt Disney World is showcased in *Destination Florida*. *Walt Disney World* then picks up the story, highlighting Orlando's changes once The Mouse showed up.

BRITTIP

Combine a visit to the History Center with lunch at the wonderfully eclectic Globe restaurant on the corner of Heritage Square nearby.

Aviation explores transportation's history, from World War II bombers to the outer reaches of space. From there, you move on to the beautifully

restored **Courtroom B** for some more real-life Orlando history.

Finally, you reach the newest permanent exhibit, **Orlando Remembered** – a journey from the 19th century to the edge of the 21st. This tells the story beyond the theme parks and is an inclusive history of Orlando's people, uncovering secrets of the past, including significant artefacts from the Historical Society of Central Florida. Find out about events like the Big Freeze of the 1890s and the area's contribution to World War II (with a replica Flying Fortress). An exhibit on African American history, featuring the achievements and tragedies of central Florida's African American community, and a series of fascinating travelling exhibits round things off, while a visit to the smart **Historium** gift shop completes your visit.

Getting there: Off Central Boulevard and Magnolia Avenue downtown (exit 83A off I-4, Amelia Street; turn right on to Amelia, 1st right on to N. Orange, then 5th left on to E. Central Blvd; see also map p214). Park at the Public Library multi-storey car park on Central Boulevard (History Center admission includes 2hrs' free parking if you show your ticket). Admission: $9 adults, $7 seniors (60+), $6 5–12s; 10am–5pm Mon-Sat, noon-5pm Sun (407 836 8500, **www.thehistorycenter.org**). AAA

Downtown Orlando

Theatre and more

Staying downtown, the free Lymmo bus service connects the central area along Magnolia Avenue, from South Street to the stunning new **Amway Center** for sports and concerts on W Church Street and up to the Centroplex area, with the old Amway Arena, and **Bob Carr Performing Arts Center** (to be replaced by the Orlando Performing Arts Center in 2012). Try **SAK Comedy Lab** at Eola Capital Loft on S. Orange Avenue, with fun improv comedy on Tues–Sat (7.30, 9, 9.30 or 11.30pm, $2–$15; 407 648 0001, **www.sak.com**). Also here is **City Arts Factory**, (11am–6pm Tues–Sat), with a huge collective of galleries under one roof from local and national artists, plus art classes and a city-wide Gallery Hop on the third Thurs each month from 6–9pm (407 648 7060, **www.cityartsfactory.com**).

The Plaza: This new multiplex in the heart of downtown boasts a state-of-the-art 12-screen cinema, 2 café bars, with a full menu and extensive beer and wine selections, and 2 Downtown Arts District galleries (407 982 5444, **www.plazacinemacafe.com**), while it is home to the Orlando Film Festival each Nov (**www.orlandofilmfest.com**).

Dining: The restaurant/bar choice is also pretty good here, too. Take your pick from the new **Frank & Steins** (with 300 craft beers, 40 on tap), **The Globe** (an eclectic lounge/café in front of the History Center, open late Thur-Sat), **Wall Street Plaza** (a lively collection of bars and lounges that are the heart of downtown nightlife) and Church Street Station, the remains of the old entertainment district, which still includes a cluster of fine restaurants and bars, notably the stylish Spanish cuisine of **Ceviche**, the elegant boutique style of **The Dessert Lady** and **Hamburger Mary's Bar & Grille**. Live music fans should make a beeline for **The Social**, 1 of Orlando's trendiest small-scale venues (407 246 1419, **www.thesocial.org**), while the artistic **Mad Cow Theatre** offers a variety of high-quality stage productions featuring highly lauded local talent.

BRITTIP

In party mode? Head for Wall Street Plaza, between Orange Ave and N Court Ave, on any Thurs, Fri or Sat night and bar-hop with the locals all night long! (**www.wallstreetplaza.net**)

Lake Eola: Once you have sampled the heart of downtown, head out here, with more restaurants and shops, plus a beautiful lakeside walk, children's play area, Swan paddle-boats and a peaceful ambience. Children can feed the birds, fish and turtles or take a paddleboat ride, while there are regular open-air concerts and storytelling at the Disney Amphitheater. The **Sunday Farmers Market** (around Lake Eola, 10am–4pm) is another focal point, with vendors including local artists as well as wonderful fresh produce.

Dining: Stop for a great meal, with a view, at **310 Lakeside** (407 373 0310, **www.310lakeside.net**) or **Spice Modern Steakhouse** (407 481 9533, **www.spicesteakhouse.com**). Continue on to the **Thornton Park** area and

Ceviche

enjoy the most happening part of Orlando, with Thornton Park Central (at the junction of Summerlin Avenue and Central Boulevard, just south-east of Lake Eola) offering a mix of unique boutiques and trendy restaurants. **Hue** is consistently rated 1 of Orlando's finest and is as stylish as they come (407 849 1800, **www.huerestaurant.com**), **Cityfish** is a more casual seafood café/bar alternative (407 849 9779, **www.cityfishorlando.com**), **Anthony's Pizzeria** is a great upmarket pizza restaurant (407 648 0009, **www.anthonyspizza.com**) and **Wildside BBQ** is a lively locals' hangout (407 872 8665, **www.wildsidebbq.com**).

BRITTIP

Don't miss the annual **Spring** and **Fall Fiestas** around Lake Eola, with hundreds of vendors, live entertainment and special fun for kids, the first weekend in April and Nov.

Loch Haven Park

Continue north and you travel the 'Cultural Corridor' to Loch Haven Park and the area's fine collection of theatres, museums and the Orlando Science Center. The **Dr Phillips Performing Arts Center** is home to the Orlando Opera and Orlando Ballet. The 34-year-old **Orlando Ballet** is central Florida's only full-time ballet company, with international dancers, plus a Family Series that accommodates children (407 426 1739, **www.orlandoballet.org**).

Also here are the extensive **Orlando Museum of Art** (407 896 4231, **www.omart.org**), the diverse **Mennello Museum of American Art**, with a permanent collection by painter Earl Cunningham (407 246 4278, **www.mennellomuseum.com**), the **Orlando Philharmonic Orchestra** (407 770 0071, **www.orlandophil.org**) and the **Orlando Shakespeare Theater** (407 447 1700, **www.orlandoshakes.org**). Parents should also note the superb **Orlando Rep**, a fabulous company specialising in family theatre, with youth academies and summer camps for kids. Their 2011 season included *Hairspray: The Broadway Musical* and *James and the Giant Peach* (407 896 7365, **www.orlandorep.com**). Highly recommended.

Orlando Science Center: Because this is Orlando, there is no such thing as a simple museum or science centre. Hence, the Orlando Science Center is more than a mere museum and far more fun than the average science centre. Here you are given a series of hands-on experiences and habitats that entertain as well as inform, and school-age children in particular will benefit greatly from it. It has 9 main permanent exhibits, a night sky observatory, an inviting café and a giant screen cinema.

NatureWorks: This is an immersion-style exhibit creating 6 typical Florida habitats, complete with native plants and animals (with field stations such as how sea turtles make their nests and a live beehive); **KidsTown**

Orlando Science Center

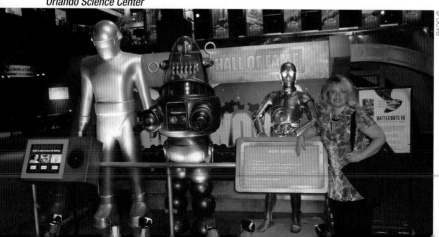

© OCVB

is for those a bit too young for the educational element, with plenty of junior-sized fun and games for under-6s (you'll be amazed at how much they can learn while having fun!); **DinoDigs** was a gift from the Walt Disney Company of its former Dinosaur Jubilee exhibit in *Disney's Animal Kingdom*, re-created in the OSC with 8 full skeleton replicas and some genuine fossils; **Science Park** is a hands-on adventure into the worlds of physical science and technology, including a hurricane simulator and Dr Dare's Laboratory; and **Our Planet, Our Universe** encourages interactive learning about planets, the sky, black holes, and cosmic collisions. Don't miss the hands-on **Mars Rover** experience and the chance to **Ask An Astronomer** (via video kiosk). Preschoolers will appreciate **All Aboard**, with child-sized trains, planes and automobiles. Watch for **Star Wars: Where Science Meets Imagination** if you visit in Autumn 2012. You will also find a handy Café and a large Science Store here. In addition, the centre has 2 separate programmes in **Dr Phillips CineDome**, a 310-seat cinema that almost surrounds its audience with large-format films and digital planetarium shows. It also boasts a 28,000-watt digital sound system that makes the experience unforgettable.

BRITTIP
Visit the Crosby Observatory (selected times only; be sure to call in advance) on top of the Science Center to gaze through the region's largest publicly accessible refractor telescope.

Getting there: On Princeton Street in downtown Orlando, just off exit 85 of I-4 (go east on Princeton; the Center is on the left but the multi-storey car park is on the RIGHT, see map p214). **Admission:** $17 adults, $16 seniors (55+), $16 Student with ID, $12 3–11s; parking $5. 10am–5pm daily (closed Wed, Easter Sunday, Thanksgiving, Christmas Eve and Christmas Day; **www.osc.org**) AAA

THE WATER PARKS

Florida specialises in elaborate water parks, and Orlando boasts the very best. Predictably, Disney has the 2 most sophisticated ones, but the opening of SeaWorld's Aquatica in 2008 provided some real competition, while Universal-owned Wet 'n Wild is also adept at providing hours of watery fun. They adopt a variety of styles that owe much to the flair of the theme park creators, and are imaginative for both the rides and imagery around them. All require at least ½ a day of splashing, sliding and riding to get full value from their rather high prices. Lockers are provided for valuables and you can hire towels.

BRITTIP
Want a day of watery fun but don't want to purchase an extra pass for a water park? Consider **CocoKey Water Resort** on International Drive. You can purchase a day pass for $15-20; (seasonally) it's great for the pre-school to 10-year-old crowd, and it's covered, to protect kids from the harsh Florida sun (**www.cocokeywaterresort.com**).

Disney's Typhoon Lagoon Water Park

When *Typhoon Lagoon* opened in 1989, it was the biggest and finest of Florida's water parks. And, although it has since been superseded, in high season it is still the busiest, so be prepared for more queues. *You should definitely arrive half an hour early if possible as entry often begins before the official opening hour.* The park's 56 acres/23ha are spread out around

Typhoon Lagoon

© Disney

© Disney

Shark Reef

the 2½acre/1ha lagoon fringed with palm trees and white-sand beaches. It is extravagantly landscaped and the walk up Mount Mayday provides a terrific overview as well as adding scenic touches like rope bridges and tropical flowers. Sun loungers, chairs, picnic tables and even hammocks are provided to add to the comfort and convenience of restful areas like Getaway Glen. However, you need to arrive early to bag a decent spot. Or, for $40 extra(!) you can reserve 2 beach loungers, 2 towels, an umbrella and a small table by stopping in at High 'n Dry Rentals. Same day only, first come first served. Really want to splash out? Opt for a **Beachcomber Shack** (cabaña), which includes a locker, drinks mug, cooler with ice, bottled water, towels, loungers and table, and waiter service. Full day rental for up to 6 guests will set you back $250 (admission not included). Reserve in advance on 407 939 7529 (we're fans of arriving early and getting your loungers for free!).

BRITTIP

While water parks provide a great way of cooling down, it is easy to pick up a 5-star case of sunburn. So don't forget the high-factor waterproof suncream, and reapply often.

Beating the crowds: To avoid the worst of the summer crowds (when the park's 7,200 capacity is often reached), Mon morning is best (steer clear of weekends at all costs) and, on other days, arrive either before opening or in mid-afternoon, when many decide to dodge the daily rainstorm. Early evening is also pleasant when the park lights up.

BRITTIP

Want to learn to surf? Typhoon Lagoon offers Surfing School 2hrs before park opening every day. Call 407 939 7529 in advance to book at $150/ person.

Slides and rides: The park is overlooked by Mount Mayday, on top of which is perched the luckless *Miss Tilly*, a shrimp boat that legend has it landed here during the typhoon that gave the park its name. Watch out for the water fountains that shoot from *Miss Tilly*'s funnel at regular intervals, accompanied by the ship's hooter, signalling another round of 6ft/1.8m waves in the **Surf Pool** (hire inner tubes to bob around on or just try body-surfing). Circling the lagoon is **Castaway Creek**, a 3ft/1m deep, lazy flowing river offering the chance to float idly along on rubber tyres.

The slides and rides are all clustered around Mt Mayday and vary from the breathtaking body slides of **Humunga Kowabunga** that drop you 214ft/65m at up to 30mph/48kph down some pretty steep inclines (make sure swimming costumes are securely fastened!) to **Ketchakiddee Creek**, which offers a selection of slides and pools for youngsters under 4ft/122cm. In between, you have the 3 **Storm Slides**, body slides that twist and turn through caves, tunnels and waterfalls, **Mayday Falls**, a wild 460ft/140m single-rider inner-tube flume down a series of banked drops, **Keelhaul Falls**, a more sedate tube ride that takes slightly longer, and **Gangplank Falls**, a family ride inside rafts that take up to 4 people down 300ft/90m of mock rapids.

The fun **Crush 'n' Gusher** is a fabulous trio of 'water-coaster' tube rides, plus a large heated pool with zero-depth entry (great for toddlers). It also has an extensive sandy beach, great for sunbathing. The 3 different slides feature tubes for 2 or 3 riders at a time that whoosh you down and UP several inclines before dropping you into the pool with a significant splash. This is busy from midday. The imaginative (but chilly) **Shark Reef** is an upturned wreck and coral reef in which you can snorkel among 4,000 tropical fish and a number of (harmless) nurse sharks. Those not brave enough to get in can still get a close-up through the underwater portholes of the sunken ship. The Reef is closed during the winter. Substantial queues build up from late morning, so do this early.

 BRITTIP

'Buy a disposable waterproof camera to tie around your wrist when you visit the water parks. We bought one cheap at Wal-Mart and have some lovely photos from Typhoon Lagoon,' says reader Judith Bingham.

Keeping out of the sun can also be a problem as there's not much shade, but a quick plunge into Castaway Creek usually prevents overheating. There are health and 4ft/122cm height restrictions on Humunga Kowabunga and Crush 'n' Gusher (not suitable for anyone with a bad back or neck, or expectant mothers).

Shopping and dining: If you have forgotten a sunhat or bucket and spade for the kids, or even your swimsuit, they are all available at

Crush 'n' Gusher

© Disney

Singapore Sal's. You CAN'T bring your own snorkels, inner tubes or rafts, but snorkels are provided at Shark Reef and you can hire inner tubes for the lagoon. For snacks and meals, **Lowtide Lou's** and **Let's Go Slurpin'** both offer a bite to eat and drinks, while **Typhoon Tilly's** and **Leaning Palms** serve a decent mix of sandwiches, burgers, salads and ice-cream. Avoid main mealtimes if you want to eat in relative comfort. You can bring your own picnic (unlike the main parks), although no alcohol or glass.

BRITTIP

As the busiest of the water parks, Typhoon Lagoon can hit capacity quite early in the day in summer. Call 407 824 4321 in advance to check on the crowds.

Getting there: On Buena Vista Drive, ½ml/800m from Downtown Disney (see map on page 69). Admission: $46 adults, $40 3–9s (under-3s free); included with Premium and Ultimate tickets; parking free; 9am (10am off season)–dusk daily. TTTT/AAAAA

Summit Plummet

Disney's Blizzard Beach Water Park

Ever imagined a skiing resort in the middle of Florida? Well, Disney has, and this is the wonderful result. This park opened in 1995 and is still the largest, with all 66 acres/27ha arranged as if it were in the Rocky Mountains rather than the subtropics! That means snow-effect scenery, Christmas trees and waterslides cunningly converted to look like skiing pistes and toboggan runs. The same 'premium' offer at Typhoon Lagoon applies here: if the price doesn't scare you off completely, you can hire a **Polar Patio** (cabaña), which includes a locker, drinks mug, cooler with ice, bottled water, towels, loungers and table, and waiter service. Full day rental for up to 6 guests is $250 (admission not included). Reserve in advance on 407 939 7529 (once again, we're fans of arriving early and getting your loungers for free).

Slides and rides: Main features are **Mount Gushmore**, a 90ft/27m

© Disney

mountain down which all the main slides run. A ski chair-lift operates to the top, providing a magnificent view of the park and surrounding areas. Don't miss the outstanding rides, including the world's tallest free-fall speed slide, the terrifying 120ft/37m **Summit Plummet**, which rockets you down a 'ski jump' at up to 60mph/97kph. For those not quite up to the big drop, the brilliantly named **Slush Gusher** is a slightly less terrifying body slide. Then there is **Teamboat Springs**, a wild family inner-tube adventure and arguably the best of all the water rides; **Runoff Rapids**, a choice of 3 tube plunges; **Snow Stormers**, a daring head-first 'toboggan' run; and **Toboggan Racers**, the chance to speed down the 'slopes' against 7 other head-first riders. All 4 provide good-sized thrills without overdoing the scare factor. The side-by-side **Downhill Double Dipper** tubes send you down 230ft/ 70m tubes in a timed race, with a real jolt half-way down! **Tike's Peak** is a kiddie-sized version of the park's slides and a mock snow-beach, and **Ski-Patrol Training Camp** is a series of challenges and slides for pre-teens. **Melt-Away Bay** is a 1-acre/0.4ha pool fed by 'melting snow' (actually blissfully warm), and **Cross Country Creek** is a lazy-flowing 1½ml/800m river round the whole park that also floats guests through a chilly 'ice cave' (look out for the ice-water waterfalls!).

BRITTIP

Adjacent to Blizzard Beach are the amazing **Winter Summerland Miniature Golf Courses** (where Santa's elves hang out!), with 2 elaborate courses that are a great diversion for children (p265).

Shopping and dining: There is a 'village' area with a **Beach Haus** shop and **Lottawatta Lodge** fast-food restaurant (pizzas, burgers, salads and sandwiches), offering a grandstand view of Mount Gushmore. Snacks are also available at **Avalunch** (ouch!), the **Warming Hut**, **Polar Pub** and **Frostbite Freddie's Frozen Refreshments**.

Getting there: Just north of Disney's All-Star Resorts off Buena Vista Drive (see map p69). **Admission:** $46 adults, $40 3–9s (under-3s free); included with Premium and Ultimate tickets; parking free; 9am (10am off-season) to dusk daily. **TTTTT/AAAAA**

Wet 'n Wild

If Disney scores highest for scenic content, Wet 'n Wild, the world's first water park in 1977, goes full tilt for thrills and spills of the highest quality, with its 2 newest rides also being highly sophisticated. This park will certainly test your swimsuit material to the limit!

Wet 'n Wild is one of the best-attended water parks in the country, and its location in the heart of I-Drive makes it a major draw. Consequently, you will encounter some crowds here, though the 15 slides and rides, Lazy River attraction, elaborate kids' park (with mini versions of many slides), Surf Lagoon, restaurant and picnic areas absorb a lot of punters before queues develop. Waits of more than ½ hour at peak times are rare, but it is busy at weekends and throughout July as well.

BRITTIP

The Kids' Park at Wet 'n Wild was built especially for those under 4ft/122cm tall – right down to having the only junior wave pool in the world.

Slides and rides: You are almost spoilt for choice of main rides, from popular group inner-tube rides of **Surge** and **Bubba Tub** to the more demanding **The Flyer**, **The Blast** and

Brain Wash

Mach 5 (head-first on a mat-slide). For body slides, try the high-energy plunge of **The Storm** and the sheer terror of **Der Stuka** and **Bomb Bay**. The latter duo are definitely not for the faint-hearted. Basically, they are 276ft/23m near-vertical body slides. Der Stuka is the straightforward slide, while Bomb Bay adds the extra terror of being allowed to free-fall on to the top of the slide. Strangely, only a minority of visitors pluck up the courage to try it! There are 4ft/122cm height restrictions on Bomb Bay and Der Stuka, while older kids can enjoy the huge, inflatable **Bubble Up**, which bounces them into 3ft/1m of water. Latest enhancement is to the old Black Hole tube ride, which is now **Black Hole: The Next Generation**, a pulsating 2-person ride down an enclosed flume, with a dynamic lighting package and other special effects.

Our favourites? We like the thrilling toboggan-like **Flyer**, which takes 4 passengers in 8ft/2m in-line tubes down more than 450ft/137m of banked curves and straights, and **The Blast**, with its 1 or 2-passenger tubes that surprise you with sudden twists and turns, explosive pipe bursts and drenching waterspouts, leading to a final waterfall plunge. And don't miss **The Storm**, a pair of identical circular slides billed as 'body coasters' – the enclosed tubes (complete with storm sound and light effects) send the rider plunging into a circular bowl, around which they spin at high speed before landing in the splash-pool below. Possibly the funniest, though, is **Disco H2O**, a superbly themed family raft ride that plunges down an

enclosed tube into a swirling 'disco bowl' (featuring lights and mirror ball!) before spitting you out through a waterfall. It is all accompanied by 1970s music and commentary to add to the fun (big queues from midday to late afternoon). Equally, **Brain Wash** is a 65ft/20m funnel ride that sends riders on 2, 3 or 4-person tubes down an enclosed flume into a huge funnel that washes the tube wildly backwards and forwards before setting it up for the final splashdown.

For those under 4ft/122cm, the **Kids' Park** has a full range of junior-sized slides, plus a sandcastle structure with 2 semicircular waterslides and a giant bucket that fills and tips up at regular intervals. Uniquely, the children can use tubes, beach chairs and tables designed specifically for their height. The neighbouring lake is also part of the fun (though not in chilly winter and spring), adding the options for cable-operated **Knee Ski**, **Wake-Skating** and the **Wild One** (large inner tubes tied behind a speedboat). Take a breather in the slow-flowing **Lazy River** as you float past palms and waterfalls, or head for one of several picnic areas (though they can be crowded). The energetic can play beach volleyball. Lockers, showers and tube and towel rentals are all available; if you bring your own equipment, you must have it checked by the lifeguards.

Shopping and dining: Sportswear, swimwear, sunglasses, hats and more can all be found at **Breakers Beach Shop**. For food, **Bubba's Bar-B-Q** serves chicken, ribs, fries and drinks, the **Surf Grill** features burgers, hot dogs, chicken and sandwiches, and **Manny's Pizza** has pizza and subs. Two additional snack bars offer ice cream, funnel cakes, kettle corn and more. You can also bring your own picnic, but not alcohol or glass containers.

Lazy River

BRITTIP

For all the water parks, it's a good idea to bring a pair of deck shoes or sandals that can be worn in water. All the local supermarkets sell them cheaply.

Getting there: Wet 'n Wild is ½ mile/ 800m north of I-Drive's junction with Sand Lake Road at the intersection with Universal Boulevard (see map p14), just off exit 75A and 74B of I-4. **Admission:** $47.95 adults, $41.95 3–9s and seniors (60+), under-3s free (also included with Orlando FlexTicket). Towels $3 ($3 deposit) and lockers $5-8, or $10 ($3 deposit); parking $10; open 9.30–9pm in summer, 10am–5, 6 or 7pm at other times (**www. wetnwildorlando.com**). **TTTTT/AAA**

Aquatica by SeaWorld

Orlando's newest and most eye-catching water park has a wonderful range of children's attractions and facilities, **small animal encounters**, innovative rides and an all-you-can-eat-meal option, spread over 59-acres/24ha of South Seas-inspired landscaping.

Slides and rides: Aquatica's signature attraction is the **Dolphin Plunge**, a twin body slide that sends riders down 300ft/91.5m of tubes and through a lagoon of playful, black-and-white Commerson's dolphins (it's a touch gimmicky as you catch only the briefest glimpse of them on the way down, but it is an exhilarating slide). You can then view the **Dolphins** at the end of the ride through the huge lagoon window, where the inhabitants often hang out to look at their human visitors! **Whanau Way** is a quadruple raft ride with 2 distinct variations that twist and turn before landing with a resounding splash, while **Tassie's Twisters** are double bowl rides that send riders down 1 and 2-person tubes into giant bowls before splashing back into the **Loggerhead Lane** lazy river (which also incorporates a cool coral reef viewing section). **Taumata Racer** is a fast-paced mat slide set up like an 8-lane racing toboggan run, partly enclosed and then with a double drop into daylight (queues can look long here but they usually move quickly). Family raft rides **Walhalla Wave** and **HooRoo Run** offer contrasting experiences: the longer Wave features a winding, enclosed section before

a big splash finale; the latter is a shorter and straighter ride – with a couple of distinctly sudden drops on the way! **Omaka Rocka** features 2 high-speed single-rider tube flumes, each with 3 sets of funnels that send you coursing up 1 side and down the other with a sensational 'feel it in your tummy' weightlessness before final splash-down. That is followed by 2 wave pools, side-by-side lagoons that create a variety of different wave patterns. **Big Surf Shores** offers the bigger, more dynamic waves, while **Cutback Cove** features gentler rolling surf (and 860,000 gallons of water!). The pools front the huge, wide sandy Beach, which offers most of the large array of sun loungers and umbrellas, and the private cabañas (which start at $70 for Standard, $100, Pool View or $120 Premium in low season; an Ultimate Cabaña is $300-600 seasonally). Roa's Island loungers (includes 2 loungers, shade umbrella, towels and locker) can be hired for $20.

BRITTIP
Head for the Beach area when you first arrive to stake out a place to base yourselves and try to grab 1 of the bigger fixed umbrellas that offer the most shade.

As well as the gentle Loggerhead Lane, you should try the dynamic **Roa's Rapids**, which provides a helter-skelter whirl along this river feature, with a series of fountains, jets and other watery boosts to keep you bobbing along with no effort at all. Free life vests are on offer here and it is worth trying 1 for the

Dolphin Plunge

feeling of floating along in high style! **Restrictions:** Taumata Racer is 3ft 6in/107cm; Walhalla Wave and HooRoo Run under 4ft/122cm must wear a life vest; Dolphin Plunge 4ft/122cm; Roa's Rapids, under 51in/129cm must wear a life vest, under 4ft/122cm on Loggerhead Lane.

Kids features: The big success of the park, though, is its extensive features for children, from the youngest to young teens. **Kata's Kookaburra Cove** is an exclusive area for those under 4ft/1.2m tall, with a whole range of scaled-down slides, rides, pools and fountains to provide a gentler experience for the young 'uns. By contrast, **Walkabout Waters** is a vast and frenzied 60ft/18m-high water play structure with every kind of climb and slide and all manner of water eruptions and outpourings, including 2 giant buckets that fill and dump in spectacular fashion over those below. The park's **small animal encounters** are also designed to appeal to children, so watch out for these around the park.

Shopping and dining: The imaginative **Kiwi Traders** is the biggest of the 4 shops, but both **Adaptations** and **Beachies** are worth a look. For dining, try **Waterstone Grill** (salads, sandwiches), **Mango Market** (pizza, chicken tenders, wraps, speciality coffees) or **Banana Beach Cookout** buffet (pizza, pasta,

sides, desserts, non-alcoholic drinks; all-day pass $16 adults, $10 ages 3–9). Aquatica also offers a pre-purchased **Family Picnic** (choose main course, side, dessert, and beverage at Mango Market) for $9 adult, $6 child, or $30 'family size,' feeding up to 6 people.

BRITTIP
Buy Aquatica tickets online for a saving on adult prices and enjoy early entry – an hour before official opening time – in summer months.

Aquatica features elements that no other park has, like Roa's Rapids and Walkabout Waters. And, if you buy the 2-park ticket with SeaWorld, it's great value in summer, as you can spend much of the day in Aquatica and then hop over to SeaWorld for the evening.

Getting there: Just across the road from SeaWorld on International Drive, exit 71 or 72 off I-4. **Admission:** $48 adults, $42 3–9s; 2-Park Ticket (with SeaWorld) $115 and $106; 3-Park Ticket (inc Busch Gardens) $122 and $130; parking $12, locker rental $10 and $5 (plus refundable $5), towels $4; 9am–10pm (summer season), 9am–7pm (Easter) or 10am–5 or 6pm (407 351 3600, **www. aquaticabyseaworld.com**) TTTT/AAAAA

That sums up the large-scale attractions on offer, but let's explore some alternatives to the mass-market experience…

Walkabout Waters

8 Off the Beaten Track

or When You're All Theme-Parked Out

Orlando's main attractions are undoubtedly a lot of fun, but they can also be extremely tiring and you may well need a break from all the hectic theme park activity. Or you may be visiting again and looking for a different experience. If either is the case, this chapter is for you.

Hopefully, you will already have noted the relatively tranquil offerings of Silver Springs and Fantasy of Flight in the previous chapter, but to enhance your view of the area further, the following are all guaranteed to take you off the beaten tourist track. This chapter could easily be subtitled 'A Taste of the *Real* Florida', as it introduces the towns of Winter Park, Celebration and Mount Dora, plus the natural delights of the area, including the state parks, day-trips, eco-tours and sports.

ORLANDO/Orange County

Foremost among the 'secret' hideaways is the elegant northern suburb of Winter Park, little more than 20mins from the hurly-burly of I-Drive yet a world away from the relentless tourism. It offers museums and art galleries, boutique shopping, numerous restaurants, walking tours, a delightful 50-minute boat ride around the lakes and, above all, a chance to slow down. Take exit 87 from I-4, Fairbanks Avenue; turn right on Fairbanks and go east

for 2mls/3km and turn left at the junction with Park Avenue.

Morse Museum of American Art: A must for admirers of American art pottery, American and European glass, furniture and other decorative arts of the late 19th and early 20th centuries, as it includes 1 of the world's foremost collections of works by Louis Comfort Tiffany. The dazzling chapel restoration from the 1893 Chicago World Expo is now on display in its original form for the first time since the late 19th century and is worth the entrance fee alone It also has special Christmas exhibitions and periodic family programmes (9.30am–4pm Tues–Sat, 1–4pm Sun, also 4pm-8pm Fri only Nov–April; adults $5, Seniors $4, students $1, under-12s free; free 4–8pm each Fri Nov–April; **www.morsemuseum.org**).

Park Avenue: The heart of Winter Park is a classy street of restaurants, fine shops and a shaded park. At 1 end is Rollins College, a small but respected arts education centre housing the beautiful Cornell Fine Arts Museum, with the oldest collection of paintings, sculpture and decorative arts in Florida (10am–4pm Tues–Fri,

12am–5pm Sat and Sun, closed Mon and holidays; $5 adults; **www.rollins. edu/cfam**).

You should also take the **Park Avenue Walking Tour**, with free maps provided by the new Welcome Center (on W Lyman Ave; 8.30am–5pm Mon-Fri; 407 644 8281). The shops of Park Avenue are a cut above most and, while you may find the prices equally distinctive, just browsing is an enjoyable experience with the charm of the area highlighted by the friendliness hereabouts. For shops both unique and fun, look for **Simmons Jewellers**, **Ten Thousand Villages** (international arts and crafts), **Bebe's** (children's clothes), the eclectic **The Doggie Door** (pet accessories), **Siegel's** (men's clothing) and **Jacobsons** (department store), plus **Peterbrooke Chocolatier**. Regular craft fairs and art festivals add splashes of colour to an inviting scenario, plus live jazz in Central Park once a month on Sun in summer. Street parking allows 3 hours free, but there is a multi-storey car park on the corner of Comstock and Park Avenue, which is a better ½-day option. Keep an eye out for the *Taste of Winter Park* in Apr and *Autumn Art Festival* in Oct (**www.winterpark.org** and **www.parkave-winterpark.com**).

Scenic Boat Tour: Started in 1938, this is located at the east end of Morse Avenue and offers a charming, 12ml/19km narrated tour around the lakes and canals, giving a fascinating glimpse of some stunning homes, boat houses and lakeside gardens (property prices start at around $1m and several top $10m!). Tours run 10am–4pm daily (closed Christmas) at $12 for adults and $6 for 2–11s, cash only; and this is 1 of the most relaxing hours you can spend in Orlando (**www.scenicboattours.com**).

Lake Tibet-Butler Preserve: For a more natural view of Florida, head to this small reserve just north of Walt Disney World on SR535 (Winter Garden-Vineland Rd). The 440-acre/178ha park features 4mls/6.5km of trails and elevated boardwalks where the cypress

A dining delight

Winter Park boasts some of the best upmarket dining in Orlando. **Park Plaza Gardens** specialises in a modern mix of American and Continental cuisines, plus a wonderful Sunday brunch. **310 Park South** offers the epitome of elegant, European café culture. We are also big fans of the pavement bistro **Briarpatch**, the Italian style of **Pannullo's**, and **Luma on Park**, a 'gastropub' featuring fresh, daily specials from simple burgers to gourmet offerings and a superb wine list (**www.lumaonpark.com**). **The Ravenous Pig** has a similar wide-ranging pub choice, from its fine micro-brewery to wonderful steaks and seafood and earns top marks from leading local restaurant critic Scott Joseph (**www.theravenouspig.com**).

swamps, freshwater marshes, scrub and pine flatwoods are home to gopher tortoises, turtles, armadillos and especially birds (it is on the Great Florida Birding Trail). Stop by the Visitor Center to pick up a map and see its wildlife exhibits and enjoy an hour or 2 of peace and quiet (10am–5 or 6pm daily).

MOUNT DORA/ Lake County

Immediately to the west and north of Orlando is this large, rural county that is home to more unspoiled Florida charms and several small-scale attractions, including a notable state park and well-known winery.

Mount Dora: This smallish town on beautiful Lake Dora is one of Florida's hidden gems; a day here is a breath of fresh air with its unique mix of pleasant shops, restaurants, bars, inns and tours. Mount Dora is also renowned as a festival city, with 17 annual galas. Visit **www.mountdora.com** to see if there is 1 during your visit (**4 July** and **Christmas** are especially notable, while the **Sail Boat Regatta** each April is 1 of Florida's finest).

Start with the **Mount Dora Trolley** from the **Lakeside Inn**, a 1-hour narrated trundle around the streets (11am, noon, 1 and 2pm Mon–Fri, $13 adults, $11 2–13s; 352 385 1023),

Mount Dora dining

Try a leisurely lunch at **Palm Tree Grille**, the excellent **Copacabana Cuban Café** or **5th Avenue Café**. **Mount Dora Coffee House** is the place for coffee and the **Windsor Rose** is a genuine English tea-room. For something stronger, try **Mount Dora Brewing**. There are notable pubs like **O'Keefe's Irish Pub** or the Icelandic flavour of **The Frosty Mug**. All the above also offer dinner, but our top 2 – especially if you arrive before the sun goes down – are **Pisces Rising**, a lovely Key West-themed restaurant, with stylish decor and a grandstand view of sunsets over Lake Dora, plus excellent fresh Florida seafood and steaks (352 385 2669, **www.piscesrisingdining.com**); and the charming **Goblin Market** bistro tucked away in a quiet corner of town (352 735 0059, **www.goblinmarketrestaurant.com**). With a small patio dining area, a conservatory-style ground floor and clubby upper floor with bar, this renovated warehouse is ideal for a refined lunch or upmarket dinner (not Mon; 11.30am–3.30pm only Sun).

a fascinating tour of 1 of the 'Top 100 Great Towns of America', and a former key stop on the now-defunct Florida railroad. Then stroll round the compact centre, which is full of quaint shops, cafés and bars. Antique hunters are spoiled for choice but should visit **Pak Ratz** and the **Village Antique Mall**, with more than 80 vendors. **Uncle Al's Time Capsule** is a must for fans of movie and celebrity memorabilia (owner Al Wittnebert also has regular celebrity signings), while other unique stores include a **Walk in the Woods** (for clothing and Crocs shoes), **Li'l Guys and Dolls** and **Thee Clockmaker Shoppe**. The town even boasts **Ridgeback Winery**, which offers tastings of its hand-crafted fruit wines (Wed–Sun, 11am–5pm). Other stops of interest include **Mount Dora Historic Museum** (the former town jail!), which displays more (free) local history, and the **Museum of Speed**, a constantly changing homage to high-powered American sports cars of yesteryear (plus other memorabilia such as vintage juke boxes and Coca-Cola machines; 10am–5pm Mon–Fri; $9/person, no under-14s; 352 385 1945, **www.classicdreamcars.com**).

Possibly the best way to see Mount Dora is with the fully narrated **Guided Tours of Segway of Central Florida**. They use unique, state-of-the-art, 2-wheel Segways to take small groups downtown, on to the iconic Mount Dora lighthouse and around scenic Palm Island Park. They pass some of the city's many fine B&Bs (including the award-winning **Magnolia Inn**

on East 3rd Avenue) and the genteel 125-year-old **Lakeside Inn**, on the National Register of Historic Places, where you can stop for a drink in Tremain's Lounge or dine in the Beauclaire Dining Room (great Sunday brunch – look at **www.lakeside-inn.com**). The Segway is easy to master (after a brief hands-on lesson) and ideal for the quiet streets. If you enjoy the 1-hour tour, there is a second guided tour of nearby Dogwood Mountain. Both cost $48/person and tours run Wed–Sun 10am, noon, and 2pm (reservations advised; 352 383 9900, **www.segwayofcentralflorida.com**). Riders must be 18 (16 with parent) and no more than 260lb/118kg. This is 1 of our favourite activities!

You can see more with **Premier Boat Tours** via the *Captain Doolittle* from the Lakeside Inn for a fascinating eco-tour of the lakes and Dora Canal. As well as gators, you may see raccoons, turtles, otters, birds of prey and other nesting birds along this beautiful waterway. There are narrated 2-hour tours daily at 11am and 2pm ($25

Mount Dora Canal Cruise

adults, $12.50 children) and 1-hour Sunset Tours (bring your favourite beverages; reservations advised on 352 434 8040, **www.doracanaltour.com**). Pontoon rentals are also available.

Getting there: On US Highway 441 north-east of Orlando, take the (toll) Florida Turnpike to exit 267A for the (toll) Western Beltway (429), and the Beltway north to its junction with 441, from where Mount Dora is 10ml/16km further north. For more info, contact the excellent Mount Dora Chamber of Commerce on 352 383 2165 or **www.mountdora.com**. The visitor centre is at 341 Alexander Street.

BRITBONUS
Take a kayak tour with **Central Florida Nature Adventures** and, when you book for 3, the fourth person paddles free! Just remember to quote the *Brit Guide* offer when you book and show your copy when you turn up.

Central Florida Nature Adventures: Head just north from Mount Dora to the town of Eustis and you find this neat local kayak tours company. And, although they are based here, they offer guided tours of the Dora Canal and the Lil' Amazon in Lake County, Rock Springs Run and the Wekiva River in Seminole County, Blackwater Lake in Marion County and the Silver River in Ocala, as well as a winter Manatee tour and even a 'paddles and saddles' experience combining a kayak trip with horse-riding. Their 2 chief guides are highly experienced kayakers but most trips (2–7hrs) require no previous experience and are wonderfully scenic. Tours vary from $59–119 (352 589 7899, **www.kayakcentralflorida.com**).

Lake Louisa State Park: Another Lake *Revolution – The Offroad Experience*

County gem just off Highway 27 (at the west end of Highway 192), this offers some beautiful countryside, with 6 lakes and rolling hills. There are over 20mls/32km of hiking trails, a picnic pavilion, swimming in Lake Louisa (with lifeguards late May–Aug), plus 20 cabins, sleeping up to 6 (8am–dusk daily, entry $5/car; 352 394 3969, **www.floridastateparks.org/lakelouisa**). Further up Highway 27 is the Citrus Tower, built in 1956, with panoramic views from its 22-storey glass observation deck (9am–5pm Mon–Sat, $4 adults $2 3–11s; 352 394 4061, **www.citrustower.com**); and **Lakeridge Winery**, a 127-acre/51ha estate producing some award-winning wines with free tours and tastings (10am–5pm Mon–Sat, 11am–5pm Sun; 1800 768 WINE, **www.lakeridgewinery.com**).

Revolution – The Offroad Experience: This newest attraction is perfect for those wanting to see more of the real Florida and anyone with kids of 16+. British-run, it is set in 230 acres/93ha of prime countryside with a private lake. They offer 4 off-road experiences – ATV, Jeep and Dune Buggy rides and a Baja racing car – plus trophy bass fishing. Their purpose-built ATV trail features 2 40-minute sessions of fab driving on these challenging but safe 4-wheel wonders (must be 16+; 12–15 can ride with an instructor). The trails and dirt tracks are all genuine wilderness but groomed for off-road activity, and you WILL get dirty, so wear old clothes (including long trousers and close-toed shoes or trainers). There is a short 'test' to ensure riders are in control, then it's off over the sand-hills and grasslands. The 4 x 4 Experience (in a Jeep Wrangler) can be driven by anyone with a driving licence and passengers are welcome, but it is primarily about skill, not speed over the steep hills and man-made stairway. The sturdy Can Am Commander X Series dune buggies are open to all with a valid driving licence, under 280lb/127kg and under 1.9m/6ft 3in, while the all-new Baja racing experience (a souped-up offroad vehicle) is over a special 6-mile/10km track (over-21s

with full licence only; or drive-along with instructor). Purely and simply, this is 1 of the best off-road drives in Florida – novel, enjoyable and highly addictive! Booking essential on 352 400 1322 or **www.revolutionoffroad.com**. ATV is $70/person; ATV & Dune Buggy or ATV & Jeep $120, or all 3 for $150. The 2 bass-fishing programmes are $200 and $275 for 4 and 6 hours, while the Baja racing experience is $000. To get there, take Highway 192 west to Highway 27; go north on 27 for 3 traffic lights; turn left on Highway 474 and go west until it hits 33, then go north (right) for 2mls/3km and Revolution Offroad is on the right.

BRITBONUS

$ Get $5/person off any activity at **Revolution Offroad** by showing your copy of the *Brit Guide* or mentioning it when booking.

OSCEOLA COUNTY
You'll find some of Florida's most scenic and nature-orientated attractions in Kissimmee area – you just need to know where to look!

Balloon trips
Florida is hugely popular for ballooning and you will often see them in Osceola County. It's a majestic experience; the utterly smooth way in which you lift off is breathtaking, but the peace and quiet, and the stunning views, are awesome. It's not cheap, but it is appealing to all but young children or those with a fear of heights. It can also be a highly personal ride, with basket capacity starting at just 4 people.

BRITTIP
Dresses are not advisable for balloon trips and hard-wearing shoes for the set-up and landing areas are essential.

Orlando Balloon Rides: The main operator in central Florida, British-run, it flies every day (weather permitting), meeting at **Orlando Sun Resort** on Highway 192 (by Marker 4) at 5.30–6.30am depending on

season (the best winds are nearly always early) then transferring to the take-off site. Here you can help the friendly crew set up the new, safety-designed balloons (for 4, 8, 10, 12 or 18 passengers) one of which is also disabled-accessible. Then you fly off for 1 hour, floating serenely or sinking to skim the treetops or one of the many lakes. After your flight enjoy a champagne landing ceremony before returning to the hotel for a breakfast buffet and your balloonist's certificate. It lasts 3–4 hours and costs $175/person (inc. tax; no under-4s or expectant mothers). Hotel pick-up is available at $10/person for the round trip, or for $20 you can be part of the chase crew and just enjoy the champagne landing and breakfast. Book well in advance on 407 894 5040 or **www.orlandoballoonrides.com**. Orlando Balloon Rides are also part of the **Orlando Adventure Collection**, a group of 6 companies with an action-themed attraction. They include Revolution – The Offroad Experience (p248), Boggy Creek Airboats (p250), Florida Eco-Safaris' zipline safari (p253), Warbird Adventures (p255) and the Sky Dive Space Center in Titusville just north of Cocoa Beach. Look up more at **www.orlandoadventurecollection.com**.

BRITTIP
Susan says: Orlando Balloon Rides has the largest balloons in the US, with 'segmented' baskets that make you feel as if you have your own space. Very comfortable, even for a height-chicken like me!

Thompson Aire: Top local pilot Jeff Thompson, a veteran with more than 30 years' flying, also flies every day (weather permitting), meeting at the **Best Western Lakeside** on Highway 192, and returning there for a hearty buffet breakfast. Fares are $185 ($105 10–15s; 1 child 5–9 can fly free with a paying adult; discounts for 4 or more adults travelling together). Call 407 421 9322 or visit **www.thompsonaire.com**. Hotel pick-ups can be arranged at $15/person.

Airboat rides

The thrill of airboat rides – like flying at ground level – can be experienced on many of Florida's waterways, but especially in Osceola County. You can explore areas otherwise inaccessible to boats, skimming over the marshes to give you an alternative, close-up view. Travelling at up to 50mph/80kph means it can be loud (you will be given headphones) and sunglasses are also a good idea to keep stray flies out of your eyes. It is NOT the trip for you, however, if you are spooked by crickets, dragonflies and similar insects that occasionally land in the boat! In summer, a good insect repellent is essential.

BRITTIP
Look out for some great discounts and special offers on Boggy Creek's website, **www.bcairboats.com**.

Boggy Creek Airboat Rides: Several operations offer airboat rides in the area but, for the most quality-conscious and friendly operation, our vote goes to Boggy Creek. It has 2 contrasting sites in different parts of Kissimmee, 1 more rural while the other has more facilities. The rural site is on Lake Toho at peaceful **Southport Park**, all the way down Poinciana Boulevard, off Highway 192 between markers 10 and 11, and across Pleasant Hill Road into Southport Road – about a 35-minute drive. Boggy Creek's ½-hour ride features the most modern 18-passenger airboats in Florida, skimming over the local wetlands for a close-up of the majestic cypress trees and wildlife including eagles, ospreys, snakes and turtles, as well as the ever-present gators. Southport Park feels like it's a million miles away from the main tourist area, and it is likely you'll see a variety of wildlife, especially in spring.

You don't need to book, just turn up, as boats go every ½ hour (9am–5pm daily; $25.95 adults, $19.95 3–10s). Don't forget the sunscreen as you can really burn on the water. It also does a 1-hour Night Tour ($49.95 adults, $45.95 3–10s, approx 9pm–10pm

mid-Mar to mid-Nov only) for a completely different and exhilarating experience (gator eyes glow red in the dark!), but you must book in advance. Or go all out with the 45-minute Swamp Excursion, exploring remote areas beyond the regular tour ($54.95/person). Round-trip hotel transport is offered (call for pricing). Boggy Creek's other (rather busier) site is at **East Lake Fish Camp** (reservations required), a completely different experience to Lake Toho, so it is worth trying both. Stay after your ride for a live alligator demonstration – and have the chance to hold a gator and have your picture taken! East Lake Fish Camp offers its own cracker-style restaurant (well worth a try, especially for breakfast) and boat rentals. To reach East Lake Fish Camp, either take exit 17 off Central Florida Greeneway – 417 – and go 3mls/5km south on Boggy Creek Road, then right into East Lake Fish Camp, or take Osceola Parkway east until it hits Boggy Creek Road. Go left and then turn right at the Boggy Creek T-junction, then right into East Lake Fish Camp after about 2mls/3km (book on 407 344 9550 or **www.bcairboats.com**).

BRITBONUS
Brit Guide readers qualify for a free souvenir with **Boggy Creek Airboats** if you mention you booked after seeing them here (souvenir choice at discretion of Boggy Creek Airboats).

Powerboat ride

Turbo's Boat Rides: Captain Turbo's motto says it all: 'Get in, sit down, shut up, hold on'! Also at East Lake Fish Camp (see above), the 1998 29ft Warlock powerboat is 1 mean water demon, topping out at 80mph/128kph during a thrilling 25–30-minute ride across East Lake Toho. The sleek Factory One class racing boat has a specially designed hull for stability, and holds several world championships from her days on the racing circuit. Accommodating 5 at a time, each ride is tailored to the rider's comfort, from mild to full-out racing speed. Turbo's

A cause for Celebration

Dining in Celebration is a real highlight. Try **Market Street Café**, a 50s-style diner serving down-home favourites such as turkey dinners or meatloaf and, or try award-winning **Café D'Antonio** for authentic Italian cuisine in a sleek, family-friendly atmosphere (407 566 2233, **www.antoniosonline.com**); Spanish-Cuban **Columbia** uses unique combinations of authentic ingredients (407 566 1505, **www.columbiarestaurant.com**); **Shannon's of Celebration** offers authentic Irish food in a pretty setting; **Celebration Town Tavern**, a casual ambiance, specialising in New England seafood; **Seito Sushi**, is the place for contemporary sushi and fusion dishes; and the **Imperium Food and Wine** is an excellent option for fine wines and cocktails, plus a tempting light bite menu, including soups, sandwiches, salads and flatbreads (407 566 9054, **www.imperiumwineroom.com**). You should also consider the **Bohemian Bar & Grill** at the Bohemian Hotel, a contemporary American steakhouse with old-world Florida charm.

powerboat is eco-friendly and feels surprisingly solid and secure for a ride all the family can enjoy. Goggles are available and will fit over your sunglasses. Find Turbo's at East Lake Fish Camp. 1–2 people $110 per person, per person; call for reservations on 407 436 4571, **www.turbosraceboatrides.com**.

BRITBONUS

Receive a $25 discount on the regular powerboat ride price of $110 with **Captain Turbo** by producing your copy of the *Brit Guide*. Remember to book in advance on 407 436 4571.

East Lake Fish Camp is itself a little gem, offering a variety of boating and fishing options (407 348 2040, **www.eastlakefishcamp.net**), a pleasant outdoor terrace and the authentic rural charm of the restaurant and gift shop (8am–9pm daily). If you're here in the morning, consider arriving early for a huge all-day breakfast, while the more adventurous will want

to try the local delicacies – catfish, frogs' legs and gator tail. For another great slice of local eating, the Fri all-you-can-eat catfish dinner is $12.95, or try the weekend breakfast buffet for $8.95.

Celebration

In 1994, the Walt Disney Company set out to build a 'new urban' neighbourhood, a model community with a friendly, welcoming spirit and strong traditional values. The result was Celebration, where picture-perfect Victorian homes mingle with smart town-houses with an array of shopping, dining and entertainment options. Today, it is a self-sufficient, bustling town with a hospital, schools, cinema and 2 distinctive hotels. Located on Disney's southern border, Celebration is easily found off Highway 192. Enter at the landmark water tower via Celebration Ave, then follow signs to Celebration Hotel in the town centre.

BRITTIP

For Celebration, don't stop at the first set of shops and services you come to off Highway 192. Keep going until you find Market Street and the centrepiece lake that lets you know you have found the proper downtown area.

Once downtown, the shops abound. Market Street shops are open 10am–9pm Mon–Sat, noon–6pm Sun, with delightful boutiques like **Market Street Gallery** (Disney collectables, Swarovski crystal, Lladro, and other fine gifts), **Confetti of Celebration** (speciality and customised gifts)

Boggy Creek Airboat Rides

and **Lollipop Cottage** (children's clothing and gifts). Besides having a wonderfully whimsical name, **Soft as a Grape** is the place to find casual wear for the family. Other specialists include **Jewel Box** and **Day Dreams** (dolls, bears, books). There are miles of bike and walking paths, with the pretty lakefront setting, children's play area and periodic festivals. A huge event is held on **4 July**, with picnics, entertainment and face-painting plus Disney-inspired fireworks over the lake (parking is at the town entrance, with a park-and-ride bus), while the Christmas period sees festive events and nightly snow on Market Street (**http://celebrationtowncenter.com**).

Segway Tours

A new feature in Kissimmee/ Celebration are 2 super opportunities to try out the fab 2-wheeled Segway transporter and get a guided audio tour of the area as well. Ideal for young and old alike (age 14 and up), they are easy to master, fun to ride and a breeze to enjoy as you trundle along Highway 192 and around the most scenic parts of Celebration in true eco-friendly style.

ZE Tours: Choose from 3 separate tours in the company of a wonderfully personable guide (9am–4.30pm daily), heading out from their store in the Rock Church plaza on Highway 192 (by Marker 10; next to the Helicopter Tours) and rolling along for 70, 100 or 130mins to discover the heart of Celebration, its many lakes, paths and byways, plus lots

Segway Tours around Celebration

of wildlife – from playful squirrels (which you can feed) to gators (which you can't!). There is a quick ride-around to get your 'Segway legs', then it is off in single-file, with the tranquil tour enabled by small walkie-talkies that clip on to your helmet. There are plenty of stops to ask questions and compare notes with your group, and your guide is a great source of knowledge about the town and the area (especially Disney). ZE Tours also offer bike rentals to tour Highway 192 at your leisure (and it's all completely flat!). The guided tours cost $55, $80 and $105/person (70, 100 and 130mins; 14-17-year-olds must be accompanied by a parent; minimum weight 100lb/45kg, max 250lb/113kg), or you can just try a ride-around on a Segway at $5 for 2mins or $15 for 10mins. Bike rental is from $5–25 (hourly or all day). Reservations are highly recommended for both on 863 512 0256 or online at **www.zetours.com**.

Old Town Segway Adventures: Based in Old Town on Highway 192, this new operation offers 2 tours, both of which visit Celebration and provide a serene look at the area. Choose from the One-Hour Guided Audio Adventure (which adds 30mins training on a Segway) or the 2½hr version, which goes into Celebration in more detail. After training, you set out along Old Town's Main Street with its many and varied shops and eateries before gliding on to Disney's carefully designed town, discovering the lakeside trails and wildlife, which can also include turtles, great blue herons and egrets as well as gators. Take in the full vista of the area for either 1 or 2 hours before returning to Old Town. The longer tour includes the training session and a rest-stop but both offer a great view of Celebration in the company of your expert guide. Tours cost $55 or $75/ person at 9am, 1pm and 4pm, and must be booked in advance, while there are riding sessions of 5mins, 1hr, 4hrs and 8hrs for $5-85 for walk-up visitors. Min age 14 or weight 100lb/45kg; max 280lb/127kg (407 749 0063 or toll-free in USA on 1866 611 9838, **www.oldtownsegway.com**).

BRITTIP
Not sure if you'd take to a Segway?
Try the 5-minute fun ride ($5) with Old
Town Segway Adventures and, if you like it,
they'll deduct the $5 cost from the price of
a full tour or rental.

Florida Eco-Safaris

For our money, this is one of the most outstanding non-theme-park attractions in Florida. Both a 4,700-acre/1,900ha wilderness preserve and working ranch, it offers a close-up of the flora, fauna and conservation issues, plus a real taste of cracker-style life ('crackers' were 19th century Florida cowboys).

Zipline Safari: Eco-safaris, horseback safaris and nature walks are all on offer, but this is the real highlight. This 2½-hour adventure starts with a short scenic hike to the launch point, which provides a breathtaking aerial view of the preserve at up to 55ft/16.8m high. The course includes 7 different zip lines, 9 observation platforms and 2 sky-bridges over 3 eco-systems. The longest run is 750ft/229m and riders reach top speeds of 25mph/40kph. The final zip brings you back to ground level and a visit to its wildlife interaction area, including a Florida panther, alligators and other animals. There are also themed 'party' events on Sat, including a Starlight Safari or Moonlight Safari on select dates, but you must book in advance (1866 854 3837, $85/person; min weight 70lb/32kg, max 275lb/125kg).

Cypress Restaurant and Visitor Center: Start here with its essential 30-minute orientation programme into the preserve's creation. Beginning as a dream of gifted biologist and ecologist Allen Broussard, it was completed after his death (from complications of Hodgkin's disease) by his parents, Dr William and Margaret Broussard as a non-profit-making memorial to their son. The education element alone is awesome, and the 2 tours feature a strong conservation message. The 2-hour **Coach Safari** is its stock-in-trade, a tranquil trundle in a large-wheeled, open-sided buggy round much of the woods, swamp and prairie that make up the Crescent J Ranch and Conservancy. Your guide gives the low-down on the fascinating history and environmental issues. A boardwalk along Bull Creek affords the chance to get up close with a typical cypress 'dome' and breathe the amazingly pure air. You are likely to encounter alligators (at a safe distance), turtles, whitetail deer, armadillos and a host of bird life – including bald eagles and wild turkeys – as well as the native cattle and horses, and you'll leave with a good understanding of the real Florida. Eco-Safaris cost $28 ($22 6–12s) and depart daily at 10am and 1pm. **Horseback Safaris** are another feature (ages 12 and over; 10 and 11 only with proven riding experience), with the chance to enjoy their Western trail rides for 1, 2 or 3 hours with a native cracker guide. Horseback Safaris cost $40, $60 or $80 (book at least 24 hours in advance on 1866 854 3837).

BRITTIP
Long trousers and closed-toed shoes
are essential for Florida Eco-Safaris'
Horse Safaris. An early morning ride here is
1 of the most enjoyable hours you are likely
to spend in Florida.

If you want to go further into cowboy country, **Rawhide Round-up** is a ½-day experience with cattle on the Crescent J Ranch, including lunch ($99). The **Horseback Safaris** can also be extended to 2 days ($199), staying in bunk-house accommodation.

Florida Eco-Safaris

Forever Florida is a good 80-minute drive out of Orlando, 40mls/64km east on Highway 192, through St Cloud as far as Holopaw, then 7½mls/12km south on Highway 441, but is well worth the journey to experience the charm and tranquillity (1866 854 3837, **www.floridaecosafaris. com**).

Green Meadows Petting Farm

This is guaranteed fun for kids 2–11 and their parents. It's the ultimate hands-on experience as, on the 2-hour guided tour, kids get to milk a cow, pet a pig, cuddle a chick or duckling, feed goats and sheep, meet a buffalo, chickens, peacocks and donkeys and learn what makes a farm tick. There are pony rides and a play area, tractor-drawn hay rides, and the Green Meadows Express train tour. Don't forget your camera! The shaded areas, free-roaming animals and peaceful aspect all contribute to another pleasant change of pace, especially as Green Meadows is barely 10mins from the hurly-burly of Highway 192. Allow 3–4 hours for your visit. Drinks, snacks and gifts are available, but it is also the ideal place to bring a picnic (on Poinciana Boulevard; 9.30am–5.30pm daily, last tour 4pm; $21/person, $17/seniors, under-2s free; 407 846 0770, **www. greenmeadowsfarm.com**).

Osceola Pioneer Museum

Only just off the beaten track in Kissimmee, but a delightful discovery, is this small-scale homage to 19th-century Florida life, with a preserved 'cracker' homestead portraying how settlers lived in the 1890s. The charming little museum traces the history of Osceola County and includes a cattle camp, nature walk, school house, country store and information centre with library. A recent addition is an 1890 citrus-packing operation from nearby Narcoossee, which was originally started by a family from the UK! The volunteers who take you round provide a fascinating view of life here more than a century ago (on N Bass Road, just off Highway 192 by the Wal-Mart Supercenter next to Medieval Times between markers 14 and 15. 10am–4pm Thurs–Sun; $5 adults, $2 children, under-5s free; 407 396 8644 **www.osceolahistory.org**).

Kissimmee Outdoor Adventures

For a more sedate view of the local flora and fauna, head to downtown Kissimmee. Under the expert guidance of a local captain, you can explore Lake Tohopekaliga for a 1½-hour circuit in a 24ft/7m pontoon boat, taking in Makinson Island and the Shingle Creek waterway (with soft drinks, water and snacks included). Your guide will point out all the wildlife, from gators and turtles to ospreys and eagles, and you will gain a valuable insight into the local ecosystems. The Miss Toho leaves the Toho Marina dock (on Lakeshore Boulevard; take Ruby Avenue off Broadway in downtown Kissimmee) at 10am, noon, 2pm and 4pm Mon–Fri, 9am, 11am, 1pm and 3pm Sat and Sun; $25 adults, $15 ages 12 and under. There is also a 2-hour Makinson Island Nature Tour, a combined cruise and guided tour of the island, daily ($50 adults, $30 children) or the hour long Birding Tour. Just want to picnic on the island? It's $15 each way for the quick trip over and back. Kayaking will be available starting early 2012 with a variety of hire options, starting at $20/hour for a tandem, $15/hour per single. Alternatively, try a fishing excursion on Lake Toho and some of the surrounding lakes. Fishing is from $250 for 2 anglers for 4 hours to

Mauiva Air Tours

$450 for a full 8-hour day, and inshore saltwater fishing $350–625 (1800 247 1309, **www.kissoutdooradventures.com**).

Warbird Adventures and Kissimmee Air Museum

This is the most exhilarating ride in town, bar none – guaranteed. It's the only place we know of where, 20mins after walking in with no previous experience, you can actually be flying a 1945 T-6 Harvard fighter-trainer plane … and doing all manner of aerobatics! It's enhanced by in-flight video and wingtip camera to record every moment. Roller-coasters? They're for wimps! Mind you, this is not cheap – a 15-minute flight costs $240, a 30-minute trip is $420 and an hour $720. Aerobatics (on 30 or 60-minute flights only) cost $35, while the DVD is $50 and photos $25. Nevertheless, the memory will last a lifetime and just the thought of it is thrilling. Max weight is 18st/ 115kg and minimum height is 4ft/122cm. Or try piloting a helicopter (15mins $125, 30 is $199, 60 $375). Scenic helicopter tours begin at $125 for 15mins (2 people), 30mins $199 (2 people), and 60mins $349 per person.

Kissimmee Air Museum: Also on the same site at Kissimmee Gateway Airport is this combination warplane showcase and restoration centre where you can get up close with the exhibits, which include a Bell 47 helicopter, an open-cockpit Ryan PT-22, a Boeing Stearman biplane, its 3 T-6 Harvards and the amazing one-off Aerocar, plus small-scale offerings like a WWII rifle collection and Luftwaffe memorabilia. Other exhibits include *Air power and Pearl Harbor – the stories behind the events*, beginning with Billy Mitchell's 1924 prediction that Pearl Harbor would be attacked to the actual attack on 7 December, 1941, plus rare photos and artefacts behind the story. In the corner of the main hangar you'll find the incredible Focke-Wulf 190 restoration project (**www.white1foundation.org**), where the volunteer mechanics will happily explain their painstaking work. It can all be found just off Hoagland Boulevard, ½ml/800m south of Highway 192, on the left (Air Museum open 9am–5pm Mon–Sat; $6/person, ages 6–12 $3, under-5s free; 407 870 7366, **www.warbirdadventures.com** and **www.kissimmeeairmuseum.com**).

Mauiva Air Tours

For more aerial thrills, superb sight-seeing and unique views of the parks (including the nightly fireworks), try this new flight-seeing opportunity. They fly every day from Kissimmee Gateway Airport and offer 4 different tours that circle the main parks and exclusive homes of the rich and famous. The 15-minute Celebration Tour (every ½-hour from 7.30am–5.30pm) covers SeaWorld and Walt Disney World from a height of 1100ft/335m, while the 30-minute Grand Tour adds an overview of Universal Orlando and the mansions of Windermere and Isleworth (where the likes of Tiger Woods and Shaquille O'Neal live). The 30-minute Sunset Tour offers a similar view at dusk while the unique Fireworks Tours offers an aerial view of 1 of the park's pyrotechnic spectaculars and other night-time views. There is a short induction film and safety briefing in their reception lounge, and then it is straight on to your 4-seater Cessna (max 3 passengers and 450lb/204kg), where your personable pilot will provide headphones so you can hear both his commentary and the control tower during the flight.

BRITTIP
Fly with Mauiva early in the morning for the smoothest flight, when winds are light and it feels like you are just floating past all the Orlando scenery.

And, once you are in clear air space, the front seat passenger (alongside the pilot) can even take the controls for a few minutes if you choose the Captain's Package. It is an exhilarating and spectacular experience, as well as being well-priced, and a portion of all fees benefit the excellent Give Kids The World charity in Kissimmee. The full experience lasts around an hour (with the 30min flight) and children are welcome (and booster seats can be provided). Bookings are not necessary for day flights but are still advisable, while the evening tours must be booked at least a week in advance. Tours cost from $60–129, while the Captain's Package is an extra $29. Mauiva are located at 3956 Merlin Drive in Kissimmee (follow the directions for Warbird Adventures but continue down Hoagland Boulvard for 1 more junction; turn left into Merlin Drive, then left again; 407 551 0577, **www.mauivaairtours.com**).

◄■■► **BRITBONUS**
$ Receive 20% off the Captain's Package with **Mauiva Air Tours** with your copy of the *Brit Guide*. Just mention this offer at the time of booking.

POLK COUNTY

Head south from Kissimmee/Osceola County and you head into Polk territory, another of Florida's oldest-established and most authentic areas. It is home to the large-scale attractions of Legoland Florida (p220) and Fantasy of Flight (p226) but also has its share of off-the-beaten-track experiences.

Bok Tower Gardens

For those wishing to experience the genuine peace, tranquillity and floral ambience of Florida, there is no better recommendation than this national monument and garden centre at Lake Wales, 50mls/80km to the south-west of Orlando (go west on I-4, then south on Highway 27). With 1 of the most unusual attractions in the state – a majestic 205ft/62.5m pink-and-grey marble Carillon Tower – set in 250 acres/101ha of unique parkland, this is a feast for the eyes and soul. Called the Singing Tower, the 1920s-built carillon is the centrepiece and concerts are given every day at 1 and 3pm. A carillon is a series of cast bronze bells played by a keyboard or clavier. There are only around 500 in the world, and this one consists of 60 bells (crafted in Loughborough) ranging from 16lb/7.2kg to nearly 12 tons. The Gardens has its own resident player, or carilloneur, and

his concerts are a real highlight. The Tower is also a work of art, a neo-Gothic and art deco mix crafted from coquina stone and marble, with superb sculptures. It is wonderfully photogenic and quite stunning on a cloudless day.

Gardens: Around the Tower are a wide moat, a pond and semi-formal gardens. At 1 of the highest points on Florida's peninsula (all of 298ft/90m above sea level), the view is inspiring and uncluttered, and retains an inherent peace and solitude that persuaded the founder, philanthropist Edward Bok, to grant the estate to the community in 1929. The gardens also provide a wildlife observatory (the **Window by the Pond**, where you can often see up to 126 species of birds, plus reptiles, butterflies, squirrels, turtles, rabbits and armadillos, as well as the endangered gopher tortoise), nature trails, an endangered plant exhibit, butterfly and woodland gardens and pine forests. The acres of ferns, palms, oaks and pines create a lush backdrop for the seasonal azaleas, camellias, magnolias and other flowering shrubs. There is a kids play area, plus brass rubbing and art classes.

Education and Visitor Center: The award-winning centre illustrates the story of Edward Bok (don't miss the film about his impact on US society), his vision for the gardens, the carillon and architecture (with a close-up of the bells), landscape design and ecology of Florida. The **Blue Palmetto Café** adds a pleasant opportunity for a light lunch and snacks (in the open air when it's not too hot – and there's often a pleasant breeze here), while the **Tower & Garden Gift Shop** offers gift and souvenir items.

Pinewood Estate: For an additional fee ($6 adults, $5 5–12s, noon and 4pm Mon-Sat, 1pm-4pm Sun), you can tour a fine example of Mediterranean-style architecture in Florida. The 20-room mansion was built as a winter retreat for a Pennsylvania steel tycoon in the early 1930s and has been lovingly maintained to show a slice of period opulence.

Getting there: Off US Highway 27 on Burns Avenue; take I-4 west to exit 55, go south on US 27 for 25mls/40km, then left on Mountain Lake Cutoff Road (2 traffic lights past Eagle Ridge Mall) and follow the signs. Admission: $10 adults, $3 5–12s (under-5s free), apart from occasional ticketed events (mainly carillon festivals and recitals). Open 8am–6pm daily (last entry 5pm; Visitor Center 9am–5pm only; 863 676 1408, **www.boktowergardens.org**). AAA½.

Lake Wales

Continue on to the Lake Wales area after Bok Tower Gardens and you encounter some other local gems.

Chalet Suzanne: A wonderfully eclectic yet classy country inn and restaurant, quietly famous throughout Florida, this family-run (since 1931) delight is a 100-acre/40.5ha estate offering 30 guest rooms, a tropical sunken wedding garden, swimming pool and private lake, plus a soup cannery (which sent its produce to the moon)! The Chalet is such a sought-after hideaway it has its own airstrip. Its restaurant, voted one of Florida's Top 20 for more than 30 years, and an amazing venue. Made up of various cast-off buildings lovingly restored and melded together, the dining rooms are built on no fewer than 14 levels! The food is another highlight – gourmet cuisine but with a semi-set menu, with specialities including broiled grapefruit, baked sugar-cured ham, Chicken Suzanne, and its own Romaine Soup – such a favourite of Apollo 15 pilot James Irwin he persuaded NASA to take it on the mission with them, hence it became known as Moon Soup. The à la carte lunch varies from $12–42 per main course, while dinner can be à la carte or the signature set meal from $59–83, depending on main course. Be aware, a 20% 'service charge' is added to every bill in lieu of a gratuity. Even if you don't dine or stay in one of its Swiss-style cottage rooms ($129–229/night), it's worth a visit for the unique charm and for the story of the Hinshaw family.

Getting there: The Chalet can be found just outside Lake Wales, off Highway 27 on Chalet Suzanne Road (1800 433 6011, **www.chaletsuzanne. com**).

Lake Wales: Head into the quaint town of Lake Wales itself and you will discover **Spook Hill** (where cars mysteriously roll uphill!), **Grove House Visitor Center** (home of Florida's natural fruit juice products – as fresh as it gets; 10am–5pm Mon–Fri; 10am–2pm Sat, seasonally. Closed Memorial Day-end of September) and the quaint **Museum and Cultural Center** (set in a restored 1928 Atlantic Coast Line railroad station; 9am–5pm Mon–Fri, 10am–4pm Sat). The **National Historic District** of the downtown area is also being restored, building by building, to its original 1920s appearance, while you can check out the exhibitions and workshops of the **Lake Wales Arts Council**, in a beautiful Mission-style 1920s church. This is also known as the world's sky-diving capital, from Lake Wales airport, with every kind of parachuting known to man. For more info, call Lake Wales Chamber of Commerce on 863 676 3445 or visit **www.lakewaleschamber.com**.

Bok Tower Gardens

SEMINOLE COUNTY

You may have flown into the airport at the historic town of Sanford and there are plenty of diversions that get you well off the beaten track. If you want to finish your holiday with a day or two in the area, there are many good hotel choices – and you can catch your breath after all the hectic theme-parking!

Black Hammock Fish Camp and Restaurant: One of the most fun and entertaining of the area's airboat rides is found off exit 44 of the Central Florida Greeneway (take SR 434 east, turn left on Deleon Street and left on Black Hammock Road). This quiet backwater on scenic Lake Jesup is home to Capt Joel Martin, whose half-hour tour takes you into every nook and cranny of either the east or west lake (which is crammed with some of the biggest gators in Florida). The standard rides leave every ½ hour (no reservation required) and are $24.95 and $20.95 (under-11s), but there are then 1-hour rides ($39.95 and $34.95) and 45-min night rides ($45/person, 4 person minimum for which reservations are required. Or try the 45-min tour, for your party only, at $45/person, 4 person minimum, reservations required. (407 365 1244 ext 106, www.theblackhammock.com). Then grab lunch or dinner at the **Black Hammock Restaurant** (fine local delicacies, especially the catfish and gator tail, plus other dishes and a kids' menu; 11am–9pm Sun–Thurs, 11am–10pm Fri and Sat; 407 365-1244 ext 105) or visit the **Lazy Gator Bar** (3pm–11pm Mon–Wed, 3pm–1am Thurs, 2pm–2am Fri, noon–2am Sat and 11am–11pm Sun), with nightly drink specials 3–6.30pm. You can also rent canoes or fishing boats.

Central Florida Zoological Park: This private, non-profit organisation puts a natural accent on the zoo theme, set in a wooded 116 acres/47ha of unspoilt countryside with boardwalks and trails around all the attractions. These include more than 100 species of animal, weekend feeding demonstrations, educational programmes, a picnic area, pony rides and a butterfly garden, plus the Zoofari Outpost gift shop and the children's water play area, Tropical Splash Ground, with animal 'fountains', raining trees, a water tunnel and bucket dump. It's good value at $11.95 adults, $9.95 seniors (60+) and $7.95 3–12s and is open 9am–5pm daily (not Thanksgiving Day or Christmas Day). Also try **ZOOm Air Adventures**, a separate series of eco-friendly rope bridges, zip lines, guide wires and other aerial challenges through the Zoo's treetops. The 2 courses can be taken separately or combined (4ft 6in/137cm to take part), while there are also 2 separate children's courses (for 3–5ft/92–152cm). It costs $26.95 for the Upland course and $17.50 for the kids' versions, while the combo Upland and Rainforest costs $45.95. ZOOm opens at 9am, last adventure 4.30pm (off exit 104 of I-4; 407 323 4450, www.centralfloridazoo.org).

◤◣▶ **BRITTIP**

Visit Central Florida Zoo at the weekend and you will be offered a series of educational and enjoyable animal encounters (ranging from gators and snakes to hedgehogs).

Rivership Romance: For a lower-key approach, this is a great choice (daily out of downtown Sanford), especially for the lunch cruises on the wildlife-rich St John's River. The old-fashioned steamer can take up to 200 in comfort and adds a fine meal, live entertainment and river narration. Choose from the 3-hour lunch cruise (11am–2pm Mon, Wed, Fri, and Sat; $38/person), 4–hour lunch cruise (11am–3pm Tues and Thurs; $48.50), or Moonlight Dinner Dance (7.30–11pm Sat; $53.75, all drinks extra) or the **Sunday Brunch Cruise**, with live entertainment (11am–2pm, $38). There is an additional $2.50 port charge for every cruise. Its dock can be found off exit 101A of I-4, east into Sanford, then left on Palmetto Ave (407 321 5091, www.rivershipromance.com).

St Johns River Cruise: At Blue Spring State Park, there's a personable 2-hour nature tour of this historic waterway, with interactive narration of the flora, fauna (including manatees in winter) and history. It leaves from Orange City marina at 10am and 1pm daily (not Thanksgiving or Christmas Day). Take Highway 17/92 north from Sanford to French Avenue and head west for 1ml/1.6km ($22 adults, $20 seniors, $16 3–12s; 407 330 1612, **www. sjrivercruises.com**).

Sanford: The heart of Seminole County, this quaint town on Lake Monroe boasts a historic centre full of brick-paved streets, antique shops and an artist colony regeneration project. It's small-town America, having lost the growth battle with Orlando years ago, but it makes a peaceful diversion with some lovely walks, notably along the **Riverwalk**. Head for **Sanford Museum** (520 East 1st Street) for an overview of the city's incorporation – in 1877 under the patronage of pioneering lawyer and diplomat Henry Sanford – as a hub on the St John's River, the 'Nile of America'. The free museum (11am–4pm Tues–Fri, 1–4pm Sat) illustrates the life and times of the city's founder, its growth into the 'celery capital of the world' and modern history as a US naval base. From there, head on to **First Street** and check out the many restored turn-of-the-century buildings, stopping for a bite at T**wo Blondes & A Shrimp** or **The Hart Sisters Café, Tea Room and Catering**. It's a pretty setting for a meal, serving sandwiches, salads, quiches and soufflés, as well as afternoon tea, on Park Avenue, 13 blocks out of the town centre (11am–3pm Tues–Fri, 11am–4pm Sat; 407 323 9448, **www. hartsisters.com**).

State Parks: You could, of course, just head for 1 of Seminole County's splendid parks and follow the well-marked trails. **Wekiva Springs State Park** offers bike rentals, hiking, canoeing, swimming, picnic areas and shelters, and **Little Big Econ** state forest has 5,048 acres/2,045ha of scenic woodlands and wetlands. **Spring Hammock Preserve** offers 1,500 acres/607ha of wilderness to explore and the **Lake Proctor** area has

6mls/10km of equestrian, hiking and biking adventures. There are more trails along the Econlockhatchee River at the **Econ River Wilderness Area**, while **Chuluota** has 625 acres/253ha and the **Geneva Wilderness Area** 180 acres/73ha, including **Ed Yarborough Nature Center**.

Where to stay: At Altamonte Springs, try the new **Embassy Suites Orlando North** (407 834 2400), while the rapidly-growing Lake Mary area (right off exits 98-101 of I-4, closest to downtown Sanford) offers the **Courtyard by Marriott** (407 444 1000), **La Quinta Inn & Suites** (407 805 9901), **Hampton Inn Suites** (407 995 9000) and the smart **Hyatt Place** (407 995 5555). Also here is the new **Westin** (407 531 3555) with **Shula's 347 Grill**, a stylish, casual eatery with exceptional Black Angus steaks, gourmet salads, speciality dishes, and full bar. Lake Mary has become an eco-traveller's delight and an overnight stay will reward visitors with a chance to unwind amid some of Central Florida's prettiest scenery. Also here are **Colonial Town Center**, a new plaza of shops and restaurants, including the Irish pub style of **Liam Fitzpatrick's**, Mexican **Vamonos Taqueria** and **Lake Mary Vineyard Wine Company**, and **Route 46**, an excellent evening entertainment/dining complex.

More info: See **www.visitseminole.com** or go to 1 of the Visitor Centers at Orlando Sanford International Airport (in the Welcome Center as you exit the main building) or the new office at the Heathrow junction of I-4 (exit 98, go west on Lake Mary Blvd, right on International Parkway and left at AAA Drive; 407 665 2900).

Wekiva Springs

CITRUS COUNTY

If you enjoy Seminole, you may want to travel a little further, in which case the 2-state park delights of Citrus County, on the Gulf Coast north-west of Orlando, are worth seeking out.

Crystal River Preserve State Park: Just north of Homosassa Springs, the Crystal River is home to the endangered manatee and it is possible to go swimming with these wonderful creatures, either on a self-guided or an organised tour. Winter and spring are ideal times for manatee sightings, but the park offers year-round adventure, with hiking and biking trails, kayaking, canoeing and fishing – or just pack a picnic lunch and enjoy a relaxing afternoon amid the natural beauty.

BRITTIP
Never touch or disturb a wild manatee. They are protected animals and there are heavy fines, strictly enforced, for harassing them.

Getting there: Take the (toll) Florida Turnpike north to I-75, then, almost immediately, take SR44 west to Crystal River. **Admission:** Free (8am–dusk; 352 563 0450, **www.floridastateparks.org/crystalriverpreserve**).

Homosassa Springs Wildlife State Park: This park also showcases the manatee (via its underwater observatory), plus whooping cranes, deer, bobcats, black bear and even a hippopotamus among an active display of rehabilitating animals. There are daily programmes on its wildlife (10.30am, 11.30am, 12.30pm, 1.30pm, 2.30pm and 3.30pm), notably snakes and birds of prey, plus a hands-on children's education centre. The park's 210 acres/85ha take in some of the state's loveliest landscape as well as the headwaters of the Homosassa River and this is extremely popular in the spring.

Getting there: As for Crystal River, but turn left on to CR490 just after Lecanta on SR44. **Admission:** $13 adults, $5 6–12s (9am–5.30pm,

last entry 4pm; 352 628 5343, **www.homosassasprings.org**).

BREVARD COUNTY

Out on the Atlantic coast you'll find the beauty of the Cocoa Beach Thousand Islands. Tranquil canals wind past mangrove stands, wildlife flourishes in the still waters and the Indian River Lagoon Estuary is 1 of the most biodiverse eco-systems in the world.

Island Boat Lines: This family-owned enterprise offers eco-tours, fishing and the wonderful **Indian River Queen** dinner boat, recalling Mark Twain's tales of paddleboats and peaceful gentility. A relaxing 2-hour **In Search of Wildlife Eco-tour** onboard Coast Guard-certified pontoon boats departs from the Sunset Waterfront Café on Highway 520 (W Cocoa Beach Causeway), passing some of the area's most impressive homes before heading into the 1,000 Islands. Here you may spot bottlenose dolphins, manatees and a variety of coastal birds. Knowledgeable guides offer a wealth of info, encouraging visitors to ask questions and move about the boat for a closer look. Tours run at 10am and 2pm Mon–Sat, 2pm Sun ($28 adults, $26 seniors and military personnel, $23 2–12s; call to book on 321 454 7414; **www.islandboatlines.com**) **Getting there:** Take the Beachline Expressway (Hwy 528) to Hwy 1 south, then Merritt Island Causeway (Hwy 520) east, approx. 2mls/3.2km with the café on the right.

BRITBONUS
$ Get $8 off the regular adult price with **Island Boat Lines** by showing your copy of the *Brit Guide*. Do remember to book in advance, though, on 321 454 7414.

Indian River Queen: Also used for private events, this beautifully appointed triple-deck paddlewheel riverboat is open to the public at weekends, with an elegant **Friday Night Dinner Cruise** featuring live music, themed dinner buffet (Traditional Riverboat BBQ, Southern, Caribbean or Italian) and full bar. Captain Georges and owners Penny and John provide memorable authentic Southern hospitality. Boarding begins at 6.30pm, sailing from 7–9pm ($44/person). On Sundays, try the Tea Buffet Cruise with live music and buffet of Southern BBQ pork sandwiches, pasta salad and homemade cookies. Boarding begins at 2pm, sailing 2.30–4:30pm ($35/person; reservations required on 321 454 7414 or www.indianriverqueen. com/events.cfm). Film buffs may also recognise the 'Queen' from the movie Out of Time starring Denzel Washington.

Getting there: To reach Cocoa Village Marina, take the Beachline (Hwy 528) east to Hwy 1, go south to Hwy 520, make a slight left at Bee Line, continue to N Cocoa Blvd, turn left at King, then left again at Delannoy.

Brevard Inshore and Nearshore Fishing: From Banana River Marina just off Highway 520 in Cocoa Beach, Captain Pete offers inshore fishing along the Indian River, Banana River and Sykes Creek, or Port Canaveral (summer only) for offshore fishing for snook, black drum, redfish and sea trout. The scenery is as exciting as the fishing, with rays and horseshoe crab skittering along the shallow flats through the clear water. Offshore catches include tarpon, cobia, kingfish and redfish. Florida native Captain Pete has been fishing here for 15 years and knows all the best spots (inshore 4-hr trip $99/ person for 2-4 anglers, additional hours $50; offshore, calm days only, 4-5-hr trip $149/person for 2-3 anglers, additional hours $50); fishing license, tackle, bait and bottled water included; call to book on 321 302 0549, http://orlandofishingadventures. com).

Cocoa Beach Sportfishing: Board the fully equipped Centerfold, a 33ft/10m Tournament-rigged boat, and get ready for big game fishing! Troll for dolphin (the fish, not the mammal), sailfish, wahoo, kingfish, grouper and more with a crew who boast plenty of experience in finding 'the big one' Captain Tim, along with Captains Beau and Brandon, share their passion for fishing with anglers of all experience levels (novice to pro), and do it with humour and professionalism. Centerfold offers 9-hour trips at $800, 5-hour trips $600, up to 6 passengers; the 24ft Center Console Killer Bee accommodates 1–4 passengers at $550 for 8 hours, $400 for 5 hours, calm weather only (fishing licence, tackle, bait, fish cleaning included; reservations on 321 848 2662, www. cbsportfishing.com). For more Cocoa Beach info, see p274.

Excursion operators

For those without a car (or wanting to put their feet up for a bit), there are tours and day trips visiting as far afield as the Everglades, Miami, Florida Keys and even the Bahamas. You can see a lot if you don't mind a long day (up to 16 hours). However, if the main attraction of a trip to the Everglades is the airboat ride, you are better off going to Boggy Creek Airboats (see p250).

BRITTIP
For more info on all tours, call 407 352 5151 or visit www. floridadolphintours.com. To enjoy our special discount, just call and say: '12½% off with the Brit Guide, please!'

Florida Dolphin Tours: Make this first on your list to check as it offers a diverse range of memorable excursions, notably its swim-with-dolphins trips to the Keys and manatee swim adventure. More to the point, as a Brit Guide partner, it offers readers a 12½% discount on all tours (see inside back cover). Choose from: Cocoa Beach and Airboat, an excellent-value all-day trip to Cocoa beach for an afternoon of fun in the sun, an exciting airboat ride in search of gators on the St Johns River, all with a wonderful lunch ($75 adults, $59 3–9s); the Kennedy Space Center trip, with transportation to both Space Center and Astronaut Hall of Fame – ask about options such as including an airboat ride, Lunch with an Astronaut, or even the

Ultimate Kennedy Experience (from $99 adult, $89 3–11s); **Swim with the Manatees**, an all-day adventure (and their No.1 attraction), featuring breakfast and a 2-hour boat trip on the picturesque Crystal River (with snorkel and mask to check out where the manatees swim). There are picnic lunches, airboat rides and trips to Homosassa State Wildlife Park, too, plus an educational briefing on manatees and a chance to see them being fed from the underwater viewing area ($119 adults, $89 3–11s); **Swim with the Dolphins**, its trademark tour, a holiday within a holiday: a 2-day excursion to the beautiful Keys with a 2-hour dolphin programme (and the choice of an organised or unstructured dolphin swim), including transport, accommodation, dolphin swim, buffet-style evening meal, continental breakfast, Everglades airboat ride, (interactive!) alligator and snake-handling show, and ½-day to see Miami with shopping at Bayside or a boat tour along the inland waterways. The dolphin programme includes a full briefing and about 30mins in the water, with dolphin contact guaranteed ($189–289; add Star Island boat tour for additional fee); **American Football**, where high-energy action is up for grabs with an all-day excursion to see the Jacksonville Jaguars of the National Football League ($109/person, Aug–Dec); **NBA Basketball**, more sporting excitement with the Orlando Magic ($119/person, Nov–Apr; playoff games $179); **Disney limo trips** give you the Grand Floridian character breakfast, Chef Mickey's character dinner buffet, or Planet Hollywood VIP ($79–119); **Clearwater Paradise**, a day-trip to the Gulf Coast for a beach adventure, including a ride on the huge **Sea Screamer** powerboat (or other boat excursions), lunch, a chance to see the local dolphins in their own environment, go deep sea fishing AND work on your tan! (from $75 and $65–$120 and $90); and a **Shopping Extravaganza**, an all-day retail adventure with stops at the top Malls and outlets like Super Wal-Mart

and Lake Buena Vista Factory Shops, breakfast and lunch included ($45 and $35; **www.floridadolphintours.com**).

Further tours and day trips can be found on **www.graylinetours.com**.

Of course, a great day-trip can also be had by heading for the superb beaches in your hire car (see Chapter 9).

SPORT

In addition to virtually every form of entertainment known to man, central Florida is 1 of the world's biggest sporting playgrounds, with a huge range of opportunities to either watch or play your favourite sport.

Golf

Without doubt, the No.1 sport is golf, with almost 200 courses in central Florida. There are numerous packages for golfers of all abilities to enjoy the weather and some spectacular courses, many designed by legends like Greg Norman, Tom Watson, Arnold Palmer and Jack Nicklaus. With an 18-hole round, including cart hire and taxes, from as little as $30 (average around $75), it's an attractive proposition and quite different from British courses. If you go in for 36-hole days, it's possible to save up to $30 by replaying the same course, while it is cheaper to play Mon–Thurs than Fri–Sun. Sculpted landscapes, manicured fairways, abundant water features and white-sand bunkers add up to memorable golf. Winter is the high season, hence more expensive, but many courses are busy year-round. Be aware some courses pair golfers with little thought for age, handicap etc., so, if 2 of you turn up, you may be paired with 2 strangers.

BRITTIP

Golf balls are inexpensive in Florida, so there's no need to bring your own. Good-quality clubs are usually available for hire, including top brands.

Virtually every course will offer a driving range to get you started, plus lockers, changing rooms and showers, while the use of golf carts is universal (including the GPS system, which gives the yardage for every shot). They feature comforts like iced-water stations and drink carts that circulate the course (don't forget to tip the trolley drivers). Some have swimming pools, and all offer a decent bar and restaurant.

Your best starting point is visiting one of the 5 **Edwin Watts** golf shops around Orlando for a free copy of the *Golfer's Guide* or the *Guide to Golf* for a handy introduction to most of the courses (and perhaps some new clubs at the Watts National Clearance Center just south of Wet 'n Wild on I-Drive; 407 397 4600 **www.edwinwatts. com**). **Tee-Times USA** (1800 374 8633, **www.teetimesusa.com**) offers excellent advice and a reservation service. Daytona Beach has an great website, **www.golfdaytonabeach.com**, devoted to local golf (1800 544 0415), while **Visit Florida** has its own golf section (**www. visitflorida.com/golf**).

Professional Golf Guides of Orlando: For a unique and personal touch, you can't beat this all-in-one service, led by owner/operator and PGA member Phillip Jaffe, who is a mine of golf knowledge, and great company. The guides take up to 3 at a time around some of the finest courses, and can supply transport and clubs. The playing lesson is high quality and includes on-course instruction, course management strategies, game analysis, improvement suggestions, shot-making demos and a wrap-up lesson. It's an eye-opening experience to play alongside Phillip and his staff and well worth it for the keen golfer who wishes to improve their game. $195/1 player, $245 for 2 and $295 for 3, while there are driving range lessons at $75/hour or a 3-lesson package at $200 (407 227 9869, **www. progolfguides.com**). The **Nick Faldo Golf Institute** on lower I-Drive (1888 463 2536) is another great place to hit a few balls.

Walt Disney World: Quick to attract the golf fanatic, Disney has 4 high-quality courses, including the 7,000yd/6,400m **Palm**, rated by *Golf Digest* in its top 25 (the 18th hole is reputedly 1 of the toughest in America), plus a 9-hole par-36 course, **Oak Trail**. Fees are $109-139 for Disney resort guests and $124-164 for visitors ($38 at Oak Trail), with a third off after 3pm. Call 407 938 4653 for tee-times. Private and group lessons are available under PGA pro guidance, with video analysis and club rentals.

BRITTIP

Some of the best tee-times at *Walt Disney World* golf courses are reserved for those staying at a Disney resort.

Champions Gate: Challenging and eye-catching, the 2 magnificent Greg Norman-designed courses to the south of Disney (exit 58 off I-4) are the International (a British-style links course) and the National (a more traditional style). The practice facilities, clubhouse, service and coaching (at the HQ of the renowned David Leadbetter Academy) are world class, and there are stay-and-play packages with the superb Omni Orlando Resort (407 787 4653, **www. championsgategolf.com**).

Dubsdread: the oldest public course In Orlando and the only municipal one, just east of the city centre, this offers a testing 18 holes featuring narrow fairways and 'postage stamp' greens. It was heavily renovated in 2008 and offers a beautiful clubhouse, restaurant and pub, where the likes of Sam Snead and Ben Hogan rubbed shoulders in the past. They also have a free shuttle from some area hotels (407 246 2551, **www.dubsdreadgolf.com**; $30-54).

Dubsdread Golf Course

BRITTIP

Visit Dubsdread Golf Course and be sure to spend some time in The Tap Room, their speciality bar and restaurant, with a great setting for a memorable meal or just a beer and a burger.

Falcon's Fire: An outstanding course in Kissimmee, featuring the ProShot digital caddy system carts. Plenty of water around the course assures a testing 18 holes, but it is highly picturesque (407 239 5445, **www. falconsfire.com**; $59-119).

Grande Lakes Orlando: This wonderful resort complex just off John Young Parkway is a Greg Norman masterpiece, offering 18 holes of Florida nature with a caddie-concierge service (call for rates, 407 206 2400, **www.grandelakes.com**).

Hawk's Landing: At the Orlando World Center Marriott, this beautiful course boasts extensive practice facilities, a superb shop, resort exclusivity and the world-class teaching of Bill Madonna's Golf Academy (1800 380 7931, **www. marriottworldcenter.com**; from $89).

Hyatt Grand Cypress: A luxury experience on Winter Garden-Vineland Road (1866 886 5053, **www. grandcypress.com/golf**; $150-175), with 3 elegant 9-hole courses and a superb 18-hole links-style offering, all designed by Jack Nicklaus.

Kissimmee Oaks: Some majestic moss-draped oaks as well as 18 holes of memorable lakeside golf, all just 3½mls/6km south of Highway 192 in the Oaks Community off John

Disney golf course

Young Parkway (407 933 4055, **www. kissimmeeoaksgolf.com**).

Legends Golf & Country Club: Just 25mins from Disney on Highway 27 towards Clermont, this has a pleasant layout with unusually rolling hills in a peaceful location (352 243 1118, **www. legendsgolforlando.com**; $39–56).

Mystic Dunes: Just off Highway 192 near the Disney entrance, this course winds through native oaks and other vegetation and is a real test. There's a wonderful menu at the clubhouse, plus the latest equipment (407 787 5678; **www.mysticdunesgolf.com**; $55–110).

Orange Lake Country Club: A massive vacation resort just 4mls/6km from Disney. It offers 2 18-hole courses, a 9-hole course and a par-3 floodlit 9 (407 239 1050, **www. orangelake.com**; $35-125).

Shingle Creek: A beauty from talented local architect Dave Harman, set in dense oaks and pines along historic Shingle Creek. Within a mile of the Convention Center, it is a world-class facility with some amazing features, at the heart of a 5-star resort. The Brad Brewer Golf Academy is highly rated by *Golf* magazine and features state-of-the-art technology (407 996 9933, **www.shinglecreekgolf.com**; $44–129).

There are dozens of others, so this is only a sample. Don't be afraid to ask if fees are negotiable, as they can be reduced at quiet times of the year or on a quiet day. There are often reductions for seniors. When you book, check the dress code, as they vary from club to club. Typically, you need a collared shirt, Bermuda shorts and no denim.

Fans: For those just looking to see the stars in action, Orlando has 2 big annual events. The **Arnold Palmer Invitational** at the Bay Hill Club off Apopka-Vineland Road in west Orlando (March) is a major tournament, with Scot Martin Laird winning in 2011 (407 876 7774, **www.rnoldpalmerinvitational. com**). The **Children's Miracle Network Classic** is another big

© Disney

date each Nov, on Disney's superb Palm and Magnolia courses (**www.childrensmiraclenetworkclassic.com**).

Mini-golf

Not exactly a sport, but definitely for fun, Orlando's many extravagant mini-golf centres are a big hit with kids and fun for all the family (if you still have the legs after a day at the park!). Several attractions and parks offer mini-golf as an extra, but for the best try the self-contained centres, of which there is a large variety. Typically, Disney has some of its own.

Disney's Fantasia Gardens: Next to the Swan Hotel just off Buena Vista Drive is a 2-course challenge over 36 of the most varied holes of mini-golf you will find. **Fantasia Gardens** – its style is taken from the classic film *Fantasia*, with a riot of visual gags as well as some tricky mini-golf. **Fantasia Fairways** is a cunning putting course, complete with rough, water hazards and bunkers to test even the best golfers. 18 holes can take more than an hour play ($12 adults, $10 children, 10am–11pm daily).

Winter-Summerland Mini-Golf: At the entrance to Blizzard Beach water park and divided into 2 18-hole courses, these mini works of art feature a 'summer' setting of surf and beach tests and a 'winter' variety of snow and ice-crafted holes. An adult round is $12 ($10 3–9s), a double round is half price (10am–11pm; Blizzard Beach admission not required).

International Drive: Mini-golf is a staple of the scene here, with no fewer than 6 courses in the vicinity. Check out the 18-hole **Congo River** in front of the Four Points by Sheraton Orlando Studio City Hotel and its 36-hole course just south of Wet 'n Wild ($10.99 adults, $8.99 under-10; see **www.congoriver.com** for money-off coupon; 10am–11pm Sun–Thurs, 10am–midnight Fri and Sat); **Hawaiian Rumble** has 36 holes next to WonderWorks on I-Drive (and in Lake Buena Vista on Apopka-Vineland Ave;) 9am–11.30pm Sun–Thurs, 9am–midnight Fri and Sat; $9.95 adults, $7.95 4–10s for 18 holes and $14.95 and $11.95 for 36; see **www.hawaiianrumbleorlando.com** for a discount coupon); **Pirates Cove** remains the original I-Drive set-up, with caves, waterfalls and rope bridges to test your skill over twin 18-hole courses (the Captain's Course and harder Blackbeard's Challenge; 9am–11.30pm daily; $10.95 adults, $9.95 4-12s, or $16.50 and $14.95 for all 36). There is a near-identical **Pirates Cove** set-up at Lake Buena Vista at the back of the Crossroads shopping plaza. Finally, the extensive **Gator Golf & Adventure Park** is just past Carrier Drive, next to Murphy's Arms Pub. With a variety of gator shows daily, you can sink your teeth into some challenging mini-golf (10am–10pm; Admission to park $4.99, golf $9.99/; $7.99 3-11s; gator shows for additional fees).

Kissimmee: Here you'll find the scenic 36-hole **Congo River Golf & Exploration Co** set-up on Highway 192 (by marker 12; $10.99 adults, $8.99 under-10s; 10am–11pm Sun–Thurs, 10am–midnight, Fri–Sat, **www.congoriver.com**). **Pirates Cove** is a 36-hole course next to Old Town (behind the Red Lobster, between markers 9 and 10; 10am-10pm); as is **Jungle Golf** (Highway 192 at markers 4 and 5; 9am–11.30pm; $8.95 adults, $7.95 4–12s, all-day play for $12.95; a second location is near Celebration at marker 8, **www.junglegolfminigolf.com**). **Pirates Island Adventure Golf** is off Highway 192 between marker 14 and 15 (10am-10pm).

Golf at Walt Disney World

© Disney

Freshwater fishing

Freshwater fishing on central Florida's abundant rivers and lakes attracts enthusiasts worldwide. The primary draw is the chance to catch giant Florida bass – which grow to record sizes in the area's grassy waters – and view some of the wildlife in its natural environment.

To fish here you need a Florida Freshwater Fishing License, from the Florida Fish and Wildlife Commission (**http://myfwc.com/License/Index. htm** to purchase online at $2.25 surcharge plus 2.5% of the total, with a credit card). You'll be issued with a temporary licence number within minutes, enabling you to fish right away. A permanent licence will be mailed within 48 hours. A 3-day licence costs $17. It's advisable to book at least 2 weeks in advance, especially at peak periods.

AJ's Freelancer Bass Guide Service: This long-running company specialises in trophy bass fishing on Lake Toho in Kissimmee. Toho is rated the best big bass lake in the USA, and AJ's holds the record for largemouth bass – 16lb 10oz/7.5kg! Saltwater trips are also offered. All guides are experienced, full-time professionals and run trips of 4–8 hours. Rates start at $250 for a 4-hr guided trip, max 3 clients per boat ($50 for 3rd person; 12 and under free). Visit the excellent **www.orlandobass.com** or call 407 3288 9670.

Ultimate Guide Service: Another personal guide and fishing service with 36 years' experience and with trophy bass the principal aim, this is led by Captain Jim Passmore and is great for novices and even better for those seeking a real challenge. It makes for a superb day or ½-day and their attitude is notably 1 of low-

Freshwater fishing

environmental impact. It costs $275 for 4 hrs of fishing, $325 for 6 or $375 for 8 hrs (extra person $50), excluding fishing licence, lunch and bait (407 572 5391, **www.fishcentralfla.com**).

For other opportunities, try **Kissimmee Outdoor Adventures** (p263, or see **www.visitkissimmee.com**, click on *Visitors*, then *Things To Do* and *Get Outdoors*). Go bass fishing (catch-and-release) at Walt Disney World for $235– $270 for 2 hours for a boat with 2–5 people. Book 24 hours in advance on 407-939-2277.

Water sports

Florida is mad keen on water sports so, on any area of water bigger than your average pond, don't be surprised to find the locals water-skiing, jetskiing, knee-boarding, canoeing, paddling, windsurfing, boating or indulging in many other watery pursuits.

Buena Vista Watersports: This is the place for jet-skiing ($55/½ hr, $98/hr), water-skiing, wakeboard and tube rides ($50/15 min, $85/30 min, $145/hr) on Little Lake Bryan by the Holiday Inn Sunspree on Highway 535 (407 239 6939, **www.bvwatersports.com**). **Orlando Watersports Complex:** Just off the Beachline Expressway (528) near Orlando International Airport, this is an elaborate facility featuring wake-boarding and water-skiing, by boat and suspended cable, for novices and experts (407 251 3100, **www. orlandowatersports.com**).

Walt Disney World: Disney offers all manner of boats (from catamarans to canoes and pedaloes) and activities (from water-skiing to parasailing) on **Bay Lake**, as well as the smaller **Seven Seas Lagoon**, **Crescent Lake** and **Lake Buena Vista**. Parasailing (from *Disney's Contemporary Resort* – see p66) comes in 2 price categories: a Regular flight, which goes to 450ft/137m for 8–10 min, and a Premium flight to 600ft/183m for 10–12 min. It costs $95–130 solo or $170-195 tandem, while boat rentals vary from $33/½ hr (21ft/6m pontoon boat) to $125/hr (personal watercraft and wave runners), and can be

found at 11 Disney resorts, plus The Marketplace at Downtown Disney. To book, call 407 939 0754.

Horse riding

For a more peaceful and scenic way to see some of Florida, take a tour on horseback.

Horse World Riding Stables: Out in rural Kissimmee, on Poinciana Boulevard (just 12mls/19km south of Highway 192), this gets you out into the wilds and you can spend anything from 1 hour to a full day enjoying the rides and lessons. The 3 main rides through 750 acres/304ha of untouched Florida countryside are the Nature Trail ($43 adults, $16.95 under-6s riding double with parent), a walking-only tour of 1 hr for beginners aged 6 and up; the Intermediate Trail (10 and up) for 1 hr ($52.95); and the Advanced Private Trail, a 11/4hr trip with a private guide for advanced riders ($74.95). There is also a picnic area with fishing pond, playing fields and farm animals to pet. Check the website for discounts (9am–5pm daily; 407 847 4343, **www.horseworldstables.com**).

Rock Springs Riding Ranch: Up in Seminole County, on wilderness property inside the state park, you can try one of 3 guided trails (1–3hrs, plus ½- and full-day treks) or pony rides for under-8s. All skill levels can be accommodated ($37–$80/person; reservations recommended; 8am-5pm daily; 352 735 6266, **www.rsrranch. com**). **Florida Eco Safaris** also offers Horseback Safaris, an excellent way to see more of the 'real Florida' (p253).

Spectator events

When it comes to spectator events, Orlando isn't as well furnished as some cities, but there's always something for those who'd like to see a local game. There are no top-flight American football or baseball teams, but there is an indoor version of gridiron called Arena Football (the **Orlando Predators** at the Amway Center), plus Spring Training (pre-season) for several baseball teams (**Atlanta** in *Disney's ESPN Wide World of Sports*™ and Houston at Osceola County Stadium in Kissimmee).

Basketball: This is the main sport in town, with the **Orlando Magic** of the National Basketball Association (NBA). The season runs Nov–May (with exhibition games in Oct), and the only drawback is the new 18,500-seat **Amway Center** where the team plays (on W Church Street, exit 82B off I-4) can be fully booked. Contact the Magic (407 896 2442, **www.orlandomagic.com**) to see if there are any tickets, but you'll have to call in person to buy them (from $10 in upper seats to $1,500 courtside), or try TicketMaster on 407 839 1630. **Florida Dolphin Tours** (407 356 4646, **www.floridadolphintours.com**) also offers Orlando Magic packages for $99 (regular season, $179 playoffs) with transport. See more at **www.nba.com/ magic/**.

🔷▶ **BRITTIP**

We rate the local sports highly if you want to experience some real Americana. You don't need to understand the game, just turn up and enjoy the excitement and fan-friendly atmosphere. Sports are a family event here.

American football: For the real thing, the nearest teams in the **National Football League** (NFL) are **Tampa Bay Buccaneers**, 75mls/120km to the west, **Miami Dolphins**, 3–4 hrs' drive south down the Florida Turnpike, or **Jacksonville Jaguars** up on the east coast past Daytona, a 3-hr drive on I-4 and I-95. Again, TicketMaster can give you ticket prices ($50–130) and availability (Sept–Dec). **Florida Dolphin Tours** (see p261) runs a limited number of trips to Jacksonville each year, and these are worth seeking out.

Baseball: For spring training each March, Osceola County Stadium for the Houston Astros is a real experience in local colour. You can book online at **www.osceolastadium. com**, or TicketMaster (**www. ticketmaster.com**). However, the best opportunity is to head to St Petersburg on the Gulf Coast where the **Tampa Bay Rays** play at indoor Tropicana Field (Apr–Sept). Tickets are nearly always available and the indoor stadium is superb (see p277).

Orlando City Soccer Club: new in 2011 was this ambitious club in the lower tier of US professional soccer. Playing at the 70,000-seat Citrus Bowl in downtown Orlando, they have quickly drawn a passionate following, even if they don't sell out the huge stadium. Home games are a fun event and there are cheerleaders and 'fan zones' to pump up the volume, while head coach is none other than former Everton and Stoke City star Adrian Heath. Ticket prices are a modest $12–25 and the United Soccer League season runs Apr–Aug (407 536 5368, **www.orlandocitysoccer.com**).

ESPN Wide World of Sports™

Inevitably, the best all-round sports facility is a Disney project, though there are only a handful of spectator events. ESPN Wide World of Sports™ is an impressive 220-acre/86ha state-of-the-art complex, featuring 30 sports. It boasts a 9,500-seat baseball stadium, a softball quadraplex, a 10-court tennis complex, 5,000-seat indoor facility, athletics and extensive sports fields.

The Ballpark: Top of the crop for a must-see visit, this is home for spring training of baseball's Atlanta Braves, where the crowds flock for 16 pre-season games late Feb–late Mar (advance tickets highly recommended; individual tickets from Ticketmaster or the box office only). This is a big deal for American sports fans and games do sell out. The centre's extensive fields also cater for soccer, lacrosse, baseball and softball, and you can often see some keen sporting action just with college and school teams. **Disney's Soccer Showcase** (Sept–Jan) is a fine example of this, with some 400 skilful teams competing under the eye of various scouts. Standard admission is $14.50 adults, $10 3–9s, but it is also an option with Premium and Ultimate tickets (excluding special events like baseball). ESPN Wide World of Sports™ is off Osceola Parkway, on Victory Way (**www.espnwwos.com**).

Disney Soccer Academy: New in 2011 and in conjunction with Virgin Holidays was this series of 4-day training camps under the supervision of Premier League stars like Craig Bellamy, Paul Robinson, Charlie Adam and Benni McCarthy. For children 6–18, it focuses on age-appropriate coaching and technical development, small-sided games and encouragement from the stars. It costs $390/child in June, and includes tuition by fully licensed coaches, an event T-shirt, special gift and lunch daily (1877 714 5575 or **www.midwestsoccer.net**).

Walt Disney World Marathon: A major annual event, its 16th running will be on 8 Jan 2012. Some 15,000 runners take part – including some of the world's leading athletes – drawing huge crowds and taking in all 4 Disney theme parks. Be aware the parks face some serious disruption but, as with the London Marathon, the Disney version is a great spectacle. The annual **half-marathon** takes place the same weekend.

Rodeo

An all-American pursuit straight out of the Old West, the **Silver Spurs Rodeo** is staged twice a year at the 8,300-seat Silver Spurs Arena. The biggest event of its kind in the south-east, it is held in Feb and early June (check website for dates). However, it sells out fast so book in advance on 321 697 3495 (**www.silverspursrodeo.com**). The event features classic bronco and bull riding and attracts competitors from as far as Canada. The arena is part of **Osceola Heritage Park**, which includes Osceola County Stadium (for baseball) and the Kissimmee Valley Livestock Show and Fair Pavilion. The Arena is a state-of-the-art facility and there isn't a bad seat in the house.

Motor sport

Richard Petty Driving Experience:
For the ultimate in high-speed
thrills, *Walt Disney World* has its own
racetrack (next to the car park for the
Magic Kingdom). Here on the 1-mile
oval, you can experience one of its
650bhp stock cars as either driver or
passenger at up to 145mph/233kph,
with programmes devised by NASCAR
legend Richard Petty. Choose from the
3-lap **Ride-Along Experience**; the 3hr
Rookie Experience (with tuition and
8 laps of the speedway); the **Kings
Experience** (tuition plus 18 laps); the
Experience of a Lifetime (an intense
30-lap programme) and the ultimate
experience of **Speedway Challenge**
(50 laps, Ride-Along, shop tour with
tech talk and lunch with instructor
and Crew Chief). The Ride-Along
will probably appeal to most (16 and
over only) – 3 laps of the circuit with
an experienced driver lasting just 37
seconds a lap but an unbelievable
blast all the way. It's a bit like flying at
ground level, is hot and noisy and you
must wear sensible clothes (you climb
in through the window), but it is
definitely the real thing in ride terms
and a huge thrill.

You don't need to book the daily
Ride-Along Experience and there is
no admission fee, so you can come
along just to watch (8am–1pm). The
3 driving programmes (not Tues or
Thurs; Sun offers Ride-Along only) all
need reservations. However, wait for
the prices: $99 for Ride-Along; $449
for Rookie; $849 for Kings; $1,299
for the Experience of a Lifetime and
$2,099 for Speedway Challenge. You
must be 18 or over for all but the
Ride-Along (min age 16; 1800 237
3889, **www.drivepetty.com**).

Indy Racing Experience: Thrill
seekers can also strap into an IndyCar
Racing machine (that has actually
been driven in the Indy 500) for an
unforgettable ride! Suit up in an
authentic fire suit, helmet, gloves
and fire shoes, then slide into the
comfortable open-wheel cockpit and
discover why Indy racing is a vastly
different experience to any other.
Your F1-style car rides just inches
above the track and the sensation
is exhilarating and undeniably
adrenalin inducing!

BRITTIP
The Indy Racing Experience does not
operate in the rain, so book your ride
or drive early in your holiday for the best
chance of rebooking.

The **Driving Program** includes a
classroom session, orientation and
8 laps for $399. Not ready to take the
wheel but still want to experience
the speed and G-forces? Opt for the
Two-Seater Ride, going 3 laps with
an experienced driver ($109). Family
and spectators are welcome at no cost
(4pm–sundown daily; 1888 357 5002,
www.indyracingexperience.com).

Daytona International Speedway:
Just up the road in Daytona (take
I-4 east, then I-95 and Highway 92),
race fans will find more big-league
thrills. The renowned Speedway
hosts more than a dozen events a
year, including motor-bike, stock car,
sports car and go-karts. Highlights
are the **Rolex 24** (a 24-hr sports car
event, late Jan), the famous **Daytona
500** (Feb), and **Coke Zero 400** (early
July). The big events attract crowds
of 200,000-plus and provide some
exhilarating sport (800 748 7467, **www.
daytonainternationalspeedway.com**).

The **Richard Petty Driving
Experience** is available here, too (but
16 and over only), and the $135 fee for
3 laps of the world-famous, steeply
banked 2½ml/4km tri-oval includes
a track tour. Or just look for the 1hr
All Access Track Tour, daily on the
hour from 10am-3pm ($22 adults, $17
6-12s, under-6s free) and a 30-min
Speedway Tour at 11.30am, 1.30pm,
3:30pm and 4pm ($15 adults, $10
6-12s, under-6 free). There is even a
special **VIP Tour** on specific dates (see
website) at $50/person. Fascinating
and fun, even for non race fans!

OK, that's the local area sorted out;
now let's take you further afield…

9 The Twin Centre Option

or To Orlando – and Beyond!

While Orlando and its surrounding areas continue to get bigger and better year by year, it is equally true there is a LOT more to see in the rest of Florida, with some magnificent twin-centre options. From St Augustine in the north-east to Key West in the extreme south (the 'Floribbean'), it's easy to find wonderful resorts, glorious beaches and more family attractions.

The beaches of the Gulf (west) coast, the Atlantic coast from Ormond Beach all the way to Miami, and the fabulous Florida Keys all feature some of the best seaside escapes in the world, while cities like West Palm Beach, Daytona, St Augustine, Fort Lauderdale, Tampa, Miami and Key West provide more Sunshine State fascination. Two-centre (or fly-drive) options are common with most tour operators, but it is also easy to arrange your own, for 1 or 2 weeks or just a night. A cruise-and-stay holiday is also a great choice, with the ports of Tampa, Port Canaveral, Fort Lauderdale and Miami within easy reach.

You can head out from Orlando in any direction in search of a great twin-centre experience. Go **East** to Cocoa Beach, New Smyrna Beach, Ormond Beach and Daytona Beach, all with terrific appeal and barely an hour's drive away; the sea is a degree or so cooler on the Atlantic side, and the surf and currents are more noticeable, hence this is good surfing territory. To the **North-East** you have historic St Augustine about 2hrs away. Go **West** for the city of Tampa and miles of pristine sands, from Clearwater Beach south to Naples and lovely Marco Island; this is better for families with younger children, while the Clearwater-St Pete Beach area is a perfect combo with Orlando (about 1½–2hrs' drive). Go **South-East** and you hit Vero Beach, West Palm Beach, Fort Lauderdale and Miami (about a 4hr drive). Continue **South** and there are the Keys, a superb 110ml/177km chain of islands linked by roads and bridges, culminating in eclectic Key West. So, heading north-east first, here's what you find.

BRITTIP
Spanish adventurer Ponce de Leon was searching for the Fountain of Youth when he arrived at the site of St Augustine in 1513. The modern day Archaeological Park tells the story of his arrival and discovery of the continent of America – and offers the chance to drink the famous waters. Visit **www.fountainofyouthflorida.com**.

St Augustine
A 2hr drive up I-4 and I-95 brings you to America's oldest city. Founded by Spanish conquistadores in 1565, St Augustine is full of authentic buildings and signs of the original

settlement around the imposing Castillo de San Marcos. Much of the original walled city still remains and 'old' is a much-revered term here, as 18th and 19th-century Mediterranean influences are everywhere. Walk the narrow, uneven streets of the Restoration Area to discover colonial architectural treasures, now home to gift shops, restaurants, pubs, ice-cream parlours, antique shops, quaint B&Bs and other attractions.

BRITTIP
The Florida Turnpike (toll) is the main route south-east from Orlando, but it is a dull drive. If time is not a factor, take the Beachline Expressway (528) east and then I-95 or, better still, Highway 1, south for a more rewarding journey.

Tours: To see as much as possible, hop on a horse-drawn carriage, the St Augustine Sightseeing Train or the Old Town Trolley Tours for a narrated tour. For a spookier experience, walk the streets with Ghost Tours of St Augustine, with your guide in period costume. Other tours reveal the architectural heritage (also the product of British and colonial American rule).

Other attractions: Florida railway mogul Henry Flagler was another big influence, building some magnificent hotels for his 'passengers to paradise'. The ornate Lightner Museum, formerly Flagler's Hotel Alcazar, is home to his turn-of-the-century treasures, including Tiffany and other glass works of art. There's a modern theatre, art galleries, Potter's Wax Museum, Ripley's Believe It Or Not Museum and Whetstone Chocolate Factory.

Restaurants: These range from The Spanish Bakery and the famous, family-owned Columbia Restaurant, where recipes have been handed down for more than a century, to a modern microbrewery, A1A Ale Works. Golf fans should visit nearby Ponte Vedra for the World Golf Hall of Fame.

Where to stay: The premier hotel is historic Casa Monica (904 827 1888, **www.casamonica.com**) and the boutique St George Inn (904 827 5740; **www.stgeorge-inn.com**) is a good choice, but there are numerous B&Bs, plus chain hotels like Best Western and Hampton Inn.

BRITTIP
Festivals are an integral part of St Augustine, from monthly art walk nights to annual costumed torchlight re-enactments of British occupation and the City Birthday on 8 Sept.

More info: St Augustine Visitors & Convention Bureau (1800 653 2489, **www.floridashistoriccoast.com**).

Volusia County
Travel south from St Augustine and you arrive in 1 of Florida's most famous beach areas.

Daytona Beach: Only 1hr from Orlando along I-4 east, this area is undergoing a transformation to a more sophisticated seaside resort, including new hotels and restaurants, but still extremely family friendly. It is busiest in summer (mid-June to mid-Aug) but there is something for everyone, especially in the quieter period around Easter when there are often some good deals. The prime attraction is the good beaches (some of which you can drive on – for a $5 toll, speed limit 10mph/16kph). From these open expanses of sands, you can go boating, parasailing, biking, jet-skiing and fishing, while there is also plenty of sightseeing. Stay in the Oceanfront area and you are at the heart of all things beach-related, with the Pier, historic Bandshell, Boardwalk and the shops and restaurants of **Ocean Walk Village**.

BRITTIP
Look out for **Speeding Through Time**, a series of memorials and plaques along Daytona's Boardwalk, highlighting the world speed records set on the beaches, including those of Britons Sir Henry Segrave and Sir Malcolm Campbell.

Here you have RC Theatres' Ocean Walk Movies 10 Cineplex, the fun of the Mai Tai Bar, Sloppy Joe's, Johnny Rockets Diner, Cold Stone Creamery, Starbucks, Ker's Winghouse and unique shopping at Maui Nix Surf Shop, Caribongo's, Point Break and Sunglass Hut. When you're hungry, our top tip is the film-themed style of Bubba Gump Shrimp Co (based on the movie *Forrest Gump*). With fun decor, wonderfully casual vibe and an excellent menu (food that lives up to its surroundings), it is ideal for a quick lunch or leisurely dinner (**www.bubbagump.com** and **www. oceanwalkshoppes.com**).

BRITTIP

Spend the day on Daytona Beach, then try some water park fun at Daytona Lagoon after 4pm, when admission is only $11.99.

Opposite Ocean Walk Village is **Daytona Lagoon**, a combination water park, go-kart track, mini-golf course, arcade and laser tag centre. The water park has a wave pool and lazy river, 10 different flumes and an area purely for toddlers (adults $27.99, children under 4ft/122cm $19.99). The 3 9-hole mini-golf courses ($7 for 18 holes), single and double go-karts ($7–9), laser tag (must be above 3ft 6in/108cm, $7), Island Hopper kiddie ride ($2) and Rock Wall ($6) are all separate items. Find out more at **www.daytonalagoon. com**.

Historic **Downtown Daytona Beach** on Beach Street is the heart of the city, with a museum of local history, restaurants, nightclubs, coffee bars and a performing arts theatre, all in a riverside setting. The **Angell & Phelps Chocolate Factory** (established 1925) is another notable curiosity. Head to the Riverfront in early evening when the street takes on a café society style. There are plenty of good places to eat, but for something different try the lively **Loggerhead Club & Marina** (right on the river at Ballough Road) or chic Chez Paul (on N Beach St with a view of the Halifax River). Similar upmarket choices are **Martini's Chophouse Restaurant** (on S Ridgewood Avenue) and **The Cellar** (on Magnolia Avenue). **Vince Carter's** (on LPGA Blvd, co-owned by the basketball star) is another smart choice, with a chic Dining Room, eye-catching Highlight Zone Sports Grill and relaxing Piano Lounge (**http:// vincecarters.com**).

Other highlights include a variety of ways to enjoy the waterways. Taking **The Manatee** scenic river voyage out of Ponce Inlet is a great choice. Their leisurely 2hr tours go year-round at 10am,1 and 4pm, plus a Sunset Cruise at 7pm Jun–Sept (on Inlet Harbor Rd; $25 for adults, $22 seniors, $16 children; reservations required on 386 761 2027, or **www.manateecruise. com**). Go south on Atlantic Avenue and you find even more choice of beaches and attractions, including **Sun Splash Beach**, **Frank Rendon Park** and **Lighthouse Point Park**, a 52-acre/21ha stretch of nature trails, fishing, observation deck, swimming and picnicking (8am–9pm; $3.50/ vehicle). The tide here can retreat up to 500ft/150m and the beaches, open to the public year-round, tend to be quieter, though there can be some serious rip-tides. At the southern end of the beaches is the wonderful **Ponce de Leon Inlet Lighthouse**, with a formidable 203 spiralling steps to the top. This well-preserved monument is a magnificent re-creation of 19th-century Florida maritime life and the view from the top of America's second tallest lighthouse is superb (10am–6pm, 9pm Jun-Aug; $5 adults, $1.50 children). It also has a lovely gift shop. Ponce Inlet has some great deep-sea fishing, too – see **www.inletharbor.com**.

BRITTIP

Try lunch or dinner at Lighthouse Landing in Lighthouse Point Park for an eclectic Floridian experience.

More family-orientated fun can be found at the **Marine Science Center** (just round the corner from the lighthouse), which showcases mangrove, manatee and sea turtle exhibits, a seabird sanctuary and turtle rehab facility. It has a huge artificial reef aquarium, plus static and interactive educational displays.

A boardwalk and nature trail extend through the Center, which also has a gift shop (10am–4pm Tues–Sat, noon–4pm Sun, closed Mon; $5 adults, $4 seniors, $2 under-13s; **www.echotourism.com/msc**).

Of course, one of the biggest draws is the Daytona Speedway (p269), with 2 great tours of this amazing facility.

Continue south on Highway 1 and you come to up-and-coming (but still largely undiscovered) **New Smyrna Beach**, with 13mls/20km of pristine white sands, great surfing, shell collecting and boating at any of the many marinas (386 428 1600, **www.nsbfla.com**).

Where to stay: You'll find some of our favourite resorts in Daytona Beach, along with a variety of Select Small Inns (**www.daytonabeach.com/ssi.cfm**). The **Wyndham Ocean Walk Resort** is a huge ultra-modern complex right on the beach at Ocean Walk Village, with versatile 1, 2 and 3-bed condos (all with kitchens and fab views). With 3 outdoor pools, waterslide and lazy river, plus a kids' water play area, 2 indoor pools, indoor mini-golf, kids' programmes, spa and an excellent lounge and food court, it is hugely family-friendly (386 323 4800, **www.oceanwalk.com**). The nearby **Hilton Daytona Beach Oceanfront Resort** is another large, recently renovated hotel with wonderfully spacious rooms, beachfront cabañas and suites, plus a terrific dining choice (notably Hyde Park Prime Steakhouse), 2 pools and a modern fitness centre (386 254 8200, **www.daytonahilton.com**). **Shores Resort & Spa** is a boutique choice on a quieter stretch of the beaches, with an elegant ambience, beautiful rooms, charming bar and fine-dining Azure restaurant. It also boasts an excellent pool, kids' pool and fitness centre, plus a heavenly Spa with Balinese and Thai treatments (386 767 7350, **www.shoresresort.com**). Try **Flamingo Inn** for a great example of the Small Inns of Daytona Beach. With a tranquil oceanfront setting, heated free-form pool, tropical Key West styling and some rooms with kitchenettes (and

all with fridges), it is a real boutique bargain hereabouts (386 252 7212, **www.daytonamotel.com**).

More info: Call 01737 643 764 in the UK, 1800 854 1234 in the US or visit **www.daytonabeach.com**.

$ BRIT BONUS

Stay 3 nights at the **Flamingo Inn** and get a 4th night free with your *Brit Guide* (excludes during special events). Just mention the book offer when booking.

Ormond Beach: Immediately to the north is another up-and-coming area with more smart resorts and beaches, notably at **Bicentennial Park** (with a nature walk, fishing dock, tennis courts and playground) and **Birthplace of Speed Park** (which commemorates the first automobile race on the beach here in 1903). Stop for lunch or dinner at the fun **Lulu's Oceanside Grill** on S Atlantic Ave, with a wonderful seafood-accented menu (try their Steamer plates or tasty Flatbreads). They also feature great cocktails, live music on Fri and Sat evenings, Happy Hour 2-6pm Mon-Fri (and 9pm-midnight Mon-Sat) and daily specials, like Mojito Monday ($5 speciality mojitos) and Fish Fry Wednesday (11am-midnight Mon-Sat, 8am-10.30pm Sun; 386 673 2641, **www.lulusoceansidegrill.com**).

$ BRIT BONUS

Dine at Lulu's **Oceanside Grill** and get 10% off your entire bill (excluding alcohol) by showing your *Brit Guide.*

Just west of Daytona Beach is **DeLand** and St Johns River Country. Located in the western half of the region, this is home to several nature preserves (**www.visitwestvolusia.com**).

New Smyrna Beach

The Space Coast

Further south on the Atlantic seaboard is the 'Space Coast', home to the iconic Kennedy Space Center (p213).

BRITTIP
For good info on all Kennedy Space Center rocket launches, especially good public viewing locations, see **www.spacecoastlaunches.com**.

Cocoa Beach: Closest to Orlando, barely 50 minutes east (on the Beachline Expressway 528, then south on Highway A1A), this area has 2 excellent public beaches plus trademark shopping at **Ron Jon's Surf Shop**, a massive neon emporium of all things water related. As it's the Atlantic, the sea can be chilly Nov–Apr, but its resort style ensures good facilities (**www.cocoabeach.com**). Cocoa Beach is also home to the excellent **Astronaut Memorial Planetarium & Observatory**, which holds daily shows in its large-screen cinema and world-class planetarium, plus an exhibition hall, art gallery and gift shop, all on Brevard Community College Campus (321 433 7373, **www.brevardcc.edu/planet**) – and don't forget Island Boat Lines (p260).

Titusville: Head here for attractions like the **US Space Walk of Fame** (a river walk with displays of memorabilia, plaques and public art depicting America's history in space), **Merritt Island National Wildlife Refuge** (a 6ml/9km driving tour adjacent to the Kennedy Space Center) and the fascinating and rather moving **American Police Hall of Fame & Museum**, with all you ever wanted to know about the history of crime and law enforcement, a tribute to police officers who have died in the line of duty, plus an indoor shooting range (see **www.aphf.org** for $3 off coupon).

Aviation fans will enjoy the **Valiant Air Command Warbird Museum**, with dozens of vintage warplanes and fully guided tours through the exhibits and history of military aviation, as well as their dedicated restoration programme (**www.vacwarbirds.org**). Look out especially for the 3-day Warbird Air Show here each March. Cape Canaveral also hosts the **Art of Sand Festival** at Space Coast Stadium in Viera every Oct (**www.artofsandus.com**).

BRITTIP
For something truly unique, Valiant Air Command Warbird Museum now offers unique flights on its beautifully restored vintage WWII C-47 paratroop transport plane for $175/person. Call 321 268 1941 or email **vacwarbirds@bellsouth.net** for full details and availability.

Melbourne: Family-friendly **Brevard Zoo** is well worth a visit here, with almost 500 animals in 5 themed areas, including the excellent Cheetah Complex in the Expedition Africa exhibit. Other highlights include Asia/Australia, La Selva (South America), Wild Florida and Paws On Play, where children can enjoy water play, a petting zoo and explore Seaside Cove and Sea Turtle Beach (9.30am–5pm; $13.75 adults, $12.75 seniors, $10.25 2–12s; 321 254 9453, **www.brevardzoo.org**).

BRITTIP
For top value at Brevard Zoo, consider a Young Explorer's Package (admission, train ride, giraffe and lorikeet feeding at $18.75, $17.75 and $14.75) or Wild Explorer's version (a choice of kayaking in Wild Florida or Expedition Africa, plus giraffe and lorikeet feeding at $20.25, $19.25 and $16.75).

Where to stay: Try lively, surf-themed **Four Points by Sheraton Cocoa Beach** (321 783 8717, **www.starwoodhotels.com**) or **International Palms Resort** (321 783 2271, **www.internationalpalms.com**). More info: call 321 433 4470 or **www.space-coast.com**.

Tampa

Going west from Orlando brings you down I-4 to the bright city of Tampa, right on a major sea bay and with some excellent attractions of its own.

Dinosaur World: Right on I-4 as you head to Tampa (and a nice stopping

Breakfast with a difference!

Just north of DeLand in DeLeon Springs State Park is the unique **Old Spanish Sugar Mill** grill and griddle house, one of Florida's little restaurant treasures. Famous for hearty cook-it-yourself breakfasts (9am–4pm; 8am at weekends), each table has an inset griddle, and you choose your ingredients and get cracking. Its speciality is pancakes (pitchers of batter provided), with all manner of fillings, but it also has bacon, eggs, ham, sausage, home-made breads, French toast, sandwiches and salads. You'll struggle to pay more than $10/person and it's great fun, as well as a local institution. However, as it is inside the State Park, there is a $6/car entry fee (386 985 5644, **www.planetdeland.com/sugarmill**). You can then try the park facilities, which include canoes, kayaks, hiking trails and boat tours (**www. floridastateparks.org**).

point by exit 17) is this family-run attraction ideal for 3–8s. With life-sized dinosaurs in a lush, natural setting, plus walking trails, picnic area, playground and gift shop, it makes a good diversion for an hour or 2. There are no rides or audio-animatronics, just set-piece models with explanatory signs, plus a cave-themed video theatre, small-scale fossil dig, museum and large 'boneyard' sand pit, while the Skeleton Garden features 6 replica skeletons. It's mildly educational, totally laid back and a nice change of pace from the main parks. There is no café (just drinks machines), but it does have picnic facilities and there are fast-food locations nearby, including a pizza delivery service (9am–6pm; 5pm Nov–Jan; $12.75 adult, $10.75 seniors, $9.75 3–12s, under-3 free; 813 717 9865, **www.dinoworld.net**).

Florida Aquarium: In the heart of Tampa (right next to the port area) is this superb 6-part journey into Florida's waterways, coast and deep-sea elements, beautifully presented and ultra child-friendly. It starts with the **Wetlands**, then moves on to **Bays & Beaches** (including Sea Turtle Corner), **Dragons Down Under** (the amazing Leafy Sea-dragons), **Coral Reef Ocean Commotion** (full of interactive touch-screens, videos and podcasts) and the outdoor **Explore A Shore** water-play area, with squirt pools, fountains and pirate ship, plus an excellent tropical-themed Bar & Grill. Highlights include the daily Penguin Promenade (where a pair of the Aquarium's penguins are brought out for a meet-and-greet), the Touch Tank, the amusing River Otters and

Shark Bay, where anyone 15 and older who is scuba-certified can join the daily dive into the lagoon ($175/person, reservations required on 813 2713 4015). Other extras include a daily 20min non-scuba 'Swim with the fishes' reef swim ($75/person), a 2hr Shark Feeding programme every Tues and Sun ($65), a twice-daily 30min Penguins Backstage tour ($25) and a new Stingray Feeding Tour ($12, 8 and over only). There's also a daily (weather permitting) **Wild Dolphin Eco-Tour** on their 130-passenger catamaran, leaving from the aquarium to explore the Bay where more than 500 dolphins live, along with the occasional manatee (9.30am–5pm daily, closed Thanksgiving, Christmas Day; parking $6; $21.95 adults, $18.95 seniors, $16.95 under-12s; with Dolphin Eco-Tour, $35.95, $31.95, $27.95; 813 273 4000, **www.flaquarium.org**).

BRITTIP

Book tickets online for the Florida Aquarium and save several dollars on their regular prices.

The Aquarium is right next to the **Channelside Bay Plaza** centre of shops and restaurants, which is well worth exploring for unique stores like Paintings of the World, Lit Cigar Lounge, Surf Down Under, White House Gear, Del Sol and Quachbal Chocolatier, plus great entertainment and dining. Choose from the fun Greek style of Taverna Opa, Hooters, Oishi Sushi, MJ's Restaurant & Brewhouse, Tina Tapa's, Howl At The Moon piano bar, Splitsville 10-pin bowling attraction, lively Wet Willie's bar, Thai Tani, Precinct Pizza and Stumps Supper Club, plus Coldstone Creamery (great ice-cream and milkshakes!). Like Ybor City, this is where Tampa parties – hence the restaurants and bars, many featuring live music, are hopping at weekends. You will also find a 10-screen cinema and the **Official Tampa Bay Visitor Center** here (**www.channelsidebayplaza. com**).

Museum of Science and Industry: More family fun (especially for 4–12s) can be found at this entertaining science centre, with 3 floors of education-tinged exhibits, activities and large-screen IMAX films. Highlights include the **Kids In Charge** science play area (under-13s), **The Amazing You** (a tour of the human body), **Disasterville** (an interactive look at natural disasters) and the **High-Wire Bicycle** (ride a bike on a steel cable 30ft/9m up). Permanent exhibits include **Gulf Coast Hurricane** and **The Saunders Planetarium**, while the **IMAX® Dome Theatre** offers a range of films daily and there are periodic travelling exhibits. Outside is the **BioWorks Butterfly Garden** and the **Historic Tree Grove**, providing more insight into natural Florida (9am–5pm Mon–Fri, 6pm Sat and Sun; $20.95 adults, $18.95 seniors, $16.95 2–12s, includes 1 standard IMAX film and Planetarium show; additional films $8.95, $7.95 and $6.95; 813 987 6100, **www.mosi.org**).

Ybor City: Tampa's other entertainment district can be found in the rejuvenated Cuban quarter of the city, where a fine mix of shops and restaurants provide a lively vibe both by day and at night. Shop at **Wear Me Out**, for signature handbags, jewellery and jackets; **Urban Outfitters** for trendy apparel and accessories; **Ybor Ybor** for visitor merchandise; **District 7 Avenue** and more. Then stop for a meal at any of **Fresh Mouth** (tempting burgers), **Hamburger Mary's** (ditto) or **Samurai Blue** (fine sushi and sake) and enjoy the lively bar scene of **Rock-N Sports Bar & Bistro**, **Centro Cantina** or (our fave) the **Tampa Bay Brewing Co**, a British-run brewpub with a varied menu, great range of beers, multiple TV screens and pool table. Find more fun at **Game Time**, an upscale arcade of games, bars and the Jax Grill restaurant, and the **Improv Comedy Theatre.** It is busiest on Fri and Sat but bustling most nights (**www.centroybor.com**). Start at the **Visitor Center & Museum**, which shows a fascinating film on the history of the city, and also try to visit the well-presented **Ybor City Museum** on East 9th Avenue for more insight into this eclectic gem (daily 9am–5pm, $4 adults, under-6s free; **www.ybormuseum.org**).

Much of downtown Tampa, including Ybor City and Channelside, is linked by the handy TECO Line Streetcar, replicas of authentic electric trams, with 1-way fares of $2.50 (cash only) and just $5 for an all-day card. A new Family All Day Ticket ($12.50, for up to 5) is available from ticket vending machines.

Where to stay: try the wonderful boutique style of historic **Don Vicente Inn** in Ybor City, a beautiful period refurbishment of a 19th-century building with just 16 individual rooms (813 241 4545, **www.donvicenteinn.com**).

BRITTIP
Have lunch or dinner at the original **Columbia Restaurant** in Ybor City, 1 of Florida's finest. Opened in 1905, it incorporates a whole city block that was gradually absorbed into this Spanish/ Cuban bar-diner. Ask at the host stand if they can give you a tour, with the story of the Gonzmart family (813 248 4961, **www. columbiarestaurant.com**).

More info: Call the Visitor Center on 813 223 2752 or **www.visittampabay. com**.

St Pete/Clearwater
Continue west and you have the gorgeous **Gulf Coast**, a 2hr drive down I-4 and through Tampa on I-275 south to **St Pete Beach** (105mls/169km) or **Clearwater Beach** (110mls/177km), with a string of beautiful resorts in between, all featuring white-sand

beaches, water sports and far fewer crowds than you would think, plus the smart new **Beach Walk** in Clearwater. The sea is a bit warmer and calmer on this side of Florida so is more suitable for small children. The 35ml/56km stretch from St Pete–Clearwater represents the heart of the Sunshine State beach experience and is one of the most popular 2-centre options. It has a wonderful array of attractions and averages 361 days of sun a year.

St Petersburg: This city, just across the Howard Frankland Bridge from Tampa, is a wonderful mix of the old and the new, with a fast-developing Art District (8 museums, dozens of galleries and counting) and a real café society feel. It boasts aspects both recent and historic and is a delight at weekends especially, when the locals are out to see and be seen. Take time especially for the world-renowned **Dali Museum** (10am–5.30pm Mon–Wed, 8pm Thurs, 5.30pm Fri and Sat, noon–5.30pm Sun; $21 adults, $19 seniors, $15 13–18s and students, $7 6–12s; **www.salvadordalimuseum.org**), now in its eye-catching new building and a real wonder in its own right. Equally, the new **Chihuly Collection** at the Morean Arts Center is a superb showcase of the American glass artist, with guided tours through the stunning series of exhibits on the hour every half-hour. There's also a separate glass studio and hot shop nearby (10–6pm Mon-Sat, 8pm Thurs, noon-6pm Sun; $15 adults, $13 seniors, $12 students and children over 5; $8 $6, $5 for Hot Shop; combo ticket $20, $16, $14; 727 896 4527, **www.chihulycollectionstpete. com**). Other highlights include the elegant **Museum of Fine Arts**, with its new Hazel Hough Wing (**www. fine-arts.org**), the recently expanded **St Petersburg Museum of History** on the Pier, the exceedingly child-friendly **International Museum** and fascinating **Great Explorations Children's Museum** (**www. greatexplorations.org**). Pedestrian-friendly streets and the Pier provide plenty of interest, while the **Bay Walk** complex adds restaurants, shops and a Muvico IMAX 20-screen cinema (**www.newbaywalk.com**). Equally worth considering is a visit to fan-friendly Tropicana Field, which hosts the **Tampa Bay Rays** baseball team (Apr–Sept) for truly terrific local entertainment ($9–210; **http:// tampabay.rays.mlb.com**). For a tour with a difference, you should try the Bayside Tours from the Museum of History on the amazing 2-wheeled Segways – 'the ride technology of the future'. They are easy to master and provide a superb view of the city's miles of waterfront parks, beaches and residences with your knowledgeable guide. Suitable for ages 12 and over (max 275lb/125kg), choose from its standard downtown tours or the off-road/beach tours at Bilmar Beach Resort on Treasure Island (Mon 12.30, 2.30 and 4.30pm; Tues–Sat 10.30am and 2pm, Sun 12.30 and 2.30pm; 1hr tour $35, 90min $50; call for reservations on 727 896 3640, **www.gyroglides.com**).

⊞ BRITTIP

Insect repellent is essential for any visit to Weedon Island Preserve as it is not sprayed for mosquitoes, and the little pests will feed on tourists!

Weedon Island Preserve: Enjoy the rich cultural history of this 3,700-acre/1,500ha seaside nature park in St Petersburg. Start at the **Natural History Center** (the main entrance, confusingly, is at the back) and learn about the prehistoric and Native American settlements here (plus periodic exhibitions), then go up to the 3rd floor observation deck. There are several miles of boardwalks and trails around the tidal wetlands, which are home to a wide variety of wildlife, like ospreys, turtles, spoonbills, turtles, mangrove crabs, raccoons and gopher tortoises, and guided hikes on Saturdays (call to register; 10am–4pm Wed–Sun, free entry; 727 453 6500, **www.weedonislandcenter.org**). The more energetic may want to try a paddle round the shallow waters with **Sweetwater Kayaks**. This close encounter with nature (stingrays, jumping mullet and the occasional manatee) takes 2–3hrs on the self-guided tour (9am and 12.30pm Sat and Sun; $40 for a half-day single-kayak rental, $56 for double, or $17 and $25 hourly; 727 570 4844 or **www.sweetwaterkayaks.com**).

Beaches: Head out to the beaches and you are spoiled for choice, from the 1,100-acre/445ha **Fort De Soto Park** in the south to stunning **Caladesi Island State Park** in the north (regularly voted in America's Top 10). There is plenty to do, too, with the likes of Treasure Island, Sand Key and St Pete Beach all receiving the Blue Wave Award for cleanliness and safety. Fort De Soto Park offers free walking tours of its Spanish-American War-era fort, while **John's Pass Village** is an eclectic shopping district and marina full of art galleries and restaurants (and home to the fun **Pirate Cruise** – a replica sailing ship offering a 2hr party cruise; $33 adults, $28 for 65 and over, $23 under-20s, inclusive of beer, wine and soft drinks; 11am, 2pm and sunset Mon–Sat; 727 423 7824). Parasailing, jet-skiing, fishing, boat rentals and tours are also popular (**www.johnspass.com**).

BRITTIP

Most public beaches will have toilets, changing facilities and picnic tables, but there is usually a parking fee.

You shouldn't miss **Dolphin Landings** in St Pete Beach, with a pair of 51ft/15.5m yachts that sail on 2hr trips along the calm inland waterway 3 times a day (usually 9.30am, noon and 2.15pm) for close-up dolphin-watch cruises and sunset sailings, plus Shell Island day trips and fishing excursions ($35 adults, $25 children; 727 367 4488, **www.charterboatescape.com**). Further north at Indian Shores is America's largest wild bird hospital, the **Suncoast Seabird Sanctuary**, caring for injured birds including birds of prey, pelicans, spoonbills and egrets. No charge to visit this non-profit-making rehabilitation centre, but it does ask for donations (727 391 6211, **www.seabirdsanctuary.com**).

BRITTIP

Don't leave Clearwater Beach without visiting the Aquarium's – and the area's – top attraction, a dolphin called **Winter**, the real-life star of the 2011 film *Dolphin Tale* with Morgan Freeman. Rescued from a crab trap, her tail had to be amputated and she was not expected to survive. Happily, she not only lived but has learned to swim with a prosthetic tail!

Continue north to **Clearwater Beach** for acres of clean, white sands and the **Clearwater Marine Aquarium**, a wonderful non-profit organisation that rescues and rehabilitates injured dolphins, turtles, river otters and more (especially good for under-12s). There are 13 main exhibits, including Turtle Cove, Otter Oasis, Shark Pass and Underwater Shipwreck Tunnel but much of the focus is on the area's Hollywood 'star', Winter the tail-less dolphin (see Brit Tip). There are dolphin presentations (into behaviour and care – not typical 'shows') 3 times a day and other animal encounters. You can also do their behind-the-scenes tour, with access to all the rehab areas and a close-up of the dolphins, or 2hr **Sea Life Safari** (great for kids) that goes out on the coastal waterway (9am–5pm Mon–Thurs, 9am–7pm Fri and Sat, 10am–5pm Sun; $14.95 adults, $10.95 seniors, $9.95 3–12s; admission plus behind-the-scenes tour $21.95, $19.95 and $18.95; plus Sea Life Safari $30.95, $28.95, $22.75; or all 3 for $37.95, $34.95 and $28.75; 727 441 1790, **www.seewinter.com**).

The new **Beach Walk** is the heart of this area, a winding beachside promenade of lush landscaping and artistic touches that links a ½-mile stretch of resorts, shops and restaurants (like the fun Frenchy's, Britt's Laguna Grill and Crabby Bill's) to **Pier 60** where the daily sunset celebration (complete with craft stalls and music) is held. Also here is the marina where you can catch the 2hr **Captain Memo's Pirate Cruise** (10am and 2pm daily; $36 adults, $31 seniors and teens, $26 under-13s) or the Sunset Champagne Cruise (at 4.30, 5, 6 or 7pm, $39, $31, $26; www.captainmemo.com). Going further north brings you to **Caladesi Island** and another of the world's most picturesque beach spots.

For those not wanting to drive, the **Suncoast Beach Trolley** is the perfect options (5.05am–10.10pm daily) both along the beaches and into St Petersburg for $2 a ride, $4.50 for an all-day pass and $20 for a week pass (727 530 9911, **www.psta.net**). The area also boasts 2,000 restaurants, of which the Key West bistro style of **Frenchy's Rockaway Grill** and **Frenchy's South Beach Café** (both in Clearwater Beach), the **Daiquiri Deck/Oceanside Grill** (Madeira Beach), **Crabby Bill's Seafood** (Indian Rocks, Clearwater Beach and St Pete Beach) and the **Moon Under Water** (St Petersburg) are all worth visiting. The chic **Parkshore Grill** in downtown St Pete is ideal for a relaxing lunch or elegant dinner (727 896 9463, **www.parkshoregrill. com**), as is the new 400 **Beach Seafood & Tap House**, which also features a fab Sunday brunch (727 896 2400, **www.400beachseafood.com**).

Where to stay: A range of **Superior Small Lodgings** combine beachfront locations with small-scale, personal service. Weekly rates can be from $800 for a 3-room apartment (727 367 2791, www.floridassl.com). Upmarket hotels include the family-friendly Tradewinds Island Resorts on St Pete Beach, a 743-room complex with great facilities and dining in a blissful location (1800 360 4016, **www.tradewindsresort.com**) and the superb **Sandpearl Resort**, a 4-star choice on Clearwater Beach, with a mix of stylish standard rooms and spacious suites. The pool, bar and grill are a beachfront sanctuary, while the modern Spa has a fab array of treatments. Caretta on the Gulf offers memorable dining with an inventive fusion cuisine, plus ceviche, sushi and a raw bar (727 441 2425, **www.sandpearl.com**). **Sunset Vistas Beachfront Suites** on Treasure Island, with 1 and 2-bed suites and fully equipped kitchens, is a good self-catering choice for a week or more (727 360 1600, **www.sunsetvistas.**

com). However, the jewel in the crown is the new **Hyatt Regency Clearwater Beach Resort & Spa**, an all-suite luxury hotel at the heart of Beach Walk. Fantastic pool facilities are superbly picturesque with great Gulf views, while the eco-friendly Sandova Spa is one of Florida's best. A state-of-the-art gym and 2 wonderful restaurants complete the line-up, along with the excellent Camp Hyatt activity programme for kids (727 373 1234, **www.clearwaterbeachhyatt. com**). By contrast, the **Vinoy Resort** (in St Petersburg) is the area's oldest formal hotel, a 1920s treasure that is well worth a look just for its Spanish Revival style. Plus, it's a great place to stop for a drink in its Lobby Bar or Promenade Lounge (727 894 1000, **www.marriott.com**). More info: Call 0208 651 4742 in the UK, 727 464 7200 in the US, or see **www. visitstpeteclearwater.com**.

> **BRITTIP**
> Don't miss the chance to dine at the **Hyatt Regency**'s SHOR Seafood Grill, with its dramatic show kitchen and superb local seafood dishes.

The south-west

Bradenton/Sarasota: Around 2hrs' drive from Orlando is this artsy area (take I-4 then I-75), which features the superb beachfronts of **Anna Maria Island** (charming and secluded beaches), **Longboat Key** and **Venice** ('the shark tooth capital of the world' and great for fossil hunters). Sarasota is year-round home to the **Ringling Circus**, and there are many circus-influenced offerings here, including the unmissable **Ringling Estate and Museum of Art**, which includes the unique Circus Museum and Tibbals Learning Center (the world's largest scale model of a classic circus). The Museum of Art features a multi-million dollar collection of Old Masters in a palatial setting while the former family home, the dazzling Ca d'Zan Mansion, grounds and gardens are also part of the entry fee (daily 10am–5.30pm; $25 adults, $20 seniors, $10 6–17s and students; **www. ringling.org**). There is superb shopping at **St Armand's Circle** in Lido Key, and the **Mote Aquarium** is also worthy of note. In Bradenton, look out for the **Village of Arts**, and the sophisticated **South Florida Museum**, which includes the Parker Manatee Aquarium and Bishop Planetarium. The Aquarium is home to Bradenton's mascot, Snooty, the world's oldest living manatee (10am–5pm Mon–Sat, noon–5pm Sun; closed Mon in May, Jun and Aug–Dec; $15.95 adults, $13.95 seniors, $11.95 4–11s; 941 746 4131, **www.southfloridamuseum.org**). Good food is always on the menu, and you should try another outlet of the excellent Spanish-Cuban **Columbia Restaurant** in Sarasota (941 388 3987, **www.columbiarestaurant.com**) and beachfront **Siesta Key Oyster Bar** (941 346 5443, **www.skob.com**).

BRITTIP

The **Londoner Inn** in Bradenton also offers an excellent British-style afternoon tea Mon–Sat, 11.30am–3pm.

Where to stay: Anna Maria Island is full of small-scale B&Bs and cute beachfront inns. The **Hyatt Sarasota** is one of the top resorts in the area (941 953 1234, **www.sarasota.hyatt. com**), while the **Ritz-Carlton** is a Gulf Coast landmark (941 309 2000, **www.ritzcarlton.com**). The **Londoner** is a sumptuous British-run B&B in Bradenton that features 6 gorgeous, individually decorated rooms, a

Chihuly Collection, St Petersburg

Seminole Central

Head west out of Fort Lauderdale to Big Cypress and you find the rewarding **Ah-Tah-Thi-Ki Museum**, home to the Seminole tribe of Florida. Here you can learn about Native American culture, from its customs to the bitter 19th century Seminole Wars and its modern face as 'guardians' of the Everglades. See the Living Village and walk the 1ml/1.6km Boardwalk over the Cypress Swamp. Then try the **Billie Swamp Safari**, a 2,200-acre/1.6ha Cypress Reservation featuring close-ups of the wildlife (including snakes and gators) via its giant-wheeled buggy, airboat rides and swamp critter shows. And you can even stay overnight in its Chickee huts (1800 683 7800, **www. seminoletribe.com**).

private 2-bed carriage house and great local hospitality (941 748 5658, **www.thelondonerinn.com**). **More info:** Sarasota, call 941 957 1877 or **www. sarasotafl.com**; Bradenton and Anna Maria Island, 941 729 9177 or **www. annamariaisland-longboatkey.com**.

Charlotte Harbor: Go further south (170mls/272km from Orlando) and you have the lower-key destinations of **Punta Gorda**, **Port Charlotte**, **Englewood** and **Boca Grande**. From here, the **Fort Myers/Sanibel** area is only a short drive. This is part of the mini tropical paradise of the **Lee Island Coast**, featuring history and nature-rich **Fort Myers** and funky **Pine Island**.

Among the many highlights of the barrier islands are bustling family-orientated **Fort Myers Beach**; **Sanibel Island**, centred around its famous shell-strewn beaches; the bird-watching Mecca at the **Darling National Wildlife Refuge**; the quirky jumble of shops and restaurants in **Captiva Island**; and **Bonita Beach**, where the **Great Calusa Blueway** paddling trail heads north for 90mls/145km. Sanibel is home to the unique **Bailey-Matthews Shell Museum**, plus a quaint Historical Village & Museum and several wildlife attractions. Canoeing, kayaking and nature tours are all featured.

Where to stay: There is a good mix of vacation homes and cottages in Fort Myers Beach and Sanibel, while the top hotels are **Lovers Key Resort** (239 765 1040, **www.loverskey.com**) and **Sanibel Harbor Resort & Spa** (1866 283 3273, **www.sanibel-resort.com**). In downtown Fort Myers, try the smart **Holiday Inn**, which boasts a stylish HI Restaurant for lunch and dinner (239 332 3232, **www.holidayinn.com/ftmyersdwntn**). More info: 239 338 3500 or **www.fortmyers-sanibel.com**.

Paradise Coast: Continue south for about 230mls/368km and you have the magnificent 'Paradise Coast' of **Naples** and **Marco Island**, 2 of Florida's lesser-known seaside treasures. Naples is a fresh, modern city with plenty of attractions (notably the **Museum of Art**, **Naples Nature Center** and **Corkscrew Swamp Sanctuary**, plus ultra-chic shopping) and a top beach destination. Its art-tinged ambience is well-evidenced in its 2 main areas of **Fifth Avenue South**, with boutique shops, sidewalk cafés and art festivals, and **Third Street South**, a mini-downtown with more distinctive stores, galleries and café society atmosphere (try the Old Naples Pub for fine food in a relaxed ambience with an outdoor patio and live music Thurs–Sat). The beaches are mere steps away; at the municipal beach, **Naples Pier** juts into placid Gulf waters, while **Lowdermilk Beach** is fully family-friendly, with volleyball and other facilities. Marco Island is the largest of the Ten Thousand Islands, consisting of 2 main communities: **Marco**, known for its wide-coved beach and fine resorts, plus a multitude of fishing charters; and **Goodland**, with its eclectic fish house restaurants, plus fishing charters into the Everglades.

BRITTIP

The Naples/Marco Island area is the perfect base from which to explore the amazing Florida Everglades, though you can also reach them from Fort Lauderdale on the east coast.

Where to stay: Pick from high-quality resorts like **Marco Island Marriott**

Beach Resort (239 394 2511, **www.marcoislandmarriott.com**), **Marco Beach Ocean Resort** (239 393 1400, **www.marcoresort.com**) and **Naples Grande Resort** (239 597 3232, **www.naplesgranderesort.com**). We also like the small-scale Caribbean-tinged **Lemon Tree Inn** in Naples (239 262 1414, **www.lemontreeinn.com**) and cosy 1 and 2-bed suites at **Marco Island Lakeside Inn** (239 394 1161, **www.marcoislandlakeside.com**). More info: 1800 688 3600 or **www.paradisecoast.com**.

Treasure Coast

Returning to the Atlantic Coast, heading south on Highway 1 brings you to an often-overlooked Florida jewel, **Vero Beach**. Nicknamed the Treasure Coast (for its history of shipwrecks), it boasts the intriguing **McLarty Treasure Museum** and the **Pelican Island National Wildlife Refuge**. Vero Beach itself is located on the barrier island of North Hutchinson but spreads to the mainland, with art galleries, smart shops, restaurants, small resorts and beach parks, including a boardwalk atop the dunes. Go south for another hour and you reach **Palm Beach** and the mainland city of **West Palm Beach**, foremost among Florida's chic cities. A playground of the rich and famous, Henry Flagler's **Whitehall** mansion is a highlight, while the many restaurants are places to go celebrity-watching. Also here is **Lion Country Safari**, with lions, elephants and giraffes (**www.lioncountrysafari.com**).

St Petersburg

Where to stay: Disney's Vero Beach Resort doesn't always have availability (it is a Disney Vacation Club hotel), but is the ideal family resort on this coast (772 234 2000, **www.dvcresorts.com**). In Palm Beach there is really only 1 place to stay (or visit) – the opulent **The Breakers**, one of America's legendary resort destinations (561 655 6611, **www. thebreakers.com**). More info: Call 561 233 3000 or **www.palmbeachfl.com**.

Miami and Fort Lauderdale

From Palm Beach, your enjoyable coast drive brings you through increasingly built-up resort territory – Delray Beach, chic Boca Raton, Deerfield Beach, Pompano Beach and **Fort Lauderdale**. This latter has become 1 of Florida's most upmarket and enjoyable destinations in recent years, with a great mix of resorts, shopping, attractions and fabulous beaches. It also has a canal and waterway network that makes it the 'Venice of America', with **water taxis** being more plentiful than the wheeled variety. Top things to see are the **Museum of Discovery & Science** (one of the state's finest), **Bonnet House Museum & Gardens**, **Old Fort Lauderdale Village & Museum** and the unmissable **Las Olas Boulevard**, full of boutiques and restaurants. Shop at **Sawgrass Mills**, Florida's largest mall, which has more than 300 outlet-style stores from big-name designers, plus the Wanadoo City role-playing park for kids. Fort Lauderdale is also a perfect stay for a few days before or after a cruise, as both Port Everglades and Miami are only a short distance away.

Where to stay: Look for their **Superior Small Lodgings** or the many high-class resorts now dotting the beachfront, like **Sheraton Yankee Clipper Hotel** (954 524 5551, **www. starwoodhotels.com**) and the dramatic 5-star **Ritz-Carlton** (954 465 2300, **www.ritzcarlton.com**). More info: 954 765 4466 or **www.sunny.org**.

Miami nice

If you see nothing else in Miami, do spend some time in **South Beach** (or SoBe as it is known) and über-cool Ocean Drive, full of open-air cafés, art galleries and pulsating nightclubs. Tranquil during the day, non-stop at night, this is where the beautiful people hang out, or just cruise in their Ferraris and Hummers. The restored Art Deco gems twinkle at night and will use up plenty of film or a spare memory card.

If you have taken the full 4hr drive south from Orlando, you will finally arrive in the state's biggest and most glamorous city, **Miami**. With superb high-rise resorts, miles of open, accessible beaches, the ultra-chic South Beach area (with its atmospheric **Art Deco District**), fantastic shopping, great sports, scintillating restaurants and nightlife, and an array of outstanding attractions, you could easily spend 2 weeks here. The city is actually 5mls/8km from the Beaches area, which runs north for almost 15mls/24km along the sprawling corridor of Collins Avenue, where you have most of the resorts and nightlife. High style is almost everywhere – a narrated boat tour (from the **Bayside Marketplace**) will show off the mansions of the rich and famous, while you should also tour **Coral Gables** and the older, neater **Coconut Grove**, with its CocoWalk shopping district and ornate **Vizcaya Museum**.

Other attractions include **Miami Seaquarium** on the island of Key Biscayne, the amazing **Venetian Pool** at Coral Gables and the surprising and entertaining family attraction **Jungle Island**, a combination of zoo, animal shows and gardens with great up-close encounters (**www. jungleisland.com**). You are spoiled for choice for shopping, from fashion-conscious **Bal Harbor Shops**, to the massive **Aventura Mall** and funky **Lincoln Road** in South Beach. Brand new is the **Village of Merrick Park** in Coral Gables, a Mediterranean-style outdoor mall with more designer style, including the iconic Nordstrom department store and superb dining, notably at fab Italian restaurant Villagio (305 529 0200, **www.villageofmerrickpark.com**).

Where to stay: There are boutique hotels and dazzling resorts aplenty; the iconic **Fontainebleau** is open again after a $1b renovation (305 538 5000, **www.fontainebleau.com**); the **Mandarin Oriental** is about as smart as it gets (305 913 8288, **www.mandarinoriental.com**); more modest but still decent is the **Best Western Atlantic Beach Resort** (305 673 3337, **www.bestwesternflorida.com**). More info: Call 305 539 3000 or **www.miamiandbeaches.com**.

Florida Keys

Leaving Miami behind on Highway 1 brings you to the unique realm of the Keys, a loose archipelago of 1,700 islands that arc down into the Caribbean. If you thought mainland Florida was easygoing, just try the laid-back 'Conch Republic', where shorts and flip-flops are official wear and the mix of influences merges into a 'Floribbean' culture. Scuba divers enjoy some of the world's best coral reefs, with renowned **John Pennekamp Coral Reef State Park** the highlight of many miles of National Marine Sanctuary. Or try **Vandenberg Artificial Reef** off Key West, an old US Navy ship intentionally sunk in 2009 to create a man-made reef. The first city you encounter is **Key Largo**, followed by **Islamorada**, where you should stop to see **Theater To The Sea**, with its dolphin and sea-lion programmes. For fishing, some of the best charters are at Islamorada, **Marathon** and **Big Pine Key**.

BRITTIP

Don't miss the opportunity to feed the hungry giant tarpon that hang around the docks by Robbie's boat rentals in Islamorada (**www.robbies.com**).

Marathon is the starting point of the amazing **Seven Mile Bridge**, the unofficial 8th wonder of the world, which connects the biggest gap between the islands, while Big Pine Key is home to **Bahia Honda State Park**, 1 of Florida's finest beaches. Finally, the 375ml/600km drive from Orlando brings you to America's southernmost city. **Key West** is possibly the most eclectic city in the US, a mix of the laid-back and outrageous, with street performers, sidewalk artists, cafes and bars (LOTS of bars!), plus the former home of **Ernest Hemingway**, whose residence and museum are essential viewing. You should also see **Key West Aquarium** and **Shipwreck Historeum**, and the wonderfully diverse array of shops. You must be on the harbour front, though, for the daily **Sunset Celebration**, when Key West's party spirit is in full force. The other great feature of Key West is its myriad of ways to get around – you can try the **Conch Tour Train**, **Old Town Trolley Tours**, **pedicabs** and **bicycles**. Just don't expect your stay to be sedate!

Where to stay: Guest houses, inns and B&Bs are plentiful in the Keys. Try **Old Customs House Inn** (305 294 8507, **www.oldcustomshouse.com**) in Key West's Old Town or charming **Banyan Resort** (305 296 7786, **www.thebanyanresort.com**). More info: 1800 352 5397 or **visit www.fla-keys.com**.

Cruise-and-stay

The options for 2-centre holidays don't end just because Florida does. Taking a cruise is a popular pick with an Orlando stay and you'll see a lot of advertising for these well-priced 3, 4, 5 and 7-day sailings out of Port

Disney's Castaway Cay island

© Disney

Canaveral, Tampa, Fort Lauderdale and Miami.

Disney has its own impressive mini-fleet sailing from a dedicated Port Canaveral cruise terminal. Classic design plus the usual Disney Imagineering have produced vessels that incorporate special features for kids, teenagers AND adults. In fact, they are a destination in their own right. With multiple restaurants (1 for adults only), a theatre, cinema, nightclub complex, choice of bars and a gorgeous spa, plus outstanding kids' facilities, they sail to the Bahamas, Key West, Caribbean and Disney's stunning private island of Castaway Cay, which has an amazing array of beach amenities. It's not a cheap option and the 3 and 4-night cruises can feel a bit frenzied but there is also a 5-night option and 7-night Caribbean voyages that offer a more relaxing style. They boast novel touches with their on-board entertainment, including dazzling theatre shows, original Disney character interaction and wonderful features like an adults-only champagne brunch. Book with many of the tour operators or direct with Disney on 1800 511 9444 (**www.disneycruise.com**).

Other Port Canaveral options (**www.portcanaveral.org**) include glitzy **Carnival Cruise Lines** (all-modern hardware, party atmosphere; 1888 2276 4825 in the US or 0845 351 0556 in the UK, **www.carnivalcruise.co.uk**) with 3 and 4-night Bahamas voyages and 7-night cruises to the east and west Caribbean; and **Royal Caribbean**

Disney Cruise Line ship

© Disney

A real Dream-boat

New Disney Cruise Line ships *Disney Dream* (2011) and sister *Disney Fantasy* (2012) have added some fantastic features to the maritime world, with a host of novel touches like the first 'water-coaster' at sea,' a 765ft/233m powered water-tube ride that actually goes OUT over the side of the vessel and features a 2-deck drop! Other highlights are a new French-themed fine-dining restaurant, Remy; sophisticated sports bar 687 and lounge-bar Pink, designed like the inside of champagne bottle; Nemo's Reef splash pool for toddlers; a mini-golf course; and 5 superb kids' clubs. Inside cabins benefit from 'virtual reality' portholes (via an outside camera), the concierge level is classically stunning and the cinema is equipped for 3-D films. The one drawback? There's too MUCH to do on a 3 or 4-day cruise!

International (also 2 modern, glamorous ships; 0844 493 4005, **www.royalcaribbean.co.uk**), similar 3 and 4-day trips to Nassau and its private island of Coco Cay and alternating 7-night Caribbean cruises.

Looking further afield in Florida, you can also catch a cruise from **Tampa** (**www.tampaport.com**), where you can choose from Carnival, Royal Caribbean, NCL, and upmarket Holland America, with 4, 5, 7 and 14-day cruises to Mexico and the western Caribbean; busy **Miami** (**www.miamidade.gov/portofmiami**), with as many as 7 cruise lines in winter throughout the Bahamas and Caribbean; and **Fort Lauderdale** (**www.porteverglades.net/cruising**), with even more choice, including the 'world's largest ships,' Royal Caribbean duo *Oasis* and *Allure of the Seas*.

For more advice, consult *World of Cruising* magazine (0870 429 2686, **www.worldofcruising.co.uk**) or specialist travel agent **The Cruise Line Ltd** (0800 008 6677, **www.cruiseline.co.uk**).

Well, that represents pretty much the full range of holiday choices. Now we need to tell you about how to enjoy all the night-time entertainment…

If Orlando and the parks are hot during the day, they positively sizzle at night, with yet more diverse and thrilling entertainment, much of it extremely family friendly. Disney and Universal lead the way, but there is much to enjoy in the live music scene generally.

The full range runs from purpose-built entertainment complexes and an amazing range of dinner shows to a unique array of bars and nightclubs. The choice is widespread and almost always high quality. Disney raised the bar for the big evening entertainment concept in 1987 when it opened *Pleasure Island*, an inspired range of clubs, discos and restaurants, but the area is largely quiet now as it goes through a redesign and becomes Hyperion Wharf. **Downtown Disney West Side** still has several evening venues worth visiting, while **Disney's BoardWalk Resort**, opened in 1996, remains a great evening option.

BRITTIP

Photo ID is essential for most bars and clubs, even if you happen to be the 'wrong' side of 30. No ID equals no alcohol, and there are no exceptions.

I-Drive caught up with this process in 1997 when **Pointe Orlando** opened. Although its prime focus is shopping and restaurants, it now has a strong evening entertainment component with an array of exceptional restaurants, BB King's Blues Club and the big Regal Cinemas 20+ IMAX multiplex. Finally, Universal Orlando got with the beat in 1998 with the opening of **CityWalk**, possibly the most elaborate and sophisticated centre of the lot. They all represent yet another slick opportunity for you to be dazzled and relieved of your cash all in the name of holiday fun!

DOWNTOWN DISNEY

Disney's big shopping, dining and entertainment district remains a 3-part adventure – The Marketplace, West Side and Hyperion Wharf – but with most of the out-and-out night-time fun weighted towards the latter 2. Hyperion Wharf is still evolving from Pleasure Island as a more mainstream area of restaurants and shops but more entertainment

Cirque du Soleil at Downtown Disney

Raglan Road

elements should be added in 2012, including a nightly light-show over the new amphitheatre and a live music stage. As things stand, the area's main nightlife attractions are as follows (see also Shopping, p325).

Hyperion Wharf/ Pleasure Island

Raglan Road: This pub features traditional live Irish music each night in its Grand Room 7pm–midnight, plus Irish dancing periodically, and dancing demonstrations on its outdoor terrace at 5pm most evenings. Enjoy its full bar, ample collection of genuine Irish whiskey, 9 European beers, plus local brews, great bartenders and an even better menu (p305) (407 938 0300, **www. raglanroadirishpub.com.**).

Paradiso 37: This expansive, split-level bar-restaurant offers a fine array of food from the Americas (all 37 countries) plus an amazing Tequila Bar featuring – 37 varieties. Live music adds to its picturesque waterfront location (p305).

West Side

Bongos Cuban Café: The 'big pine-apple' restaurant with Latin flair has great dining, 3 bars with bright mosaics and bar stools shaped like conga drums, salsa music and a live band Fri and Sat nights. Sit on the outdoor balcony on a balmy evening (407 828 0999; **www.bongoscubancafe. com**).

House of Blues: Free live music every night at the Front Porch bar, with full concerts at the separately accessed music venue next to the restaurant, plus an entertaining Gospel Brunch (10.30am and 1pm every Sun). The main venue offers a mix of big-name headliners (including the likes of Duran Duran, My Chemical Romance and Cheap Trick), up-and-coming bands and local acts. All concerts are standing room only. Tickets required, no discounts for children ($8–$35 and up; 407 934 2583, **www.hob.com**).

AMC® Dine-In Theaters Complex: With 24 screens and 6,000 seats and inspired by the grand movie theatres of the 1920s, this superb cinema multiplex shows first-run films in state-of-the-art surroundings, including the Enhanced Theatre Experience (a bigger screen, with 3D technology, 12-channel audio and digital projection) and the new feature Dine-In option, with 6 of the auditoriums converted to serve meals and drinks while you watch. The menu includes starters like wings, potato skins and onion rings, then salads, fish and chips, chicken pasta, sandwiches and burgers and yummy desserts, plus wine, beer and cocktails (tickets $6-20, prices vary by show; food and drink extra; call 1-888-262-4386 for show times; under 18s must be accompanied by an adult in Dine-In theatres). Disabled accessible; assisted listening devices available at Guest Services.

BRITTIP

Some films have added features, such as enhanced sound, larger screen, or 3-D, that will increase your ticket price. However, you can save $2 on adult tickets at the AMC® cineplex by visiting before 3.55pm.

DisneyQuest: The most unusual element to the West Side, DisneyQuest is described by one Cast Member as 'a theme park in a box'. It houses 11 major adventures, such as **CyberSpace Mountain** (design and ride your own roller-coaster), **Mighty Ducks Pinball Slam** (a fun life-size pinball game), **Ride the Comix!** (a virtual-reality battle, this time with super-villains), **Virtual Jungle Cruise** (shooting the rapids, prehistoric style) and **Aladdin's Magic Carpet** (more virtual-reality fun in best cartoon fashion), a host of old-fashioned video games in **Replay Zone**, the latest sports games, a test of imagination in **Animation Academy** and 2 cafés – **Wonderland Café**, with computers and internet tables, and **Food Quest**, straight out of a space-age comic book.

BRITTIP

A combined annual pass for DisneyQuest and Disney's water parks at $129 adults and $99 3–9s can work out good value for multiple visits.

Two more interactive experiences are **Pirates of the Caribbean: Battle for Buccaneer Gold** (a 3-D immersion in a swashbuckling quest for pirate treasure) and **Buzz Lightyear's Astro Blasters** (inter-galactic bumper cars

with cannonball action! Restrictions: 4ft 3in/129cm). You enter via the clever Cybrolator to Ventureport and then have 4 main areas to explore: **Score Zone** (for most of the game-playing); **Explore Zone** (role-playing and virtual-reality games); **Create Zone** (hands-on activities to be your own 'Imagineer'); and **Replay Zone** (a 'moonscape' of classic games and rides). Admission: 11.30am–10pm Sun–Thurs, 11.30am–11pm Fri and Sat. But, if you want to avoid the queues (the building admits only 1,500), go during the day. A 1-day ticket costs $42 ($36 3–9s). It's a bit too elaborate for most youngsters, but teenagers will love it.

Cirque Du Soleil: The greatest show we've seen anywhere is Cirque du Soleil's **La Nouba™**. Twice a day, 5 times a week, the company's purpose-built, 1,671-seat theatre stages the most stupendous combination of dance, circus, acrobatics, comedy and live music in a 90min show by more than 60 performers. Unique styling, outrageous costumes and captivating sounds make this a stunning multi-dimensional assault on the senses.

La Nouba™

© Cirque du Soleil

The show title comes from the French *faire la nouba*, to live it up, and this it does in grand style. It features trampolines, acrobatics, trapezes, juggling and even mountain bikes, woven with comedy, innovative dance, spellbinding music and magnificent staging. Some of the stunts are truly jaw-dropping, notably the Chinese diabolo acrobats, world-record juggler Anthony Gatto and the mind-boggling final act, Power Track/Trampoline. But the overall effect of the constant flow of movement, sublime timing and multitude of different characters is a masterpiece. A kaleidoscopic explosion of talent that never fails to amaze, it is just as exciting as when it opened in 1998. It is not cheap, but we believe it is worth every cent and a highlight of any visit to Orlando. Booking is vital and can be done up to 6 months in advance on 407 939 7600 (or **www.cirquedusoleil.com**). Shows are at 6pm and 9pm Tues–Sat, but try to be early for some excellent pre-show fun. Admission: there are 5 pricing groups, Front & Center at $124 for adults and $91 for 3–9s; Cat 1, $109 and $87; Cat 2, $87 and $70; Cat 3, $71 and $57; and Cat 4, at just $57 (but there is hardly a bad seat in the house).

Disney's BoardWalk

Disney's other big evening entertainment offering is part of its impressive *Disney's BoardWalk Resort*, where the waterfront entertainment district contains several notable venues (not counting the excellent micro-brewery and restaurant of the Big River Grille and Brewing Works, the thrilling ESPN Club for sports fans and 5-star Flying Fish Café). **Jellyrolls** is a variation on the duelling piano bar, with the lively pianists conjuring up a humorous and often raucous evening of audience participation (7pm–2am; $10 cover charge; 21 and over only). The **Atlantic Dance** club features mainly modern dance music with both house and guest DJs, plus occasional live music, all with a huge dance floor and a great bar service and ambience. It's especially popular on Fri and Sat nights (9pm–2am; closed Sun and Mon). It's strictly 21 and over, so bring your ID (no ID, no entry, no exceptions). The Boardwalk also features some amusing stalls and live entertainers, which add to the carnival atmosphere, while the **ESPN Club** features regular celebrity (American) sports guests.

Disney's Boardwalk

UNIVERSAL'S CITYWALK

As part of the big Universal Orlando development, this 30-acre/12ha spread offers a bustling expanse of restaurants, snack bars, shops, open-air events and nightclubs. It offers a huge variety of cuisines, from fast food to fine dining, an unusual blend of speciality shops and an eclectic nightclub mix, from reggae and rock 'n' roll to salsa, jazz and high-energy disco, plus the superb Blue Man Group show and a karaoke theatre/bar. There's a $7 entry fee at the 6 clubs but you can buy a **CityWalk Party Pass** ($11.99) or **Party Pass with Movie** (1 free film at the 20-screen **Universal Cineplex**; $15.00) for entry to all of them, while most multi-day tickets include a Party Pass. The area splits into 3, the Main Plaza (shopping and dining), Lagoon Front (dining, live music and theatre) and the Promenade (dining and nightclubs).

BRITTIP
Park in Universal's multi-storey car park for all CityWalk venues – only $3 after 6pm. For more info, call 407 363 8000 or visit **www.citywalkorlando.com**.

Main plaza

Shopping: Among the most original of the 10 shops are **Endangered Species**, with products designed to raise eco-awareness; **Quiet Flight**, for radical surf and beachwear; the retro-American decor of **Fossil** for leather goods, watches and sunglasses; **Fresh Produce** for swimwear, casual clothing and accessories; **Cigarz**, for cigars, accessories and a full bar; the large **Island Clothing Store** for Tommy Bahama clothing and merchandise; **Katie's Candy Company** sweet shop, **Hart & Huntington Orlando Tattoo Shop** with an array of permanent tattoos, as well as clothing and accessories, the skate-boarding chic of **Element**, and the huge **Universal Studios Store** for souvenirs.

Restaurants: Take your pick from a wide dining choice. **Bubba Gump's Shrimp Co.** has a full *Forrest Gump* theme, from the Southern-inspired menu to the decor and the little flip-sign on your table to tell your server whether you need something (Stop Forrest Stop!). The menu is heavy on seafood but also includes chicken, sandwiches, ribs, salads and more, with catchy names like Bubba's After the Storm 'Bucket of Boat Trash'. The gift shop carries Shrimp beanies, Gump Gear clothing, lots of miscellanea and, of course, A Box of Chocolates. Open 11am–12am.

BRITTIP
Mention you are celebrating a birthday at Bubba Gump's and you'll find you quickly become the centre of attention!

Emeril's: This is a sophisticated and vibrant, 5-star journey into the cuisine of New Orleans with master chef Emeril Lagasse. Fine wines and a cigar bar enhance Emeril's Creole-based gourmet creations, and if you don't try the Louisiana oyster stew you'll have missed a real treat (lunch 11.30am–3pm; dinner 5–10pm Sun–Thurs, 5–10.30pm Fri and Sat). It books up well in advance at weekends, so try for a weekday (407 224 2424, **www.emerils.com**).

Jimmy Buffet's Margaritaville: An island homage to Florida's laid-back musical hero, with 'Floribbean' cuisine (a mix of Key West and Caribbean), live music and 3 bars (11.30am–2am), with the Volcano Bar, which 'erupts' margarita mix (!) when the blender needs filling. There is a cover charge ($7) starting at 10pm, when the live band hits the stage.

Emeril's

© OCVB

NASCAR Sports Grill: A must for motor-racing fans (11am–midnight), with full-size stock cars and racing memorabilia, tableside plasma screens, videos and interactive games while you dine on burgers, steaks, ribs, pasta and grilled shrimp. The interior has a smart, sophisticated look, with a balcony and patio seating for a taste of the 'Tailgating' experience (the American 'picnic in the car park' phenomenon).

Pastamore: A delightful indoor/outdoor Italian diner, with the choice of full-service dining (5pm–10pm) for pizza, pasta, grilled chicken and steaks, or try the counter-service Marketplace Café for breakfast (pizza, egg dishes, pastries to 11am), pastries and snacks.

BRITTIP

The Kids Buffet at **Pastamore** is $9.95/child for their 10-item spread. No children? Try the Chef's Table for a special dining experience, seating up to 6 (book at least 2 days in advance, 407 224 3663).

Lagoon front

Blue Man Group: The most entertaining element here at the Sharp AQUOS Theatre offers a unique brand of comedy, music and multi-media theatrics, adding something completely novel to the Universal line-up. In the hands (or mouths!) of the Blue Men, mundane items like pipes, paintballs, cereal and even

NBA City

audience members become the instruments of wild creativity with sometimes stunning, occasionally slightly gross but always hilariously gratifying outcomes. There is a strong live music element and it can feel like a rock concert. Their ability to drum up a tune on various bits and pieces is truly amazing. The wild finale, involving the whole theatre, is a real corker, and don't worry if you're seated in the 'poncho section'; the Blue Men will make sure you have adequate protection. It all adds up to an unforgettable evening of family entertainment starting at $64 adults, $25 3–9s. Tickets are available at **www.universalorlando.com** or from the theatre box office.

Hard Rock Café and Hard Rock Live: The largest example of this worldwide chain, with its collection of rock 'n' roll memorabilia (including a pink 1959 Cadillac) and full concert venue is hugely popular, so try to get in early for lunch or dinner (11am–midnight). You'll also find prices in the gift shop friendlier than in the UK. **Hard Rock Live** is the massive mock-Coliseum styled 2,500-seat theatre with high-tech staging and sound. Big-name bands and performers are on stage several times a week (Earth, Wind and Fire, Jeff Beck, Kylie Minogue and ZZ Top all appeared in 2011) in this slightly retro rock 'n' roll venue (407 351 7625, **www.hardrock.com**).

NBA City: Across the CityWalk waterway is the 2-storey Lagoon Front location of NBA City, another huge dining experience that is sure to thrill basketball fans with its Cage dining room, interactive playground area and Club lounge where you can watch live and classic games (11am–10.30pm Sun–Thurs; 11am–11.30pm Fri and Sat).

BRITTIP

CityWalk too crowded? Can't get in any of the restaurants? Jump on one of the boats to the Hard Rock Hotel or Portofino Bay Hotel and you can usually dine without a wait at The Kitchen (Hard Rock), Trattoria del Porto or Mama Della's (Portofino Bay).

Promenade

The Promenade area offers a choice of nightclubs and more fine dining, plus the ubiquitous **Starbucks** and a **Fat Tuesday** bar for frozen drinks and New Orleans-inspired cocktails.

Bob Marley – A Tribute to Freedom: A clever re-creation of Marley's Jamaica home is turned into a courtyard live music venue, restaurant and bars. The bands are excellent, the atmosphere authentic and the place comes alive at night (dining 4pm–10pm Sun-Thurs, 4pm-11pm Fri-Sat; bar open until 2am, 21 and over only after 9pm; cover charge $7 after 9pm).

Latin Quarter: South America is the vibe for this wonderful venue/restaurant that serves up vibrant music, dance, decor and outstanding cuisine – a combination of beef, fresh fish and poultry with spicy salsas and mouth-watering marinades (open 5–10pm). A new upscale Brazilian churrascaria upstairs added even more delight in 2011, with fresh-carved meats, plus there's an Express window if you'd like a bite on the go.

Pat O'Brien's: This is a reproduction of the famous New Orleans bar and restaurant (4pm–2am), with its Flaming Fountain courtyard, main bar and duelling piano bar (5pm–2am, with a $7 cover charge after 9pm; 21 and over only). Excellent Cajun food and world-famous Hurricane cocktails!

Rising Star Karaoke: It's karaoke taken to the next level, with a live band, back-up singers and a host who makes every volunteer singer feel like the latest star. There is also a full bar with speciality cocktails, appetisers and a large selection of songs (21 and over; 18 and over on Thurs only; 8pm–2am nightly; $7 cover charge, no additional charge to sing). Tues–Sat live band, back-up singers and host; back-up singers and host only on Sun and Mon.

Red Coconut Club: This retro dance club has a trendy, tropical vibe. With live music, signature cocktails, tapas-style menu and eclectic South Seas décor, it is a popular venue (8pm–2am Sun–Thurs; 6pm–2am Fri and Sat; cover charge $7, free admission for ladies on Thurs; 21 and over only). DJ daily, live music Thurs–Sat.

The Groove: For club-minded visitors this is a high-tech dance venue designed like a Victorian theatre but with the latest in club music, lighting and special effects (9pm–2am; 21 and over only; cover charge $7; attire casual chic, no hats, no tank-tops). Teen Nights periodically, check **www. universalorlando.com** for dates.

Not breathless yet? Well, there's still the 20-screen **Universal Cineplex** with a capacity of 5,000 and the latest in movie comfort. There's also a Meal & Movie Deal for a film and dinner at one of the 8 restaurants for $21.95.

Hard Rock Café

POINTE ORLANDO

This eye-catching development on I-Drive, almost opposite the Convention Center, is a mix of shops, cinema, restaurants, live entertainment and the **WonderWorks** fun centre (with its magic-themed dinner show). The Pointe is open all day but has notable evening appeal. The shops (12pm–10pm Mon–Sat, 12pm–8pm Sun) are all upscale and include some imaginative touches (p343–4). Here is the full choice of night-time entertainment.

Adobe Gila's: On the upper level, you have a fine Mexican cantina, home of the 64oz margarita and more than 70 tequilas (!), plus some south-of-the-border dining delicacies like the signature Gila Wraps. Especially popular with locals and often packed at weekends, it stays open late and features live outdoor music and DJs several days a week. On Fri and Sat the place should be kicking from 6.30pm: on weekdays, it's likely to be 8.30pm (407 903 1477; **www.adobegilas.com**).

Capital Grille

BB King's Blues Club: Live jazz and blues make this a fine choice for a meal or drinks and a show in this imaginative venue, featuring a main 2-storey concert hall, a variety of bars, an open-air terrace and a gift shop. If what you want is a real party, BB King's takes some beating. A Southern comfort-food menu features items such as Fried Shrimp Po Boy and (Simon's favourite) Southern Fried Catfish, and there's a full bar. There is live music nightly from 7pm with one of its 2 excellent house bands, plus guests (407 370 4550, **www.bbkingclubs. com**).

Capital Grille: An elegant dining option, with an extensive wine menu, chops, dry-aged steaks, plus seafood and complimentary valet parking (407 370 4392, **www.thecapitalgrille. com**).

Cuba Libre: This bar/club/restaurant adds a touch of 1940s Havana, with Latin floorshows, salsa dancing – and some wicked cocktails! The energetic tropical open-air atmosphere lends itself to the party spirit, with the architecture, music and art to match. It serves Latin-inspired cuisine,

BB King's Blues Club

combining beef, pork, seafood and chicken with exotic fruits, vegetables, herbs and seasonings (5pm–11pm daily, bar open until 2am weekends; 407 226 1600, **www.cubalibrerestaurant. com**).

Funky Monkey: The menu is Asian-American fusion, featuring locally grown organic beef, fresh seafoods, and hand-rolled sushi, but the big highlight is their extensive wine list (lunch 12pm–4pm; dinner 5pm–11pm Mon-Sat, 5pm–midnight Fri and Sat; 407 351 5815, **www. funkymonkeywine.com**).

Hooters: The local party place, with its famous 'Hooter Girl' waitresses and 'soon to be relatively famous' wings, burgers and seafood; **Johnny Rockets** provides a 1950s diner-style, with a burger-and-milkshake menu; **Maggiano's Little Italy** is a journey into family-style Italian dining in a relaxed, friendly atmosphere; the **Oceanaire Seafood Room** offers a classic 1930s ocean liner vibe and a heavenly range of fresh fish and shellfish, ideal for a special night out; **Taverna Opa** is a chance to go Greek and enjoy some lively taverna society, where impromptu table dancing may erupt all around you with paper napkins thrown at all and sundry (cheaper than breaking plates!); and **Tommy Bahama's Tropical Café**, a laid-back Island setting for an impressive array of food, wine and cocktails, for lunch and dinner (plus a huge emporium of home furnishings, accessories and clothing).

Orlando Improv Comedy Club and Fat Fish Blue: New at the Pointe, the Improv pulls in top name comedians from across the country, with shows ranging from mildly risqué to downright raucous. The theatre is intimate, making it easy for entertainers to interact with guests (often with hilarious results!) and it is a terrific change of pace for a grown-up night out. Seating is first-come, first-seated, full food and drinks menu available, all shows 21 and over. No shows on Tues. Connected to the Improv is the bistro-style **Fat Fish Blue**, featuring American fare

with a New Orleans accent. Full bar, a good range of speciality beers, and live music 5 nights per week. All ages welcome (407 480 5233, **www. theimprovorlando.com**).

The POINTE Performing Arts Center: Off-Broadway plays and musicals are the highlights here, with new shows monthly. Past shows include Xanadu, Blithe Spirit and Equus. Also featured are family oriented and Young Audience performances geared toward children ages 3–10 (for current shows, 407 374 3587, **http:// fantasylandtheatrical.com**.

Also here is the **Regal Cinema**, a 21-screen movieplex (1 an IMAX) with a vast and cleverly themed foyer, state-of-the-art stadium seating and sound systems, where you can often see a new film several months before it arrives in the UK. Look for the ticket office on the ground level (407 248 9228). For more on Pointe Orlando, 407 248 2838, **www.pointeorlando.com**. For more on the restaurant choices, see p319.

DINNER SHOWS

Another source of evening entertainment comes in the many dinner shows that are a major Orlando phenomenon. From murder mysteries to full-scale medieval battles, it's all wonderful, imaginative fun, even if the food is usually quite ordinary. As the name suggests, it is live entertainment coupled with dinner and free wine, beer and soft

Disney's Spirit of Aloha

Hoop-Dee-Doo Musical Revue

drinks in a fantasy-type environment, where even the waiters and waitresses are in costume. They have strong family appeal and you are usually seated at large tables where you get to know other people, too, but, at $35–60, they are not cheap (especially with taxes and tips). Be aware, too, of the attempts to extract more dollars from you with photos, souvenirs, upgrades, etc.

BRITTIP

American cinema popcorn is invariably SALTED! Sweet popcorn in the US is usually called Kettle Corn.

Disney shows

Walt Disney World's offerings are often overlooked by visitors unless they are staying at one of the hotel resorts, but they are certainly worth considering.

Disney's Spirit of Aloha: For an excellent night of South Seas entertainment, go to Luau Cove at *Disney's Polynesian Resort*. It's a bit expensive – $65.99 for adults (Category 1 main floor centre seating) and $33.99 for under-10s; or Cat 2 upper floor and sides $60.99 and $29.99; Cat 3 extreme sides $56.99 and $28.99 – but good value as the

2hr show features some splendid entertainment, such as Hawaiian singers and dancers, and an amazing Samoan fire juggler. The food is plentiful, with salad, roast chicken, ribs, salad, vegetables, pineapple, and rice, plus a chocolate mousse Volcano Dessert (limited kid-friendly menu). Beer, wine and soft drinks are included, and shows are at 5.15 and 8pm Tues–Sat. Make reservations up to 180 days in advance, with full payment when booking.

Hoop-Dee-Doo Musical Revue: At *Disney's Fort Wilderness Resort & Campground*, this is a popular nightly dinner show that maintains the resort's Western theme, and has great food (all-you-can-eat ribs, fried chicken, seasonal vegetable, baked beans, corn bread and strawberry shortcake, plus unlimited beer, wine, sangria and soft drinks). Especially loved by children, it features the amusing song and dance of the Pioneer Hall Players in a merry American hoedown. Okay, it's corny, but it is performed with great gusto! The Revue plays nightly at 5, 7.15 and 9.30pm at the Pioneer Hall, Category 1 seating (main floor centre) is $61.99 for adults, $31.99 for under-10s; Cat 2 (back and balcony) $56.99 and $27.99; Cat 3 (side balconies) $52.00 and

$26.99 (under-3s free; Cat 3 pricing is seasonal; all prices include tax and gratuity) and the show lasts almost 2 hours. Reservations are ALWAYS necessary and can be made up to 180 days in advance (full payment at booking).

Mickey's Backyard Barbecue: If you can't get enough of the Disney characters, try this twice-weekly dinner show, usually Thurs and Sat, Mar–Dec at 6.30pm and 8pm, at *Disney's Fort Wilderness* resort. It features Mickey and the gang in a country buffet-style dinner at picnic tables under an open-air pavilion with live music, line dancing, rope tricks and other entertainment, and plenty of character interaction (great for younger children). The all-you-can-eat buffet offers barbecued pork ribs, baked chicken, hot dogs, hamburgers, watermelon and more. Like all Disney dining, this is a no-smoking environment. The show may be cancelled if bad weather threatens ($44.99 adults, $26.99 3–9s). To book a Disney show, call 407 939 3463.

Electrical Water Pageant: An alternative is the nightly (and free!) pageant that circles Bay Lake and the Seven Seas Lagoon, passing by each of the **Magic Kingdom** resorts in turn. It lasts just 10 minutes, but it's almost a waterborne version of the Main Street Electrical parade, with thousands of twinkling lights on a floating cavalcade of boats and mock sea creatures. The usual schedule is 9pm at *Disney's Polynesian Resort*, 9.15 at *Disney's Grand Floridian*

Resort & Spa (get a grandstand view in Narcoosee's restaurant), 9.35 at *Disney's Wilderness Lodge*, 9.45 on the shores of *Disney's Fort Wilderness Resort* and 10.05pm at *Disney's Contemporary Resort*. It can also be seen from outside the *Magic Kingdom*.

> **BRITTIP**
> Most dinner shows can be quite chilly, especially those with animals, such as Arabian Nights and Medieval Times, so bring a jacket or sweater to beat the air-conditioning.

Arabian Nights

This lovingly maintained, family-owned attraction, now in its 24th year, is a large-scale production and one of the most popular with locals as well as tourists. And you don't need to be an equestrian expert to appreciate the spectacular stunts, horsemanship and marvellous costumes as some 70 horses perform a 20-act show. The show is staged in the huge arena at the centre of this 1,200-seat 'palace'. Daring gypsy acrobats, magical genies, square-dancing cowboys, exotic Latin Garrocha riding and a thrilling chariot race all add up to a memorable show that kids, especially, adore. A special **Christmas Holiday Show** takes over for the winter season (Nov–Jan), and there is also some impressive pre-show entertainment, featuring magician Michael Baron. The food is above average too, with a choice of sirloin steak, Black Angus chopped steak with gravy, pork

Arabian Nights

© OCVB

tenderloin with Marsala sauce, grilled chicken breast with steakhouse mashed potatoes, plus salad, seasonal vegetables, and choice of Oreo fudge brownie or cheesecake. A veggie lasagne is also available and children have the option of chicken tenders with macaroni and cheese. Hot tea on request. Located ½ml/1km east of I-4 on Highway 192 (on the left, just to the side of the Parkway shopping plaza, at marker 8), Arabian Nights runs every evening at 6 or 8.30pm (often both), with occasional matinees. It lasts almost 2hrs (and includes a preshow with belly dancer, henna tattoos, caricature artist and children's games) and you can buy tickets ($49 adults, $31 3–11s; VIP experience $15 extra adults, $12 extra child; Backstage tour $20 extra per person; Horse Lover Package $40 extra per person) at the box office 8am–10pm or by credit card on 407 239 9223, **www.arabian-nights.com**.

Medieval Times

Spain in the 11th century is the entertaining setting for this 2hr extravaganza of medieval pageantry, sorcery and robust horseback jousts that culminate in furious hand-to-hand combat between 6 knights. It's worth arriving early to appreciate the clever mock castle design and the staff's costumes as you are ushered into the pre-show hall before being taken into the arena. The Knights of the Realm show features fast-paced skills tests, all set to a dramatic musical score by the Prague Symphony Orchestra. The weapons are all real and used with great skill, and there are some neat special effects. You need to be in full audience participation mode

as you cheer on your knight and boo the others, but kids (and adults) get a huge kick out of it and they'll also love eating without cutlery (the soup bowls have handles!). The elaborate staging is backed up by an excellent chicken dinner and the serfs and wenches who serve you make it a fun experience. Prices, which include the **Medieval Life** exhibit (see below), are $59.95 for adults and $35.95 for 3–12s. A basic Royalty Package upgrade for $10/person includes preferred seating, knight's cheering banner, commemorative programme and behind-the-scenes souvenir DVD. The King's Royalty Package adds VIP first-row seating all sections or second row in the centre seating area ($20) and the Celebration Package adds the framed group photo and a slice of cake ($16 more). Doors open 90mins prior to showtime. Times vary seasonally, so call 1866 543 9637 or visit **www.medieval times.com** for reservations and details. The recently renovated Castle is on Highway 192, 5mls/8km east of the junction with I-4. If you have 45mins to spare before the show, the **Medieval Life** exhibit is an interesting diversion. This mock village portrays the life and times of 900 years ago (with some gruesome dungeon and torture chamber scenes not for young children!). Stay on after the show (the 2nd show only on busy nights) for **The Knight Club**, with bar service, music, dancing and the chance to meet royalty and knights for autographs and photos.

Pirates' Dinner Adventure

This show (revamped in 2011) features one of the most spectacular settings, with a life-size pirate ship 'anchored' in a huge indoor lagoon. It also delivers good value with its pre-show elements, plentiful food and drink, and after-show Buccaneer Bash disco. Coffee is served at the Buccaneer Bash and a kids' choice (chicken fingers or vegetarian) if the hearty main meal of pork and chicken with rice and roasted potatoes doesn't appeal. The all-new story sees the

Pirates' Dinner Adventure

Curse of Poseidon's Treasure invoked in historical style by the Treasure Bay Archaeological Society, landing the audience a close encounter with the mythical *Emerald Shark* and her feuding pirate crew. That is the cue for much swashbuckling and derring-do, with the audience divided into 6 sections and encouraged to cheer 'their' pirate through various challenges, swordfights and noisy mayhem. Comedy, acrobatics, trapeze acts and songs keep the action energetic, fast-paced and eye-catching, even if the story is a bit hard to follow at times. Highly family friendly and a big hit with kids ($61.95 adults, $41.95 3–11s; see website for savings).

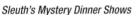

BRITTIP

When there are 2 or more shows of The Pirate's Dinner Adventure in 1 night, opt for the last 1 if you want the disco bash afterwards.

There is a **Governor's VIP Upgrade** ($25; available in advance or at the ticket window) with an exclusive pre-show lounge, restroom and bar, front-row seating, guaranteed audience participation, special appetiser buffet, champagne toast, opportunity to upgrade dinner fare to Filet Mignon or Lobster Tail (add $14.99), and chicken breast instead of leg; or a **Captain's Upgrade**, with enhanced seating ($15; row 2 and 3), and pirate hat and beads. It is located on Carrier Drive between I-Drive and Universal Boulevard, and runs at 6pm, 7.30pm or 8.30pm, with appetisers served for 45mins prior to seating (407 248 0590, **www.piratesdinneradventure.com**). There is a $3 fee for parking but also a special **Pirates Christmas Dinner Adventure** show, that adds suitably festive themes.

Sleuth's Mystery Dinner Shows

This is a real live version of Cluedo acted out before your eyes in hilarious fashion while you enjoy a substantial meal (with a main course choice of honey-glazed Cornish hen, prime rib or lasagne with or without meatballs) and unlimited beer, wine and soft drinks. You can choose between 3 theatres and no fewer than 14 different plot situations (several of which have amusing British settings), including Joshua's Demise, Roast 'Em

Sleuth's Mystery Dinner Shows

Outta Control Magic Comedy

& Toast 'Em and Lord Mansfield's Fox Hunt Banquet (mayhem at an English banquet), that add up to some elaborate murder mysteries. The action takes place all around you and members of the audience can take some cameo roles. The quick-witted cast keep things moving and keep you guessing during the theatrical part

Al Capone's

of the 2½-hour show, then during the main part of dinner you think up questions for interrogation (but the real murderer is allowed to lie!). Solve the crime and you win a prize, but that is pretty secondary to the overall enjoyment and this is a show we enjoy a lot, plus it's a terrific choice with teens ($53.95 adults, $23.95 3–11s; times vary; 407 363 1985, **www.sleuths.com**). Also check out their periodic **Stand Up Comedy Spotlight** (see website for dates, times, and comedians). Sleuth's is in the plaza just past Ripley's Believe It Or Not on I-Drive, with 3 different theatres, a smart pre-dinner bar area and gift shop.

WonderWorks: Outta Control Magic Comedy

On a smaller scale but no less fun, this dinner show is at WonderWorks on I-Drive (on one corner of Pointe Orlando). A novel mixture of improvised comedy and magic, the show is accompanied by all-you-can-eat pizza, salad, popcorn and dessert, plus beer, wine and coke. Set in the intimate Shazam Theater, it features live music, special lighting effects and some slick magic tricks from illusionist (and funny guy!) Tony Brent. The tricks are routine, but the show is served up in terrific style and involves plenty of audience participation. Beware of sitting too close to the stage – you WILL end up as part of the act! Twice nightly at 6pm and 8pm, it costs $24.95 adults, $16.95 4–12s and seniors. A Magic Combo ticket for the show and access to WonderWorks afterwards (open until midnight, p230) is $38.95/$28.95 (407 351 8800, **www.wonderworksonline. com**).

Capone's Dinner & Show

The setting is 1930s gangland Chicago and, although prohibition is still in full swing, the drinks flow freely at Al's speakeasy. Enter Capone's comedy show and you enter a mixed-up world of song-and-dance acts loosely fitted around the nefarious dealings of local gangster 'Bugs' Moran and ditzy Bunny-June and her new husband, Fingers Salvatorio. The snappy one-liners keep coming and the servers join in at key moments to ensure the momentum never lags. Although it leans slightly toward the risqué, the show still remains in family-friendly territory. A huge Italian-American

buffet offers 3 types of pasta, ham, turkey, pot roast and side dishes. Unlimited Bud Light, a selection of wines and cocktails, plus soft drinks, juice, Kiddie Cocktails and Mama Capone's 'dessert surprise' round out the all-you-can-eat-and-drink menu ($54 adults, $34, 4–12s, 3 and under free; 407 397 2378, **www.alcapones. com**; see the website for money-off coupons).

Live music

Orlando's live music scene is always lively and always changing but several venues can be relied on for quality entertainment. As already noted, the House of Blues and Hard Rock Live provide regular big-name concerts, while international acts appear at the state-of-the-art **Amway Center** in downtown (as well as the Orlando Magic and Orlando Predators sports teams), including Lady Gaga and Bon Jovi in 2011 (**www.amwaycenter.com**). On a smaller scale but just as engaging, **The Social** is downtown's premier venue for up-and-coming live music, with a wide range of bands and great bar vibe (on Orange Avenue). Look up the latest info at **www.thesocial.org** (or call 407 246 1419).

Downtown Disney

© Disney

Sports bars

The Sports Bar is a particularly American invention and is well served hereabouts if you'd like to sample the way the locals follow their sport (American football is usually the biggest at weekends Sept–Jan, but basketball is also popular, along with baseball and ice-hockey). Among the multitude of sports bars are our favourites, the **Orlando Ale House** group, with a fine example on Kirkman Road, opposite Universal Studios (407 248 0000) at Lake Buena Vista on Highway 535 near *Downtown Disney* (407 239 1800), and the newest location, Miller's Ale House on I-Drive (407 370 6688). The Ale Houses feature more than 30 TVs (each!), classic American bar food, including their signature spicy 'chicken zingers' and an above-average range of beers (**www.millersalehouse.com**).

Another chain worth noting is **Buffalo Wild Wings**, with 3 Orlando locations (notably on I-Drive just south of Wet 'n Wild, 11am–2am daily, 407 351 6200 and Lake Buena Vista near Downtown Disney, 11am-2am, 407 827 0444), where masses of chicken-orientated dishes (watch out for the Blazin' sauce – it's seriously hot!) are served up in a casual, lively atmosphere, highlighted by its Buzztime Trivia System at each table and multiple big-screen TVs (**www.buffalowildwings.com**).

Disney boasts the excellent **ESPN Club** at *Disney's BoardWalk Resort*, a full-service restaurant with sports broadcast facilities, video games, more than 70 TV monitors, giant scoreboards and even a Little League menu for kids. Universal CityWalk boasts the **NBA City** (for basketball fans) and **NASCAR Sports Grille** (for motor-racing followers), with more big-screen TV style. The various British-style pubs also offer sports bar style. Try the **Cricketers' Arms**, formerly in Festival Bay, now in the Dellagio plaza on Sand Lake Drive (**www.cricketersarmspub.com**), **Orlando George & Dragon** on International Drive next to Wet 'n Wild (**www. britanniapubs.com**), the football-focused **Best of British Pub**, also on I-Drive (**www.bestofbritishpub.com**) and the **Shamrock Pub & Grille** (**www. theshamrockpub.net**) on Highway 27 in Davenport (See more on these 'home-from-home' pubs p314).

Put a Cork in It

Ice Bar

Something different

Icebar: Spend 45 minutes surrounded by 50 tons of carved ice while sipping a chilled vodka beverage, then warm up in the Nordic-inspired Fire Lounge, at Orlando's ICEBAR on I-Drive just north of WonderWorks. Ponchos and gloves are provided (wear a warm shirt as the ponchos don't cover your arms), and entry fee is $19.95 (drinks not included; save $5 by booking online). Open 7pm–midnight, with the first ICEBAR entry time at 7:15pm; ages 8 and up allowed 7:15pm and 8pm time slots only. No cover charge for Fire Lounge, but no children (407 426 7555 or **www. icebarorlando.com**).

BRITBONUS

Pay for entry to the **Icebar** and receive a FREE pint in the Fire Lounge afterwards. Just show your copy of the *Brit Guide* for the free drink.

Howl at the Moon: If you're looking for a serious party, try Howl at the Moon on I-Drive, where the live music doesn't stop until the wee hours! An energetic piano-playing duo pound out a rockin' good time, highlighted by 'Showtime', when the whole bar joins in a choreographed dance-fest. Signature cocktails are available by the glass or the bucket (!), with drink specials nightly (21 and over only; 7pm–2am Sun–Thurs, 6pm–2am Fri, 6pm–2am Sat; $10 cover charge, free Sun; cover charge after 8pm Mon-Thurs; 5pm Fri, 6pm Sat; 407 352 5999, **www.howlatthemoon. com**).

Put A Cork In It: Not so much a live venue, as a relaxed place to enjoy a glass of wine or beer. They have great all-day wine-tasting sessions, wine classes, private tasting parties and wonderful themed wine dinners in partnership with some of the excellent local restaurants. Located in the Rialto plaza on Sand Lake Road (next to the Ocean Prime and JR Alexander's), they mix cabaret, comedy, jazz and open-mic nights. British owners Alan and Gwen offer both a wine store (by day) and wine bar by night, also serving micro-brew beers, sodas, coffees, cheese platters and tapas, with 'room service' delivery from Alexander's and Ocean Prime. A place to kick back and relax with friends, old and new, and try a few new wines from their trendy Enomatic serving system (open from mid-day until late; 407 351 8400).

BRITBONUS

Buy 1 glass of House Wine at **Put A Cork In It** and get a second free by showing your copy of the *Brit Guide*. Offer limited to 1 per customer per visit and valid until 31 Dec 2012.

Now you'll want to know a lot more about where, when and how to tackle that other holiday dilemma – where to eat. Read on…

Dining Out

or Man, These Portions are HUGE!

The options for dining out are omnipresent and large scale, which is excellent news as it means it's impossible to go hungry and easy to feed the family – without breaking the bank.

Variety

The variety, quantity and quality of restaurants, cafés, fast-food chains and snack bars is in keeping with the local tradition of convenience and value.

As a rule, food is plentiful, relatively cheap, available 24 hours a day, and nearly always appetising and filling. You will encounter an increasing number of fine-dining possibilities, but the basic emphasis is on value. Portions are large, service is efficient and friendly, and it's hard to come by a bad meal. The 1 real exception is if you dine mainly at fast food places and the likes of Dennys and Co, you won't find much fresh veg. But if you look up the vegetarian options, visit outlets like Sweet Tomatoes and ask for the vegetable option instead of fries or potatoes at other restaurants, you will find a more balanced choice. Plus salads are almost always on the menu.

Exceptional deals

Most restaurants tend towards the informal (T-shirts and shorts are nearly always acceptable) and cater readily for families; you will always find a kids' menu, and many have activity packs. Many hotels and restaurants offer Kids-eat-free deals (from under-10 to under-14), provided parents are also dining. The age limits vary. The all-you-can-eat buffet is another common feature, where you can probably eat enough at breakfast to keep you going to dinner! Some places offer early-bird specials – a discount to dine before 6pm. Be aware that 5.30–7.30pm is peak time for many restaurants, though, and you may have to wait for a table if you arrive between 6 and 8pm.

BRITTIP

Portions are often so large, you can save money by sharing a main course. Your waiter or waitress should be happy to oblige (if you keep their tip up to the full rate).

Don't be afraid to ask for the leftovers 'to go' and don't hesitate to say if something isn't right; the locals will readily complain (politely) if they are not happy, so restaurants are keen to ensure everything is to their diners' satisfaction. And, please, don't forget to tip; the basic wage for waiters and waitresses is low, so they rely heavily on tips as part of their income and are taxed on an assumed level of tips. Unless service really is shoddy (in which case mention it), the usual tip rate is 10% of your bill at buffet-style restaurants and 15% at full-service restaurants. Check whether service is already added to your bill, though this is not common.

You will encounter a huge array of food types. Florida is renowned for its seafood, which comes much cheaper than in the Mediterranean: crab, lobster, shrimp (what we call king prawns), clams and oysters, as well as several dozen varieties of fish, many unusual (like mahi mahi and grouper). Latin-style cuisines, notably Cuban and Mexican, are common, and the South American influences mean the delicious citrus-marinated seafood called ceviche is often featured. There is also plenty of Asian fare, from Chinese and Indian to Japanese, Thai and Vietnamese. The big shopping malls all offer good food courts, which are often particularly good value. 'Cracker' cooking is original Floridian fare, and the speciality is alligator, either stewed, barbecued, smoked, sautéed or braised. Fried gator tail 'nuggets' are a local favourite, as are catfish and frogs' legs. And you must try key lime pie!

How to order

Ordering food can be an adventure in itself. The choice for each item is often the cue for an inquisition! You can never order just 'toast' – it has to be white, brown, whole wheat, rye, muffin or bagel; eggs come in a baffling variety (order them 'sunny side up' for a traditional British fried egg; 'over easy' is fried both sides but still soft); an order of tea or coffee often brings the response 'Iced, lemon, green, herbal or English? Regular or decaf?'; and salads have more dressings than the NHS. Ask to see a menu if what you fancy isn't displayed.

BRITTIP
An excellent section of the All Ears Net website run by Deb Wills lists places that cater for special diets, including veggie, at **www.allearsnet.com/din/special.htm**.

Vegetarian options

In a country where beef is king, vegetarians often find themselves hard done by. However, there are some bright spots. First, there are several largely veggie restaurants, like the Indian cuisine of **Woodlands** on S Orange Blossom Trail (407 854 3330, **www.woodlandsusa.com**), the popular Chinese of the **Garden Café** on Highway 50 (407 999 9799, **www.gardencafevege.com**), **Black Bean Deli** on S Orlando Ave in Winter Park (try its tamales platter; 406 628 0294, **www.blackbeandeli.com**) and the trendy **Ethos Vegan Kitchen** on N Orange Ave, just north of downtown (407 228 3898, **www.ethosvegankitchen.com**). The tapas-style **Café Tu Tu Tango** on I-Drive also serves a good variety of veggie dishes. However, most upmarket restaurants can offer a vegetarian option and will be happy for you to ask in advance. In *Walt Disney World*, the **California Grill** (in *Disney's Contemporary Resort*), **Citricos** (*Grand Floridian Resort and Spa*), **Le Cellier** (Canada pavilion in *Epcot*) and **Jiko** (*Animal Kingdom Lodge*) feature good vegetarian choices, while the seafood-orientated **Flying Fish** (*Disney's Boardwalk*) and **'Ohana** (*Disney's Polynesian Resort*) also serve up decent veggie fare if asked. Two good Mediterranean-style choices are **Anatolia** (p313) and **Cedar's** (p314). Most full-service restaurants (notably **Bongos Cuban Café™** and **Wolfgang Puck® Café** in *Downtown Disney*; p307) and even some counter-service outlets can cater for non-menu requests. It's always worth asking.

BRITTIP
Sweet Tomatoes is a restaurant chain we recommend highly, and you can benefit from its enhanced dinner menu by arriving a little before 4pm but still paying only the lunch buffet price.

However, **Sweet Tomatoes** (with 4 outlets in the area, notably on I-Drive by the Kirkman Road junction and a new location in the Crossroads Plaza at Lake Buena Vista) is notably the most popular vegetarian-friendly regular outlet. A buffet restaurant with some great meal deals, it has an all-you-can-eat lunch for $8.59 ($9.99 at dinner, after 4pm) that includes a vast salad counter, a choice of freshly made soups, pizza, pasta, bread and pastries, plus fruit and frozen yoghurt. The menu as a whole is health conscious and the quality is consistently first class, while its website lists all the nutrition info. Drinks are $2.75 (refills free) and kids' meals are $3.99 3–9s and $4.99 9–12s (11am–10pm, **www.soupplantation. com**). **Chamberlin's Market & Café** (with 6 Orlando outlets, notably in the Dr Phillips Plaza just off Sand Lake Rd) is another enlightened choice, with home-made soups, salads, sandwiches and fruit smoothies (**www.chamberlins.com**). The **Panera Bread** chain also offers some decent veggie options (plus free wi-fi).

BRITTIP

American bacon is always streaky and crisp fried, and sausages are chipolata-like and slightly spicy. Very different from the British versions.

Eating 24/7

It's not unusual to find restaurants open around the clock (or 24/7, as they say). So here is where you can go for a snack or even a full-scale meal at 4 in the morning. **Chain restaurants:** Denny's, Waffle House, Steak & Shake, some McDonald's. Individuals: B-Line Diner (Peabody Hotel, I-Drive), Planet Java (Gaylord Palms Resort), Sundial 24-7 (Regal Sun Resort) and Mainstreet Market (Hilton at Walt Disney World Resort).

Drinking

A big complaint from Brits on holiday in the US is about the beer. With the exception of a handful of English-style pubs and micro-breweries, American big-label brewery beer is generally ice cold lager, bottled or on draught (though smaller scale breweries have a more European flair). It goes down great when it's hot, but is weaker and fizzier than our own. Of course, there are exceptions (try Killian's Red, Michelob's Amber Bock, Leinenkugel's or Sam Adams beers for a fuller flavour), but don't expect a good, old-fashioned British pint. You should also look out for **The**

Big River Grille at *Disney's BoardWalk Resort* and **Orlando Brewing** (on Atlanta Ave, just south of downtown Orlando), an organic micro-brewery with a range of distinctive brews, plus free brewery tours Mon–Sat at 6pm (407 872 1117, **www.orlandobrewing. com**). Spirits (called 'liquor') come in a large selection, but beware of ordering just 'whisky' as you'll get bourbon. Specify if you want Scotch or Irish whiskey and demand it 'straight up' if you don't want it with a mountain of ice. When you order a soft drink from a counter-service outlet, ask for 'no ice' or 'light ice' unless you want a drink with 50% ice.

If you fancy a cocktail, there is a massive choice and most bars and restaurants have lengthy happy hours with good prices. Good-quality Californian wines are better value than European. If you stick to soft drinks ('sodas') or coffee, most bars and restaurants give free refills. You can also run a tab in the majority of bars and pay when you leave. But be aware US licensing laws are stricter than ours and **you must be 21 to drink alcohol in a bar or lounge**. You'll often be asked for proof of age before you are served (or allowed into a club), so take your passport or photo driving licence. Don't bother to argue – no photo ID, no beer!

Where to eat

That gives you the inside track on HOW to eat and drink like the locals. Now you need to know WHERE. There are 4,000-plus restaurants in the area, so the following selection covers the main ones, grouped by style. You'll find the Fast Food and Family Favourite type in all the main areas. We also indicate a budget:

$ = most main courses under $10
$$ = most main courses $10–15
$$$ = most main courses $15–20
$$$$ = most main courses $20–30
$$$$$ = most main course $30-plus

We also have a special section on each of the three main areas of I-Drive, Highway 192/Kissimmee and Lake Buena Vista. But, as ever, we start with *Walt Disney World.*

Belly up to the bar!

If you'd like just a snack or sample of a restaurant's fare, many places offer a bar or appetiser menu, including Capital Grille, Fishbones, Bar Louie, Big Fin Seafood, Bravo, Bonefish Grill, City Fire, Emeril's Tchoup Chop, House of Blues, Morton's, Ravenous Pig, Roy's, Seasons 52, The Oceanaire, McCormick & Schmick's, Luma on Park, Carrabba's, Fulton's Crab House, Fleming's, Samba Room, Old Hickory and Moonfish, plus The Crab House (for its Mon–Fri Happy Hour, 4–7pm), Brio Tuscan Grille (3-7pm Mon–Fri), Landry's Seafood House (4–6.30pm) and The Palm (5–7pm and 9pm–close).

DOWNTOWN DISNEY DINING

While the parks and resorts hold their share of dining delights, the heart of Disney dining can be found at *Downtown Disney* with 17 outlets.

BRITTIP

If there are several of you drinking beer, ordering a pitcher will work out cheaper than buying it by the glass.

Hyperion Wharf/ Pleasure Island

Raglan Road: This Irish-themed pub, with lively music, food to match and a genuine Emerald Isle style, is where you really can enjoy the craic. Much of the restaurant's interior was shipped over from Ireland (including 4 reclaimed 130-year-old bars, plus 9 European beers on draft), establishing an authentic backdrop to an original menu created by celebrity master chef Kevin Dundon. Fresh, simple ingredients with an imaginative twist make the likes of shepherd's pie, mussels, beef stew, Irish sausages and bread pudding a wake-up call for the senses (along with 2 new curries which are our current favourites). Stop in at the gift shop and check out Kevin *Dundon's Full On Irish* cookbook ($$–$$$;11am–2am, 407 938 0300, **www.raglanroadirish pub.com**).

Paradiso 37: This 'Taste of the Americas' offers a wide variety of foods, much with a Latin-tinged flavour, and live music nightly. A tempting menu includes Argentinean skirt steak, Chilean salmon, Mexican fare, plus signature cocktails and tequila. The lively style, split-level restaurant, chic bar area (inside and out) and lakeside setting mark this out for a relaxing lunch or upbeat dinner, or just somewhere to kick back with a drink or speciality coffee ($$–$$$$; 11.30am–midnight Sun–Thurs, 1am Fri and Sat; 407 934 3700).

Portobello: Don't overlook this Tuscan-country trattoria on the edge of the Marketplace and Hyperion Wharf. From the fresh bread with oven-baked garlic to the family-style menu and full wine list, there's everything from pizza to zucchini ribbons in a tomato seafood broth. Add a great wine list, speciality beers and seasonal prix fixe menus ($39.95 for a 3-course dinner) completes an impressive picture, with reservations not always necessary. The recent addition of a fun Meatball Bar and new dishes like Biramisu (Tiramisu with a local porter ale!) help to keep everything fresh and inviting, too ($$–$$$$; 11.30am–11pm; 407 934 8888; **www.portobellorestaurant.com**).

Portobello

BRITTIP

For a great lunch at **Portobello**, try the Misti antipasti platter and then 2 of their signature sandwiches (say, Beef Brisket and Meatball Sub). Great value at just $32 for 2. Their Cafe Shakerato (Italian iced coffee) is also a real treat.

Fulton's Crab House: Good seafood is not hard to come by, but great seafood is the preserve of a handful – like Fulton's. This mock riverboat has 6 dining rooms (each with the same menu), plus the Stone Crab Lounge, which features a busy raw bar. The recently refurbished interior is filled with nautical props, photos and lithographs, giving it an eclectic atmosphere, but the real attraction is some of the freshest and most tempting fish, crab and lobster dishes in Florida, including fresh daily specials and a kid's menu. Recent additions are an excellent calamari steak and a pan-roasted mussels pasta. The Stone Crab Lounge serves lunch and dinner 11.30am–11pm, while the restaurant is open for dinner only ($$$–$$$$$; 4–11pm; 407 394 2628; **www.fultonscrabhouse.com**).

BRITTIP

Don't miss the Tollhouse Cookie dessert at **Fulton's Crab House**, as the cookies are all made fresh daily.

T-Rex Cafe: Enter the audio-animatronic world of the people who created the Rainforest Café chain: a vast series of themed areas like the Ice Cave and Jurassic Forest, which are home to all manner of roaring dinos, with meteor strikes and thunderstorms for good measure! The food is straightforward (albeit with

Fulton's Crab House

fancy names like Woolly Mammoth Chicken and Boneyard Buffet) but portions are suitably large ($$–$$$; 11am–11pm, midnight Fri and Sat, 407 828 8739, **www.trexcafe.com**).

Other choices: To one side of Raglan Road is **Cooke's of Dublin**, a chippie serving up real chips, beer-battered fish, gourmet battered sausages and 'Do bars' (deep-fried Snickers bars!). **Fuego Cigars by Sosa** is an upmarket lounge offering premium cigars and wines.

BRITTIP

For reservations at any Disney restaurant, call 407 939 3463 (407 WDW DINE), or book online at **www.disneyworld.co.uk**.

The Marketplace

While The Marketplace is largely the shopping heart of *Downtown Disney* (p338), it also offers tempting dining.

Rainforest Café: With its safari-style 'adventures' under a volcano-topped exterior, this is the place to entertain the family while they fill up on huge platefuls of chicken, pasta, steak, seafood and burgers, surrounded by audio-animatronic animals and periodic 'rainstorms', with an excellent menu for 10s and under ($$–$$$; 11.30am–11pm; 407 827 8500, **www.rainforestcafe.com**).

Cap'n Jack's Restaurant: Head here for great chowder, crab cakes, shrimp and many other fine seafood offerings, as well as its trademark 'fishbowl' margaritas. Open for lunch and dinner, it makes a relaxing choice in a busy area with great lake views ($$–$$$$,11.30am–10pm).

Other choices: Ghirardelli Ice Cream & Chocolate Shop is a great location for dessert or just a milkshake while you wander. The **Earl of Sandwich** is an excellently priced café for a quick bite or a lighter meal, while the **Pollo Campero** is a Latin American chicken-based food court café (a healthier option than the McDonald's that used to be here) and a **Wolfgang Puck Express** for quick-service Californian cuisine.

West Side

Back in the more hip night-time district of *Downtown Disney* are another 5 options.

Planet Hollywood: The largest and busiest of this worldwide chain offers lashings of its film-related fun style, with a widely varied menu (if heavy on American diner fare) and some wonderful cocktails ($$–$$$; 11am–1am; 407 827 7827, **www. planethollywood.com**).

Bongos Cuban Café: Co-owned by Gloria and Emilio Estefan, the sounds and tastes of Old Havana enliven this imaginative setting, with red-hot Latin music and excellent Cuban fare ($$–$$$$, 11am–10.30pm, Sun–Thurs 11.30pm Fri and Sat; 407 828 0999, **www.bongoscubancafe.com**).

House of Blues®: This cavernous combination live music venue and restaurant in backwoods Mississippi style is a must for anyone even vaguely interested in blues, rock 'n' roll, R&B, gospel and jazz – while its trademark Gospel Brunch on Sundays serves up some fab food with a full gospel show (10.30am and 1pm; $33.50 adults, $17.25 3–9s). The big restaurant (11am–11pm) offers some fine fare, including seafood jambalaya, fresh fish and a host of Cajun delicacies, with live music Thurs–Sat ($$–$$$$; 11.30am–11pm, 1am Thurs–Sat; 407 934 2583, **www. houseofblues.com**).

Wolfgang Puck® Café: A rich 4-option experience from the top Californian chef: the Café, gourmet food in a casual setting; Wolfgang Puck Express, the fast-food version; the Sushi Bar for seafood and pizzas; and the Dining Room, an upscale restaurant featuring top international cuisine. It caters for just about every taste (the sushi is to die for) and is highly family friendly ($$–$$$$$; 11.30am–11pm, 6–10.30pm in Dining Room; 407 938 9653, **www.wolfgangpuck.com**).

Other choices: Grab a snack at **Wetzel's Pretzels**, with the choice of pretzels, hot dogs, lemonade and Haagen-Dazs ice-cream.

FAST FOOD

While it's hard to fault Disney's quality, the prices can be tough on the wallet. Thankfully, it is possible to eat a lot cheaper outside *Walt Disney World* and we'll now take a look at the rest of your options, starting with some familiar names. This first section is primarily fast-food outlets, all in the $ category.

The big names: There are around 70 **McDonald's**, from small drive-through types to a mega, 24-hour establishment on Sand Lake Road (near the I-Drive junction) that also has the biggest Play Place for kids of any McDonald's in the world. Look for the Bistro option in some outlets, as this features some genuinely healthy, fresh choices of salads, sandwiches, pizza and wraps. **Burger King** is well represented, as is that other burger bastion, **Wendy's**. **KFC** also has many outlets throughout the area, and you'll find plenty of **Pizza Huts** and **Domino's Pizza**, both of which deliver locally – even to your hotel room.

Local variations

Check out **Checkers** or **Hardees** for burgers, **Popeye's Famous Fried Chicken & Biscuits** or **Chick-fil-A** as a KFC alternative, **Taco Bell** if you'd like the cheap and cheerful Mexican option, or **Arby's** for a range of hot roast beef sandwiches that make a nice change from burgers. **Dairy Queen** offers burgers, hot dogs, pork sandwiches and ice-cream dishes, while **Papa John's**, **Little Caesar's** and **Hungry Howie's** make a decent alternative to Pizza Hut. The 'sub', or torpedo-roll sandwich, is what they serve at **Subway**, **Sobik's**, **Quiznos** and **Miami Subs**. An even better bet is health-conscious **Tijuana Flats**, which started in central Florida and now has more than 70 outlets in the US, notably in Winter Park and Thornton Park. Its Tex-Mex style is geared around fresh, hand-made food in a lively atmosphere. Check out its burritos, quesadillas, enchiladas, tacos and salads – and you'll struggle to spend more than $10/person (**www.tijuanaflats.com**).

The big up-and-coming brand is the award-winning **Five Guys Burgers & Fries**, with a dozen Orlando outlets and also a more healthy approach. Using only fresh-ground beef (never frozen), peanut oil and no trans fats, they serve up just 4 basic burgers (plus Little Burgers), hotdogs and sandwiches, and you can add your own extras from a 16-item toppings bar (**www.fiveguys.com**).

Yes, you *can* find proper chips in the States. They are called 'steak fries', and you will find them in most grocery stores and on some restaurant menus, (notably at Outback Steak House).

FAMILY FAVOURITES

After all the fast food choices, there is a huge selection that specialises in more regular fare, still with an all-American flavour but with greater variety and ultra family friendly. They vary from buffet to fairly sophisticated, and you'll find them in multiple locations.

The breakfast specialists

Need to start the day by stoking up with a big breakfast? Look no further.

Bob Evans: Notable for its friendly, country-style, hearty menus (plus low-carb options) and delicious desserts, it also offers takeaway and country store choice ($; 6 or 7am–10pm; **www.bobevans.com**).

Cracker Barrel: Delightful old country store style, with mountainous breakfasts, well-balanced lunch and dinner menus, Kid's Stuff choices and an old-fashioned charm that belies the usual tourist frenzy ($; 6am–10pm Sun–Thurs, 6am–11pm Fri and Sat; **www.crackerbarrel.com**).

Friendlys: A cheerful diner, with a typical array of American fare, plus delicious ice-cream-based desserts ($; 7am–11pm; **www.friendlys.com**).

Denny's: Another traditional 24hr restaurant, its wide selection makes a traditional bacon-and-egg breakfast seem ordinary and it does an

Drive through

Now we've imported the drive through, we know you drive up to the voice box to give your order, then carry on around the building (don't wait by the voice box!) to pay and receive your food at a side window. A neat variation on this theme is **Sonic**, a modern version of the drive-in diner, where you stay in your car and the 'carhop' comes to take the order. The fare – burgers, hot dogs, wraps, salads and sandwiches – won't win any awards, but the style is fun. Try its I-Drive location just north of Kirkman Rd (7am–11pm; **www.sonicdrivein.com**).

excellent range of toasted sandwiches and dinner meals, like grilled catfish, as well as a Senior Selections menu, with smaller portions for over-55s ($; **www.dennys.com**).

International House of Pancakes (or IHOP) and Waffle House: You will struggle to spend more than $8 on a full meal, whether on 1 of their huge breakfast platters or a hot sandwich with fries. Waffle Houses are open 24hrs a day ($; www.wafflehouse.com) and IHOPs 6am–midnight ($; **www.ihop.com**).

Perkins: Also a great breakfast choice; for a hearty meal try Perkins Eggs Benedict (2 eggs and bacon on a toasted muffin with hash browns and fresh fruit), while its bread-bowl salads are equally satisfying (some branches open around the clock; **www.perkinsrestaurants.com**).

Village Inn: Massively popular with the tourist crowd is this unassuming outlet on Westwood Boulevard, just off I-Drive near SeaWorld. Unpretentious but fab value for breakfast, lunch and dinner, it serves up heaps of basic fare with friendly service, plus some of the most decadent desserts (we dare you to try their Boston Cream, French Silk or Key Lime pies!). Huge breakfast plates (all at around $6.59), great kids' menus and salads, sandwiches and burgers ($–$$; 6am–midnight; **www.villageinn.com**).

Susan's choice

A chain that provides a good balance between tasty and healthy is the **Panera Bread** counter-service option (dine in or takeaway). As well as wonderful pastries and fresh-baked breads, it serves terrific sandwiches, soups and salads, including vegetarian options (7am–10pm; **www.panerabread.com**).

Buffet style

The value of the all-you-can-eat restaurants is much in evidence here.

Ponderosa Steakhouse and **Sizzler:** These 2 popular, identikit, consistent but unspectacular big-chain offerings feature huge breakfast, lunch and dinner buffets. You order and pay as you enter and are then seated, before being unleashed on the help-yourself serveries. You'd be hard pushed to tell whose food was whose, but there IS a difference in price depending on location, with I-Drive tending to be a dollar or 2 dearer. Standard dinner fare includes chicken wings, meatballs, chilli, ribs, steaks (for a small supplement) and seafood, plus immense salad bars ($–$$; 7am–late evening, **www.sizzler.com** and **www.ponderosasteakhouses.com**).

Golden Corral and **Shoney's:** The buffet theme is served rather better by these 2, where you may pay a bit more but the extra quality is undeniable. Golden Corral impresses for its fresh style and Carver's Choice of roast meats plus an excellent vegetable selection and dessert bar (around 20 choices!). There is a weekend supplement at some outlets as they add steak to the main choices ($–$$; 7.30am–10pm; **www.goldencorral.com**). Shoney's has an à la carte menu as well as excellent buffets, all with a Southern accent ($; 7am–11pm; **www.shoneys.com**).

BRITTIP
A buffet breakfast at Golden Corral or similar should keep you going until tea-time and is a good way to start a theme-park day.

The big chains

Moving up into the next price and facilities are the following choices.

Applebee's: Self-styled 'neighborhood bar and grill', this offers a rather more health-conscious menu with good salads and weight-watchers' choices as well as an array of steaks and chicken dishes ($–$$; 11am–midnight; **www.applebees.com**).

Bahama Breeze: Lively Caribbean food and surroundings, there is a pleasing individual touch and you will get good value for money here. The decor is refreshing and entertaining, and it's worth popping in just for a drink. On the menu, try the West Indies Patties, calypso shrimp linguine or jerk chicken pasta for a memorable meal ($$–$$$$; 4pm–2am Mon–Sat, 4pm–midnight Sun; **www.bahamabreeze.com**).

BRITTIP
The Bahama Breeze restaurants don't take reservations and are extremely popular in the evening. Try to arrive before 5.30pm to avoid a wait or try the Lake Buena Vista location, which can be a bit quieter.

Boston Market: Typical home cooking, café style, they specialise in fresh-carved meats, rotisserie chicken, decent vegetables and excellent value ($–$$; 11am–10pm; **www.bostonmarket.com**).

Buffalo Wild Wings: A huge sports bar and grill, featuring chicken wings, tenders, wraps, salads, burgers and ribs. Simple but tasty, and popular with its many large-screen TVs ($–$$; 11am–1am Mon–Fri, 2am Fri & Sat, noon–midnight Sun; **www.buffalowildwings.com**).

Café Tu Tu Tango: Another original local restaurant high on style and quality, the accent is artist-colony Spanish, with an original tapas-style menu, live music and artwork on the walls that changes daily. Vegetarians are well catered for, and you can try some succulent pizzas, seafood, salads and soups plus imaginative Mexican dishes and a well-thought-out kids' menu (11.30am–11am, midnight Fri and Sat; **www. cafetututango.com**).

Cheesecake Factory: While its prime feature is desserts (including more than 30 cheesecakes), the rest of a huge menu is impressive in an eclectic, high-tech setting. Mexican dishes jostle with pizza, pasta, seafood, burgers, steaks and salads, plus it offers a great brunch. Beware – portions are LARGE! ($$–$$$; 11am– 11pm; **www.thecheesecakefactory.com**).

Chevy's: A healthy slice of Mexicana while still providing American selections, its salsa is fresh-made every hour and the tortilla chips, fajitas and tortillas are delicious ($–$$; 4–11pm Mon–Thurs, 4pm– midnight Fri, 11am–midnight Sat, 11am–11pm Sun; **www.chevys.com**).

BRITTIP

Take advantage of **Chevy's** Kids-eat-free Tues (free kids' meal with any regular entrée purchase). Chevy's also has a 3–7pm Happy Hour in its Cantina bar, with a $3 drink menu and half-price appetisers.

Chili's: Also in Tex-Mex territory, it places the emphasis more on steak and ribs and less on tortillas and spices. Service is usually highly efficient ($–$$; 11am–1am Mon–Sat, 11am–11pm Sun; **www.chilis.com**).

Don Pablo's: A fairly elaborate Mexican offering with clever theming, a fun, lively atmosphere (especially round the Cantina bar) and classic, well-explained menus ($$; 11.30am– 10pm Sun–Thurs, 11.30am–11pm Fri and Sat; **www.donpablos.com**).

Fuddruckers: Some of the best burgers you'll find, with a huge choice (including veggie and ostrich!) and a kid-friendly style. Make your selection, find a table and wait for your burger to be cooked fresh, or choose from salad and sandwich options, plus tempting shakes, cookies and desserts ($–$$; 11am–10pm Sun–Fri, 11pm Sat; **www. fuddruckers.com**).

Hooters: A lively place that makes no bones about its style – 'delightfully

tacky yet unrefined' – this is popular with the beach-party crowd, and for the famous Hooter Girl waitresses. The entertaining menu features seafood, salads and burgers, plus Hooters Nearly World Famous Chicken Wings in 8 strengths – beware of the Samurai! ($–$$; 11am– midnight Mon–Thurs, 11am–1am Fri, Sat, noon–11pm Sun; **www.hooters. com**).

Houlihan's: Classic bar-restaurant with plenty of style, cheerful service, an extensive and appetising menu (try its Down Home Pot Roast) – and huge portions (but also a mini-dessert option; $–$$; 11am–1am; **www.houlihans.com**).

Logan's Roadhouse: A fun, rustic atmosphere includes masses of peanuts in their shells (which are meant to end up all over the wooden floor!), plus a menu featuring burgers, chicken, steaks and ribs, $3.99 kids' meals and express lunch selection ($$; 11am–10pm Sun–Thurs, 11pm Fri and Sat; **www.logansroadhouse.com**).

Lone Star Steakhouse: Head to Texas for its mesquite-grilled steaks, ribs, chicken and fish, with a friendly welcome and roadhouse ambience (plus more huge portions! $$-$$$; 11am–10pm Sun-Thurs, 11pm Fri and Sat; **www.lonestarsteakhouse.com**).

Longhorn Steakhouse: The newer, fancier version of the Texas steakhouse and 'Flavour of the West', this features fresh-grilled steaks, chops and ribs, plus chicken and seafood that is hard to beat at the price, with a good menu for under-

Pop into our 'local'

The nearest thing to a typical pub in these parts is the **Orlando/Miller Ale House** chain. Hugely popular with the locals, it features pool tables, multiple TV screens for all the sports action and a friendly, efficient style with a varied menu. It can be rowdy on weekend big-game days but is a great place to hang out with friends, bring the family or just pop in for a drink. The Ale House in Lake Buena Vista on Winter Garden-Vineland Road is also our 'local', and the new-style Miller's Ale House on I-Drive is positively vast ($–$$; 11am–2am; **www.millersalehouse.com**).

10s ($$–$$$$; 11am–10pm, 11pm Fri and Sat; **www.longhornsteakhouse.com**).

Olive Garden: One of America's big successes, bringing Italian food into mass-market territory. The light, airy dining rooms create a relaxing environment and it does a modest menu well and in generous portions. Pasta is the speciality but there is also chicken, veal, steak and seafood, plus great salads and garlic breadsticks (with unlimited refills) ($$–$$$; 11am–10pm Sun–Thurs, 11pm Fri and Sat; **www.olivegarden.com**).

Outback Steakhouse: An Australian slant on American steakhouse style, with some of the best fare – and biggest portions. Its thick, juicy, well-seasoned steaks, ribs and seafood selections are all above average, while its trademark is the Bloomin' Onion, a large fried onion with a dipping sauce, and all at moderate prices. Good kids' menu, and a real Brit visitor favourite in recent years ($$–$$$; 4–10.30pm Mon–Thurs, 4–11.30pm Fri, 3.30pm– 11.30pm Sat, 3.30–10.30pm Sun; **www.outback.com**).

Smokey Bones: With a rustic, log-cabin touch and succulent, deep-smoked BBQ, it serves up fire-grilled steaks, salmon, chicken, burgers and salads. Try the BBQ platters and rib combos especially. Sports fans can also enjoy a huge array of TVs ($–$$$; 11am–11pm Sun–Thurs, midnight Fri and Sat; **www.smokeybones.com**).

Sonny's Real Pit Bar-B-Q: A national chain with no great pretensions, just masses of food of the slow-cooked barbecue persuasion served up in friendly, let's-get-messy style. The good kids' menu makes it ideal for families, and you should definitely try the ribs and its own-recipe coleslaw ($–$$; 11am–10pm; **www.sonnysbbq. com**).

TGI Fridays: Lively, eclectic style, Orlando boasts multiple offerings of this popular chain. The drinks menu is the size of a book and the main menu is heavy on wings, ribs, burgers and steaks ($–$$; 11am–2am; **www. tgifridays.com**).

Tony Roma's: 'Famous for ribs', the airy decor and ambience, clever kids' menu, junior meals and melt-in-the-mouth ribs are a winning combo. You can still get chicken, burgers and steaks, but why ignore a dish that's done this well? ($$–$$$; 11am–11pm Sun–Thurs, 11am–midnight Fri and Sat; **www.tonyromas.com**).

Uno Chicago Grill: The place to go if you're bored with Pizza Hut, it specialises in deep-dish pizzas plus pastas, chicken dishes, steaks and salads, ($–$$; 11.30am–midnight; **www.unos.com**).

Urban Flats: An upmarket chain of flatbread grills, specialising in creative dips, salads, wraps and a wide variety of tempting toppings for its flatbreads. They offer more than 30 wines by the glass and 100 by the bottle, and their trademark Wine Down Wednesdays offer a range of wines to sample, along with appetisers and flatbreads, (5-8pm at $20/person. ($–$$; 11am–10pm Sun–Wed, 11am–11pm Thurs–Sat, **www. urbanflats.net**).

TGI Fridays

INTERNATIONAL FLAVOURS

Your food choice extends beyond the obvious to an international array, featuring Chinese and Indian, but also Thai, Japanese and Italian. Some are still chains, others are one-offs.

Indian, Chinese and more

There's a wide range of Asian restaurants in Orlando, from ordinary Chinese to 5-star Japanese. Take your pick from this recommended selection.

Aashirwad: A decent Indian choice, with an excellent lunch buffet and some seriously spicy Mughlai dishes ($–$$$; 11.30am–3pm and 5.30–10.30pm; 407 370 9830; **www. aashirwadrestaurant.com**).

Dragon Court Buffet: This locals' Chinese favourite in Lake Buena Vista serves a huge spread of fresh, appetising dishes at a terrific lunch price. With 100 items, including sushi, this is well worth trying ($$–$$$; 11am–11pm; 407 238 9996, **www. dragoncourtorlando.com**).

India Palace: An unassuming location tucked in a small shopping plaza in Lake Buena Vista, this serves good food in large amounts and with family-friendly service ($–$$$; 11.30am–11pm Tues–Sun, 5–11pm Mon; 407 238 2322).

Kobe: This brings a touch of Americana to its Japanese-themed dining, but still achieves individuality with the chef preparing the food at your table ($$$; 11.30am–11pm; **www. kobesteakhouse.com**).

Ming Court

The cream of America

Orlando boasts outstanding ice-cream parlours: check out Carvel, Baskin Robbins, Dairy Queen, Marble Slab Creamery and Cold Stone Creamery, all of which make Mr Whippy seem extremely ordinary. But our gold medal for la crème de la crème of iced delights goes to trendy new **Pinkberry** frozen yoghurt, which has 3 locations here (including Mall at Millenia and Orlando Premium Outlets on I-Drive) and offers a superlative array of 5 luscious flavours to which you add various toppings and fresh fruits. Healthier than ice cream and a true taste sensation, see more at **www.pinkberry.com**.

Memories of India: Well-recommended Indian on Turkey Lake Rd, also a good choice for vegetarians. Its Goan fish curry is a particular speciality, but it also offers great biryanis, tandoori dishes and fresh breads, and a novel Champagne Sunday Brunch ($$; 11.30am–2.30pm and 5.30-10pm Mon-Sat, 9pm Sun; 407 370 3277, **www.memoriesofindiacuisine.com**)

Ming Court: The Rolls-Royce of Chinese is this beautiful place on I-Drive, opposite Pointe Orlando, with its magnificent setting and live music most evenings. The menu is extensive and beautifully presented by friendly servers. Many dishes can be had as a side order rather than a full main course and there are extensive dim sum and even sushi and sashimi choices, plus an imaginative kids' menu. The basil chicken is 1 of our all-time favourites and, after 23 years in business, this is I-Drive's longest-serving restaurant ($$–$$$; 11am–2.30pm, 4.30pm–midnight; **www.ming-court.com**).

BRITTIP

Check out **Ming Court**'s website for a print-at-home 10% money-off coupon or an Early Bird special (4.30-6.30pm) offering 50% off a 2nd entrée (click 'Menus').

New Punjab: Another decent Indian on I-Drive, with fine tandoori dishes and good vegetable selection

A Florida steak-out

America serves great steaks and it is hard to get a BAD sirloin, T-bone or filet. For those who really want to indulge, the following (totally unofficial) ranking should help (NB: the US Dept of Agriculture grades its meat quality Standard, Select, Choice and, for the top 2%, Prime).

Standard: Ponderosa, Golden Corral, Sizzler, O'Charley's, Beef O'Brady's, Great Western, Western Sizzlin', Shamrock Pub. **Select:** Black Angus, Applebee's, TGI Fridays, Cattleman's Steakhouse, Chili's, Logan's Roadhouse, Lone Star, Tony Roma's, Uno Chicago Grill, Cricketer's Arms, Colorado House of Beef, Smoky Bones, Rainforest Café, Chevy's, Ruby Tuesday, Miller's Ale House, Red Lobster, Copper Canyon Grill. **Choice:** Outback, Longhorn Steakhouse, Kobe, Shogun, Brio Tuscan Grill, Vito's Chophouse, The Oceanaire, J Alexander, Texas de Brazil, The Venetian Room, Le Cellier (Epcot), Jack's Place, Amura's, Carrabba's, Cantina Laredo, Bergamo's, Johnnie's Hideaway. **Prime:** Charley's, A Land Remembered, Old Hickory, Fleming's, The Palm Restaurant, Spencer's, Ruth's Chris, Del Frisco's, Everglades, Morton's, Capital Grille, Antonio's, Christini's, Timpano's, Shula's, The Yachtsman (*Disney's Yacht Club resort*).

($–$$$; 5–11pm Mon, 11.30am–11pm Tues–Sun; 407 352 7887; **www. punjabindianrestaurant.com**).

PF Chang's China Bistro: This mixes classic Chinese fare with American bistro style that makes fans of virtually all who sample it. You should try the spicy ground chicken and eggplant (aubergine), Cantonese roasted duck or Oolong marinated sea bass. There is also a good veggie selection ($$–$$$$; 11am–11pm, 10pm Sun; **www.pfchangs.com**).

Red Bamboo: Authentic Thai flavours and contemporary décor, with soups and curries to die for. House speciality Smokey Pot is a superb stew of marinated prawns, vegetables and glass noodles in chilli ($$–$$$$; 11am–2.30pm and 5–10pm Mon–Fri, noon–10pm Sat, closed Sun; 407 226 8997; **www.redbamboothai.com**).

Seito Sushi: Another Japanese offering from this great chain, with a formal sushi bar and a more inviting, small-scale approach ($$–$$$$; 11.30am–2.30pm, 5–10pm; 407 644 5050; **www.seitosushi.com**).

Shogun Steakhouse: This national chain, which is ideal for those a little unsure of Japanese food, opts for the Teppanyaki-style service, at long, bench-like tables with the chef cooking in front of you. But you can still order a no-nonsense steak or chicken ($$$–$$$$; 6–10pm Sun–Thurs, 6–10.30pm Fri and Sat; 407 352

1607, **www.shogunorlando.com**).

Sizzling Wok: A cheerful budget-orientated offering on Sand Lake Road (by the Florida Mall), it features a massive Chinese buffet at a reasonable price ($–$$; 11am–10pm Sun–Thurs, 11am–10.30pm Fri and Sat; 407 438-8389).

Tastes of the Med

Italy, Turkey and Greece are all represented in this selection.

Anatolia: For something exotic, head for the Turkish flavours in the Dr Phillips Plaza off Sand Lake Road. With a delicious range of authentic breads, hot and cold appetisers, salads, soups, pides (Turkish pizzas), kebabs and specialities like moussaka and baklava, you can dine royally without breaking the bank. Try the babaghanoush (char-grilled aubergine with fresh herbs and spices), tabouli, kofte kebab or chicken adana ($$–$$; 11am–10pm Sun–Thurs, 11pm Fri and Sat; 407 352 6766, **www.anatoliaorlando.com**).

Antonio's: This impressive local chain goes distinctly upmarket, with 3 outlets (including 1 with a café, deli and superb wine shop) that feature an individual style as well as outstanding cuisine – sensational risottos are a signature dish, while veal and New York strip steak are equally good ($$$–$$$$$; 5–10pm Mon–Sat; **www. antoniosonline.com**).

Bravo Cucina Italiana: This fresh, inviting twist on classic Italian fare features home-made pasta, pizza, flatbreads, steaks, chops and seafood in an inviting 'Roman-ruin' decor. Casual and chic, and fun for the grown-up crowd ($$–$$$$; 11am–10pm, to 11pm Fri and Sat; 407 351 5880; www.bravoitalian.com).

Carrabba's: Direct from Sicily, here's casual-but-elegant dining in a festive atmosphere. House specialities include crispy calamari, chicken marsala, pasta and hand-made pizzas. The kids' menu is 1 of the best and the style is very child friendly ($$–$$$; 4–10pm Sun–Thurs, 3–11pm Fri and Sat; **www.carrabbas.com**).

Cedar's: Lebanese cuisine is the name of the game here, and it's some of the best chicken and lamb in town. In 'Restaurant Row' on Sand Lake Rd, this family-run Middle Eastern delight offers the full range of kebabs, falafel and hoummus as well as specialities like fish tajine, grilled quail and baked kibbeh. A really different alternative and an aromatic treat ($$–$$$$; 407 351 6000; http://cedarsorlando.com).

Greek Flame Taverna: New in 2011 was this stylish offering in the Dr Phillips plaza off Sand Lake Rd. Saganaki (flamed cheese), dolmades (stuffed vine leaves) and spanakopita (spinach pie) are joined by other classic Greek dishes, including salads, gyros and souvlaki, ensuring a smooth taste of the Med ($$–$$$; 407 370 4624; **www.greekflametaverna.com**).

Macaroni Grill: Another slice of Little Italy, its spacious restaurants are stylish, comfortable and well served,

with excellent à la carte and family-style menus (serving 8–10). The pasta and wood-oven pizzas are first class and the wine list is impressive ($$–$$$$; 11.30am–10pm Sun–Thurs, 11.30am–11pm Fri and Sat; **www.macaroni grill.com**).

HOME FROM HOME

Having extolled the virtues of the all-American choices, there is an array of British-style pubs that should appeal to UK visitors. All offer predictable pub grub and beers and you can happily take the kids into any of them.

Best of British: This fresh choice (opposite Ripley's Believe It Or Not on I-Drive) goes for a footy-themed style, with 12 flat-screen TVs, plus a giant theatre-style screen for all the big games. It boasts 8 British beers on tap, plus pool and darts, Curry Nights, a traditional roast on Suns (noon–5pm), karaoke, live music and even 2 internet terminals, as well as a private meeting room (ideal for football fan club meets). Typical menu items include shepherd's pie, fish 'n' chips, ploughman's, burgers, steak and kidney pies and kids' specials, while its full breakfast really is the Best of British (8am–midnight; 407 264 9189; **www.bestofbritishpub.com**).

Bistro UK: Half pub, half bistro but all British is this family-run offering at Champions Gate (just off exit 58 of I-4). A pleasant retreat after the bustle of the theme parks, it features traditional pub fare (notably roast beef and Yorkshire pud, bangers and mash and fish and chips) plus a good range of wines, and specials on various evenings ($–$$$, 5–9pm, 10pm Sun, closed Tues; 863 852 4300, http://bistrouk.weebly.com).

Cricketers Arms: The area's oldest-established British pub closed down at its Festival Bay location in April 2011 but was due to open up again in a new location close to Sand Lake Rd, later in the year. Look for them to maintain their offering of 17 beers (including 4 real ales), appetising food, live evening entertainment, stylish indoor and outdoor seating

The Dellagio complex on I-Drive

International Drive

The majority of restaurants in this busy tourist area are of the Fast Food or Family Favourite type, but there are several individuals.

The **North** section (from Prime Outlets International to Sand Lake Road) features *Fast Food:* Baskin Robbins, Burger King, Cold Stone Creamery, Dairy Queen, Dunkin' Donuts, Five Guys Burgers & Fries, KFC, McDonald's, Quiznos, Pizza Hut, Popeye's Chicken, Sonic, Starbucks, Subway and Taco Bell. *Family Favourites:* Buffalo Wild Wings, Chili's, CiCi's Pizza, Denny's, Fuddruckers, IHOP, Perkins, Sizzler, Sweet Tomatoes, TGI Fridays. *International Flavours:* Aashirwad, New Punjab Indian Restaurant, Red Bamboo, Shogun Steakhouse. *Home From Home:* Orlando George & Dragon. *Seafood Specials:* Red Lobster. *Deluxe Dining:* Texas de Brazil.

The **South** section (from Sand Lake Rd to Orlando Premium Outlets) has *Fast Food:* McDonald's, Pizza Hut, Subway. *Family Favourites:* Bahama Breeze, Café Tu Tu Tango, Cattleman's Steakhouse, Denny's, Don Pablo's, Friendlys, Golden Corral, Houlihan's, IHOP, Miller's Ale House, Olive Garden, Outback Steakhouse, Ponderosa, TGI Fridays, Tony Roma's, Uno Chicago, Village Inn. *International Flavours:* Kobe Steakhouse, Ming Court. *Home From Home:* Best of British Pub. *Seafood Specials:* Boston Lobster Feast, Crab House, Red Lobster. *Deluxe Dining:* Charley's Steakhouse, Everglades, Vito's Chophouse, Spencer's. Plus, **B-Line Diner:** inside the Orlando Peabody Hotel is a fab art deco homage to the traditional 1950s diner. You sit at a long counter or in one of its booths with a good view of the chefs at work and a menu that changes during the day. The food is way above usual diner standards, but the prices aren't. Desserts are displayed in a huge glass counter and you just can't ignore them! ($$; 24 hours; 407 352 4000; **www.peabodyorlando.com**).

and lots of live football. For the latest info, look up Cricketer's Arms Pub and Eatery on Facebook.

Frankie Farrell's: Inside the Lake Buena Vista Resort Village & Spa is this smart pub-style restaurant and bar with an imaginative menu, excellent range of beers and live entertainment ($$–$$$; 9am–2am daily; 407 597 0214).

Hagan O'Reilley's: Rather off the beaten track in Winter Garden (about 20mins north of Disney) is this genuine Irish pub, boasting good beers, classic fare and traditional entertainment most nights. With 15 beers on tap and Happy Hour from 4–7pm, you could easily be in the Emerald isle, although the beer garden is pure Florida! ($–$$$; 11.30am–11pm; 407 905 4782; **www.haganoreillys.com**).

Orlando George & Dragon: Another all-British operation, this serves a hearty traditional breakfast as well as pub fare. It stocks Guinness, Stella, Boddingtons, Fosters, Newcastle Brown, Bass, Grolsch and Carlsberg,

and features darts, pool, karaoke, Sky Sports and live entertainment on its outdoor patio. A good option for Christmas dinner, Sunday lunch, and St George's Day, celebrated in style; $–$$$; 9am–2am; 407 351 3578; **www.britanniapubs.com**).

Stage Door: Another friendly, family-run pub and restaurant, this has also been a local fixture for years and still draws a good crowd of locals and tourists, with typical fare (including a Sunday roast) and a good range of beers, plus live entertainment or karaoke most nights ($–$$; 11am–2am Tues–Sat, 11am–midnight Sun and Mon; 863 424 8056; **www.stagedoorpub.com**).

The Shamrock Pub & Grille: on Highway 27 in Davenport (at the junction with I-4, exit 55), this has a great range of beers, excellent food, multiple HD TVs and a family-friendly touch. Its beer garden offers live karaoke and other entertainment Wed–Sat ($–$$; 11am–2am Mon–Sat, 11am– midnight Sun; 863 424 4242; **www.theshamrockpub.net**).

SEAFOOD SPECIALS

The choice of seafood eateries is equally wide and features some fun chains and excellent individuals.

Big Fin Seafood: One of Orlando's most imaginative and award-winning seafood options, in the Dellagio complex just off Sand Lake Rd. Refined but relaxed, this is a big-scale experience that offers special-occasion atmosphere, from the entrance seafood kitchen to the elegant outdoor bar (the Bar-A-Cuda – *groan!*). The main dining room features a grand salon style but 2 smaller rooms are more intimate, while the Trophy Bar is a fun first stop for a pre-dinner drink.

BRITTIP

Big Fin Seafood has possibly 1 of the best meal deals in town, with its Monday Lobster Dinner special, featuring a whole Maine lobster at just $13.95.

The menu is an impressive collection of sushi, sashimi, oysters and ceviche; classic salads and chowders; meat, chops and chicken; their exclusive crab and lobster dishes; fresh fish; and tempting pastas. You can push the boat out with the $40 Alaskan king crab dinner or opt for a modest burger ($10.95). Notable are the succulent signature swordfish steak, lobster mac-n-cheese, crab cakes and Bonner's famous fish and chips. A good kids' menu, delectable desserts (don't miss the bread pudding) and superb service all add up to a high-quality experience – but without the price tag. There is Happy Hour 5–7pm with $5 appetisers and select wines and cocktails ($$–$$$$; 5–10pm Sun–Thurs, 11pm Fri and Sat; **www. bigfinseafood.com**).

BRITBONUS

Show your copy of the *Brit Guide* at **Big Fin Seafood** and receive a 10% discount off your entree. Not valid with any other offers/specials.

Bonefish Grill: This chic choice can be found throughout Florida and offers both casual dining and an upmarket dinner experience, with some of the freshest fish and a terrific range of martinis and other cocktails. Non-fish fans can choose from chicken, chops, steak and main-course salads ($$–$$$$; 4–10.30pm Mon–Thurs, 11.30pm Fri and Sat, 10pm Sun; **www.bonefishgrill.com**).

Boston Lobster Feast: The place for a real blow-out on an unlimited lobster and seafood buffet. There are usually early-bird specials (4–6pm Mon–Fri, 2–4.30pm Sat and Sun), and, while it is not gourmet fare, its 40-item Lobster Feast is guaranteed to stretch the stomach ($$–$$$$; 4–10pm Mon–Fri, 2–10pm Sat and Sun; **www. bostonlobsterfeast.com**).

The Crab House: Self-explanatory: garlic crabs, steamed crabs, snow crabs… you could try its prime rib, pasta or seafood, but it'd be a shame to ignore the house speciality ($$–$$$$; 11.30am–11pm Mon–Sat, noon–11pm Sun; **www. crabhouseseafood.com**).

Flying Fish: At *Disney's BoardWalk Resort*, the menu of this superb seafood experience is select but brilliantly presented. Its Chardonnay-steamed mussels starter is a taste sensation. Steak and beef short ribs, plus a vegetarian option, are also available (4–11pm Mon–Sat, 4–10pm Sun; 407 939 3463).

Joe's Crab Shack: Part of Crab House chain but more inventive and less seafood-based. Very family friendly with its kids' play area and ideal if you don't want the whole shellfish thing ($–$$$; 11am–11pm Sun–Thurs, 11am–midnight Fri and Sat; **www. joescrabshack.com**).

Landry's Seafood: From the same company but with a more elegant touch, there is a fresh catch of the day, seafood platters and excellent salad bowl with each dish, while the service is top-notch ($$–$$$$; 11am–10pm Sun–Thurs, 11am–11pm Fri and Sat; **www.landrysseafoodhouse.com**).

McCormick and Schmick's: Easily one of the most eye-catching of the seafood chains, the chef creates a daily menu based on product, price and availability. Oysters are a speciality, along with soups and salads, and you'll be hard pushed to find better prawns, scallops and salmon ($$–$$$$$; 11am–10pm Mon–Thurs, 11am–11pm Fri and Sat, 11am–9pm Sun; **www.mccormickandschmicks.com**).

Moonfish: Another great place for seafood, you could make a feast of its appetisers alone, while its sushi, sashimi and raw bar are inspired. It's a touch avant-garde but it works well ($$–$$$$; 4.30–10.30pm, 11pm Fri and Sat; 407 363 7262; **www.talkofthetownrestaurants.com**).

BRITTIP

For something different, check out **Moonfish** on its Sushi Sundays, with $4 selections all day long. It also has a Happy Hour Mon–Sat (4.30–6.30pm) with bar specials and half-price sushi.

Red Lobster: Part of the Olive Garden chain and for the family market, with a varied menu, lively atmosphere and one of the best kids' menu/activity books. While lobster is the speciality, the wood-fired steaks, chicken, salads and other seafood are equally appetising, and it does a variety of combination platters ($$–$$$$; 11am–10pm Sun–Thurs, 11am–11pm Fri and Sat; **www.redlobster.com**).

DELUXE DINING

This is where you can really go to town with your dining choice.

Bohème Restaurant: A magnificent menu at this tucked-away gem at the Grand Bohemian hotel in downtown Orlando. Fine seafood mixes with superb lamb, duck and seafood, with some eclectic twists and a great Sunday Brunch ($$$–$$$$; 5.30–10pm, 10.30pm Fri and Sat 407 313 9000; **www.grandbohemianhotel.com**).

Cala Bella: At the stylish Rosen Shingle Creek Resort is this superb Italian-influenced restaurant, heavy on pasta and seafood, but with signature dishes like its sensational Cala Bella Lamb, veal piccata and Mediterranean pork. Save room for

dessert – the pastry chefs are among the best in America ($$$–$$$$; 5.30–10.30pm; 407 996 3663; **www.calabellarestaurant.com**).

Charley's Steak Houses: Cooking over a specially built wood-fire pit earns high marks from US meat-lovers. All the meat is specially aged, hand-cut and seasoned, making for a superb array of steaks and chops and, while it also offers fine seafood, you'd be foolish to overlook its stock-in-trade ($$$–$$$$$; 5–11pm; **www.talkofthetownrestaurants.com**).

City Fire: Brand-new in 2011 and an eye-catching addition to the upscale Dellagio complex on Sand Lake Rd, this can be a special-occasion night out or just a friendly, low-key lunch or dinner, with their signature stoneflat pizzas from just $8 or a superb filet for $22 (plus side dishes). The eclectic decor, feature open-flame, stone-fired oven, elegant bar, outdoor patio and Martini list (plus some fine draft beers) makes for a flexible array of highlights to suit most styles (and pockets), and their daily Happy Hour (4.30–6.30pm) adds good drink specials and $3 snacks ($–$$$$; 407 722 8888; **www.cityfirerestaurants.com**).

BRITTIP

We rate **City Fire** the most impressive new restaurant for its different style and well-grooved oven-fired menu. Try the chicken thumbits for starters, chicken vesuvio lasagna or braised short ribs for main and chocolate bread pudding for dessert for a truly memorable night out.

Big Fin Seafood

Del Frisco's: Locals consistently rate this unprepossessing restaurant (on Lee Rd in north Orlando) their favourite steakhouse and the more formal dining experience is enhanced by prime steaks and lobster, beautifully cooked and presented ($$$$–$$$$$; 5–10pm, closed Sun; 407 645 4443; **www.delfriscosorlando.com**).

Everglades: Tucked away inside the Rosen Centre Hotel is this beautiful Florida speciality restaurant, specialising in great steaks and fine seafood. Don't miss the Broiled Florida Grouper and melt-in-the-mouth Filet Key Largo ($$$–$$$$$; 5.30-10.30pm; 407 996 2385; **www. evergladesrestaurant.com**).

Fleming's: Check in here for finest aged prime beef and an inventive array of fresh seafood, chops, generous sides and salads, plus tempting desserts. Its award-winning wine list features 100 wines by the glass and a magnificent Reserve List for the real connoisseur ($$$–$$$$$; 5–10pm Sun–Thurs, 11pm Fri and Sat; 407 352 5706; **www. flemingssteakhouse.com**).

J Alexander's: Chic venue on Sand Lake Road for a relaxing lunch or upmarket dinner, with a varied menu that covers the basics (burgers, salads and sandwiches) and the more gourmet (filet mignon béarnaise, ahi tuna and cilantro shrimp), plus an excellent wine list and range of martinis ($$–$$$$; 11am–10pm, 11pm Fri and Sat; 407 345 1039; **www. jalexanders.com**).

Johnnie's Hideaway: Chic lakefront supper club in the Crossroads plaza at Lake Buena Vista, serving a rich mix of salads, premium seafood, stone crabs, veal and succulent, dry-aged steaks. The menu is colossal, and there is also a raw bar and some of the biggest desserts we have ever seen, along with a charming bar area and outdoor terrace ($$$–$$$$$; 5–10pm, 11pm Fri and Sat; 407 827 1111; **www. talkofthetownrestaurants.com**).

Luma on Park: Head to Winter Park for this trendy 'gastropub', where the cuisine can be as simple as a well-cooked burger or pizza or a fabulous filet mignon. The mix of outdoor patio, lounge bar and restaurant makes it a chic and lively venue, with fresh contemporary cuisine. Fine lamb, duck and fish are among the highlights, along with a great wine cellar, serving by the bottle, ½-bottle, glass or ½-glass! It also features a 3-course prix fixe menu Sun–Tues, and a special Chef's Table that should be booked in advance ($$–$$$$$; lounge bar 4.30–midnight, dining room 5.30–10.30pm; 407 599 4111; **www.lumaonpark.com**).

Morton's of Chicago: A more upmarket style following a recent refurbishment, with a lively ambience that adds to the enjoyment of its trademark steaks, cooked on an open range. Memorable, although not cheap, especially as vegetables are extra ($$$$; 5pm–11pm Mon–Sat, 10pm Sun; **www.mortons.com**).

> **BRITTIP**
>
> American restaurant terminology calls a starter an 'appetizer' and a main course an 'entrée'. 'Broiled' means 'grilled'.

Old Hickory Steakhouse: In the Gaylord Palms Resort with elaborate Everglades theming, their steak needs few gimmicks as the house speciality of certified prime-aged beef is cooked to perfection. Side dishes are extra, but the attentive service and alternatives such as oven-roasted swordfish and Maine lobster provide a memorable experience ($$$–$$$$$; 5.30–10.30; **www.gaylordhotels.com**).

Roy's: Go upmarket Hawaiian at this grand choice, where the Asian-Pacific fusion cuisine is as spectacular as the decor and service. Creator and celebrity chef Roy Yamaguchi displays his sense of style ($$$$–$$$$$; 5.30–10pm, 10.30pm Fri and Sat; **www.roysrestaurant.com**).

Ruth's Chris Steak House: Another major chain, this also offers prime beef in a mouth-watering variety. It isn't cheap, but you'll be hard pushed to get a better steak. Simply seared, seasoned and served, they are the reason it has more than 80 locations worldwide, including in the Sand

Try it all at Pointe Orlando

Dining choice doesn't come more varied than at Pointe Orlando on I-Drive.

Fast Food: **Johnny Rockets** 1950s-style diner for burgers and shakes ($; 11am–9pm Sun–Thurs, 11am–11pm Fri and Sat; 407 903 0762, **www.johnnyrockets.com**); **Pizza Valdiano**, for café-style pizza, salads, subs and panini ($–$$; 11am–10pm Sun–Thurs, 11pm Fri and Sat; 407 903 5855, **www.pizzeriavaldiano.com**). *Family Favourites:* **Hooters**; and **Copper Canyon Grill**, which appeals to hearty appetites with its wood-fired rotisserie chicken, hearty chicken pot pie, steaks and succulent barbecued ribs ($$–$$$$; 11am–10.05pm Sun–Thurs, 11.05pm Fri and Sat; 407 363 3933; **www.ccgrill.com**). *International Flavours:* the lively bar and Mexican-restaurant style of **Adobe Gila's**, with more than 50 tequilas (!) and live music and karaoke most nights of the week, plus happy Hour specials 4–7pm weekdays ($–$$; 11.30am-2am, 11pm Sun; 407 903 1477, **www.adobegilas.com**). **Funky Monkey Wine Company** is a fun-style wine bar, featuring tapas-like appetiser plates, great steaks and seafood, stylish Sushi Mondays and a superb wine list, many available by the glass ($$–$$$, 407 418 9463, noon–11pm Mon–Thurs, noon–midnight Fri and Sat, 5–11pm Sun, **www.funkymonkeywine.com**). **Maggianos Little Italy** serves exceptional family-style Italian dining in a relaxed, friendly atmosphere with vintage 1940s Chicago decor and ambience. Portions are huge (even by Orlando standards!). The Bombalina appetiser platter will feed a family of 4, while the Family Style meals feature all-you-can-eat refills – and no one leaves hungry ($$–$$$$; 11am–10pm Mon–Thurs, 11pm Fri and Sat, noon–10pm Sun; 407 241 8660; **www.maggianos.com**); **Taverna Opa** is a lively Greek option, with a thoroughly traditional and appetising menu, from hot and cold meze to moussaka, souvlaki and stewed lamb, but much more besides, like fine steaks and fresh seafood – plus dancing on the tables and a great ouzo bar! ($$–$$$$; 11am–11pm Sun–Thurs, 2am Fri and Sat; 407 351 8660, **www.opaorlando.com**). *Deluxe Dining:* **Capital Grille**, a wonderfully upmarket and elegant restaurant featuring dry-aged steaks, seafood and tantalising desserts – perfect for that special night out ($$$$–$$$$$; 11.30am–3pm Mon–Fri, 5–10pm Sun–Thurs, 11pm Fri and Sat; 407 370 4392, **www.thecapitalgrille.com**); **Cuba Libre Restaurant and Rum Bar** is a highlight dining and entertainment spot, featuring traditional Cuban cuisine with an exciting twist, from tasty ceviche to pan-seared sugarcane-skewered jumbo shrimp. Great cocktails (notably mojitos and caipiranhas) and smooth service entice visitors to just stop by the bar and graze on its appetisers. The interior setting is magnificent, while it offers live Latin music in the evening at weekends ($$$–$$$$$; **www.cubalibrerestaurant.com**); The **Oceanaire** (see Top 10, page 322); **Tommy Bahama's Tropical Café** offers inspired dining in a laid-back, tropical setting. The menu is refreshing for lunch or dinner, with highlights being its Loki Loki Tuna appetiser and shrimp entrées, plus sandwiches, chicken, fresh fish and fab salads ($$–$$$; 11am–11pm Sun–Thurs, to midnight Fri and Sat; 321 281 5888, **www.tommybahama.com**).

Other options include **BB King's Blues Club**, with a Louisiana-tinged menu and some excellent chicken, ribs, catfish, Cajun pasta carbonara and steak, as well as standard burgers and salads ($$–$$$$; 4pm–midnight Sun–Fri, 11am–1am Sat; 407 370 4550, **www.bbkingclubs.com**).

Lake Rd 'restaurant row' ($$$$–$$$$$; 5–10pm Mon–Sat, 9pm Sun; **www.ruthschris.com**).

Samba Room: A memorable Cuban experience in an elegant lakefront restaurant. The menu exhibits an exotic touch, with the likes of Argentinean skirt steak and Chilean sea bass, and its range of cocktails is Cuban-laced. Popular, though a touch pricier than others, so reservations are advised ($$$–$$$$; 4–10pm Sun–Thurs, 11pm Fri and Sat: 407 266 0550; **www.sambaroom.net**).

Sanaa: The latest dining experience at *Walt Disney World*, this is in the new Kidani Village resort next to *Animal Kingdom Lodge* and features a novel take on Indian cuisine, with some imaginative variations, many served as sampler platters and, for once, not the usual huge portions. It also offers great animal savannah views ($$$$; 11.30am–3pm, 5–9pm; 407 939 3463).

Shula's Steak House: Expansive and expensive, the porterhouse and prime rib steaks are outstanding, and this chain (owned by ex-American football coach Don Shula) is popular with locals at the Walt Disney World Dolphin Hotel ($$$$$; 5–11pm; 407 934 1362; **www.donshula.com**). Less formal but equally stylish is **Shula's 347** bistro in the swish Westin Hotel at Lake Mary, near Sanford (right on exit 101A of I-4), a nice balance of casual diner with upmarket menu. It still features the signature Shula Cut steaks, but also burgers and salads, as well as great fish dishes. As part of the hotel, it is open for breakfast, lunch and dinner and is fun for big sports events with its multiple TVs ($$–$$$$; 6.30am–midnight; 407 531 3567).

Spencer's: The Hilton by the Convention Center on I-Drive is home to this beautiful restaurant that features magnificent steak, chops and seafood. Side dishes are extra, but the natural steaks are all pasture-raised without hormones or antibiotics, aged for 21 days and cooked in a custom-made grill. The prime porterhouse for 2 is outstanding, as are the loaded hash browns ($$$$–$$$$$, 5-10.30pm Tues–Sat; 407 313 4300; **www.thehiltonorlando.com**).

BRITTIP

Non-Hilton guests who dine at Spencer's Steakhouse benefit from free valet parking. Its monthly Culinary Class, featuring select wine pairings, is worth checking out on the first Sat every month.

Sanaa

Texas de Brazil: An unusual but delicious Brazilian-style steakhouse, or churrascaria, with a wonderfully upmarket touch. Its variety of meats – every one carved at the table off sword-like skewers – is superb, all beautifully cooked over its open-flame grill ($$$–$$$$$; 5–10pm Mon–Thurs, 5–10.30pm Fri, 4–10.30pm Sat, 4–9.30pm Sun, plus brunch noon–3pm Sat and Sun; 407 355 0355; **www.texasdebrazil.com**).

The Palm Restaurant: Inside Universal's Hard Rock Hotel is this upmarket New York original, famous for prime-aged steaks and jumbo lobsters, served in elegant surroundings. The house speciality, jumbo Nova Scotia lobster, is spectacular. All this is reflected in the prices, and vegetables are extra, but non-hotel guests qualify for free valet parking ($$$$–$$$$$; 5–10pm Mon–Thurs, 11pm Fri and Sat, 9pm Sun; 407 503 7256; **www.thepalm.com**).

Timpano Italian Chophouse: Step back in time here as the dark, elegant interior is bustling and convivial 1950s New York. From its trademark Martini Bar to the tiramisu dessert, everything is served with style , with live music at its baby grand Tues–Sat. ($$$–$$$$; 11.30am–11pm Sun–Wed, midnight Thurs–Sat; 407 248 0429; **www.timpanochophouse.net**)

Our Top 10

Finally, if you fancy really splashing out, why not book in advance at one of our suggestions for venues with that je ne sais quois.

A Land Remembered: This is just the best steakhouse we've visited. Inside the golf clubhouse of the Rosen Shingle Creek Resort (but open to non-residents), it is a superbly refined venue boasting exquisite service and an outstanding wine list. The menu oozes class and even features local specialities like frogs' legs, gator stew, a fresh fish selection and key lime pie. But, while the lamb, chicken and short ribs are outstanding, the steak choice is out of this world (featuring all-natural prime black Angus beef from the Harris Ranch in

Kissimmee/Highway 192

The long stretch of this tourist corridor offers the greatest density of restaurants in Central Florida. Here's how they line up, starting with the **East** section from the junction with I-4 to John Young Parkway: *Fast Food:* Arby's, Burger King, Chick-Fil-A, Domino's, Dunkin' Donuts, KFC, McDonald's, Pizza Hut, Quiznos, Subway, Taco Bell, Wendy's. *Family Favourites:* Applebee's, Bob Evans, Cattleman's Steakhouse, Chevys, Chili's, CiCi's Pizza, Cracker Barrel, Denny's, Friendlys, Golden Corral, IHOP, Logan's Roadhouse, Longhorn Steakhouse, Olive Garden, Perkins, Ponderosa, Ruby Tuesday, Shoney's, Smokey Bones, TGI Fridays, Uno Chicago, Waffle House. *International Flavours:* Kobe Steakhouse, Punjab Indian Restaurant. *Seafood Specials:* Boston Lobster Feast, Joe's Crab Shack, Red Lobster. *Deluxe Dining:* Charley's Steakhouse. Plus, **Pacino's:** a well-established, family-friendly Italian choice, offering suitably healthy portions in a themed setting. Highly traditional and with an emphasis on pasta and seafood, plus good steaks ($$–$$$$; 4–11pm; 407 396 8022; **www.pacinos.com**).

In the **West** section (from I-4 all the way to Highway 27) you have: *Fast Food:* Burger King, Chick-Fil-A, Dunkin' Donuts, McDonald's, Pizza Hut, Subway, Taco Bell, Wendy's. *Family Favourites:* Black Angus, Bob Evans, Carabba's, Cracker Barrel, Denny's, Golden Corral, IHOP, Longhorn Steakhouse, Miller's Ale House, Olive Garden, Outback Steakhouse, Perkins, Ponderosa, Shoney's, Sizzler, TGI Fridays, Waffle House. *International Flavours:* Passage to India. *Home From Home:* Stage Door. *Seafood Specials:* Red Lobster.

California). Filet mignon, New York strip, ribeye, porterhouse, prime rib, chateaubriand and a surf & turf (with lobster) are among the most succulent meat dishes you will find and, while it is pricey, it is worth every cent ($$$$–$$$$$; 5.30–10pm; 407 996 3663; **www.landrememberedrestaurant. com**).

Bice: Anyone looking for the most authentic Italian dining experience outside Italy should head to the Portofino Bay Hotel at Universal Orlando where this is as smart and smooth as they come. Genuine Tuscan style oozes out of every facet, from the formal welcome, the classic dining room, live balcony music and authentic menu, overseen by executive chef Alessandro Lozzi and general manager Francesco Fiore. Lozzi insists on only the freshest ingredients, with everything made from scratch, and it shows in dishes like the buffalo mozzarella and vine-ripened tomato starter, marinated seafood salad, papardelle pasta and braised veal shank. His signature risottos are superb and chicken pallard a masterpiece, while Lozzi's soft chocolate soufflé cake is heavenly. The wine list is impressive and Italian-orientated and the whole experience 1 to be savoured slowly thanks to exceptional wait staff. A

3-course meal will top $120 for 2, but it's worth it for a special occasion ($$$$–$$$$$; 407 503 1415; **http:// orlando.bicegroup.com**).

bluezoo: One of the hippest places in town (at the Walt Disney World Dolphin Hotel), bluezoo not only looks the part, but it also serves some of the finest food in the Disney realm, thanks to celebrity chef Todd English. With an undersea theme that benefits from superb lighting (dine later

Bice

for the full effect), it has a soothing feeling, whether you are just at the bar or in one of the 3 main restaurant areas. Both the service and the staff's knowledge are impeccable, so feel free to let them steer you around a mouth-watering menu, which includes ceviche and a raw bar. Fish is the signature dish (though rotisserie chicken, beef filet and pork loin are also on offer) and seafood lovers will struggle to narrow down the choice: miso-glazed black cod, Basque-style tuna, swordfish, Cantonese lobster and more, or just try your choice of freshly caught fish, whole-roasted on its Teppenyaki grill with a choice of sauces. There's also a daily fresh pasta selection and Chef's 5-course Tasting Menu ($$$$–$$$$$; 3.30–11pm; 407 934 1111; **www.thebluezoo.com**).

Brio Tuscan Grille: With 2 Orlando locations (Mall at Millenia and Winter Park Village, plus another 5 in Florida), this stylish Italian offering makes for a superb casual lunch or romantic dinner. A mouth-watering menu – featuring delicious flatbreads, luscious salads, superb steaks and surf & turf, creative pastas and regional specialities like chicken limone and gorgonzola lamb chops, plus daily fish specials – is complemented by a well-balanced wine list and superior service. The Tuscan country-style, quality-

Wolfgang Puck's

conscious ambience and fresh kids' menu all add up to memorable dining. Great weekend brunch, too (10am–3pm). ($$–$$$$; 11am–10pm Mon–Thurs, 11pm Fri and Sat, 10am–10pm Sun; 407 351 8909/622 5611; **www.brioitalian.com**).

BRITTIP

At **Brio Tuscan Grille**, don't miss the melt-in-the-mouth beef carpaccio starter, the bistecca insalata and sensational shrimp and scallop risotto as a superb dinner combination.

Jiko: This great favourite of ours is at *Disney's Animal Kingdom Lodge* and is possibly Disney's most imaginative culinary offering. Maintaining the hotel's African theme, Jiko ('the cooking place') features twin wood-burning ovens, a masterful menu and an exclusive selection of South African wines. The menu has Indian, Asian and African influences, with dishes like Swahili curry shrimp, Chermoula tanglewood chicken and maize crusted wreck-fish, plus a couple of excellent vegetarian choices and a cheese plate that can be ordered as a main course or dessert. Its flatbreads are also a speciality and the dessert selection is totally decadent. The personal service and ethnic ambience underline the adventure of eating here, and it's the perfect venue for a romantic meal (5–11pm; 407 939 3463).

The Oceanaire: Step back in time at this relaxed and stylish seafood room at Pointe Orlando. The decor, reminiscent of a classic 1930s ocean liner, and mood music lead you into a fish and shellfish wonderland, complete with a superb oyster bar. Shrimp, crab, scallops, clams, lobster and as many as 15 types of fish all jostle for attention on a sumptuous menu that also offers great salads, steaks and chicken (though you'd be crazy to ignore the seafood here). The selection varies daily according to the freshest produce available, but typical examples include 'Black & Bleu' Ecuadorian swordfish, cioppino (a delightful fish and shellfish stew), stuffed Atlantic flounder and stuffed

Lake Buena Vista

The third main tourist area, this features the broadest range of choice. Looking first at the area **East** of I-4: *Fast Food:* Subway, Dunkin' Donuts, Wendy's. *Family Favourites:* Bahama Breeze, Carraba's, CiCi's Pizza, Golden Corral, Lone Star Steakhouse. *Home From Home:* Frankie Farrell's. *Seafood Specials:* Landry's Seafood.

To the **West** of I-4 (in the Crossroads area, SR 535 and Palm Parkway) there is: *Fast Food:* McDonald's, Pizza Hut, Quiznos, Steak 'n Shake, Subway, Taco Bell. *Family Favourites:* Black Angus, Buffalo Wild Wings, Chevys, CiCi's Pizza, Denny's, Fuddruckers, Hooters, IHOP, Macaroni Grill, Olive Garden, Orlando Ale House, Perkins, Shoney's, Sizzler, Sweet Tomatoes, TGI Fridays, Uno Chicago, Waffle House. *International Flavours:* Dragon Court Buffet, India Palace, Kobe Steakhouse. *Seafood Specials:* Crab House, Joe's Crab Shack. *Deluxe Dining:* Johnnie's Hideaway. Plus: **Giordano's**, a fabulous Chicago-style pizzeria serving some of the best deep-dish pizza pies, plus salads, sandwiches and pasta ($–$$$, 11am-10pm; 407 377 0020, **www.giordanos.com**).

DINING OUT

Caribbean lobster tail, as well as a surf & turf option and a dozen types of oyster. Its grand shellfish platter (at $30 per person) is an extravaganza of shrimp, crab, lobster and oysters and it has an impressive wine list. Service is top-notch and there is also a seasonal fixed 3-course menu at a reasonable $35/person ($$$$–$$$$$; 5–10pm Sun–Thurs, 11pm Fri and Sat; 407 363 4801; **www.theoceanaire.com**).

Seasons 52: A trendy national chain (in the Plaza Venezia on Sand Lake Road next to the Altamonte Mall), this presents some of the best fine dining in the state. The name reflects the creative, seasonal, health-conscious menu. All appetisers, salads and soups range from 100–250 calories, the majority being either grilled or oven-roasted, and all mains are less than 475 calories. Its fish and seafood are a highlight but lamb, chicken and steaks are equally tempting and there are good vegetarian choices. The 'mini indulgence' desserts are ideal to finish a meal in style. Your server will offer advice – not least with an extensive wine list – while the bar area and outdoor terrace are equally stylish, ideal for a romantic occasion ($$–$$$$; 11.30am–2.30pm and 5–10pm Mon–Fri, 11.30am–11pm Sat, 11.30am–10pm Sun; 407 354 5212; **www.seasons52.com**).

Wolfgang Puck's: At *Downtown Disney*, this unusual mix of styles and restaurants – 4 under 1 roof –

represents some of the best family dining, with a great upmarket option in the Dining Room. The main Café is smart enough, but head upstairs and you are in seriously romantic territory, with a great view of Pleasure Island and service to match. The contrast with the fun hubbub below is striking, while the menu is well thought out and varied – try the Chinois-style lamb rack or lobster risotto, or just opt for one of their superb steaks. Fans of exceptional German cuisine will want to try the signature pork Wiener schnitzel while there are also 2 fixed-priced menus, a 4-course for $60/head and a 3-course for $50. ($$$–$$$$ Café 11.30am–11pm; $$$$–$$$$$ Dining Room 6–10.30pm; 407 938 9653; **www. wolfgangpuck.com**).

◀▶ BRITTIP

Need expert local advice on dining? Check out our good friend, restaurant critic and keen foodie Scott Joseph for up-to-date news, views and insight at **www.scottjosephorlando.com**. Not only is his 'Flog' (a Food Blog) essential reading, he also offers periodic special deals for ½-price coupons at a great range of restaurants. His *Orlando Restaurant Guide* is great reading and has a free app. for iPhone, iPod and iPad at the iTunes store. Just look up Scott Joseph Orlando.

Zen: Find a fine hotel and you will find a fine restaurant, and that is true of the Omni Orlando resort at

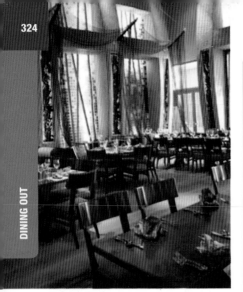

Tchoup-Chop

Champions Gate, where Zen is a wonderful Asian-themed restaurant. With a sake bar, sushi bar and elegant main restaurant, this is an oasis of oriental charm and style. Highlights are the mouth-watering Beijing Spare Ribs and Sautéed Shrimp with Chile Pepper Sauce and Glazed Walnuts. Or just opt for the superb Zen Experience, a multi-course feast. ($$–$$$$, 6–10pm Tues–Sun; 407 390 6664; **www.omnihotels.com**).

And our No 1…

While it's practically impossible to single out one restaurant from this vast wealth of culinary delight, if pushed we would have to plump for what we consider the most amazing restaurant experience in central Florida, at Universal's Royal Pacific Resort. **Tchoup-Chop** (pronounced 'chop chop'), from the gourmet stable of New Orleans master chef Emeril Lagasse, offers Asian-Pacific fusion cuisine in the most eye-catching setting. Service is a team effort at each table and the superb menu is well presented and explained. Blending aromatic and flavoursome elements of Thai, Chinese, Japanese, South Seas and other Pacific Rim cuisines, Lagasse has conjured up a delectable array of dishes. Start with steamed vegetable dumplings or Polynesian crab cake

(with mango-habañero butter sauce and caramelised pineapple compote), then graduate to furikake-crusted Atlantic salmon (with coconut purple sticky rice, cucumber namasu and sweet sake yuzu soy jus), Mongolian barbeque grilled pork tenderloin or smoked sea salt grilled filet of beef tenderloin (with garlic potatoes in a green peppercorn sake). The desserts are equally fragrant and the whole experience is a 5-star treat ($$$–$$$$$; 5.30–10.30pm Sun–Thurs, 11pm Fri and Sat; 407 503 2467; **www.emerils.com**).

Or…take a tip from Scott Joseph, who rates the **Ravenous Pig** in Winter Park his No. 1 (and he's hard to argue with!). Taking the British gastropub idea, local restaurateurs James and Julie Petrakis have crafted a cozy hideaway that oozes charm and style, and with a menu that is superbly simple or simply superb, depending on if you just want great pub food or the full gourmet experience. Creative salads jostle with fresh pastas and a Raw bar, as well as standards like a Pub Burger, Devilled Eggs, and a Fish Sandwich. Bookings here are highly advisable though, as its popularity is spreading ($$–$$$$; 11.30–2pm and 5.30–11pm Tues–Sat; 407 628 2333; **www.theravenouspig.com**).

But now on to another of our favourite topics – shopping…

Tchoup-Chop

12 Shopping

or How to Send Your Credit Card into Meltdown

As well as being a theme park wonderland, this vast area of Florida is a shopper's paradise, with a dazzling array of specialist outlets, malls, flea markets and discount retailers. New centres spring up all the time, from smart malls to cheap gift shops – and you can't go a few paces in the tourist areas without a shop insisting it has the 'best bargains' of 1 sort or another.

With so much good shopping to be had for UK visitors, there's a danger of exceeding your baggage allowance for the flight home – or your duty free allowance. American stores are genuinely fun just to browse, let alone splash out in, and you can expect to pay roughly the same in dollars as you do in pounds for items like clothes, books and CDs, and real bargains are to be had in jeans, trainers, shoes, sports equipment and cosmetics. Virtually everywhere offers free, convenient parking, while American shop assistants are all polite and helpful.

Sales tax: Be aware of the hidden extra costs of shopping. Unlike our VAT, Florida sales tax is NOT part of the displayed purchase price, so you must add on 6% or 7% (it varies by county) for the final price. Also, some shops will ask for photo ID with credit card purchases, so have a photo driving licence or other ID with you.

Allowances: Your limit in the catch-all duty category of 'gifts and souvenirs' is only £390 per person. If you exceed that, you need to keep your receipts and go through the 'goods to declare' channel (though paying the duty and VAT can still be cheaper than buying the same items at home). Some items, such as clothing and footwear for children, do not incur a VAT rate. However, restrictions apply to all reduced-rate VAT items, so be sure to check details with HM Revenue & Customs. Your ordinary duty-free allowances from America include 200 cigarettes and 1 litre of spirits or 2 litres of fortified wine or sparkling wine and 4 litres of still wine.

Customs duty: You pay duty (which varies depending on the item) on the total purchase price (i.e. inclusive of Florida sales tax) once you have exceeded £390, plus VAT at 20%. You CANNOT pool your allowances to cover 1 item that exceeds a single allowance. Hence, if you buy a digital

Tren-D at Downtown Disney

camera that costs £400, you have to pay the duty (at 4.9%) on the full £400, taking the total to £419.60 and then VAT on that figure. However, if you have several items that add up to £390, and then another that exceeds that, you pay the duty and VAT only on the excess item (and customs officers usually give you the benefit of the lowest rate on what you pay for). Duty rates are updated regularly and vary from 2.2% (e.g. video games) to 14% (e.g. a computer monitor) bearing in mind VAT rates are subject to change. For more info, contact the Customs and Excise National Advice Service on 0845 010 9000, **www.hmrc. gov.uk**.

> ### BRITTIP
> Pick up the *Orlando Sentinel* newspaper on Sun and you will get the full local lowdown on all the great sales for the coming week.

Alligator products, which still constitute those of an endangered species (to UK authorities), require an import licence, and you should consult the Global Wildlife Licensing and Registration Service for more info.

> ### BRITTIP
> Don't buy electrical goods in the US – they won't work in the UK without an adapter. Most games systems (notably X Box, Wii and PS3) are also NOT compatible with UK players. Hand-held games are fine, though.

Downtown Disney

In many ways, the heart of Walt Disney World is its **Downtown Disney** district, split into 3 linked sections: Disney Marketplace, Hyperion Wharf/ Pleasure Island and West Side. This is typical Disney, a beautiful location, imaginative architecture and a host of one-off elements that make shopping a pleasure, with 48 shops and dining opportunities. A handy water-taxi links the 3 main elements of this 120-acre/48.5ha plaza.

Downtown Disney can be found off exits 67 and 68 of I-4 and is well signposted (exit 68 can be congested at peak periods). You can also rent boats at Cap'n Jack's Marina (Marketplace), including the fun 2-person Sea Raycers ($32 per ½ hr) and the 21ft/6.5m Sun Tracker pontoons, which take up to 10 ($45 per ½hr).

Bibbidi Bobbidi Boutique

Up, up and away!

A recent addition to *Downtown Disney*, in the West Side across the bridge from Hyperion Wharf, is **Characters In Flight**, a wonderful tethered balloon ride that gently soars up to 300ft/91.5m high carrying up to 30 at a time in a 19ft/5.7m gondola on 6min rides. It provides a fab panorama of much of the huge extent of *Walt Disney World* and is a great photo opportunity by day or night (10.30am–11pm, to midnight Fri and Sat). It costs $18/adult and $12/3–9s. In certain weather conditions the number of passengers is limited, while it is grounded in high winds or heavy rain.

Disney Marketplace: (9.30am–11pm) Don't miss the **World of Disney** store, the largest of its kind, which includes **Bibbidi Bobbidi Boutique** (where young girls can have hair, make-up and nails done in true Princess style, the all-new **Lego Imagination Center** (an interactive playground and shop), the amazing **Art of Disney** and **Team Mickey's Athletic Club**. **Once Upon A Toy** is a gigantic toy emporium complete with a host of classic games, many with a Disney theme, for kids to try. Other worthwhile one-offs are the blissful **Basin** (for toiletries) and **Disney's Wonderful World of Memories** (for all scrapbook fans, plus the only place to get a Disney postmark for your postcards home!).

BRITTIP
Young girls in the princess mood may want to take part in the daily **Princess Parade** from the World of Disney store. Held at 2pm weekdays (noon at weekends) each day, it marches in full pomp from the Princess Hollow end of the store through the Marketplace, finishing at the Carousel, where all children get a free ride. Girls can dress up (or not) as they wish, and there is NO fee to take part.

Marketplace Dining: For the lowdown on where to eat in this part of *Downtown Disney* – Rainforest Café, Pollo Campero, Wolfgang Puck Express, Cap'n Jack's Restaurant, Ghirardelli's, Earl of Sandwich and T-Rex Café – see p306.

BRITTIP
Parents beware! The Bibbidi Bobbidi Boutique hair and make-up shop is hideously expensive. Packages range from $50-$240, so you may want to steer your Princess gently away!

Arribas Brothers is a big, attractive gift store. Those keen on the pin-trading hobby should check out **Pin Traders**. Then there's **Disney Design-A-Tee, Tren-D**, a cutting edge Disney fashion store for women, **Little Miss Matched** for fun and funky socks, bedding and more (popular with young girls), and **Disney's Days of Christmas**. For bargain-hunters, a section by **Goofy's Candy Company** offers **Marketplace Fun Finds** – everything at reduced prices. Dancing fountains and squirt pools (where kids tend to get seriously wet), the lakeside setting and boating opportunities all add to the appeal.

Hyperion Wharf (formerly Pleasure Island): This area is still being revamped, with new shops and restaurants being added to make it lively during the day as well as by night. Parts will see ongoing construction through the end of

World of Disney Store

© Disney

© OCVB

Pointe Orlando

2011 and into 2012 but the entire area is now a more continuous part of *Downtown Disney*, with a large bridge to the West Side, wider walkways and a water-taxi dock. The cornerstone **Harley-Davidson** store has temporarily moved to the West Side to accommodate part of the re-build, but there is still **Curl by Sammy Duvall**, a surfing, apparel and accessories shop, and F**uego Cigars by Sosa**, an upmarket cigar emporium and lounge. Both **Raglan Road** and **Paradiso 37** restaurants have their own gift shops here.

Hyperion Dining: For dining choice in Hyperion Wharf/Pleasure Island – Fulton's Crab House, Portobello, Paradiso 37, Raglan Road and Cookes of Dublin – see p305.

West Side: Continuing into West Side (10.30am–11pm) gives you the superb **AMC 24** cinema complex (p000), plus another 16 retail and dining outlets. The **Hoypoloi Gallery** is one of our favourites for an eclectic range of artwork from metal to glass, while **Magic Masters** (a wide variety of tricks and souvenirs, with demonstrations), **D Street** (Vinylmation figurines and collectables) and **Pop Gallery** are all highly original. **Goofy's Candy**

Cauldron is a big hit with kids and the temporary outlet of the **Harley-Davidson** store can be found here, along with gift shops for **House of Blues**, **Bongos Cuban Cafe**, **Cirque du Soleil** and **DisneyQuest** (p287).

West Side Dining: For the lowdown on all the great dining in this part of *Downtown Disney* – Planet Hollywood, House of Blues, Bongo's Cuban Café and Wolfgang Puck Café – see p307.

International Drive

This core tourist area is awash with shopping of all kinds, from the cheapest and tackiest plazas, full of tourist gift shops, to 3 clever, purpose-built centres. Some of the shops just north of the Sand Lake Road junction are best avoided, while the northern end of I-Drive has undergone a major redevelopment. This area is also renowned for discount outlet shopping – a local speciality – offering name brands at heavily reduced prices.

Premium Outlets International Drive (formerly Prime Outlets): At the top of I-Drive, this attractive 175-shop 'lifestyle centre' has gone all out for the big, semi-open-air style that encourages people to wander the long interior promenades full of shop fronts and big-name brands. Boasting a landscaped canal running through the centre, outdoor seating, cafés, a Market Place food court and a Guest Services centre, it provides a luxury touch. Major brands include the **Neiman Marcus Last Call Clearance Center**, which will attract the fashion-conscious, as will the **Hugo Boss Factory Store**, **White House/ Black Market**, **Esprit** and **Jones New York Outlet**. Other familiar names include **Nike Factory Store**, **Tommy Hilfiger**, **Crabtree & Evelyn**, **Banana Republic**, **Bath & Body Works**, **Ted Baker**, **Coach and Brooks Brothers**, plus, inevitably, a **Starbucks**. New in 2011 were an **Eddie Bauer**, **PS from Aeropostale** (for kids) and the exotic taste of **Pinkberry** frozen yoghurt. With its attractive food court and 2 smart full-service restaurants, Italian-styled **Vinito** and the Caribbean flair of **Kafe Kalik**, you have 1 of the area's brightest shopping centres (10am–11pm Mon–Sat, 10am–9pm Sun; **www.premiumoutlets.com/orlando**).

Festival Bay: Due to undergo a major redevelopment in 2012, it was unclear at the time of writing what stores will remain. We believe Bass Pro Shop, Vans Skate Park, Ron Jon Surf Shop and the Cinema will stay open during Festival Bay's transformation from a covered mall to an open-air style village, but check the website for the latest details **www.shopfestivalbaymall.com**.

Pointe Orlando: Following a massive redevelopment in 2009, the dramatic rebuild added a new entrance plaza directly from I-Drive, as well as new shops and especially restaurants, making this a good choice for an evening out with a bit of retail therapy. Among 20-plus smart stores, you can indulge your passion for fashion at **Victoria's Secret**, **Armani Exchange**, **Chico's** and **Hollister** or stock up on gifts and souvenirs at **Bath & Body Works**, eclectic **Artsy Abode**, **Tommy Bahamas**, **SGH sunglass hut**, **Brighton** gifts and accessories and the excellent **Tharoo & Co** jewellery. Don't miss **Baterbys**

Art Auction Gallery for artworks by Masters such as Dali and Picasso, as well as contemporary artists.

Pointe Dining: For the full rundown on where to eat at Pointe Orlando – Capital Grille, The Oceanaire, Johnny Rockets, Pizzeria Valdiano, Maggiano's, Cuba Libre and Taverna Opa – see p319.

You will also find plenty of entertainment by night here at **BB King's Blues Club**, **Adobe Gila's** and the **Regal Cinemas Stadium 20 + IMAX Cineplex**, which shows first-run movies in large screen format. Parking is at The Pointe's multi-storey car park, but several stores and restaurants will redeem your parking ticket if you shop there. It's open noon–10pm Mon–Sat, noon–8pm Sun, later at the bars and restaurants (407 248 2838, **www.pointeorlando.com**).

BRITTIP

While you may not be able to afford some of the art on offer at **Baterbys** at Pointe Orlando – which includes the likes of Dali, Picasso, Miro and Peter Max – its huge gallery offers superb viewing. Named Best Art Gallery by *Orlando Style Magazine*, it features periodic fund-raising auctions, while its website previews many of its offerings at **www.baterbys.com**.

Festival Bay

Kissimmee

Down along the tourist territory of Highway 192, you will again find a complete mix of outlets, with a profusion of the cheap and cheerful, but also several highly enticing possibilities.

Old Town: This is Kissimmee's version of the purpose-built tourist shopping centre, an antique-style offering with an eclectic mix of shops, restaurants, bars and fairground attractions, set out along brick-lined streets. The shops range from standard souvenirs, novel T-shirt outlets and Disney merchandise to sportswear, motorbike fashions and other collectables (check out the **Old Town General Store** for a step back in time, or the **Old Town Portrait Gallery** for period-style photos). The individual style of **Out Of This World Embroidery** offers a 'you name it, we'll stitch it' service, while **Black Market Minerals**, **Kandlestix**, **Andean Manna** and **Magic Max** are all great for novel gift ideas. There are also 16 restaurants or snack bars.

A Kissimmee tradition

Old Town is home to some weekly events that appeal to locals and tourists alike and are well worth catching. The **Saturday Nite Cruise** at 8.30pm is a trademark drive-past of 300-plus vintage and collector cars (the biggest in America; viewing starts at 1pm). A **Friday Nite Cruise** features cars built between 1964 and 1979, while Wed night's 5pm **Little Darlin' Street Party and Cruise In** brings out the pre-1987 cars. There is live music, fairground-type stalls and prizes, and it can get fairly raucous later on, with plenty of alcoholic libations (witness the Sun on the Beach bar!).

For pampering, head to **Vivian's Day Spa**, for lunch or dinner try **Tex Mex** Mexican cuisine or **Kool Katz Grill & Pub** featuring American favourites in a casual atmosphere reminiscent of the Friday and Saturday Nite car cruises, while the **Blue Max Tavern** is another fun alternative. **Flippers Pizzeria** and **Old Town Chippy** are also worth trying, while there are other snack outlets, with offerings from popcorn to candy and the wonderful **Old Town Ice Cream Company**. **Sun on the Beach** is a good nightclub in evenings. Parking is free (10am–11pm daily; rides open noon–11pm; 407 396 4888; **www.old-town.com**).

Kissimmee Old Town

© OCVB

Mural in Downtown Kissimmee

Downtown Kissimmee offers the more local, authentic face of shopping in Florida, with the charming Main Street area featuring a range of antique shops, one-off boutiques, cafés and restaurants. Much attention has been paid to the historic district in recent years, and it is now a relaxing place for a wander and a meal. The **Welcome Station** on Main Street (formerly an old-fashioned petrol station) is a great place to start, and even has local crafts, keepsakes, and books focusing on Floridian history (9am–5pm Mon–Fri; 10am–2pm Sat). Then look into the likes of local landmarks **Lanier's**, **Makinson Hardware** (the oldest hardware store in Florida), and **Gallery One Artists**. The authentic Mexican family style of **Azteca's** is worth trying, along with the casual sports-bar style of **Broadway Pizza**, while we're fans of the smart **Chef John's Dockside Inn** (try the Grouper sandwich!). Every Thurs (7am–1pm) you can also sample the local **Farmers' Market** on the corner of Pleasant St and Darlington Ave. Look up **www.kissimmeemainstreet.com**.

The Kissimmee area is largely short of quality shopping otherwise, but head up to the Osceola Parkway (at the junction with John Young Parkway), which runs parallel to Highway 192, and you find the extensive developments of **The Loop** and the recently added **Loop West**,

which help redress the balance. This double open-air plaza offers a unique mix of shops and restaurants, plus a 16-screen **Regal Cinema**, in a pedestrian-friendly setting, with the shops grouped around 2 large car parks. Many of the shops may not be familiar but are worth visiting. Of note at The Loop are **Ross** (a huge discount warehouse of clothes, shoes, linens, cosmetics and more), **Kohl's** (a well-priced department store), **Bed, Bath & Beyond** (household wares), **Pacific Sunwear** (beach and casual wear), **Old Navy** (clothing), **Michaels** (arts and crafts), **Sports Authority** and **Famous Footwear** (discounted shoes). There is also a hairdresser, nail salon, chemist (**CVS**). At The Loop West, look for the big department stores of **JC Penney** (clothing and housewares) and **Belk** (home goods), plus **Ulta** (cosmetics), **Christopher & Banks** (women's clothing) and **DSW** (shoes), plus 15 additional shops.

In all, The Loop and Loop West boast 65 shopping and dining outlets and this has quickly become a major proposition, especially for the extensive dining choice. Take your pick from classic 1950 diner **Johnny Rockets**, **Red Brick Pizza**, the counter-service of **Pei Wei Asian Diner**, Mexican choice **Abuelo's**, **Tropical Smoothie Cafe** and the big-name chains of **Macaroni Grill** (p314), **Chili's** (p310), **Panera Bread** (p304) and **Bonefish Grill** (p316) to name just a few. The shops are open 10am–9.30pm Mon–Sat, 11am–6pm Sun, later at the restaurants and cinemas (407 343 9223; **www.attheloop. com**).

Downtown Kissimmee

Lake Buena Vista

The Lake Buena Vista area offers 2 of the best discount outlet centres, with great range and great prices!

Orlando Premium Outlets: High on your 'must visit' list, this is a huge hit with UK visitors – and it's still growing. With a fresh look and style, and a legion of big-name designers, it can be found on Vineland Avenue between I-Drive and I-4 (just south of SeaWorld; or exit 68 off I-4).

BRITTIP

Don't try to battle with the crowds in the main open-air car park at Orlando Premium Outlets. Instead, head towards the back of the centre where you will find the 1,600-car multi-storey car park.

In all, it offers 150 stores of well-known brand names (like **Timberland**, **Diesel**, **Burberry**, **Giorgio Armani**, **Kenneth Cole**, **Banana Republic**, **French Connection** and **Calvin Klein**) in a semi-covered pedestrian plaza, with free parking and the convenience of being at the south end of the I-Ride Trolley (main line). Other signature shops are **Samsonite Company Store**, **Ecko Unltd** (jeans and sportswear), **Fendi** (stylish women's clothing and handbags), **OshKosh B'Gosh** (baby/toddler clothes), **Factory Brand Shoes** (a mini-warehouse of footwear fashion) and **Perfumania**. Watch out

Orlando Premium Outlets

also for big Disney bargains at the **Character Première**. In all, there are 75 clothing and fashion stores, 25 for shoes, 10 jewellers, 9 for children's clothing and 6 for luggage. A big 2008 expansion added another 38 upmarket shops, including **J Crew**, **Hurley** and **Wolford**, while new in 2011 were the handbags and accessories of **Vera Bradley**, women's fashions at **Final Cut BCBG Max Azria**, **Rockport** and **Steve Madden** shoes and the designer fashions of **Tory Burch**.

BRITBONUS

Brit Guide Itinerary Planner Service clients will receive Orlando Premium Outlets' special **Premier Platinum VIP Passport** voucher, for significant extra savings at many shops (p45).

The food court is quite tempting, too, with 10 outlets, from **Villa Fresh Italian Kitchen** and **Maki of Japan** to **Starbucks**, **Taco Bell** and **Subway**. There is even a beer and wine café. For those without a car, there is a daily free shuttle service from 15 hotels in Lake Buena Vista ($11/person from Highway 192 in Kissimmee). Call 407 390 0000, extension 2, for reservations, which are required at least 2 hours in advance. The Lynx bus service also stops here (407 841 2279), while Maingate Taxi as on-site taxi stands, or you could try **Star Taxi** (407 857 9999). Premium Outlets is open daily 10am–11pm (9pm Sun; 407 238 7787; **www.premiumoutlets.com/orlando**).

Lake Buena Vista Factory Stores: Get ready for more big-name products at discount prices here, from Fossil, Converse, Reebok, Liz Claiborne and Van Heusen to a budget-priced **Disney Character Outlet**, **OshKosh B'Gosh** superstore and (the better-priced) **Carter's For Kids**. It is another open-air plaza, with almost 50 stores spread over 6 acres/2.5ha and with plentiful parking. It's slightly off the beaten track and therefore not quite as busy as some of the others. New shops are opening all the time, and recent additions include stylish **Ann Taylor Loft Outlet**, **Under Armour**,

Florida Mall

Tommy Hilfiger, funky **Aeropostale**,
Ecko Unltd, **Izod**, **Avanti Sunglass
Boutique**, **Eddie Bauer Outlet** and
Rawlings Factory Store for sporting
goods. There is also a decent food
court with a pleasant outdoor
deck, and a kids' playground. Some
of the stores and brand names
may not be well known to us, but
the likes of **Old Navy** (excellent-
value casual clothing), **Perfume
Smart** (discounted fragrances and
cosmetics), **SAS Shoes** (think Hush
Puppies, only cheaper!), **Travelpro**
(luggage) and **Rack Room Shoes** (big
names at serious savings) are worth
discovering. **Book Warehouse** offers
great bargain books, **Camera Outlet**
carries a large selection of European
PAL systems, and **World of Coffee** is
both an internet café and one of the
best places you could find to sip a
latte and enjoy a cake or pastry, with
its outdoor terrace and bird cages.
Worth noting at the neighbouring
Lake Buena Vista Resort Village and
Spa are the luxurious **Reflections Spa**
for a bit of pampering after your day
of shopping, and **Frankie Farrells
Irish Pub** (p000).

BRITTIP
Those who enjoy scrapbooks or other
arts and crafts, should find one of
Orlando's 8 **Michaels** stores are heaven!

The Factory Stores are on SR 535
(2mls/3km south off exit 68 on I-4)
and are open daily 10am–9pm (to
7pm Sun). Their shuttle service
picks up at hotels and condos in a
10ml/16km radius (407 238 9301,
www.lbvfs.com).

BRITTIP
Go to **www.lbvfs.com** for up to
$400 in discount coupons.

Malls
Head out slightly beyond the main
tourist territory and you will discover
the further choice and style of the
area's many malls. They contain a
huge range of shops and, if you take
advantage of their periodic sales, you

Florida Mall

will be firmly back on the bargain trail. The top 2 locally are the Florida Mall and the Mall at Millenia, and both offer a contrasting experience.

BRITTIP

Need a good book? Make a beeline for **Barnes & Noble**, on West Sand Lake Road in the Venezia Plaza, on the South Orange Blossom Trail opposite the Florida Mall, or at the new Winter Garden Village shops. Each has a great coffee shop, too.

Florida Mall: The largest in central Florida, this features more than 260 shops, with 6 large department stores and a 22-counter food court, plus a children's play area, the lively bar-restaurant **Ruby Tuesday**, the popular fresh offerings of **Nature's Table**, **California Pizza Kitchen** and hearty **Buca di Beppo**. Located on the South Orange Blossom Trail, on the corner of Sand Lake Road, this spacious and smart mall is open 10am–9pm Mon–Sat, noon–6pm Sun. Highlights are the department stores, led by the upmarket (but expensive) **Saks Fifth Avenue** and **Macy's**, plus **JC Penney**, **Nordstrom** (with a sit-down café), **Sears** and **Dillard's**. Other shops worth looking out for are **Bath & Body Works**, **Williams-Sonoma** (the place for cooks), **PacSun** (beachwear and more) and, for kids, the **Build-a-Bear Workshop**, **Game Stop** and the fun **M&M's World** store, plus trendy **Gap** and a **Zara** outlet. New in 2011 were women's fashion store **Francesca's Collections**, chic **Brighton Collectibles**, **Soma**

The Mall at Millenia

Intimates, **Rockport** shoes and **Flip Flop Shops**. Guest services offers a discount booklet with a handy international size chart to help with American sizing, while there is also free wheelchair use, pushchair rental and foreign currency exchange. There are even spa and beauty treatments in the Lancôme Institut de Beauté in Dillard's, and the JC Penney styling salon (407 851 6255; **www.simon. com**). The Mall also benefits from the integral **Florida Hotel**, with Cricket's Grille & Bar. Nearby on Sand Lake Road, you'll find warehouse-like **Old Time Pottery**, a vast emporium of home goods of all kinds, from crockery to linens (**www.oldtimepottery. com**).

BRITTIP

Kids – let your parents take you to the Florida Mall, then insist on visiting the huge **Toys 'R Us** store at the front and then **M&M World** inside the mall!

Mall at Millenia: If the Florida Mall is the biggest shopping venue, this is the smartest. Opened in October 2002 just off I-4 to the north of Universal Orlando (exit 78), it is the most upmarket, dramatic and technologically advanced shopping complex in Florida, with New York's most famous department stores – Bloomingdale's, Neiman Marcus and Macy's – among a select number of other top-name boutiques such as Louis Vuitton and Tiffany & Co. The entrance features a 60ft/18m glass rotunda with a flowing water garden theme and a concierge desk (valet parking is available). Then you can head in 1 of 4 directions over the marble and terrazzo floors or go upstairs to the high-quality 12-outlet food court, **Bistro Sensations** (salads, soups, wraps), F**irehouse Subs**, **Haagen-Dazs** (decadent ice cream), the authentic Mandarin-style of **Chinatown**, the fresh Greek **Jalapeno** (tacos and burritos – but nothing Greek!) and **Southwest Grill** (succulent chicken, barbecue beef and salads), plus **Tony's & Bruno's** for Italian specialities (pasta, pizza, salads and cheesecake).

The Mall at Millenia

BRITBONUS

$ Visit the concierge office at Mall at Millenia, in the lower level, opposite the Cheesecake Factory and show this book to receive a complimentary gift and savings book.

The grand architecture is also focused on 5 separate courts along a flattened, serpentine S-shape, topped by an arched glass roof like a gigantic conservatory. On 2 airy levels (3 in Bloomingdale's and Macy's) and with 8 Juliet balconies connecting the 2 sides, the mall consists of a colossal amount of glass, plus a stunning Grand Court, featuring a dozen 20ft/6m columns capped by curved plasma video screens. And, while around 20% of the 150 stores are upmarket (**Cartier**, **Chanel**, **Jimmy Choo**, **Burberry** and **Gucci**), there are many unexpected options, such as **Urban Outfitters**, **Apple**, **MAC Cosmetics** and **Anthropologie**. You will also find plenty of mainstream names like **Abercrombie & Fitch**, **Hollister**, **Gap**, **Banana Republic** and **Victoria's Secret**. The 4 main restaurants are also first class:

gourmet seafood **McCormick & Schmick's**, heavenly **Cheesecake Factory**, **PF Chang's China Bistro** and the stylish Italian of **Brio Tuscan Grille** (p322). On top of that there is the excellent fresh sandwich style of **Panera Bread**, the **California Pizza Kitchen** and a **Johnny Rockets** diner. This is also the only mall with a US post office inside (NB: Standard postcards to the UK cost 98c). A currency exchange is available, as are international phone cards. Chic **Blue Martini**, a speciality martini bar, restaurant and music venue, is worth trying for a special occasion. With more than 32 unique martinis,

Blue Martini

© OCVB

AMC Cineplex at Downtown Disney

plus premium cigars, an extensive wine list and a tapas-style menu, this is the current trendy hangout, with an outdoor terrace and indoor stage room. There's live music (8–11.30pm Mon–Thurs, 7.30–11.30pm Fri and Sat), then dance music with the house DJ (4pm–2am Mon–Fri, 1pm–2am Sat and Sun, Happy Hour 4–7pm Mon–Fri; **www.bluemartinilounge.com**). All in all, this takes the Florida shopping experience to a new level (10am–9pm Mon–Sat, 11am–7pm Sun; 407 363 3555; **www.mallatmillenia.com**).

Other malls: There are 3 alternatives to these popular (and busy – especially at weekends) malls. The **Altamonte Mall** is on Altamonte Avenue in the suburb of Altamonte Springs (take exit 92 off I-4 and head east for ½ml/800m on Route 436, then turn left); **Seminole Towne Center**, just off I-4 to the north of Orlando on the outskirts of Sanford (exit 101C off I-4); and **Oviedo Marketplace**, to the east of Orlando (right off exit 41 of Central Florida Greeneway, 417). The Altamonte Mall is the best of the bunch and well off the beaten tourist track, featuring 160 speciality shops, 4 major department

stores – Macy's, Dillard's, JC Penney and Sears – and 22 eateries, including the fun **Bahama Breeze** (p309), upmarket **Seasons 52** (p323) and pub-style **Orlando Ale House** (p300). An 18-screen cinema and children's soft- play area round out the offerings. Open 10am–9pm Mon–Sat, 11am–6pm Sun, the Customer Service Centre offers a VIP savings book to visitors (**www.altamontemall.com**). Shop during the week and you'll feel as if you have the place to yourself!

Winter Garden Village: One last major shopping recommendation is this more offbeat offering, 5mls/8km north of *Walt Disney World* on Highway 535 at the junction with toll road 429, which is primarily a new locals' centre but still has visitor appeal. The expansive open-plan design, set around key stores like **Super Target**, **Best Buy**, **Ross**, **Marshall's** and **Beall's**, features a mix of the big names and smaller boutiques, as well as a tempting array of 21 cafes and restaurants sprinkled throughout. Look for the upmarket seafood choice of Bonefish Grill, the elegant Longhorn Steakhouse, family-style Chili's, Cracker Barrel, UNO

Chicago Grill and Mimi's Café, or the counter-service options like 5 Guys Burgers, Urban Flats, Panda Express, Coldstone Creamery and Chick-Fil-A (**www.wintergardenvillage.com**).

Specialist shops

Wal-Mart: High on many people's lists, this warehouse-like store sells just about everything. There are 21 Wal-Marts in central Florida, 16 of which are 24hr Supercenters. The main tourist area stores are on Highway 27 (just north of 192); Highway 192 by Medieval Times (between markers 14 and 15); Osceola Parkway (at Buenaventura Lakes); John Young Parkway (at Sand Lake Road); on Kirkman Road (north of Universal Boulevard); by Highway 535 and Osceola Parkway; and on Turkey Lake Road.

Other supermarkets: There are plenty of other supermarkets and you will find better-quality produce at the likes of **Publix** (throughout the main tourist areas, notably on Highway 192 and 27) and **Winn-Dixie** (a major south-east US chain). But the real Rolls-Royce of food stores, **Whole Foods Market** (our favourite), opened an Orlando branch on Turkey Lake Road, with its signature superb fresh produce emporium and plenty of chances to sample, plus a

magnificent hot-food counter to grab a meal (**www.wholefoodsmarket.com**). For clothes, DIY, home furnishings, electrical goods, household items, gifts, toys and groceries, visit **Target** (its superstores on Highway 192 just west of Highway 535, near Mall at Millenia and Winter Garden Village are fine examples). The big chemists ('drug stores') of **Walgreens** and **CVS** also carry a surprisingly wide range of goods and almost resemble mini-supermarkets in their own right.

BRITTIP

If you shop at any US Wal-Mart store, you can return faulty or wrong-size goods to your local Asda for a refund, as long as you present the receipts.

Flea World: The locals also have a passion for flea markets, highlighted by America's largest covered market, with 1,700 stalls spread over 104 acres/42ha, including 3 massive (air-conditioned), themed buildings and a 7-acre/2.8ha amusement park, **Fun World**. Flea World is open 9am–6pm

Winter Garden Village

Fri, Sat and Sun (Fun World 9am–6pm Sat and Sun only), and can be found a 30min drive away on Highway 17/92 (best picked up from exit 90 on I-4) between Orlando and Sanford (to the north). The stalls include all manner of market goods (nearly all new or slight seconds), from fresh produce to antiques and jewellery, while there is a full-scale food court and a 300-seat pizza and burger eatery, the **Carousel Restaurant**, plus free entertainment on the Fun World Pavilion stage (407 330 1792; **www.fleaworld.com**).

> **BRITTIP**
> Wal-Mart offers 1hr photo processing at great savings on UK prices, as do branches of Walgreens.

Individual outlets: Keen shoppers will want to check out other unfamiliar options. Ross (10 in Orlando, see **www.rossstores.com**) carries a huge range of discounted brand-name clothes, shoes, linens, towels etc. (9.30am–9.30pm Mon–Sat, 10am–9pm Sun), while **Marshalls** (5 in Orlando, **www.marshallsonline. com**) and **TJ Maxx** (also 5, **www.tjmaxx. com**) are similar. For American sports gear visit **Sports Authority** stores

(**www.sportsauthority.com**) or **Sports Dominator** (**www.sportsdominator. com**), while golfers should visit the **Edwin Watts Golf** stores (including the I-Drive clearance centre; **www. edwinwatts.com**), or any of the **Special Tee Golf & Tennis** shops. You can pick up some great deals on golf clubs in particular. By the same token, anglers can stock up on the latest gear at bargain prices at **Bass Pro Shops Outdoor World** (at the Festival Bay centre; **www.basspro.com**).

As a final recommendation, those staying in villas, condo-hotels or just wanting a taste of home should check out the **British Supermarket** (on Vineland Rd just east of its junction with Kirkman Ave, north of Universal Orlando). From Walkers Crisps to Daddies Sauce, Lucozade to Ribena, and proper British bacon to Irish sausages and meat pies, this is a genuine Union Jack grocery, with UK owners who stock everything for those picky eaters (not just kids!) who can't quite take American fare (10am–4pm Mon–Sat, 11am–3pm Sun; 407 370 2023, **http://britishsupermarket.com**).

But now the shopping is done, it's time to think about the journey home…

Downtown Disney's World of Disney Store

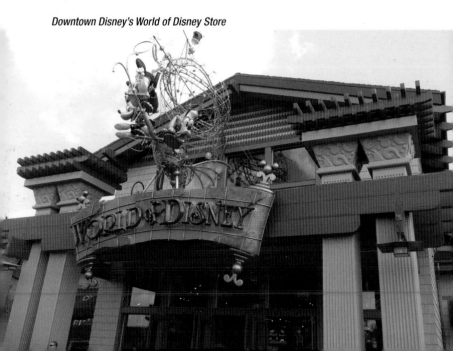

13 Going Home

And so, dog-tired, lighter in the wallet but (hopefully) blissfully happy and with enough memories to last a lifetime, it's time to deal with that bane of all holidays – the journey home.

Now you have come through the last 2 weeks relatively unscathed, here's how to avoid any last-minute pitfalls.

The car

Returning the hire car can take time if you used an off-airport car depot, so allow an extra ½ an hour; the process is much slicker with firms that operate directly from the airports, as nearly all now do. Most airlines require you to arrive 3hrs before an international flight, so don't be tempted to leave your check-in until the last minute. The off-airport check-in facilities for Virgin Holidays (at *Downtown Disney* by Cirque du Soleil®) are a major bonus in making this process smoother. Now you'll have time to kill, so here is a guide to the 2 main Orlando airports.

Orlando International Airport

Orlando International is 46mls/74km from Cocoa Beach and 54mls/87km from Daytona Beach on the east coast, 84mls/135km from Tampa and 110mls/177km from Clearwater and St Petersburg to the west, 25mls/40km from *Walt Disney World*

and 10mls/16km from Universal Orlando; so always allow plenty of time for the return journey, check-in and security procedure. The Beachline Expressway (528) can get congested in late afternoon, for example, and the Central Florida Greeneway (417) is often better.

This modern airport is the 3rd largest in size in the USA, the 10th for number of passengers (No 1 in Florida) – and top rated for passenger satisfaction. It handles more than 34 million passengers a year (or 90,000 a day), busier than Gatwick and San Francisco. It can get busy at peak times, but its 1,000-acre/405ha terminal complex usually handles crowds with ease, and this is one of the most comfortable airports you could find. It boasts great facilities and its wide, airy concourses make it feel more like an elegant hotel (1 end is actually the airport-owned Hyatt Hotel).

Set off home with plenty of great memories

© Disney

Ramps, restrooms, wide lifts and large open areas ensure easy wheelchair access, and there are features like TDD and amplified telephones, wheelchair-height drinking fountains, Braille lift controls and companion-care restrooms to assist any travellers with disabilities.

The airport always aims to stay a step ahead, and is often engaged in a development project or 2, including ongoing environmentally friendly enhancements. It boasts a major food court, extra restaurant options and some superb shops. There is an emphasis on the 'green' aspect to Orlando International, as its latest fleet of shuttle buses are hydrogen powered, with zero emissions. A convenient 'quick turnaround' area for hire cars allows 96% of hire car companies to have onsite locations, a huge boon to visitors' ease in pick-up and drop-off.

Should you have more than 3hrs to spare, it's worth taking the 15min taxi ride to the Florida Mall, or checking in early, keeping the car and visiting Gatorland about 20mins away (p224).

BRITTIP

You are advised to leave all luggage unlocked (no combination locks or padlocks) when you check in for your flight, as the TSA security staff open a LOT of bags during screening and have the right to access any case, locked or not. TSA-approved locks are suggested, if you prefer to lock your cases.

Orlando International Airport

Landside

As with all international airports, there is a division between LANDSIDE (for visitors) and AIRSIDE (where you must have a ticket). There are 3 levels to Orlando's Landside.

• 1 is for ground transportation, tour operator desks, parking, buses and car rental agencies.

• 2 is for Baggage Claim, which you negotiated on your arrival, and private vehicles meeting passengers.

• 3 is where you enter on your return journey, as it holds the check-in desks, shops and restaurants.

The main area of Level 3 is then further divided into interconnected sections:

Landside A: This houses the check-in for **Gates 1–29** and **100–129**. Here you'll find American Airlines, Air Canada, Martinair, Southwest, JetBlue and Virgin (though Virgin departs from Gates 60–99).

Landside B: Check-in here for **Gates 30–99** and the likes of Aer Lingus, Air France, BA, Continental, Delta, United, Spirit, US Airways and AirTran.

Once you've checked in, you can explore the **East** and **West Halls** of the Level 3 concourse. These house a good mix of shops and restaurants, plus currency exchange, information desks and ATMs, while the Hyatt Hotel is in the East Hall. The East and West Halls are linked by the restaurants, shops and services of the **North** and **South Walks**. In total, there are 47 places to shop and eat, including a handy food court, and it's almost like being in a smart shopping mall. There's a **Suntrust** bank, **post office** and even the fun new **King of Kong arcade** (keep the kiddies busy before your flight!). Many shops feature outstanding design and even photo opportunities: see the 2 **Disney** stores, **Harley-Davidson, Universal, SeaWorld/Busch Gardens** and **Kennedy Space Center**. Other notable shops are **Lush** bath products, **L'Occitane** cosmetics, the unique apparel of **Del Sol, Borders Books** (with its Seattle's Best coffee bar), **Ron Jon Surf Shop**, **Perfumania**, **Johnston & Murphy** (clothing) and **Hudson Booksellers**.

Dining is another pleasure here. The 8-counter food court features **McDonalds**, **Carvel** ice-cream, **Krispy Crème** and **Nathan's Famous Hot Dogs**, as well as the slightly healthier option of **Chick-Fil-A**. **Macaroni Grill** is a tasty full-service Italian restaurant option, while **Fox Sports Sky Box** adds a multi-screen TV set-up plus counter and table service. Upstairs at the West Hall is **Chili's Too**, a cheerful, quick-service Tex-Mex bar-diner.

The **East Hall** tends to be quieter and more picturesque as it is dominated by the 8-storey Hyatt Hotel atrium. Up the escalator is the main entrance, and to see out your visit in style, **McCoy's Bar and Grill** (up and turn right) is a smart bar-restaurant with a grandstand view of the runways. To go really upmarket, take the lift to the 9th-floor **Hemispheres** restaurant (breakfast and dinner only). You'll have an even more impressive view, and its superb Continental cuisine and wine-tasting evenings offer some of the best fare in the city. It's pricey, but 5-star.

BRITTIP
Save some film or card space for the excellent photo opportunities at the airport: outside the Disney stores, the 2 Harley-Davidson shops and the Kennedy Space Center outlets.

Airside

Once it's time to move to your departure gate, be aware of the 4 satellite 'arms' that make up the airport's Airside. This is where you will probably need to queue as the security screening takes time, and you should allow AT LEAST 30 minutes. The arms are divided into Gates 1–29 and 30–59 at the West end, and 60–99 (international departures) and 100–129 (all American domestic flights) at the East. All the departure gates are here, plus duty-free shops and more cafés.

The 4 satellites are each connected to the main building by an automated tram, so you need to be alert when it comes to finding your departure gate. There are no Tannoy announcements for flights, so you should check your departure gate and time when you check in. However, there are large monitors in the terminal with all the departure info. The usual gates are:

- **1–29:** Aer Lingus, American, Air Canada, Martinair and JetBlue.

- **30–59:** Continental, Spirit, United and US Airways.

- **60–99:** AirTran, British Airways, Delta and Virgin.

- **100–129:** Southwest.

BRITTIP
Orlando International Airport offers **free wi-fi** throughout its main concourse and satellite arms.

Although there isn't as much choice as at the main terminal, you should find the Airside areas just as clean and efficient, with the bonus of 2 duty-free shops (your purchases are delivered to the departure gate for you to collect as you board). Both stores include designer sunglasses, jewellery, handbags, fashion watches, new perfumes and a selection of travel retail exclusives.

Gates 1–29: Here you will find the first **duty-free shop**, a newsagents (the **Keys Gift Shop**), 2 **Cibo Express** gourmet markets, **Za-Za's** Cuban café and a mini food court featuring **Starbucks**, **Burger King**, **Cold Stone Creamery**, **Brioche Doree** and **Famous Famiglia**.

Airside at Orlando International Airport

ORLANDO INTERNATIONAL AIRPORT

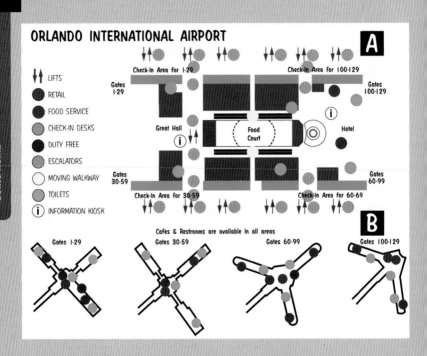

ORLANDO SANFORD INTERNATIONAL AIRPORT

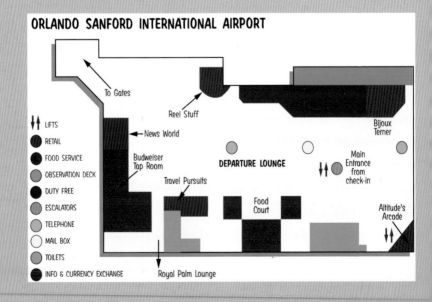

Your chance to give something back

After having the holiday of a lifetime, all being well, you might like to know about 2 charities helping children with serious illnesses to have a memorable time here. **Give Kids the World Village** is an amazing organisation in Kissimmee, providing a week's holiday in central Florida for children with life-threatening illnesses. GKTW works with more than 250 wish-granting foundations worldwide to provide an unforgettable Wish Vacation for children and their families. It is set up as a resort and includes meals, accommodation, transportation, whimsical venues, donated theme park tickets and many other thoughtful touches in a magical setting. It's a charity we are happy to support ourselves, and we hope you will, too. You can make a donation through its website – **www.gktw.org** – or send it to: Give Kids The World, 210 South Bass Road, Kissimmee, Florida 34746, USA.

Equally, **Dreamflight** is a registered UK charity taking seriously ill children aged 8–14 to Florida annually, often with the help of British Airways. It costs around £3,000 per child and, while many people generously donate their time to help, cash donations are essential. You can contribute by post: Dreamflight, 7C Hill Avenue, Amersham, Bucks HP6 5BD (01494 722733), online at **www.justgiving. com**, or by email to **office@dreamflight.org**. Look up more at **www.dreamflight.org**.

Thanks in advance for any contributions to these worthwhile organisations.

Gates 30–59: These have **Cibo Express**, **Pancho's Spanish Bakery and Deli**, **Natures Table**, **Wendy's**, **Freshens Treats**, **Za-Za's Cuban Coffee**, full-service **Ruby Tuesday** and **Hudson News**.

Gates 60–99: The main satellite for UK flights offers a good **duty-free shop**, currency exchange, **Stellar News & Gifts**, the speciality **Zoom System** shop, and a mini play area. A food court contains **Burger King**, **Nathan's Hot Dogs**, **Carvel**, **Starbucks** and **Fresh Attractions** deli, plus the excellent table-service **Outback Steakhouse** and bar.

Gates 100–129: Offer 2 **Johnny Rivers Smokehouse Express** outlets, a food court with **Freshens Treats**, and **McDonald's**, plus **Starbucks** coffee shop, **Au Bon Pain** café, **Kafe Kalik** bar/lounge and 9 shops. For more details, see **www.orlandoairports.net**, which includes live flight departure and arrival info.

Orlando Sanford International Airport

Returning to what is now the main Orlando gateway for British charter flights should be relatively simple, providing you retrace your route on the Central Florida Greeneway (following signs for Orlando Sanford Airport, NOT Orlando International) and come off at exit 49. Turn first right at the lights, then first right again on to Lake Mary Boulevard and follow it to the airport. The efficiency of Alamo and Dollar's car return adds to the simplicity.

NB: the airport turn-off sign is right after the toll plaza before exit 49 and is easy to miss; once you go through that toll plaza, take the very next turn-off.

Orlando Sanford was created as a full international airport in 1996, as an initiative between the airport authorities and several British tour operators. Thomson, Monarch and Thomas Cook, plus the scheduled services of Icelandair, all now go for this simpler option. Of course, you are further north, so your journey time is 45 minutes longer and you have to pay an extra $3.50 in tolls compared with the journey to and from Orlando International, but providing you follow the simple directions, you should have no problem retracing your steps here.

And, while this charter gateway is smaller than Orlando International, it boasts a spacious check-in area and works hard to make the departure as painless as the arrival, especially with its Royal Palm Lounge facility.

Icelandair usually uses Terminal B for check-in; the other UK airlines check in at Terminal A. But all passengers use the same international departure lounge in Terminal A. It continues to grow, and has finished a major facility upgrade, notably in Terminal B.

There are no food or beverage outlets at the check-in level at Terminal A, but you can walk across to Terminal B where there is a **Ritazza Café** and a food court. Once checked in, you need to pass through security (allow at least 30mins) to reach the International Departure Lounge. Here you have the **Budweiser Tap Room**, which serves a good selection of international beers, and the handy food court. The 4-part outlet offers **American Grill**, **Daily Specials**, **Sweet Endings** and the aptly named **Grab-N-Go** (soft drinks, bottled water and snacks). There is then an extensive **duty-free store** (also with an increased range of merchandise), a **Discover Orlando Sanford** shop (gifts and artwork with a 'local' flair), **Hudson News** for sundries, **KidWorks** for educational games, books, and toys, plus **Indulgences** for home, bath and body products. Neatly located in a corner, **Altitudes Arcade** is guaranteed to appeal to kids, while there is also an **information** and **currency exchange** kiosk. Smoking is not permitted inside the lounge, but there is an extensive outdoor deck for smokers.

Royal Palm Lounge: The big extra here, this premium space is available

See you soon!

to all passengers for a modest fee. It's in a separate annexe from the main lounge and is an oasis of comfort and quiet, perfect for relaxing for the last few hours of your holiday (the only things it doesn't have are beds and shower facilities!). Split into 2 distinct halves, it boasts a pleasant café bar, where you can enjoy unlimited tea, coffee, soft drinks and snacks (plus 2 glasses of beer or wine per over-21). It also provides 2 home theatre lounges, with widescreen TV and surround-sound, for recently released films; 2 quiet reading rooms; 11 computer terminals for internet access and email; a youth entertainment centre with 14 Sony PlayStation 2 consoles; a separate toddlers' playroom with soft toys and games; a smoking lounge; and a left-luggage area. The Royal Palm Lounge is billed as an airport lounge with the comforts of home and it is well worth the extra cost ($30 per adult, $20 4–20s, under-4s free) if you're likely to be here for an hour or more. Most tour operators offer it in advance at a discount, or you can book on arrival or through your reps at the resort. With its extra capacity and facilities, this is a very satisfying way to conclude a holiday. See the Royal Palm Lounge, and more about the airport, at **www. orlandosanfordairport.com** or email **royal. palm@tbiusinc.aero**.

Whether you are using Orlando International or Orlando Sanford, you can also expect the return flight to be about an hour shorter than the journey out, thanks to the tailwinds provided by the Atlantic jetstreams. Nevertheless, you'll land back home rather more jetlagged than on the trip out because the time difference is more noticeable on eastward flights, and it may take a day or so to get your body clock back on local time. It is important not to indulge in alcohol on the flight if you will be driving when you land. By far the best way to beat Florida jetlag is to enjoy the memories from this trip – then start planning your next Orlando holiday!

Believe us, the lure of this theme park wonderland is hard to resist – you WILL be back!

© Disney

Your Holiday Planner

Example: 2 weeks with Disney's 5-Day Premium Ticket and Orlando FlexTicket

(Disney's 5-Day Premium Ticket gives 5 days at their 4 main theme parks, plus 5 visits to *Blizzard Beach, Typhoon Lagoon, DisneyQuest* and/or *Disney's ESPN World Of Sports*™, valid for 14 days from first use. The Orlando FlexTicket is valid for Universal Orlando's 2 parks, plus SeaWorld, Wet 'n Wild and CityWalk for 14 days from first use.)

Day	Our Example	Your Planner
1 (Sun)	Arrive 2.40am local time, Orlando Sanford airport; transfer to resort – check out local shops and restaurants	
2 (Mon)	Attend tour operator Welcome Meeting; rest of day at UNIVERSAL STUDIOS	
3 (Tues)	Chill-out day at *Disney's Blizzard Beach* water park	
4 (Wed)	All day at MAGIC KINGDOM Park (Wishes fireworks at 9pm)	
5 (Thurs)	All day at DISNEY'S HOLLYWOOD STUDIOS (Fantasmic! show at 8.30pm)	
6 (Fri)	All day at EPCOT Park (IllumiNations at 9pm)	
7 (Sat)	Have a lie-in, then try some shopping at Orlando Premium Outlets and Lake Buena Vista Factory Shops	
8 (Sun)	DISNEY'S ANIMAL KINGDOM Park Eve: Medieval Times Dinner Show (8pm)	
9 (Mon)	ISLANDS OF ADVENTURE Eve: CityWalk and dinner at Hard Rock	
10 (Tues)	Kennedy Space Center Eve: International Drive	
11 (Wed)	All day at SEAWORLD ADVENTURE PARK (Mistify at 10pm)	
12 (Thurs)	Have a chill-out day; head for the new Aquatica water park	
13 (Fri)	Enjoy a UNIVERSAL ORLANDO highlights day. Eve: Sleuth's Mystery dinner show	
14 (Sat)	Have a lie-in, then head for MAGIC KINGDOM Park (Wishes fireworks at 9pm)	
15 (Sun)	Gatorland/Back to airport; return flight at 5.30pm	

Busy Day Guide

NB: These days can change on a month-by-month basis. This is an EXAMPLE ONLY. For the most up-to-date information, please check our website, **www.venesstravelmedia.com**.

Day	Busiest	Average	Lightest
Mon	*Magic Kingdom; Disney's Animal Kingdom; Islands of Adventure*	*Disney's Hollywood Studios*	*Epcot;* Universal Studios; Busch Gardens; Kennedy Space Center; SeaWorld; water parks
Tues	*Epcot; Magic Kingdom*	*Disney's Animal Kingdom;* Universal Studios	*Disney's Hollywood Studios;* Busch Gardens; IoA; Kennedy Space Center; SeaWorld; Water Parks
Wed	*Disney's Hollywood Studios* (high season)	*Disney's Animal Kingdom;* Islands of Adventure; SeaWorld; water parks	*Magic Kingdom; Epcot;* Busch Gardens; Kennedy Space Center; Universal Studios
Thurs	*Magic Kingdom;* Universal Studios	*Epcot;* Busch Gardens; SeaWorld; water parks	*Disney's Hollywood Studios; Disney's Animal Kingdom;* IoA; Kennedy Space Center
Fri	*Disney's Hollywood Studios* (high season) SeaWorld; IOA; Water Parks	*Disney's Animal Kingdom;* Busch Gardens; Kennedy Space Center	*Magic Kingdom; Epcot* Universal Studios
Sat	*Disney's Animal Kingdom;* Busch Gardens; IoA; Kennedy Space Center; SeaWorld; Universal Studios; water parks	*Magic Kingdom; Epcot*	*Disney's Hollywood Studios* (high season)
Sun	*Epcot; Magic Kingdom;* IoA; Kennedy Space Center; SeaWorld; water parks	*Disney's Hollywood Studios;* Busch Gardens; Universal Studios	*Disney's Animal Kingdom*

Only here for a week? Here's our suggestion for an action-packed 7 nights in Orlando:

Day 1: Arrive; visit *Epcot* in evening for IllumiNations

Day 2: Up early for Magic Kingdom

Day 3: All day at Universal and Islands of Adventure

Day 4: Epcot for the day; Disney's Hollywood Studios for evening

Day 5: Disney's Animal Kingdom park day; Epcot evening

Day 6: Aquatica and SeaWorld

Day 7: Disney's Hollywood Studios & Magic Kingdom

Day 8: Shopping and return flight.

Index

Page numbers in *italics* refer to maps or tables. Those in **bold** refer to major references. (A) = Animal attraction, (D) = Dinner shows, (R) = Restaurant, (T) = Tour company, (W) = Water park

accommodation 18–20
  American-style 60
  camping 68–70
  golfing resorts 87, 90, 93, 94, 96
  green 70
  holiday homes 19, 21, 22, **96–100**
  holiday resorts 90–6
  International Drive 19, **82–5**
  Kissimmee 20, 75, **87–8**
  Lake Buena Vista 19, 69, 71–2, **86–7**
  motel-style 60
  rental accommodation 96–100
  self-catering 90–6
  suite hotels 61
  timeshares 92, 95, **102**
  Universal Orlando 80–2
  Walt Disney World Resort 18–19, **61–73**
  see also hotels
adults, entertainment in Orlando 35
Advantage Vacation Homes 98
adventure tours *see* eco-tourism
air conditioning 60
airboat rides 250, 258
aircraft attractions 8, **226–7**, 255–6, 274
  see also flying, recreational
airports *see* Orlando International
  Airport; Orlando/Sanford Airport
Alamo (Car hire) 48, 49, 53–4
alcohol 285, **304**
Alexander Holiday Homes 99
alligators 222, **224–6**
Altamonte Mall 336
Altamonte Springs 259
ambulance emergency number 29, 44
American
  banknotes 42
  clothes and footwear 38
  English 39
  football 262, 267
  holidays 18
  measurements 38
aquarium 275, 278
Aquatica (W) 8, **243–4**
Arabian Nights (D) 295–6
art galleries 329
arts
  festivals 246
  museums 245–6, 277
Astronaut themed attractions **213–20**, 274
Atlantic coast 20, **270**
Atlantic Dance 288
ATMs 42
attractions 7–8, 14
  Downtown Orlando 233
  free 30
  maps 214
  must-do 25
  new for 2012; 16–17
  repeat visitors 43
  smaller 26
  see also individual attractions

baby centres 28, 33
babysitting 33
baggage allowance 325
Bahama Bay Resort 90–91
Bahama Breeze (R) 309
Bahamas 284
ballet 236
balloon trips 227, **249**
Barefoot'n Resort 91
bars 300–301
baseball 267–8

basketball 262, 267
Baterbys Art Auction Gallery 329
Bay Lake Tower at Disney's
  Contemporary Resort 71
beaches 261-2, **270**, **276–9**, 281–2
Beachline Expressway (Route 528) 48, 49
beer 304
Best of British (R) 314
Best Western Lake Buena Vista 71–2
Bibbidi Bobbidi Boutique 327
Bice (R) 321
Big Fin Seafood (R) 316
bike hire 259
birds
  seabirds 278
  watching 225, 247
birthday celebrations 40–2, 82, 200
Bistro UK (R) 314
Black Hammock Fish Camp and
  Restaurant 258
Blue Heron Beach Resort 91
Blue Man Group 290
Blue Martini (R) 335–6
Bluezoo (R) 321–2
boats
  glass-bottomed boat rides 222–3
  tours 222–3, 246–8
  see also airboat rides; cruises; fishing
Boggy Creek Airboat Rides 250
Bohemian Hotel 87–8
Bok Tower Gardens 256–7
botanical gardens *see* Bok Tower Gardens;
  State Parks
Brevard County 7, **260–61**
Brevard Zoo (A) 274
Brio Tuscan Grille (R) 322
Brit Bonus 16
British Airways Holidays (T) 20
British Consulate 44
Bubba Gump's Shrimp Co. (R) 289
Buena Vista Palace Hotel & Spa 72
Busch Gardens (A) 8, 17, **201–12**
  at-a-glance 201
  Bird Gardens 205–6
  character dining 206
  Cheetah Hunt 204
  Congo 208
  Edge of Africa safari 210
  Egypt 211
  getting there 203
  Gwazi Coaster 205
  Jungala 207–8
  Kumba Coaster 208
  Montu Coaster 211
  Morocco 204–5
  Myombe Reserve 204
  Nairobi 210
  night time entertainment 212
  places to eat 203, 206–7, 208, 211
  planning visit 203–4
  queuing 203
  Rhino Rally 210
  Serengeti Plain 210
  Sesame Street Safari of Fun 206
  SheiKra 206–7
  shops 206, 208, 211
  Shuttle Express 203
  Stanleyville 206–7
  tickets 203
  Timbuktu 209
  tours 203, **211–12**
Busch Shuttle Express 51
buses 50–51
Busy Day Guide 346

cabarets *see* dinner shows
Café Tu Tu Tango (R) 309–10
Caladesi Island 278
camping 68–70

canoeing 254, 259, 260
Capone's Dinner & Show (D) 299
car hire 53–5
  insurance 54
  need for credit cards 42
  Orlando International Airport 48
  Orlando Sanford Airport 49
  returning the car 339
  see also driving; fly-drives; roads
Caribbean 284
Carnival Cruise Lines 284
cars 44–5, 55
  off-road driving 248–9
  vintage 30, 330
  see also car hire
cash machines 42
Cast Members (Disney) 105
Castaway Cay 284
Celebration Town (Disney) **251–2**
Central Florida Zoological Park (A) 258
Chalet Suzanne 257
Channelside Bay Plaza 275–6
characters
  autographs 103
  meals **103, 104**, 114–15
  see also individual theme parks
Charlotte Harbour 280
Cheesecake Factory (R) 310
chemists (drug stores) **29**, 337
children 31–3
  in cars 57
  child swap 105
  height restrictions on rides 37
  kids deals 21, 23, 31, 302
  kidsuites 65
  planning holiday for 25–6, **31–3**
  theme park services 33, 103
  travel company services 22
Christmas time 88, 252
cinemas 168, 235, 291, 293, 331
  dining in 286–7
  Imax 213, **216–17**, 329
  see also Disney's Hollywood Studios;
  Universal Studios
circuses 279, 287–8
Cirque du Soleil 287–8
Citrus County 260
City Fire (R) 317
CityWalk
  evening entertainment 285, **289–91**
  Lagoon Front 290
  Main Plaza 289–90
  Promenade 291
Clearwater Beach 262, **276–9**
climate 12, 18
clothing 27–8, 38
CoCo Key Hotel & Water Resort Orlando 79
CoCo Key Water Resort (W) 237
Cocoa Beach 261, 274
Columbia Restaurant, Ybor 276
comedy (live shows) 290, 293
Complete Orlando (T) 24
Continental Airlines Vacations (T) 23
coral reefs 283
Cornell Fine Arts Museum 30, **245–6**
Cosmos Holidays (T) 20–21
cowboys 253, 268
Cracker Barrel (R) 308
credit cards 42–3
Cricketer's Arms (R) 314–15
crime prevention 43–5
crocodiles 222–3, **224–6**
cruises
  Caribbean 284
  cruise-and-stay options 20, 22,
    270, **283–4**
  rivers and waterways 222–3, 258–9
  see also airboat rides; split holidays
Crystal River Preserve State Park 260

INDEX

Customs and Excise advice 325–6
customs forms 12–15
Cypress Restaurant and Visitor Center 253

Dali Museum 277
day trips 52, **261–2**
Daytona 271–3
 Beach 271–2
 Lagoon (W) 272
 Speedway 269
dehydration, avoiding 28
dining out
 24/7; 304
 airports 341, 343, 344
 Asian 312–13
 breakfasts 308
 British-style pubs 223, 305, **314–15**
 buffet-style 309
 Cajun 291, 307
 Celebration 251
 chain restaurants 309–11
 character meals **103**, **104**, 114–15
 and children 32
 Chinese 312–13
 CityWalk 289–90
 Creole 289
 Cuban 292–3, 319
 deals 302–3
 deluxe dining 317–20
 dinner shows 26, 229, **293–9**
 Disney Dining Plan 23, **62**
 'doggy bags' 302
 Downtown Disney 286, **305–7**, 327, 328
 drinking 304
 drive-through 308
 family favourites 308–11
 fast food 307–8
 Floribbean cuisine 289
 Greek 293, 313–14
 Hyperion Wharf 305–6
 ice cream 312
 Indian 312–13, 319
 International Drive **315**, 329
 Italian 305–6, 311, 313–14
 Kissimmee 321, 330–31
 Lake Buena Vista 323, 332–3
 Latin American 291
 Mall at Millenia 334–6
 McDonald's 307
 Mexican 292, 310
 Mount Dora 247
 ordering 303
 pancakes and waffles 308
 Pleasure Island 305–6
 Pointe Orlando 292–3, 319
 portion sizes 15
 prices 15
 seafood 316–17
 steakhouses 310–11, **313**, 317, 318, 320
 themed cuisine 289–90
 tipping 302
 top ten restaurants 320–4
 top ten romantic 41
 Turkish 313–14
 variety 302, 303
 vegetarian options 131, **303–4**
 Winter Park 246
 see also individual attractions
dinner shows 26, 229, **293–9**
Dinosaur World 274–5
disabled travellers **34–5**, 198, 216
 access to buses 50
 airport facilities 340
 travel company services 35
discos *see* evening entertainment
Discovery Cove (A) 8, **197–200**
 disabled visitors 198
 Dolphin Swim 199
 entrance fees and costs 197–8
 Explorer's Aviary 199
 getting there 198
 Grand Reef 199–200

special occasions 200
 Trainer For A Day Programme 198
 Wind-away River 199
Disney cruises 284
Disney Dining Plan 23, **62**
Disney Hollywood Studios
 ABC Sound Studio 138
Disney Hotel Plaza 71–3
Disney resorts 70–3
 benefits of 61–3
 character dining 103, **104**
 deluxe 65–8
 moderate 64–5
 value 63–4
 see also individual resorts
DisneyQuest 287
Disney's All-Star Resorts 63–4
Disney's Animal Kingdom Lodge 65
Disney's Animal Kingdom Lodge – Kidani Village 71
Disney's Animal Kingdom Theme Park (A) 7, 147
 Africa 151–2
 Asia 153–4
 at-a-glance 146
 best time to see animals 148
 Camp Minnie-Mickey 151
 characters 104, 149, **151**
 children's attractions 155
 DinoLand USA 154–6
 DINOSAUR! 154–5
 Discovery Island 149–51
 environmental message 146, **152**
 Expedition Everest 153–4
 Festival of the Lion King 151
 Finding Nemo the musical 155
 getting there 148
 It's Tough To Be A Bug! 150
 Kali River Rapids 153
 Kilimanjaro Safaris 148, **151–2**
 Maharaja Jungle Trek 153
 The Oasis 149
 Pangani Forest Exploration Trail 152
 parades 156
 places to eat 149, 150–2, 154, 156
 planning your visit 148–9
 shopping 149, 150, 152, 154, 156
 tours 156
 The Tree of Life 149–50
Disney's Art of Animation Resort 17, 63–4
Disney's Blizzard Beach Water Park (W) 7, 240–41
Disney's BoardWalk Inn and Villas 65–6
Disney's BoardWalk Resort 30, 285, **288**
Disney's Caribbean Beach Resort 64
Disney's Contemporary Resort 66
Disney's Coronado Springs Resort 64
Disney's Extra Magic Hours 19, 26–7, 63
Disney's Fort Wilderness Resort & Campground 68–70
Disney's Grand Floridian Resort & Spa 66–7
Disney's Hollywood Studios 7, 136
 American Idol Experience 138
 Animation Courtyard 142–4
 at-a-glance 134
 Beauty and the Beast 143
 Character dining 104
 children's attractions 143
 Christmas 145
 Commissary Lane 141
 Echo Lake 138–9
 Fantasmic! 143–4
 Great Movie Ride 137
 Hollywood Boulevard 137
 Honey I Shrunk the Kids 139
 Indiana Jones™ Epic Stunt Spectacular 138
 Journey into Narnia: Prince Caspian 142
 Lights! Motors! Action!™ 139–40
 Magic of Disney Animation 143
 main attractions 135–7
 Muppet Vision 3-D Show 139
 parades 145

 Pixar Place 141–2
 places to eat 137, 139, 141, 145
 planning your visit 134–7
 Rock'n Roller Coaster 135, **144**
 shops 135, 137, 139, 141, 145
 Skywalker and Co. 145
 Star Tours 135, 138–9
 Streets of America 139–41
 Sunset Boulevard 144–5
 tours 140, **145**
 Toy Story Mania 135–6, 141–2
 Twilight Zone™ Tower of Terror 135, **144**
 Voyage of the Little Mermaid 142
 Walt Disney: One Man's Dream 142–3
Disney's Old Key West Resort 70
Disney's Polynesian Resort 67
Disney's Pop Century Resort 63
Disney's Port Orleans Resort 64–5
Disney's Saratoga Springs Resort & Spa 70
Disney's Spirit of Aloha (D) 294
Disney's Typhoon Lagoon Water Park (W) 7, 237–40
Disney's Vacation Club resorts **70–71**, 102
Disney's Wilderness Lodge 67
Disney's Yacht and Beach Club Resorts 67–8
dolphins 133, 187, 189, 243, 275
 Dolphin Landings 278
 swim with **199**, 262
Doubletree Guest Suites 72
Downtown Disney 7, **285–6**
 Cirque du Soleil 287–8
 DisneyQuest 287
 evening entertainment 285–8
 Hyperion Wharf 327–8
 Marketplace 306
 Pleasure Island 285
 restaurants 286, **305–7**, 327, 328
 shopping 326–8
 West Side 286–8, 307, 328
Downtown Orlando 233
drinking 28
 alcohol 285, **304**
 beer 304
 dehydration 28
 and driving 57
 licensing laws 285, 304
 photo ID needed 285, 304
 water 27
driving 14, 44–5, 47, **55–9**
 AA member discounts 57–8
 accidents 58
 disabled visitors 34–5
 road map 6
 see also car hire; motor sport
duty-free allowances 325–6

East Lake Fish Camp 250
eBookers (T) 23
eco-tourism 253, 272–3
electrical appliances 76, 326
Electrical Water Pageant 67, **295**
emergency services 29, 44, **46**
Epcot 7, 121
 at-a-glance 120
 character dining 104
 characters 127
 children's attractions 131
 cruises 132–3
 Ellen's Energy Adventure 122
 festivals 133
 fireworks (IlumiNations) 132–3
 Food and Wine Festival 133
 Future World 120, **122–7**
 Imagination 124
 Innoventions 126–7
 The Land 124–5
 IlumiNations 132–3
 Mission: Space 122–3
 places to eat 125, 126, **128–32**
 planning your visit 120–2
 The Seas with Nemo and Friends 125–6
 shops 127, **128–32**
 Soarin' 125

Spaceship Earth 126
Test Track 123–4
tours 133
Universe of Energy 122
World Showcase 122, **127–32**
ESPN Club 300
ESPN Wide World of Sports
Complex 7, **268**
ESTA forms **12–13**, 47
evening entertainment 26, **285–301**
excursions 52, **261–2**
Expedia (T) 23
Extra Magic Hours 19, 26–7, 63

Fantasy of Flight 8, **226–7**
Farmers' Market 235, 331
FastPass rides 102–3
Festival Bay 329
festivals 271
fingerprints and ID 13
First Choice (T) 21
fishing 249, 250, 251, 254–5, **261**, **266**
flea markets 337–8
flights
scheduled 24
see also travel companies
Florida 6
Florida Aquarium (A) 275
Florida Choice Vacation Homes 99
Florida Dolphin Tours 261
Florida Eco-Safaris (A) 253–4
Florida Keys 270, 283
Florida Leisure Vacation Homes 99
Florida Mall 334
Florida Sales Tax 325–6
Florida Vacation Shop 99
Floridays Resort Orlando 92
fly-drives 20–21, 22
flying, recreational
helicopter rides 232
iFLY Orlando 231–2
Mauiva Air Tours 255–6
Waldo Wright's Flying Service 227
Warbird Adventures 255
see also aircraft attractions;
balloon trips
food
British Supermarket 338
see also dining out
football, American 267
football (soccer) 268
footwear, American 38
Fort Christmas Historical Park 30
Fort Lauderdale **282**, 284
Fort Myers 280
Fountains Resort 92
Frankie Farrell's (R) 315
free attractions 30
fuel 54, 55
Fulton's Crab House (R) 306
Fun Spot Action Park 17, 229–30
Fun Spot USA 232–3
Funway Holidays (T) 23

gardens *see* Bok Tower Gardens;
State Parks
gas stations 55
Gatorland (A) 224–6
Gaylords Palms Resort 88
go-karts **229–30**, 232–3
Go Orlando Card 9–10
golf 262–5
resorts 87, 90, 93, 94, 96
see also mini-golf
Grand Bohemian Hotel 89
Grande Lakes Orlando 89
Green Meadows Petting Farm (A) 254
Greeneway (Route 417) 48, 49
Gulf Coast 276–9

hair dryers 76
Hapimag Resort 92
Hard Rock Café (R) 290
Hard Rock Hotel 80–81

Harry Potter 174, **176–80**
health
care 29
insurance 30–31
heatstroke, avoiding 28
helicopter rides 232, 255
Hemingway, Ernest 283
Highway 192: 59, 321
Highway 27: 59
accommodation 20
hiking 30
Hilton at Bonnet Creek Resort 86
Hilton Orlando 82–4
Hilton Orlando Resort 72
history museums 233–4, 254, 259, 277
holiday homes 19, 21, 22, **96–100**
Holiday Inn 73, 76
Holiday Planner 345–6
Homosassa Springs Wildlife State
Park (A) 260
Hoop-Dee-Doo Musical Revue (D) 294–5
Hooters (R) 293, **310**
horses
Horseback Safaris 253
riding 267
rodeo 268
hospitals 29
hotels 60–8
air conditioning 60
airport 48
American-style 60
budget 73–4
chains 74–6
condo-hotels 85, 90–6
deluxe 79–80
Disney 61–3
green 70
kidsuites 65
moderate 76–7, 80
prices 61
room sizes 60, 70
security 44
suite hotels 61, 76, **82**
telephone calls from 33, 60
upmarket 77–9
value **74–6**, 77
see also accommodation
House of Blues (R) 307
hovercraft *see* airboat rides
Howl at the Moon 301
hurricanes and storms 40
Hyatt Regency Grand Cypress 87
Hyperion Wharf 16–17, 285–6
restaurants 305–6
shops 327–8

ice cream 312
Icebar 301
iFLY Orlando 231–2
immigration forms **12–15**, 47
Independence Day 170, 212, 252
Indian River Queen 260–61
information 46
see also visitor centres
insect repellents 29
insurance
car 54
health and travel 30–31
International Drive 58–9
accommodation 19, **82–5**
attractions 228–32
I-Ride Trolley 50–51
mini-golf 265
restaurants **315**, 329
shopping 328–9
see also Pointe Orlando
internet
cafés 333
search engines 24
travel agents 23–4
websites 46
Interstate 4: 58
Islands of Adventure 8, **171–84**
Amazing Adventures of Spider-Man 184

at-a-glance 171
children's attractions 183
Discovery Center 181
Dr Doom's Fearfall 183–4
Dragons Challenge 177
Dudley Do-Right's Ripsaw Falls 182
Eighth Voyage of Sindbad 175
guest services 173
Harry Potter and the Forbidden
Journey 177–9
Incredible Hulk Coaster 183
Jurassic Park 181
the Lost Continent 175–6
Marvel Super-Hero Island 182–4
places to eat 173, 175–6, 179–82, 184
planning visit 173–4
Port of Entry 173–4
Poseidon's Fury 175
Seuss Landing 174–5
shops 173, 175, 179–82, 184
Toon Lagoon 181–2
Wizarding World of Harry
Potter 174, **176–80**

Jellyrolls 288
jet-lag, avoiding 27, 344
Jetsave (T) 23
Jiko (R) 65, **322**

karaoke 291
kayaking 254, 259, 260, 277–8
Kennedy Space Center 8, **213–19**, 261–2
Key West 283
kids deals 20–21, 22, 31, 302
Kissimmee 59
accommodation 20, 75, **87–8**
Air Museum 255
Downtown 331
Loop West 331
mini-golf 265
Old Town 30, 232–3, 330
Outdoor Adventures 254–5
restaurants 321, 330–31
shopping 330–31

La Nouba™ 287–8
Lake Buena Vista
accommodation 19, 69, 71–2, **86–7**
Factory Stores 332
Resort Village & Spa 92–3
restaurants 323, 332–3
shopping 332–3
shuttle service 51
Lake County 7, **246–9**
Lake Eola Park 30, 235
Lake Louisa State Park 248–9
Lake Tibet-Butler Preserve 30, 246
Lake Tohopekaliga 254
Lake Wales 257
Lakeridge Winery and Vineyards 30
Lakeside Inn 247
Land Remembered (R) 320–21
LastMinute (T) 23
Legoland Florida 17, **220–2**
licensing laws 285, 304
Lighthouse Point Park 272
Liki Tiki Village 93
limousines 52
Loch Haven Park 236–7
Loyalty Homes 100
luggage 15, 43, 340
Lymmo Bus Service 233
Lynx Bus System 50

Magic Kingdom Park 7, **106–19**
Adventureland 109–11
at-a-glance 106
Big Thunder Mountain Railroad 111
Buzz Lightyear's Space Ranger
Spin 115–16
character dining 103, 104, 114–15
characters 109
children's attractions 117
Christmas 119

City Hall (information bookings) 109
Fantasyland 16, **112–15**
Frontierland 111
getting there 107
Halloween 119
Haunted Mansion 112
It's a Small World 112
Jungle Cruise 110
Liberty Square 112
Main Street USA 107–9, 118
Mickey's PhilharMagic 113
Monsters Inc Laugh Floor 116
night-time 118
parades 116–19
parking 107
Pirates of the Caribbean 110
places to eat 109, 110–12, 114–16
planning visit 107
shopping 110–12, 114–16
Space Mountain 115
Splash Mountain 111
Stitch's Great Escape 115
Tomorrowland 115–16
tours 119
Wishes Cruises 118
Magic Your Way tickets 9
Magical Midway 230
MagicCity National Transportation 51
Maingate Transportation 51
Mall at Millenia 334–6
manatees 190, 260, 262
maps 54, 55, 56
marathon 268
Marco Island 281
Mardi Gras 170
Marine Aquarium (A) 278
Marine Science Center (A) 272–3
markets 235, 331, 337–8
Marriot hotel chain 78, 89
Mauiva Air Tours 255–6
McDonald's (R) 307
Mears
    coach shuttle service 51
    taxis 53
measurements, American 38
medical treatment 29
Medieval Times (D) 296
Miami **282**, 284
Mickey's Backyard Barbecue (D) 295
mini-golf 241, **265**
mobile phones
    apps 105
    hire 38
Mona Lisa Suite Hotel 88
money 42–3
Moonfish (R) 317
Morse Museum of American Art 30, 245
mosquitoes 29
motor sport 269
    see also Daytona
Mount Dora 246–9
multi-centre holidays **20**, 270, **283–4**
museums
    aircraft 226–7, 255, 274
    art 245–6, 277
    cars 247
    cowboys 254
    history 233–4, 254, 259, 277
    Native Americans 280
    police 274
    science 236, 276
    shells 280
music, live 16–17, 81, 286, 289–90,
    292, **299**
    see also evening entertainment
Mystic Dunes Resort and Golf Club 93

Naples 281
Native Americans 280
NatureWorks 236–7
New Smyrna Beach 273
Nickelodeon Family Suites 82

night-clubs 291

observatories 237
Ocean Florida (T) 23
Oceanaire (R) 322–3
Old Hickory Steakhouse (R) 318
Old Spanish Sugar Mill (R) 275
Old Town, Kissimmee 30, 232–3, 330
Omni Orlando Resort at Champions
    Gate 90
Orange County 7, **245–6**
    History Center 233–4
Orange Lake Resort 93
Orlando 5–7
Orlando FlexTickets 9
Orlando George & Dragon (R) 315
Orlando International Airport 47–9,
    339–40
    airside 341–3
    car hire at 48
    disabled access 340
    driving from 48–9
    driving to 339
    landside 340–41
    security 340, 341
Orlando Premium Outlets 332
    shuttle service 51
Orlando Remembered 234
Orlando/Sanford Airport 49, 343–4
    driving from 49
    driving to 343
Orlando Science Center 236
Orlando World Centre Marriot 86
Ormond Beach 273
Osceola County 7, **249–56**
Osceola Parkway 331
Osceola Pioneer Museum 254
Oviedo Marketplace 336

pacing yourself 27
Palisades Resort 93–4
Palm Beach 281–2
Palm Restaurant (R) 320
Paradise Coast 281
Paradiso 37 (R) 305
Park Avenue 245–6
Park Square Homes 100
parking 15, 57
    disabled visitors 34
parks see Bok Tower Gardens;
    State Parks
passports 13
Peabody Duck March 30, 84
Peabody Orlando 84
pensioners see senior citizens
performing arts 235–6
phones 33, 38, 60, 105
PhotoPass 103–4
Pirates Dinner Adventure (D) 296–7
Planet Hollywood (R) 307
planning your holiday 5, 15
    avoiding theme park busy times 26
    Busy Day Guide 346
    busy time of year 18
    flights 24
    must-do-experiences 25
    online agencies 23–4
    pacing yourself 27
    Personalised Itinerary Planner 45
    split holidays 20, 270, **283–4**
    travel companies 20–4
    what to do when 26–7
    what to take 24–7
    when to go 12, 18
    your day 27
Pleasure Island see Hyperion Wharf
Pointe Orlando 285, **292–3**
    restaurants 292–3, 319
    shopping 329
police 44
    museum 274
Polk County 7, 256

Ponce de Leon Inlet Lighthouse 272
Ponderosa Steakhouse (R) 309
Portobello (R) 305–6
Portofino Bay Hotel 81
post offices 38–9
powerboats 250–51
pregnant women, rides to avoid 32
Premier Vacation Homes 100
Premium Outlets International 328–9
prescription drugs 29
Prestiege Vacations Direct 100
public transport 50–51
pubs 311
    British 305, **314–15**
    Irish 286, **305**, **314–15**, 348
pushchairs 15, 33, 103
Put a Cork In It 301

queuing 27, 109, 135
    FastPass rides 102–3
    Single Rider Queues 157
    Universal Express Plus 157, 173
Quick Transportation 52

Raglan Road (R) 286, **305**
rain 12, 18, 19
Rainforest Café (R) 306
Ravenous Pig (R) 324
Regal Oaks at Old Town 94
Regal Palms Resort 94
Renaissance Orlando Resort 84–5
repeat visitors 43
restaurants see dining out
Reunion Resort & Club 94–5
Revolution Offroad 248–9
rides 102
    FastPass rides 102–3
    height restrictions 37
    and pregnant women 32
Ripley's Believe It Or Not 228
Ritz-Carlton 89–90
river cruises 222–3, 258–9
    see also airboat rides; boats; cruises
Rivership Romance 258
roads 6, 14, 56
    key routes 58–9
    toll roads 48, 54, 56
rodeo 268
Rosen Hotels & Resorts **78**, 80
Rosen Shingle Creek Hotel 85
Royal Pacific Resort 81–2
Royal Palm Lounge 344
Royal Plaza Resort 73

safety and security 43–5
Sandpearl Resort 279
Sanford 259
    Museum 259
Sarasota 279–80
SatNav 55
science museums 236, 276
scuba-diving 283
SeaWorld (A) 8, 185–96
    at-a-glance 185
    Atlantis Bayside Stadium 196
    Blue Horizons 190
    character meals 188
    children's attractions 195
    getting there 188
    Journey to Atlantis 190–91
    Key West at Sea World 189
    killer whales 194
    Kraken 191
    Manta 191
    night time entertainment 196
    Penguins and Sea Lions 191–2
    places to eat 188, 189, **191–3**, 194–6
    planning your visit 188–9
    Ride Central 190–91
    Shamu Central 194–6
    sharks 193

Sharks and Co. 193–4
shops 189, 191, **192**, 194–6
tours 187–8
The Waterfront 192–3
Whale and Dolphin Theater 190
Wild Arctic 195
see also Discovery Cove
security 43–5
Segway Tours 247
Seminole Central 280
Seminole County 7, **258–9**
Seminole Towne Center 336
senior citizens 36–8
Seven Mile Bridge 283
Sheraton Vistana Resort 95
Sheraton Vistana Villages 95
Sherlock's (R) 315
shopping 26, 325–6
airports 340, 341, 343
antiques 247, 331
arts and crafts 333
books 333, 334
British food 100, **338**
cameras 333
Celebration 251
character souvenirs 332
CityWalk 289
clothes and footwear 331, 332–3, 334
day excursions 262
department stores 334
Downtown Disney 326–8
duty free allowances 325–6
electrical goods 326
Factory Stores 332
farmers' markets 235, 331
Festival Bay 329
flea markets 337–8
Florida Sales Tax 325–6
food 100, 331, 338
golf shops 263, 338
Hyperion Wharf 327–8
International Drive 328–9
Kissimmee 330–31
Lake Buena Vista 332–3
malls 333–7
Mount Dora 247
Park Avenue 245–6
Pointe Orlando 329
shuttle buses 51
specialist shops 337–8
sports shops 333, 338
supermarkets 100, **337**
tips 337
toys 327, 334
Winter Garden Village 336–7
see also individual attractions
Shores Resort and Spa 273
Shuttle launches 213, **215–16**, **219–20**
shuttle services (transport) 51–2
Silver Springs (A) 222–4
Silver Spurs Rodeo 268
single travellers 23
Sky Hotels & Resorts 79
skydiving 231–2, 257
Skyline Tours 30, 233
Skyy Limousines 52
Sleuth's Mystery Dinner Shows (D) 297–8
smoking 102
South West Orlando 279–81
Southport Park 250
space *see* astronaut themed attractions;
Kennedy Space Center
Space Coast 274
spectator sports 267–9
speed cameras 58
speed limits 57
split holidays 20–21, 22, **270**, **283–4**
sports bars 300
sports, spectator 267–9
St Augustine 270–71
St John's River Cruises 258–9
St Petersburg 277
Stage Door (R) 315

stamps and post offices 38–9
State Parks 259–60
State Tax 325–6
stock car racing 269
Summer Bay Resort 95–6
sun, protection against **28**, 32, 238
SunPass 54
supermarkets 100, **337**
surfing 238
Sweet Tomatoes (R) 303–4

T-REX Café (R) 306
Tampa 274–6
tax offices 34
taxes 325–6
taxis 52–3
Tchoup Chop (R) 324
tea-making facilities 73
TGI Fridays (R) 311
theatre 235–6
theme parks
busy day guide 346
busy times 26
disabled visitors 34–5
Disney 101–56
height restrictions 37
planning your visit 25–6
and pregnant women 32
prices 15
rides, rating of 102
security 105
see also individual parks
Thomas Cook (T) 21
Thomson (T) 21
Thornton Park 236
tickets **8–11**, 101–2
see also individual attractions
timeshares 92, 95, **102**
Timpano Italian Chophouse (R) 320
tipping 12, 76
Titanic – The Experience 228–9
Titusville 274
toll roads 48, 54, 56
tourism 7
tourist information *see* information;
visitor centres
tours
airboats 250, 258
boat 222–3, 246–8, 254, 260–61
day trips and excursions 52, **261–2**
kayak 277–8
powerboats 250–51
Skyline Tours 233
walking 246
see also cruises; eco-tourism
town cars 52
traffic lights 56
Trailfinders (T) 24
travel accessories 38
Travel City Direct (T) 21–2
travel companies 20–4
travel insurance 30–31
Travel Supermarket 24
travellers' cheques 42
Treasure Coast 281–3
Treehouse Villas 70
Turbo's Boat Rides 250–51
Tuscana (Resort) 96

Universal Orlando 8, 17, 27, 157
accommodation 80–2
Single Rider Queues 157
tickets 157
Universal Express Plus 157, 173
see also CityWalk; Islands of Adventure;
Universal Studios
Universal Studios 8, **158–70**
at-a-glance 158
and children 169
Despicable Me 161
Disaster 165
ET Adventure 168
Fear Factor Live 165

getting there 158
Hollywood 169–70
Hollywood Rip, Ride, Rockit! 161–2
Jaws 165
KidZone 167–8
Men In Black – Alien Attack 166–7
New York 163–4
places to eat 162, 164, 166-8, 170
planning visit 158–9
playgrounds 167–8
Production Central 159–62
Revenge of the Mummy 163–4
San Francisco/Amity 165–6
shopping 162, 164, 166-8, 170
Shrek 4-D 159–61
The Simpsons Ride 166
special programmes 170
Terminator 2: 3-D Battle Across
Time 169
Twister 163
Universal 360; 170
Woody Woodpecker's Nuthouse
Coaster 168
World Expo 166–7
wrestling 159
US Astronaut Hall of Fame 219–20

Valiant Air Command Warbird
Museum 274
VAT 325–6
Vero Beach 282
Villa Direct 100
villas *see* holiday homes
Villas at Grand Cypress 96
vineyards 30
Vineyards 248
Virgin Holidays (T) 22–3
visas 12–15
visitor centres 46, 102, 233
Vista Cay Resort 96
Volusia County 7, **271–3**

Wal-Mart stores 337
Waldo Wright's Flying Service 227
Waldorf-Astoria 86–7
walkie talkies 42
Walt Disney World Resort 7–8
accommodation 18–19, **61–73**
Swan and Dolphin Resort 68
see also individual theme parks
Warbird Adventures 255
water
drinking 27
parks 237–44
sports 266–7
weather 12, 18–19, 40
weddings **39–40**, 200
Wedding Pavilion 7, 40
Weedon Island Preserve (A) 277
West Side 307, 328
Western Beltway 59
Westin Imagine Orlando 85
Wet 'n Wild (W) 8, 241–3
Wild Waters (W) 224
wilderness areas 253, 259
Windsor Palms Resort 96
Winter Garden Village 336–7
Winter Park 245–6
Wolfgang Puck's (R) 307, **323**
WonderWorks **230–31**, 291
WonderWorks Dinner Show (D) 298–9
Wyndham Lake Buena Vista Resort 73
Wyndham Ocean Walk Resort 273

Ybor City 276

Zen (R) 323–4
ziplines 258
Zipline Safari 253
zoos 258, 274
see also Busch Gardens

Copyright notices

Acknowledgements

The authors wish to acknowledge the help of the following in the production of this book: Visit Orlando, Visit Kissimmee, Walt Disney Attractions Inc., Universal Orlando, SeaWorld Parks & Entertainment, St Petersburg/Clearwater Area Convention and Visitors' Bureau, Daytona Beach Area Convention & Visitors' Bureau, Seminole County Convention & Visitors' Bureau, Florida Huddle, Mount Dora Chamber of Commerce, Greater Orlando Aviation Authority, Orlando Sanford International Airport and Alamo Rent A Car.

In person: Danielle Courtenay, Amy Voss (Visit Orlando), Larry White, Sylvia Oliande, Chris Long (Visit Kissimmee), Todd Heiden, Sarah Hodson, Dave Coombs, Jason Lasecki, Geoff Pointon, Marilyn Waters (Walt Disney), Sharon Sears, Patrick Harrison (Seminole County CVB), Mary Haban (St Petersburg/Clearwater CVB), Tangela Boyd (Daytona Beach CVB), Cathy Hoechst, (Mount Dora), Nina Stemson (Alamo Rent A Car), Tom Schroder, Alyson Lundell, Kristen Clarke, (Universal), Andrea Farmer (Kenney Space Center), Jackie Wallace, Emily Kruse (Legoland Florida), Carolyn Fennell, Rod Johnson (Orlando Aviation Authority), Lorraine Ellis (Get Married In Florida), Andy James, James Brown (Florida Dolphin Tours), Nick Gollattscheck, Susan Flower, Jill Revelle (SeaWorld Parks & Entertainment), Brooks Jordan (Silver Springs), Christine Foley (Bok Tower Gardens), Laura Richeson (Richeson Communications), Scott Joseph (ScottJosephOrlando.com), Treva Marshall (TJM Communications), Mary Kenny (Mary C Kenny & Associates), Michael Caires, Greg Dull (Orlando Sanford International Airport), Allan Oakley (Alexander Homes & Associates), Nigel Worrall (Florida Leisure), Brad Conner, (Mauiva Air Tours), Sandy Marshall (Sky Resorts), Jason Schulke (Orlando Balloon Rides), Wrenda Goodwyn (International Drive), Mark McHugh, Michelle Harris, Bret Chism (Gatorland), Donna Ernbro (Sleuths), Gene Columbus (The Orlando Rep), David Walker (Titanic: The Experience), Mary Deatrick (Deatrick PR for Rosen Hotels), Margie Long (Boggy Creek Airboats), Phil Coppen (Cricketers Arms), Kevin and Audrey Jowett (Revolution Offroad), and Jennie and Paul Skingley (Best of British Soccer World).

Reader feedback via email: John Hidle, Hayden Robinson, Sandra Leaney, Alan Day, Hayley Burnett, Julie Brown, John Tanner, The Maze family, Rod Hellawell, plus many 'regulars' on the Attraction Tickets Direct forums, wdwinfo.com and thedibb.co.uk. You know who you are!

Other publications: Check out *Orlando Attractions Magazine* for information and features on this great destination – **www.attractionsmagazine.com**.

Got a red-hot Brit Tip to pass on? We want to hear from YOU to keep improving the guide each year. Drop us a line at: Brit's Guide (Orlando), W. Foulsham & Co. Ltd, Capital Point, 33 Bath Road, Slough, Berkshire SL1 3UF. Or e-mail britsguide@yahoo.com.